The pharmaceutical industry

The pharmaceutical industry

A guide to historical records

Edited by
LESLEY RICHMOND, JULIE STEVENSON AND ALISON TURTON

ASHGATE

© Lesley Richmond, Julie Stevenson and Alison Turton 2003

All rights reserved. No part of this publication may be reproduced, stored in a retrieval system, or transmitted in any form or by any means, electronic, mechanical, photocopying, recording or otherwise without the prior permission of the publisher.

Published by
Ashgate Publishing Limited
Gower House
Croft Road
Aldershot
Hants GU11 3HR
England

Ashgate Publishing Company
101 Cherry Street
Burlington, VT 05401-4405

Ashgate website: http://www.ashgate.com

British Library Cataloguing in Publication Data
The pharmaceutical industry : a guide to historical
  records. - (Studies in British business archives)
  1.Pharmaceutical industry - Great Britain - Archival
  resources
  I.Richmond, Lesley II.Stevenson, Julie III.Turton, Alison
  338.4'7615'0941

Library of Congress Cataloging-in-Publication Data
The pharmaceutical industry : a guide to historical records / edited by
  Lesley Richmond, Julie Stevenson, and Alison Turton.
       p. cm. -- (Studies in British business archives)
  Includes bibliographical references and index.
  ISBN 0-7546-3352-7 (alk. paper)
    1. Pharmaceutical industry--Great Britain--History--Sources. I.
Richmond, Lesley. II. Stevenson, Julie. III. Turton, Alison. IV. Series.

HD9667.5 .P465 2002
338.4'76151'0941--dc21

2002026134

ISBN 0 7546 3352 7

This book is printed on acid free paper

Printed and bound in Great Britain by MPG Books Ltd, Bodmin, Cornwall

Contents

Foreword by Peter Haggett — *vii*

Acknowledgements — *ix*

The early years of the pharmaceutical industry — *1*

The British pharmaceutical industry since 1851 — *14*

Archives of the pharmaceutical industry: their scope and use — *33*

Select chronology of pharmaceutical legislation — *49*

Select bibliography — *53*

User's guide — *61*

Select glossary of pharmaceutical terms — *66*

Pharmaceutical businesses: lists of records — *73*

Trade organisations and pharmacy schools: lists of records — *388*

Appendix 1: Geographical guide to minor collections — *431*

Appendix 2: Guide to public records — *488*

Index of names — *491*

Index of places — *534*

Index of subjects — *546*

Index of archive repositories — *556*

Foreword

Writing guides to archives and sources is both of one of the more arduous and one of the more rewarding of historical tasks. Arduous because it means tracking down, sorting and codifying a host of diverse and sometimes difficult materials; rewarding because it holds the promise of opening up new research topics for the next generation of researchers.

By many yardsticks, the pharmaceutical industry has proved itself one of the critically important engines of British industrial growth since the Second World War. Given its key role in providing the materials for medical treatment, the industry has also for some years been one of the areas identified by the History of Medicine Panel of the Wellcome Trust as deserving closer attention by historians. It is therefore pleasing to see this critical guide to historical sources in the UK pharmaceutical industry edited by Lesley Richmond, Julie Stevenson and Alison Turton. The volume grew out of work directed by Professor Derek Oddy on behalf of the Business Archives Council and supported by a research grant from the Trust over the period 1995 to 1997. It was also the subject of a successful symposium held at the University of Westminister in May 1997.

This clear guide to historical records within the pharmaceutical industry should prove itself a *vade-mecum* which will attract more historians to explore this complex but rewarding field. The success of volumes of this kind is measured less by immediate impact than by the long-term encouragement they give to find new trackways through previously unknown, but potentially exciting, terrain. This timely guide to the archives of the pharmaceutical industry deserves to be widely used.

Peter Haggett

Acknowledgements

First and foremost the authors and the Business Archives Council would like to thank The Wellcome Trust for funding the archive survey on which this guide is based. We hope that the information the book contains about hitherto unknown archives relating to the history of Britain's pharmaceutical industry will stimulate further research into the origins and development of this important sector. We would also like to thank the many company executives, archivists, librarians and museum curators throughout the country who have provided information about historical records in their care or who have allowed access for listing purposes. Without their enthusiastic and generous support this book would not have been possible.

We are particularly indebted to Dee Cook, now archivist of The Worshipful Society of Apothecaries, who as the first survey officer undertook much of the initial work on the project. A number of the entries are based on her early research. We would also like to thank Dr Trevor Jones, Director General of the Association of the British Pharmaceutical Industry and President of the Royal Pharmaceutical Society of Great Britain, who supported the survey enthusiastically from the outset. Edwin Green, former Chairman of the Business Archives Council, and Derek Oddy, Chairman of the Council's Survey Committee, have also been closely involved with the project from the beginning. Dr Peter Worling, former managing director of Vestric Ltd, gave a lot of time to the project particularly assisting in the compilation of a number of the company histories, and we are also very grateful for the help and support given by members of the British Society for the History of Pharmacy. To all the other individuals and organisations who offered support and advice we extend our grateful thanks. The preparation of the text for publication was undertaken by Rita Hemphill who undertook the work with her usual speed, accuracy and good humour.

Any further information on the archives or histories of British pharmaceutical businesses which would update or supplement the book's contents would be welcome and should be sent to the authors at Business Archives Council, 101 Whitechapel High Street, London E1 7RE.

Lesley Richmond
Julie Stevenson
Alison Turton

The early years of the pharmaceutical industry

J BURNBY

The eminent pharmaceutical historian, George Urdang, once entitled an article, 'Retail Pharmacy as the Nucleus of the Pharmaceutical Industry', and the more one studies the subject, the more correct one sees this to be. As early as the seventeenth century, some medicinal substances were manufactured on a relatively large scale, as, for example, Nehemiah Grew and the Moult brothers with their rival productions of Epsom salts. In the eighteenth century a man practising pharmacy, whether apothecary or chemist and druggist, made his 'back shop' the centre of his manufacturing activities, even if it were on but a small scale.

Many pharmaceutical manufacturers of today are able to trace their origins to a small shop. The well-known firm of Allen & Hanburys, for example, dates back to the pharmacy established in Plough Court by the newly qualified apothecary Silvanus Bevan in 1715, and forward to the present giant of Glaxo Wellcome. Likewise, Arthur Hawker Cox, aged twenty-six, in 1739, opened a pharmacy in Ship Street, Brighton, which, after considerable manufacturing expansion, moved to Barnstaple, Devon, and was then taken over by the German firm of Hoechst. The latter soon afterwards set up the German/French consortium of Hoechst/Roussel-Uclaf, and in 1995 bought the American company Marion Merrell Dow. One can, with some justice, say that the age of the global company has arrived.

The term 'the little technology' is often used to describe the small-scale work of the back shop. Pills and boluses could be made by hand, tinctures by the simple process of maceration or the slightly more complex one of percolation, infusions were no more than making a cup of tea, and ointments merely used mortar and pestle. Few chemists and druggists were content with just dispensing, but developed what has been termed 'own lines', that is the pharmacist's own formulation for a soothing cough mixture, a worm eradicator, an ointment for scabies or an effective, but not too griping purge. Many hoped to make a fortune, as did Beecham, Holloway or Morison, with the aid of extensive advertising, but at best had to be content with something on the scale of Steedman's Children's Soothing Powers. John Steedman established his pharmacy at 272 Walworth Road, London, in 1812 and became a well-known proprietary medicine manufacturer in the nineteenth century. His Soothing Powders were still being sold in the 1950s, until the link between 'pink disease' and mercury preparations was made.

Where photographs exist of the 'elaboratories' of what appear to be quite small pharmacies, one is surprised at the amount of equipment displayed, forgetting how self-sufficient they aimed to be. Recently a survey was done of the preparations made at a pharmacy in Birkenshaw, Yorkshire, which used a 254-page formulary containing 545 handwritten formulae and 409 printed cuttings. Admittedly, this was of the 1880s, but it is not thought to have differed significantly from those of earlier years. Of the handwritten entries there were 316 medicinal, sixty-nine cosmetic, seventy-eight veterinary and eighty-two domestic entries, and the cuttings were of about the same order. Mixtures and pills were the dominant dosage-forms as compressed tablets did not as yet dominate the scene. A few proprietories, such as Phosferine and Squire's Cold Cream were imitated, but there were also lotions for insect bites, essence for smelling salts, a baking-powder and ginger-beer powders, as well as raspberry brandy. The pharmacist had formulae for a glove cleaner, a non-mercurial plate powder, artificial ivory, cockroach bait and a highly dangerous silvering solution which used Scheele's Prussic Acid.

Nor was this pharmacist unusual. William Davison of Alnwick (1781–1858) stocked at least thirty-one oils and sixteen gums, fresh leeches, Lucifer matches, invalid foods, seeds of all sorts, besides paints, varnishes and dyes, stomach pumps, lancets, syringes and trusses, and, of course, the usual proprietary medicines. Some of these items obviously he did not make, but at least he had to be knowledgeable enough to select them. Furthermore, he dispensed prescriptions and made up family recipes. He was also a printer of some renown. Rather unexpectedly there was a close link in the eighteenth century between the stationer, bookseller, printed and newspaper owner, and the seller of 'patent' medicines.

The chemist and druggist was infinitely versatile. Many, besides practising pharmacy, were oil and colourmen, others specialised in veterinary preparations or even became veterinarians. Two men, Peter Squire of Oxford Street and William Hooper of Pall Mall East, were able at short notice to make the first apparatus in England for ether anaesthesia in 1847; others at a later date were pioneers in X-ray work. Perhaps the commonest side-line of all was the production of aerated waters. R T Taylor, who founded his pharmacy in Sheffield in 1824, developed this business and then later specialised in the manufacture of laboratory and medical equipment. Another was A J Caley of Norwich before he moved into the manufacture of chocolate, Caley's Marching Chocolate attaining fame in the Great War. The previously mentioned William Hooper set up in partnership in the 1830s with a Dr Friedrich Struve, proprietor of the Royal German Spa in Brighton, so forming the mineral water concern of Hooper, Struve & Co, which was granted a royal warrant in 1835. There was widespread mineral water production in the first half of the nineteenth century, nearly all of it by chemists and druggists as it was regarded as therapeutic. It was continued in pharmacies into the twentieth century, but for retail only as the days of the small factory were over.

Another valuable activity, but one practised by comparatively few, was the fitting out of portable medicine chests. The apothecary and chemist, William Randall, who moved from London to Southampton in 1792, was one such who also compiled a useful accompanying booklet. Others were the flamboyant Alexander Dalmahoy of Ludgate Hill, Blake & Son of Piccadilly, and George Allen of Rochester.

All of these men were not only retailers, but wholesalers as well. In the eighteenth and early nineteenth centuries there was little or no division between the two branches of the drug trade. William Jones was first established in 1746 in Little Russell Street, London, and then ten years later moved to 24 Great Russell Street, taking over the pharmacy of Elim Walker. It was a retail shop, but by far the most extensive portion of Jones's trade was wholesale, in which he dealt with apothecaries and surgeons who dispensed, hospitals, such as Chester Infirmary, and with other druggists. He also supplied Newberys of St Paul's Churchyard, London, with the antimony and cream of tartar required for making Dr James's powder of which they had the monopoly. At first the costs were counter-balanced by the powders which Jones took from them, but, in time, he came to accumulate as much as £100 of credits.

From an inventory of 1761, it is learnt that the Great Russell Street premises consisted of the shop, a counting house, a laboratory, warehouses, vaults, cellars, a cock-loft, and living quarters for family, guests and servants. The front shop had a brass chandelier, three desks, two stools, a bookcase and a safe. The dispensing was done at two counters under which were nests of drawers with weights, labels, containers and plaster leather. Each had its own beam scale and eight hand balances. There was a *Pharmacopoeia Londinensis* and the centre of the shop was stacked with hundredweight sacks of drugs and casks of senna, Peruvian bark, Glauber's Salts, etc. Behind the counters in dry goods were fifty-three shop boxes and ten more casks, nests of drawers under both windows and 130 species glasses; liquids were on six shelves and in a large glass case 150 glass stoppered bottles. In the laboratory was a still, a retort and a digester, presses, syrup and plaster pans, oil jars, sand-baths and a wind furnace. The chemicals which Jones obtained from manufacturing chemists, such as Henry Durbin of Bristol and Matthew Saunderson of Sheffield, were kept in a large vault, and the vegetable drugs in the warehouses, complete with pulley and tackle.

Jones made twice yearly rides to the Midlands, the West Country and the Welsh borders. To a limited extent he also traded overseas, principally to the West Indies and Nova Scotia. William died in 1789 and his son, John, who had worked with him for many years, continued the business. In 1837 it came into the hands of a William Hooper, who is not to be confused with the man of Pall Mall East, although they were contemporaries. Hooper had gained much experience with Godfrey & Cooke of Southampton Street, names which are famous in the annals of pharmaceutical history. Ambrose Godfrey Hanckwitz, born in Germany in 1660, came to Britain in about 1681. After a period as Robert Boyle's assistant and, it is thought, as a chemical operator in the laboratory of Apothecaries' Hall, he started his own laboratory where he made a pure phosphorus and preparations such as English Salts. He worked as a manufacturing chemist, analyst and consultant, in which he was followed, not too satisfactorily, by his two sons.

Unusually, both these two firms, Jones now Hooper, and Godfrey, ultimately gave up manufacturing. The former moved out of London to Letchworth in 1908 when the old shop was demolished, and the latter, after a move or two, was acquired by Savory & Moore in 1916, which could, in its turn, be dated back to 1794 when a surgeon and apothecary, Thomas Paytherus, leased 136 New Bond Street for eleven years at an annual rent of £200, and so started a famous retail pharmacy. His business flourished, and in 1806 he took in two partners, Thomas Moore, apothecary, and Thomas Field Savory. The partnership agreement shows that he both made and sold proprietary medicines, and that the stock-in-trade, the house with lease, utensils, furniture and fixtures were valued at £3,427. A branch was set up in the High Street of Cheltenham by 1809 and, only two years later, Paytherus decided to retire. In order to buy him out, Savory and Moore had to find a further £21,700 – and this did not include the Cheltenham shop.

In about 1814, Thomas Savory invented his enormously successful Seidlitz Powders which he patented in the October of the following year. Other partners were taken in, but did not stay long. More branches were opened in London and Brighton. Thomas Savory retired in 1830 and was followed by his nephew, John Savory, apothecary and pharmacist, who, after Moore's death, carried on alone until 1854 when his two sons were admitted. The Crimean War widened their outlets and in the years 1855 and 1856 the firm had government contracts worth over £50,000. Afterwards they became one of the main suppliers of medicine and equipment to British troops all over the world. Manufacturing was by now at least as important as the busy retail side, which, however, was by no means neglected, as in the early twentieth century they acquired the goodwill, prescription books and formulae of Godfrey & Cooke, Charles Dinneford and John Lloyd Bullock.

In 1927 the amalgamation took place with perhaps the most famous pharmaceutical concern of all, John Bell & Co, Oxford Street, London. As in all the other cases, with the exception of Godfrey, the firm started as a small pharmacy in 1798, but from at least 1840 was increasingly involved in wholesale and manufacturing and acquired laboratories and warehouses. The 'elaboratory' was totally rebuilt in the late 1850s, when it was fitted as a pharmaceutical manufacturing plant capable of making everything except chemicals on a large scale. By 1908 it was deemed advisable to divide the two activities, the wholesale and manufacturing becoming John Bell, Hills & Lucas Ltd and the retail side John Bell & Croyden Ltd.

Two houses which showed a different emphasis between manufacturing and retail outlets were the well-known and well-documented firms of Allen & Hanburys and Corbyn, Stacey & Co. The latter's origins may with certainty be traced back to 1707 when Benjamin Morris, citizen and apothecary in High Holborn, London, took Joseph Clutton as an apprentice. Clutton undoubtedly practised both medicine and pharmacy, the governors of the County Hospital in Winchester to which he was a supplier, referring to him as 'Mr Clutton, Chymist'. He died in 1743, but his widow continued the business, both retail and wholesale, with the aid of her excellent journeyman, Thomas Corbyn, who had begun his apprenticeship with Clutton in 1728.

Corbyn forsook medicine entirely and concentrated on the manufacture and sale of drugs. On the death of Morris Clutton in 1755 he bought out the whole Clutton interest. Trade had already started with the American colonies in Clutton's day and as the eighteenth century progressed, the firm became one of the principal suppliers of drugs to America and the West Indies. This was by no means a new feature of pharmaceutical trading as may be seen from the letters of Joseph Cruttenden from 1710 to 1717.

Cruttenden hailed from Cranbrook, Kent, but gained his freedom of the London Apothecaries' Society by redemption in 1687. The bulk of his trade was in simples, elixirs and cordials with but a few chemicals. He had some English wholesale trade, but the overseas one seems to have been more important to him. He always stoutly defended the quality of his goods and tried to maintain his prices, but bad debts were a bigger risk to him than losses at sea. In a letter to William Arbuckle of Jamaica in 1716 concerning mercurials, he related that he had bought them at the Apothecaries' Hall where they were more expensive but '... where I can depend on the goodness of them.' Often his buyers did not pay in sterling but in colonial currency which was more expensive for them – £100 sterling in 1710 being equivalent to £133.75 (Barbados) or £155 (Massachusetts). Cruttenden would often warehouse and sell his customers' commodities in London, crediting their account with the proceeds minus the costs of transport and customs dues, something which the Bevans tried to avoid, although the Corbyns would accept goods in kind such as cotton, sugar and skins.

The catalogues, stock lists, warehouse records and recipe books of Corbyn & Stacey are still extant, and are revealing as to the size of the drug trade in the mid-eighteenth to early nineteenth centuries. Corbyns sold good quality simples such as senna, rhubarb, arrowroot, and compounded preparations as, for example, Hungary Water or the complex theriacs. They experimented in improving manufacturing techniques, tried alternative methods for removal of impurities and always itemised the costing details.

Thomas Corbyn, his partners and successors, traded from the well-known 300 High Holborn, but there was a separate laboratory and a very large warehouse in Cold Bath Fields which, in 1761, according to the stock book, had over 2,500 separate items, some of them in large quantities, including 276 pounds of senna and 806 pounds of magnesia alba. They also worked on a large scale, the recipes frequently calling for hundredweight quantities. An example is extract of cinchona which required 150 pounds of the bark and 90 gallons of spirit. It has been noted that the cost of producing some compound medicines was as much as £50 or more per batch, and the wholesale value could be at least doubled.

Drug manufacture was labour intensive, the refining of 73 pounds of ambergris requiring 40 operators, 20 bushels of coal and one man's time for seven weeks. In the 1760s at any one time, Corbyns employed ten or twelve employees. It is nevertheless difficult to obtain reliable figures for the capital involved. It is known, however, that when Morris Clutton and Thomas Corbyn went into partnership in 1747, the business was worth some £4,000, but that forty years later it was about £20,000. Only for the year 1770 is there a clear profit and loss account. During this year the firm laid out about £9,500 on raw materials, plus some £2,000 for wages, leases, rates, taxes, etc. It had already in hand about £5,500 worth of the total stock in January, but sales amounted to just under £14,000, so the final clear profit amounted to £2,114 on the year which had to be split between the four partners.

Like many reputable firms in those days, Thomas Corbyn & Co acted as a bill-broker, discounter and banker, and would consign merchandise other than drugs, such as haberdashery. Indeed, Joseph Gurney Bevan of the Plough Court Pharmacy, seems to have derived up to a third of his income as an agent for woollen goods in his early days. Corbyn comprised four separate sections, each with its own ledger in the 1750s and 1760s. The town apothecaries which represented a steady business and included the London hospitals of St George's, Guy's and St Thomas's; the provincial or 'country' wholesale trade which comprised a large part of their activities and included surgeons, apothecaries and general shopkeepers; the retail shop for over-the-counter sales and those sent by post, which was of little importance; and the foreign overseas trade, principally to America, Nova Scotia southwards to Jamaica, the customers being surgeons, apothecaries, physicians and general merchants. In size the overseas trade was about half of the domestic one. It could result in losses due to breakages and bad debts, but unlike Allen & Hanburys, Corbyn seemed content to continue and even expand their overseas business well into the nineteenth century.

George Atkinson & Co used to advertise that it had been founded in 1654; proof so far is lacking though it is not impossible. The first really secure date is that of April 1711 when John Maud claimed his freedom of the Weavers'

Company by patrimony, his father being a Gamaliel Maud who is probably the 'Mr Maud – the Chymist in yr Street' to whom Richard Myddleton Massey referred when he wrote to James Petiver in 1703. Within two years John Maud became the master of Nathaniel Primatt, son of a druggist and grandson of a drug-grinder. The firm was to be found at 66 Aldersgate Street until 1884, when the manufacture of certain chemicals was forbidden by the City authorities, so causing the factory to be moved to Southall. Unlike the other businesses we have considered, there is no indication that a retail shop was ever present.

Primatt soon rose to become a partner with John Maud whose son, of the same name, after apprenticeship and election to Fellow of the Royal Society in 1738, also joined the firm. In due course a third generation, John Maud, joined Nathaniel's son, Lacey Primatt, and took over the running of the firm in the 1770s. For these later years some useful business archives have survived, including an invoice book listing the drugs imported from France, Germany, Holland, Italy and Spain, with their freight charges, accounts, drafts of letters, rough notes and calculations. There are also recipes for the preparation of chemicals and medicines which include methods of manufacture and costings devised by John Maud II, such as those for mercury sublimate and nitric acid in 1752.

John Maud III was forward-looking and in 1797 had installed a Boulton & Watt rotative engine at Aldersgate Street which continued working until 1885 and can still be seen in the Science Museum. The letters and invoices to John Maud & Co show that the firm imported considerable quantities of cochineal (15 bags costing over £700), 'chymical oils' such as oils of origanum, lavender and spike from Cette (£133), Stibium Bergamot (£590), vermilion, aniseed oil, sassafras, juniper berries and camphor. Letters from Leghorn in 1803 refer to essence of lemons and to bergamot, and those from Hamburg in the same year relate that borax was in very short supply. Nevertheless, the agents were advised to send only three tons of it and none of the oil of cassia. In 1806 John Maud bought 1,000 pounds of quicksilver and nine casks of vermilion, and later in the year more mercury and antimony, the whole amount costing £518. The agent wrote that the price was high, but the goods were of good quality and fresh supplies would be impossible.

Maud weathered the storms of the Napoleonic War but retired in about 1820 when the firm was taken over by Biggar, Atkinson & Dale, which, in turn, became known as George Atkinson & Co. Then in 1887 it was acquired by Thomas Whiffen and his two sons. It was in 1854 that Thomas Whiffen had joined Edward Herring and Jacob Hulle in making alkaloids and fine chemicals in the Borough, London. They moved to Battersea five years later where quinine and strychnine were manufactured in the garden of Whiffen's house. During its history, Maud & Primatt, later Whiffens, were close neighbours of two other historically important firms.

A very close neighbour in Aldersgate had been Thomas Fynmore, druggist, at No.65, said to have been there since 1741. By the end of the century Edward Palmer was a partner and Fynmore had retired from active work. In 1812 Richard Hotham Pigeon, first treasurer of the Pharmaceutical Society, was admitted to partnership. Both he and his son died within a year or so of each other, so that the firm soon became named Burgoyne, Burbridge, well-known for more than a century. They made pills and salines, and, as they were introduced to pharmacy, capsules and tablets, and what was more, successfully made the move to the manufacture of the newer synthetic drugs, as for example, chloral hydrate which was introduced into medicine in 1869 by Oscar Liebreich.

Better known to the world is May & Baker. In 1834 the partners John May, Joseph L Prickett and Thomas Ship Grimwade started as manufacturing chemists in Battersea, the men having known each other as apprentices in Ipswich. Prickett died shortly afterwards and then Grimwade resigned to take up farming in Harrow where, years later, he took out patents for the evaporation and drying of milk. Grimwade's place was taken by William Garrard Baker, and thus was born the famous initials of M & B. The firm originally made acids, bismuth salts, magnesium carbonate and oxide, mercurials and ceramic chemicals, but later moved on to chloroform, ether, lithium salts, iodides and molybdates, cocaine, strychnine, santonin and ephedrine. Although it is believed that all the young men had obtained their training in retail pharmacies, the age of increasingly large-scale pharmaceutical manufacture had arrived, and it was with this development that they placed their careers.

It is particularly interesting to note that price-rings were organised between these early manufacturers. Robert Biggar of John Maud wrote on a number of occasions to Luke Howard suggesting price-rings. On 17 July 1812 he pointed out that the price of rough camphor had advanced and that it should not be sold at less than 19d per pound, and on 3 December 1818 felt that refined camphor should be priced at not less than £4 10s for a pound weight. Camphor was an important item for both Howards and Maud. The two firms were close collaborators, consulting each other frequently in order to maintain prices. Mercurials were also important to the two of them. Robert Biggar in July 1816 brought up the problem of some new mercurial makers which he dubbed 'The Battersea Chymists' and they agreed on a strategy of how to deal with the newcomers.

Howards also had private agreements with Thomas Henry of Manchester, an apothecary turned chemical manufacturer, and Mander, Bacon & Weaver of Wolverhampton. The cosy arrangements with the latter firm to whom Luke Howard sold mercurials were also being damaged by Cleaver & Walker. In 1808 Luke had come to a price agreement with John Towers of Warner Street, Cold Bath Fields, London, relating to potassium salts. Towers was on the point of separating from Samuel and Thomas Huskisson, all three of them having inherited the manufacturing firm from John's father, George Towers. They had a number of products for which they were famous, including Rochelle Salts, bicarbonate of soda, and aromatic spirit of ammonia. Even in the very early days of the Towers they were well-known for their oxalic acid, one buyer alone taking thirteen hundredweight weekly. John Towers, nevertheless, did not have his father's enthusiasm for the pharmaceutical and chemical industries, so it is not surprising that in 1816 he sold out to Howards. The Huskissons on the other hand went from strength to strength.

Perhaps John Towers was wise, as from 1816 price-cutting was rife and competition fierce. Howards weathered the storm but suffered considerably from the rivalry of MacMurdo & Co in the sale of sodium and potassium carbonates and oxalic acid, whilst Cope & Biddle of Birmingham posed a problem for ammonia. Nevertheless, Luke could write proudly to Goethe in 1821 that he now employed 'over thirty workmen', a figure which rose nine years later to forty-three.

For many years Thomas and William Henry had taken large quantities of tartaric acid from Howards, but were now reluctant. Luke Howard, however, bought much of his Epsom Salts from Henrys so he could fight back – and did. Associated firms often entered into agreements to secure exclusive markets and to exclude potential rivals. Howards began to produce iodine compounds on a large scale in the 1830s, and made an arrangement with Patrick Miller of Glasgow. On 21 July 1832 Miller wrote 'In answer to yours of 18th, [it was agreed that] provided you took from me 4,000 ozs of Iodine at 10½ per oz [sic] every 3 months for a year, I would undertake not only that no Hydriodide of Potash would go to London, but that none would be made in this part of the country as I'm the only maker.'

New dosage forms, new processes, new equipment, new chemicals and new products began to arrive in the 1820s, and rapidly increased in number as the decades went by. A price list of 1841 has 1,300 drugs and galenicals, which included oils, spirits and ointments, 125 'patent' medicines (which was quite modest as Barclay & Son of Farringdon Street who specialised in their manufacture had a list of nearly 500), vegetable dyes and dry powdered colours such as chrome yellow and cobalt blue, sixteen sauces and twenty pickles, some of which like that of Lea & Perrins came to be known the world over.

Allen & Hanburys developed their process of making tinctures *in vacuo* which preserved their active principles; A H Cox devised a pearl-coating for pills which was tasteless; George Meggeson in his pharmacy in Cannon Street, London, was a pioneer in sugar-based lozenges and was one of the first to make medicated pastilles; Alfred Bishop, soon after he started in 1857 at Whitechapel, introduced the more palatable effervescent granules of magnesium citrate, caffeine, iron and arsenic, etc. which proved most successful. Wholesalers of the calibre of Thomas Herring in the Barbican and Aldersgate Street, determined not to be at the mercy of the drug-grinders and their only too frequent adulteration, had powerful drug-mills installed; both ointments and the bulk manufacture of pills began to be made in large mills.

Cocoa butter was introduced in 1852 as a base for suppositories which greatly increased the prescribing of this medication. The soft gelatin capsule arrived on the scene in 1834 and the hard capsule some twenty-five years later, though it was not an instantaneous success, any more than was the compressed tablet. The subcutaneous injection appeared in 1855 which in time led to the ampoule and the tablet triturate.

An important development occurred in 1821 with the arrival of the relatively pure alkaloids and their salts. T N R Morson was the first to make them in this country having learnt the processes whilst gaining further experience in Paris. His 1821 price list shows him to be manufacturing quinine sulphate, morphine acetate as well as emetine, strychnine and brucine amongst other preparations.

In this survey of the early pharmaceutical industry mention must be made of what were named 'Apothecaries' Companies', usually started by a group of doctors, ostensibly to ensure themselves a source of pure drugs. Luke Howard did a fair amount of reciprocal trading with the Glasgow Apothecaries' Company. In January 1819, the Glasgow Apothecaries Company paid Howards just under £213 and at the same time ordered 1¼ hundredweights of mercurials, 28 pounds of antimony tartrate and a hundredweight of tartaric acid; twelve years later, Glasgow sent an invoice for goods supplied of £404.

It can be seen these were not small concerns. The Liverpool Apothecaries Company was founded in May 1836 with a capital of £100,000, its premises comprising a warehouse, chemical and pharmaceutical laboratories, and a retail shop. In about 1855 the General Apothecaries Company in London was founded with, for a short time, a branch in Birmingham, and in 1860 amalgamated with the Liverpool company.

Finally, the manufacturing activities of the London Society of Apothecaries at Blackfriars must be noted. Following the Great Fire of London and its re-building activities, some seventy apothecaries of the Society in 1672 subscribed £1,205 to establish their own manufacturing 'elaboratory'. Society members could buy their requirements at discounted rates, and subscribers received a dividend. After the College of Physicians of London had tried to break the Society's pharmaceutical monopoly with the setting up of its dispensaries, a second joint stock company was formed, known as the Navy Stock. It had a capital of £6,000 and in 1703 was supplying not only the Royal Navy's medicines but was fitting out the naval surgeons' medicine chests. In the later eighteenth century it also supplied the medical needs of the East India Company and the Army for long periods. Manufacture of medicines did not cease until 1922.

Nor must the patent and proprietary medicine trade be totally ignored for in the eighteenth and nineteenth centuries it was big business. The three largest dealers during most of the eighteenth century were probably Diceys in Bow Churchyard, Newberys of St Paul's Churchyard, and Wrays of Birchin Lane, London. Other important London wholesalers who placed their advertisements all over Britain were Thomas Jackson of 95 Fleet Market and his successors the Barclay family, John Wye of 59 Coleman Street, once a partner of Diceys, and Shaw & Edwards who had started out in Borough High Street.

Some of these firms were merely distributors who stocked well-advertised medicines drawn from several manufacturers, but the Sun Fire insurance records show that others were engaged in the actual production. In January 1786 Thomas Barwis of Wandsworth and Hilton Wray of 14 Birchin Lane, London, druggist, became the assignees to the estate of Joseph Gattey and William Waller at 16 Cloak Lane, 'druggists & chymists'. The property included six houses (and the wearing apparel and household goods in two of them), utensils and stocks, a 'madder stove house', 'an iron liquor house', two brewhouses, offices, two drying houses, four warehouses and an 'elaboratory', the whole being insured for £5,900. This may be compared with Joseph Gurney Bevan's insurance policy of £1,000 for Plough Court in January 1783 which comprised 'his now dwelling house, being two houses laid into one', utensils, stock, vaults, counting house, cellar and 'elaboratory'.

The 'quack' medicines would have had little, if any, therapeutic value, but then neither had most of those prescribed by physician or surgeon apothecary; indeed there was often little to tell between them. The 'patent' medicine trade at least had the merit of passing on a knowledge of how to manipulate equipment and mix ingredients in bulk.

William Garrard Baker could claim in 1897 that he was struck by the continuity in manufacturing processes, but much in fact had changed in the pharmaceutical industry. George Schacht of Clifton, North Somerset, correctly bewailed the fact that so few items were made on the premises of English pharmacies in the 1870s because the pharmaceutical industry was becoming increasingly dominant. It had already begun with the isolation of many of the alkaloids in the first decades of the nineteenth century. T N R Morson was innovative enough to make these newly discovered drug entities in the 'back-shop' of his pharmacy at 65 Fleet Market, London. It was not long before its limitations were apparent and he moved to 19 Southampton Row. A close parallel, though a little later, is that of J F Macfarlan and of T & H Smith, both of Edinburgh. They too had begun manufacturing morphine hydrochloride and other opium alkaloids in their back shops and basements in the 1830s, but ten years later had set up factories away from the centre of the town and extended their range of products.

The arrival of the organic synthetics such as acetanilid and phenacetin, the local anaesthetics and the biologicals, the antitoxins and the sera, made it inevitable that the pharmaceutical industry had to move, not only out of the pharmacy to the factory, but into a highly complex organisation with its research, pharmacological and quality control laboratories.

NOTES ON SOURCES

Manuscripts

Archives & Manuscripts, Wellcome Library for the History & Understanding of Medicine: Corbyn, Stacey MSS; Maud, Primatt, Atkinson, Whiffen MSS; Morson MSS
Royal Pharmaceutical Society: Huskisson MSS
London Metropolitan Archives: Howards MSS
Guildhall Library: Records of Sun Fire Insurance, Grocers' Company and Weavers' Company
Library of the Society of Friends: material relating to Jacob Bell.

Monographs

R E W Maddison, 'Studies in the Life of Robert Boyle, FRS', Part V; 'Boyle's Operator: Ambrose Godfrey Hanckwitz, FRS', in *Notes & Records of the Royal Society of London*, 1953, 159-87; Anthony Morson, *Operative Chymist* (Clio Medica, Amsterdam, 1997) – T N R Morson; D F S Scott (ed), *Luke Howard (1772–1864): His correspondence with Goethe and his journey of 1816* (Sessions, York, 1976); A W Slater, 'Howard's Chemical Manufacturers, 1797–1837: A study in business history' (MSc dissertation, London University, 1955); J A Slinn, *Pills and Pharmaceuticals: A H Cox & Co Ltd, 1839–1989* (A H Cox, Barnstaple, 1989); S S Stander, 'A History of the Pharmaceutical Industry with Particular Reference to Allen & Hanbury, 1775–1843' (MSc dissertation, London University, 1965); I K Steele (ed), *Atlantic Merchant Apothecary: Letters of Joseph Cruttenden, 1710–1717* (Toronto University Press, Toronto, 1978); G M Watson, 'Some Eighteenth Century Trading Accounts' in F N L Poynter (ed), *The Evolution of Pharmacy in Britain* (Pitman Medical, London, 1965).

Journals

Chemist and Druggist: 'Thomas Henry, FRS, Inventor of Calcined Magnesia', 1 Dec 1934; 'Development of Burgoyne, Burbridges & Co', 15 Mar 1941; 'The Pharmaceutical Houses of London', 6 Jun 1953; 'An Historic House Removes', 14 Apr 1934 – May & Baker; 'A Tyneside Business Celebrates its Bicentenary', 16 Nov 1968 – Mawson & Proctor; 'London Pharmaceutical Industries', 24 Jun 1933; A Duckworth, 'Rise of the Pharmaceutical Industry', 10 Nov 1959; 'Friends of a Lifetime', 10 Nov 1959; 'More Friends of a Lifetime', 2 Jan 1960; 'The Oldest Pharmacy in London', 31 Jan 1903 – Hooper & Co; 'A Coming Centenary', 30 Jul 1898 – John Bell & Croyden Ltd.

Pharmaceutical Historian: C O'Leary, 'The Elaboratory and Stocks of the Society of Apothecaries', 27, Jun 1997; W E Court, 'The Formulary of a West Yorkshire Pharmacy', 27, Mar 1997; J Burnby, 'The Origin and Development of Pharmacy in North-Eastern England', 25, Sept 1995; A F P Morson, 'Iodine and Pharmaceutical History', 24, Jun 1994; T R Irwin, 'Marion Merrell Dow: Historical perspective of a "merging" company', 24, Jun 1994; G D Hopkinson, 'An Establishment Unique', 13, Mar 1983, 24, Jun 1994; G D Hopkinson, 'Alexander Dalmahoy, Chemist to Her Majesty', 14, Dec 1984; P M Worling, 'Pharmaceutical Wholesaling', 22, Dec 1992; J Burnby, 'Pharmacy in the Mid-nineteenth Century', 22, Jun 1992; A F P Morson, 'Pharmacy in the 1840s: The wholesale chemists & druggists', 21, Nov 1991; W E Court, 'General Practice Pharmacy in the 1840s', Parts I & II, 21, Jun & Sep 1991; R Porter, 'Manufacturing Drugs in the Early Consumer Society: The case of the Corbyns', 20, Jun 1990.

Pharmaceutical Journal: J Burnby, 'The Towers and the Huskissons', 21 Jun 1980; J Burnby & Whittet', 'The Firm of Corbyn & Stacey', 9 Jan 1982; J Burnby, 'Printers Ink and "Patent" Medicines: The story of the Diceys', 14 Aug 1982; L Matthews, 'The Bond Street Apothecaries', Parts 1-8, 27 Aug, 12 Nov, 24 & 31 Dec 1983, 3 Mar, 18 Aug 1984, 5 Jan, 27 Apr, 13 Jul 1985; Savory & Moore; 'Retail Pharmacy Over One Hundred Years', 12 Apr 1941; H E Chapman, 'A Century of Proprietary Medicines', 12 Apr 1941; A O Bentley & F R Mumford, 'Developments in Pharmaceutical Apparatus', 12 Apr 1941; 'Established One Hundred Years', 12 Apr 1941; J Burnby, 'The Family History of Jacob Bell', 21 May 1983.

Others: D Bolton, 'The Development of Alkaloid Manufacture in Edinburgh, 1832–1939', *Chemistry and Industry*, 4 Sep 1976; E Booth, 'The History of the Seaweed Industry, Part 3, Iodine', *Chemistry and Industry*, 20 Jan 1979; J Burnby, 'Common Roots', *Dental Historian*, 12, Oct 1986; J Burnby, 'The Preparers and Distributors of English Proprietary Medicines', *Dental Historian*, 32, May 1997; J Schwitzer, 'The Soda Water Site Explored', *Hornsey Historical Bulletin*, 26, 1985 – T H Dunn of Highgate; R Palmer, 'Thomas Corbyn, Quaker Merchant', *Medical History*, 33, 1989; R & D Porter, 'The Rise of the English Drugs Industry: The role of Thomas Corbyn', *Medical History*, 33, 1989; G Sonnedecker, 'The Rise of Drug Manufacture in America', *Emory University Quarterly*, 21, 1965.

The British pharmaceutical industry since 1851

T A B CORLEY

Centre for International Business History, University of Reading

Britain's pharmaceutical industry, like its petroleum industry, is one which possesses a national comparative advantage both technologically and in the balance of overseas trade; yet it is not easy to delineate. Until quite recently, some member companies also made ranges of different products such as foodstuffs, household goods and heavy chemicals. Moreover, many producers in the UK are subsidiaries of overseas pharmaceutical corporations. Even so, the companies involved do form a recognisable industry, competing among themselves in the field of high-technology health care.

The outlines of such an industry began to emerge in the 1930s but became far more distinct after 1948 when the National Health Service (NHS) was set up. Official policies of actively encouraging the technological leaders – foreign as well as British – at the expense of the less adventurous followers, through its pricing and clinical testing rules for prescription drugs, allowed those comparative advantages to be built up. Vigorous competition flourishes also in marketing and in distribution to retail chemists and to other outlets for both ethical drugs and over-the-counter remedies.

This essay outlines some of the principal changes that have taken place from 1851 onwards in the systems of manufacture and distribution of these medicines. It also addresses the question of how and why the transformation occurred from low- to high-technology production, from small to large scale, and from dependence on imports of advanced drugs to a high degree of self-sufficiency at home.

THE INDUSTRY'S ORIGINS 1851–1914

While the term 'pharmaceuticals' was used as early as the 1880s to describe the core products treated here, successive UK Censuses of Production from 1907 to 1935 classified them as 'drugs, medicines and medicinal products'. Since the first post-war census of 1948, the adjective 'pharmaceutical' has been included in the sub-group of 'Order V. Chemicals and allied industries'. The earlier terminology indicates that during the pre-1939 era, firms making these products fell into three, sometimes overlapping, categories. The first group, comprising makers of galenical or simple compounds of vegetable substances such as aloes or ginger, served the many people in Britain who sought to avoid having to visit doctors for their ills and instead preferred self-medication. In earlier centuries, 'wise women' had often provided alternative health care with herbal remedies. That important role was hijacked by men once doctors and apothecaries began to offer for general sale their own pills and concoctions.[1] Few of these patent or proprietary medicines were in fact patented, but the owners kept their formulae secret.

Among the earliest of such products were Dr Patrick Anderson's Scotch Pills from the 1630s onwards. The most widely known eighteenth-century nostrum was Dr Robert James's Fever Powders, containing antimony and vigorously marketed by the London wholesale chemists and publishers Newbery & Co, of St Paul's Churchyard. By contrast, Dr Samuel Solomon's restorative Balm of Gilead, made of brandy and herbs, enjoyed a few decades of considerable popularity. Then sales plummeted after his death in 1819, mainly because he had not employed a reliable wholesaler.

In 1851, UK patent medicine firms had a combined home turnover of about £250,000.[2] The market leader was Thomas Holloway in London, who that year produced for domestic sale some £25,000 worth of pills and ointment. Claiming to spend £20,000 annually on advertising world-wide, he sold to all outlets with a medicine licence. He had decisively overtaken the pills of James Morison, which for a while in the 1830s achieved annual turnovers of £65,000 but which had been discredited following all too many fatalities attributed to excessive pill doses.

As Table 1 shows, demand thereafter grew spectacularly for these and less well-known patent remedies. As real wages began to rise above the subsistence level from the early 1860s onwards, ordinary people increasingly spent on nostrums for improving or maintaining good health. In 1884 there were estimated to be between 800 and 1,000 makers of 4-5,000 such medicines in Britain, about 19,000 people being employed in their manufacture and distribution.[3] Six years later, according to a separate estimate, no fewer than 2,060 million – mainly digestive – pills were being taken annually in the UK, or one a week for every man, woman and child.[4] Half came from patent medicine manufacturers. The firm of Thomas Beecham, then the acknowledged leader, made 250 million pills in 1890, rising to 308 million in 1915 and close on 500 million in the early 1920s. Many of these firms advertised extensively; Beecham in 1890 spent over £100,000 on all forms of publicity.

The other 50 per cent of pills were made by the second group, the wholesale drug firms. Their pills were generic products, using the formulae from the *British Pharmacopoeia*, published since 1863 under the auspices of the British Medical

Association. These firms dealt in a range of raw drugs and preparations, and extracted alkaloids, such as morphia, from vegetable sources. About the only chemicals they processed were alcohol and acetic acid. A few of their products could act effectively against specific illnesses, as for example quinine – made from cinchona bark – did against malaria, but most were intended to clear the bloodstream or ease pain, and thereby help to build up the body's resistance to disease.

Some of these wholesalers were very old-established 'universal providers' for the medical profession, dealing even in surgical instruments. They included Allen & Hanburys, founded in 1715, Howards of Ilford which dated back to 1797, and Thomas Morson of London, T H Smith of Edinburgh and May & Baker of Battersea to 1821, 1827 and 1834 respectively. They bought their – often imported – ingredients at drug auctions, principally in London. Their laboratories were in the main concerned with drug testing, but they did carry out some limited research: Allen & Hanburys made repeated attempts to improve the process of extracting cod-liver oil. May & Baker as early as the 1880s was assisted by a scientist of King's College, London, in the development of new products such as a cod-liver oil and iron compound.

The third group of firms was dominated by Burroughs Wellcome, a London company established in 1880 by two American entrepreneurs, Silas Burroughs and (Sir) Henry Wellcome. In three respects Wellcome, in sole charge from 1895, operated on very different principles from his more traditionally-minded rivals. He introduced a high standard of quality control, more sophisticated sales techniques – being the first in Britain to arrange personal calls on doctors and to distribute free samples – and laboratories specifically for primary research. The Wellcome Physiological Laboratory of 1894 developed sera and vaccines, most notably against diphtheria, while its chemical research laboratory (1896) evolved a range of fine (refined or specialised) chemicals, including a drug to treat leprosy. In 1914 the newly-established Wellcome Bureau of Scientific Research began investigating cures for a range of tropical diseases.[5]

The British company Evans Sons, Lescher & Webb Ltd (later Evans Medical Ltd), founded in 1902 by merging earlier Evans wholesale drug firms in Liverpool and London, about that date began to make biological medicines for humans and animals; these included sera and antitoxins for diphtheria, tetanus and meningitis. It worked closely with Liverpool University Medical School, with whom it jointly administered the Incorporated Liverpool Institute of Comparative Pathology. The company took over the Institute as a branch when the latter was faced with closure in 1911.

The Production Census of 1907 (see Table 1) found that the combined output of these three groups, in the 'drugs and medicines' category, accounted for only one-third of 1 per cent of the UK's manufacturing production.

Table 1
Pharmaceutical Production in the UK 1851–1992

	Proprietary Medicines (£m)	Other (£m)	Total Pharmaceutical (£m)	Total UK Manufacturing Production (£m)	Pharmaceutical Total UK Manufacture (%)
1851	0.2				
1875	0.6				
1900	1.5				
1907	1.5	3.4	4.9	1,428	0.34
1924	6.7	9.7	16.4	3,336	0.49
1935	7.9	11.8	19.7	3,034	0.65
1951	21.1	88.6	109.7	15,287	0.72
1963	na	na	234.9	27,826	0.84
1970	na	na	512.6	46,304	1.11
1981	na	na	2,618.1	163,937	1.60
1992	na	na	8,531.8	318,568	2.68

Sources: Proprietary medicines 1851–1907. Based on patent medicine duty returns (Inland Revenue); Pharmaceuticals 1907–1970, Business Statistics Office, *Historical Record of the Census of Production 1907 to 1970* (H M Stationery Office, London, 1978); Pharmaceuticals 1981–1992 from Censuses of Production for those years (H M Stationery Office, London, 1983 and 1994 respectively.)

Note: na = not available.

Less than a third comprised proprietary medicines, the rest being fine chemicals and allied products. Most firms traded internationally; exports that year came to nearly 40 per cent of their total output, or almost £1.9 million out of £4.9 million. As retained imports were valued at less than £1.1 million, the industry was a net contributor to Britain's balance of trade.

However, many of these imports were of more advanced drugs, which came largely from Germany, then the world leader in this field. German scientists were carrying out fundamental research on a large scale, often in conjunction with university departments. The most celebrated scientist was Paul Ehrlich, who effectively combined physiological with synthetic chemistry to create a new science of chemotherapy: in those non-intrusive days defined as treating diseases with chemical substances that attacked the harmful parasites without adversely affecting the body as a whole. Ehrlich in 1909 developed the synthetic anti-syphilitic drug *Salvarsan*, marketed by the German firm Hoechst. German firms exerted weight as dominant members of international cartels for a number of widely-used chemicals.

By 1914, the drugs and medicine industry in the UK also included a number of foreign-owned firms, including Hoechst UK Ltd. Although the Patent Act of 1907 gave foreigners protection only if they worked their patents in Britain, German pharmaceutical firms somewhat half-heartedly set up manufacturing branches, using obsolete plant brought over from home.[6] Likewise, the Swiss Hoffmann-La Roche made only slow and limited progress in Britain after arriving in 1909. US firms were then technologically behind the Germans and came a poor third to Germany and Britain in world drug exports. The activities of the UK branches of Parke Davis (1902) and United Drug (1912) were on a relatively modest scale.

Most member firms sold in Britain to chemists and druggists, whose professionalisation was well under way by 1907. Legislation in 1852 had provided for registration of pharmaceutical chemists and an Act of 1868 for qualifying examinations to be set by the (Royal) Pharmaceutical Society of Great Britain, formed in 1841, and for the compilation of a register of chemists and druggists; in 1905 they totalled 15,000.[7] Their work was regulated by the Sale of Food and Drugs Acts of 1875 and 1899.

By the 1890s, a number of multiple chemists' chains had been established, such as Boots of Nottingham and Taylor's Drug Company of Leeds, later part of the Timothy Whites group which in 1968 merged with Boots, to offer cut-price medicines. Their rivals set up the Proprietary Articles Trade Association (PATA) in 1896 to combat price-cutting, and the controversy over prices rumbled on for decades. Many were also members of the London Wholesale Drug and Chemical Protection Society of 1867, subsequently the Drug Club (1891), governing relations with raw drug suppliers and brokers.

For deliveries to retailers, wholesalers used common carriers, sending small consignments through the royal mail; some undertook to fulfil orders on the day of receipt. Many wholesalers started as regional operators, but the leading London firms such as Barclay & Sons (1770) and Sangers (1803) began national distribution once Britain had a comprehensive railway network. These and other large wholesalers such as Evans built up a considerable export trade, through the major ports, most notably London and Liverpool. Speedy responses to orders became increasingly in demand as the number of drugs, especially those required in emergencies, grew; the telephone, and overseas the cable, proved useful here. All these interlocking production and distribution arrangements were to be seriously disrupted in 1914 by the arrival of what soon turned into a total war.

FIRST WORLD WAR AND INTER-WAR PERIOD 1914-1939

The outbreak of war in 1914, while stimulating the demand for patent medicines – often used as placebos to ease stress – brought grave problems to the other sectors of the industry.[8] Heavy exporters, such as May & Baker of bismuth and mercury salts, found their trade decimated when the government, to safeguard home supplies, banned the export of many fine chemicals. London rapidly declined as the world centre of trade in raw drugs. Even more crippling were the shortages of many synthetic and other advanced pharmaceuticals after the cessation of imports from Germany.

An official Committee on the Supply of Drugs set about identifying those available from alternative sources, and the ones whose manufacture would have to be organised from scratch at home, most notably *Salvarsan* and the local anaesthetic *Novocain*. As Britain's technological leader, Burroughs Wellcome offered to the government its entire productive capacity; within a year it had developed a substitute for *Salvarsan*, vital at a time when the numbers of civilians and soldiers infected with venereal disease were soaring. It also manufactured versions of aspirin and of *Urotropine*, used in typhoid cases. The Wellcome Physiological Laboratory made sera and vaccines for the army, while its scientific research bureau stepped up work on antidotes to tropical diseases. Its North American and Australian branches contributed much-needed supplies.

The Royal Society urgently enlisted the aid of university chemical laboratories, which embarked on the production of essential drugs such as *Novocain* and other anaesthetics. From 1917 onwards manufacture was transferred to commercial firms, including Boots and Parke Davis. By then the largest chain of retail chemists in Britain, Boots began to extend its manufacturing capacity from proprietary to pharmaceutical drugs, thanks to the single-minded efforts of the founder Jesse Boot. In 1915 he had set up a fine chemicals department, employing a research team poached from Burroughs Wellcome. Within three years Boots had launched products ranging from antiseptics and anaesthetics to aspirin and saccharin, as well as the tonic *Sanatogen*. Boots thus placed itself on a par with the longer-established manufacturers in the industry.

Evans' wartime activities, while not known in any detail, included a crash programme for drugs. By 1916 it had in operation a new and extensive chemical works, where in the following year it was making its own brand of *Salvarsan*. In 1914 May & Baker began production of the anti-malarial quinine, and shortly afterwards entered the field of synthetic organic arsenicals through an agreement with Poulenc Frérés of Paris to market the latter's *Salvarsan* equivalent. Two years later, having recruited a scientist formerly with Burroughs Wellcome, it started up production of this drug itself.

By the armistice of November 1918, these and other British firms could claim to have overcome, despite plentiful difficulties, the problem of replacing the range of German advanced drugs. However, although the demands of war had introduced many of them to novel techniques and had stimulated in-house research, most were reluctant to remain in these new areas as they feared the renewal of post-war competition from lower-cost German imports. In spite of the efforts made by the Drug Club, they failed to set up an industry-wide research association which would have undertaken collaborative work on common scientific issues. They thus lost out on funds from the Department of Scientific and Industrial Research, created in 1917 to promote applied research throughout industry.

The 1914–1918 war and the UK's subsequent economic troubles did not lead to the creation of an industry dominated by a few giant companies. Instead, firms remained small and family-run. Those business leaders who might have effected large-scale mergers had their attention elsewhere. Jesse Boot had offered to sell his Boots firm to Selfridges & Co Ltd, which had a pharmacy department, and did so in 1920 to the US-based United Drug Company, whose Rexall pharmacies were beginning to invade Britain. Henry Wellcome was heavily involved in an internal reorganisation; in 1924 his firm became part of the newly established Wellcome Foundation. May & Baker, by then claiming to be the UK pharmaceutical leader, was occupied in consolidating its links with Poulenc Frérés. The great national inter-war combines, such as ICI, Unilever and Associated Electrical Industries, each had workforces well in excess of the total number of those manufacturing drugs and medicines. Of the 200 firms in the latter industry in 1935, only thirteen employed more than 500 people. The three leading companies accounted for only 18 per cent of total output.

However, individual firms were tending to build on the Research and Development (R & D) expertise they had acquired in the war. The Wellcome Foundation promoted further innovations in the field of vaccines and sera. Allen & Hanburys expanded its laboratory, and in 1923 began production of insulin jointly with the manufacturing side of British Drug Houses, founded in 1908 as a wholesaler for private chemists. Joseph Nathan & Co, then part of the food industry as maker of the Glaxo milk powder, in 1919 recruited the scientist (Sir) Harry Jephcott to run a small laboratory. He developed types of vitamins, both as additives to the milk products and as medicines in their own right. In 1935 he established Glaxo Laboratories Ltd, which soon began to manufacture liver extract for anaemia.

The most impressive pharmaceutical innovations between the wars came from May & Baker, using French know-how from Poulenc. In 1934 Rhône-Poulenc, as it had become, acquired control of May & Baker, but used its UK laboratories to develop the first sulphonamide drug, *M & B 693*, a pioneer in treating bacterial pneumonia. May & Baker tested this drug in the Middlesex Hospital's laboratory and also in that of the Pharmaceutical Society.[9] ICI initiated a programme of pharmaceutical research in 1936, as part of a diversification plan out of dyestuffs into the discovery of new drugs. In 1944, it set up Imperial Chemical (Pharmaceuticals) Ltd, although for some years the latter's work was hampered by inadequate finance.

Meanwhile Beecham, the only UK patent medicine maker of note which transformed itself into a pharmaceutical giant, was taking the first steps in this lengthy transition process. After the ending of family control and its first registration as a limited company in 1924, its new entrepreneurs set up a laboratory and two years later launched the analgesic Beecham's Powders. The chairman, Philip Hill, thereafter acquired a number of household goods and drugs firms, including those making veterinary medicines. As consultants he engaged scientists of the calibre of (Sir) Jack Drummond and Sir Charles Dodds. Having unsuccessfully bid for research-based companies such as May & Baker (1928) and Boots on its return to UK ownership (1933), in 1937 he endowed the Beecham laboratory in the Royal Northern Hospital, London, for product testing and research and development. In 1938 he purchased Macleans, of toothpaste and stomach powder fame, which had some valuable research facilities.

To allay fears of the UK industry that foreign competition would be damagingly revived after the war, in 1921 the government replaced wartime controls with a key industry duty on imports of synthetic and other fine chemicals; many overseas firms therefore opened branches in the UK. The Swiss CIBA had already established a laboratory here in 1919, and Sandoz came to Britain two years later. American arrivals included Wyeth (1926), Merck Sharp & Dohme (1927), W R Warner (1932) and Eli Lilly (1934). Smith Kline & French entered via an agency agreement with the British A J White Ltd, in 1927, acquiring it in 1956. After the wartime expropriations, German firms were reluctant to set up branches again, and instead marketed their drugs through agents.

By 1939 Britain could be said to have a pharmaceutical industry, with member firms interacting with one another in a more structured way than in the past. Top managers regularly met on specialist committees of the Chamber of Commerce or in the former Drug Club, since 1930 the Wholesale Drug Trade Association. Even so, closer collaboration proved elusive. Two attempts after 1918 to form a joint research body failed as firms were reluctant to share their secrets. Instead, they competed in all aspects except price, most notably in intense publicity and maximising the range of products on offer. UK advertising outlay in 1935 on 'medical goods', including health salts and tonic wine, came to nearly £5.8 million, or 37 per cent of their manufacturers' net sales, exclusive of duty.[10] These arm's-length attitudes came under pressure when war broke out again in 1939.

SECOND WORLD WAR AND ITS AFTERMATH 1939–1950s

Britain's pharmaceutical industry was not caught unprepared at the onset of the new war as it had been twenty-five years earlier. In 1938 the Medical Research Council had compiled a list of essential wartime medicines, such as pain-reducing analgesics and antipyretics to combat fevers. From 1941 onwards the Directorate of Medical Supplies in the Ministry of Supply both oversaw the supply of drugs and arranged for the output in Britain of those most needed. Producers, who had already devoted scarce resources to analysing German drugs, were unhappy at being expected to bear the development costs of possible substitutes.

A synthetic drug to treat malaria being a very urgent requirement, early in 1940 *Mepacrine* was developed as identical with the German *Atebrin*. At the end of 1941, the Japanese conquests in the Far East deprived the allies of cinchona bark for quinine, and with official encouragement May & Baker, ICI and Boots collaborated to make improved anti-malarial drugs, notably ICI's *Paludrine*. Once the Far East became a major theatre of war after 1943, a vaccine against scrub or mite-borne typhus was evolved within six months.[11]

Two other pharmaceutical products received high priority. One was sulphonamide, of which companies at home tripled their output between 1942 and 1945. The other was penicillin.[12] In 1941 Britain's five leading pharmaceutical firms, namely Boots, British Drug Houses, Wellcome, Glaxo and May & Baker, jointly set up the Therapeutic Research Corporation (TRC), to co-ordinate and expand their research capabilities. ICI became a member in the following year. A major task of the TRC was to achieve the government target of meeting the armed forces' entire needs for penicillin, at a time when production still took the form of slow surface culture in pilot plants. At last, official subsidies became available. From December 1943 onwards, six new factories were built with £2 million of government money. As a result, whereas in 1944 penicillin supplies from the US exceeded British output ten-fold, by the end of the war in 1945 production in the UK had overtaken US imports.

British scientists, companies and the government have been criticised for letting slip the opportunity to develop the far more efficient deep-fermentation process for penicillin. However, it was American enterprise and know-how that achieved the critical breakthrough, which allowed the drug to be mass-produced; for a number of years British companies using the new process had to pay royalties to the US companies concerned. The fundamental truth was that for the beleaguered Britain, the paramount aim was 'to win no matter what the cost'.[13] As the historians of Glaxo put it, 'Critics under-estimate the desperate pressure [in the UK] for other drugs to be produced with the limited available facilities, and also neglect the difficulties of the war economy haunted by bombs, manpower shortages, lack of materials and accommodation.'[14]

Instead, other wartime successes of the industry deserve attention. Glaxo, building on its expertise in vitamins, produced vast quantities of Vitamin B2 to enrich imported white flour which lacked the vitamin but took up less shipping space than the whole-wheat variety. In 1941, all British insulin manufacturers combined to maximise insulin yields from the limited quantities of pancreas glands then available. Inter-firm collaboration and improvisation allowed output of pharmaceuticals to continue when plants were damaged by bombing. Raw material supplies, a constant worry for all firms, were allocated by a distribution system agreed between the industry and the Ministry of Supply, and generally held to be both effective and fair. In 1940, on government prompting, a Pharmaceutical Export Group of twenty-seven – later more than 100 – companies was established, to maintain the flow of exports: the annual value of these grew from £3.3 million in 1939 to £4.5 million on average over the next five years. The Finance Act of 1944 at last actively encouraged R & D by allowing such expenditure to be fully offset against tax.

As Table 1 makes clear, the pharmaceutical industry's output grew over five-fold in money terms between 1935 and 1951, or more than two and a half times allowing for inflation. Its stake in UK manufacturing production rose marginally from 0.65 to 0.72 per cent. The leading firms were beginning to pull ahead at the expense of a long 'tail' of lower-technology followers; the proportion of the industry's output from the three largest companies increased by 1951 from 18 to 27 per cent, with workforces averaging 4,400 as against 1,400 in 1935. While 192 of the total population of firms made pharmaceutical *preparations*, of which the top three firms made only 19 per cent, no more than eighteen made the technologically more advanced pharmaceutical *chemicals*, the top three contributing 66 per cent of output.[15] To signify the industry's growing cohesion, in 1948 the Wholesale Drug Trade Association was re-named the Association of British Pharmaceutical Industry, and soon merged with the Pharmaceutical Export Group of 1940. In 1961 it became the Association of the British Pharmaceutical Industry.

In the 1950s Britain was probably second to the US in the size of its pharmaceutical workforce, but no data exist for Switzerland or West Germany. The UK share of large plants, with over 1,000 employees, was 33 per cent of the total, compared with America's 44 per cent. It was during that decade, one of substantial US direct investment in European industry generally, that American companies became significant. The twenty-five firms between them contributed nearly a quarter of Britain's total pharmaceutical output, almost all antibiotics except penicillin, and a range of other ethical drugs and household products. They supplied nearly a third by value of the drugs purchased by the National Health Service (NHS).[16] There were also three Swiss-controlled firms and one (May & Baker) partly financed by French capital.

BEGINNINGS OF THE INDUSTRY TRANSFORMATION 1950s –1970

The rate of structural change in Britain's pharmaceutical industry accelerated markedly in the next few decades. A principal cause was the government's strategy for both pricing and drug safety, which astutely used market forces that induced firms to adopt more advanced technology. As a single (monopsonistic) buyer of prescription drugs for the NHS, the Department of Health aimed to keep the cost to the taxpayer as low as possible, without thereby impeding the flow of new and improved drugs. Under the Voluntary (in 1978 renamed the Pharmaceutical) Price Regulation Scheme from 1957 onwards, it fixed drug prices at levels to allow manufacturers a reasonable return on investment.[17] Its formula encouraged expenditure on innovative R & D that promised to yield good returns, and large exporters received added incentives. It also penalised firms that were merely followers. A number of the latter went under, but the foreign companies, which had previously become used to poaching for their overseas laboratories well-trained scientists coming out of UK universities, were pressured into carrying out more of their R & D in Britain.

Likewise, after a tragic mishap, the government strengthened procedures for the testing of drugs, in a way that benefited the more progressive firms. After the sedative *Thalidomide*, made by the Distillers Company Biochemical, was in 1962 found to be responsible for birth defects, a Committee on Safety of Drugs was set up, beginning work two years later. Its members were academic experts on behalf of the industry. In 1967 the Sainsbury committee on the relationship of the industry with the NHS recommended that quality control and testing should be undertaken by an independent official body; the Committee on Safety of Medicines took over in 1971.[18] Because these successive committees adopted the rigorous standards of the industry leaders, often with American regulations in mind, many surviving smaller firms either ceased to develop ethical drugs or were taken over by more powerful rivals.

In consequence, the number of new drugs launched in Britain fell sharply. However, the proportion of innovative drugs rose from 25 to 70 per cent, at the expense of local or derivative drugs. The former represented a higher percentage of the total flow than in either the United States or France. These deliberate official policies helped to transform the shape of the whole industry.

From 1957 onwards ICI's pharmaceutical division, having been given greater autonomy, stepped up its R & D effort, discovering the anaesthetic *Fluothane* and the anti-convulsant *Mysoline*. By that year, the three largest indigenous companies all had very gifted entrepreneurs who took full advantage of the opportunities created by government.

Sir Harry Jephcott, chairman of Glaxo from 1946 onwards, invested heavily in R & D, by 1955 achieving the synthesis of cortisone and launching a new generation of immunological drugs. He also built up overseas markets across the world except in the US and Japan where he was hampered by earlier agreements. Concerned as they were about the encroachment of foreign rivals, between 1958 and 1967 he and his successor acquired Allen & Hanburys, Evans Medical and British Drug Houses among others, so as to create a British giant capable in due course of challenging the world leaders.

The second entrepreneur was Sir Michael Perrin, a chemistry graduate who in 1953 became chairman of the Wellcome Foundation. Although Sir Henry Wellcome had in his later years promoted some useful innovations, a lack of day-to-day control had led to a period of drift, exacerbated after he died in 1936 by a cash shortage resulting from his substantial death duty bill. It was the largely autonomous American branch which until the 1950s kept the company afloat by earning nearly three-quarters of the profits and developing new products itself. Perrin now ploughed into R & D at home no less than 70 per cent of all Wellcome's profits up to 1970, and like Jephcott vigorously opened up markets overseas.

Unlike the other two men, Leslie Lazell of Beecham was not a trained scientist but an accountant, originally with the R & D-minded Macleans. Philip Hill had died in 1944 after authorising the creation of a central laboratory, but his successor as chairman unwisely diversified into low-earning food companies. When Beecham's profits slumped, Lazell in 1951 was appointed chief executive. By skilful marketing, he built up the profits of household products such as *Brylcreem* and *Lucozade* so as to finance a massive R & D programme, costing £5 million a year by 1970. In 1954 he introduced a plan to make semi-synthetic penicillins; these came on stream from 1959 onwards, among the best known being *Penbritin*. He also invested heavily overseas, at first in the US and later in Europe.

Equally far-reaching developments were taking place in pharmaceutical wholesaling and distribution. Improved punchcard systems helped to cope with the ever higher throughput and stocks arising from the rapidly expanding range of ethical drugs. Now that chemists were dispensing a greater volume of prescriptions, they demanded more frequent deliveries of medicines. A further impetus to reorganisation among distributors was provided by successive official steps to free up competition. In 1956 the government outlawed restrictive trade practices, and eight years later abolished individual resale price maintenance.

To protect their interests, regional trade associations amalgamated in 1966 to become the National Association of Pharmaceutical Distributors, from 1991 the British Association of Pharmaceutical Wholesalers. Not until 1970 did the Restrictive Practices Court give a ruling that administered prices of medicines were legal. Glaxo's acquisitions since 1958 of Allen & Hanburys and other companies had brought extensive wholesaling interests into the group, and in 1966 these were hived off into the newly-established Vestric Ltd. The latter created a network to cover much of Great Britain, and set up custom-built warehouses as hubs of rationalised distribution areas.

MEETING GLOBAL CHALLENGES 1970–2000

During the final three decades of the twentieth century, Britain's pharmaceutical leaders increasingly looked overseas for their future growth. A basic problem for all of them was their small domestic market. As late as the 1990s, only 3.5 per cent of the world's pharmaceutical sales took place in Britain: a far lower percentage than the 33 per cent in the US, 17 per cent in Japan and 9 per cent in Germany. The UK leaders therefore had to compete with their overseas rivals globally, despite the latters' advantages through larger markets and greater financial power. In 1982, no UK leader was anywhere near the top of the world pharmaceutical sales league. Glaxo was eighteenth and ICI, Wellcome and Beecham twenty-third to twenty-fifth respectively; Boots was only forty-second.[19]

Glaxo responded to this problem by selling off the 30 per cent of its assets unconnected with ethical medicines. It was greatly assisted by having, from 1981 onwards, as its best-selling drug *Zantac*, an anti-ulcerant which contributed two-fifths of its turnover, and by ranking fifth in the world market for antibiotics. In 1978 it was at last able to invest directly in the US. By 1994 its US stake comprised 43 per cent of its turnover, as against 36 per cent from Britain and continental Europe.

Beecham, on the other hand, continued to rely on the 70 per cent of output in non-pharmaceutical products to help finance R & D and further expansion. Its attempt in 1972 to acquire Glaxo, which attracted a counter-bid by Boots, foundered after the UK Monopolies and Mergers Commission rejected its argument that only a company with substantial assets could compete in R & D with overseas rivals. The Commission's view was that British companies suffered no handicap from their relatively small size, since research teams of any reasonable scale could throw up worthwhile ideas.[20] Beecham's subsequent policy of further diversification only led to unsatisfactory results. After a radical change in direction, in 1989 it amalgamated with the American company Smith Kline Beckman, partly to spread the escalating costs of R & D. Moreover, marketing costs could be shared, as the SmithKline Beecham combine would become the world's second largest supplier of over-the-counter proprietary medicines.

As for ICI, whereas in the late 1980s pharmaceuticals represented only 10 per cent of the group's total turnover, the success of its anti-hypertension drug *Tenormin* made the pharmaceutical division into ICI's highest profit earner. In 1993 the ICI bioscience group, consisting of the pharmaceutical, agrochemical and specialities division was split off into Zeneca plc. Four years later, Zeneca merged with Astra of Sweden which made the popular anti-ulcer drug *Prilosec*. Wellcome, while still relying on its US subsidiary for much of its profits, in 1981 launched in Britain its anti-viral *Zovirax*, the most successful drug in its history. Then in 1986 Wellcome plc was floated in London, the previous foundation thus becoming a commercial organisation. However, it relied heavily on *Zovirax* and on *Retrovir*, a treatment for HIV and AIDS, and a sequence of disappointing clinical trials failed to turn up satisfactory replacement drugs. In 1995 Glaxo made a successful hostile bid for the company, making the merged Glaxo Wellcome into the world pharmaceutical leader in terms of sales, just ahead of the American Merck. Also that year Rhône-Poulenc took over Fisons, which had already disposed of most R & D operations to overseas buyers, and Boots sold its prescription drug-making interests to BASF of Germany. In one year, therefore, the six top British companies were reduced to three.

In 1998 SmithKline Beecham, then ninth in the world pharmaceutical league, opened merger talks with American Home Products, manufacturer of some useful brand-name drugs. However, these were overtaken by a proposal to merge SmithKline Beecham with Glaxo Wellcome. Huge economies were forecast, both in R & D and in marketing, for example as Glaxo Wellcome's anti-ulcer *Zantac* could be sold jointly with SmithKline Beecham's *Tagamet*. Because important management questions proved impossible to resolve, this most ambitious of all the industry's merger proposals was called off.

For pharmaceutical distributors, the process of change was no less rapid. The Medicine Act of 1968 had required wholesalers to obtain licences, a move that encouraged new entry by outsiders who could well have been less committed to the industry. Particularly affected were the 'comprehensive' wholesalers, standing ready to supply all the listed drugs, many of which were slow movers and therefore more expensive to stock. However, some firms responded positively by seeking greater efficiency. UniChem had been founded in 1938 as a supplier of independent pharmacies and had grown steadily ever since. In 1975 it was the first British wholesaler to introduce the computer system WOLF, or warehouse on-line facility.

When resale price maintenance at the wholesale level broke down in 1979, suppliers attempted to defend themselves through offering favourable terms to chemists who bought all their requirements from them. One casualty of this trend was Sangers, which sold virtually all the businesses it had acquired since 1803 and then closed. A major response, however, was increased merger activity. In 1985 Vestric was sold to AAH plc, originally an anthracite firm with a small health services division. The combine thus created was developed into the first truly national wholesaling organisation. Ten years later, it was acquired by a German firm in the same line, GEHE AG. In 1997 UniChem merged with Alliance Sante SA to create Europe's second largest pharmaceutical distribution company, all customers of which would have access to French, Italian and Spanish, as well as British, drugs. If international amalgamations at the manufacturing level were becoming more common, distribution combines over frontiers were clearly expected to yield considerable economies of scale.

In the latest Census of Production report, that of 1992 (see Table 1), the total value of the pharmaceutical industry's output was seventeen times that of 1970. Its contribution to national manufacturing output had over those years more than doubled. Whereas the industry had spent only £2.5 million in 1949 and £22 million in 1970 on R & D, that expenditure rose in 1995 to £2,000 million, nearly a quarter of the country's total R & D outlay. Of the world's top twenty prescription drugs in 1995, five had been discovered and developed in British laboratories, as had ten of the top thirty-five drugs.[21]

The UK's revealed technical advantage in pharmaceuticals is measured by the national share of patenting in this sector relative to the national share of all non-US patents. If an industry is just pulling its weight technologically in an economy's overall industrial activities, the ratio will be one. The ratio for UK pharmaceuticals was 0.61 in 1890–1896. It then declined to 0.31 in 1920–1924 but recovered in 1940–1959 to 0.62. Then in 1973–1977 it rose to 1.15 and in 1987–1990 was as high as 1.92, nearly double the 1.06 for Germany.[22]

As noteworthy was Britain's international trading advantage in pharmaceuticals. In the mid-1990s their exports were worth no less than £6,000 million, second in size only to North Sea Oil. The pharmaceutical trade surplus with the rest of the world was as high as £2,000 million. The industry employed nearly 75,000 people directly, and about a quarter of a million indirectly. A proportion of this output, employment, R & D and overseas trade came from the subsidiaries of foreign companies, and the present survey should properly address the consequences for the industry and the British economy of this overseas presence in the UK. The Association of the British Pharmaceutical Industry and the Office of Health Economics possess no data. However, the American Pharmaceutical Group, representing all relevant US-owned companies operating in Britain, in 1992 contributed 13.5 per cent of UK pharmaceutical sales, 16 per cent of R & D and 18 per cent of total drug sales in the National Health Service.

CONCLUSION

The pharmaceutical industry in Britain has thus progressed at a rate and in directions that could not have been foreseen in 1851. Substances of vegetable, or occasionally animal, origin have been very largely swept aside as its tools, in favour of synthetic drugs. Named 'magic bullets' by Paul Ehrlich, those have in the twenty-first century improved out of all recognition in their capacity to target specific disorders, while causing as little harm as possible to the patient's system. Yet by the millennium, the industry's capacity to deliver a succession of really novel 'blockbuster' drugs had tended to slow down. Recently, each of the top ten global firms had been introducing less than one such pioneering drug on average every two years. If more and ever larger-scale mergers did not always speed up this flow, an alternative course was that of outsourcing, or purchasing highly specialist know-how from outside. In the mid-1990s, such bought-in fruits of research made up nearly one-fifth of the industry's total R & D expenditure.

In the increasingly vital area of biotechnology, a number of smaller – mainly American – firms had sprung up since the 1980s, particularly concerned with isolating the molecules that could regulate the body's metabolism and eliminate harmful organisms. SmithKline Beecham had been the first giant in the industry to grasp the value of such work, and linked up with the Human Genome Sciences Co. This 'genome' research, into the composition of people's genes, has gone hand-in-hand with 'combinatorial chemistry', to assemble in the most effective way groups of health-providing molecules. In 1994 Zeneca bought into certain disease management and technology firms. Glaxo, in the wake of its merger with Wellcome, followed suit by acquiring its own biotechnological subsidiary.[23]

Early in 2000, the amalgamation of Glaxo Wellcome with SmithKline Beecham was finally announced, to create the largest drug company in the world, responsible for 7.5 per cent of global output. Registered in Britain, it would have its operational headquarters in the United States. The merger would above all help exploit the UK's comparative advantage in the biological field. As, during the century's first decade, pharmaceutical companies world-wide raced to complete the cataloguing of the entire human genome, thus identifying genes and proteins that influence the cause and progress of diseases, the Glaxo SmithKline combine could use its considerable resources and know-how to evolve appropriate new drugs.[24]

Such economic developments would allow the industry to move progressively from curing ills to predictive medicine, or using diagnostic methods to monitor and treat patients, especially those predisposed to certain diseases. When the chairman of Glaxo Wellcome mused on his company's future name being changed to 'Glaxcare', he was looking forward to a time when the industry might well become a true partner, rather than largely a handmaid, in the labour of delivering long-term health care to the nation and to the world.

NOTES ON SOURCES

General surveys: C J Thomas, 'The pharmaceutical industry', in D Burn (ed), *The Structure of British Industry*, Vol II (Cambridge University Press, 1958), 331-75;

A Duckworth, 'Rise of the Pharmaceutical Industry', *Chemist and Druggist*, 172, 1959, 127-39; J Liebenau, 'The Rise of the British Pharmaceutical Industry; *British Medical Journal*, 301, 1990, 724-33; C A Hill, 'The Changing Foundations of Pharmaceutical Manufactoring', *Pharmaceutical Journal*, 134, 1935, 533-5. See also A W Slater, 'Fine chemicals', in C Singer, E J Holmyard, A R Hill & T I Williams (eds), *A History of Technology*, Vol V (Clarendon Press, Oxford) Chap. 14, esp. 317-18.

Censuses of Production: See Table 1. The censuses until 1958 provided lists of the industry's various products; the subsequent absence of such data is to be regretted.

Distribution: E H Shields, 'Pharmacy in Britain from 1859', *Chemist and Druggist*, 172, 1959, 171-9; J B Jefferys, *Retail Trading in Britain 1850–1950* (Cambridge University Press, 1954), 379-99; P Worling, 'Pharmaceutical Wholesale Distribution' (unpublished PhD thesis, University of Bradford, 1988, quoted by kind permission); *Census of Distribution 1950*, Vol I (H M Stationery Office, London, 1976) Table 9A gives data of the outlets; P M Worling, *Vestric: The first twenty years 1966–86* (Vestric, Runcorn, 1986); *NAPD 25th Anniversary* (National Association of Pharmaceutical Distributors, Farnham, 1992).

Patent Medicines: T A B Corley, 'Interactions Between the British and American Patent Medicine Industry 1708–1914', *Business and Economic History*, 2nd series, 16, 1987, 111-29.

Pharmaceutical histories: Allen & Hanburys: G Tweedale, *At the Sign of the Plough* (John Murray, London, 1990). **Beecham:** T A B Corley, 'The Beecham Group in the World's Pharmaceutical Industry', *Zeitschrift für Unternehmensgeschichte* 39 Heft 1, 1994, 18-30; H G Lazell, *From Pills to Penicillin: The Beecham story* (Heinemann, London, 1975); R P Bauman, P Jackson & J T Lawrence, *From Promise to Performance: A journey of transformation at SmithKline Beecham* (Harvard Business School Press, Boston MA, 1997). **Boots:** S Chapman, *Jesse Boot of Boots the Chemists* (Hodder & Stoughton, London, 1974). **Evans Medical:** A E Smeeton, *The Story of Evans Medical 1809–1959* (Evans Medical, Liverpool and London, 1959); C W Robinson, *Twentieth-Century Druggist* (Galen Press, Beverley, 1983); *Chemist and Druggist*, 26, 1884, 326-7; 38, 1891, 148-51; 66, 1905, 46-7; 87, 1916, 57-8. **Glaxo:** R P T Davenport-Hines & J Slinn, *Glaxo: A history to 1962* (Cambridge University Press, 1992); P Girolami, 'The development of Glaxo' (paper presented to seminar at LSE, 1985). **ICI:** W J Reader, *Imperial Chemical Industries: A history*, Vols 1-2 (Oxford University Press, 1970, 1975); A M Pettigrew, *The Awakening Giant: continuity and change in Imperial Chemical Industries* (Blackwell, Oxford, 1985). **May & Baker:** J Slinn, *A History of May & Baker* (Hobson, Cambridge, 1984). **Wellcome:** H Turner, *Henry Wellcome: The man, his collection and his legacy* (Heinemann, London, 1980); R Rhodes James, *Henry Wellcome* (Hodder & Stoughton, London, 1994).

Biographies: Much useful information, and some statistics, can be obtained from entries in *the Dictionary of Business Biography* (Butterworths, London, 1983–86), including the biographies of Thomas and Sir Joseph Beecham, Jesse Boot, James C Eno, Philip Hill,

Thomas Holloway, Sir Harry Jephcott, Leslie Lazell, Sir Michael Perrin and Sir Henry Wellcome. A list of the 'pharmaceutical and toiletries' biographies is in the *Dictionary of Business Biography Supplement* (Butterworths, London, 1986). T A B Corley has written entries on many of these worthies for the *New Dictionary of National Biography* (Oxford University Press, 2004), including Patrick Anderson, Thomas and Sir Joseph Beecham, James C Eno, Philip Hill, Thomas Holloway, Robert James, Leslie Lazell, James Morison and Samuel Solomon.

[1] L Davidoff & C Hall, *Family Fortunes: Men and women of the English middle class 1780–1850* (Hutchinson, London, 1987), 307.

[2] The home turnover is calculated from annual data of the yield from the patent medicine tax, introduced in 1783. Figures of tax receipts 1850–1914, the sources and retail value (not turnover) are given in S Chapman, *Jesse Boot of Boots the Chemists* (Hodder & Stoughton, London, 1974), 203-5.

[3] *Hansard*, 26 March 1884, Vol 807.

[4] *Chemist and Druggist*, 36, 1890, 367; 50, 1897, 125.

[5] J Liebenau, 'Industrial R & D in Pharmaceutical Firms in the Early Twentieth Century', *Business History* 26, 3, 1984, 335-40; idem, 'Ethical Business: The Formation of the pharmaceutical industry in Britain, Germany and the United States before 1914', ibid, 30, 1, 1988, 116-29.

[6] A Hagen, *Deutsche Direktinvestitionen in Grossbritannien 1871–1918, Beiträge zur Unternehmengeschichte*, 97/3 (Franz Steiner Verlag, Stuttgart, 1997), 62-103, 329-38. This supplements the account in L F Haber, *The Chemical Industry 1900–1930* (Clarendon Press, Oxford, 1971), 135-50.

[7] C A Russell, N G Coley & G K Roberts, *Chemists by Profession* (Open University Press, Milton Keynes, 1977), 44-54.

[8] M Robson, 'The British Pharmaceutical Industry and the First World War', in J Liebenau (ed), *The Challenge of New Technology: Innovation in British business since 1850* (Gower, Aldershot, 1988), 83-105.

[9] M Robson, 'The Pharmaceutical Industry in Britain and France 1919–39' (unpublished PhD thesis, University of London, 1989).

[10] N Kaldor and R Silverman, *A Statistical Analysis of Advertising Expenditure and of the Revenue of the Press* (Cambridge University Press, 1948), 147.

[11] M M Postan, *British War Production* (H M Stationery Office, London, 1952), 356-8.

[12] J Liebenau, 'The British Success with Penicillin', *Social Studies of Science* 17, 1987, 69-86, should be read in conjunction with R P T Davenport-Hines & J Slinn, *Glaxo: A history to 1962* (Cambridge University Press, 1992), 138-49.

[13] A S Milward, *The Economic Effects of the Two World Wars on Britain* (Macmillan, London, 1970), 9.

[14] Davenport-Hines & Slinn, *Glaxo*, 143. For vitamin enrichment see ibid, 138.

[15] H Leak and A Maizels, 'The structure of British industry', *Journal of the Royal Statistical Society* (Series A) 108, 1945, 194; R Evely & I M D Little, *Concentration in British Industry* (Cambridge University Press, 1960), 297.

[16] J H Dunning, *American Investment in British Manufacturing Industry* (Routledge, London, revised edition, 1998), 40.

[17] L G Thomas, 'Implicit Industrial Policy: The triumph of Britain and the failure of France in global pharmaceuticals', *Industrial and Corporate Change 3*, 1994, 451-89; G Owen, *National Environment and National Competitiveness: A comparison of the British pharmaceutical and electronics industries* (Foundation for Manufacturing and Industry, London, 1994). I am grateful to Sir Geoffrey Owen for a copy of this very helpful book.

[18] Lord Sainsbury, *Report of Committee of Enquiry into the Relationship of the Pharmaceutical Industry with the National Health Service* (H M Stationery Office, London, Cmd 3410, 1967).

[19] M L Burstall, *The Community's Pharmaceutical Industry* (Commission of the European Communities, Brussels, 1985), 20.

[20] Monopolies Commission, *Beecham Group and Glaxo Group Ltd (and Boots-Glaxo) Report on Proposed Mergers* (H M Stationery Office, London, 1972), 67-9.

[21] For present-day structure of industry see D Hale & A Towse, *Value of the Pharmaceutical Industry to the UK Economy* (Office of Health Economics, London, 1995); A Archer & P M Marshall (eds) *Pharmaceuticals International Year Book 1996* (Cartermill Publishing, London, 1996), v-viii and company profiles; *Association of the British Pharmaceutical Industry Annual Review 1996* (ABPI, London, 1996)

[22] J A Cantwell, 'The Globalisation of Technology: What remains of the product cycle model?' *Cambridge Journal of Economics*, 19, 1995, 155-74. I am grateful to Professor Cantwell for the unpublished data quoted in the text.

[23] *Economist*, 24 January 1998, 76-9; 7 February 1998, 85-6; 21 February 1998 (Survey of the Pharmaceutical Industry), 14-16; 28 February 1998, 81-82; 12 December 1998, 82-7.

[24] *Financial Times* 17 and 18 January 2000, *Economist* 22 January 2000, 77-8.

Archives of the pharmaceutical industry: their scope and use

GEOFFREY TWEEDALE
Manchester Metropolitan University

The modern pharmaceutical industry has a high-technology image. The manufacture of drugs now conjures up glossy pictures of research laboratories, computers, genetic engineering, designer drugs, and miracle cures. This image has been enhanced by the pharmaceutical industry's business performance, which has made it the UK's fastest growing high-technology industry in recent years. The drugs industry − whether it be publicity about the latest advances in cancer therapy, headlines about new drug combinations to combat AIDS, or controversy over the side-effects of certain drugs − is constantly in the news.

The impression is usually given that this so-called chemotherapeutic revolution is a very recent event − say from the 1940s or 1950s − when antibiotics made their great impact and scientists began unravelling cell biology and the physiological mechanisms that underlay disease. However, a closer examination of the pharmaceutical industry reveals that its history extends much further. Pharmacy began when primitive man first employed herbs for dressing wounds, treating infection and relieving pain. As an industry, drug manufacture can be traced to the activities of the apothecaries, who mixed and compounded drugs for the physicians and general populace in the fifteenth and sixteenth centuries. This lineage can be traced through to the activities of those apothecaries who became chemists and druggists in the seventeenth and eighteenth centuries. Some of the latter, when they decided to concentrate on the dispensing and manufacturing of drugs (instead of following careers in medical practice), created a new profession of pharmacy. The pharmaceutical establishment at that time, as represented by the Pharmaceutical Society of Great Britain (founded in 1841), contained men such as William Allen, Jacob Bell, Luke Howard, Thomas Morson, and John Savory. These chemists and druggists provided the springboard for later advances in drug manufacture and the businesses they operated became the forerunners of some of today's pharmaceutical giants.

The archives relating to the history of the pharmaceutical industry, therefore, cover a greater period than one might initially suppose. The records listed in this volume reflect something of the industry's great ancestry, beginning with the roots of the industry in the era of the apothecary and extending to the modern era of multinational enterprise. They also reflect its variety, covering both retailing and manufacturing. Of course, other British industries have roots that go back at least as far as pharmaceutical manufacture – for example, brewing – and they too have left similarly rich collections of records. However, some aspects of the drug industry were different and need emphasis. In particular, very few industries have experienced such a dramatic transformation in either scale or in technological innovation. This in itself makes the industry worthy of attention and increases the value of its surviving archives.

The survival rate of those archives has been somewhat uneven. Historical records for the pharmaceutical industry have suffered their share of neglect and many documents have been lost due to the usual depradations of time and fire. Before the twentieth century, drug manufacture was a small industry, especially when compared to textiles, engineering and coal, and so there has been less documentary material to collect. Since the last war, the industry has experienced controversy as well as success and this has sometimes bred a secrecy that has been inimical to the survival of certain types of records. It should be emphasised at the outset that the image historians have of the industry is very much one that accords with the industry's own view of itself – one unsullied by debates over excessive profits, distasterous drug side-effects, and unethical marketing behaviour. Documentary evidence on these themes has yet to surface and it may never come into the public domain. On the other hand, this has been balanced partly by a good deal of continuity in the industry, despite (or perhaps because of) the number of mergers. Many of the older firms were taken over as going concerns after friendly merger (rather than by bankruptcy) and, while their records often changed location and sometimes disappeared from view for a time, some archives did at least survive. The merger in 1995 that formed the UK's largest pharmaceutical company, Glaxo Wellcome, was also an amalgamation of one of the country's largest group of archives: the records included, *inter alia*, those of Glaxo's root business Joseph Nathan, of companies that Glaxo had absorbed (such as Allen & Hanburys), and also the records of Burroughs Wellcome.

Another factor that has also influenced the survival of records has been the nature of the pharmaceutical business. Even from the earliest days of the apothecary and chemist and druggist, the industry has been typified by a practice of committing things to paper. The apothecaries and chemists who made up drugs would record their ingredients carefully. There would be much weighing, measuring and mixing – all recorded in the firm's laboratory logs and prescription books. This was especially so in the nineteenth and early twentieth centuries, when certain drugs were classed as 'dangerous' and each recipe and order needed to be carefully noted. In the inter-war period, legislation required that a qualified pharmacist should be in charge of the manufacturing and other departments in a business. The Dangerous Drugs Act of 1922, which affected the manufacturing, wholesale and retail sides of pharmacy alike, necessitated the employment of trained and qualified people for carrying out many of its exacting provisions. The Pharmacy and Poisons Act of 1933 further tightened the regulations concerning the selling and dispensing of listed poisons and controlled drugs, which could now only be done by registered members of the Pharmaceutical Society. Regulation meant paperwork: firms now had to keep registers of dangerous drugs and poisons and many of them have survived. Nowadays, the dispensing and licensing controls for drugs are even more extensive. In particular, detailed information on the profile of drugs is amassed and retained, as a precaution against future toxic side-effects. Drug development can take years, proceeding from numerous animal experiments through to human trials, then to complicated licensing applications. Innumerable files are created as a drug is brought to market, which should make interesting reading for future historians, if the records are ever made available.

Other aspects of the industry fostered systematic record-keeping. Both on the buying and selling side, firms had dealings with large numbers of people. An examination of some of the early letter-books of the chemists and druggists reveal the complexity of the trade, even in the eighteenth century. In Britain, firms could find themselves dealing with customers throughout the country: returns came in, usually in cash, from a large number of small accounts. Systematic book-keeping was essential if a business was to prosper. Even as early as the seventeenth century raw materials for drugs often came from abroad. Perhaps the best example is 'Fever Bark' or 'Jesuits' Powder', an anti-malarial drug that was derived from South American tree bark. There were many others: ipecacuanha from Brazil, jalap from Mexico, senna from North Africa and storax from the Far East. Importing raw materials and exporting drugs increased a business's paperwork, as transactions brought with them all the problems of loans, credit, and international exchange.

Finally, many chemists seem to have been attached to their old prescription books, royal letters, and other archives. They were aware of their publicity value and often put them in their shop window or used them for anniversary histories and booklets.

The type of records generated by the pharmaceutical industry have changed as it has evolved. Some documents have survived from the earliest days of the industry, when apothecaries were amongst a gamut of medical personnel available to treat diseases. In the fourteenth and fifteenth centuries, apothecaries held a position somewhat subservient to the physican, who regarded the apothecary as his underling. The apothecary compounded and dispensed medicines which had been prescribed by the physician. Perhaps the most ancient records extant from this early period of pharmacy are fourteenth century apothecaries' medical receipt books, which list the medicines that they compounded and sold. Orginally, apothecaries had been a sub-group within the Spicers, Pepperers & Grocers' Company: however, in 1617 the apothecary's calling was sufficiently important for it to be recognised as an art rather than a mere trade. The Worshipful Society of Apothecaries was formed, which had powers to control the quality of drugs and also – like many trade guilds at that time – to regulate entry into the trade. The Society could grant a formal qualification as an apothecary. This was usually after a laborious seven years' apprenticeship at the end of which the candidate would have been examined about his knowledge and 'Election of Simples', and his preparation, dispensing, handling, commixing and compounding of medicines. Successful candidates would be entered into the court minutes of the Society. These records, now at the Guildhall Library in London, are an important source and continuous record from 1617 onwards. The minutes provide information on individual apothecaries and also the 'genealogy' of the early industry.

Formulating and making up medicines may have smacked of mere 'trade' – a 'mechanical' art distinctly below the education and status of a physician – but this was no drawback to making money. Qualification as a freeman of the Company of Apothecaries led naturally for many into a partnership and business, either as an apothecary or chemist and druggist. Partnership records are amongst the earliest survivals of the pharmaceutical industry and are a sign that a particular business was already becoming too complex to be controlled by one individual. The earliest partnership documents date from about the eighteenth century: a partnership document drawn up for the Corbyn family in 1743 is an example of one of the oldest. Thereafter such agreements become more plentiful, partly because they were legal documents and were therefore kept in a safe place, and also because they were often revised as a partner died, or as new partners joined the business. For example, a run of articles of co-partnership has survived for the London dispensing chemists, Savory & Moore Ltd. These date from 1806, when Thomas Field Savory (who had been apprenticed to a Cheltenham apothecary) became a partner; and there are several others extant that were drawn up as other family members joined the firm. Partnership agreements set out the terms of the business arrangement and typically included the names and status of the partners, their roles within the business, and information on capital and respective shares. In the eighteenth century, these documents could be brief and relatively straightforward; by the nineteenth century, partnership agreements could be more extensive. The other side of the coin are dissolution documents, which again contain a variety of information: valuations of the business and the shares of the partners; inventories of assets and office equipment; and details of the circumstances of the winding up of the partnership. In the case of Savory, there are some half dozen different deeds of dissolution between 1814 and 1851, as various partners came and went.

It is important to remember that until at least the 1890s, pharmacy was essentially a retail trade. Manufacture was not yet a speciality and most enterprises were mainly involved with selling. They were therefore subject to the laws of the market-place and vigorous competition. In the early days of the industry, everyone from the high-street apothecary to the old village crone who brewed herbs in her garden competed for the trade of the sick. In William Hogarth's 'Marriage-a-la-Mode', painted in the 1740s, the French quack (with his exotic – and often painful – nostrums for venereal diseases), the apothecary (with his clyster syringe and bottle of medicament), and the licensed physician (his status apparent from his cane and sword) all make their appearance.

By far the most successful at this time were the quacks – men such as Robert James, Joshua Ward, James Morison and Thomas Holloway – who achieved fame and sometimes notoriety by inventing a proprietary medicine. Although the contribution of these individuals to the development of pharmacy should not be underestimated – indeed many famous manufacturers, such as Beecham can trace their roots to proprietary medicine – it was advertising rather than science that was their forte. Original documents about quacks survive more precariously than company records or laboratory archives. No substantial body of business records is known to have survived for any seventeenth- or eighteenth-century mountebank – the intinerant nature of their trade meant that most probably did not keep many formal records. Likewise, business archives for the subsequent period are scanty. On the other hand, the quacks were good at generating other types of records, which trumpeted their miracle-working nostrums. These included handbills, testimonials and newspaper advertisements. Some collections of these materials survive. The British Library is known to have an excellent collection of handbills from the late seventeenth century. The more prominent proprietary medicine manufacturers also accumulated similar records. For example, Thomas Holloway (1800–1883), the maker of various digestive pills and ointments, left a collection of advertisements and press cuttings. J C Eno, the Newcastle pharmacist, also created similar publicity for his famous stomach-settling drink. These records are often devoid of any hard business information, so that the sales and wealth of the quacks remain difficult to substantiate. However, handbills and advertisements do reveal the role of publicity in pharmacy, the evolution of various treatments, and the nature of public demand. They also provide amusement for the historian, with their hair-raising remedies and extravagant claims and promises.

Some drug formulae were patented (hence the other term by which proprietary drugs were known – patent medicines) and these can provide some information on individual quacks or chemists and druggists. Besides patenting, branding and trade marking were popular. Makers of proprietary medicines and prominent chemists and druggists often registered a mark. By 1875 trade marks had been given statutory protection, with a register of marks and the protection of the laws to counter infringement. The information in trade mark registers is rather narrow: however, court actions over infringement, which generated letters to trade mark attorneys and correspondence relating to counterfeiting can provide information on drug manufacture and the nature of competition. One of the best examples was the action Burroughs Wellcome took against Thompson & Capper in 1903 in the 'Tabloid' case, when Henry Wellcome was victorious against an infringer of his trade name. The case generated a good deal of publicity and correspondence, which can still be read in the company archives.

Some of the more prominent apothecaries and chemists and druggists sold medicines over the counter at their own shops. Like the quacks, they too catered, to a certain extent, for the public's desire for balsams, purges, vomits, pain-killers and the latest patent medicines. But their business practices and compounding methods were more conventional and, though they often charged the customer a premium, their approach was marked by greater honesty. Probity and quality were the selling points, rather than wonder-cures. Quaker druggists in particular – of which there were several – traded much on their ethical stance at a time when swallowing a specific could be a risky undertaking for the patient. These enterprises generated more formal record-keeping and a wider spread of archives; and as the industry began to develop in the nineteenth century these records began to proliferate. New categories of documents came into existence that the more personally-managed business might do without. If the chemist and druggist had a shop, then leases and deeds would be required; and plans would often be drawn up. Partnerships would also generate letter-books, annual valuations of stocks and sales, notes of meetings amongst the partners, financial records between the business and financial institutions such as banks, employment records, and invoices.

In the late eighteenth and early nineteenth centuries, business letters are often the most revealing documents available. Some of the earliest that have survived relate to the more prominent London chemists and druggists, such as Corbyn, Allen & Hanburys and Howard. They reveal that these concerns were relatively small-scale. In the early nineteenth century, business would be run by one of the partners and a clerk, with perhaps a couple of warehousemen and an assistant or two dispensing the medicines. Even by the 1860s, it was unusual for chemists and druggists to employ more than twenty or so. In those days, business was often relatively leisurely and sometimes no more than a dozen letters or so would be despatched in any given day (sometimes less). Sometimes the original letter would be transcribed into a book by a partner and then a copy made for actual transmission by a clerk. Both the Bevans (forerunners of Allen & Hanburys) and Savory & Moore followed this method. More often, letters would be written in a letter-press book – a copy being made by damping an interleaving tissue sheet, which picked up an impression from the ink. Anyone familiar with such press copies will know that they are often very flimsy and difficult to decipher.

Business letters can be frustratingly brief, but at their best they provide information on sales, customers, sources of raw materials, and the ingredients of drugs. Depending upon the idiosyncrasies of the writer and the intended recipient, they can often be discursive and include information on religion, politics and personal life. A feature of early chemists' and druggists' letters is the variety of customers and the wide spread of products. A London chemist and druggist would deal with other druggists and merchants, hospitals, as well as a large number of customers around the country – often supplying them with raw materials as well as drugs. It is important to remember that business in the early nineteenth century was not only confined to drugs, but to all aspects of the chemical trade. Business letters at this time might record the making of fireworks, the manufacture of fluoric acid for glass stainers, ships' chests for seafarers, mineral waters for physicians, essential oils for confectioners, chemicals for professors and laboratories, and photographic chemicals for professional and amateur alike. The pharmacists' technical expertise sometimes meant that they were able to offer chemical analysis for a wide range of other industries. Surgical instrument manufacture was another speciality that can be seen emerging at this time. The trade was already international, with consignments to Continental Europe and also to the West Indies and America. Both the Corbyn and Bevan collections of records contain letters to foreign customers, documenting an overseas trade that was already active by the 1740s.

The more important chemists and druggists were led logically into the manucture of chemicals and drugs. They often had a chemical laboratory on the premises, though it would initially be quite a rudimentary affair with furnaces, a still, a workbench and various bottles and shelves for storing and mixing chemicals. A laboratory would also have a book in which each day's work was carefully noted. Early laboratory notebooks for these firms are rare, but provide invaluable information on the scale of operations and methods of manufacture. Typically, a laboratory notebook provides information on each batch of medicine or chemicals. Each entry would note the source, the date, the ingredients, the quantity and their price. A major factor in drug manufacture, then as now, was the invisible input: the time, knowledge and experience needed to make a medicine. Entries usually therefore indicate the cost for 'attendance' – labour. Chemists and druggists were still rooted in the empirical age of pharmacy which involved the preparation of natural medicaments from plants. Partners in these businesses were much concerned with plants: importing them, researching them and cataloguing them. This interest spilled over into their notebooks, personal letters and published articles.

Most drug formulations were taken from a pharmacopoeia. In 1618 the first *London Pharmacopoeia* was issued by the Royal College of Physicians and was enforceable on all apothecaries. These books were regularly revised and each laboratory would usually have several of these volumes, many of which have been passed down to us. Occasionally, they would contain annotations or the compounder's own variations. Sometimes, too, the druggist would have his own volume of formulae.

Overlapping with laboratory records are formularies and prescription books, which have survived in relatively large numbers. In these books, the chemist and druggist recorded each prescription as it was made up. The survival of these records may relate to a number of factors. First, they were sometimes large (and occasionally massive) bound volumes that were not easily mislaid. Second, they were an important source of reference for future prescriptions and also a record of past transactions, which could be quickly cross-checked if something went wrong. Third, even as their usefulness declined, they were often passed down through a business because of their historical interest. Pharmacists themselves have sometimes developed a fascination with the early history of their trade and methods of compounding drugs.

Whatever the reason for their survival, prescription books often provide an important run of information. At a more general level, they give some indication of the activity and the direction of a business. It is sometimes possible to analyse the number of prescriptions dispensed each year. Patients or customers are often identified by name, trade or profession, and sometimes addresses are provided. These could include members of the ordinary public, prominent institutions, the Army and Navy, titled personages, even royalty (as some of the London firms, such as Savory, dealt directly with the Royal family). Other questions can be posed and sometimes answered. Was the business or shop mainly concerned with making up proprietary medicines or its own range of drugs and galenicals? Were the recorded formulae medical, cosmetic, veterinary or domestic? What type of preparations were dispensed: mixtures and draughts, pills, powders, or lotions? What type of diseases were being treated predominantly: stomach complaints, fevers, sore throats, toothache or skin disorders? From where did the prescriptions originate: physicians, textbooks and journals, or the chemist's own formulation? Although there is a certain sameness about prescribing and manufacturing drugs in the nineteenth and early twentieth century the detailed nature of the entries in prescription books enables pharmaceutical historians to estimate the efficacy of many treatments and also the knowledge of the industry's early practitioners. Much work remains to be done on early prescription books, but some that have been examined in detail show that considerable skill was needed in the formulation of medicines. Chemists, despite their lack of formal medical training, were able to use their own experience to provide both their customers and patients with a wide range of mostly useful medicines that laid the modern foundation of the pharmaceutical industry.

This does not exhaust the different type of records that are available from the early days of the industry. Circulars and business cards told customers about changes of location or partnership. So-called 'waste-books' were used for recording details of wholesale and overseas sales. Day-books, such as one might find for any manufacturing or retail business, recorded retail sales from the shops. Weight-books recorded – as one might suppose – the weights of articles received from other firms. Where they survive, such records can provide many insights into a business. Even something as mundane as a selection of company invoices can be useful, providing information on prices, products and customers – perhaps even an illustration showing the exterior of the shop or factory layout.

Occasionally, diaries, letters and personal notebooks have survived relating to the leading members of the firm. Many chemists and druggists were involved in the scientific movements of the day and also took part in pharmaceutical politics, as their trade became professionally organised. Some professed an interest in subjects such as chemistry and botany: they corresponded with leading scientific figures, attended lectures, and filled their notebooks and letters with references to the latest scientific advances or new drugs. Others described their foreign travels or searches for rare plants and drug treatments in distant countries. For example, the personal and private letter-books of Henry Wellcome provide information on the development of his business, his interest in scientific research, and his activities as a philanthropist and collector. Occasionally, the manuscript memoirs of a partner shed light on the early history of a company. Letters from scientists not directly employed by the business can occasionally surface in company records: thus Humphry Davy ordered chemicals for his experiments from William Allen; Joseph Lister corresponded with companies about antiseptic materials.

By the late nineteenth century, the modern pharmaceutical industry can be seen to be emerging more clearly. This was due less to brilliant scientific advances, than a rising population and standard of living, which greatly increased the customer base. Chemists and druggists transformed the scale of their operations in the period between 1850 and 1914; while the retailing sector of the industry also expanded dramatically. Business documentation was also transformed as partnerships (with unlimited liability) gave way to incorporated companies with limited liability. The latter continued to generate many of the same type of documents as had the previous business – articles of partnership, minutes, letters, ledgers, and financial reports. This is not so surprising as many firms remained under the same control (usually under one family), even after the shareholding of a firm became more dispersed. However, the legal form of incorporated business did foster the introduction of new sets of records and greatly increase the scope of old types of documentation. Limited companies generated articles of association, board minutes, registers of ordinary and preference shareholders, proxies, annually published accounts and reports, notices of meeting and chairmens' speeches. It is no coincidence that the bulk of the records listed in this volume date from the late nineteenth century onwards.

Board minutes usually became more formal and more detailed once a business adopted limited liability status. Full board meetings would take place at regular intervals – say once every month or two. The minutes would note the date of the meeting, list those present, and sometimes recap on the details of the last meeting. 'Matters arising' would then be dealt with systematically. The range of subjects would typically be very wide and could include anything that came within the scope of that business, from the important to the mundane. Sales and financial returns might be discussed; the opening of new offices and extensions; costs of raw materials for drugs; employment problems; retirements; wages and labour turnover; foreign competion – the list is almost endless. At their best, company minutes can provide a detailed overview of the business, with easily-found information on company growth and finance. However, much depended on the energy and thoroughness of the individual who kept the minutes. The number of richly detailed board-minute volumes is easily outweighed by others which are frustratingly short and tedious and merely list matters that had been 'resolved', with only a very brief commentary. Even the most voluminous nineteenth-century minutes often become much briefer by the inter-war period.

In this case, the most illuminating documents are the board papers – the documents prepared before each meeting, so that the company directors were satisfactorily briefed. These are potentially more useful than the minutes: not only are they usually much more voluminous, but they also give some idea of the various options that were considered before major decisions were taken. They therefore often give some clue as to why certain strategies were adopted, and others discarded. Unfortunately, board papers have not survived as well as company minutes: they were more bulky and were rarely bound. Usually, it is the board minutes which provide the data from which the business historian has to reconstruct a business.

Linked to the board minutes are other bound volumes and papers that show how ownership and control was spread. Share issues generated a large amount of paperwork. Various share registers show in great detail who owned the business; dividend lists show the share-out of profits; new share issues resulted in Stock Exchange papers and correspondence about debentures.

Not all companies were successful and some were eventually dissolved. If they were registered under the Companies Act, then a record of the dissolution of such companies would be made to the Board of Trade. The company files for England and Wales are now located at the Public Record Office (BT41 and BT31) and for Scottish firms in the National Archives of Scotland (BT2). These files can contain the constitution and articles of association, registered address, data on nominal share capital, information on directors, share capital and shareholder returns, annual balance sheets, and documents detailing the liquidation. Unfortunately, tracing an individual company, especially if it was private, is made difficult by the Public Record Office's policy of heavily weeding files. Even in the twentieth century, pharmaceutical manufacture remained a very diverse business. Firms could be involved in both retailing and manufacturing; and even those that specialised sometimes had little in common with each other. Some concentrated on household medicines, such as cough syrups and embrocations; others on malted foods and drinks; and some on veterinary products. Some of the leading chemists and druggists – firms such as Evans Sons, Lescher & Webb (later Evans Medical) – were self-styled 'universal providers', who aimed to supply *everything* for the prevention and treatment of disease 'in man or beast.' Such firms not only provided medicaments, but also chemists' sundries (i.e. everything that was not practically a medicine, such as bedpans, scales, scalpels and even complete operating theatres). Separate product divisions evolved: some were involved in retailing, some in drug manufacture, and others in some linked business. Surgical instrument manufacture was for some firms a logical step for a business which was closely linked with the medical profession. These divisions would be at a separate locations, have their own managers, and generate their own records – though progress reports would often be included in the board papers.

More importantly, before 1914 the UK pharmaceutical industry had taken its first steps towards multinational status with the opening of overseas subsidiaries. Colonial markets – Canada, South Africa and Australia – were the favourite destinations before the First World War, though some firms were also active in Russia, South America and India. Usually, British multinational activity involved the opening of selling agencies rather the launch of manufacturing operations. The trade can often be tracked in letters from agents, or the overseas reports of UK directors after they had paid the occasional visit. In the twentieth century, the scale of operations overseas began to increase and eventually some firms did begin manufacturing overseas. Foreign subsidiaries now began providing their own annual reports and financial data. It is important to emphasise that this process had a mirror-image: the creation of subsidiaries in the UK by foreign firms or entrepreneurs. Glaxo and Burroughs Wellcome are examples of this trend. International agreements were also important to the emerging British industry. Cross-licensing was popular amongst some firms, who until after the 1950s often needed overseas expertise to market competitive products.

Also in the twentieth century, merger played a significant role in the evolution of the industry, especially after 1945. At the end of the Second World War, the British pharmaceutical industry still had a Victorian air. Many of the old names were still operating with their popular pastilles, cough syrups and ointments; the industry was still highly fragmented; and it was still very reliant on licensing from the world leaders, the USA and Germany. Scientific advances and the growth of the UK market (triggered, *inter alia*, by the birth of the National Health Service) attracted American drug companies which soon shouldered aside the British competition. One defensive reaction was a merger movement amongst the leading firms, which saw the birth of a few leaders with the ability to switch to research-based drug manufacture. Merger activity provides a rich crop of records for the business historian, both published records and those generated within the business. Papers relating to a merger provide information on the negotiations prior to the transaction, besides detailed valuations of assets, and estimates of the future prospects for the merged company. Sometimes detailed reports have to be submitted to the government, especially if the Monopolies and Mergers Commission takes an interest in the proceedings. If a merger is successful, detailed rationalisation plans are often executed, with closures, fresh capital expenditures (or cost-cutting) and job re-deployments.

A significant feature of the modern UK pharmaceutical industry – and some would say the major reason for its success in recent years – has been the development of science-based research. It was not always thus. Germany and America made most of the major scientific advances before the Second World War and only a few firms – such as Burroughs Wellcome and Glaxo – had a significant interest in research and development. After 1945, this picture was transformed. Recently, the British pharmaceutical industry has emerged as one of the world leaders in pharmaceutical research, with a number of major technical and commercial successes to its credit. The story of this transformation is to be found in a variety of research reports and laboratory notebooks. Research into drugs usually began quite modestly at most companies, with perhaps a few trained staff in a small laboratory. Details of experiments and other data would be recorded in chemist's and pharmacist's diaries; and also various laboratory logbooks. Henry Wellcome's business, which was a pioneer in pharmaceutical research (its Physiological Research Laboratories were founded in 1894), generated a number of such diaries and notebooks, which are extant from about the turn of the century. By the inter-war period, research in some of the leading companies was becoming more formal and extensive. Wartime work on penicillin undoubtedly gave the industry a push in this direction.

The collection of May & Baker (now part of Rhône-Poulenc) gives an indication of the type of archives that can be generated by the research activities of a leading firm. These include: committee minutes and research reports relating to the chemotherapeutic research division between 1943 and 1947, especially concerning chemists engaged in penicillin synthesis; documents on research programmes between 1946 and 1963; files on the appointment of research associates and research grants; and material relating to the design of overseas research laboratories.

Within the last decade or two, research and development has become the dominant and best-publicised activity by the industry leaders. Thus pharmaceutical archives, which up to the 1950s, are heavily slanted towards various aspects of marketing, advertising, patenting and production, now tend to be filled with documents involving research and development. As more funding was poured into the search for new drugs, the status of research and development rose and separate research divisions began operating, which had their own budgets, research plans and strategies. Beecham Research Laboratories, founded in 1945, is a good example. Historians can track the development of this initiative through the proposals and correspondence in 1943 relating to the Laboratories' formation; through the memoranda and papers relating to the organisation and costs; through the register of members and share ledger; the research committee minutes between 1948 and 1949; and the general meeting minute books between 1945 and 1982. Schedules of the research programmes; conference memoranda; papers on research fees; an address by Sir Alexander Fleming at the official opening in 1947 – these are a few of the miscellaneous documents that help build up the picture.

On the other hand, it is important to emphasise that the pharmaceutical industry has retained an important retailing sector. For many of us, our point of contact with pharmaceutical products remains the local chemist's shop or chain store. Sales of indigestion remedies, pain-killers, throat-pastilles, vitamin pills, and first-aid items are still a major sector of the market. Hundreds of retail outlets sell and dispense these medicines and hygiene products. The records of the retailing side of the industry have a different flavour than the high-technology wing. There is, for one thing, more emphasis on property. Opening a shop involved tenancy agreements and leases, such as those that survive for Savory & Moore. Boots has property deeds relating to many of its premises; there are architects' plans and drawings (even archaeological records) relating to various branches of the Boots' firm; and staff records, prescription books, and price lists abound. Papers relating to other aspects of branch management survive for the Portsmouth retail chemists, Tremletts: these include insurance, branch purchase, and building and repair work.

All pharmaceutical businesses – whether in retailing or manufacturing – generated a good deal of other materials useful for the historian. One can include under this head old photographs, volumes of press cuttings, celebratory brochures, cartoons, display cards, personal reminscences and retirement presentations. Academic historians may consider these less high-grade than primary manuscript materials, such as old letter-books and board papers. However, they are still 'archive' material and their ephemeral nature should not be allowed to belie their usefulness. It should be stressed that the pharmaceutical industry was a pioneer in advertising techniques. Firms led by Beecham, Holloway, Eno, and Boot became experts at running advertising promotions, devising striking brochures and trade advertisements. Many of these survive in company archives or at institutions such as the History of Advertising Trust. To give only one example, The Sequah Medicine Co, a London manufacturer of patent medicines, published a penny newspaper, *Sequah Chronicle*, in 1890–1891, which contained advertisements, short stories and jokes.

Trade catalogues also had a promotional element and were produced in some number. They varied in size from the slim booklet to the heavyweight tome, with hundreds of pages and thousands of illustrations. Often they were never copyrighted and so they may only be found in a company archive. Old pharmaceutical trade catalogues contain a greater spread of information than one might suppose. The introductory sections can give details and illustrations of company agencies and trading outlets, with perhaps brief historical details; product lists can be invaluable for comparing prices with those of competitors; and the illustrations can provide important background on everything from, say, the recipes for nerve tonics to the evolution of surgical instruments.

Other ephemeral archives are no less important for illuminating the social history of pharmaceutical companies. Labour records are still a much neglected source and tend to be overshadowed by the data emanating from the men 'on the bridge' or in the research laboratories. Wages and salary books, pension scheme data, personnel records, office and staff rules, and materials on workers' safety and occupational health are all important sources to be considered. The Boots archive, for example, contains information on an athletic club, various welfare and sporting activities, Boots college and the booklovers' library, and staff training programmes. Many of the larger companies – in common with firms in other British industries – ran a staff magazine. Allen & Hanburys, for example, published *Plough Magazine* (named after its trade mark) in the 1920s. It featured descriptive tours of the branches, reminiscences, news of the latest products, photographs, obituaries, and details of staff events, such as holiday outings and staff promotions. If the historian is lucky, then a company archive may also have archive film of its past activities or influential personalities.

Researchers delving into the history of the pharmaceutical industry are also likely to encounter oral history sources. Historians of pharmacy are lucky in having a wide range of reminscences available in pharmaceutical journals. The *Pharmaceutical Journal* (founded in 1841) has a tradition of publishing recollections of retired chemists and (sometimes) industrialists. Published descriptions of 'notable pharmacies' have also appeared in the *Chemist and Druggist*. The Pharmaceutical Society of Great Britain launched a series of tape-recorded interviews with prominent pharmaceutical personalities in 1970. By 1996, some forty-five recordings had been made, including several leading industrialists and research directors, such as Sir Harry Jephcott and Sir David Jack. In 1991, when the Royal Pharmaceutical Society celebrated its 150th anniversary, members of the Nottingham branch commemorated the occasion by interviewing and taping local pharmacists. A more extensive project, a twentieth-century 'Oral History of British Community Pharmacy Practice,' was launched in 1995 by the London School of Hygiene & Tropical Medicine with the aid of

Wellcome funding. Oral history often promises much, but can sometimes disappoint. The quality of the recording, the skill of the interviewer, the candidness of the subject, the reliability of memory, and the length of the recording – all these can vary greatly. Nevertheless, this medium has much to offer and more recordings are needed.

Underpinning the rise of pharmacy as major industry was its emergence as a profession. This involved the establishment of a number of organisations designed to regulate and raise the status of the chemist and drug manufacturer. Overlapping with these professional organisations were several bodies which aimed to regulate the industry and protect it from the competition.

The first organisations that represented the emergent pharmaceutical profession – the Worshipful Society of Apothecaries and the Royal Pharmaceutical Society of Great Britain – have already been mentioned. The Society of Apothecaries still exists and still offers diplomas in pharmacy; however, the main body for registering and regulating pharmacists is the Royal Pharmaceutical Society. It contains a wealth of records on the industry (indeed it has its own extensive archives and library). Many of these are of a formal nature relating to charters, grants of arms, registration and class lists, prizes and leases and inventories. However, the Society has played an important role in pharmaceutical education, law, ethics, and science. Operating through a host of committees and specialist departments, the Society has generated a large number of working party reports.

The Proprietary Articles Trade Association, since its founding in 1896, has promoted resale price maintenance. Its activities are recorded in its minute books, which contain annual reports and accounts; a journal, *The Anti-Cutting Record*; and correspondence with various government departments, such as the Board of Trade. Meanwhile, the Proprietary Association of Great Britain, founded in 1919, looks after the interests of proprietary medicine and food manufacturers. It has a similar spread of records to the Royal Pharmaceutical Society of Great Britain, covering its committees and submissions to government enquiries. Representing the interests of the retail chemists is the National Pharmaceutical Association, established in 1921, the records of which provide information on topics as diverse as trade marks, sickness insurance, marketing, price-setting and industrial relations.

Beyond company and trade association archives, details about pharmacists themselves are found in wills and other civil registration records in local and national repositories. Additional information can be found in sources such as the ledgers of the Sun Fire insurance companies, now held at the Guildhall Library, London. Local directories and rate books; local plans and antique maps; and photographs offer other kinds of documentation. The trade press is another extremely valuable, and often neglected source, which provides a mine of information. The *Chemist and Druggist*, for example, published advertisements, obituaries, trade news, company profiles, illustrations, details of new drugs and processes – even articles on pharmaceutical archives.

Here we are drifting away from purely 'archive' material into the realms of printed and published work, though often with uncopyrighted material – such as company magazines and trade catalogues – the line is not clear cut. Many of these external business sources are also, of course, not unique to the pharmaceutical industry. However, the latter does have one characteristic which it does not share with other industries: historians have still to research extensively the available archive material. More company histories are needed as well as more thematic works; and, as yet, there is no single-volume on the history of the British pharmaceutical industry. This guide demonstrates that the lack of writing on the subject is not entirely due to the paucity of archives.

Select chronology of pharmaceutical legislation

1617 Apothecaries Act: Allowed apothecaries to break away from the Grocers' Company of the City of London and to establish their own guild, The Worshipful Society of Apothecaries of London. The Society was charged with the duty of improving the quality of drugs available to the public and regulating the qualifications of dispensers.

1815 Apothecaries Act: Allowed apothecaries to trade as medical practitioners and stipulated that they must serve a seven year apprenticeship. The Worshipful Society of Apothecaries was charged with the duty of regulating the qualifications of medical practitioners. Made way for a new group, chemists and druggists, legitimately to prepare and dispense medicines.

1851 Arsenic Act: Required vendors of arsenic to keep a register of sales of the poison. (In theory the seller was supposed to know the buyer and to mix soot or indigo with the arsenic to prevent its use in food.) The act was, however, poorly enforced.

1852 Pharmacy Act: Enforced compulsory registration of pharmaceutical chemists (those who had passed the major examination of the Pharmaceutical Society of Great Britain, or who were members of the Society prior to 1852), and introduced a statutory annual register of pharmaceutical chemists.

1858 Medical Act: Established the General Medical Council, which replaced the Worshipful Society of Apothecaries as the chief regulator of general practitioners, and which was charged with the duty of producing the first *British Pharmacopoeia*.

1868–1869 Pharmacy Acts: Regulated the sale of poisons through the introduction of a *Poisons List*, and compulsory labelling of poisons. Unlawful for anyone other than a pharmaceutical chemist or chemist and druggist to sell poisons. (A loophole in this law meant that limited liability companies, which used the titles pharmaceutical chemist or chemist and druggist falsely, could not be prosecuted, due to their status.)

Enforced compulsory registration of chemists and druggists (those who had passed the minor examination of the Pharmaceutical Society of Great Britain, the minimum requirement necessary to practise as an assistant), and introduced a statutory annual register of chemists and druggists.

1908 Poisons and Pharmacy Act: Decreed that limited liability companies were liable to the same legal action as other business if they used pharmaceutical titles falsely in order to sell medicines or poisons.

1917 Venereal Diseases Act: The first of a series of acts which attempted to reduce the number of expensive and rarely effective secret remedies on the market. Prevented the sale and advertising of remedies for venereal diseases, except by medical practitioners.

1920 Dangerous Drugs Act: The first in a series of acts which decreed that an individual had to hold a prescription provided by a physician or other health official in order to be supplied with a dangerous drug such as cocaine, morphine or the opiates.

1925 Therapeutic Substances Act: Stipulated that vaccines, sera and toxins had to be tested and deemed safe before they could be licensed and sold. Manufacturers of such substances were required to hold a licence.

1933 Pharmacy & Poisons Act: Established an annual register of pharmaceutical premises, and created a statutory committee of the Pharmaceutical Society of Great Britain which was endowed with the power to remove offending pharmacists from the registers of pharmaceutical chemists and chemists and druggists, and to reinstate individuals formerly barred. Membership of the Society became a compulsory feature of registration as a pharmacist.

Established a government advisory committee, the 'Poisons Board', and isolated a new class of 'medical poisons' which could be sold only by a registered pharmaceutical chemist or chemist and druggist. Regulations concerning the sale of agricultural and horticultural poisons were relaxed so that they could be sold by any shopkeeper.

1939 Cancer Act: Prevented the sale and advertising of remedies for cancer, except by medical practitioners.

1941 Pharmacy & Medicines Act: Prevented the sale and advertising of remedies for Bright's disease, cataracts, diabetes, epilepsy, glaucoma, paralysis and tuberculosis. Decreed that the contents of medical containers must be disclosed.

Select chronology of pharmaceutical legislation 51

1947 Penicillin Act: Decreed that the antibiotic penicillin could be supplied only by medical practitioners or on prescription.

1953 Therapeutic Substances (prevention of misuse) Act: Decreed that a further range of antibiotics could be supplied only by medical practitioners or on prescription.

1953 Pharmacy Act: Abolished the minor examination of the Pharmaceutical Society of Great Britain which led to qualification as a chemist and druggist, and decreed that intending pharmacists must pass the major examination of the Society or a degree in pharmacy. Separate registers of chemists and druggists and pharmaceutical chemists were replaced by one annual register of pharmaceutical chemists.

1956 Therapeutic Substances Act: Replaced the 1947 Penicillin Act and the 1953 Therapeutic Substances (prevention of misuse) Act, bringing regulations concerning the manufacture and supply of antibiotics together.

1963 Report of the Dunlop Committee: Introduced a scheme whereby pharmaceutical companies voluntarily tested their own products and presented the results before a sub-committee of the Dunlop Committee. This committee decided whether the testing method justified a clinical trial, and if so, following the trial, decided whether the drug was safe for public release. Companies were not obliged to participate, but details of those that did not were presented to doctors and prescribers of drugs with a warning. Until the 1960s there had been no body which had to be satisfied on standards before a pharmaceutical product could be launched. The *Thalidomide* tragedy of 1962 focused public attention on the potential hazards of this lack of control.

1964 Drugs (prevention of misuse) Act: Decreed that it was an offence to unlawfully possess amphetamines and some other drugs and narcotics.

1968 Medicines Act: Repealed the 1933 Pharmacy and Poisons Act and decreed that scientists must hold a product licence before launching a new pharmaceutical drug. Such a licence could be acquired only by satisfying the licensing authority of the quality and safety of the product. Manufacturers of such products were obliged to hold a manufacturer's licence and to have their premises inspected by government inspectors. Wholesalers had to hold a dealer's licence to demonstrate that their premises were suitable for the storage of medicines.

Prohibited the advertisement of specific products for the treatment of named diseases and decreed that all medicinal containers, labels and advertisements must be inspected and approved by the Pharmaceutical Society of Great Britain and by local authorities. Retail pharmacists were obliged to keep a register of every sale or supply of a prescribed drug (unless a contraceptive), and to retain these registers for two years after the date of the last entry.

Select bibliography

This bibliography contains general histories relating to the pharmaceutical industry. It does not contain histories of individual companies or businesses which are to be found at the end of the main record entries of the company or business concerned.

Books and articles

F J Anderson, *An Illustrated History of the Herbals* (Columbia University Press, New York, 1977)
S Anderson, 'I Remember it Well: Oral history in the history of pharmacy', *Social History of Medicine*, 10, 2, 1997
K Arnold-Forster & N Tallis, *The Bruising Apothecary: Images of pharmacy and medicine in caricature* (Pharmaceutical Press, London, 1989)
J K Aronson, *An Account of the Foxglove and its Medical Uses 1795–1985* (Oxford University Press, London, 1985)
J Bartle, *Pills, Potions and Powders: A short history of Penrith pharmacy from 1600* (Whin Brow, Penrith, 1990)
J Bell & T Redwood, *Historical Sketch of the Progress of Pharmacy in Great Britain* (Pharmaceutical Society of Great Britain, London, 1880)
M Bliss, *The Discovery of Insulin* (Harris, Edinburgh, 1983)
P Boussel, H Bonnemain & F Bove, *The History of Pharmacy and the Pharmaceutical Industry* (Askelepios Press, Paris, 1983)
W W Breckon, *The Drug Makers* (Eyre Methuen, London, 1972)
D R Browning, 'The Pharmaceutical Industry' in C A Heaton (ed), *The Chemical Industry* (Blackie, Glasgow, 1986)
J G L Burnby, *John Sherwen and Drug Cultivation in Enfield: A re-examination* (Edmonton Hundred Historical Society, Enfield, 1973)
J G L Burnby, *Plague, Pills and Surgery: The story of the Bromfields* (Edmonton Hundred Historical Society, Enfield, 1975)
V Coleman, *The Medicine Men* (Arrow Books, London, 1977)
M H Cooper, *Prices and Profits in the Pharmaceutical Industry* (Pergamon Press, Oxford, 1966)
D L Cowen & W H Helfand, *Pharmacy an Illustrated History* (Harry N Abrams, New York, 1990)

J K Crellin, 'Pharmaceutical History: The growth of professionalism in the nineteenth century', *Medical History*, 11, 3, 1967

C G Drummond, 'Assistants, 1862, Shorter Working Hours', *Chemist and Druggist*, 189, 1968

C G Drummond, 'Pharmacy in Victorian Edinburgh', *Pharmaceutical Journal*, 200, 1968

M Facklam, *Healing Drugs: The history of pharmacology* (New York, Oxford, c.1992)

A Gilbertus, *Healing and Society in Medieval England* (University of Wisconsin Press, c.1991)

J M Good, *The History of Medicine, so far as it relates to the profession of the apothecary;...the origin of druggists, their gradual encroachment on compound pharmacy, and the evils to which the public are from thence exposed* (General Pharmaceutic Association of Great Britain, London, 1795)

S F Gray, *The Elements of Pharmacy and of the Chemical History of the Materia Medica* (London, 1823)

J A Grier, *A History of Pharmacy* (Pharmaceutical Press, London, 1937)

B Griggs, *Green Pharmacy: A history of herbal medicine* (Hobhouse, London, 1981)

B Griggs, *New Green Pharmacy: The story of western herbal medicine* (Vermilion, London, 1997)

M B Hall, 'Apothecaries and Chemists. First BSHP Lecture', *Chemist and Druggist*, 188, 1967; *Pharmaceutical Journal*, 199, 1967

C V Hammond, *Pack Up Your Medicines 1939–1947: An account of the work of pharmacists during the Second World War* (Purnvic Books, Basingstoke, 1998)

D W F Hardie & J Davidson Pratt, *A History of the Modern British Chemical Industry* (Pergamon Press, Oxford, 1966)

R Hare, *The Birth of Penicillin and the Disarming of Microbes* (George Allen & Unwin, London, 1970)

D C Harrod & E J Shellard, *Pharmacy at Chelsea, 1919–1979* (Chelsea College of Science and Technology, London, 1979)

W H Hughes, *Alexander Fleming and Penicillin* (Priory Press, London, 1974)

C L Huisking, *Herbs to Hormones: The evolution of drugs and chemicals that revolutionised medicine* (Pequot Press, Essex, c.1968)

J Hunt, 'Oral History Interviews With Elderly Pharmacists', *Wellcome Trust Annual Record*, 1995

B Inglis, *Drugs, Doctors and Disease* (Andre Deutsch, London, 1965)

W A Jackson, *The Victorian Chemist and Druggist* (Shire, Princes Risborough, 1981)

Select bibliography

E Kremers & G Urdang, revised by G Sonnendecker, *The History of Pharmacy* (J B Lippincott, Philadelphia and London, 4th edition, 1976)

C H La Wall, *Four Thousand Years of Pharmacy: An outline history etc.* (J B Lippincott, Philadelphia and London, 1927)

J Liebenau, 'The Rise of the British Pharmaceutical Industry', *British Medical Journal*, 301, 1990

J Liebenau, 'The British Success with Penicillin', *Social Studies of Science*, 17, 1987

J Liebenau, G J Higby & E C Stroud (eds), *Pill Peddlers: Essays on the history of the pharmaceutical industry* (American Institute of the History of Pharmacy, Madison, 1990)

G Macfarlane, *Alexander Fleming: The man and the myth* (Oxford University Press, Oxford, 1985)

A G M Madge, *A Brief History of Pharmacy: With some observations on alchemy* (Marshalle, Plymouth, c.1986)

R R Mathison, *The Eternal Search: The story of man and his drugs* (Frederick Muller, London, 1959)

L G Matthews, *Antiques of the Pharmacy* (Bell, London, 1971)

L G Matthews, *The History of Pharmacy in Britain* (E & S Livingstone, London, 1962)

L G Matthews, *Milestones of Pharmacy* (London, 1980)

L G Matthews, *Pharmacists in the Wider World* (Merrel Pharmaceuticals, London, 1981)

L G Matthews, *Regional Guide to Pharmacy's Past* (Merrel Dow Pharmaceuticals, London, 1985)

L G Matthews, *The Royal Apothecaries* (Wellcome Historical Medical Library, London, 1967)

L G Matthews, 'The Spicers and Apothecaries of Norwich', *Pharmaceutical Journal*, 198, 1967

A Maurois, translated by G Hopkins, *The Life of Sir Alexander Fleming: Discoverer of penicillin* (Jonathan Cape, London, 1959)

L Mez-Mangold, *A History of Drugs* (F Hoffman-la-Roche, Basle, Switzerland, 1971)

S Miall, *A History of the British Chemical Industry* (Ernest Benn, London, 1931)

W D Moore, *An Outline of the History of Pharmacy in Ireland* (Hodges & Smith, Dublin, 1848)

S M Palliser, *The Use of Plants in English Folk Medicine 1600–1800* (University of Leeds, Leeds, 1984)

R Porter & M Teich, *Drugs and Narcotics in History* (Cambridge University Press, Cambridge, 1995)

R Potzch (ed), *The Pharmacy: Windows on history* (Roche, Basle, Switzerland, c.1996)

F N L Poynter, *Chemistry in the Service of Medicine* (Pitman, London, 1963)
F N L Poynter, *The Evolution of Pharmacy in Britain* (Pitman Medical, London, 1965)
H Redwood, *The Pharmaceutical Industry: Trends, problems and achievements* (Oldwicks Press, Felixstowe, 1988)
J M Riddle, *Dioscorides on Pharmacy and Medicine* (University of Texas Press, Austin, 1985)
J M Riddle, *Quid Pro Quo: Studies in the history of drugs* (Variorum, Aldershot, 1992)
B Robinson, *The History of Pharmaceutical Education in Manchester* (Manchester, 1986)
T Rogers Forbes (ed), *The Admiral Secrets of Physick and Chyrurgery* (Yale University Press, New Haven, 1984)
G Sonnendecker, *History of Pharmacy* (3rd edition, 1963)
C Stockwell, *Nature's Pharmacy: A history of plants and healing* (Century, London, 1986)
S G B Stubbs, *Sixty Centuries of Health and Physick: The progress of ideas from primitive magic to modern medicine* (Sampson Low, London, c.1931)
D Symonds, *Dusting and Dispensing: Tapes of reminiscences* (Splendid Productions, Nottingham, 1992)
J Taggart, *The World Pharmaceutical Industry* (Routledge, London, 1993)
N Tallis & K Arnold-Forster, *Pharmacy History: A pictorial record* (Pharmaceutical Press, London, 1991)
G Teeling-Smith (ed), *The Pharmaceutical Industry and Society: A study of the changing environment and economics of the pharmaceutical industry* (Office of Health Economics, London, 1972)
C J S Thompson, *The Mystery and Art of the Apothecary* (John Lane, London, 1929)
G E Trease, *Pharmacy in History* (Balliere, Tindall & Cox, London, 1964)
T E Wallis, *History of the School of Pharmacy, University of London* (Pharmaceutical Press, London, 1964)
M Weatherall, *In Search of a Cure: A history of pharmaceutical discovery* (Oxford University Press, Oxford, 1990)
C Webster (ed), *Biology, Medicine and Society 1840–1940* (Cambridge University Press, Cambridge, 1981)
N E J Wells, *Pharmaceutical Innovation: Recent trends, future prospects* (Office of Health Economics, London, c.1983)
T D Whittet, 'Dorset Apothecaries' Tokens and their Issuers', *Proceedings of the Dorset Natural History and Archaeology Society*, 107, 1985
T D Whittet, 'From Apothecary to Pharmacist', *Chemist and Druggist*, 189, 1968
J R Wood, *Tablet Manufacture: Its history, pharmacy and practice* (J B Lippincott, Philadelphia and London, 1906)

A C Wootton, *The Chronicles of Pharmacy* (Macmillan, London and Basingstoke, 1910)

Theses

A Batrinou, 'Development, Location and Global Expansion of the Pharmaceutical Industry' (MSc thesis, Imperial College, London, 1990)

C M Bond, 'Prescribing in Community Pharmacy: Barriers and opportunities' (PhD thesis, Aberdeen University, 1995)

J G L Burnby, 'A Study of the English Apothecary 1660–1760' (PhD thesis, University of London, 1979)

D G Burt, 'A Study of Factors Contributing to the Development of a Uniform System of Pharmacy Education' (MPhil thesis, University of Wales, Cardiff, 1991)

V Chi, 'Pricing Regulation of the Pharmaceutical Industry' (MSc thesis, Imperial College, London, 1986)

M P Earles, 'Studies in the Development of Experimental Pharmacology in the Eighteenth and early Nineteenth Centuries' (PhD thesis, University of London, 1961)

J D G O'Hare, 'The Development and Function of Pharmaceutical Services in Psychiatric Hospital Practice' (PhD thesis, Queen's University, Belfast, 1989)

C W Peters, 'Innovation in the Pharmaceutical Industry: A study of the effects of regulation on the UK pharmaceutical industry' (PhD thesis, Aston University, 1986)

M Robson, 'The Pharmaceutical Industry in Britain and France 1919–39' (PhD thesis, University of London, 1989)

M T Robson, 'The Pharmaceutical Industry in Britain and France 1919–1939' (PhD thesis, London School of Economics, 1993)

F Sapolyo, 'Market Structure and Competition in the British Pharmaceutical Industry' (PhD thesis, Manchester University, 1981)

P M Worling, 'Pharmaceutical Wholesale Distribution: The influence of the National Health Service and growing market competition on the development of the wholesale distribution of pharmaceuticals in the United Kingdom' (PhD thesis, University of Bradford, 1988)

Pharmaceutical practice

The Art of Dispensing (*Chemist and Druggist*, London, 1888)

Chemist's Windows: The art of displaying pharmaceutical goods with chapters on ticket writing (*Chemist and Druggist*, London, 1915)
The Pharmaceutical Pocket Book (Pharmaceutical Press, London, 1970)
H Beasley, *The Druggist's General Receipt Book* (Churchill, London, 1852–1907)
H Beasley, *The Pocket Formulary* (Churchill, London, 1842–99)
A J Cooley, *Cyclopedia of Practical Receipts* (Churchill, London, 1845–82)
H G Moss, *The Retail Pharmacist's Handbook* (George Newnes, London, 1962)
J P Remington, *The Practice of Pharmacy* (Phillip Lippincott, London, 1885–1985)
C J S Thomson, *The Chemist's Compendium* (Whittaker, London, 1898)

Laws and legislation

The Pharmacy and Poison Laws of the UK, their history and interpretation (*Chemist and Druggist*, London, 1892)
G E Applebe & J Wingfield, *Dale and Applebe's Pharmacy Law and Ethics* (Pharmaceutical Press, London, 1993)
I H Harrison, *The Law on Medicine* (MTP Press, London, 1986)

Sources and methodology

Select Bibliography for Pharmacy History (Museum of the Royal Pharmaceutical Society of Great Britain, London, 1993)
'A Selective Index of Entries in Local Newspapers Relating to Winchester Pharmacies c.1772–1870', *Index to Hampshire Newspapers*, 1, 197
A L Brunn, *How to Find Out in Pharmacy: A guide to sources of pharmaceutical information* (Pergamon Press, Oxford, c.1969)
J G L Burnby & D A Hutton, *A Guide to Sources in Pharmaceutical History* (British Society for the History of Pharmacy, Edinburgh, 1990)
E Clarke, *Modern Methods in the History of Medicine* (Athlone Press, London, 1971)
A B Davis & M S Dreyfuss, *The Finest Instruments Ever Made: A bibliography of medical, dental, optical and pharmaceutical company trade literature, 1700–1939* (Medical History Publishing Associates, Arlington, c.1986)
G J Higby & E C Stroud, *The History of Pharmacy: A selected annotated bibliography* (Garland, London and New York, 1995)
W R Pickering (ed), *Information Sources in Pharmaceuticals* (Bowker-Saur, London, 1989)

B Strickland-Hodge & M H Jepson, *Keyguide to Information Sources in Pharmacy* (Mansell, London and New York, 1989)

Historical periodicals and series

Pharmaceutical Historian (British Society for the History of Pharmacy), 1967 on
Pharmacy in History (American Institute of the History of Pharmacy), 1959 on
J K Crellin & M P Earles, 'The History of Pharmacy. Its study and its application', a series in the *Pharmaceutical Journal*
K Holland, a series of business history profiles in the *Pharmaceutical Journal*, 1986 on

Trade journals and registers

The Annual Register of Chemists and Druggists, 1869–1954
The Annual Register of Pharmaceutical Chemists, 1841 on
British and Colonial Druggist, 1886–1915, continued as *British and Colonial Pharmacist*, 1915–1951, *British and Overseas Pharmacist*, 1952–1957, and *British and Overseas Pharmacy and Medicine*, 1958–1960
British Journal of Pharmacology and Chemotherapy, 1946 on
Chemist and Druggist, 1859 on
The Chemist and Druggist Diary, 1886, 1892, 1896, 1900–1935, continued as *Chemist and Druggist Diary and Yearbook*, 1935–1969, *Chemist and Druggist Yearbook and Buyers Guide*, 1969–1970, *Chemist and Druggist Yearbook* 1970–1972, and *Chemist and Druggist Directory*, 1972 on
Chemists and Druggists Yearbook and Directory for Scotland, 1914–1939
Journal of Pharmacy and Pharmacology, 1928 on
Manufacturing Chemist, 1892–1998, 1935 on
Pharmaceutical Journal, 1841 on
Post Office Directory of Chemists and Druggists, 1869–1876, *Kelly's Directory of Chemists and Druggists*, 1880–1916, and *Kelly's Directory of the Chemical Industry*, 1919–1938
Retail Chemist, 1929 on

Pharmacopoeias

British National Formulary (Pharmaceutical Society of Great Britain and British Medical Association, London), 1957 on
British Pharmaceutical Codex (Pharmaceutical Press, London), 1907–79

The British Pharmacopoeia (General Medical Council, London), 1864 on
The Edinburgh Pharmacopoeia (Royal College of Physicians of Edinburgh, Edinburgh), 1699–1841
The London Pharmacopoeia (Royal College of Physicians of London, London), 1618–1851
Martindale: The Extra Pharmacopoeia (Pharmaceutical Press, London), 1883 on
P Squire, *A Companion to the British Pharmacopoeia* (Whittaker, London), 1864–1916

User's guide: arrangement of the book

This guide to the surviving records of the British pharmaceutical industry defines the industry as any business or company which manufactured, dispensed, distributed or sold ethical pharmaceutical preparations, patent medicines, drugs or galenicals primarily intended for human use. The archive survey upon which the guide is based focused on businesses established between 1750 and 1968, although some records pre- or post-dating this period are included. The survey also covered trade associations, trade unions and employers' organisations allied to the pharmaceutical industry.

Users should note that it was not possible to compile entries for every pharmaceutical company or business currently trading in the United Kingdom. Some companies professed to have no surviving archives, and others did not wish to allow the Business Archives Council, which undertook the survey, access to their records. A number of companies and trade associations established since 1960, were also excluded from the survey as they were deemed unlikely to hold significant archive collections.

PHARMACEUTICAL BUSINESS RECORD ENTRIES

Entries have been arranged by the name of the company, partnership, or proprietor to which they relate. Each entry comprises the name and address of the pharmaceutical business, a note describing its principal business activity, a brief history of its development, a bibliography of publications relating to its history and a list of the extant historical records which it generated with details of their location.

Business name

The title of each entry is generally the most recent name under which the business operated, but on some occasions, where it was widely known under a previous name, or where the records relate only to the earlier years of a business, exceptions have been made. All previous and subsequent names are included in the history section and are also included in the name index at the end of the book.

Business address

The address is the last known location at which the company or business was trading, or for currently operating companies or organisations, the address from which it was trading in January 1998.

Business activity

The business activity section indicates the main business of the company, partnership or sole trader, whether trading as a pharmaceutical manufacturer, retailer or wholesaler. It has not proved possible to standardise descriptions of business activities, except in the case of registered chemists and druggists and pharmaceutical chemists and the guide generally employs the description used by the business itself. Business activity is included in the subject index at the end of the book.

History

The history section is a short chronological account of the development of the company or business which outlines origins, name changes, trading activity, geographical location and corporate status. The histories are intended to aid the user in understanding the records generated, and should not be considered definitive in their own right. They were compiled using a number of sources, which, apart from the published histories cited in the bibliography sections, included *The Chemical Trade Directory* (London, 1928 on); *Chemist and Druggist* (London, 1859 on); D W F Hardy and J Davidson Pratt, *A History of the Modern British Chemical Industry* (Oxford, 1966); *Kelly's Directory of Chemists and Druggists* (London, 1880–1916); *Kelly's Directory of the Chemical Industry* (London, 1919–1938); *Pharmaceutical Historian* (Edinburgh, 1967 on); *Pharmaceutical Journal* (London, 1841 on); *Post Office Directory of Chemists and Druggists* (London, 1869–1876); and *Registers of Pharmaceutical Chemists and Chemists and Druggists* (London, 1869 on).

Bibliography

The publications section lists books, articles, leaflets and pamphlets relating to the history of the company or business. Whilst many of these histories were commercially published, others were unpublished or privately printed and may only be available through the holder of the record collection.

Records

The records section for each entry is headed by the location of the records in October 2000, whether they were held by the parent company, at a branch office or in a public record repository. The Business Archives Council will aim to update this information from time to time, but changes in the addresses of many archive repositories can be ascertained by reference to the Royal Commission on Historical Manuscript's *Record Repositories in Great Britain* (HMSO, London) or on ARCHON (URL http://www.hmc.gov.uk/archon). In many entries, as a result of the division of collections, more than one location is given. These locations are numbered as Records (1), Records (2), and so on. Separate collections of the same company's records held in one repository, have been amalgamated as single entries. Record office and company references to collections are listed at the end of the records section. Records have been listed in the following order: partnership and corporate records; financial records; legal records; manufacturing records; distribution and sales records; property records; staff records; and miscellaneous other records. Record summaries have been standardised as far as possible, but due to the inevitable diversity of cataloguing practices in different repositories, it has been impossible to ensure uniformity.

TRADE, PROFESSIONAL AND EMPLOYMENT ORGANISATION ENTRIES

The historical records of professional bodies, trade associations, trade unions and employers' organisations allied to the pharmaceutical industry have been arranged in a similar manner to those of pharmaceutical companies and businesses.

APPENDICES

Minor collections: lists of records

Appendix 1 lists relevant miscellaneous items relating to pharmaceutical companies, businesses or trade associations, or those of unknown provenance which do not merit a separate entry. Records are listed under the name of the archive repository at which they are held, and each archive repository is listed under the name of the country and county in which it is situated.

Public records

Appendix 2 indicates some categories of public records which are of relevance to the pharmaceutical industry and to the pharmacy profession.

ACCESS TO RECORDS

Users should be aware that the records of currently operating businesses, companies and trade organisations included in this guide are in private ownership, and that access to them is at the discretion of the owning company, association or individual. The co-operation of such bodies or individuals with the survey does not imply that access will automatically be given to those who request it, especially if the records are confidential in nature, or facilities can not be provided to accommodate researchers. Researchers should write, asking to consult records, to the Company Secretary, if a company, or to the Secretary, if a trade association, at the address given in the relevant records section, unless a named official to whom enquiries should be directed is indicated. Research enquiries should be as specific as possible.

Publicly deposited records should be accessed by first writing to the County or Chief Archivist at the repository named in the relevant records section. Some such records are governed by conditions of access, and may have closure periods not indicated in the guide. Further information on hours of opening and conditions of access may be found in: J Foster and J Sheppard, *British Archives: A guide to archive resources in the United Kingdom* (Macmillan, Basingstoke, 2001), *London Local Archives: A directory of local authority record offices and libraries* (Greater London Archive Network, London, 1994) and L Richmond and A Turton, *Directory of Corporate Archives* (Business Archives Council, London, 1998) and on ARCHON (URL http://www.hmc.gov.uk/archon). Researchers should contact the relevant repository well in advance of any visit.

If, for any reason, a researcher cannot contact a company or trade association named in the guide he or she should write for advice to the Business Archives Council, 101 Whitechapel High Street, London E1 7RE. If unable to contact a repository, researchers are advised to contact the National Register of Archives, Royal Commission on Historical Manuscripts, Quality House, Quality Court, Chancery Lane, London WC2A 1HP.

ABBREVIATIONS USED IN THE GUIDE

b.	born
c.	circa
cent(s).	century(ies)
Co	company
d.	died
Inc	Incorporated
incl.	including
Ltd	Limited
(m)	microfilm copy
n.d.	no date
(p)	photocopy
plc	public limited company
re	concerning
Ref:	reference number
UK	United Kingdom of Great Britain and Northern Ireland
USA	United States of America
Vol(s).	volume(s)
(w)	wanting, i.e. record series incomplete

Select glossary of pharmaceutical terms[1]

Ampoule: A sealed container, usually a glass vial, containing a sterile medicinal solution, or powder to be made up in solution. Primarily for administration by injection.

Apothecary: From the Latin *apothecarius*, from the Greek *apotheke*: a store or repository, a store keeper. Obsolescent term for a pharmacist or druggist. Apothecaries were first recognised by law in 1617, when they were enabled to break away from the Grocers' Company and establish their own guild. Until 1815 they were chiefly dispensers of medicines, but following the Apothecaries Act of that year were recognised as medical practitioners.

Balsam: A mixture of volatile oil and resin obtained from trees of the family *Leguminosae*, for external use as a stimulant and antiseptic, or internal use as an expectorant.

Capsule: A hard or soft soluble gelatinous shell containing a dose of a drug.

Chemical, fine: A chemical used in small amounts and of fairly pure origins.

Chemical, pharmaceutical: A chemical used in the production process of a pharmaceutical drug.

Chemist, dispensing: One who composes, weighs and distributes drugs to patients, normally from a pharmacy; or a pharmacy.

Chemist, manufacturing: One who produces pharmaceutical drugs.

Chemist, pharmaceutical: Correct term for a pharmacist. The first statutory register of pharmaceutical chemists was established in 1852, following the Pharmacy Act of the same year. Registration was achieved by passing the major examination of the Pharmaceutical Society of Great Britain. Following the

---

[1] Definitions are derived from several sources, but mainly from *Churchill's Illustrated Medical Dictionary* (Churchill Livingstone, New York, 1989), *Stedman's Illustrated Medical Dictionary* (Williams & Wilkins, Baltimore and London, 1982) and *Oxford English Dictionary* (Clarendon Press, Oxford, 1989).

phasing-out of the minor examination in 1954, chemists and druggists ceased to exist and all trained pharmacists were termed pharmaceutical chemists.

Chemist, retail: One who sells pharmaceutical preparations; or a store from which pharmaceuticals can be purchased.

Chemist, wholesale: One who buys products in bulk from a pharmaceutical manufacturer, and distributes those products to retail and dispensing chemists.

Chemist (chymist) and druggist: Term for a pharmacist in use before 1954. Chemists and druggists were first recognised as dispensers of medicines in the 1815 Apothecaries Act. Compulsory registration for chemists and druggists was introduced in the Pharmacy Act of 1868. Registration was achieved by passing the minor examination of the Pharmaceutical Society of Great Britain, the minimum legal requirement to practice as a pharmacist.

Chemotherapy: The treatment of disease with chemical compounds or drugs.

Cinchona: The dried bark of the root and stem of several species of *Cinchona* (a genus of evergreen trees native of South America), and their hybrids. A rich source of the quinoline alkaloids, including quinine and cinchonidine. Also known as *Cinchona bark, Peruvian Bark, Jesuits' Bark.*

Collodion: From the Greek *kollodes*: 'gluelike'. Nitro-cellulose dissolved in a solution of alcohol and ether, used as a protective for cuts or as a vehicle for the local application of medicinal substances.

Compound: A pharmaceutical preparation composed of two or more ingredients.

Confection: From the Latin *conficere*: to make or bring together, to prepare. A medicinal preparation that has been made sweet by the addition of sugar, honey or syrup.

Cordial: A sweet aromatic liquor.

Cream: From the Latin *cremor*: a thick juice or broth. A thick ointment-like emulsion, applied to the skin for protective or medicinal purposes.

Drug: Any therapeutic agent other than food used for the treatment or diagnosis of diseases, or for the prevention of pathological states.

Drug, crude: An unrefined, natural source of a therapeutic substance, usually of plant origin.

Drug, dangerous: Defined by various Acts of Parliament, the first of which was the Dangerous Drugs Act 1920, which determined that dangerous drugs could not be supplied without prescription. Usually refers to narcotics and highly addictive substances, which when correctly prescribed have medicinal properties.

Drug, generic: A non-proprietary drug which can be substituted for a proprietary brand in a prescription.

Drug, homeopathic: A therapeutic agent which contains minute dosages of a medicinal substance, which in a larger dosage would produce symptoms of the disease being treated. Homeopathy follows the concept of the law of similia, 'fighting fire with fire'.

Druggist: One who prepares and dispenses drugs, a pharmacist. Used interchangeably with the term chemist, except in Ireland where before 1951 a druggist was untrained and held lower status.

Drysalter: A dealer in chemical products such as drugs and gums, and occasionally in oils, sauces and pickles.

Elixir: A clear, sweetened, hydroalcoholic solution, containing flavouring substances or medicinal ingredients.

Embrocation: The application of a liquid medicinal material, usually a liniment, to the body surface.

Emulsion: The dispersion of an insoluble liquid in another liquid in the form of suspended globules (for example, fat in water). Emulsions are used in creams and liniments.

Essence: A volatile plant oil, concentrated tincture or spirit that imparts a distinctive quality to perfume or flavour.

Extract: A concentrated vegetable or animal drug preparation obtained by the removal of the active constituent of that drug. Extracts are produced as semiliquids or syrups, solids and powders.

Select glossary

Formula(-e): A recipe or prescription containing ingredients and directions for the compounding of a medicinal preparation.

Formulary: A list of drugs available through a pharmacy or a published collection of formulas for the compounding of medicinal preparations. Examples of the latter are the *National Formulary* and the *British Pharmacopoeia*.

Galenical: Taken from Galen, a Greek physician c.130–200 AD given to compounding remedies of organic origin. A crude drug of herbal or vegetable origin and the tinctures, decoctions and other preparations made from it, as distinguished from a mineral or chemical medicament.

Herb: From the Latin *herba*: small plant, grass. A prepared drug that consists of plant or plant parts.

Herbal remedy: A medicinal product consisting of dried or crushed plants, or plants which have been mixed with water or some other inert substance.

Herbalist: A dealer in, or manufacturer of, medicinal herbs or simples.

Infusion: A solution containing the water-soluble extract of a vegetable drug.

Injection: A pharmaceutical preparation for intravenous administration.

Ipecacuanha: The dried root of *Cephaelis Ipecacuanha*, a Brazilian shrub, which contains emetine, cephaeline emetamine and ipecacuanhic acid. It has expectorant, emetic and antidysentric properties.

Liniment: An oily, liquid preparation applied externally to the gums or skin by friction or upon a surgical dressing. It may be a solution, suspension or emulsion, and is used as a counter-irritant or cleansing agent.

Liquor: An aqueous solution of a non-volatile substance or gas.

Lotion: A liquid preparation for external application without friction, containing suspended or emulsified medicinal ingredients.

Lozenge: A medicated tablet in a flavoured and sweetened base for local treatment of the mouth and throat. The medicine is slowly released whilst the tablet dissolves.

Materia medica: Rarely used term for pharmacology

Medicine: Any substance used to treat disease or ease pain; a drug.

Medicine, ethical: A prescription-only medicine, which requires the approval of a physician or other health-care official before purchase, and which must be obtained from a pharmacy.

Medicine, over-the-counter: A pharmaceutical preparation which requires no prescription to obtain, and which need not always be purchased from a pharmacy.

Medicine, patent: A pharmaceutical product protected by trade-mark or patent, and usually of secret composition.

Medicine, proprietary: A medicinal compound whose formula and rights to manufacture are controlled by an owner through patent or copyright. Such products can not be manufactured by another party without the consent of the patent holder.

Medicine, 'quack': A compound of little therapeutic value advertised and sold falsely as curative of certain or all diseases.

Mixture: A blend of two or more substances without chemical reaction, so that the properties of the components are retained. Pharmaceutical mixtures usually contain a solid component dispersed in a liquid solution.

Nostrum: A therapeutic agent, sometimes patented and usually of unknown composition, offered to the public, with exaggerated claims about its healing powers as a remedy for specific diseases.

Ointment: A semi-solid preparation of one or more medicinal substances, in a suitable base, for external application. Bases include water-in-oil for good absorption, creams which can be washed off and greaseless substances.

Pastille: A lozenge with a gelatine base.

Pharmaceutical: From the Greek, *pharmakon*: a drug or relating to drugs. Relating to pharmaceutics, pharmacy or medicinal drugs.

Pharmacist: One qualified by education and training to prepare and dispense prescription drugs, and who has knowledge of their properties. In Britain used interchangeably with the term chemist. Other terms for a pharmacist include druggist, pharmaceutist and apothecary.

Pharmacopoeia: A formulary, usually official and revised from time to time, which has legal force in pharmacies. It contains a description of all drugs used in current medical practice with their composition and formulae and gives instructions as to their preparation, and directions for regulating purity and quality, for example the *British Pharmacopoeia*.

Pharmacology: The science concerned with drugs, including their origin, appearance, preparation, isolation, chemistry, actions and uses.

Pharmacy: The science and practice of preparing, preserving, compounding and dispensing medicinal drugs, and advising on their usage; or a place where pharmacy is practised, a drug store.

Physician: A licensed practitioner of medicine or osteopathy, who is licensed to examine and care for the sick.

Pill: A solid but soluble medicine in the form of a tablet with a coating that protects the medicament and disguises the taste. Intended to be swallowed intact.

Powder: A single dose of a dry, finely ground drug in a packet.

Prescription: From the Latin *praescribere*: to set before in writing. A written direction for the preparation and release of a drug for the treatment of disease or injury; or a drug prepared according to the directions provided in a prescription.

Recipe: From the Latin *recipio*: to receive. A prescription or formula.

Remedy: Any medicament that cures a disease or relieves its symptoms.

Serum: From the Greek *oros*: whey. The watery liquid obtained after removal of clotted blood cells, distinguished from the plasma in circulating blood; or a blood serum that has been injected with toxins and has developed antibodies to them.

Simple: A medicament consisting of a single constituent, usually of one herb or plant.

Solution: A liquid phase containing at least two substances, usually an aqueous solution of a non-volatile substance. Also known as a liquor.

Spiritus vini rectificatus (SVR): Prior to 1953 the official designation of all spirits was *spiritus*. An alcoholic or hydroalcoholic solution containing a volatile substance.

Surgeon: Current usage, a practitioner of medicine or osteopathy who treats disease and illness by surgical operation. Obsolescent usage, a practitioner without the degree of MD, but with the licence of the Royal College of Surgeons.

Syrup: An aqueous solution of a sugar such as sucrose. Usually used as a flavouring agent for other drugs. When the syrup contains a medicinal substance it is referred to as a medicated syrup.

Tablet: A solid medicament composed of one or more drugs, a disintegrating agent and a binding agent. It is taken orally and may vary in shape, size and weight and may be in moulded or compressed form.

Tincture: An alcoholic or water-alcoholic solution containing animal, vegetable or chemical ingredients. Prepared by percolation or maceration. Compound tinctures are made according to long established formulas.

Vaccine: From the Latin v*acca*: cow. A living microbe or variant strain of a virus or bacteria which, when injected into or ingested by a patient, causes a clinically insignificant infection. The original vaccine was a preparation of the cowpox (vaccinia) virus by Edward Jenner, to immunise against smallpox.

Pharmaceutical businesses: lists of records

ABBOTT LABORATORIES LTD
Queenborough, Kent

Pharmaceutical manufacturer and distributor of pharmaceutical, nutritional, hospital and diagnostic products

History: During the 1880s Wallace Calvin Abbott, an American physician, established a small pharmaceutical manufacturing business on his own account, trading from his house in Chicago, USA. He prescribed liquid alkaloid extracts to his patients, but due to dissatisfaction with their performance, began producing alkaloid pills in 1891. In 1900 his business was incorporated as a limited liability company, Abbott Alkaloidal Co Inc, Chicago. In 1937 the company, renamed Abbott Laboratories Inc, incorporated Abbott Laboratories (England) Ltd as a UK subsidiary, at 3 Wadsworth Road, Perivale, Ealing, London. In addition to importing American manufactured products and marketing them locally, Abbott Laboratories Ltd manufactured some drugs, chiefly *Nembutal* and *Pentothal*. In 1946 Abbott Laboratories Inc incorporated Abbott Laboratories Eire Ltd, to market and distribute, but not to manufacture its pharmaceutical products in the Republic of Ireland. In 1965 this company was re-named Abbott Laboratories Ireland Ltd. After the Second World War, Abbott Laboratories (England) Ltd re-located to a factory and offices at Bede Trading Estate, Jarrow, South Tyneside, and in 1949 was renamed Abbott Laboratories Ltd. In the early 1950s it began manufacture of a rat poison, *Ratero*, and a subsidiary company, Tobal Products Ltd, was incorporated in 1952 to promote this product. In 1957 Abbott Laboratories Ltd established a London office at Berk House, 8 Baker Street, and around the same time launched a cough medicine, *Antussin*, which was also marketed by Tobal Products Ltd. The *Antussin* trademark was sold to Unilever in 1966. Tobal Products Ltd was renamed Abbott Chemical Co Ltd in 1966, and was wound up in 1980. During the 1940s and 1950s Abbott Laboratories Ltd consolidated its export business and opened storage and distribution depots in Birmingham, Bristol, Glasgow, Manchester, and Sydenham and Ealing, London. Between 1959 and 1962 new works and offices were built at Queenborough, Kent. All Abbott Laboratories Ltd operations were transferred to this site in 1962, and the depots and London office closed down. The principal business of the company was the manufacture and sale of ethical pharmaceuticals, including antibiotics, and the manufacture of chemicals, barbiturates and anti-epileptic drugs. In 1987 offices were acquired at Norden Road, Maidenhead, Windsor & Maidenhead, to accommodate the sales, marketing and medical divisions. In 1999 these offices were relocated to Norden Road. The company was still trading in 1999.

Anon, *The Abbott Almanac: One hundred years of commitment to quality health care* (The Benjamin Company, New York, 1988); 'Abbott Laboratories', in T Derdak (ed), *International Directory of Company Histories*, Vol. 1 (St James's Press, London, 1988); H Kogan, *The Long White Line: The story of Abbott Laboratories* (Random House, New York, 1963); J Slim, *Abbott Laboratories in the UK – celebrating 60 years of commitment to health care* (Granta Editions, London, 1999)

Records 1: Abbott Laboratories Ltd, Queenborough ME11 5EL

Directors' and general meetings minutes 1937 on; memorandum and articles of association 1958; combined registers of members and share ledgers 1937 to date; share certificates 1937–65; seal book 1954–65; annual reports and accounts 1966 to date; annual accounts 1937–41, 1945–51, 1954, 1965; manufacturing, trading and profit and loss accounts 1942–54 (w); balance sheets: 1941–46, Southern Rhodesia branch 1947; ledgers: nominal 1937–40, general 1940–64; tax computations based on annual accounts 1965; drug information leaflets, some from representatives' presentation packs 1970s; clinical trial booklet, blank forms n.d., c.1980s; product labels and price stickers n.d., c.1960s–70s; title deeds 19th–20th cents; Queenborough construction site and plant plans, drawings and photographs 1959–62; pensioners' records 1937 to date.

Abbott Laboratories Ireland Ltd: directors' and general meetings minutes 1946–63; combined register of members and share ledger 1946–61; annual reports and accounts 1966–79; annual accounts 1965.

Abbott Chemical Co Ltd: directors' and general meetings minutes 1952–80; combined register of members and share ledger 1952–78; annual reports and accounts 1966–80; annual accounts 1952–54, 1965.

Records 2: F Maltby & Sons Ltd, Dunston House, Portland Street, Lincoln LN5 7NN

Product index 1960.

R & T ADAM LTD
8 Roseneath Street, Edinburgh

Retail chemist

History: R & T Adam Ltd, a retail chemist's business, based at 8 Roseneath Street, Edinburgh, was incorporated as a limited liability company in 1947, by John Cruikshank Adam, Thomas Chalmers Adam and Richard Dickson Adam, all chemists, and Jeanie Whitson Adam. In 1975 it was acquired by Raimes, Clark & Co Ltd, wholesale and manufacturing chemists of 17 Smith's Place, Leith, Edinburgh, and thereafter continued to trade under its own name. The company was dissolved in 1990.

Records: The Secretary, National Register of Archives (Scotland), H M General Register House, Princes Street, Edinburgh EH1 3YY

Minutes 1947–86; annual returns 1952–68; combined register of members and share ledger 1954–73; directors' reports, balance sheets and accounts 1963–74. (Ref: NRA(S) 2974)

JOHN ADAMS (CHEMISTS) LTD
4-5 Market Street, Shrewsbury, Shropshire

Chemist

History: In 1873 William Adams registered as a pharmaceutical chemist. He traded in Great Malvern, Worcestershire, until 1882, when he established himself in business at 30 High Street, Shrewsbury, Shropshire. In 1938 the business was named William Adams & Son, and in 1944 William Adams ceased to be registered. Following this, the business passed to Hubert Adams, who had registered as a pharmaceutical chemist in 1906, and had previously operated a business at 1 Russell Ridge, Roman Road, Shrewsbury. In 1948 John Hubert Adams registered as a pharmaceutical chemist and in 1955 replaced Hubert Adams in the business at 30 High Street. He re-located the business to 3 Market Street, Shrewsbury, in 1957, and later to 4-5 Market Street, trading as J H Adams. In 1966 the business was incorporated as a limited liability company, John Adams (Chemists) Ltd, and was acquired by Dudley Taylor, a Warwickshire pharmacist who owned a chain of retail pharmacies around the country. In 1993 Dudley Taylor (Holdings) Ltd was incorporated as a limited liability company, with offices at Harris Road, Wedgnock Industrial Estate, Warwick, Warwickshire, as a holding company for these many concerns. John

Adams (Chemists) Ltd was still trading from 4-5 Market Street in 1997 but in 1998 it was absorbed into Dudley Taylor (Kenilworth) Ltd.

Records 1: Dudley Taylor Holdings Ltd, Unit 2B, Harris Road, Wedgnock Industrial Estate, Warwick CV34 5GH

Directors' reports and annual accounts 1983-96 (w).

Records 2: Shropshire Records & Research Centre, Castle Gates, Shrewsbury SY1 2AQ

Prescription books 1872-75, 1911-78; formulae book c.1900. (Ref: 6232/1-16, 76232/17/1)

ADCOCK LTD
53 High Street, Alcester, Warwickshire

Chemist and druggist

History: Isaac Dickson Adcock was in business before 1868, at 97 Lorrimore Road, Walworth, Southwark, London. In 1868 he registered as a chemist and druggist and in 1871 re-located to 25 Albert Street, Newington, Southwark. In 1873 he moved to Swan Street, Alcester, Warwickshire, and in 1876 to 53 High Street, Alcester, where he traded as a chemist and druggist. In 1890 he was replaced in the business by Herbert Dickson Adcock, who had registered as a chemist and druggist in 1885. In 1929 Walter James Adcock registered as a chemist and druggist at 15 Holly Road, Edgbaston, Birmingham, and in 1931 joined Herbert Dickson Adcock in the business at High Street, Alcester. In 1951 Herbert Dickson ceased to be registered, and Walter James continued to trade from High Street, under the business name Adcock. He incorporated the business as a limited liability company, Adcock Ltd, in 1954. In 1975 the business at 53 High Street, Alcester, was acquired by Savory & Moore Ltd, and Walter James Adcock moved to Perrymill, Evesham Street, Alcester, and in 1984 ceased to be registered.

W J Adcock, *Adcock – Chemist, Alcester*, 1872-1972 (Ebineezer Bayliss, Worcester, 1972)

Records 1: Warwickshire County Record Office, Priory Park, Cape Road, Warwick CV34 4JS

Day book 1861-82; purchase agreement 1872; prescription books 1872-96; poisons register 1872-76; diaries 1879-89; correspondence 1896-1926; memoranda relating to work n.d. (Ref: CR2368, MI281, MI285)

Records 2: The Museum Curator, Royal Pharmaceutical Society of Great Britain, 1 Lambeth High Street, London SE1 7JN

Account book 1860-82. (Ref: IRA.1996.003)

A H ALLEN & PARTNERS
Sheffield

Analytical chemist and public analyst

History: A H Allen came to Sheffield, from London, in 1864 to work as analytical assistant to Dr James Allan. By 1871, following the death of James Allan, A H Allen had established a business on his own account, as an analytical chemist, at 1 Surrey Street, Sheffield. Shortly afterwards he was appointed Professor of Chemistry and Physics at Sheffield School of Medicine, and Public Analyst for Sheffield in 1873. The business remained at Surrey Street until 1984.

Records: Sheffield City Archives, 52 Shoreham Street, Sheffield S1 4SP

Balance sheets with profit and loss accounts 1918-42 (w); ledgers 1959-82; day books 1900-82; cash books 1922-81; bank books 1904-29; samples book 1968-76; professional notebook 1898-1922. (Ref: 600/B1-8)

ALLEN & HANBURYS LTD
Stockley Park West, Uxbridge, Hillingdon, London

Pharmaceutical manufacturer

History: In 1715 Silvanus Bevan established a pharmacy at the Old Plough Court, Lombard Street, London. His younger brother, Timothy, joined him as an apprentice in 1725 and in the early 1730s became a partner. The business was named Silvanus & Timothy Bevan, apothecaries, Lombard Street. On the death of Silvanus in 1765, the firm became known as Timothy Bevan & Sons, 'druggists and chymists', Plow Court. The 2 'sons' were from Timothy's first marriage, but they did not play an active role in the business, and when Timothy died in 1786, the business passed to Joseph Gurney Bevan, his youngest son by his second marriage, who had been charged with the running of the business since 1775. Under his ownership, the firm manufactured and sold drugs wholesale and retail to druggists, merchants and surgeons, both in London and the colonies. It also sold surgical instruments and medical books. Bevan retired in 1794 and sold the business to Samuel Mildred, who took into partnership William Allen, a former clerk to Bevan, and renamed the business Mildred & Allen in 1795. In 1797 Allen bought Mildred out and entered into partnership with Luke Howard, naming the business Allen & Howard. Howard assumed control of the laboratory side of the business which was based at a site in Plaistow, Newham, London, whilst Allen took charge of the Plough Court business. This partnership was dissolved in 1807, Howard developing a chemical manufacturing business on his own account, Howard & Sons, whilst Allen assumed total control of the Plough Court retailing business and concentrated on the production of galenicals. In 1804, John Thomas Barry was taken on as Allen's confidential clerk and aided the winding-down of the largely non-profitable transatlantic trade. By the 1830s this trade was essentially discontinued whilst the retail business had expanded significantly. After the death of his first wife, William Allen married Charlotte Hanbury in 1806, and brought 2 of her nephews into the business, Daniel Bell Hanbury in 1808, and Cornelius Hanbury in 1813. In 1818 Barry, who was by then in charge of the manufacturing laboratory, which had moved from Plaistow to Stratford, London, in 1805, was made a partner, and the title of the business became William Allen & Co. In 1824 Daniel Bell and Cornelius were also taken into partnership, and the firm became Allen, Hanburys & Barry. All 4 were influential in the foundation of the Pharmaceutical Society of Great Britain in 1841, William Allen being elected its first president. In 1856 Barry retired, followed in 1858 by Cornelius, and the firm was renamed Allen & Hanburys. Two new partners were admitted, Daniel Hanbury, eldest son of Daniel Bell Hanbury, in 1841, and Cornelius Hanbury, son of the retired Cornelius. In 1868 Daniel Bell Hanbury retired and was succeeded in 1874 by Cornelius Hanbury's only other surviving son, Frederick Janson Hanbury. Daniel and Cornelius Hanbury, junior, expanded the retailing side of the business and enlarged the dispensing and manufacturing premises at Plough Court during the 1860s. In 1874 part of an old match factory at Bethnal Green, Tower Hamlets, London, was leased, and by 1907 the whole premises had been acquired. Frederick Janson was in charge of this factory and recruited a number of pharmaceutical chemists. One of Allen & Hanburys' first successes was the manufacture of refined cod-liver oil, and from 1860 the firm established oil refining factories in Newfoundland, Canada; Norway; Aberdeen; and Kingston upon Hull. During the 1880s, Allen & Hanburys also began to produce malted extract, throat pastilles, compressed tablets and infant milk. In 1884 a second retail outlet was acquired at 7 Vere Street, Cavendish Square, London, and in 1893 the business was incorporated as a limited liability company, Allen & Hanburys Ltd. In 1896 the company acquired a mill at Ware, Hertfordshire, where it immediately began the production of malted food, pastilles and bulk galenicals. The Bethnal Green factory became essentially a packaging, distribution and administration centre. In 1894 further premises were acquired at 48 Wigmore Street in the west end of London, where production of surgical instruments for the medical community in Harley Street commenced. A number of overseas subsidiary companies were also established. Allen & Hanburys Co Ltd (Canada) was incorporated in 1902, Allen & Hanburys (South America) Ltd in 1909, and Allen & Hanburys (Russia) Ltd in 1913. After the First World War, the Hanbury family still controlled the company, with Frederick Janson Hanbury as chairman and his sons, Capel and Reginald, as senior directors. Between 1918 and 1922 the factory at Bethnal Green was rebuilt as a result of bomb damage, and the freehold was purchased. An analytical laboratory was established on site, and as early as 1923 Allen & Hanburys Ltd had become one of the first producers of the diabetic drug *insulin*. This drug was marketed as *Insulin A B* and represented a joint production venture with British Drug Houses Ltd, through a jointly owned company, Insulin A B Ltd. By the end of 1923 this company accounted for 95 per cent of the UK's production of the drug. In contrast, Allen & Hanburys Ltd's production of dried food products declined. Glaxo Laboratories Ltd produced an infant milk product, in 1924, which was rich in vitamin D, and began production of cut-price milk foods. As a result, Allen & Hanburys Ltd acquired a creamery near Glastonbury, Somerset, in 1931, in order to increase milk supplies for manufacture, but competition was fierce and the company's profits suffered. In 1934 it introduced *Haliborange* and *Halibol*, halibut-liver oil, which was found to be richer in vitamin A than cod-liver oil, and along with the production of a laxative, *Lixen*, the company was able to compensate for some of the damage done to the dried milk trade. Finally, in 1953, the production of milk products was discontinued. In 1937 Capel Hanbury succeeded his father as chairman, and in 1958 Allen & Hanburys Ltd was acquired as a wholly-owned subsidiary of Glaxo Laboratories Ltd, which was known as Glaxo Group Ltd by 1961. In 1963 a factory was purchased in Portsmouth, to manufacture hospital furniture. This was registered under the name Swanbrig Engineers Ltd until, in an attempt to bring this and other Glaxo subsidiaries which produced surgical equipment together, Allen & Hanburys (Surgical Engineering) Ltd was incorporated in 1963. During the 1960s Allen & Hanburys Ltd acquired the business of Allied Laboratories Ltd, a London-based company which had been acquired by Edinburgh Pharmaceutical Industries Ltd in 1959. Other subsidiaries of Allen & Hanburys Ltd included Eschmann Bros & Walsh Ltd and W H Deane (High Wycombe) Ltd, both manufacturers of surgical instruments. Allen & Hanburys Ltd continued to manufacture drugs and in 1969 introduced *Ventolin*, and in 1972 *Becotide*, both treatments for asthma. John C Hanbury retired as chairman in 1973, and was succeeded by David Smart, a non-family member. In the same year the pharmacy at Vere Street was closed. In 1974 Allen & Hanburys Ltd introduced *Beconase*, a treatment for hay fever. Research activities at Greenford, Ealing, London, the Glaxo Group Ltd site, and Ware, were unified as Glaxo Group Research Ltd in 1979, and in 1982 Allen & Hanburys Ltd's administration was transferred to Greenford, and the Bethnal Green site closed. In 1997 the company continued to trade under the name Allen & Hanburys Ltd.

P Baker, 'London origins of the Glaxo Group', *Supplement to the Pharmaceutical Journal*, 30, 1983, 12-13; D Chapman-Huston & E C Cripps, *Through a City Archway: The story of Allen & Hanburys*, 1715–1954 (John Murray, London, 1954); E C Cripps, *Plough Court: The story of a notable pharmacy, 1715–1927* (Allen & Hanburys, London, 1927); J C Hanbury, 'Early Developments in the Fine Chemical Industry: an historical survey', *Chemistry and Industry*, 1952, 300-8; R L Hanbury, 'The History and Development of Allen & Hanburys Ltd, 1715–1965' (Unpublished typescript, 1965); K Holland, 'Sir John Hanbury', *Pharmaceutical Journal*, 28 Nov 1992; A A Locke, *The Hanbury Family*, 2 Vols. (A L Humphreys, London, 1916); C S Stander, 'A History of the Pharmaceutical Industry With Particular Reference to Allen & Hanbury, 1775–1843' (Unpublished MSc thesis, London University, 1956); G Tweedale, *At the Sign of the Plough: Allen & Hanburys and the British pharmaceutical industry 1715–1990* (John Murray, London, 1990); M E Weeks, 'The Chemical Contributions of William Allen', *Journal of Chemical Education*, 35, 1958, 70-3

Records 1: Archivist (Historical Records), Records Centre, Glaxo Wellcome plc, 891-995 Greenford Road, Greenford UB6 0HE

'Journal handwritten 1814–1816' relating to New Lanark Co; 'Private ledger no 3' c.1822–43; correspondence 19th cent.; letterbook of Joseph Gurney Bevan; orders addressed to Mildred and Allen, early 19th century; letterbook n.d.; family letters n.d.; letters 1830s; notebooks of D and R Hanbury n.d.; journal 1863 (with Glaxo babies poster); 'William Allen's preparation book' n.d.; Daniel Hanbury's notebooks 1842–78; letterbooks 19th cent.; Cornelius Hanbury's letterbook 1896–99 and deed 1890s; general ledger 1783–1804 ('Silvanus Bevan deceased'); prescription books n.d.; papers, incl. William Allen's letters, 19th cent.; trial balance 1826, W A Hanbury's teenage journal 1836–39, lab notebook 1881; deeds 19th cent.; letters and other papers of Cornelius Hanbury 1880s on; letters of Cornelius Hanbury 1890s incl. documents re probate of W A Hanbury and estate of A W A de Hanbury 1898 on; trust deeds, other legal documents and papers relating to debentures n.d.; deeds etc. n.d. (Ref: Acc 96/14:3, Acc 96/55:1, Acc 96/66, Acc 98/20:6, Acc20/11, Acc 98/20:12, SP54, SP 300, SP 697 pt, SP 815 pt, SP 1387 pt, SP 1389, SP 1390/1-7, SP 1391/1-5,

SP 1392/1-6, SP 1394, SP 1396/4, SP 1405/1-5, SP 1406/1-3, SP 1617 pt, SP 2274 pt, E1X 036 - GGA 36, E1X 463 - GGA 463, E1X 435 G61 - GGA 435, GGA 664)

Directors' and general meetings minutes 1894 on; memoranda and articles of association 1951-60; board papers 1955-78 (w); directors' papers 1971-72; executive committee minutes and papers 1966-78; committee meeting minutes: research and development (finance and policy) 1955-61, new products 1950-61, marketing 1967-76; share registers 1926-35, 1941-69; dividend lists 1912-25; share valuation 1938-49; stock exchange papers 1920-62; papers and correspondence re debentures 1894-65; share purchases 1964-66; annual reports and accounts 1921-68; accounting schedules and papers 1934-74; budget sheets 1974-76; accounts 1953-78; journals: private 1948-72 (w), reserves and provisions 1956-58, export 1965, 1970; cash books 1960-70; financial registers: assets 1970-71, 1974-75, capital 1971-72, plant 1946-70, motor 1970-73; capital control statements 1974-77; capital expenditure papers 1969-78; investment grant applications 1966-76; papers re taxation 1921-54, 1961-75; audit papers 1940-75 (w); papers re acquisition n.d.; commercial papers, negotiations and correspondence 1953-74, n.d.; papers re merger with Glaxo Laboratories Ltd 1958; papers re subsidiary companies 1954-58, n.d.; production rationalisation papers 1964; research papers and correspondence 1940, 1949-50; licence agreements 1968; papers re surgical division 1947-49; overseas representatives' papers n.d.; correspondence: orders and papers re export business 1793-1823, 1925-50s, Cornelius Hanbury 19th cent., investments 1966-69, Midland Bank re overdraft facilities 1947-56; valuations of plant and equipment, Bethnal Green 1950; papers re property 1948, 1954-63; papers re overseas subsidiaries 1904-08, 1931-57; historical notes and articles 1965-66, n.d.; records unlisted 18th-20th cents.

Allen & Hanburys (Farms) Ltd: directors' meetings minutes 1956-85; register of directors' shares 1967-68.

Allen & Hanburys (Research) Ltd: annual reports and accounts 1958, 1964-70.

Allied Laboratories Ltd: directors' meetings minutes 1937-n.d.; chairman's meetings minutes 1960-64; combined register of members, directors and share ledger 1937-61; annual reports and accounts 1938-63 (w); trading and profit and loss accounts n.d.; journals: 1959-65, private 1964-65; accounting papers 1956-65; audit papers 1965; papers re acquisition by Edinburgh Pharmaceutical Industries Ltd and Allen & Hanburys Ltd n.d.; payroll papers 1963-65; statutory documents and correspondence 1957-80.

Insulin A B Ltd: register of shares 1967–69; annual reports and accounts 1963–68; ledger 1961–68; auditor's reports 1963–67; finance directors' papers 1958–69; directors' attendance book 1964–68; statutory forms 1964–78.

Records 2: Museum of the History of Science, University of Oxford, Old Ashmolean Building, Broad Street, Oxford OX1 3AZ

Prescription books 1840–94 (w); pharmaceutical and chemical supplies, orders and invoices 1795, 1802, n.d.; scrapbook, containing autographed prescriptions from distinguished physicians collected by, and some written for, the Hanbury family 1790, 1822–73, n.d. (Ref: MSS Allen & Hanbury 1-9)

Records 3: Royal Botanic Gardens, Library & Archives, Kew, Richmond TW9 3AE

Correspondence and miscellaneous reports of Daniel Hanbury, Cecil Hanbury, Frederick Janson Hanbury and Sir Thomas Hanbury re drugs and plants 19th cent. (Ref: Directors' correspondence 26, 29, 31-9, 41, 87, 109, 121, 134, 142, 146, 148, 152, 214, 218; R Melville – Drugs – Misc.)

Records 4: Archives & Manuscripts, Wellcome Library for the History & Understanding of Medicine, 183 Euston Road, London NW1 2BE

Out-letterbook of Daniel Hanbury to overseas correspondents 1858–60. (Ref: MS 5304)

Records 5: The Museum Curator, Royal Pharmaceutical Society of Great Britain, 1 Lambeth High Street, London SE1 7JN

Laboratory calculation book 1795–98; drug notebooks 1920–49; stock book 1810–11; cost price book 1824–44; price list of drugs 1844–46; correspondence, notes and papers: William Allen 1824, 1833, Daniel Hanbury 1856–75, n.d.; Quaker House marriage entry for Silvanus Bevan and Elizabeth Quare 1715. (Ref: IRA.1996.037, 090, 230-31; IRA.1997.008-10, 021, 044, 072, 134)

Records 6: Society of Friends, Library of the Religious Society of Friends, Friends House, 173-177 Euston Road, London NW1 2BJ

William Allen, diary fragments 1815. (Ref: Temp MSS 57/13)

Records 7: History of Advertising Trust, HAT House, 12 Raveningham Centre, Raveningham NR14 6NU

Advertisements for *Haliborange* 1976–79. (Ref: MEAL collection 1976–78, R75)

STAFFORD ALLEN & SONS LTD
20-42 Wharf Road, Shoreditch, Hackney, London

Medicinal herb grower, extractor, miller and manufacturer

History: In 1833 Stafford Allen, the nephew of William Allen of Allen & Hanburys, established, in partnership with Charles May, a drug milling business at Ampthill, Bedfordshire. Later new premises were purchased in Cowper Street, City Road, London, and the site at Ampthill was used as a herb growing farm which supplied the London business with raw materials. The firm engaged in grinding, extracting, processing and distilling these materials into semi-manufactured products such as liquid extracts and emulsions, which were supplied to pharmaceutical manufacturers and wholesalers. In 1843 Charles May left the partnership to join a firm of engineers, Ransome, Sims & May, in Norwich, Norfolk, and George Allen, Stafford's brother, who had been made a partner in 1841, replaced him. This partnership was styled S & G Allen. In 1857 the partnership agreement between George and Stafford Allen was dissolved and George Allen left to conduct the Ampthill business on his own account as George Allen & Co. In 1861 Edward Ransome Allen, Stafford's son, joined his father in partnership, followed in 1863 by his younger brother, William Clarkson Allen. Following this the London business was renamed Stafford Allen & Sons and in 1893, on the death of George Allen, the business, George Allen & Co, was acquired by Stafford Allen & Sons. In 1898 the Cowper Street premises were expanded to incorporate new pepper mills, but in 1910 were destroyed by fire and rebuilt a year later. The firm was incorporated as a limited liability company, Stafford Allen & Sons Ltd, in 1899 and in 1902 a factory and farm at Long Melford, Suffolk, were purchased, the plant and farm stock from Ampthill transferred, and the Ampthill premises sold. The company acquired 3 drug grinding businesses, Horner & Sons in 1907, Ferris & Williams in 1913 and J & E Barringer Ltd in 1931. The latter was established in 1846, and incorporated as a limited liability company in 1907, with head offices at Hackney Wick, Hackney, London. In 1938 Stafford Allen & Sons Ltd's headquarters were moved to new premises in Wharf Road, Shoreditch, Hackney, London, and following further destruction of the Cowper Street buildings during the Second World War, the decision was taken to vacate these premises in 1958. The company specialised not only in drug milling and grinding, but also in oil distillation and the manufacture of galenicals. In addition it produced non-pharmaceutical products such as food flavourings, perfumery compounds and insecticides, and established a subsidiary company, during the early 1950s, Allen Chlorophyll Co Ltd, to manufacture chlorophyll. In 1964 the business of Stafford Allen & Sons Ltd was acquired by Albright & Wilson Ltd, a phosphorus manufacturer, and continued to trade under its own name. In 1966 the company acquired the business of Warrick Bros Ltd, Lavender House, Seymour Road, London, a supplier of pastilles and lozenges to retail pharmacists. In the same year Stafford Allen & Sons Ltd, W J Bush & Co Ltd, a fine chemical and toiletries manufacturer, and A Boake Roberts & Co Ltd, an industrial chemical manufacturer, merged to form Bush Boake Allen Ltd, a subsidiary of Albright & Wilson Ltd.

'Centenary of Stafford Allen & Sons', *Chemist and Druggist*, 1 July 1933; *A Century of Service 1833–1933: Achievement through a century* (Stafford Allen & Sons, London, 1933); W G Norris, 'Visit to Stafford Allen & Sons Ltd, Long Melford Factory', *Manufacturing Chemist*, Nov 1957; 'Stafford Allen', *Pharmaceutical News*, April 1959; *Stafford Allen & Sons Ltd* (Stafford Allen, London, c.1930s); 'Stafford Allen to Join A & W Group', *Albright Magazine*, Feb 1964, 2-3; *The History of 'Allen's English': Eighty years of progress* (Stafford Allen, London, 1911)

Records 1: Bush Boake Allen Ltd, Blackhorse Lane, Walthamstow, London E17 5QP

Articles of partnership, Stafford Allen and George Allen 1841; minutes: directors' and general meetings 1899–1907, directors' meetings 1908–53; papers re acquisition by Albright & Wilson Ltd 1964; register of members, directors, shares and mortgages 1899–1973; share register 1940–59; annual report and accounts 1948–58; balance sheet, profit and loss account and general accounts 1908–53 (w); accounts with correspondence 1954–58; ledgers: expenses 1961–66, private 1888–90s; day book, Cowper Street 1833–37; audit programme 1938–41; certificate of contract re land taxation 1876; formulae books 1920s–30s; still books 1909–60 (w); galenical production record books 1900–16; manufacturing production costs 1857–84; order books 1941–50; export order 1935; product leaflets 1935, 1959, 1964, n.d.; price lists 1952–66; market report and news 1964; quality control instructions booklet 1964; advertisements 1910–17, c.1943, n.d.; title deeds and deeds relating to property 19th–20th cent., 1847, 1866–79, 1904, 1919–72; statutory declaration 1982; mortgage papers 1839, 1882, 1893; leases and tenancy agreements 1839, 1923–45, 1974–75; grant of right of way 1875; property assignments 1849, 1934; conveyances 1839,

1862–72, 1904–72; agreements re land 1919, 1933–58, 1975–82; licence agreement with Grand Union Canal Co 1937; inventory and valuation: Cowper Street 1863, Wharf Road and Long Melford 1962; location map, Long Melford n.d.; memoranda re property 1877, 1972–78; papers re admissions to property: William Byford 1867, Edward J Bence 1918; photographs, production at Wharf Road and Long Melford 1950s–60s, 20th cent.; register of employees 1931–56; career prospectus n.d.; *Stafford Allen Pharmaceutical News* 1959–61, 1963; *Spice News* 1962; lectures re chlorophyll 1951–52; research papers by staff 1911, 1950s; stationery guardbook n.d.

George Allen & Co: accounts 1894–1901; statement of affairs, schedules of debtors and creditors, sundry receipts and payments 1893–94.

Allen Chlorophyll Co Ltd: share certificates book 1952; transfer journal 1959–67; ledgers: overseas accounts 1952–66, payments 1961–66, nominal 1962–64; production leaflets c.1952, n.d.; *Allen Chlorophyll Bulletin* 1952, 1953.

J & E Barringer Ltd: directors' and general meetings minutes 1907–74; combined register of members and share ledger 1907–74; balance sheet and profit and loss accounts 1941–57; bought ledger 1936–67; nominal ledger 1959–67.

Warrick Bros Ltd: combined register of members and share ledger 1949–73; share certificate books 1944–68; share transfer forms 1952–60; journal 1964; stock lozenges formulae book 1877.

Records 2: William Ransom & Son plc, 104 Bancroft, Hitchin SG5 1LY

Articles of association 1907; special resolutions re articles of association 1907, 1920; directors' annual report 1925; balance sheets 1918–24; statement of sales 1915–20; deeds of declaration re sales with William Ransom & Son and William Phene Neal 1910, 1915; price regulation agreement with William Ransom & Son and William Phene Neal 1910; price lists: wholesale 1940, 1952, pharmaceutical 1959, export 1965; advertisements 1952–56; correspondence: agreement with William Ransom & Son re shared business 1933, A B Lucas re accounts 1950.

ALLIANCE UNICHEM PLC
UniChem House, Cox Lane, Chessington K79 1SN

Wholesaler of pharmaceuticals and chemists' sundries and retail chemist

History: UniChem Ltd was incorporated as a limited liability company at 219 Upper Tooting Road, London, in 1938. It was a pharmaceutical wholesaling company, inspired by Ernest Skues, which was financed and controlled solely by pharmacists and which served independent pharmacies. During the Second World War the number of pharmacies with membership of UniChem Ltd increased steadily. In 1944 UniChem Ltd acquired the business of Broadwater Properties Ltd, and in 1946 established warehouse premises on site at Broadwater Road, Tooting, Wandsworth, London, in order to keep pace with increased demand. A van delivery service was established in the following year. During the 1940s UniChem Ltd began to specialise in the supply of branded ethical drugs, galenicals and generic bulk tablets as opposed to over-the-counter medicines, and published an *Ethical Products List* and a *Prescriber's List*. A second warehouse was acquired at Fortescue Road, Colliers Wood, Merton, London, during the 1950s, to enable the company to distribute chemists' sundries, and in 1958 and 1961 further sites were established at Walthamstow, Waltham Forest, London and Nuneaton, Warwickshire. In 1962 UniChem (Investments) Ltd was incorporated as a subsidiary of UniChem Ltd at Crown House, Morden, Merton, London, which became the new headquarters of UniChem Ltd. Its purpose was to buy and sell shares in the parent company. It ceased trading in 1972 and was wound up in 1982. In 1963 UniChem Ltd acquired the business of 2 wholesale companies, P D S (Leeds) Ltd and P A S (Yorks) Ltd, and established a subsidiary company, UniChem (Northern) Ltd, which traded until 1973 and was dissolved in 1986. In 1969 UniChem Ltd converted its status from a limited liability company to an industrial and provident society, thereby maintaining its membership-only base. It also began production of its own-label pharmaceutical range. Retail pharmacists still represented a majority on the board of directors, but a professional executive team was charged with the running of the organisation. Regional branches were established by 1973, at Sheffield; Swansea; Preston, Lancashire; and Newcastle upon Tyne, and a Scottish branch was established at Livingston, West Lothian, in 1974. UniChem became the first British wholesaler to introduce the computer system WOLF (Warehouse-On-Line-Facility) in 1975 and in 1976 a branch was opened in Exeter, Devon. From the 1980s UniChem began offering loans and guarantees to independent pharmacists, to enable them to open new premises or to expand existing businesses, and also offered insurance and pension policies. By 1987 it was clear that the benefits of industrial and provident society status were limited, preventing expansion into new markets, for example, the hospitals sector. In 1990 the society was re-converted to a public limited liability company, UniChem plc, and its shares floated on the London Stock Exchange. Following this, the company embarked upon a programme of retail pharmacy acquisition, purchasing E Moss Ltd, with 92 pharmacies, and Scott Chemists Ltd, a Scottish retail and wholesale company, in 1992. It also acquired 2 wholesale businesses,

Bradford Chemists' Alliance in 1993 and Hall Forster & Co in 1994. At the end of 1997 UniChem plc merged with Alliance Sante SA to become Alliance UniChem plc. This move consolidated its position as a distributor, wholesaler and retailer of pharmaceutical, medical and healthcare products in Europe.

'UniChem: fifty years of service 1938–1988', *Chemist and Druggist*, supplement to mark company's golden jubilee, 21 May 1988, 3-14; 'The UniChem Report', *Pharmaceutical Journal*, supplement, to mark company's 40th anniversary, 9 Sept 1978; G White & K Hide, 'UniChem's Golden Jubilee', *Pharmaceutical Journal*, 2 Jan 1988, 32-7

Records 1: Alliance UniChem plc, UniChem House, Cox Lane, Chessington KT9 1SN

Minutes: directors' meetings, incl. trading accounts 1938 to date, general meetings 1940 to date; memoranda and articles of association 1938–64; certificates of incorporation 1938, 1969, 1990; application for company registration: declaration of compliance 1938, statement of nominal capital 1938; papers re registration as industrial and provident society 1969; society rules 1969–90; committee meeting minutes: 1938–69, formula 1942–57, extension 1942–45, staff 1945–69; registers of seals 1969–89; register of directors' shareholdings 1948–69; register of members and share ledgers 1938–69; registers of share transfers: cumulative preference 1952–69, ordinary 1952–71, noteholders 1954–69; applications for conversion of loan notes to loan stock and loan stock to member shares 1969–80; annual reports and accounts 1939 to date; press cuttings book 1938–64; executives' employment agreements 1946–64; pension fund, trustees' accounts 1966–72; pension and assurance scheme, correspondence and membership applications 1907–80s; UniChem magazine, *News and Views* 1954–66 (w); silver jubilee dinner menu and seating plan 1964.

Broadwater Properties Ltd: directors' and general meetings minutes 1944–53; memorandum and articles of association 1944; liquidation and amalgamation agreement 1951.

Scott Chemists Ltd: memorandum and articles of association 1975; certificates of incorporation 1975, 1992.

UniChem (Investments) Ltd: directors' and general meetings minutes 1952–82; memorandum and articles of association 1962; certificate of incorporation 1962; combined register of members and share ledger 1962–70; accounts 1969–80.

UniChem (Northern) Ltd: directors' and general meetings minutes, incl. share applications and annual trading reports 1963–83; memorandum and articles of association 1963; certificate of incorporation 1963; register of directors and secretaries 1963–75; combined register of members and share ledger 1963; share certificates 1963–70; share prospectus 1964; share issue register 1964–67; register of share transfers 1963–70; annual reports and accounts 1966–67; annual accounts 1965–82 (w).

Records 2: Dr Peter M Worling, The Grange, 29 Fernielaw Avenue, Edinburgh EH13 0EF

Report 1959.

Records 3: The Museum Curator, Royal Pharmaceutical Society of Great Britain, 1 Lambeth High Street, London SE1 7JN

Tape recorded interview with Marion Rawlings, community pharmacist 1996. (Ref: IRT.1996.82)

PHILIP J ANNISON
15 North Bar Street, Beverley, East Riding of Yorkshire

Chemist

History: In 1830 the business at 15 North Bar Street, Beverley, East Riding of Yorkshire, was trading as William Pipes. Thomas Marshall was in business as a chemist and druggist in Beverley prior to 1868, and by 1876 was operating from North Bar Street and Toll Gavel. He was still registered as a chemist and druggist in 1895. Ownership of the business later passed to T H Gabbetis and John Stanser. Philip J Annison acquired the business some time after the First World War.

Records: East Riding of Yorkshire Archives & Records Service, County Hall, Beverley HU17 9BA

Thomas Marshall: ledgers 1857–65, 1875–91, day books 1859–82 (w), bill book 1871–73, prescription books 1850–73; John Stanser: ledger 1914–24, prescription book 1932–45; Philip J Annison: prescription book 1937–47, bottle label, 'Annison's Carbolic Seed Dressing' n.d.; photograph of the premises n.d. (Ref: DDX 186, DDX 278, Acc 2073)

APLIN CHEMIST
1 Silver Street, Trowbridge, Wiltshire

Dispensing chemist

History: John Henry Aplin was registered as a chemist and druggist in 1888, and in 1889 established a business at 6 Silver Street, Trowbridge, Wiltshire. He traded from these premises on his own account until 1926, when he ceased to be registered. In 1907 a relative, also named John Henry Aplin, was registered as a chemist and druggist at Clematis Cottage, Yerbury Street, Trowbridge. In 1928 he was trading from 41 Hilperton Road, Trowbridge, and in 1935 re-located to 1 Silver Street. In 1938 his business was styled Aplins, and in 1953 was incorporated as a limited liability company, Aplins (Chemists) Ltd. In 1965 John Henry Aplin retired from the business, moving to 39 Hilperton Road, Trowbridge, and the business was continued by Robert John Aplin, who resided at Arvonia, Trowle, Trowbridge, and traded from 1 Silver Street. Aplins (Chemists) Ltd was dissolved, and the business traded as Aplin Chemist from 1968 until 1993, when it was acquired by Kingswood Chemists Ltd. In 1994, it was acquired by Lloyds Chemists Ltd, and renamed Lloyds Retail Chemists Ltd. It was still trading in 1997.

Records: Wiltshire & Swindon Record Office, County Hall, Trowbridge BA14 8JG

Profit and loss accounts and balance sheets 1921–43; account book, shop payments 1943–50; accounts, Mr Perry's dental practice above Aplin's shop 1913–19; cash books 1939–53; spirit stock books 1919–31; artificial limb order book 1916–43; recipe book c.1900–60; prescription books 1861–1975; monthly record book, doctors' prescriptions 1915–69; rental agreement and inventory re 41 Hilperton Road, Trowbridge 1897. (Ref: 2152)

E ASHLEY LTD
4 Cheapside, Derby

Chemist

History: William Ashley was in business as a chemist and druggist at Cheapside, Derby, prior to 1868. He traded from this address until 1902. In 1911 the business was incorporated as a limited liability company, E Ashley Ltd, operating from 4 Cheapside. It ceased trading in 1982, and was dissolved in 1985.

Records: Derby Local Studies Library, 25B Irongate, Derby DE1 3GL

Ledgers: accounts, incl. stock, wages, fixtures and fittings 1921–42, goods supplied to customers 1884–1924; day book 1919–21; cash books 1921–69; recipe book n.d.; prescription books 1820–99 (w); sale of poisons register 1926–36; explosives register 1876–1924. (Ref: DL 280)

JOHN ASKER LTD
12 Bridge Street, Stratford-upon-Avon, Warwickshire

Pharmacist, later photographic chemist

History: Thomas Cheney New was in business in Evesham, Worcestershire, before 1868. In 1873 he registered as a chemist and druggist and in 1887 established a business at 12 Bridge Street, Stratford-upon-Avon, Warwickshire. Between 1892 and 1893 he moved to 2 Prospect Place, Stratford-upon-Avon, and the Bridge Street premises were acquired by Francis Cole, who had been in business since before 1868 at Claughton, Wirral. In 1904 the business was acquired by B M Preston, who traded from 12 Bridge Street until 1912, when it was acquired by Alan Foster Brownlow, who was in business there from around 1927 until 1961. In 1962 the business was incorporated as a limited liability company, John Asker Ltd.

Records: Shakespeare Birthplace Trust Records Office, The Shakespeare Centre, Stratford-upon-Avon CV37 6QW

Prescription books c.1876–1954; dangerous drugs register 1954–63; sale of poisons register 1960–62. (Ref: DR 301, DR 332)

ASTRAZENECA PHARMACEUTICALS LTD
Alderley House, Alderley Park, Macclesfield, Cheshire

Pharmaceutical manufacturer

History: In 1926 Imperial Chemical Industries Ltd (ICI Ltd) was incorporated as a limited liability company following the merger of Brunner Mond & Co Ltd, manufacturer of alkalis, Nobel Industries Ltd, explosives manufacturer, United Alkali Co Ltd, manufacturer of chlorine, disinfectants and fine chemicals, and British Dyestuffs Corporation Ltd, manufacturer of dyestuffs. A head office was located at 9 Millbank, London, and the company established a number of specialist divisions, one of which was Dyestuffs. In 1916 it had been discovered that acriflavine, a yellow dye, could be used to disinfect wounds. Following this, further research was conducted which demonstrated that there were medicinal properties to a number of dyestuffs. During the 1930s this relationship became widely recognised, and in 1936 ICI Ltd established a medicines section within its Dyestuffs Division, based at Blackley, Manchester. This section, among whose staff was the prominent chemist, Dr Frank Rose, conducted research into synthetic organic pharmaceuticals. In 1939 *Mepacrine* was produced as a treatment for malaria, and during the 1940s was replaced by a superior treatment, *Paludrine*. The section was also one of the first in Britain to manufacture penicillin, at the company's fermentation plant at Trafford Park, Trafford. As a result, in 1942, ICI Ltd was requested to conduct research into 20 essential drugs. This led to the incorporation of a subsidiary company, Imperial Chemical (Pharmaceuticals) Ltd, in the same year, as a marketing company for these new products. The medical section began production of antiseptics during the Second World War, and in 1957 launched *Fluothane* as a safe alternative anaesthetic to ether and chloroform. By 1957 work conducted by the section, and Imperial Chemical (Pharmaceuticals) Ltd, had expanded to such an extent, that both were removed from the Dyestuffs Division and redefined as an independent Pharmaceuticals Division of ICI Ltd, based at Alderley Park, Macclesfield, Cheshire. In 1960 a beta-blocker used in the treatment of heart disease, *Alderlin*, was introduced, and was later replaced by improved versions of the drug, *Inderal* and *Tenormin*. ICI Ltd also manufactured the proprietary antiseptic *Savlon*. In 1966 building extensions took place at Alderley Park, and a new pharmaceuticals production plant was opened at nearby Hurdsfield industrial estate, Macclesfield. A further plant was opened at Avlon Works, near Bristol, in 1971. In 1978 ICI Ltd received the Queen's Award for Technology, for *Novadex*, an anti-oestrogen cancer drug, and in 1991 for *Zoladex*, a treatment predominantly for male cancers. By 1990 the Pharmaceuticals Division comprised 21 production sites and 150 sales offices across the world. The parent company, ICI plc, housed many divisions, 3 of which were grouped together as the 'biosciences': pharmaceuticals, agro-chemicals and specialties. In 1993 these 3 divisions demerged from ICI plc, to consolidate their businesses within a newly incorporated, wholly-owned subsidiary company, Zeneca plc. Each of the former bioscience divisions was incorporated as a subsidiary of Zeneca plc, the Pharmaceuticals Division becoming Zeneca Pharmaceuticals Ltd. This company was the most successful, accounting in 1993 for 40 per cent of sales and 83 per cent of profits. In 1997 its headquarters remained at Alderley Park, and the company continued to manufacture cardiovascular, anti-cancer and anaesthetic products. In 1998 it merged with the pharmeceutical company Astra of Sweden and changed its name to AstraZeneca Pharmaceuticals Ltd.

ICI In Focus (ICI, London, 1965); 'ICI' in T Derdak (ed), *International Directory of Company Histories*, Vol. 1 (St James Press, London, 1988) 351-3; *Pharmaceutical Research in ICI 1936–57* (ICI Pharmaceuticals, 1957); P Brodie, *Crescent over Cathay: China and ICI, 1898 to 1956* (Oxford University Press, 1990); K Holland, 'ICI Pharmaceuticals', *Pharmaceutical Journal*, 12 Sept, 1987, 286-8; C Kennedy, *ICI: The company that changed our lives* (Hutchinson, London, 1986); W J Reader, *Imperial Chemical Industries: A history. Volume I: 1870–1926* (Oxford University Press, Oxford, 1970); W J Reader, *Imperial Chemical Industries: A history. Volume II: 1926–1952* (Oxford University Press, Oxford, 1975); W A Sexton, 'The Research Laboratories of the Pharmaceutical Division of ICI', *Chemistry and Industry*, 1962, 372-7

Records 1: ICI plc, The Library, Imperial Chemical House, 9 Millbank, London SW13JF

Annual report 1993; report on the company 1993; magazine, *Zeneca Pharmaceuticals* 1993 to date.

ICI plc: memoranda and articles of association 1926, 1949, 1987; chairman's general meeting speeches 1949, 1958, 1967; annual reports 1927–94; directors' report and accounts 1927; annual review and summary financial statement 1993; in-house magazines: *ICI Magazine* 1928–39, 1947–87, *ICI Magazine Supplement* 1955–75 (w), *The Roundel* 1988–93, *Head Office News Headline* 1976–77, *Headline* (subsequently *Newsline*) 1978–88, *ICI Today* 1988–91.

ICI Pharmaceuticals Division: divisional board papers 1957–62; papers re liquidation of subsidiary companies 1957–59; divisional organisation papers 1957–60; pharmaceuticals policy papers 1933–44; papers re Pharmacy and Poisons Act 1933–44; papers re potential acquisitions and mergers 1930–49, 1957–59; divisional directors' papers: H Mond 1933–35, W H Coates 1933–50; papers of H Gaskell, director of post-war works committee 1940–49; production papers: venture with Dupont, Metropolitan Vickers and British Drug Houses Ltd 1933–39, products, technical development 1935–44, manufacture of *Atebrin* by Trafford Chemical Co Ltd 1938, manufacture in time of national emergency 1938–43, anti-malarial drugs 1938–44, proposed collaboration with Bayer Products 1939–40, manufacture by Dyestuffs Group 1939–43, negotiations with Wellcome Foundation Ltd re manufacture and sale 1940, sulphanilamides 1940–44, Trafford Park penicillin plant 1942–44, pharmaceuticals finishing factory 1944, Thailand manufacture 1956; pharmaceutical research papers: chemotherapeutic research, British Drug Houses Ltd 1926–27, cancer research 1930–34, British Dyestuffs Corporation 1934, general 1935–40, molecular distillation for pharmaceuticals and vitamins in USA 1936–44, chemistry of immunisation 1937-38, immunisation and marketing of vaccine with Burroughs Wellcome & Co Ltd 1938-43, collaboration with Boots Pure Drug Co Ltd 1939-43, Therapeutic Research Company of Great Britain Ltd 1941-44, proposed veterinary research field station 1942-43, collaboration with American companies 1943-44; booklet re pharmaceutical research at ICI Ltd 1936-57; sales papers: agreements with British Dyestuffs Group and British Drug Houses Ltd re sales of flavines and antrypal 1933-40, Dyestuffs Group products 1939-41, joint selling company with Bayer Products Ltd and Winthrop Co 1939-40, Export Council pharmaceuticals group 1940-43, ICI (China) Ltd 1941, USA pharmaceuticals 1943-44, agencies abroad 1944-49, 1956-60, USA-Dupont purchases 1945-46, registration of pharmaceuticals abroad 1945-47, ICI mission to East Africa re pharmaceuticals 1947, sales agreements, Belgian Congo 1947; reports: pharmaceutical fine chemical industry 1930, companies in the British pharmaceutical industry 1955; papers re *British Pharmacopoeia* Commission 1936-41; property papers: storage accommodation 1943-44, offices 1944; magazines: *Pharma World* 1990-94, *ICI Pharmaceuticals* 1990-92; photographs of factories, offices, production, products and staff 1986, n.d.; booklet re first 74 years of pharmaceuticals business 1990; historical research files 1930-57.

Imperial Chemical (Pharmaceuticals) Ltd: memorandum and articles of association 1942; organisation chart 1951; files re pharmaceutical chemicals 1941-44; labour arrangements under essential work order of 1941, 1941-43.

Records 2: AstraZeneca Pharmaceuticals Ltd, AstraZeneca Library Centre, Merside, Alderley Park, Macclesfield SK10 4TG

ICI Pharmaceuticals Division: papers re reorganisation of division 1960s-70, 1979, 1982-86; company code books 1939, 1945; report re development of chemical group 1960; organisational charts 1949, 1953-78 (w); re-valuation of assets 1961; papers and correspondence re expenditure 1957; library ledgers 1956-71; scientific meetings minutes and committee papers: chemotherapeutic research committee 1936-44, 1947-54, penicillin technical conference 1942-59, pharmaceuticals conference 1943-54, joint pharmaceuticals division and biological department 1943-54, research panel 1945-55, medicinal products technical conference 1947-48, 1952-58, development memorandum 1954-60, research director's conference 1954-57, management committee 1955-63, biological hazards committee 1955-63, penicillin management committee 1957-63, laboratory safety committee 1957-81, advisory committee 1962, biological research committee 1962-69, re research collaboration with Glaxo and Cyanamid 1960-61, 1963-71; scientific period reports: biochemicals section 1936, 1939-47, medicinal chemicals section 1937-47, medicinal process section 1939-54, research department 1946-80, pharmaceutical research and service laboratory

1946–52, medicinals division 1947–54, antibiotics process section 1951–57, joint chemical, organic and biochemical sections 1954–57, statistical research section 1954–57, biological group 1954–57, organics division 1955–82, medicinals formulation section 1956, organic chemicals division 1956–57, intermediates pioneer section 1956–57, research experimental plant 1956–57, physical chemical division 1958–62, general organic chemicals division 1958–62, plant and process division 1958, development department 1958–63, 1987, productivity services department 1959–68, research and development 1962–63; research papers and correspondence re drugs development 1959–60; research reports 1964, 1975; programmes for experimental work 1955–58; fermentation plant: minutes and memoranda 1958–81, reviews and reports 1952–81, customs and excise files 1968–81, ledgers 1957–68, 1970–71, 1975, costing and accounting reports 1943–46, 1957–71, accounts 1945–46, 1954–81, policy and development files 1951–53, 1957–80, production planning files 1962–80, production sheets 1967–69, works results 1961–81, *Oxytetracycline* files 1943–74, *Griseofulvin* batch record books, suspension sheets and files 1960–81, penicillin suspensions record books 1962–74 (w), purity test record books 1968–79, exposure plate records 1978–80, batch record books 1945–75, recipe sheets 1960s–70s, pass-on books 1968–71, papers re infections 1962–78, papers re abnormal occurrences 1958–81, technical reports 1966–81, register of process literature 1940–49, papers re stocks 1956–81, materials files 1944–46, 1965–80, raw materials sampling registrations book 1975–77, effluents files 1963–81, equipment files 1959–81, papers re expansion programme 1959–61, site plans 1950s–70s, papers re plant 1964–81, personnel files 1957–81, accident statistics 1964–81, health and safety files 1961–81, services files 1962–81, quality control files 1962–80, correspondence 1962–81; personal papers of Dr F L Rose: committee minutes and papers 1933–50, 1954–56, research papers and reports 1940–46, 1954–56, research plans 1937–45, 1948–49, photograph of conference delegates 1951; papers re drugs: monographs 1961, notebook re developments 1939–42, tables 1958, booklets 1971, 1976, 1983; booklets re illnesses 1976; handbook for epileptics 1968; technical handbook 1978; technical report 1949; technical service notes 1960–84; notes re index to reports 1958; product reviews 1944–47, 1983; catalogue of stockable items 1965; product handbooks 1961–62, 1969–70; product information and promotional literature 1950s–86; sales catalogue 1938; advertisement n.d.; promotional booklets 1949, 1955, 1960–86; press cuttings books re products 1977–86; press cuttings: drug development and costs 1973, William H Perkins' discovery of 'mauve' 1856, premises 1959–75, research laboratories 1970, pharmaceutical industry n.d.; poster re malaria parasite 1952; maps and plans of Alderley Park estate 1842, 1871–72, 1938–72 (w), n.d.; map of Macclesfield 19th cent.; architectural plans: Trafford Park fermentation plant n.d., building extension work 1970, modifications to laboratory block 1976; reports re Alderley Park 1979–89; insurance valuations,

Alderley Park 1956, 1959; purchase orders for premises and fittings 1961–64; site rules n.d.; list of works 1972; poster re new laboratories at Alderley Park 1957; invitation to opening of research laboratories, Blackley 1938; laboratories visitors books 1943–64; correspondence re libraries 1950s–70s; managing directors' instructions 1954–57, 1963; managing directors' memoranda 1957–58; managers' remits 1964; staff lists 1936–67, 1970–72, 1979; telephone directories and staff lists 1971–76, 1983–85; staff representation report 1970; staff information book 1972; careers booklets 1955, 1961; papers re staff induction courses 1965–66; training manuals 1977; safety regulations for chemical laboratory assistants 1962; memoranda re staff: appointments 1977–79, transfer to Pharmaceuticals Division 1957; central labour department code book 1953; guides: management services 1974–75, technical information services 1969; long service awards: list of recipients 1965, catalogue 1972; company magazines: *ICI Magazine* 1935, *Fulshaw Times* 1949–65, *SCAN* 1966 to date, *Pharma World* 1989 to date; correspondence: transfer of reports and records to Pharmaceutical Division 1956, staff salary increases 1966, War Office 1919; computer information systems handbooks 1975–82; information news sheets 1963–68; catalogues of medical films and videotapes 1978–86; cinefilms and videotapes re company 1973–86, n.d.; photographs: board of directors 1926, staff c.1900, 1946–63, n.d., buildings and laboratories c.1912–86, n.d., drugs n.d., conferences and awards 1963–73; cartoons: senior management 1973, laboratory n.d.; Butterwick Club: list of members 1951, programme 1951; social club: honours lists 1978 89, minutes and papers of motoring section 1963–72; historical notes 1938, 1951–87, n.d.; biographical notes: Dr F L Rose 1927–74, Mr I Levinstein 1845–1916; company publications and papers 1937–86; published reference works and lectures 1961–63, 1984–85.

Records 3: The Royal Society, 6 Carlton House Terrace, London SW1Y 5AG

Correspondence between ICI and Sir Henry Hallett Dale 1943–57; correspondence and reports of Howard Walter Florey, scientific adviser n.d. (Ref: 93 HD/48.3, HF 194)

Records 4: The Museum Curator, Royal Pharmaceutical Society of Great Britain, 1 Lambeth High Street, London SE1 7JN

Howard Walter Florey: notes re honorary fellowship of Pharmaceutical Society of Great Britain 1966–68, obituary 1968. (Ref: IRA.1996.375)

Records 5: History of Advertising Trust, HAT House, 12 Raveningham Centre, Raveningham NR14 6NU

Papers and memoranda with agents re advertising 1988–91; advertisements for *Savlon* 1974–89. (Ref: Leo Burnett research material; MEAL collection 1974–89, R10-80)

GEORGE ATKINSON & CO
66 Aldersgate Street, London

Chemical manufacturer

History: In 1654 a Mr Primatt began compounding drugs at 66 Aldersgate Street, London. During the early eighteenth century, his son, Humphrey Primatt, was joined in partnership by John Maud, and the business was styled Primatt & Maud by 1744 and Maud & Primatt, Chymists, by 1753. The firm's product range included iodine, bromides and camphor. Following the death of John Maud in 1782, his son, also named John Maud, assumed control of the business on his own account from 1798 to 1820. From 1821 the business passed through a succession of partners, including Biggar, Atkinson, Dell and Chippendale, until 1865 when it was styled George Atkinson & Co. In 1884 the production of certain kinds of chemicals was banned in the City of London and the firm moved to factory premises at Southall, Ealing, London, which were named Aldersgate Chemical Works, and warehouses and offices at 31-32 St Andrews Hill, London. The firm was acquired by Whiffen & Sons, fine chemical manufacturers of Lombard Road, Battersea, Wandsworth, London, in 1887 but continued to trade under its own name.

R S Law, *The End of a Chapter: The story of Whiffen & Sons Limited, fine chemical manufacturers* (Fisons, London, c.1973); J T W Mann & P R E Lewkowitsch, 'A Short History of Whiffen & Sons Ltd 1654–1947' (reprinted from *Fisons Journal*, Jan 1948); G McGuire, 'Whiffen & Sons Limited', *Fisons Journal*, 73, Aug 1962, 19-23

Records 1: London Metropolitan Archives, 40 Northampton Road, London EC1R 0HB

Ledger, supplies of herbs, berries and spices for use in production of oils and essences 1794–99; cash books 1822–40, 1852–59; bank book 1843–56; record books re procedure and costing for manufacture of mercury sublimate and nitric acid, invoice for foreign drugs and foreign exchange rates for Spanish dubloons 1752, 1761; price lists 1865, 1870. (Ref: B/WHF)

Records 2: Archives & Manuscripts, Wellcome Library for the History & Understanding of Medicine, 183 Euston Road, London NW1 2BE

Invoice book, imported *materia medica* from European countries and recipes for chemical and medical preparations 1749–1806; invoices, accounts, draft out-letters, notes and calculations 1768–1800, 1819, n.d.; bank passbook 1819–27; notebook, product costings and stock records 1877–84; monthly delivery books 1886–1932; letters to John Maud from trading partners in Hamburg and Leghorn 1803–06; miscellaneous papers, incl. lease agreement on warehouse in Charterhouse Buildings 1886, n.d. (Ref: MSS 5878-86)

AYRTON, SAUNDERS & CO PLC
Liverpool

Manufacturing chemist, pharmaceutical wholesaler and export dealer

History: This business was established in Liverpool in 1868 by A H Saunders, a retired partner in a firm of chemists at Walworth Road, London, and F Ayrton, a Liverpool doctor, to manufacture cod-liver oil emulsion, dyestuffs and surgical instruments. The partnership was based at Cornwallis Street, Liverpool, later relocating to Duke Street then to Parr Street and in 1898 to Hanover Street. A H Saunders died in 1889, leaving the firm to his 2 sons. The business was incorporated as a limited liability company, Ayrton Saunders Ltd, in 1902. In 1903 2 chemists' businesses, Henry Gilbertsons Ltd, London, and W H Kemp & Sons, Lincolnshire, were acquired. The company was renamed, Ayrton, Saunders & Kemp Ltd, and in 1908 was re-styled, Ayrton, Saunders & Co Ltd. During the First World War new chemical laboratories were acquired in Duke Street. During the 1950s the company expanded into pharmaceutical wholesaling, establishing depots in Stoke-on-Trent, and Prenton, Wirral. In 1982, the company was converted to a public limited liability company, Ayrton, Saunders & Co plc, and in 1987 the majority shareholding was acquired by AAH plc, a holding company for a chain of pharmaceutical wholesale and retail companies based at Runcorn, Halton. AAH plc was acquired in 1995 by GEHE AG and by 1999 was trading under its parent company's name GEHE UK plc.

'Ayrton, Saunders & Co Ltd', *Liverpool Daily Post Supplement*, 21 Nov 1968

Records 1: National Museums & Galleries on Merseyside, Maritime Records Centre, Merseyside Maritime Museum, Albert Dock, Liverpool L3 4AA

Registers of members and share ledgers 1903–51; transfer registers 1903–54; preference share issue prospectuses 1912, 1919; circular to shareholders 1878; annual reviews 1925–38; annual reports and accounts 1970–86 (w); sales sheets 1892; sales aids 1961–70; annual list and summary 1913–18; bank passbook 1886–87; formulae 1933–56; product catalogues c.1905, c.1950–60; price lists 1885–1985, n.d.; export review 1962–63; sales and publicity material 1954–70; advertising budgets 1954–65; advertising material 1921, 1961–64, n.d.; lease agreement 1888; deed of covenant 1905, 1910; company magazines: *Ayrton Link* 1925, 1928, 1954–59, *Ayrton's Quarterly* 1930, *The Ayrton Touch* 1931, *Ayrton Review* 1960–67, n.d., miscellaneous 1878–1957; papers re pay, machinery, review and management 1955–71; correspondence 1888–1917, 1961–71; photographs: directors late 19th cent.–1950s, staff and laboratories 1920–25, 1961, n.d., buildings 1920s, n.d., products 1961–64, vehicles c.1920s–30s, sales n.d., social c.1920; souvenir publication, 50th anniversary 1918; notice of staff dance 1924; Christmas record 1957; *Roving the world*, by W H Saunders 1924; postcards sent by W H Saunders whilst on world tour 1900; historical notes n.d. (Ref: B/AS 1-25)

Records 2: GEHE UK plc, Retail Branch, Atherstone, Warwickshire. Enquiries to GEHE UK plc, Sapphire Court, Walsgrave Triangle Business Park, Coventry CV2 2TX

General meetings minutes 1957–96; register of directors and managers 1921–85; advice booklet re stocking a pharmacy n.d.

Ayrton Saunders (Midland) Ltd: general meetings minutes 1966–96, combined register of members, directors and share ledger 1966–89. (Ref: Box S11, current minutes, box 4)

Records 3: Dr Peter M Worling, The Grange, 29 Fernielaw Avenue, Edinburgh EH13 0EF

Price lists: 1936–56 (w), 1985, patents and proprietaries 1938, drugs and tablets 1954, 1957, 1960, druggists sundries 1960, 1963, export 1931, 1985; press cutting 1968; *Round the World*, by W H Saunders 1938.

BAKER & SON (CHEMISTS) LTD
42 & 44 High Street, Cosham, Portsmouth

Chemist

History: Following an apprenticeship to John Parkinson of Southsea, Portsmouth, Thomas B Baker, a surgeon and apothecary, chemist and druggist, established a retail chemist business on his own account in the High Street, Cosham, Portsmouth, in 1845. Around 2 or 3 years later he built new premises across the road where he continued in business until his death in 1901. He was succeeded in the business, styled Baker & Son (Chemists), by his nephew, Cyril Baker, who incorporated the business as a limited liability company, Baker & Son (Chemists) Ltd, in 1946. In 1953 the firm was acquired by the Barlow family, who had been chemists in Southsea, Portsmouth, since 1909. The company was dissolved in 1975.

'A Cosham Pharmacy. History of two generations', *Pharmaceutical Journal*, 6, 4, 1957 (reprint); 'A Pharmacist Looks at Portsmouth. Its pharmacies and pharmaceutical activities', *Chemist and Druggist*, 176, 16 Sept 1961, 300

Records: City Museum & Records Office, Museum Road, Portsmouth PO1 2LJ

Ledgers: clients 1847–54, 1873–74, suppliers 1898–1907; customers' credit account books 1899–1914 (w); invoices of goods supplied to Baker & Son 1867; prescription/recipe books: Thomas Baker 1847–49, Henry and John Barlow 19th cent., Cyril Baker 1907–11; menu card for British Pharmaceutical Conference dinner, Portsmouth 1911. (Ref: 1439A)

BANNISTER & THATCHER LTD
11 Upper Brook Street, Rugeley, Staffordshire

Pharmacist

History: Charles Murfleet Bass was registered as a chemist and druggist in 1893, and traded from 11 Upper Brook Street, Rugeley, Staffordshire, on his own account. In 1929 he was joined in the business by Wilfred Raymond Bass, who had registered as a chemist and druggist in 1928. In 1933 Charles Murfleet Bass ceased to be registered, and Wilfred Raymond Bass continued the business, trading as W R Bass, until 1938, when the business was renamed C M Bass & Son. It traded under this title until 1968, when Wilfred Raymond Bass moved to 12 Elm Close, Great Haywood, near Stafford, Staffordshire, and the business at 11 Upper Brook Street was acquired by Alfred Melvin Brunton, who traded as Bass & Son until 1980 when the business was acquired by Bannister & Thatcher Ltd, and ceased to trade under its own name. Bannister & Thatcher Ltd ceased trading in 1992, following its acquisition by AAH plc, a holding company for a chain of pharmaceutical wholesale and retail companies, based at Runcorn, Halton.

Records 1: Staffordshire Record Office, Eastgate Street, Stafford ST16 2LZ

Ledgers 1878–1924, 1937–52; cash books 1892–1904, 1916–37; day book 1912–41; prescription books 1874–n.d., 1920s–53; sale of poisons register 1937–43; memorandum book 1958–68. (Ref: D4766)

Records 2: Gwent County Record Office, County Hall, Cwmbran NP44 2XH

Newport branch: formulae books 1914–29, prescription ledgers 1882–1937, prescription books 1893–1912. (Ref: D1495)

BARNES & CROMPTON LTD
Ribble Bank Mills, River Street, Bow Lane, Preston, Lancashire

Manufacturing and wholesale chemist

History: James Barnes registered as a pharmaceutical chemist in 1852, followed in 1866 by his son, Lawrence Robert Barnes. By 1876 they were in business as James Barnes & Son, chemists and druggists of 114A Fishergate, Preston, Lancashire. The business was in the hands of Harold Williams by 1920, when it was incorporated as a limited liability company, Barnes & Crompton Ltd, to manufacture patent and proprietary medicines and to trade as a wholesale and retail chemist and druggist. The business expanded quickly and by 1922 the company had acquired the businesses of H G Crompton, Bamber's Yard, Preston, where it opened a wholesaling warehouse facility, and of H H Gourlay at Lytham, Leyland, Lancashire. By 1929 Barnes & Crompton Ltd was trading in drugs, galenicals, chemists' sundries, medical products, patent medicines, proprietary articles, chemicals and bottles. In 1973 it was acquired by UniChem Ltd and ceased trading in 1974. It was dissolved in 1986.

Records: Alliance UniChem plc, UniChem House, Cox Lane, Chessington KT9 1SN

Directors' and general meetings minutes 1920–83; general meetings: minutes 1968, notices 1929, 1965, special resolution 1970; memorandum and articles of association 1920; certificate of incorporation 1920; acquisition papers 1972–74; annual returns 1929–33 (w); register of directors' holdings and interests 1931–64; register of directors and secretaries 1973; combined register of members and share ledger 1920-73; share transfer forms 1921-73; annual dividend lists 1922-28; annual report and statement of accounts 1968-72; accounts 1973-81; ledger, containing balance sheets, trading and profit and loss accounts 1920-70; *Lanconide* trademark renewal certificate 1956; Customs and Excise licence for supply of methylated spirits 1949; staff assurance scheme, papers and policies 1960s-78.

ROBERT BATTISCOMBE
Windsor, Windsor & Maidenhead

Apothecary

History: Robert Battiscombe was born in around 1754 and served his apprenticeship in Crewkerne, Somerset, later moving to Windsor, Windsor & Maidenhead, to establish himself in business as an apothecary. Amongst his patients were King George III, King George IV and other members of the royal household. He died in 1839 aged 85.

Records: Dorset Record Office, 9 Bridport Road, Dorchester DT1 1RP

Apprenticeship to George Hailes, Middlesex, apothecary 1769; papers re appointment as Apothecary in Ordinary to King George III 1805; accounts incl. entries re the royal family 1780-1835; memorandum re treatment of members of the royal family, incl. the King 1782-1835. (Ref: D.239:F2-5, 8)

BATTLES LTD
Stonebow, Lincoln, Lincolnshire

Wholesale druggist, colour merchant, optician and photographic dealer

History: Battle, Son & Maltby, a partnership between Joseph Maltby and William Battle Maltby, both in business prior to 1868, and John Scoley Battle, who registered as a pharmaceutical chemist in 1867, was trading from 294 High Street, Lincoln, Lincolnshire, from at least 1876. In 1885, Joseph Maltby registered as a chemist and druggist and established a business on his own account at Stonebow, Lincolnshire. In 1936, the Stonebow business was incorporated as a limited liability company, Battles Ltd, to trade as a wholesale distributor to chemists, doctors and hospitals. The company was operational until at least 1958.

Records: Lincolnshire Archives, St Rumbold Street, Lincoln LN2 5AB

Ledgers 1950–69; prescription books 1865–66.

BAYER PLC

Pharmaceutical Division, Bayer House, Strawberry Hill, Newbury RG14 1JA

Marketing of Bayer pharmaceutical chemicals and some pharmaceutical manufacturing

History: In 1863 Friedrich Bayer and Johann Friedrich Weskott joined in partnership to establish the synthetic dye business, Friedr Bayer et Comp, Elberfeld, West Germany. In 1884 Carl Duisberg joined the company as a research chemist and, with Dr Oskar Hinsberg, successfully synthesised acetophenetidine from the dyestuff benzoazurine. The end product was marketed as *Phenacetin*, the world's first synthetic pharmaceutical drug. In 1899 another Bayer chemist, Dr Felix Hoffmann, discovered an acetylated compound which was marketed under the trade name *Aspirin*. This 'miracle drug' was a worldwide success and ensured Bayer's continued growth. In 1906 Bayer Products Ltd was incorporated as a UK subsidiary of Friedr Bayer et Comp in London. An American subsidiary was also incorporated, but was sold to Sterling Products Inc, New York, during the First World War. Stirling Products Inc acquired the rights to use the Bayer name and trade marks, including *Aspirin*, not only in the USA, but also in the UK and South America, thus diminishing control of Bayer Products Ltd by Friedr Bayer et Comp. A compromise was reached in 1923, through the Weiss agreement, whereby Friedr Bayer et Comp and Stirling Products Inc, by then renamed Stirling Drug Inc, each took a 50 per cent share in the profits of Bayer Products Ltd. This lasted until 1949, when the Custodian of Enemy Property instructed the German parent to sell its shares in Bayer Products Ltd to Sterling Drug Inc, which became sole parent. During the 1950s Bayer Products Ltd manufactured a range of medicines and veterinary products, and was the only British company to manufacture the hormone cortisone. Friedr Bayer et Comp was incorporated as Farbenfabriken Bayer AG in 1952, and successfully incorporated a pharmaceutical sales company in Britain, Levmedic Ltd, in 1958. In 1959 this company was renamed FBA Pharmaceuticals Ltd and in 1962 moved to Haywards Heath, West Sussex. It was renamed Bayer Pharmaceuticals Ltd in 1972. Its main business was to market imported German pharmaceutical products, and in addition, to manufacture some products such as *Iversal*, *Aspirin*, *Fabahistin* and *Autan gel*. In 1974 Bayer Pharmaceuticals Ltd merged with Bayer AG's other UK subsidiaries, including Bayer Dyestuffs Ltd and Bayer Chemicals Ltd, to form Bayer UK Ltd, a holding company for Bayer

AG's British affiliates. Bayer Pharmaceuticals Ltd became a division of Bayer UK Ltd, named Pharma. In 1977 Bayer AG, acquired Miles Laboratories Inc, USA, a long established pharmaceutical company, incorporated as Dr Miles Medical Co Inc in Indiana in 1885, and renamed Miles Laboratories Inc in 1922. During the 1930s this company successfully launched the painkiller *Alka-Seltzer* and in 1946, incorporated a UK subsidiary company, Miles Laboratories Ltd. By 1959 Miles Laboratories Ltd was located at Stoke Court, Stoke Poges, Buckinghamshire, and in 1988 was renamed Miles Ltd. Thereafter, its various divisions were renamed Bayer UK Ltd, with the exception of the diagnostic division, located at Bridgend, Wales, which retained the title Miles Ltd, until 1996, when it was renamed Bayer Diagnostic Production Ltd. Bayer UK Ltd was based at Richmond, Richmond upon Thames, until 1983 when it moved to new headquarters in Strawberry Hill, Newbury. Pharma re-located there from Haywards Heath, and Miles Ltd vacated Stoke Court, and also moved to Strawberry Hill during the 1980s. In 1997 Stoke Court was used as a library and conference centre, and Bayer Diagnostic Production Ltd, remained at Bridgend. Pharmaceutical products which were successfully launched by Bayer UK Ltd during the 1970s and 1980s included *Alrheumat*, *Canesten* and *Adalat*, the cardiovascular agent. In 1986 *Ciproxin* the first full quinoline was launched, and is now one of the leading antibacterials in the world. In 1992 Bayer UK Ltd was converted into a public limited company, Bayer plc, and Pharma remained a division of this holding company. Bayer plc in 2000 employed 2,300 people in the UK and Ireland at 13 major sites.

'Bayer AG', in T Derdak (ed), *International Directory of Company Histories*, Vol. 1 (St James Press, London, 1988); K Holland, 'Bayer AG', *Pharmaceutical Journal*, 20 July 1991; P Lindsay & J Philpot, *The Story of Stoke Court* (Miles, 1990); 'Pharmaceutical Houses of London', *Chemist and Druggist*, 159, 1953, 575; E Verg, *Milestones: The Bayer story 1863–1988* (Bayer AG, 1989)

Records 1: Bayer plc, Pharmaceutical Division, Bayer House, Strawberry Hill, Newbury RG14 1JA

Memorandum and articles of association 1958; certificate of incorporation 1972; seal register 1944–71; balance sheets and profit and loss accounts 1958, 1965–66; ledgers 1958–67; purchase ledgers 1958–68; purchase accounts 1958–59; cash books 1958–64, 1969; staff expenditure accounts 1965–83; analysis of sales 1959; exchange cheques booklet 1977–83; patents and trade mark licences n.d.; price lists, pharmaceutical products 1964, 1967–71; advertisements: *Ospolot* n.d., *Canesten* n.d., *Alka-Seltzer* n.d., 'heart and circulation' n.d.; schedules of leases and transfers 1973; service and maintenance agreements n.d.; employment agreement, Dr H B Allen 1971; sales and salaries book 1976–82; staff shop receipt books 1983; staff bulletin 1968; memorandum to representatives 1967; *Crosstalk*, staff magazine 1970–96; *Crosslink*, company journal 1990–96; photographs: Sir Derrick Dunlop and J B Miller 1962, staff and social events c.1960s–90s, Pharma Divisions A, B and C, staff and laboratory work 1975–90s, headquarters at Strawberry Hill 1984–95, Stoke Court site n.d., other UK locations c.1970s–80s, events and visitors at Strawberry Hill 1970s–80s, corporate presentations and exhibitions 1980s, drugs, health aids and display cabinets n.d., 'Bayer Tapestry' outlining the history of the company 1980–90, drugs n.d., *Adalat* campaign 1994; slides illustrating 'The Pharmaceutical Industry and the Nation's Health' c.1987; postcards of medicinal plants, drug jars and paintings of apothecaries 1975.

Miles Ltd: front cover of *Dr Miles' Almanac*, an advertisement for Dr Miles' 'anti-pain pills' 1930.

Records 2: Bayer Diagnostic Production Ltd, Western Avenue, Bridgend Industrial Estate, Bridgend CS31 3TY

Miles Ltd: financial statements 1948–49.

Records 3: History of Advertising Trust, HAT House, 12 Raveningham Centre, Raveningham NR14 6NU

Guardbooks of advertising material: Bayer plc 1963, Alka-Seltzer 1970–81; advertising proofs and artwork, Alka-Seltzer 1979; advertisements: *Autan* 1976–77, *Alka-Seltzer* 1977–89. (Ref: Leo Burnett guardbooks 4, 20, proofs, shelf 2; MEAL collection 1976–77 R80, 1977–89 R10-80)

BEECHAM FOODS LTD
SmithKline Beecham House, Great West Road, Brentford, Hounslow, London

Patent medicine manufacturer

History: Hazelwell Products Ltd was incorporated as a limited liability company in 1929 to manufacture and retail pills and patent medicines from 55-56 Pall Mall, London. Later in the same year it re-located to 420 Chester Road, Old Trafford, Manchester, and in 1931 was acquired by Beecham Pills Ltd, whereupon it moved to 51 Westfield Street, St Helens. In 1934 it was renamed Products (Beechams) Ltd, and in 1945 re-located to 68 Pall Mall, London. In 1946 it was renamed Beechams Pills Ltd, its parent having changed its name to Beecham Group Ltd in the previous year, and in 1955 was renamed Beecham

Foods Ltd. In spite of its new title, the company continued to manufacture pills and patent medicines as well as foodstuffs. In 1961 it re-located, along with a number of other Beecham Group Ltd subsidiaries, to Beecham House, Great West Road, Brentford, Hounslow, London. It was dissolved in 1993.

Records: St Helens Local History & Archives Library, Gamble Institute, Victoria Square, St Helens WA10 1DY

Memorandum and articles of association 1934; schedule of agreements 1929; trade mark papers, product costings and advertising leaflets 1920s–65; historical notes 1965.

BEECHAM PROPRIETARY MEDICINES LTD
Great West Road, Brentford, Hounslow, London

Proprietary medicine manufacturer

History: Yeast Vite Ltd was incorporated as a limited liability company in 1927, and was acquired by Beecham Pills Ltd during the early 1930s. It manufactured the proprietary medicine *Yeast Vite* from a factory and offices at Watford, Hertfordshire, and distributed its products to chemists. In 1959 it became part of Beecham Group Ltd's Proprietary Medicines Division, which became the Pharmaceuticals Division in 1962, and was renamed Beecham Proprietary Medicines Ltd. From 1966 *Yeast Vite* was manufactured from the Products Division of Beecham Group Ltd at Great West Road, Brentford, Hounslow, London. Beecham Proprietary Medicines Ltd was still trading in 1997.

Records 1: St Helens Local History & Archives Library, Gamble Institute, Victoria Square, St Helens WA10 1DY

Private ledger 1940–50; litigation with S Oskotsky re unlawful sale of *Yeast Vite* 1934; papers re foreign rights 1931–35. (Ref: BP/4/12)

Records 2: SmithKline Beecham plc, SmithKline Beecham House, Great West Road, Brentford TW8 9BD. Enquiries to SmithKline Beecham plc, 1 New Horizons Court, Great West Road, Brentford TW8 9EP

General meetings minutes 1928–39; papers re countries holding *Yeast Vite* trade marks 1939; promotional leaflet 1954.

Records 3: History of Advertising Trust, HAT House, 12 Raveningham Centre, Raveningham NR14 6NU

Guardbook of advertising material for *Yeast Vite* 1955; press cuttings of advertisements for *Yeast Vite* 1974–89. (Ref: Leo Burnett guardbooks, 56; MEAL collection 1974–89, R10-80)

BELL'S CHEMISTS
Ambleside, Cumbria

Chemist and druggist

History: This chemist and druggist's business was established in 1839, in Ambleside, Cumbria, by Thomas Bell. His son, Thomas, was registered as a chemist and druggist in 1872, and traded from Lake Road, Ambleside until at least 1895.

Records: Cumbria Record Office (Kendal), County Offices, Stricklandgate, Kendal LA9 4RQ

Purchase ledger 1918–21; prescription books 1892–1947. (Ref: WDB/48 (microfilm JAC 166, 167 and 168))

JOHN BELL & CROYDEN LTD
50 Wigmore Street, London

Retail pharmacist

History: In 1908 John Bell & Croyden Ltd was incorporated as a limited liability company by John D Marshall, who had formerly been dispenser at the Chapel Street branch of Savory & Moore. It was the product of an amalgamation of 2 long-established pharmacies in the west end of London: John Bell & Co, of 338 (re-numbered 225) Oxford Street, and Croyden & Co, of 45 Wigmore Street, Cavendish Square. John Bell & Co was founded in 1798 by a Quaker, John Bell, who had been apprenticed to an eminent chemist and druggist, Frederick Smith, 20 Haymarket, London. In 1819 he took Thomas Zachary and John H Walduck into partnership, and established a manufacturing laboratory at the rear of his shop where he manufactured galenicals and chemicals used in his dispensing business, and proprietary medicines which he sold to dispensing apothecaries and other pharmacists. Zachary and Walduck retired in 1836 and Bell's 2 sons Jacob and Frederick John joined their father. On his father's death in 1849, Jacob Bell became sole proprietor, his brother having left the business 2 years earlier. Jacob was one of the founder members of the Pharmaceutical Society of Great Britain, and its president at the time of his death in 1859. Thomas Hyde Hills joined the business as an assistant in 1837, became laboratory superintendent, entered into partnership with Jacob in 1852 and, when Jacob died, assumed control of the business, which by then was concerned chiefly with dispensing. Hills' nephew, Walter Hills, took charge on his uncle's death in 1891, in partnership with Samuel Gale. E W Lucas was later appointed to manage the laboratory and to expand the wholesaling side of the business. In 1908 the wholesale and retail operations were separated. The wholesale branch was incorporated as a limited liability company, John Bell, Hills & Lucas Ltd, with Walter Hills as chairman. It moved in 1909 to Oxford Works, Tower Bridge Road, London, and by 1910 was trading as a wholesaler and manufacturer. In 1938 it re-located to a larger factory at Sydenham, Lewisham, London. The retail chemist's business was merged with Croyden & Co Ltd, 55 Wigmore Street, London, in 1908 to form John Bell & Croyden Ltd. Croyden & Co Ltd had been established in 1832 by Charles Croyden, formerly Bell's assistant. Around 1886 the firm was acquired by F W Hyde and J H Cartwright who traded under the name Croyden. The premises comprised a sales department, dispensing room and laboratory, where powders, tinctures, pills and infusions were compounded and medicated water for dispensing purposes was distilled. John Marshall acquired the firm at the turn of the century and incorporated the business as a limited liability company, Croyden & Co Ltd. In 1908 John Bell & Croyden Ltd, was incorporated as a limited liability company, to manage the retail business. The directors were John Marshall, who was managing director, Walter Hills, E W Lucas and J R Wretts. In 1912, John Bell & Croyden Ltd moved from 45 Wigmore Street to a new pharmacy, which had been opened by the Lord Mayor of London, at 50 Wigmore Street. Marshall publicly avowed that the shop would remain open 24 hours a day, 365 days a year. The pharmacy met this promise, throughout both world wars, until 1966. By 1914 he had 20 professionally qualified pharmacists on his staff. About the same time John Bell & Croyden Ltd acquired Uxbridge Cotton Mills Ltd for the purposes of manufacturing lint, absorbent cotton and medicated gauzes, all essential for war dressings. The works were re-named the Army Dressings Factory. In 1921 the company acquired Langham Bros, Perivale, Ealing, London, which was a manufacturing chemists and perfumers business. By this time John Bell & Croyden Ltd was running a motorised delivery service for hospital operating equipment as well as hiring out surgical appliances. In 1923 John Bell & Croyden Ltd acquired a leading surgical instruments and equipment and hospital furniture manufacturing firm, Arnold & Son, Giltspur Street, London, which was established in 1819 in Smithfield, and was a royal warrant holder. By the 1950s Arnold & Son had been incorporated as 2 limited liability companies: Arnold & Sons Veterinary Instruments Ltd, 54 Wigmore Street, London, which was responsible for retail sales, and Arnold & Sons Basildon Ltd, Honywood Road, Basildon, Essex, which manufactured veterinary and surgical instruments. In 1928 John Bell & Croyden Ltd was acquired by Savory & Moore Ltd, which in turn was acquired by Macarthys Pharmaceuticals Ltd in 1967. The latter was acquired by Lloyds Chemists plc in March 1992. John Bell & Croyden Ltd has continued to trade under its own name throughout the takeovers, its business organised into the following areas: community pharmacy, surgical appliances, invalid aid and external sales to both home and overseas customers.

'A Coming Centenary', *Chemist and Druggist*, 30 Jul 1898, 160-5; 'A Business Bell Founded. Origins, growth and present activities of John Bell, Hills & Lucas Ltd', *Chemist and Druggist*, 6 June 1959, 614-16; 'A Day at Bell's', *Chemist and Druggist*, 25 June 1921, 128-9; J Burnby, The Family History of Jacob Bell', *Pharmaceutical Journal*, 21 May 1983, 582-4; R Donald, *From Ancient Alchemy to Modern Pharmacy: Bond Street 150 years ago* (Savory & Moore, c.1940); 'John Bell & Croyden. Its relationship to John and Jacob Bell', *Chemist and Druggist*, 6 June 1959, 609; 'Legacy of Jacob Bell', *Pharmaceutical Journal*, 4 July 1970, 37; L Matthews, 'Jacob Bell 1810–1859', *Chemist and Druggist*, 6 June 1959, 610-13; G Parkes, 'John Bell & Croyden – 75 Years of Professional Service', *Pharmaceutical Journal*, 231, 30 July 1983, 119; K Sabbagh, 'Shop Talk', *Punch*, Nov 1980

Records 1: John Bell & Croyden Ltd, 50-54 Wigmore Street, London W1H 0AU

Formulations books 1919–55; dispensing records book, prescription analyses 1956; unsourced prescription books n.d.; *John Bell & Croyden News*, company newsletter 1977–78 (w); J D Marshall: obituaries n.d., c.1932, personal scrapbook containing cuttings, labels, photographs, articles, correspondence, booklets, staff instructions and rules and advertisements 1914–[31]; personal notebooks: 'Notices at the Sink', containing miscellaneous jottings re the business 1891–1903, 'Meteorological' 1881–92, recording the writer's weight [1889]–97 and miscellaneous notes 1881–97; catalogue and price list of invalid and nursing requisites, incl. pictures of laboratories at Lawrence Road, Tottenham, and showroom at 50-52 Wigmore Street, London, n.d., c.1920s; architectural plan of 50 Wigmore Street c.1970s; photographs: John Bell's pharmacy n.d., shop window displays n.d., c.1940s, leeches on hands n.d., shop interior n.d.

Arnold & Sons Ltd: catalogue of surgeons' instruments 1927; catalogue of orthopaedic appliances n.d., c.1930s; photographs of shop window displays n.d.

Records 2: GEHE UK plc, Retail Branch, Atherstone, Warwickshire. Enquiries to GEHE UK plc, Sapphire Court, Walsgrave Triangle Business Park, Coventry CV2 2TX

Address to be delivered by the President of the Pharmaceutical Society of Great Britain and exhibition catalogue to mark the centenary of the death of Jacob Bell 1959; photographs, leaflets and cards of shops, Arnold & Sons Ltd and laboratories c.1890–1950; list of historical artifacts held at Wigmore Street n.d.

John Bell & Co: receipt for payment of goods bought by The British Hospital, Porto 1861; recipe book 1897.

Records 3: The Museum Curator, Royal Pharmaceutical Society of Great Britain, 1 Lambeth High Street, London SE1 7JN

Partnership articles between Walter Hills, John Robert Wretts and Edward William Lucas 1903; laboratory journals 1873–1901; recipe books c.1839–1904; miscellaneous papers re Jacob Bell, 18th–19th cents; marriage entry for James Bell, nephew of Jacob Bell to Ann Spencer 1858.

John Bell, Hills & Lucas Ltd: journal 1903–08; cash ledgers 1872–89, 1903–08; formulae receipt book 1875; press cuttings re gas warfare 1915–18. (Ref: IRA.1996.067, 132, 163; IRA.1997.014-17, 076, 150; LDPHA.LIB.37324-30)

BELLAMY & WAKEFIELD LTD
1 Easy Row, Birmingham

Chemist

History: In 1839 John Harrison & Co, druggist and tea dealer, occupied premises at 1 Easy Row, Birmingham. By 1849 the firm was renamed Harrison & Scott, and in 1865/66 was acquired by John Bellamy. The tea dealing side of the business appears to have been wound up in 1878. John Wakefield, who was registered as a pharmaceutical chemist in 1879, had been made a partner by 1882, when the firm was trading as Bellamy & Wakefield. During the 1890s a branch of the business was established in Hagley Road, Birmingham, and remained operational until the 1920s. In 1922 the firm was incorporated as a limited liability company, Bellamy & Wakefield Ltd, and, although John Bellamy and John Wakefield were no longer associated with the business, the established name was retained until the company was dissolved in 1973.

Records: Birmingham City Archives, Central Library, Chamberlain Square, Birmingham B3 3HQ

Directors' meetings minutes 1923, 1938–45; annual returns and related papers 1931–55; share transfer certificates 1934–55. (Ref: MS 1831)

H BELLRINGER LTD
1 Elton Street, Great Clowes Street, Salford

Manufacturing chemist

History: H Bellringer Ltd was incorporated as a limited liability company at 1 Elton Street, Great Clowes Street, Salford, in 1962, by John Noble, the proprietor of J Noble, dispensing chemists, 20 Great Clowes Street, Salford, and his wife. It ceased trading in 1972, and was dissolved in 1973.

Records: Salford City Archives, 658-662 Liverpool Road, Irlam, Manchester M44 5AD

Directors' meeting minutes 1962–72; general meetings minutes 1963–72; memorandum and articles of association 1962; register of directors and secretaries 1962; register of members and share ledger 1962; list of share allotments c.1962; share certificates 1962, n.d.; annual return 1963; draft directors' report 1968; ledger, incl. trading and profit and loss account 1962–72; account book 1962–72; cash book 1962–72; petty cash book 1962–72; tax papers 1970, n.d.; insurance papers 1963, n.d.; correspondence and papers re suppliers 1968–69, 1971; papers re Dunlop Committee on Safety of Drugs 1963. (Ref: U39)

BENCARD PHARMACEUTICALS LTD
4 New Horizons Court, Great West Road, Brentford, Hounslow, London

Pharmaceutical manufacturer

History: In 1930 Clotabs Ltd was incorporated as a limited liability company, to manufacture basic pharmaceutical products. It was renamed C L Bencard Ltd in 1949, when it was acquired by Macleans Ltd, a wholly-owned subsidiary of Beecham Group Ltd. In 1959 C L Bencard Ltd merged with Beecham Research Laboratories Ltd, to concentrate on the production of penicillin. In 1973 it was renamed Bencard Pharmaceuticals Ltd, and in 1997 was in liquidation.

Records: SmithKline Beecham plc, SmithKline Beecham House, Great West Road, Brentford TW8 9BD. Enquiries to SmithKline Beecham plc, 1 New Horizons Court, Great West Road, Brentford TW8 9EP

General meetings minutes 1949–83; share certificates 1959–73; share transfer certificates 1956–73; directors' annual report 1953; auditor's report 1949.

BENGERS LTD
Holmes Chapel, Cheshire

Pharmaceutical manufacturer

History: This company was established as Mottershead & Co in Manchester in 1790. It was acquired by Frederick Baden Benger in 1870, and in 1891 was incorporated as a limited liability company, F B Benger & Co Ltd. The company was renamed Bengers Food Ltd in 1903, and in 1939 re-located to Holmes Chapel, Cheshire, after which it was renamed Bengers Ltd. It manufactured ethical pharmaceuticals including *Auralgicin*, a treatment for ear infections, and *Bengers Food*, a milk supplement. In 1947 it was acquired as a wholly-owned subsidiary of Fisons Ltd, producers of agricultural products and fertilisers of Ipswich, Suffolk. Thereafter it continued to trade under its own name. In 1946 Genatosan Ltd, a proprietary medicines and fine chemicals manufacturer of Loughborough, Leicestershire, was acquired by Fisons Ltd, and in 1947, Genatosan Trust Ltd, was incorporated as a limited liability company by Fisons Ltd, to acquire the business of Whiffen & Sons Ltd, fine chemical manufacturers of London. In the same year Genatosan Trust Ltd was renamed British Chemicals & Biologicals Ltd (BCB Ltd), a co-ordinating company for Bengers Ltd, Genatosan Ltd and Whiffen & Sons Ltd. In 1951 it was made dormant and Bengers Ltd, Genatosan Ltd and Whiffen & Sons Ltd regained control of their respective businesses. In 1964 Bengers Ltd and Genatosan Ltd were merged to form one operating company, Fisons Pharmaceuticals Ltd, a subsidiary of Fisons Ltd, with research laboratories at Loughborough and a manufacturing plant at Holmes Chapel.

M S Moss, 'Fertilisers to Pharmaceuticals: Fisons – the biography of a company 1720–1986' (Unpublished typescript, 1996, copy at Ipswich Record Office)

Records 1: Rhône-Poulenc Rorer Ltd, Rhône-Poulenc Rorer House, 50 Kings Hill Avenue, Kings Hill, West Malling ME19 4AH

Directors' meetings minutes 1948–51; memorandum and articles of association 1948; balance sheets 1974–75; advertisement 1895; product advertising booklets 1960s; papers re transfer of property to Fisons Pharmaceuticals Ltd 1964–69; photograph of doctors' hobbies exhibition n.d.

Records 2: History of Advertising Trust, HAT House, 12 Raveningham Centre, Raveningham NR14 6NU

Advertising material re Bengers foods late 19th–early 20th cents. (Ref: Ogilvy & Mather collection; AA1/2/6r; MEAL collection 1974–89, R10-80)

EDWARD BEVAN
19 Nelson Street, Swansea

Chemist and druggist

History: Edward Bevan was registered as a chemist and druggist at 19 Nelson Street, Swansea, in 1876. He worked in partnership with John Thompson Williams, who had registered as a pharmaceutical chemist in 1855. Edward Bevan acquired the business on the death of John Thompson Williams in 1896.

Records: University of Wales Swansea, Library & Information Services, Singleton Park, Swansea SA2 8PP

Edward Bevan: annual balance sheet with related accounts 1896, day books 1896–99, 1924–30, cash books 1897–1901, bank passbooks 1896–98, 1923–31, bills from W S Phillips, decorator 1921–25, bills from Edwin Bevan, builder 1928–29, delivery driver's log book 1956; John Thompson Williams: account book, bills and personal expenses 1859–64, cash book 1881–88, income tax and house duty papers 1889–96, estate duty forms 1896–97, executors' bank passbook 1896–1905, combined pharmaceutical notebook and address book c.1875, pocket book, personal and farming receipts and expenditure 1880–86.

BILSON & FRIENDSHIP LTD
Bournemouth

Pharmacist

Records of pharmaceutical businesses 113

History: Frederick Eastall Bilson was registered as a chemist and druggist at 1 Landsdowne Crescent, Bournemouth, from 1880 until at least 1895. In 1948 the business was incorporated as a limited liability company, Bilson & Friendship Ltd. The company was dissolved in 1974.

Records: Department of Western Manuscripts, Bodleian Library, University of Oxford, Broad Street, Oxford OX1 3BG

Account book 1941–52; cash book 1942–47; prescription day books 1878–1948 (w). (Ref: MSS. Top. Hants. c.8-60)

BIOREX LABORATORIES LTD
2 Crossfield Chambers, Gladbeck Way, Enfield, London

Research, manufacture and marketing of pharmaceutical preparations

History: Biorex Laboratories Ltd was incorporated as a limited liability company in 1944, but did not begin trading until 1950. The aims of the company, under the direction of Dr Siegfried Gottfried, a medical doctor from Romania, and Lily Baxendale, a research chemist, were to carry out research into the discovery and development of new drugs in the areas of dermatology and gastroenterology and to manufacture and market pharmaceutical preparations. Initially the company opened 5 retail pharmacies in London between 1950 and 1955, a wholesale department and a small unit preparing stock mixtures, ointments, creams, lotions, ampoules and tinctures, to supply the needs of the shops. All the profits from the retail operations, which traded as Kendale Dispensing Chemists, were used to finance the company's research activities. During the 1950s, the central research of Biorex Laboratories Ltd was into the uses of liquorice root, of which the main constituent is glycyrrhizin. Investigations discovered that glycyrrhetic acid had anti-inflammatory properties, and clinical trials demonstrated its usefulness in treating several skin complaints. In 1956 a subsidiary company, Biorex (Marketing) Ltd, was incorporated to market products containing this compound under the trademark *Biosone*. Between 1957 and 1960 this company organised a novel advertising campaign whereby promotional material was sent to doctors featuring cartoons drawn by *Punch* magazine artists: Anton, Emett, Ffolkes and Thelwell. In 1957 research scientists at Biorex Laboratories Ltd discovered, through the synthesis of carbenoxolone, a possible treatment for gastric ulcers. Initial pharmacology and toxicology testing was carried out at university departments on behalf of the company, and in 1959 Dr Richard Doll at the Medical Research Council Unit, Central Middlesex Hospital, London, conducted trials which showed that carbenoxolone significantly accelerated the healing of gastric ulcers. These findings were published in the *Lancet* in 1962. As Biorex's primary interest was in research, the compound was out-licensed, to Berk Pharmaceuticals, under the trading name *Biogastrone*, and marketing commenced in 1963. Income received in royalties allowed the company to purchase a public house in the City Road, London, and to convert it into a chemical research facility in the early 1960s. The premises incorporated chemical production rooms, laboratories, a conference room and animal houses. By this time Biorex Laboratories Ltd had secured a number of contracts to supply hospitals with tablets, capsules, gels, sterile products and water for injections. By 1967 the company required more space and a lease was taken out on premises at Canonbury Villas, Islington, London, subsequently named Biorex House. In June 1968 the offices and manufacturing unit were re-located to Biorex House, and the research departments followed in 1969–70. Biorex (Marketing) Ltd became a wholly-owned subsidiary of Biorex Laboratories Ltd in 1970, and in 1972 Biorex Laboratories Ltd won the Queen's Award to Industry for the technical development of carbenoxolone. Further research led to the development of a number of other dosage forms, including *Bioral gel* for mouth ulcers, *Duogastrone* for duodenal ulcer, *Pyrogastrone* for oesophagitis (1974) and *Bioplex* mouthwash granules (1985). All of these products were out-licensed for marketing in the UK and overseas. To enable research to expand further, the manufacturing unit was moved to Biopharm House in Queensland Road, Islington, London, in 1980. Pharmaceuticals manufactured there included capsules and tablets, creams, ointments and gels. The premises also housed analytical and quality control laboratories and a packaging department. The company's chain of retail pharmacies, Kendale Dispensing Chemists, was gradually sold between the 1970s and 1986, in order to concentrate on pharmaceutical research and manufacture. Dr Gottfried died in 1983 and Lily Baxendale took over his duties. Research continued in the 1980s and a compound, balsalazide, was synthesised for possible use in the treatment of ulcerative colitis. Clinical trials were conducted and results were published in 1988. After this the decision was made to close down the research departments but to continue the development of balsalazide and some other compounds using external resources. The laboratories closed in January 1989 and in November of the same year the company moved from Biorex House to an office in a small business unit in Enfield, London. In 1997, the company was granted a marketing authorisation for balsalazide under the trade mark *Colazide*, which was launched for sale in the UK by Astra Pharmaceuticals Ltd. The manufacturing, packaging and analytical unit in north London continued to operate in 1999, supplying drugs to hospitals and to short- and main-line wholesalers.

Records: Biorex Laboratories Ltd, 2 Crossfield Chambers, Gladbeck Way, Enfield EN2 7HT

Directors' and general meetings minutes 1944 to date; memorandum and articles of association 1944; certificate of incorporation 1944; combined registers of members and share ledgers incl. some annual returns 1944 to date; share transfer forms 1950s–60s; share certificates: ordinary 1954–85, preference 1954–68; papers relating to proposed re-construction of company 1969; ledgers: nominal 1974–88, bought 1983–88; cash book and journal 1944–87; royalties book 1965–91; managing director's/company secretary's work diaries 1986 to date; use of barbiturates and dangerous drugs record books 1976–89; radioactive materials: diary of use 1975–89, stock record 1975–89, compounds record book 1971–73, disposal of waste record book 1981–89; inspectors' business cards, Drugs Branch, Home Office n.d.; mailshots to doctors featuring cartoons by famous artists, samples and original artwork 1957–60; record book for equipment in operation out of normal working hours 1977–88; plant records for inspection and insurance purposes: boiler reports 1968–81, lifting gear reports 1968–89; factory register 1968–81; accidents books 1969–89; correspondence re purchase of Italian capsule-filling machine 1965–72; Biorex Staff Pension and Life Assurance Scheme, correspondence and related papers 1970 to date; photographs: Dr S Gottfried 1982, shop facias 1950s, Apsley House laboratories 1960s, capsule-filling machine 1963, march on Biorex House by anti-vivisectionists 1983, demonstration outside Biorex House 1987; photograph albums: Carbenoxolone Sodium Symposium 1967, 21st birthday celebration 1971, Queen's Award for Industry presentation, incl. laboratories 1972; Queen's Award for Industry certificate 1972.

Biorex (Marketing) Ltd: directors' and general meetings minutes 1956 to date; memorandum and articles of association 1956; certificate of incorporation 1956; combined register of members and share ledger 1956–76; share certificates 1956–77; nominal ledger 1963 to date; purchases day book 1956 to date; sales day book 1963 to date; cash book 1972 to date.

BLADES CHEMIST LTD
88 Mostyn Street, Llandudno, Conwy

Dispensing chemist

History: James Sinclair established a chemist and druggist's business at 88 Mostyn Street, Llandudno, Conwy, in 1876. After his death in 1880, his wife, Matilda Anne Sinclair, who registered as a pharmaceutical chemist in 1884, carried on the business. She was still operating from Mostyn Street in 1895. During the twentieth century, the business passed through a succession of owners and names, including Cocker, and Blades Chemist. In 1950 the firm was incorporated as a limited liability company, Blades Chemist Ltd. It was dissolved in 1987.

'Pharmacies in Llandudno', *Chemist and Druggist*, 170, 19 July 1958, 62-3

Records 1: Gwynedd Archives & Museums Service, Caernarfon Area Record Office, Victoria Dock, Caernarfon. Enquiries to County Offices, Shirehall Street, Caernarfon LL55 1SH

Ledger 1919–25; cash summary books 1947–50; account book, incl. analysis of NHS prescriptions 1948–54; prescription books, incl. oral contraceptives 1896–1975 (w); reference list, surgical instruments, appliances and hospital equipment 1930. (Ref: XD/53)

Records 2: Department of Manuscripts, The Library, University of Wales, Bangor LL57 2DG

Prescription books 1900–03. (Ref: 25748)

WILLIAM BLAIN & SONS LTD
25 Market Street, Bolton

Wholesale and manufacturing chemist

History: This business was founded by William Blain of Bolton, who undertook his pharmacy training in Preston, Lancashire, and gained further experience in Guernsey, Channel Islands, under Thomas Millais, cousin of the artist John Millais. He returned to Bolton in 1851 to establish a business on his own account in Deansgate and later in Newport Street. He acquired premises at 25 Market Street in 1854. In 1868 he was registered as a pharmaceutical chemist and, shortly afterwards, was joined in the business by his sons, Alfred Lucas Blain and William Rushton Blain, who registered as pharmaceutical chemists in 1881 and 1883 respectively. The business was styled William Blain & Sons. In 1947 the business was incorporated as a limited liability company, William Blain & Sons Ltd. James Hart, who formerly traded in Newport Street, Bolton, acquired the business in 1974. It was removed from the register of companies in 1978.

'A Hundred Years in One Family', *Chemist and Druggist*, 156, 17 Nov 1951, 660; 'An Old Established Lancashire Business', *Chemist and Druggist*, 121, 1 Sept 1934, 279

Records: Bolton Archive & Local Studies Service, Central Library, Civic Centre, Le Mans Crescent, Bolton BL1 1SE

Ledgers 1948–82; cash book 1948–52; prescription books 1946–74; notebook containing prescription totals 1976–78; unofficial lists of formulae from National Formularies and National War Formularies 1933–57, 1955, 1961; advertisements: 50th and centenary anniversaries 1901, 1951, illustrated price list and brochure for Badger shaving brushes 1968; labels and letterheads c.1900–60; photograph of shop, 25 Market Street, Bolton c.1980. (Ref: ZHR)

BLEASDALE LTD
York

Wholesale and manufacturing chemist

History: John Dales, an alderman of the City of York, established a chemist's manufacturing and wholesale business at 23 Colliergate, York, in 1780. In 1838 it was acquired by James Moore Butterfield, who took Joseph Clarke as his partner, and named the firm Butterfield & Clarke. James Butterfield died in the early 1850s and his share of the business was acquired by William Bleasdale in 1856. Shortly afterwards, William Henry Bell and Richard B Tollington, both pharmaceutical chemists, joined the firm, which manufactured and sold a range of pharmaceutical preparations including emulsions, oils and syrups. As a result of 2 fires, in 1863 and 1864, the premises were completely rebuilt in 1866, by which time the firm operated a drug grinding mill and manufacturing laboratory in addition to a distribution warehouse. William Bleasdale became sole proprietor following the deaths of Clarke and Tollington and the retirement of Bell, and traded under the name W Bleasdale & Co until his death in 1888. The business operated under trust until 1891 when G A Grierson was appointed manager. In 1894 the firm was incorporated as a limited liability company, Bleasdale Ltd, with Grierson as managing director. Following the introduction of the National Health Service in 1948, the company reduced its manufacturing activities and concentrated on wholesaling. In 1982 Bleasdale Ltd moved from Colliergate to a warehouse at 2 Birch Park, Huntingdon Road, York. During the 1980s the company was acquired by Lloyds Chemists plc which was acquired later by AAH plc which now trades as GEHE UK plc.

Yorkshire Herald, 3 Sept 1910, 11

Records: York City Archives Department, Art Gallery Building, Exhibition Square, York YO1 2EW

Ledgers: 1886–1913, 1955–58, bought 1871–96; town ledgers: 1884–93, sales 1902–05, purchase 1905–12; extracts from ledgers used in Bleasdale v Bell 1886–87; day book 1956–60; cash books 1894–1908, 1915–57 (w); cost books, purchases from suppliers 1821–83; milling book 1866–76; pill books 1880–90; pill recipe book c.1910–27; prescription books 1871–82, c.1900–45, n.d.; perfume recipe book 1893–1930; warehouse book 1857–87; staff attendance register 1865–73. (Ref: Acc 83 & 302)

A BOAKE ROBERTS & CO LTD
Blackhorse Lane, Walthamstow, Waltham Forest, London

Manufacturer of industrial and pharmaceutical chemicals

History: In 1869 Arthur Boake travelled from Dublin, Ireland, to London, where he established a business on his own account at Stratford, Newham, styled A Boake & Co, to manufacture chemicals for use in the brewing and wine industries. In 1876 he was joined in partnership by Francis George Adair Roberts, and the business was restyled A Boake Roberts & Co in 1888. In 1897 the business was incorporated as a limited liability company, A Boake Roberts & Co Ltd, and began manufacture of flavouring essences and essential oils. Its headquarters moved to Carpenters Road, Stratford, in around 1900 and during the 1940s and 1950s, factories were established at Walthamstow, Waltham Forest, London; Rainham, Havering; Letchworth, Hertfordshire; and Widnes, Halton. In 1953 a holding company, A Boake Roberts & Co (Holding) Ltd, was incorporated, and A Boake Roberts & Co Ltd became its trading and manufacturing subsidiary. The latter was briefly renamed A Boake Roberts & Co (Manufacturing) Ltd in 1953, but later in the same year reverted to its original title. The main products of A Boake Roberts & Co Ltd were industrial chemicals and concentrates for use in the perfumery, cosmetics and foodstuffs industries, and also some chemicals for use in the pharmaceutical industry. In 1960 A Boake Roberts & Co (Holding) Ltd, its overseas subsidiaries and home subsidiary, A Boake Roberts & Co Ltd, were acquired by Albright & Wilson Ltd, a phosphorus manufacturer. All retained their established names. In 1966 A Boake Roberts & Co Ltd merged with Stafford Allen & Sons Ltd, a drug milling and grinding company, and W J Bush & Co Ltd, a manufacturer of flavourings and essential oils, to form Bush Boake Allen Ltd, a subsidiary of Albright & Wilson Ltd, with headquarters at the A Boake Roberts & Co Ltd site at Blackhorse Lane, London.

Records: Bush Boake Allen Ltd, Blackhorse Lane, Walthamstow, London E17 5QP

Partnership deed between Arthur Boake and Frederick George Roberts 1876; minutes: directors' meetings 1907–54 (w), general meetings 1897–1954, debenture stockholders' meetings 1921–53; general meetings attendance book 1916; certificates of incorporation 1897, 1953; change of name certificate 1953; power of attorney to company director 1930; combined register of members and share ledger 1905–74; registers: shares 1951–64, debentures 1916–54, transfers 1897–98, 1948–59, mortgages and charges 1965; transfer forms: preference shares 1930–47, debentures 1917–48; share certificates books 1897–1935, 1953–64; cancelled share certificates 1930s–40s; debenture certificates book 1915–32; redeemed debentures 1954; annual report and accounts 1947; balance sheets and profit and loss accounts 1910, 1933–40; trial balances 1934–49; private ledgers 1876–81, 1897–1908; patent specifications and trademarks books 1885–1938; manufacturing formulae book 1924–30, n.d.; stock control and production planning report 1955; product brochures and leaflets 1922, 1940, 1950s–64, n.d.; price lists 1930–40, 1962–64, n.d.; price survey 1935; property plans, applications, licences, deeds and related correspondence 1925–73; mortgage papers 1959–70; tenancy agreements and leases 1931–79; statutory declaration 1965; leasehold and capital redemption policies 1900, 1953; conveyances 1923–71; maps and drawings n.d.; inventory and valuation of land, plant and buildings 1950–69; correspondence with local authorities and British Waterways Board re property 1945, 1965–67; senior staff salaries and income tax calculations 1930s–50s; salary ledger 1932–42; departmental staff salary sheets 1936–41; staff statement of gratitude on inauguration of pension and life assurance scheme 1936; pension scheme information booklet n.d.; sickness and benevolent friendly society booklet n.d.; personnel papers 1958; staff bonus receipts 1945; staff information booklet c.1960; staff study booklet n.d.; safety manuals 1950s, 1963, n.d.; visitors book 1956–69; sports and social club: constitution and rules booklet n.d., balance sheet 1964, ledger 1960–65; general correspondence 1870s–90s; photographs 19th cent.; labels booklet n.d.; historical notes 1947, 1956–57.

A Boake Roberts & Co (Holding) Ltd: directors' meetings minutes 1954–82; general meetings minutes 1954–67; change of name certificate 1953; agreement re transfer of assets 1953; papers re proposed sale to Albright & Wilson Ltd 1960; registers: seals 1932–67, directors 1897–1983, directors' holdings and interests 1957–60, ordinary stock 1947–60, preference shares 1930–60; trust deeds 1957–64; agreement re debentures 1953; certificate of mortgage registration 1957; share transfer forms and certificates 1948–68; annual reports and accounts 1956–63; historical notes 1960s.

R L BOOTH
Kirkby Lonsdale, Cumbria

Chemist

History: This business traded initially at 56 Main Street, Kirkby Lonsdale, Cumbria, under the ownership of C Parker, George W Thexton, John B Foggitt and W T Foggitt. It later moved to 2 Market Square and was acquired by R L Booth.

Records: Cumbria Record Office (Kendal), County Offices, Stricklandgate, Kendal LA9 4RQ

Cash registers 1922–40; bank book, John B Foggitt 1922–26; formula books 1892–1959; prescription books 1905–18, 1930–60; sale of poisons registers 1909–49; diaries used as jotters for small orders 1949–61; letters 1932–33, n.d.; page of *Chemist and Druggist*, 12 November 1938 with label for W T Foggitt's Balsamic drops attached. (Ref: WDB/46)

THE BOOTS CO PLC
Nottingham

Retail chemist and pharmaceutical manufacturer

History: In 1849 John and Mary Boot operated a herbalist shop in Goosegate, Nottingham. In 1877 their son Jesse took control of the family business. In addition to the preparation of herbal remedies, he sold patent medicines at lower rates than his competitors, causing much consternation amongst the pharmaceutical community which maintained high prices through local agreements. Boot began advertising in the local press from 1880 as 'Boots Cash Chemists'. In 1883 his business was incorporated as a private limited liability company, Boot & Co Ltd, and a pharmacist, E S Waring, was appointed to allow the company to trade as a chemist and druggist store. Branches were opened subsequently in High Street, Lincoln, Lincolnshire, in Snig Hill, Sheffield, and in various towns around the East Midlands. In 1888 a public limited liability company, Boots Pure Drug Co Ltd, was incorporated to manufacture pharmaceuticals and to act as a holding company for the local retail branches, which by 1893 numbered 33 and by 1897 126. Jesse Boot was knighted for his achievements in 1909. In 1915 John Lawson joined Boots Pure Drug Co Ltd as a manager, after studying and working in Leeds, Manchester, and Dublin, Ireland. He became chairman of the formula committee and manager of the specialities, packed goods and proprietary articles departments. In 1920 Jesse Boot sold the company to the United Drug Co Inc, USA, after which it remained under American ownership until 1933, when, following the death of Jesse Boot in 1931, John Boot, his son, successfully spearheaded a British buy-back of the shares. In the late 1920s a 300-acre site was acquired at Beeston, Nottingham, and in 1933, the year in which the company opened its thousandth store, 'D10', the factory designed by Owen Williams, was officially opened there. The vast manufacturing plant, designed in concrete and glass, was so efficient that the company introduced a 5-day week for workers. In 1968 the company acquired Timothy Whites & Taylors Ltd and its chain of chemist shops. The company was renamed The Boots Co Ltd in 1971 and The Boots Co plc from 1982. Its most successful product during the 1970s was *ibuprofen*, marketed as *Brufen*, a treatment for rheumatoid arthritis and osteoarthritis, which was launched in the UK in 1969. The company was awarded the Queen's Award for Exports in 1974, and for Technological Achievement in 1985, for this product. In 1983 *ibuprofen* was introduced as an over-the-counter medicine under the trade name, *Nurofen*. After a period of company restructuring, in 1995, the pharmaceutical research and development operation, Boots Pharmaceuticals, was acquired by BASF AG, a German chemical company founded in 1865. The main subsidiary businesses, Boots the Chemists, Boots Opticians, Boots Contract Manufacturing, Boots Healthcare International, Boots Properties and Halfords, remained operational in 1999.

'Boots Pure Drug Co Ltd: chemists to the nation', reprinted from *Financial News*, 22 Nov 1934; S Chapman, *Jesse Boot of Boots the Chemists: A study in business history* (Hodder & Stoughton, London, 1974); J E Greenwood, *A Cap for Boots: An autobiography* (Hutchinson, London, 1977); C Roberts, *Achievement: A record of fifty years progress of Boots Pure Drug Co Ltd* (Boots, Nottingham, 1938); E Walker, *Boots 1877–1977: 100 years of shopping at Boots* (Boots, Nottingham, 1977); C Weir, *Jesse Boot of Nottingham* (Boots, Nottingham, 1994)

Records 1: Company Archivist, The Boots Co plc, Company Archives (D31), Nottingham NG2 3AA

Committee meeting minutes: formula committee 1921–39, product committee 1939–45, merchandise committee 1950–72; annual reports and circulars to shareholders 1892 to date; private ledger 1885–93; copyright registrations 1880s–1920s; formulae 1907–15; drug books 1887–1916; tincture reference book 1898–1917; price lists and catalogues 1903 to date; product literature 1930 to date; sales brochures 1932–90; merchandise bulletins 1924–80s; Christmas catalogues 1936 to date; overseas visits reports 1929–49; advertisements

1908–80; packaging designs 1900 to date; press cuttings re company 1950s–80s; property deeds re Nottingham premises 1851–83; miscellaneous store deeds (unlisted); architectural plans and drawings re stores 1920s to date; archaeological reports re Thurgarton Priory 1940–61; branch address books 1920 to date; salary books 1895–98, 1902–03, 1909–10; branch wage book 1914–17; assistants record books 1889–1908; staff training literature 1940s to date; careers information papers 1940s–80s; staff magazines: *Comrades in Khaki* 1915–16, *The Beacon* 1919–35, 1948–69, *The Bee* 1921–39, 1948–66, *The Mixture* 1939–47, *Boots News* 1970–95, *Blueprint* 1995 to date; papers: Boots College 1900 to date, Booklovers Library 1900 to date, athletic club, welfare and sporting activities 1900 to date, hobbies and social activities 1900 to date; book department catalogues 1920s–88; 'Scribbling Diaries' 1898–1989; 'Home Diaries' 1900–84; papers re international retail development 1930s; photographs of stores, factories, laboratories, staff, products and transport 1890s to date; company publications 1930s to date; historical notes and publications 1876 to date; records unlisted 19th–20th cents.

Records 2: Department of Manuscripts & Special Collections, Hallward Library, University of Nottingham, University Park, Nottingham NG7 2RD

John Lawson papers: education, professional training and early career 1892–1917, correspondence 1896–1905, printed material re advertising and publicity of merchandise 1890–1913; papers re John Lawson's employment with company: formula committee papers incl. reports, policy documents, correspondence and blueprints for formulae 1921–28, n.d., reports re medicine stamp duties and trade marks 1925–1943, n.d., sales figures and values 1923–42, price lists 1914–19, c.1940, memorandum on the organisation of pharmacy 1943, correspondence and miscellaneous papers 1915–43, 1963; press cuttings re Sir Jesse Boot's funeral and the opening of the 1000th Boots store 1931, 1933; company employees' magazines 1915–44 (w); private papers of John Lawson: association with Methodist Church 1932–58, position as a public figure 1938–39, correspondence 1912, 1927–32, 1953, library books 1888–1964. (Ref: Ln/1-8)

Records 3: Nottingham City Library, Local Studies Library, Angel Row, Nottingham NG1 6HP

Annual reports and accounts 1941–42, 1963 to date; reports to staff 1976, 1992 to date; staff magazines: *The Beacon* 1919–39 (w), 1949–69, *The Bee* 1921–69 (w), *Staff Magazine* 1942–68 (w), *Boots News* 1970–95, *Blueprint* 1995 to date; investors' magazine, *Boots Shareholder* 1995 to date; news supplement for retired staff 1995 to date; summary of community and charitable activities 1995 to date; fact files 1995 to date. (Ref: L66.8, fL66.8, qL66.8)

Records 4: Nottinghamshire Archives & Southwell Diocesan Record Office, County House, Castle Meadow Road, Nottingham NG2 1AG

Shop site deeds: Stodman Street, Newark-on-Trent, Nottinghamshire, 1720–1894, Radford Road and Bright Row, Nottingham 1825–1917; Charles Edward Coulthard: historical notes and reminiscences re bacteriological laboratories, research and fine chemicals departments, apprenticeship and employment with company 1915–19; special contributions by Boots staff members re history of company c.1963. (Ref: Ref: DD 1565, M 24, M 531)

Records 5: Buckinghamshire Record Office, County Hall, Aylesbury HP20 1UU

Aylesbury, Buckinghamshire branch: prescription registers 1933–74, dispensing record books 1969–78, sale of poisons register 1962–70. (Ref: D 142)

Records 6: Bury Archive Service, 1st Floor, The Derby Hall Annexe, Edwin Street, Bury BL9 0AS

Bury branch: prescription books 1900–73, sale of poisons register 1958–78. (Ref: BBT)

Records 7: Cumbria Record Office (Kendal), County Offices, Stricklandgate, Kendal LA9 4RQ

Ambleside, Cumbria branch: prescription books 1934–40, 1953–70; Bowness-on-Windermere, Cumbria, branch: cash book 1923–25, day books 1931–35, prescription books 1902–31, repeat prescription books 1912–31, poisons register 1936–50; Windermere, Cumbria, branch: prescription books 1933–61. (Ref: WDB/39-40, 47)

Records 8: Gloucestershire Record Office, Clarence Row, Alvin Street, Gloucester GL1 3DW

Cheltenham, Gloucestershire branch: prescription book 1923–24. (Ref: D7700)

Records 9: Lancashire Record Office, Bow Lane, Preston PR1 2RE

Burnley, Lancashire branch: prescription book 1920–37. (Ref: DDX 1101 acc 7803 (unlisted))

Records 10: The Museum Curator, Royal Pharmaceutical Society of Great Britain, 1 Lambeth High Street, London SE1 7JN

Station Road, Horley, Surrey branch: prescription book 1940–43. (Ref: LDPHA.MANUSCOL.17.1)

Records 11: Stockport Archive Service, Central Library, Wellington Road South, Stockport SK1 3RS

Stockport branch: sale of poisons register 1929–36. (Ref: B/II/6/23)

Records 12: Surrey History Centre, 130 Goldsworth Road, Woking GU21 1ND

Dorking, Surrey branch: prescription books, incl. customers' names and addresses, prescriptions and prices, with emergency prescriptions at the back, and a record of purchases of industrial methylated spirit 1945–89. (Ref: 6237)

Records 13: Warwickshire County Record Office, Priory Park, Cape Road, Warwick CV34 4JS

High Street, Warwick, Warwickshire branch: prescription books 1934–35, 1939–42. (Ref: CR2196)

Records 14: The Royal Society, 6 Carlton House Terrace, London SW1Y 5AG

Correspondence with Sir Henry Hallett Dale 1940–52. (Ref: 93 HD/48.2)

Records 15: Public Record Office, Ruskin Avenue, Kew, Richmond TW9 4DU

Medical Research Council committees re company c.1913–54. (Ref: FD1/13/930, 2261, 2516, 2518)

Records 16: History of Advertising Trust, HAT House, 12 Raveningham Centre, Raveningham NR14 6NU

Papers and memoranda with agents re advertising 1987–90; advertisements: *Nurofen* 1985, vitamin tablets 1985. (Ref: Leo Burnett research material; MEAL collection 1985 R10, R75)

Records 17: Somerset Archive & Record Office, Obridge Road, Taunton, Somerset TA2 7PU

Weston-super-Mare, North Somerset branch: prescription books 1925–56. (Ref: A/AKH 1/1-9)

Records 18: North Devon Record Office, Tuly Street, Barnstaple, Devon EX31 1EL

1-2 High Street, Ilfracombe, Devon branch: prescription books 1926–96; record of dangerous drugs sold or supplied 1937–83. (Ref: B483/1-21, B483/22)

BRADFORD CHEMISTS' ALLIANCE LTD
Alliance House, York Street, Fairweather Green, Bradford

Wholesale distribution of ethical medical products, dressings and proprietary goods

History: The Bradford Chemists' Alliance Ltd was incorporated as a limited liability company in 1917 by 5 pharmacists from Bradford, who aimed to secure cheap medical supplies from the large drug houses by consolidating their buying power. Initially storage facilities were informal, but as the volume of stock increased it became necessary to find warehouse accommodation, and buildings were acquired at Union Street, Bradford. In 1952 the company moved to larger premises in East Parade, Bradford, and established a weekly delivery service to pharmacies in the locality. Subsequently the company moved twice more, to Scoresby Street, and Thornton Road, before settling in a purpose-built warehouse in York Street, Bradford. The company's distribution area covered the whole of west and parts of north and south Yorkshire and north east Lancashire. In 1987 the company was renamed Bradford Chemists' Alliance Ltd and in 1993 was acquired by UniChem plc which merged with Alliance Sante SA in 1997. By 1999 the company was dormant, its business and assets having been transferred to E Moss Ltd.

'Bradford Chemists' Alliance Ltd' in *NAPD 25th Anniversary* (NAPD, 1991); 'Gentleman's Agreement That Grew and Grew', *Bradford Telegraph and Argus*, 18 Sept 1963

Records: Alliance UniChem plc, UniChem House, Cox Lane, Chessington KT9 1SN

Directors' and general meetings minutes 1968–79; directors' meetings minutes 1994; change of name certificate 1987; acquisition papers 1993–94; combined register of members and share ledger 1917–93; title deeds and legal papers re purchase of land and buildings on south side of York Street 1889–1911, 1959, 1973–76.

BRADLEY & BLISS LTD
Reading

Wholesale and retail chemist

History: In 1817 George Cooper established a wholesale and retail chemist and druggist's business in Fisher Road, Reading, relocating shortly afterwards to 31 Market Place. By 1837 the business was styled George Cooper & Co, but following its purchase by George Bradley, a chemist and druggist of Ashbourne, Derbyshire, and William Thomas Bliss, a chemist and druggist of Birmingham, in 1872, it was renamed Bradley & Bliss. In 1882 the firm moved to King's Road, Reading, and in 1907, to London Street. In 1909, following the death of George Bradley, the business was acquired by his son, Charles Reginald Bradley, and incorporated as a limited liability company, Bradley & Bliss Ltd. From 1947 the company expanded its wholesale business, opening branches in St Leonards, East Sussex, in 1952 and Sandwich, Kent, in 1957. In 1964 it was acquired by British Drug Houses Group Ltd. In 1966 following the merger of the wholesaling interests of Glaxo Group Ltd and British Drug Houses Group Ltd, and the incorporation of a new limited liability company, Vestric Ltd, Bradley & Bliss Ltd became the Reading and Bexhill, East Sussex, branch of Vestric Ltd, and ceased to trade under its own name.

'The South of England, Reading and Bexhill' in P M Worling, *Vestric: The first twenty years 1966–86* (Vestric, Runcorn, 1986)

Records 1: Archivist (Historical Records), Records Centre, Glaxo Wellcome plc, 891-995 Greenford Road, Greenford UB6 0HE

Minutes 1949–55; accounts 1956–73. (Ref: CA331, 493)

Records 2: The Museum Curator, Royal Pharmaceutical Society of Great Britain, 1 Lambeth High Street, London SE1 7JN

Prescription books 1941–68. (Ref: IRA.1996.442)

Records 3: Dr Peter M Worling, The Grange, 29 Fernielaw Avenue, Edinburgh EH13 0EF

Price list 1963; press cutting re new warehouse 1959; historical article 1969.

BRITISH CAMPHOR CO LTD
Ilford, Redbridge, London

Camphor manufacturer

History: In 1906 British Camphor Co Ltd was incorporated as a limited liability company by Howards & Sons Ltd, to synthesise turpentine to produce camphor, using Behal's process. In that year a factory was built at Howards & Sons Ltd's site, off Uphall Road, Ilford, Redbridge, London, adjacent to the premises of Hopkin & Williams Ltd, another of its subsidiaries. British Camphor Co Ltd was liquidated in 1909.

Records: London Metropolitan Archives, 40 Northampton Road, London EC1R 0HB

Memorandum and articles of association 1906; certificate of incorporation 1906; share certificate 1906; correspondence re camphor manufacture and purchase of stock in the company 1906; annual report 1907; legal papers and correspondence 1909–10; building works agreements and lease 1906; letter of agreement re divided responsibility with Howards & Sons Ltd for payment of chemists 1906; letter from Howards & Sons Ltd re payment of staff and expenditure at Ilford 1908; correspondence and receipt re receivership and liquidation, incl. letter from Behal 1908–09. (Ref: Acc 1037/150-51, 743-53)

BRITISH DRUG HOUSES GROUP LTD
Graham Street, City Road, London

Wholesale chemist

History: British Drug Houses Ltd was incorporated as a limited liability company in 1909. It was established as a result of a series of amalgamations, fostered by Charles Alexander Hill of Arthur S Hill & Sons, wholesale chemists of London since 1755. In 1896 Arthur S Hill & Sons merged with Davy, Yates & Hicks to form Davy, Hill & Co, which in turn merged with Hodgkinson, Clark & Ward to form a limited liability company, Davy, Hill & Hodgkinson Ltd. In 1909 this company amalgamated with Hearon, Squire & Francis, a firm of wholesale druggists dating back to 1650, and Barron Harvey & Co, established in Giltspur Street in 1792, to form British Drug Houses Ltd. In 1910 new premises were acquired at Graham Street, City Road, London, and the many separate concerns which formed British Drug Houses Ltd were brought together on one site. Graham Street became a major distribution centre, servicing London and the south east of England with drugs, chemicals and patent medicines for over 50 years. During this period British Drug Houses Ltd was renamed British Drug Houses Group Ltd and acquired a number of pharmaceutical wholesale businesses, including J R Gibbs, Bristol, in 1923 and Bradley & Bliss Ltd, Reading, in 1964. In 1966 British Drug Houses Group Ltd and Glaxo Group Ltd amalgamated their wholesaling interests, resulting in the incorporation of a new limited liability company, Vestric Ltd. Following this the Graham Street premises were closed and the business conducted by the company was transferred to branches in London at Ruislip, Hillingdon; Enfield; and Foots Cray, Bexley. In 1968 the shareholding in British Drug Houses Group Ltd which was held by Mead Johnson Inc, USA, was acquired by Glaxo Group Ltd and Vestric Ltd became a wholly-owned subsidiary of Glaxo Group Ltd. In 1973 Merck Ltd, the UK subsidiary of Merck KgaA, Darmstadt, Germany, founded in 1668 by Fredrish Jacob Merck, acquired British Drug Houses Group Ltd from Glaxo Group Ltd. Merck Ltd became the sole UK company in 1991 and British Drug Houses Group Ltd ceased to trade.

'Distribution in London, The British Drug Houses, London' in P M Worling, *Vestric: The first twenty years 1966–86* (Vestric, Runcorn, 1986)

Records 1: Archivist (Historical Records), Records Centre, Glaxo Wellcome plc, 891-995 Greenford Road, Greenford UB6 0HE

Directors' meetings minutes 1965–74; general meetings minutes 1968–70; agendas, minutes and papers 1940–71; memorandum and articles of association 1908; papers: sale of company 1973–76, liquidation 1973, merger 1960–68; attendance register 1960–67; report to directors 1967–74; rights issues 1970–81; dividend warrant 1967–85; preference and ordinary share register 1970; lists of shareholders 1967–85; share dividends 1946–67; papers re shares 1964–68; share issue correspondence 1920–61; shareholder correspondence 1967–69; seal register 1973–76; annual reports and accounts 1926–66; reports on profit and loss accounts 1950–55; cost accounts 1950–57; accounts and merger proposals 1965; agreements with Glaxo Group Ltd 1966–73; reports: physiological laboratory 1936–46, chemical research department 1962–63; product literature 1928–46; promotional calendars 1932–61; memoranda to secretary 1970–76;

papers re overseas subsidiaries 1931–63; miscellaneous papers 1969–78; records unlisted 19th–20th cents.

Records 2: Gwynedd Archives & Museums Service, Caernarfon Area Record Office, Victoria Dock, Caernarfon. Enquiries to County Offices, Shirehall Street, Caernarfon LL55 1SH

Invoice to J L Williams for consignment of drugs 1945. (Ref: XM3522)

Records 3: Dr Peter M Worling, The Grange, 29 Fernielaw Avenue, Edinburgh EH13 0EF

Pharmaceutical price list 1964.

E A BROCKLEHURST LTD
27 Bridgegate, Howden, East Riding of Yorkshire

Pharmaceutical chemist

History: From the 1930s Brocklehurst's chemist's business was trading from 214 Willerby Road, Kingston upon Hull. In 1952 the business was incorporated as a limited liability company, E A Brocklehurst Ltd. By 1994, the year in which the company was acquired by E Moss Ltd, the retail subsidiary of UniChem plc, it operated 10 chemist's shops. 7 of these were purchased by E Moss Ltd, whilst the remaining 3, of which one was 214 Willerby Road, were still trading as E A Brocklehurst Ltd in 1997. By 1999 the company was dormant, its remaining business and assets having been transferred to E Moss Ltd.

Records: Alliance UniChem plc, UniChem House, Cox Lane, Chessington KT9 1SN

Directors' and general meetings minutes 1981 to date; acquisition papers 1993–94; combined register of members and share ledger 1952–94; register of directors' shareholdings 1952–92; share certificate book 1978–94; report and financial statements 1994; title deeds and documents: Howden, incl. copy will of William Selley of Howden, chemist and druggist 1853, 132-134 Chanterlands Avenue, Kingston upon Hull 20th cent.; architectural plan of Howden 19th–20th cents.

J BROWN & SON CHEMISTS (WALKER) LTD
2/4 Byker Street, Walker, Newcastle upon Tyne

Dispensing and family chemist

History: In 1946 the chemist and druggist's business of Nancy Rust and Murray Dinsdale Oubridge at 2/4 Byker Street, Walker, Newcastle upon Tyne, was incorporated as a limited liability company, J Brown & Son Chemists (Walker) Ltd. The company was acquired by UniChem plc in 1992 (which merged with Alliance Sante SA in 1997 to become Alliance UniChem plc) and assigned to E Moss Ltd as a dormant subsidiary.

Records: Alliance UniChem plc, UniChem House, Cox Lane, Chessington KT9 1SN

Directors' and general meetings minutes 1946–61 (w), 1970–73, 1980–91; memorandum and articles of association 1946; certificate of incorporation 1946; combined register of members and share ledger 1946–92.

BROWN'S PHARMACY
159 Woodhouse Lane, Leeds

Chemist

History: Edward Brown was registered as a pharmaceutical chemist in 1867, residing at 66 Woodhouse Lane, Leeds. His son, Edward Oliver Brown, was registered as a chemist and druggist in 1875. The business of Edward Brown was registered at 159 Woodhouse Lane, Leeds, in 1876, and both were still residing at 66 Woodhouse Lane in 1895.

Records: West Yorkshire Archive Service, Leeds, Chapeltown Road, Sheepscar, Leeds LS7 3AP

Pharmaceutical memorandum book 1882–1903; prescription book 1897–1900. (Ref: Acc 1373)

BURROWS & CLOSE LTD
Melton Mowbray, Leicestershire

Chemist and druggist

History: James Attenburrow traded as a chemist and druggist from before 1868 at Pall Mall, Melton Mowbray, Leicestershire. In 1869 Joseph Attenburrow was also registered as a chemist and druggist in Melton Mowbray, relocating in 1878 to Cornhill in that town. James Attenburrow continued to trade from Pall Mall. In 1889 a second James Attenburrow registered as a chemist and druggist in Melton Mowbray. In 1890 James Attenburrow, the elder, joined Joseph Attenburrow in the Cornhill business and in 1902 ceased to be registered. In 1914 Joseph Attenburrow also ceased to be registered. James Attenburrow, the younger, continued to trade from Melton Mowbray and by 1935 was operating from 1 High Street as J Attenburrow. In 1941 he was joined in the business by Ellen Attenburrow who continued the business after he ceased to be registered in 1947 on her own account, trading as J Attenburrow until 1952 when the business was renamed E Attenburrow. It continued to trade under this name until 1976, when it was incorporated as a limited liability company, Burrows, Graham, Ltd. In 1977 it was renamed Burrows & Close Ltd. In 1985 Ellen Attenburrow ceased to be registered and in 1988 the company ceased trading.

Records: Record Office for Leicestershire, Leicester & Rutland, Long Street, Wigston Magna, Leicester LE18 2AH

Ledger 1914–24; account book 1925–29; day books 1918–29; statement of sums payable re drugs and appliances ordered 1927–31; price list 1923; correspondence: proposed shop alterations 1900, general 1868–72; estimate of proposed shop alterations 1897. (Ref: DE1955, 3160, Misc1205, 1341)

BUSH BOAKE ALLEN LTD
Blackhorse Lane, Walthamstow, Waltham Forest, London

Manufacturer of essences, fragrances and flavourings

History: Bush Boake Allen Ltd was incorporated as a limited liability company in 1966, following the merger of Stafford Allen & Sons Ltd, a drug milling and grinding company, W J Bush & Co Ltd, a manufacturer of flavourings and essential oils, and A Boake Roberts & Co Ltd, a producer of industrial chemicals. Bush Boake Allen Ltd was incorporated as a subsidiary of Albright & Wilson Ltd, a phosphorus manufacturer, with headquarters at the former A Boake Roberts & Co Ltd site at Blackhorse Lane, Walthamstow, Waltham Forest, London. It was acquired by Union Camp Corporation Inc, New Jersey, USA, in 1982, and was still trading in 1999 as a manufacturer of essences, fragrances and flavourings, some for use in the pharmaceutical industry.

Records: Bush Boake Allen Ltd, Blackhorse Lane, Walthamstow, London E17 5QP

Directors' and general meetings minutes 1966–82; certificates of registration 1968; minutes: executive committee meetings 1967–71, flavours division, committee of management meetings 1966–68, banking committee meetings 1974–83; dividend cards 1944–55; report re company profitability 1960s; insurance schedules 1970; court orders 1983–84, 1990–93, n.d.; registers of trademarks 1883–1965; lapsed trademarks and patents 20th cent.; research laboratory report 1967; incubation room registers 1968–78; stock control manuals 1976, 1982; product and price lists 1960s–70s; information brochures re flavourings 1960s–70s, n.d.; representatives' handbook n.d.; order book 1977; world-wide contracts 1960s to date; corporate design manual 1967; advertisements 1966; package code book 1975; product labels 1966–71; promotional brochure n.d.; title deeds 1973–94, n.d.; mortgage registration certificates 1992–94; leases and agreements 1971–94; applications, licences and assignments 1973–94; site plan n.d.; maps and drawings n.d.; land certificates n.d.; legal charge certificate 1993; contract for sale 1978; property inventories and valuations 1966–69; memoranda re property 1982–90; personnel chart 1977–78; terms of employment 1972; staff information booklet 1984; safety manual c.1972; office procedures manual 1975; magazines: *Bush Review* 1973–75, *Bush Telegraph* 1983–93; staff and social club correspondence 1960–71; visitors books 1975–93; correspondence: Achille Serre Ltd 1972, Garfield Glass Ltd 1979, Newham Borough Council 1985, Martin-Thomas Ltd 1987; photographs: visit of Princess Margaret 1975, staff and personnel late 20th cent.; staff research papers and lectures 1969; historical notes 1970s–95.

W J BUSH & CO LTD
Ash Grove, Hackney, London

Manufacturer of perfumes and flavourings, some for use in the pharmaceutical industry

History: In 1851 William John Bush established a business on his own account at Bishopsgate, City of London, styled W J Bush & Co. From factory premises he prepared herbs, spices, tinctures and essences. In 1885 the firm re-located to Ash Grove, Hackney, London, and the following year acquired the business of Potter & Moore, a herb distiller, established in Mitcham, Merton, London, in 1749, which was incorporated as a limited liability company, Potter & Moore Ltd, in 1928, and renamed Ash Grove Perfumery Ltd in 1969. William Bush died in 1889, and was succeeded in the business by his son, William Ernest Bush, who, on his death in 1903, was replaced by his brother James Mortimer Bush. In 1897 the firm was incorporated as a limited liability company, W J Bush & Co Ltd. During the First World War the company manufactured large quantities of chloroform, salicylic acid and *Aspirin*, and during the Second World War provided pharmaceutical manufacturing companies with essential chemicals required in their production processes. In addition it manufactured perfumery products and flavourings, fruit bases and essential oils, many of which were prepared to flavour and colour pharmaceutical products. W J Bush & Co Ltd was acquired by Albright & Wilson Ltd, a phosphorus manufacturer, in 1961, but continued to trade under its own name. In 1966 W J Bush & Co Ltd, Stafford Allen & Sons Ltd, a drug milling and grinding company, and A Boake Roberts & Co Ltd, an industrial chemical manufacturer, merged to form Bush Boake Allen Ltd, a subsidiary of Albright & Wilson Ltd, with head offices at Blackhorse Lane, London.

A Pictorial Record of Bush World-Wide Development, Establishments and Personalities During One Hundred Years Of Progress 1851–1951 (W J Bush, London, 1951)

Records: Bush Boake Allen Ltd, Blackhorse Lane, Walthamstow, London E17 5QP

Minutes: directors' meetings, incl. annual reports and accounts 1897–1966, general meetings 1897–1966, committee of directors' meetings 1940–66; certificate of incorporation 1897; change of name certificate 1966; chairman's general meeting statement 1947; notice re merger 1964; registers: directors 1904–15, directors and secretaries 1915–63, shareholders 1958–64, ordinary shares 1897–1966, preference shares 1897–1961, debentures 1897–1929, transfers 1897–1921; annual reports and accounts 1897–1959 (w); ledgers: private n.d., warehouse 1952–73; interim and final dividends cash book 1936–56; trademark certificates 1906; laboratory journal 1898; formulae books c.1900–40, n.d.; experiments book 1947–50; drug department log book 1901–04; batch record book 1954–57; product specifications 1955–56, n.d.; technical reference book 1971–73; code index 1940s; buyers' guide 1953; representatives' manuals 1952–53, 1961; product and price lists early 20th cent., 1936, 1949–63; drawback book 1946–72; advertisement press cuttings 1910–17, 1930s–40s; centenary album 1951; souvenir programme 1951; labels and packaging samples 1909–10; Ash Grove: title deeds 1856–74, 1896, 1947–51, rent redemption 1881, 1917; Mitcham: title deeds 1854–1912, purchase objections 1868, plan of plant and works 1966, inventory and valuation 1969, land registry certificate 1919; wages and salaries books 1944–50; superannuation booklet 1960s; pension fund rules 1960–63; rules and conditions of employment n.d.; Ash Grove, joint advisory council constitution and rules n.d.; staff booklet n.d.; staff roll of honour 1977; staff outing souvenir programme 1939; agreements: English *Aspirin* Makers Convention 1930, use of trade mark *Sobenife* 1962; photographs: James Bush n.d., Ash Grove early 20th cent., staff and plant c.1930s, containers n.d.; portrait of William Ernest Bush n.d.; sports club constitution and rules 1919–38; *The Sports Bulletin*, magazine 1936–38; memorial service programmes 1953–54, 1967; company publications 1898, 1924, 1961; historical notes 1951, 1960s, n.d.

Ash Grove Perfumery Ltd: directors' meetings minutes 1929–76; general meetings minutes 1930–66; certificate of incorporation 1928; change of name certificate 1969; combined register of members and share ledger 1928–71; private ledger 1929–64; development report 1963; valuation 1965; papers and plans re sale of site 1973; photographs: drug fields and workers c.1920s–30s, product promotion n.d.

W J Bush Pension Trustees Ltd: directors' and general meetings minutes 1948–69; voluntary liquidation book 1970; share certificate book 1948–62; memorandum re stocks and shares transfers 1959–65; ledger 1966–70; list of investments to be transferred to Albright & Wilson Ltd 1968; schedules of investments 1964–66.

Cameron Pharmaceuticals Ltd: directors' and general meetings minutes 1944–74; combined register of members and share ledger 1944–71.

E H BUTLER & SON LTD
Galen House, 66 Commercial Square, Freemen's Common, Leicester

Pharmaceutical manufacturer and wholesaler, retail chemist and financial advisor

History: In 1827 John Butler established a chemist and druggist's business in Wharf Street, Leicester, on his own account. He supplied and compounded medicinal preparations including citric acid, dragon's blood, Iceland moss, ipecacuanha root and Spanish flies. By 1869 the business was controlled by John's son, Edward Henry Butler, in partnership with William Beckett and Henry Pickering, and was styled Butler, Pickering & Beckett. The firm operated from premises in Halford Street, Leicester, relocating in 1870 to 93 Humberstone Gate, Leicester. Pickering died in 1871 and, on Beckett's retirement in 1877, E H Butler assumed sole charge of the business. He was joined in partnership by his son, Edwin Henry Butler (1868–1954) in 1888, and the business was styled E H Butler & Son. From 1904 until 1924 E H Butler & Son was the UK distribution agent for the dyes of the Swiss company, Geigy, of Basle. In 1923, following the death of his father in 1903, Edwin Henry took his son, Edwin Harold Butler (1898-1970), into partnership. By this time the firm was manufacturing galenicals, some chemicals and compressed tablets. By the mid-1930s E H Butler & Son was wholesale agent to many major manufacturing companies in Britain, including Allen & Hanburys Ltd, British Drug Houses Ltd, May & Baker Ltd and Parke, Davis & Co Ltd. In 1934 the accommodation at Humberstone Gate was extended into Vestry Street. In 1936 the business was incorporated as a limited liability company, E H Butler & Son Ltd, and expanded into the wholesale distribution of prescription medicines. In 1949 the company acquired additional premises in Thornton Lane, Leicester, and in 1958 in Brunswick Street, Leicester, after which Humberstone Gate and Thornton Lane were closed. By the 1950s a twice-daily wholesale distribution service was offered to retail chemists within a 50 mile radius of the company, and later to towns as far afield as Nottingham, Birmingham, and St Albans, Hertfordshire. A second wholesale depot was opened in Northampton, Northamptonshire, in 1966, and closed in 1980. During the early 1950s Edwin Hugh Butler, the son of Edwin Harold, joined the company. Between 1962 and 1966 he was secretary of the Northern Wholesale Druggists' Association and, in 1965, was instrumental in the incorporation of Onward Pharmaceutical Services Ltd, as a joint venture with Ridley (Wholesale Chemists) Ltd, Carlisle, Cumbria, and Raimes, Clark & Co Ltd, Edinburgh. The company was established to offer a national distribution service to manufacturers, and by the end of the 1960s it had 16 members. In 1967 E H Butler & Son Ltd was the first pharmaceutical distributor to operate a computerised invoicing and accounting system. As a result, a subsidiary company, Inter City Computer Bureau Ltd, was incorporated in 1969, to market the system. It was acquired by Mayne Nickless in around 1977. In 1976 Charnwood Pharmaceuticals Ltd was incorporated as a joint venture limited liability company, by E H Butler & Son Ltd and Richard Daniel & Son Ltd of Derby, to manufacture and package generic pharmaceuticals, and to supply them to wholesalers. It operated from Abbey Lane, Leicester, until 1981 when it was sold to Fisons Ltd, and became a dormant company. In 1990 the wholesale distribution interests of E H Butler & Son Ltd were sold to Medicopharma Ltd, North Street, Romford, Havering, London, and the family company was renamed Galen Management Services Ltd. From 1980 to 1994 the company operated a number of retail pharmacies, through a wholly-owned subsidiary, Bullalow Ltd. This company was acquired by E Moss Ltd in 1994.

'Charnwood Generic Venture', *Pharmaceutical Journal*, 217, 1976, 90-1

Records 1: Galen Management Services Ltd, Galen House, 66 Commercial Square, Freemen's Common, Leicester LE2 7SR

Directors' and general meetings minutes 1936 to date; memorandum and articles of association (p) 1936; balance sheets 1898–99, 1936; trading and profit and loss accounts and balance sheets 1937–95; invoice 1893; formulae book, human and veterinary preparations 1848; recipe book 1896; price lists 1931–35, 1947–66 (w); labels book, packed goods late 1940s; advertising business notice 1827; product advertising slides 1930s; wages book 1926–27; Ministry of Health staff insurance receipt 1927; press cuttings re long-service employees 1971, 1994; photographs, incl. depots, vans and sale of wholesale business 1970s, 1990; British Pharmaceutical Conference, Leicester, official programme, and photograph 1926.

Onward Pharmaceutical Services Ltd: minutes of inaugural meeting 1965; directory of members 1967; letter of resignation of E H Butler as chairman 1990; price lists 1968, 1970–72; promotional leaflet late 1980s.

Charnwood Pharmaceuticals Ltd: directors' and general meetings minutes 1975–82; directors' report and accounts, incl. profit and loss account and balance sheet 1977–80.

Bullalow Ltd: directors' and general meetings minutes 20th cent.; trading, profit and loss accounts and balance sheets 1980–94; photographs of branches 1991.

Records 2: Dr Peter M Worling, The Grange, 29 Fernielaw Avenue, Edinburgh EH13 0EF

Onward Pharmaceutical Services Ltd: price lists 1968, 1970–71, pack list n.d.

BUYCHEM (S W LONDON) LTD
Crown House, Morden, Merton, London

Wholesale and retail chemist

History: Buychem (S W London) Ltd was incorporated as a limited liability company in 1964, by member pharmacists of UniChem Ltd, to carry on the business of wholesale, retail and manufacturing chemists and druggists. The company was wound up in 1982, and dissolved in 1985.

Records: Alliance UniChem plc, UniChem House, Cox Lane, Chessington KT9 1SN

Directors' and general meetings minutes 1964–82; memorandum and articles of association 1964; certificate of incorporation 1964; combined register of members and share ledger 1964–71.

THE CAPSULOID CO LTD
Chapelle Court, Borough, Southwark, London

Proprietary medicine manufacturer

History: The Capsuloid Co Ltd was incorporated as a limited liability company in 1902, to acquire George E Dixon's business, The Capsuloid Co, which had traded for some years, from 31 Snow Hill, London, manufacturing the proprietary medicine, *Capsuloids*. George E Dixon was appointed as manager in the same year. In 1905 the company moved to 47 Holburn Viaduct, London, and in 1910, to Chapelle Court, Borough, Southwark, London. The Capsuloid Co Ltd was dissolved in 1913.

Records 1: Public Record Office, Ruskin Avenue, Kew, Richmond TW9 4DU

Memorandum and articles of association 1902; certificate of incorporation 1902; certificate of registration 1902; agreement to purchase The Capsuloid Co 1902; company prospectus 1902; special resolutions 1906, 1908; copies of registers of directors or managers 1902–07, 1909–10; consent to act as directors 1902; list of consenting directors 1902; consent of directors to take pay for qualification shares 1902; annual return 1903; declaration of compliance with Companies Acts 1902; statements of capital and shares 1902–03, 1909; return of allotments 1902–04; notice of situation of registered office 1902; notices of change in situation of registered office 1905, 1910; notice of dissolution 1913. (Ref: BT31/10026/74985)

CAPSULOIDS (1909) LTD
Watford, Hertfordshire

Proprietary medicine manufacturer

History: In 1909 Cicfa Co Ltd was incorporated as a limited liability company. It was later acquired as a wholly-owned subsidiary of Beecham Group Ltd, and renamed Capsuloids (1909) Ltd. It manufactured and distributed the proprietary medicine *Cicfa* from a factory and offices in Watford, Hertfordshire, until at least 1953, after which it was dissolved.

Records: St Helens Local History & Archives Library, Gamble Institute, Victoria Square, St Helens WA10 1DY

Minutes 1909–53; memorandum and articles of association 1909; special resolutions 1923; annual returns 1918–53; share certificate book 1909–51; share transfers book 1909–49; private ledger 1936–50; miscellaneous papers incl. financial information and correspondence 1935–36; letter to G B Simpson enclosing dividend cheque 1931; correspondence re trade marks *Cirfa* and *Cicfa* c.1959–64; papers re manufacture and packaging of tablets 1951–53.

CARTER & SONS (SHEFFIELD) LTD
Sheffield

Pharmaceutical chemist

History: This business was established around the turn of the twentieth century as Carter & Sons, manufacturing chemists of Pond Hill, Sheffield. By 1919 the business had moved to Attercliffe Road, where it remained until at least 1973. In around 1926 it was renamed Carter & Sons (Sheffield). The business was incorporated as a limited liability company, Carter & Sons (Sheffield) Ltd, in 1966, having changed its trading activity to that of cocoa, chocolate and confectionery manufacturer. In 1997 it was still trading, and had registered offices at Fairview Trading Estate, Kingsbury Road, Curdworth, Warwickshire.

Records: Sheffield City Archives, 52 Shoreham Street, Sheffield S1 4SP

Ledgers: nominal 1933–41, purchases 1951–52, accounts with firms supplied 1954–57, cash analysis 1954–56; day book, receipt and despatch of goods 1940–44; invoices 1922; inventory and valuation of machinery and equipment 1922–39; weekly stock books: laboratory 1937–42, 1945, packaging materials 1947–48; display cards and cartons 1930s. (Ref: MD 6094-104)

J R CAVE LTD
Southport, Sefton

Chemist

History: James Righton was registered as a chemist and druggist at 229 Lord Street, Southport, Sefton, in 1873. He was still trading from this address in 1895. By 1943 the business was trading at 511 Lord Street, Southport, and in 1951 was acquired by the Sheldon family. J R Cave Ltd, established in 1922, was first situated at 15 Leyland Avenue, Southport. By 1953 it had moved to 52 Nevill Street and 15 Burton Arcade, Southport, and appears to have owned additional premises at 13 & 21 Burton Arcade during the 1960s and 1970s. J R Cave Ltd later acquired the business owned by the Sheldon family.

Records: Merseyside Record Office, Central Library, William Brown Street, Liverpool L3 8EW

Cash book 1966–77; recipe books c.1885, c.1919; prescription books 1876–87, 1936–78; surgical appliance books 1954–65. (Ref: 380CAV)

CEPHOS LTD
SmithKline Beecham House, Great West Road, Brentford, Hounslow, London

Proprietary medicine manufacturer

History: Cephos Ltd was incorporated as a limited liability company in Blackburn, in 1917, to manufacture the proprietary medicines *Cephos* and *Cephaids*. It was acquired by Beecham Group Ltd in 1959 and production was transferred to the Beecham Group Ltd site at St Helens.

Records: St Helens Local History & Archives Library, Gamble Institute, Victoria Square, St Helens WA10 1DY

Minutes: directors' meetings 1959–60, general meetings 1959–60; memoranda and articles of association 1917, 1948; notice of resolution to raise more capital 1951; annual returns c.1957–60; share transfers 1917–51, 1959; profit and loss accounts 1953–57; trading accounts n.d.; private ledgers 1914–33, 1942–49; accounts 1950s; auditor's reports 1953–60; deed of assignment re use of trade marks *Cephos* and *Cephaids* n.d.; papers re sales, advertising and packaging 1958–67; notes re product pricing 1958–59; correspondence with Leamington Spa public health department re advertising 1962; papers re transfer of operations to St Helens 1958–60; correspondence re disposal of Blackburn premises 1959; notes re redundancy payments c.1959.

CHEERS & HOPLEY LTD
Northgate Street, Chester, Cheshire

Dispensing chemist

History: A chemist's business appears to have been established at Northgate Street, Chester, Cheshire, by Thomas Lloyd and John Grindley in 1817. By 1876 William Grindley, who registered as a pharmaceutical chemist in 1861, was trading from 146 Northgate Street as Grindley & Son. In 1891 Samuel Cheers, who registered as a chemist and druggist in 1890, and John Henry Hopley, who registered as the same in 1889, acquired the business in partnership under the style of Cheers & Hopley. In 1939 the business was incorporated as a limited liability company, Cheers & Hopley Ltd, and in 1973 was acquired by Owen Owen Ltd. The shop was closed in 1979.

Records: Chester Archives, Town Hall, Chester CH1 2HJ

Business registers 1939–59; account books, goods purchased 1955–68; journals, goods sold 1956–67; day books 1940–55; prescription books 1888–1971. (Ref: CR 154, CR 154/2)

CHEMISTS HOLDINGS LTD
London

Holding company for a chain of pharmaceutical wholesale and retail companies

History: Chemists Holdings (London) Ltd was incorporated as a limited liability company in 1958. In 1976 it was acquired by AAH Holdings plc, a holding company for a number of wholesale and retail pharmaceutical companies based in Lincoln, Lincolnshire, and renamed Chemists Holdings Ltd. Purchased in order to acquire a number of pharmaceutical wholesale and retail concerns on its parent's behalf, the main operating subsidiaries of Chemists Holdings Ltd were Hills Pharmaceuticals Ltd, a pharmaceutical wholesaler, and Hill-Smith (Warrington) Ltd, a group of 10 retail pharmacies. After 1976 the company continued to operate under its own name and acquired, amongst others, Mawson & Proctor Pharmaceuticals Ltd in 1983, and Herbert Ferryman Ltd and Northern Pharmaceuticals Ltd, in 1985. It ceased trading in 1986, when it was absorbed by Vestric Ltd, which had been acquired by AAH plc in 1985. AAH plc was acquired in 1995 by GEHE AG.

Records: GEHE UK plc, Retail Branch, Atherstone, Warwickshire. Enquiries to GEHE UK plc, Sapphire Court, Walsgrave Triangle Business Park, Coventry CV2 2TX

General meetings minutes 1958–96; memorandum and articles of association 1958; change of name certificate 1976; seal register 1972–88; combined register of members, directors and share ledger 1958–88; loan agreement 1976. (Ref: Boxes S18, A4, current minutes, box 5)

J F CHESTER (ROUGHTON) LTD
4 New Horizons Court, Great West Road, Brentford, Hounslow, London

Pharmaceutical manufacturer

History: J F Chester (Roughton) Ltd was incorporated as a limited liability company in 1953, to manufacture basic pharmaceutical products. It was subsequently acquired by Beecham Group Ltd, and continued to trade under its own name until 1997 when it went into voluntary liquidation.

Records: SmithKline Beecham plc, SmithKline Beecham House, Great West Road, Brentford TW8 9BD. Enquiries to SmithKline Beecham plc, 1 New Horizons Court, Great West Road, Brentford TW8 9EP

Meeting minutes: directors' 1953–83, general 1953–83; register of members and share ledger 1953–83; seal register 1983–91.

CHIDDINGFOLD PHARMACY
Chiddingfold, Surrey

Pharmacy

History: In around 1907 E Gane Inge & Co established a retail pharmacy at Chiddingfold, Surrey. In 1910 the business was acquired by Wiles & Holman, who operated a chemist's business in Haslemere, Surrey, prior to 1909, which continued to trade. Between 1920 and 1922 the Chiddingfold pharmacy was purchased by J Rees Jones, chemist, who sold the business to Samuel Edwards & Sons in around 1934. Samuel Edwards & Sons had been trading as pharmacists from Godalming High Street, Godalming, Surrey, since around 1909. From 1949, the Chiddingfold pharmacy was managed by Gordon Cooper, who purchased the business in the early 1960s, and was still trading there in 1975.

Records: Surrey History Centre, 130 Goldsworth Road, Woking GU21 1ND

Account books, incl. weekly sales, expenses, salaries, insurance and NHS prescription totals 1909–22, 1964–75; Gordon Cooper's business expenses account book 1964–77; customer accounts ledgers c.1907–40 (w); stock ledgers, purchases and accounts with suppliers 1909–26 (w); Surrey Insurance Committee and West Sussex Insurance Committee invoices for drugs and appliances supplied 1916; prescription books: first series 1907–81, second series 1913–34; sale of poisons registers 1907–20, 1941–52; poisons booklets, purchase and sale 1943–59; dangerous drugs register, purchase and sale 1929–40. (Ref: 5223/1-56)

CLARK & HOWES LTD
15 West Street, Fareham, Hampshire

Dispensing chemist

History: Charles Batchelor was registered as a pharmaceutical chemist in 1853, and operated from 90 West Street, Fareham, Hampshire. In 1877 Alfred Ernest Batchelor was registered as a chemist and druggist, trading from 15 West Street, Fareham, until at least 1895. Around 1931 the business was incorporated as a limited liability company, Batchelors Ltd. It was acquired by Clark & Howes Ltd during the 1950s, and was dissolved in 1976.

Records: Hampshire Record Office, Sussex Street, Winchester SO23 8TH

Ledger, customers' purchases 1945–n.d.; cash book 1941–45; cash daily totals sheets 1958–68; cash analysis books 1948–51; supplies book 1957–58; prescription books 1923–50 (w), 1961–77. (Ref: 33M77)

CORBYN, STACEY & CO LTD
London

Wholesale and manufacturing chemist and druggist

History: In 1728 Worcestershire-born Quaker Thomas Corbyn (1711–91) was apprenticed to Joseph Clutton, a London apothecary. After serving his apprenticeship he worked for 6 years as Clutton's journeyman. On Clutton's death in 1743, Corbyn entered into partnership with his widow, Mary, until 1747, when he took Clutton's son, Morris, as a partner. On Morris's death in 1754, Thomas Corbyn became sole owner of the business, styled Thomas Corbyn & Co, at 300 High Holborn, London. The premises housed a warehouse, laboratory and retail outlet. A succession of partners joined Corbyn in the business. John Brown and Nicholas Marshall were taken into partnership in 1762, followed by Corbyn's son John, John Brown and John Beaumont. In 1772 he was joined in the business by George Stacey. The business continued to trade as Thomas

Corbyn & Co until 1789, when it was renamed Corbyn, Stacey & Co. Stacey died in 1816. The firm's domestic trade was vast, and its export trade, especially with North America, grew significantly, with substantial outlets in Boston, Connecticut, New York, Rhode Island, and Philadelphia and throughout the West Indies. In 1850 Corbyn, Stacey & Co acquired the businesses of Winstanley & Son, 7 Poultry, London, and George Butler, Cheapside, London. Winstanley & Son was sold to A W Waring in 1894. During the 1870s the firm acquired 2 chemist's businesses, W H Bucklee, 68 New Bond Street and 308A Oxford Street, London, and Taylor Brothers, manufacturing and dispensing chemists, 4 Vere Street, London. These purchases enabled Corbyn, Stacey & Co to increase its retail outlets in the west end of London, and to establish a large store at 86 Bond Street. This store was sold to F A Rogers in 1894. In the same year the firm acquired offices at 22 Great St Helen's in the City of London, and shortly afterwards a large warehouse near Dorrington Street, Cold Bath Fields, London. The last of the retail outlets was sold in 1897, after which the firm operated solely as a wholesale and manufacturing druggist. In 1898 it was incorporated as a limited liability company, Corbyn, Stacey & Co Ltd. The wholesale laboratories moved from 300 High Holborn to 673 Commercial Road, London, in 1908. In 1927 the company was wound up.

'A Chapter in Drug History', *Chemist and Druggist*, 48, 1896, 164-6; 'London Wholesalers in 1863 and Now', *Chemist and Druggist*, 83, 26 July 1913, 145; R Palmer, 'Thomas Corbyn, Quaker Merchant', *Medical History*, 33, 1989, 371-6; R Porter, 'Manufacturing Drugs in the Early Consumer Society: the case of the Corbyns', *Pharmaceutical Historian*, 20, 2, June 1990, 2-5; R Porter & D Porter, 'The Rise of the English Drugs Industry: the role of Thomas Corbyn', *Medical History*, 33, July 1989, 277-95; A L Short, 'Corbyn Stacey & Co – a note on their antiques', *Pharmaceutical Journal*, 2 Sept 1967, 211; T D Whittet & J G L Burnby, 'The Firm of Corbyn and Stacey', *Pharmaceutical Journal*, 228, 9 Jan 1982, 42-8

Records 1: Archives & Manuscripts, Wellcome Library for the History & Understanding of Medicine, 183 Euston Road, London NW1 2BE

Co-partnership agreements 1762–1890; co-partnership papers 1738–1910; private account books 1772–1857; stock inventories and valuations 1761–70, n.d.; manufacturing recipe books 1748–1851; drugs catalogues, re sales and also used in stock-taking 1747–73 (w), n.d.; trade correspondence and papers re North America and Caribbean c.1745–1831; letterbooks re foreign customers 1741–55, 1809–51; title deeds and papers re Cold Bath Fields, High Holborn, Bucklersbury, Poultry and New Bond Street 1726–1891; wages books 1762–1825; Clutton family papers, incl. partnership papers 1738–54; executors' papers: Josiah Messer I 1783–1820, George Stacey I 1768–1829, Thomas Corbyn 1754–69; biographical research notes by Dr T D Whittet n.d., c.1982. (Ref: MSS 5435-60)

Records 2: The Museum Curator, Royal Pharmaceutical Society of Great Britain, 1 Lambeth High Street, London SE1 7JN

Catalogues: chemical and galenical remedies 1789, 18th cent., chemical and pharmaceutical preparations 1792–93, 1795–99; bills, Margaret Tailour, Edinburgh 1796, 1799. (Ref: IRA.1996.288; 50614-23 LIB)

Records 3: Museum of the History of Science, University of Oxford, Old Ashmolean Building, Broad Street, Oxford OX1 3AZ

Itemised bill of Joseph Clutton, for creating a *materia medica* cabinet 1729. (Ref: Museum 25-44)

HORACE COULSON & SONS LTD
71 Bridge Street, Cambridge, Cambridgeshire

Dispensing chemist and pharmacist

History: Horace Coulson & Sons, dispensing chemists, was established in 1937 at 37 Bridge Street, Cambridge, Cambridgeshire. It was incorporated as a limited liability company, Horace Coulson & Sons Ltd, in 1939. The company later moved to premises at 71 Bridge Street, Cambridge, and in 1990 was acquired by AAH Holdings plc. It became a dormant company in 1991.

Records 1: Cambridgeshire Record Office (Cambridge), Shire Hall, Castle Street, Cambridge CB3 0AP

Ledgers: 1937–39, university clients 1937–41; day books 1941–42; prescription books 1892–1969. (Ref: R80/60: 888, and R84/30)

Records 2: GEHE UK plc, Retail Branch, Atherstone, Warwickshire. Enquiries to GEHE UK plc, Sapphire Court, Walsgrave Triangle Business Park, Coventry CV2 2TX

General meetings minutes 1939–96; combined register of members, directors and share ledger 1939–91. (Ref: Box S19, current minutes)

ARTHUR H COX & CO LTD
Whiddon Valley, Barnstaple, Devon

Pharmaceutical manufacturer

History: After serving his apprenticeship to a Brighton doctor, Arthur Hawker Cox established a chemist and druggist's business at 32 Ship Street, Brighton, Brighton & Hove, on his own account in 1839. He compounded medicines on the premises and in 1854 successfully patented a unique pearl coating for pills, which improved the quality of tablets taken orally, by removing their unpleasant taste. In 1871 Arthur H Cox separated his retail and manufacturing operations, presenting his son, Homersham Edward, with the Ship Street pharmacy, and conducting the manufacturing business himself from new premises at 10a St Martin's Place, Brighton. During the late 1880s Arthur H Cox's son, also named Arthur H Cox, joined his father in partnership, and in the 1890s, his younger son, Edward Edwards Cox, also became a partner. On Arthur H Cox the elder's death in 1903, the business was incorporated as a limited liability company, Arthur H Cox & Co Ltd. In 1909 the company acquired the patents for soured milk products called 'massolettes', which led to the incorporation of a subsidiary company, Lactic Ferments Ltd, in 1910 to manufacture them. This was a short-lived venture, and the company was liquidated in 1911. Between 1910 and 1911 Arthur H Cox & Co Ltd moved to larger premises in Lewes Road, Brighton, and in 1921 A H Cox the younger's son, Tom, and Edward's son, Valentine, joined the company, and were themselves succeeded by Tom's brother, Roy, and Valentine's brother, Anthony, in 1930. The company was granted a licence in 1931 as sole manufacturer of *Bile Beans* for C E Fulford Ltd, Leeds, which had hitherto been made in the USA. This contract was maintained until the 1950s, although sales were diminishing from 1949. In 1938 Arthur H Cox & Co Ltd established a sickness and benevolent fund for staff, and during the 1950s, expanded its range of products to include sulphamezathine, sulphanilamide and *Pauldrine* tablets, for which it received large contracts to supply ICI Ltd and Boots Pure Drug Co Ltd. It also introduced a new range of chemists' own brand products, which were manufactured and packaged by Arthur H Cox & Co Ltd, but labelled with the names and addresses of independent pharmacists. During the 1960s Continental Laboratories Ltd, incorporated as a limited liability company in 1924, was acquired by Arthur H Cox & Co Ltd, to market and promote sales of Arthur H Cox & Co Ltd's products, in particular its *Co-Tab* range, one of which was marketed under the trade-name *Kloref*. The company was renamed Cox Continental Ltd in 1966. The *Co-Tab* range had been produced from the 1950s by Contabs Ltd, a limited liability company incorporated by Arthur H Cox & Co Ltd to manufacture commonly prescribed ethical drugs branded with a code mark for easy identification. Contabs Ltd was renamed

Co-Tabs Ltd in 1965. In 1971 Arthur H Cox & Co Ltd acquired the business of Thomas Marns & Co Ltd, a manufacturer of medicated smelling salts, which had been incorporated as a limited liability company, Lestar Laboratories Ltd, in the late 1950s. In 1965 it was renamed Dr MacKenzies Laboratories Ltd, and in 1968, Thomas Marns & Co Ltd. This company operated from a site at Rustington, West Sussex. In 1976 Arthur H Cox & Co Ltd moved to new premises at Whiddon Valley, Barnstaple, Devon, and in 1984 was acquired by Hoechst UK Ltd, Hounslow, London, retaining its registered name and trading as a subsidiary under the title, Cox Pharmaceuticals. The company manufactures a wide range of medical products in tablet, cream and liquid form, which were marketed throughout the UK and overseas. In May 1998 Arthur H Cox & Co Ltd was acquired by Alpharma Inc, New Jersey, USA, and in 1999 continues to trade under its established name.

'Arthur H Cox & Co Ltd', *Pharmaceutical Journal*, 146, 12 April 1941; 'Arthur H Cox & Co of Barnstaple', *Chemist and Druggist*, 21 July 1979; C Fearon, 'The History of A H Cox & Co Ltd', *Pharmaceutical Historian*, 23, 2, 1993; J Slinn, *Pills and Pharmaceuticals, A H Cox & Co Ltd 1839–1989* (Arthur H Cox, Barnstaple, 1989)

Records 1: Arthur H Cox & Co Ltd, Whiddon Valley, Barnstaple EX32 8NS

Minutes: directors' and general meetings 1904–11, directors' meetings 1917–82, general meetings 1912–38; memoranda and articles of association 1903, 1950, 1976; certificate of incorporation 1903; papers re acquisition by Hoechst UK Ltd 1984; seal books 1941–59, 1971–84; register of directors' shareholdings 1904–70; registers of members and share ledgers 1936–67; annual reports 1931–39, 1970, 1974; statement of accounts 1976–83; ledgers: manufacturing 1949–65, bought 1938–60, insurance valuation 1966; private journal c.1910–40; schedule of papers deposited with bank 1970; agreement with Industrial and Commercial Finance Corporation Ltd re secured loans 1971, 1978, 1983; letters patent and royal seal for 'pearl coating' 1854; formulae books 1922, 1928–70s; pearl coaters colour formulary n.d.; recipe book 1828; contract for assorted bulk tablets n.d.; price lists 1875–1989; customer listings 1963, 1968; label books 1957, n.d.; pill tile late 19th–early 20th cent.; promotional literature 1950s–70s, 1983, 1989; press cuttings 1879, 1952, 1964–66, 1989; property deeds, plans and papers: Brookside Industrial Estate, Rustington, West Sussex, 1970–71, Whiddon Valley, Barnstaple, Devon, 1970s; lease of 6 D'Aubigny Road, Brighton, Brighton & Hove, to E E Cox 1930; architectural plan of new factory 1910; return under War Damage Act and memorandum re insurance valuation 1941; agreements: National Telephone Co Ltd 1888–1905, London, Brighton & South Coast Railway Co 1912–49; certificate of membership of National Union of Manufacturers 1953; Sickness and Benevolent Fund: trust deed and rules 1838, journal 1938–69, bank and building society passbooks 1942–83; *Hoechst UK News*, company news sheet 1988; correspondence: Crown Agents for the Colonies 1913, company history 1980s; photographs: directors 1970s, premises and laboratories 19th cent., 1920s–87, n.d., delivery vans 1940s, representatives presentation items 1930s–40s, social activities 1930s–89; reports and papers re computing programmes 1968; programmes: male staff outings 1960–66, n.d., coronation year outing to London 1953; Christmas book, gifts to staff 1911–34; 125th anniversary dinner dance invitation 1964; cricket club fixture list 1962; will of A H Cox 1896–1900; historical notes 1979; book of cartoons and poems n.d.

Lactic Ferments Ltd: directors' meetings minutes 1910–11.

Cox Continental Ltd: minutes: directors' meetings, incl. annual reports and accounts 1942–78, 1982, general meetings 1943–78, certificate of incorporation 1924, 1966; register of members and share ledger, incl. stock transfer forms, share certificates and correspondence 1924–80; *Kloref* manual outlining stages of manufacturing 1970s.

Co-Tabs Ltd: directors' and general meetings minutes 1956–65; register of members and share register 1957–65.

Thomas Marns & Co Ltd: directors' meetings minutes 1970; certificate of incorporation 1965; notification of change of directors 1970; annual returns 1961–65, 1971–72; register of members and share ledger 1959–77; combined register of applications and allotments, incl. directors' meetings minutes 1965–77; stock transfer forms 1970–71; directors' report and balance sheet 1973, 1977.

Records 2: F Maltby & Sons Ltd, Dunston House, Portland Street, Lincoln LN5 7NN

Product information guide n.d.

CROSS & HERBERT LTD
47 Blue Boar Row, Salisbury, Wiltshire

Dispensing chemist

History: James Read & Co, a wholesale and retail druggist, was operating at Blue Boar Row, Salisbury, Wiltshire, in 1855. The business was renamed a number of times, to become Higgins Chemists, possibly owned by William Clement Higgins, Read & Orchard and later Cross & Herbert Ltd.

Records: Wiltshire & Swindon Record Office, County Hall, Trowbridge BA14 8JG

Supplies and prices book c.1926; prescription books: day books 1870–74, incl. instructions to patients 1878–1915 (w), Dr Ord's 1897–1914, 1921–27; prescription book indexes 1887–88, 1914–50. (Ref: 1701)

R CUNDALL & CO
5-7 Market Street, Pocklington, East Riding of Yorkshire

Manufacturing chemist, druggist and seed merchant

History: Robert and Edward Cundall were both in business as chemists and druggists in Pocklington, East Riding of Yorkshire, prior to 1868. In 1894 Thomas Bowser Cundall was registered as a chemist and druggist, and traded from 5-7 Market Street, Pocklington. In 1902 Edward Cundall retired, followed in 1912 by Robert Cundall. Thomas Bowser continued to trade from 5-7 Market Street, under the business name T B Cundall, until 1938, when the business was renamed R Cundall & Co. Thomas Bowser retired in 1940, and the business ceased to operate under its own name.

Records: East Riding of Yorkshire Archive & Records Service, County Hall, Beverley HU17 9BA

Account book 1891–1902; invoice books containing invoices, receipts and accounts pasted into trade magazines 1878–1933 (w); invoice books 1880–83, 1896; carriage book re parcels delivery 1889–1900; correspondence 1894. (Ref: Acc 2850)

H DAVY'S EXORS LTD
19 Bridgegate and 30 High Street, Rotherham

Chemist and druggist

History: Humphrey Davy (1829–1908) was trading as a chemist and druggist at 19 Bridgegate, Rotherham, from around 1852. In 1863 he acquired a similar business belonging to James Crowther at 20 High Street, Rotherham. Some time between 1898 and 1902 the High Street business re-located to 42 and, by 1905, to 30 High Street. By 1912 the business was styled Exors of Humphrey Davy, and in 1921 was incorporated as a limited liability company, H Davy's Exors Ltd, with Humphrey Davy's son, Edward Josiah Davy (1854–1923), and Cecil Alexander Wain as directors. The company continued to trade from Bridgegate until its closure in 1980, and from premises at 1 Clifton Grove, Rotherham, from around 1932 until 1952. The Clifton Grove shop was run by Davy's grandson, Douglas Edward (1901–1974), whilst the 30 High Street business was managed by another of Davy's sons, Percy (1865–1955), who was assisted by his daughter, Kathleen, and Alfred E Thomas. This business closed some time between 1965 and 1967. A related manufacturing chemist (and later wholesale druggist) business, Humphrey Davy & Son Ltd, was operating between 1881 and 1973 at Victoria Works, Masbrough Street, Rotherham. H Davy's Exors Ltd was removed from the register of companies in 1982.

Records: Rotherham Metropolitan Borough Archives & Local Studies Section, Brian O'Malley Central Library, Walker Place, Rotherham S65 1JH

Memorandum and articles of association 1921; annual accounts 1942–55 (w); ledgers: private, incl. capital and trading accounts, balance sheets and bank accounts 1921–50, suppliers' accounts 1858–64, 1914–45 (w), customers' accounts 1914–19, 1937–42; day books: supplies purchased 1888–1907, business customers 1920–21, 1940–46 (w); cash books 1942–49; account book: stocktaking, 20 High Street 1864–67, balance sheets 1859–67, cash accounts and other payments 1863–73; account from Frederick Mason 1903–04; sales registers: 1944–45, Clifton Grove 1941–42; income tax notice and assessments 1941–42; formulae books 1853–late 19th cent.; recipe book, incl. veterinary remedies late 19th cent.; valuation of fixtures and fittings with related correspondence re 42 High Street 1899–1903; genealogical charts of Davy family 1980. (Ref: 85/B)

DEANE & CO
17 The Pavement, Clapham, Lambeth, London

Chemist

History: James Deane was registered as a pharmaceutical chemist in 1871 at 17 The Pavement, Clapham, Lambeth, London. In 1876 his business was registered as Henry Deane & Co, and traded under that name until at least 1886, when James Deane ceased to be registered. The business continued to trade into the twentieth century, although sometime before 1936 it changed its name to Deane & Co.

Records: Lambeth Archives Department, Minet Library, 52 Knatchbull Road, London SE5 9QY

Account books 1927–56, prescription books 1908–10, 1925–73. (Ref: IV/143)

DOWNER & WALKER
25 West Street, Buckingham, Buckinghamshire

Chemist

History: In 1921 Harold George Heathfield was registered as a chemist and druggist at 158 Lower Richmond Road, Putney, Wandsworth, London. In 1926 he re-located to 25 West Street, Buckingham, Buckinghamshire, and traded there as a chemist and druggist. In 1928 he moved to Colchester, Essex, and the business at West Street was acquired by George Frederick Arthur Downer, who had registered as a chemist and druggist in 1920. He traded as G F A Downer and in 1954 was joined in the business by Helen Emily Walker, who had registered as a pharmaceutical chemist in 1939 and also traded from 46 Well Street, Buckingham. In 1962 the 25 West Street business was renamed Downer & Walker. In 1978 George Downer retired, and Downer & Walker was acquired by R W Pattison, who traded under his own name until 1985, when the business closed. Helen Walker was still trading from 46 Well Street in 1997.

Records: Buckinghamshire Record Office, County Hall, Aylesbury HP20 1UU

Account books 1927–33; prescription books 1923–48. (Ref: D 149)

R B DREIFUSS LTD
63 London Road, Morden, Merton, London

Retail chemist

History: This family firm of retail chemists was incorporated as a limited liability company, R B Dreifuss Ltd, in 1965 with Richard Dreifuss, chemist, Moritz Dreifuss and Patricia Dreifuss the first appointed directors. It was acquired in 1994 by E Moss Ltd, the retail subsidiary of UniChem plc that became Alliance UniChem plc in 1997. By 1999 the company was dormant.

Records: Alliance UniChem plc, UniChem House, Cox Lane, Chessington KT9 1SN

Directors' and general meetings minutes 1965–94; annual returns 1969–93; acquisition papers 1994–95; combined register of members and share ledger 1965–94; stock transfer forms 1992; directors' report and accounts, incl. balance sheets, trading and profit and loss accounts 1969–92; abbreviated accounts 1993.

JAMES DUDGEON LTD
134 Duke Street, Leith, Edinburgh

Retail chemist

History: James Dudgeon Ltd was incorporated as a limited liability company in 1970, by Raimes, Clark & Co Ltd, wholesale and manufacturing chemists of Smith's Place, Leith, Edinburgh. It was a retail chemist's business, based at 134 Duke Street, Leith. The company was dissolved in 1990.

Records: The Secretary, National Register of Archives (Scotland), H M General Register House, Princes Street, Edinburgh EH1 3YY

Minutes 1970–86; combined register of members and share ledger 1970–72; directors' reports, balance sheets and accounts 1963–74. (Ref: NRA(S) 2974)

DUNCAN FLOCKHART & CO LTD
Edinburgh

Manufacturer of pharmaceuticals and anaesthetics

History: The founder of this business, John Duncan, was born in 1780 in Kinross, Perth & Kinross, Scotland. In 1794 he entered into an apprenticeship agreement with a druggist in Lawnmarket, Edinburgh, for a period of 5 years. After successfully completing his apprenticeship he remained with this firm to serve his improvership. The exact year in which Duncan moved to London is not known, but by 1804 he was in the employment of Kernoth, druggists of Bear Street, Leicester Square. After a brief stay in London he returned to Scotland and in 1806 established a business on his own account in Perth, Perth & Kinross, where he received both admiration and criticism for his innovatory packaging methods. He dispensed pills in small boxes rather than in paper, and ointments in pots as opposed to the traditional receptacle, the mussel shell. By 1812 the business was sufficiently successful to allow a move to larger premises in Parliament Close, High Street, Perth, where Duncan concentrated on drug manufacture, and began with the extraction of morphine. In 1818 Duncan took a young man, Ogilvie, as a junior partner and the firm was named Duncan & Ogilvie. In 1820 a second shop was opened at 52 North Bridge, Edinburgh. The management of the Perth shop was left to Ogilvie whilst Duncan moved to Edinburgh and took on an assistant, James Robertson, to assist with the running of the North Bridge shop. Both premises traded under the name Duncan & Ogilvie until 1832, when Ogilvie took over the Perth business on his own account and Duncan entered into a new partnership agreement with one of his apprentices, William Flockhart, and another young man named Anderson. The new firm traded from 52 North Bridge and was renamed Duncan, Anderson & Flockhart. Due to the untimely death of Anderson, the business was renamed Duncan & Flockhart in 1833 and styled Duncan Flockhart & Co from 1836. In 1839 the firm began to manufacture lactucarium, a substitute for opium, and in 1847 was commissioned by Sir James Young to manufacture chloroform, for his historic experiment of the same year in which he established chloroform as a more effective anaesthetic than ether. Duncan Flockhart & Co was thus the first British manufacturer of chloroform and, from this point, received world-wide recognition, exporting to the colonies almost immediately. In 1851 the firm exhibited chloroform at the Science Exhibition and during the Crimean War of 1854–56 production of chloroform became its main work, although it also manufactured cod-liver oil. The need for more laboratory space at North Bridge prompted the establishment of a separate retail establishment at 139 Princes Street, Edinburgh, in 1846, and 4 new partners were taken on. Duncan remained senior partner with the firm until his retirement in 1853 and Flockhart remained the chief managing partner. As a result of pressure by Sir James Murray, inventor of fluid magnesia, the firm received a royal warrant between 1862 and 1875. Duncan and Flockhart died within weeks of each other in 1871 and the firm, although no longer in family hands, continued to trade under its own name and business expanded under a succession of partners. In 1876 a factory at Holyrood Road, Edinburgh, was acquired and in 1896 a branch of Duncan Flockhart & Co was established at 155 Farringdon Road, London. The London branch was concerned chiefly with the distribution of goods manufactured in Edinburgh, both at home and abroad, and with marketing and public relations. The First and Second World Wars encouraged further expansion in the production of chloroform and also anaesthetic ether and ethyl chloride which were supplied to the British and Allied forces, the Ministry of Supply and the Red Cross. During the early months of the First World War a drug-growing farm was established at

Warriston, Edinburgh, to maintain a steady supply of raw materials. The firm also branched out into the production of regional anaesthetics, vaccinations and protein therapy. The business was incorporated as a limited liability company, Duncan Flockhart & Co Ltd, in 1948 and in 1953 was acquired by Edinburgh Pharmaceutical Industries Ltd, although it continued to manufacture specialist drugs and anaesthetics under its own name. Edinburgh Pharmaceutical Industries Ltd was acquired by Glaxo Group Ltd in 1963, and thereafter its constituent companies, including Duncan Flockhart & Co Ltd, traded under their former names. In 1965 Duncan Flockhart & Co Ltd was renamed Duncan Flockhart Evans Ltd and in 1968 was integrated with British Drug Houses Group Ltd, when the latter was acquired by Glaxo Group Ltd.

Anon, *The History of Duncan, Flockhart & Co: Commemorating the centenaries of ether and chloroform* (Duncan, Flockhart & Co, Edinburgh, 1946); S Blackden, *A Tradition of Excellence: A brief history of medicine in Edinburgh* (Duncan, Flockhart & Co, Edinburgh, 1981); L G Matthews, *History of Pharmacy in Britain* (Livingstone, Edinburgh, 1962) 224-5

Records 1: Archivist (Historical Records), Records Centre, Glaxo Wellcome plc, 891-995 Greenford Road, Greenford UB6 0HE

Minutes: directors' meetings 1948–65, directors' private meetings 1952–61, general meetings 1949–64; memorandum and articles of association 1948; change of name certificates 1965, 1968; board papers 1948–79; directors' reports and instructions 1962–64, 1968–74; papers re company organisation 1951; registers: seals 1949–73, directors' attendance 1954–75, directors' shares and debenture interests 1964–68, shares 1948–64, assets 1971–72; annual reports and accounts 1946–55; balance sheets and profit and loss accounts 1948–66; statement of accounts 1851; accounting schedules 1972–74; accounting papers 1957–63; sales statistics 1923–38; land tax receipts and assessments 1849–78; audit papers 1965, 1968–71; papers re patents and royalties, overseas patents of *Duncaine/Xylocaine* 1961–63; papers re promotion of overseas agreements for *Romotal/Tackine Hydrochloride* 1961–62; products booklets 1964; notes and correspondence re drugs 1833–60, 1932–47; prescriptions 1833–47; agreements: Royal College of Physicians, Edinburgh, re supply of vaccines 1915, manufacture of polyaminostyrene n.d., manufacture of soap n.d.; promotional papers 1959, 1962; Warriston Plant Garden, plans, accounts and photographs 1915–17; property papers and plans 1948–56, 1960; salary register 1956–57; wages book 1876–88; staff papers: appointments and pensions n.d., motor accident n.d.; staff record cards 1919–64; memorandum on wage payments during illness 1939; letters of acceptance and terms of employment 1832–58; local air raid precautions 1938; correspondence: chloroform 1844–60, n.d., drugs

1961–63, Charles Dickens 1854, J A Hiddleston 1952, home and overseas agents 1960–64, cabinet maker 1851; correspondence and licensing agreements with overseas countries 1958–63; account of symposium 1959; statutory forms 1967–78; historical notes 1843–47, 1957–64. (Ref: Macfarlan Smith Historical Collection)

Records 2: Macfarlan Smith Ltd, Wheatfield Road, Edinburgh EH11 2QA

Research reports 1950–70; development papers 1958–80; production papers 1957–64, 1974–86, n.d.; product lists n.d.; photographs: plant and buildings 1950–97, staff 1950–97, miscellaneous n.d.

EASTGATE PHARMACY
15 Eastgate, Chichester, West Sussex

Pharmacist

History: In 1858 Robert Wright established a chemist's business on his own account at 15 Eastgate Street, Chichester, West Sussex. In 1863 the business was acquired by Edward Baker, who was succeeded by a family member, Samuel Baker, in 1871. By 1874 the business was trading under the name Edward Baker, and by 1880 had been renamed Baker & Son. The firm rarely used this title preferring to trade under the name Eastgate Pharmacy. In 1910 it was acquired by George Bevis and in 1938, by his son, also named George Bevis. The firm continued to be registered as Baker & Son until 1939, when it was renamed Bevis. In around 1950 the business was incorporated as a limited liability company, G F Bevis Ltd. It continued to trade as Eastgate Pharmacy until around 1989, when it was renamed Eastgate Pharmacy. It was still trading in 1998.

Records: West Sussex Record Office, Sherburne House, 3 Orchard Street, Chichester. Enquiries to County Hall, Chichester PO19 1RN

Customers' ledgers 1935–52; general account books 1904–37 (w); day book, retail sales 1936–38; stock inventories 1919–21; formula book c.1900; prescription books: general 1905–47, Dr A H Bostock 1918–27, National Health Insurance 1920–24; trademarks, correspondence and certificates 1884–1912; advertising material and related papers c.1880, c.1920; lease of house and shop, Samuel Baker to George Bevis 1913; label collection 1858–1968. (Ref: Add MSS 20, 113-20, 155)

EDINBURGH PHARMACEUTICAL INDUSTRIES LTD
Edinburgh

Pharmaceutical wholesaler and manufacturer

History: Edinburgh Pharmaceutical Industries Ltd was incorporated as a limited liability company in 1953 to acquire a number of large Scottish pharmaceutical manufacturing and wholesale concerns, the first of which was Duncan Flockhart & Co Ltd, Edinburgh, acquired in 1953. During the 1950s and 1960s Edinburgh Pharmaceutical Industries Ltd purchased a number of other businesses including William Paterson & Sons Ltd, Aberdeen, T & H Smith Ltd, Edinburgh and W & R Hatrick & Sons Ltd. In 1963 Edinburgh Pharmaceutical Industries Ltd was acquired by Glaxo Group Ltd, and thereafter the wholesaling activities of the group were centred at Holyrood Road, the former premises of Duncan Flockhart & Co Ltd. In 1966 these premises became the Edinburgh branch of Vestric Ltd, and Edinburgh Pharmaceutical Industries Ltd ceased to trade under its own name.

'Vestric Edinburgh' in P M Worling, *Vestric: The first twenty years 1966–86* (Vestric, Runcorn, 1986)

Records 1: Archivist (Historical Records), Records Centre, Glaxo Wellcome plc, 891-995 Greenford Road, Greenford UB6 0HE

Minutes: directors' meetings 1953–86, general meetings n.d.–1968, chairman's committee meetings 1957–64, private meetings 1957–63; agendas, board papers and minutes 1963–68; corporate papers: company re-organisation 1963–71, merger with Glaxo Group Ltd 1962–63; registers of shareholders 1952–83; list of ordinary shareholders 1955–61; share capital returns forms 1944–69; certificates and forms on transfer of shares to Glaxo Group Ltd 1963–64; correspondence re shareholding 1959–65; quarterly financial reports 1960–64; profit and loss accounts and budgets 1965–66; accounts 1959–64; ledger 1962–68; accounts analysis book 1964–67; return on capital 1961–69; financial returns 1963; stocktaking methods and returns 1957–64; memorandum on operating profits 1964; bank loan 1963; record of bank guarantees given to customers 1953–65; papers re insurance and merger with Glaxo Group Ltd 1962–64; papers re licencing, trade marks and patents 1957–63; licences to use dangerous drugs and correspondence with Home Office 1960–64; research and development papers 1962; research information 1963; press releases 1962–63; papers re warehouse at Killearn Street, Glasgow, 1963–65; list of procedures at Holyrood site 1964; surveys and reports re expansion of company overseas 1957–64; staff papers: salary lists 1949–65, papers re management 1956–65, appointments and promotions 1953–62, organisation and welfare 1954–65, retirements and redundancies 1958–65, fringe benefits enquiry 1961–62, general files 1960–63; staff magazines: *The Bulletin* 1964–66 (w), *Bulletin International* 1967–72 (w); Queen's Award to Industry certificate 1975; annual sales conferences, photographs and menus 1950–64. (Ref: Macfarlan Smith Historical Collection)

Records 2: Macfarlan Smith Ltd, Wheatfield Road, Edinburgh EH11 2QA

Papers re Glaxo Group Ltd acquisition 1960–64; accounts 1962–69; research reports 1950–70; development papers 1958–80; agreements n.d.; deeds and licence agreements n.d.; leases and warrants n.d.

EDMONDSON & VOGT LTD
Kendal, Cumbria

Chemist

History: William Edmondson was registered as a chemist and druggist in 1873. He was in business at 30 Highgate, Kendal, Cumbria, until at least 1895. In 1914 the business was incorporated as a limited liability company, Edmondson & Vogt Ltd, and was removed from the Register of Companies in 1978.

Records: Cumbria Record Office (Kendal), County Offices, Stricklandgate, Kendal LA9 4RQ

Account book 1914–15; stock books 1960s; counterfoil book 1972–73; prescription books 1929–75; post book 1974; book of surgical hosiery supplies 1968–71; index cards for surgical hosiery and trusses 1959–71. (Ref: WDB/38)

WILLIAM ELMHIRST
Oustlethwaite, Worsbrough, Barnsley

Surgeon and apothecary

History: William Elmhirst (1721–73) of Genn House, Darfield, Worsbrough, Barnsley, came from a wealthy family. He completed his apothecary surgeon's apprenticeship in 1743 and in 1746 succeeded to the estates of his father William. His large practice earned him a annual income of around £250, and in 1769 he purchased Ouslethwaite in the parish of Worsbrough. His business passed to his son William following his death in a riding accident in 1773.

E M Sigsworth, 'William Elmhirst 1721–1773. Surgeon-apothecary – and medical frontiersman', *Pharmaceutical Historian*, 14, 3, Sept 1984, 6-7

Records: Sheffield City Archives, 52 Shoreham Street, Sheffield S1 4SP

Medical ledger, incl. names and addresses of patients, details of drugs, treatment and charges 1769–73; list of taxes and assessments 1783–1831; notes on tithes 1770–1806; wages accounts book 1783–1802; transcript of ledger 1993; will and probate papers 1715–88. (Ref: EM863-4, EM888)

J C ENO LTD
St Helens

Pharmaceutical manufacturer

History: James Crossley Eno was apprenticed to a pharmacist at Sandhill, Newcastle upon Tyne, after which he was pharmacist to the city's Royal Infirmary before establishing himself in business as a chemist and druggist at Groat Market, Newcastle upon Tyne, during the 1850s. He began compounding medicines, and soon achieved success with a stomach settling drink, *Fruit Salt*. During the 1870s he moved his business to a factory in Pomeroy Street, New Cross, Lewisham, London, and in 1879 the business was incorporated as a limited liability company, J C Eno Ltd. The company manufactured a number of products, including anti-bilious pills, digestive granules and iron and quinine tonic. In 1907 *Fruit Salt* was recognised as a trade name. In 1920 the company was voluntarily liquidated and a new limited liability company of the same name, J C Eno Ltd, was incorporated to acquire the business. It was acquired by International Proprietaries Ltd in 1928, but was reconstituted in 1934 as an independent concern, Eno Proprietaries Ltd. Later in 1938 it was acquired by Beecham Pills Ltd and renamed J C Eno Ltd. From 1940 to 1946 *Fruit Salt* was produced at the factories of Macleans Ltd at Great West Road, Brentford, Hounslow, London, after which its production moved to Watford, Hertfordshire. In 1953 production of *Fruit Salt* briefly returned to Macleans Ltd, following which all Eno trade name brands were produced by Beecham Pharmaceuticals Ltd at St Helens.

J C Eno, 'A Birthday and Some Memories, 1868–1928' (Unpublished typescript, 1928); 'Famous British Firms, J C Eno Ltd', *The Indian and Eastern Druggist*, Aug 1921

158 The pharmaceutical industry – a guide to historical records

Records 1: SmithKline Beecham plc, SmithKline Beecham House, Great West Road, Brentford TW8 9BD. Enquiries to SmithKline Beecham plc, 1 New Horizons Court, Great West Road, Brentford TW8 9EP

Directors' and general meetings minutes 1918–92; register of members and share ledger 1972–74; indenture re issue of preference shares 1935; share certificates and share transfer certificates 1955–73; seal register 1991; trade marks registered in Germany (p) n.d.; applications to register *Fruit Salt* as a medicinal product 1921, n.d.; patent papers re company ashtray and ornament 1926–31; memorandum re use of words *Eno* and *Fruit Salt* 1953; advertisement for *Fruit Salt* 1891; report re advertising appraisal 1966; papers re *Eno/Alka-Seltzer* advertising controversy 1967; agreement re electric light installation 1928; letter from Queen Mary 1924; general correspondence 1960–75; treatise by J C Eno n.d.; photograph of bust of J C Eno n.d.; historical notes and articles 1928, 1961, n.d. (Ref: Box 97-016, unlisted)

Records 2: St Helens Local History & Archives Library, Gamble Institute, Victoria Square, St Helens WA10 1DY

Letters patent for *Fruit Salt* 1877; report re application for registration of trade mark *Eno* 1919; advertisements 1877–1901, 1930, n.d.; *Eno Staff News and Messenger* 1910, 1948; correspondence re *Fruit Salt* 1943–46; historical notes 1961. (Ref: BP/4/13)

Records 3: Proprietary Association of Great Britain, Vernon House, Sicilian Avenue, London WC1A 2QH

Presentation folder, publicity campaign, showcard and counter card 1940s.

Records 4: History of Advertising Trust, HAT House, 12 Raveningham Centre, Raveningham NR14 6NU

Advertising material re *Fruit Salt* late 19th–early 20th cents; press cuttings of advertisements for Eno's preparations 1976–78; papers, memoranda and advertising campaign material 1965–66. (Ref: AA1/1/8; AA1/2/13r, 31r, 57r; MEAL Collection 1976 R60, 1977 R55, 1978 R55-60; JWT 107 (1965) 302 (1966) 428)

EVANS HEALTHCARE LTD
10 St James's Street, London

Holding company for a group engaged in the development and marketing of pharmaceutical products

History: This company was incorporated in 1986 as Precis (497) Ltd, but was renamed Evans Healthcare Ltd later in the same year. It was formed to purchase the entire issued and allotted share capital of Evans Medical Ltd from Glaxo Holdings plc, to act as the holding and co-ordinating company of Evans Medical Ltd and Evans Medical Pensions Ltd and to carry on the associated business of pharmaceuticals manufacturer and distributor through its subsidiaries. In 1990 it was acquired by Medeva plc of Jermyn Street, London, a pharmaceutical manufacturer which was incorporated in 1986 as Fineasset plc and began operations in 1987 under the name Medirace plc. Its name was changed to Medeva plc when it acquired Evans Healthcare Ltd in 1990 in an attempt to reflect and give recognition to the respective businesses of Medirace plc and Evans Healthcare Ltd.

K Holland, 'Evans Healthcare Ltd', *Pharmaceutical Journal*, 23 Jan 1988

Records: Medeva plc, 10 St James's Street, London SW1A 1EF

Directors' and general meetings minutes 1986 to date; directors' meetings minutes, agenda, board papers and reports 1986–89; memorandum and articles of association 1995; certificates of incorporation and change of name certificates 1986, 1995; combined register of members and share ledger 1986–90; share certificates 1990, 1991; share transfer forms 1990; nominee's deed 1993; annual returns, correspondence and related papers 1986–92; directors' reports and accounts 1987–94; papers re acquisition by Medirace plc, background and offer papers 1987–90.

RONALD H EVANS
36 Hilton Crescent, West Bridgford and Portland Road, Nottingham

Retail chemist

History: This business was first registered at Portland Road, Nottingham. By 1953 Ronald Evans had an additional outlet in Hilton Crescent, West Bridgford, Nottingham.

Records: Nottinghamshire Archives & Southwell Diocesan Record Office, County House, Castle Meadow Road, Nottingham NG2 1AG

Ledger 1954–57; cash books, weekly takings and expenses 1963–66; balance sheets: 1965–66; correspondence with accountants re annual accounts and income tax 1963–65. (Ref: DD 813/1, DD 1741/1-16)

FARQUHAR
Princes Street, Perth, Perth & Kinross

Dispensing chemist

History: In 1874 James Farquhar registered as a chemist and druggist, and traded from 76 St John Street, Perth, Perth & Kinross, until 1903, when he moved to 11 Princes Street, Perth. In 1911 James Marshall Farquhar was registered as a chemist and druggist, and traded from 13 Princes Street, Perth, until 1936, when he moved to 15 Princes Street. James Farquhar ceased to be registered in 1934. In 1949 James Marshall Farquhar was joined in business by a second James Farquhar, who had registered as a chemist and druggist in 1948. James Marshall Farquhar ceased to be registered in 1952, and James Farquhar continued the business on his own account, trading as J M Farquhar, until 1968, when he ceased to be registered.

Records: Perth Museum & Art Gallery, George Street, Perth PH1 5LB

Account book extract 1871–81; sale of poisons register 1936–68; prescription book c.1950. (Ref: 813-14, 815, 816)

FENNINGS PHARMACEUTICALS
46 London Road, Horsham, West Sussex

Pharmaceutical manufacturer

History: This business was founded in 1840 when Dr Alfred Fennings opened the Golden Key Pharmacy in Hammersmith Broadway, London. He formulated and sold medicines on the premises for the treatment of typhoid and cholera, and also for lesser ailments such as coughs, colds and teething problems. In 1850 the business moved to factory premises in Cowes, Isle of Wight, in order to increase the output of formulae manufactures. Dr Fennings died in 1900, and thereafter the business was administered by trustees and all profits bequeathed to a national children's charity. By 1984 the firm operated from Horsham, West Sussex, with a manufacturing plant in Mabelthorpe, Lincolnshire, and a distribution depot at Ashton-under-Lyne, Tameside.

'Formulae for Success', *The Grocer*, March 1984, 43

Records 1: Proprietary Association of Great Britain, Vernon House, Sicilian Avenue, London WC1A 2QH

'Every Mother's Book' with advertisements c.1840s, 1935–55, 1975; 'Everybody's Doctor' with advertisements c.1934–39; advertising booklets c.1938, 1940; publication by Alfred Fennings n.d.

Records 2: Isle of Wight & Diocesan County Record Office, 26 Hillside, Newport, Isle of Wight PO30 2EB

Promotional literature 1939–40. (Ref: 96/4)

HERBERT FERRYMAN LTD
Galen House, 1 Oakley Road, Shirley, Southampton

Pharmaceutical wholesaler

History: In 1887 Herbert Ferryman qualified as a chemist and druggist and established a chemists' business on the corner of Bellevue Road and St Mary Street, Southampton. The business was incorporated as a limited liability company, Herbert Ferryman Ltd, in 1915. In 1926 the company, which traded as both a retail and wholesale chemist, was divided into 2 businesses. The retail pharmacy was taken over by R Leeson, a former director of Herbert Ferryman Ltd, who traded thereafter under his own name, whilst Herbert Ferryman took control of the wholesale side of the business, which continued to trade as Herbert Ferryman Ltd. In 1940 the company's premises were destroyed by enemy action, and Herbert Ferryman Ltd re-located to Highfield Farm, Hilldown Road, Southampton. In 1941 further premises at Cobden Bridge, formerly the Lyric Cinema, were acquired and became the registered offices of the company. In 1940 W M Cox, a director of Randall & Wilson Ltd, wholesale druggists of Southampton, became a director of Herbert Ferryman Ltd and in 1951 Galen House, Priory Road, was acquired as a manufacturing plant for drugs and galenicals. In 1963 the Cox family acquired the business of Herbert Ferryman Ltd, which continued to trade under its own name. In 1977 Peter Cox, son of W M Cox, established Cranfordian Ltd, which was incorporated as a wholly-owned subsidiary of Herbert Ferryman Ltd, to offer financial advice and support to independent pharmacists. In 1981 Herbert Ferryman Ltd re-located to new premises at 1 Oakley Road, Shirley, Southampton, purchasing the building from Eucryl Ltd, a company of manufacturing chemists established in 1900. The name Galen House was transferred to the Oakley Road premises. In 1985 Herbert Ferryman Ltd was acquired by AAH Holdings plc's wholly-owned subsidiary, Chemists Holdings Ltd, and became a constituent part of AAH Pharmaceuticals Ltd which itself became part of GEHE UK plc. By 1999 Herbert Ferryman Ltd was a dormant company.

Records: GEHE UK plc, Retail Branch, Atherstone, Warwickshire. Enquiries to GEHE UK plc, Sapphire Court, Walsgrave Triangle Business Park, Coventry CV2 2TX

General meetings minutes 1966–96; articles of association 1985; combined register of members, directors and share ledger 1915–85; ledger 1956–64; papers and correspondence re acquisition by AAH Holdings plc 1984–85; annual reports and accounts 1976, 1980; ledger 1944–55; combined ledger and dispensing book 1910, 1964–73; price lists: general and revised 1940s, 1954, 1962, proprietary articles 1936, 1954, packed pharmaceuticals 1953, 1964, *Cortisone* 1957, seasonal and Christmas goods 1951–62; product labels booklets, Randall & Wilson Ltd and assorted manufacturers n.d.; Herbert Ferryman, certificate of qualification as chemist and druggist 1887; pension scheme papers and correspondence 1968–93. (Ref: Box A2, S9, current minutes, box 7)

FISONS PHARMACEUTICALS LTD
Fison House, Princes Street, Ipswich, Suffolk

Pharmaceutical manufacturer

History: In 1929 3 companies, Joseph Fison & Co Ltd, Packard & James Fison (Thetford) Ltd and Prentice Bros Ltd, all agricultural merchants of Suffolk from the late eighteenth century and manufacturers of fertilisers from the 1840s, merged to form Fison, Packard & Prentice Ltd, at Ipswich, Suffolk. Packard & James Fison (Thetford) Ltd had been formed by the merger of James Fison & Sons Ltd and Edward Packard & Co Ltd in 1919, both producers of fertilisers and dealers in agricultural products. From 1929 Fison, Packard and Prentice Ltd traded predominantly as fertiliser manufacturers, being renamed Fisons Ltd in 1942. In 1946 the company acquired Genatosan Ltd, manufacturers of proprietary medicines and fine chemicals, Loughborough, Leicestershire, in which it had owned a part share since 1937. This company was established in

1906 at Chenies Street, London, as a wholly-owned subsidiary of Wulfing AG of Germany, manufacturers of the nerve tonic *Sanatogen*. In 1919 the company was incorporated as Genatosan Ltd, an anagram of *Sanatogen*, to avoid any unpopular Germanic associations. In 1947 Genatosan Trust Ltd, a limited liability company, was incorporated by Fisons Ltd to acquire the business of Whiffen & Sons Ltd, fine chemical manufacturers of London. From this point onwards, Fisons Ltd began to diversify into pharmaceutical manufacture. Bengers Ltd, producers of ethical pharmaceuticals including *Auralgicin*, a treatment for ear infections, and *Bengers Food*, a milk supplement, based at Holmes Chapel, Cheshire, was also acquired by Fisons Ltd in 1947. This company was established in Manchester, in 1790, as Mottershead & Co. It was acquired by Frederick Baden Benger in 1870, and in 1891 was incorporated as a limited liability company, F B Benger & Co Ltd. The company was renamed Bengers Food Ltd in 1903, and in 1939 re-located to Holmes Chapel, after which it was renamed Bengers Ltd. Following the acquisition of this company by Fisons Ltd, Genatosan Trust Ltd was renamed British Chemicals & Biologicals Ltd (BCB Ltd), a co-ordinating company for Genatosan Ltd, Whiffen & Sons Ltd and Bengers Ltd. At the same time, a number of companies specialising in the manufacture of cosmetics and shampoos were acquired by Fisons Ltd. In 1951 BCB Ltd was made dormant and Genatosan Ltd, Whiffen & Sons Ltd and Bengers Ltd regained control of their respective businesses. However, BCB Ltd was reinstated as a fine chemical manufacturer, renamed Fisons Chemicals Ltd, in 1952. In 1953 Bengers Ltd launched an iron supplement, *Dextraven*, which was developed in 1954 and marketed as *Imferon*, an intramuscular injection. In 1955 Fisons Ltd was divided into 5 divisions: fertilisers and heavy chemicals, agricultural chemicals, industrial and pharmaceutical chemicals, ethical pharmaceuticals and proprietary medicines. In 1964 the businesses of Genatosan Ltd, Bengers Ltd and C E Fulford Ltd and Vitapointe (UK) Ltd, both producers of toiletry products, were merged to form one operating company, Fisons Pharmaceuticals Ltd, a subsidiary of Fisons Ltd, with research laboratories at Loughborough, and a manufacturing plant at Holmes Chapel. In 1966 Whiffen & Sons Ltd was renamed Fisons Industrial Chemicals Ltd, from then onwards having little connection with the pharmaceutical businesses. Fisons Ltd's fertiliser business was sold in 1982, and thereafter the company concentrated primarily on the manufacture of pharmaceuticals and fine chemicals, becoming a market leader in the production of anti-allergic drugs by 1985. In 1995, in a major company restructuring, staff at the Ipswich and Loughborough sites, and at a small Manchester site, were re-located to new head offices in London. Later in the same year, Fisons Ltd (now plc) was acquired by Rhône-Poulenc Rorer Inc, a French-owned pharmaceutical manufacturer, and renamed Rhône-Poulenc Rorer Ltd.

P A C Moore, *Fisons* (Scrimgeour Research, London, 1973); M S Moss, 'Fertilisers to Pharmaceuticals: Fisons – the biography of a company 1720–1986' (Unpublished typescript, 1996, copy at Ipswich Record Office); *Two Sides of the Same Coin: Fisons profile special* (Fisons, Ipswich, c.1973)

Records 1: Rhône-Poulenc Rorer Ltd, Rhône-Poulenc Rorer House, 50 Kings Hill Avenue, Kings Hill, West Malling ME19 4AH

Directors' meetings minutes 1967; memorandum and articles of association 1964; directors' resignation letters 1972–75; supplemental trust deeds 1964, 1970s; share certificate book n.d.; stock transfer forms 1967; papers and correspondence re stocks, shares and mortgages 1960s–80s; annual accounts and correspondence 1964–69; product booklet re *Imposil 200* 1968; advertising literature and booklets 1968–69; press cuttings 1969; title deeds, Loughborough and Leicester premises 1965–67; correspondence: conveyances of premises 1965–67, overseas subsidiaries 1982–83.

Fisons plc, pharmaceutical division: directors' meetings minutes 1967–94; board papers and correspondence 1969–70, 1977–84; board meetings agendas and papers 1991–92; inter-company trading committee minutes and papers 1978–81; divisional operations reports 1991–95; annual accounts and correspondence 1970–76; year end accounts 1983; budgets and plans 1971–80; forecasts 1983; papers re fixed assets 1985–89; trading results 1982; accounting working papers 1991–92; papers re finances 1981–92; papers and correspondence: UK taxation 1989, corporation tax 1977–90; papers re acquisitions: 1986–91, USA 1970–78; contracts with overseas agents 1985–86; contract negotiations 1986; operations monitoring papers 1986; research and new products plan 1977–85; manufacturing validation reports 1992; scientific equipment report 1989–90; papers and correspondence: *Intal* 1966–78, projects with other pharmaceutical companies 1990s; report re market trends 1995; data presentations and market analyses 1990s; papers re Wrexham expansion 1985–87; construction work at Willow Works, Loughborough 1970s; general papers re Loughborough 1991; *Gen*, staff newsletter 1972–73; correspondence: pricing and third party distributors 1976–82, general 1970s, 1991–92; photographs of Loughborough site n.d.; British Chemicals & Biologicals (Export) Ltd, price list 1952.

Fisons plc: minutes: directors' meetings 1929–61, 1980–87 (w), executive committee of directors' meetings 1929–32, 1958–61, 1992, general meetings 1929–77, 1980, 1990–95, group secretarial meetings 1967–78; papers re formation of Fison, Packard & Prentice Ltd 1929; memoranda and articles of association 1949, 1974, 1977; board of directors' agendas 1980–87; board papers 1957–71, 1985; abstracts from board papers 1951–69; papers re registration of company overseas 1969; executive committee papers 1983–89, 1991–93; annual returns 1930–38; committee minutes: sealing transfer meetings 1929–48, 1953–58, pension fund meetings 1946–86, group development meetings 1967–80, terms of employment meetings 1969–73, 1976–77, group finance meetings 1969–78, trustee investment meetings 1975–77, communications policy meetings 1977, public policy meetings 1978, consumer affairs and legal aspects meetings 1978–79, group operations meetings 1978–81, share bonus scheme meetings 1980–86, appeal meetings 1983–85; attendance books 1929–44, 1974–81; agendas: technical advisory committee 1978–80, group operations committee 1978–81, group development committee 1980, group environmental health committee 1980; special resolutions 1949–71; extraordinary resolution 1959; chairman's addresses 1969–70s; registers: seals 1949–81, 1985–86, directors or managers 1930–42, directors' interests 1960s–87, combined members, directors and share ledger 1932–40, members 1934–42, 1948–55, debenture stockholders 1950–94, preference shares 1940–65, ordinary shares 1929–65, shares 1986, probates 1941–48, 1964–78, transfers 1939–43, 1979, members of share incentive scheme 1976; share prospectus 1985; trust deeds 1934–92; rights issues 1974–88, 1992; minute sheets: debenture meetings 1972–78, ordinary, transfer meetings 1972–78, loan stock meetings 1972–78, convertible stock meetings 1970; annual reports re debenture redemption 1962–64; chairman's statement to stockholders 1969; shareholders' reports 1982, 1986; stock exchange quotations booklets 1947–63, 1969–81; share registration certificates 1982–84; shareholders' accounts 1953–73; scheme of arrangement re share capital 1969; guarantee bonds 1987; loan for bond investments 1988–92; dividends 1960–80; share incentive scheme: resolutions 1970–83, papers and correspondence 1971–75; share bonus scheme: first appropriation letters 1980–81, lists 1984–85; share options scheme papers 1980s; analysis of shareholder survey 1979; shareholder brochures advising rejection of Rhône-Poulenc Rorer bid 1995; papers and correspondence re stocks and shares 1965–90; annual reports and accounts 1939, 1947–93 (w); balance sheets and profit and loss accounts 1930–37, 1949–51, 1982–83; annual accounts 1922–80 (w); reports on annual accounts 1958–62; directors' reports: 1986, overseas policy committee 1974–75; ledgers: 1929–46, 1957–77 (w), nominal 1957, 1963–64, n.d., expenses 1974, 1980, fixed assets 1988, control 1982; ledger sheets 1969–80 (w); journals: 1968–71, credit transfer 1961; cash books 1956–75, 1983; accounting reports 1951–52; interim financial statements 1951–54, 1967–93 (w); final accounts 1951, 1961–76 (w); year end accounts 1961–89 (w); budgets 1968–85; investment accounts 1968–73; accounts schedule 1956, 1982; papers re accounting procedures 1953–74; internal control reports 1983–85; news bulletins re accounting procedures 1983–87; accounting working papers 1965–92; papers: group finance committee 1969, 1971, capital expenditure committee 1968–72, capital control committee 1966–67, capital projects committee 1973–78, capital expenditure 1967–90, capital control scheme 1967, company finance 1969–85, fixed assets 1959–79, 1992, profit sharing 1981–90, price commission 1973–78, inter-company loans 1973–81; papers re departmental costs: general 1980–89, archives 1977–78; scheme and loan files 1978–80; work order payment cards 1970–71; purchase and sales contracts 1987–92; papers re purchases 1975; report data 1959; forecasts 1967–71, 1981; invoice registers 1978; debit notes from customers 1978–81; bills receivable 1959; stock accounts 1962; standing orders and instructions book 1955–64; banking papers 1976–92; Fisons charity trust: accounts 1964–89, correspondence 1980–81; general accounting papers and correspondence 1970–94; audited accounts 1958–69 (w); auditors reports and accounts 1965–91 (w); audit planning 1986; audit fees 1988; asset and insurance valuations 1987; papers: insurance 1977–90, group taxation 1967–94, corporation tax 1975–85, stamp duty 1968–80, Inland Revenue 1968, national insurance 1988; tax deduction certificates 1978–89; tax income certificates 1964–78; schedule of rates 1989; litigation papers 1975; legal papers, agreements and correspondence 1958–92; legal claims 1971; paper re local authority tendering 1987; trade marks and patents 1985, 1987; patent licence agreements 1984; trade mark agreement with Reckitt & Colman 1987; papers and correspondence re patents of Astra Pharmaceuticals Ltd 1991–92; secretarial papers 1960s–90s; treasury papers, purchase and sale agreements 1954–94; acquisition papers: Charnwood Pharmaceuticals Ltd 1980, CP Pharmaceuticals Ltd 1983–84, general 1974, 1986; agreements and papers re projects concerning third parties 1960s–90s; group manuals 1952, 1965–67, 1986; organisation charts 1965; manufacturing agreements and correspondence 1961–79, 1990s; project files 1982; extended product contracts 1968–75; corporate design manuals 1984–86; promotional brochures 1951–79, n.d.; promotional audio and visual cassettes n.d.; information bulletins 1978–80; programme re visit of directors to Immingham site 1949; press cuttings 1960–81; press cutting and advertisement album 1970s; advertising material 1968; Fisons Property Ltd, accounts and correspondence 1959–71; property leases: New Cardinal Street, Ipswich 1955–69, Wine Street, Bristol 1957, general 1987; papers re leases 1978–88; conveyances and papers re conveyancing 1968; legal papers, licences and agreements re property 1960s–70s; property accounts 1955–57; report re structural condition of Fison House, Princes Street 1979; property papers: Fison House 1960–91, Plymouth Harbour 1969, land at Bramford 1970, sale of land at Eling Quay 1970–76, Manchester premises 1985, new office block, Derby Road 1989, general 1968–69; Uxbridge factory projects 1979; construction contracts 1985; land building valuation 1968; property re-evaluation 1989; booklets re Levington research station 1957; guide to the move to Loughborough 1968; papers and correspondence re property 1978–82; papers re directors' salaries and employments 1968–78; salary tables 1979; Fisons Pension Trust Ltd: memorandum and articles of association 1946, 1986, meetings' agendas 1958–

60, 1983, 1988, register of seals 1951–74, ledgers 1963–66, 1969, ledger sheets 1971, 1978–80, cash book 1982, accounts 1965–74, 1984–88, audited accounts 1985, papers re accounts 1988–89, actuarial valuation 1986, invoices 1971–80, papers re supplementary funds 1977–84, deeds 1980–86, contract notes 1973–77, guide to the fund 1988, charts 1980, papers and correspondence 1980s; pension authorities' papers 1979–83; booklets and papers re pension fund 1966–79, 1985; board correspondence re pension rules 1979–84; employee mortgage loans 1958–70s; employee report 1977; accounts re former staff 1974; careers booklet n.d.; papers re industrial training 1966–69; *Fisons Journal*, staff magazine 1930–80; *Fison News*, staff newsletter 1966–69; Fisons press releases 1991–92; papers re sports and social clubs 1976–96; health and safety papers 1985–86; papers re security at headquarters 1985; emergency procedures, Loughborough 1982; sickness returns and correspondence 1978–79; papers re charitable donations 1986; correspondence: group administration 1974–90, 1993–94, registrars 1983–88, finance director 1983, executive committee 1978–82, health and safety committee 1981–84, Ian Wormald re company support of Conservative Party 1963, research enquiries 1970s–80s, Princes Street premises and regulations 1979–83, internal 1980s–90s, general 1976–90; photographs: Sir Clavering Fison 1961, directors 1960, n.d., presentation 1958; lists of recipients of annual reports 1981–85; papers re organisational changes 1981; subscription to Chemical Industries' Association 1970; papers re new telephone system 1988; profile of Lord Netherthorpe and George Burton c.1972; historical notes 1972; records unlisted 20th cent.

Records 2: London Metropolitan Archives, 40 Northampton Road, London EC1R 0HB

Fison's Chemicals (Export) Ltd: memorandum and articles of association 1951; special resolution on change of name 1953; file containing correspondence, circulars and press cuttings 1948–51. (Ref: B/WHF/1-245)

Records 3: History of Advertising Trust, HAT House, 12 Raveningham Centre, Raveningham NR14 6NU

Guardbooks of advertising material 1942, 1955–63. (Ref: Ogilvy & Mather collection; AA1/2/6r; MEAL collection 1974–89, R10-80)

FITZHUGH & CARR
21 Long Row East and 32 Derby Road, Nottingham

Chemist

History: During the 1820s William Brothers, chemists and druggists, of Long Row, Nottingham, and William Williams, surgeon of Bridlesmith Gate, Nottingham, joined in partnership to form Brothers & Williams, chemists and druggists, of 60 Long Row. By 1844 the firm was operating from 18 Long Row East. By 1853 William Williams, chemist and druggist, was trading on his own account at 22 Long Row East, and in 1864, formed a partnership, Williams & Fitzhugh, chemists and druggists, at both 22 & 32 Long Row East. Elizabeth Williams, chemist, was also registered at the latter address. Richard Fitzhugh, another Nottingham chemist, was registered at Shakespeare Street in 1864. By 1877 he had qualified as a pharmaceutical chemist, trading from 21 Long Row East and Greyhound Street, Nottingham. From 1908 this business was styled Fitzhugh & Carr, pharmaceutical chemists. The business retained this name until around 1957, when E F Burr, of 317 Musters Road, West Bridgford, Nottingham, acquired the business, closed the premises and re-located the business to Derby Road, Nottingham, where he was proprietor of S H Plattin, a firm of dispensing and photographic chemists. Fitzhugh & Carr continued to trade under its own name.

Records: Nottinghamshire Archives & Southwell Diocesan Record Office, County House, Castle Meadow Road, Nottingham NG2 1AG

Ledgers: E A Wright 1845–56, 1882–84, customers' accounts 1871–84 (w), 1925–39, customers' daily purchases 1916–17, 'small' 1941–63, itemised sales, with customer and price details 1942–49; cash book 1964; purchases invoice book 1946–57; invoices and credit notes 1958–59; prescription books: G E Burr 1844–65, 1900–03, 1913–14, Mr Burr, chemist, Halam 1858–1928, detailed 1885–1916 (w), private 1936–60. (Ref: DD 687 and DD 687 add)

FRANCIS & CO (WREXHAM) LTD
Hope Street, Wrexham

Chemist

History: John Francis was registered as a pharmaceutical chemist in 1865 and was in business at 53 Hope Street, Wrexham, in 1876. He was succeeded in the business by John Herbert Francis, who registered as a chemist and druggist in 1886 and James Bridge Francis, who registered as a chemist and druggist in 1884. James Bridge Francis left the business in 1901, moving to Brooklyn, Wrexham, leaving John Herbert Francis in sole charge. He continued to trade from 53 Hope Street until 1935, when he ceased to be registered. Following this, the business was incorporated as a limited liability company, Francis & Co

(Wrexham) Ltd, continuing to trade from 53 Hope Street until 1976, when it closed.

Records: Denbighshire Record Office, 46 Clwyd Street, Ruthin LL15 1HP

Draft stock book 1932; private receipt book, incl. remedies 1901–23; sales registers: dangerous drugs 1929–53, methylated spirits 1927–56, poisons 1935–57; prescription books 1889–91, 1911–75. (Ref: DD/DM/196)

GEHE UK PLC
Sapphire Court, Walsgrave Triangle Business Park, Coventry CV2 2TX

Holding company for a chain of pharmaceutical wholesale and retail companies

History: In 1923 Amalgamated Anthracite Collieries Ltd was incorporated as a limited liability company to distribute solid fuel around Lincoln and the East Midlands. The company was based at 186 High Street, Lincoln, Lincolnshire, but its head office was in London. After the Second World War the company acquired a large number of fuel and building materials companies, including the Lincoln Brick Company Ltd in 1949. An unusual sideline was a small health services division which, after the acquisition of Vestric Ltd, a pharmaceutical wholesaler, from Glaxo Holdings plc in 1985, became a major group activity. By 1985 the company, renamed AAH Holdings plc in 1981, had moved its headquarters to South Park, Lincoln. In 1988 the company sold its fuel distribution interests and, thereafter, its main business activities became healthcare services, environmental services, builders' supplies, consumer products and distribution services. Healthcare services was the largest of these, and provided wholesale distribution of drugs, medical products and toiletries through AAH Pharmaceuticals Ltd, and its wide range of countrywide distribution centres. AAH Pharmaceuticals Ltd was incorporated as a limited liability company in 1987 following the merger of a number of pharmaceutical wholesale companies which were acquired by AAH Holdings plc's wholly-owned subsidiary, Chemists Holdings Ltd, during the 1970s and 1980s. These included, Hills Pharmaceuticals Ltd, acquired in 1976, Mawson & Proctor Pharmaceuticals Ltd, acquired in 1983, and Herbert Ferryman Ltd and Northern Pharmaceuticals Ltd, both acquired in 1985. By the 1990s, the healthcare division also owned more than 200 retail pharmacies, including Hill-Smith (Warrington) Ltd, a group of 10 pharmacies, through AAH Retail Pharmacy Ltd. These companies traded under the name Vantage Chemists. In 1995 AAH plc was acquired by GEHE AG, the German wholesale distribution company, although it continued to trade under its own name. It re-located to Hampton

Court, Manor Park, Runcorn, Halton, in the same year. By 1999 AAH plc continued to trade but under the name of its parent company, GEHE UK plc, which was formed to unite all of AAH's and GEHE's activities in the UK. All the AAH plc and AAH Pharmaceutical Ltd offices in Runcorn were closed and those in Dosthill, Staffordshire, and Southampton were relocated to the new GEHE UK plc head offices in Coventry. In 1999 GEHE UK plc had 1,800 branches in the UK.

J R B Davies, 'AAH in Lincoln', *Centenary Echo*, 6, 17 April 1993

Records: GEHE UK plc, Retail Branch, Atherstone, Warwickshire. Enquiries to GEHE UK plc, Sapphire Court, Walsgrave Triangle Business Park, Coventry CV2 2TX

Minutes: general meetings 1923–85, executive committee meetings 1925–29, technical committee meetings 1942–46; memorandum and articles of association 1923; directors' attendance book 1947–62; register of directors' holdings 1950–67; seal books 1927–49, 1969–78; trust deed 1929; register of mortgages n.d.; annual reports and accounts 1949–94; legal charge 1935; papers re restructuring of pharmaceuticals division 1987–88; papers re acquisition of Herbert Ferryman Ltd and Northern Pharmaceuticals Ltd 1984–85; staff pension scheme papers 1944–79, 1985–96; register of pension trustees n.d. (Ref: Boxes S1-2, S21, A2, A4)

Subsidiary companies: minutes: Acklam & Wood Ltd 1984–96, Actons Chemists Ltd 1988–96, George Alan (Chemists) Ltd 1994–96, M & J Barr Ltd 1965–96, D F Brint (Portishead) Ltd 1987–96, J C N W Burr Ltd 1972–96, C P Caplan & Sons Ltd 1990–96, P & J Carr (Chemists) Ltd 1958–96, Castlereagh Pharmaceuticals Ltd 1924–96, A H Clark (Allington) Ltd 1972–96, A H Clark (Maidstone) Ltd 1964–96, A H Clark (Park Wood) Ltd 1951–96, E & F Cummins Ltd 1987–96, D E Davies Ltd 1981–96, A S Davy Ltd 1986–96, R J Dawe (Park Parade) Ltd 1964–96, Dobson & Stokoe Ltd 1993–96, Elliotts Pharmacy Ltd 1988–96, Foster Pharmaceuticals Ltd 1984–96, Gilchrists (Chemists) Ltd 1966–96, F Alistair Glenn Ltd 1977–96, Gordon's Pharmacy Ltd 1957–96, Gwynfa's (Bont) Ltd 1992–96, Gwynfa's (G C G) Ltd 1992–96, Gwynfa's (Hounslow) Ltd 1992–96, Gwynfa's Ltd 1992–96, Hammond Hopkins Ltd 1989–96, Hartleys Chemists Ltd 1938–96, S Haydock & Co Ltd 1970–96, Hillcross Pharmaceuticals Ltd 1948–96, F Holroyd (Garforth) Ltd 1976–96, F A A Jones Ltd 1986–96, Arthur Kendrick Ltd 1980–96, Lewin Peplow Ltd 1973–88, Lockwoods (Chemists) Ltd 1969–96, G W McKenzie Ltd 1986–96, A F Marshall Ltd 1969–96, H B Mattion Ltd 1937–96, K Newberry (Chemists) Ltd 1951–96, H E Niblett Ltd 1986–96, R G Nicklin Ltd 1973–96, O T C

Supplies Ltd 1967–96, Pharmagen Ltd 1964–96, Pharmed Ltd 1967–96, Walter F Pickup Ltd 1987–96, Reappage Ltd 1984–96, Roundthorn Ltd 1980–96, Shipman Davies Ltd 1957–96, Smallwood Chemists Ltd 1919–96, Solomian Ltd 1985–96, M W & A Taylor Ltd 1991–96, G H Trott Ltd 1976–96, F B Vickers Ltd 1983–96, Charles W Waddington Ltd 1973–96, R W F Wilson & Co (Arbroath) Ltd 1992–96, R W F Wilson & Co (Inverness) Ltd 1977–96; memoranda and articles of association: E & F Cummins Ltd 1967, 1987, Gordon's Pharmacy Ltd 1957, 1992, Lockwoods (Chemists) Ltd 1987; combined registers of members, directors and share ledgers: Acklam & Wood Ltd 1973–94, Actons Chemists Ltd 1988–89, George Alan (Chemists) Ltd 1971–90, M & J Barr Ltd 1965–93, D F Brint (Portishead) Ltd 1990–92, J C N W Burr Ltd 1972–88, C P Caplan & Sons Ltd 1990, P & J Carr (Chemists) Ltd 1977–93, Castlereagh Pharmaceuticals Ltd 1924–89, A H Clark (Allington) Ltd 1971–90s, A H Clark (Maidstone) Ltd 1952–91, A H Clark (Park Wood) Ltd 1965–93, E & F Cummins 1967–87, D E Davies Ltd 1979–90, 1993, A S Davy Ltd 1986–93, R J Dawe (Park Parade) Ltd 1974–88, Dobson & Stokoe Ltd 1978–93, Elliotts Pharmacy Ltd 1982–91, Foster Pharmaceuticals Ltd 1993, Gilchrists (Chemists) Ltd 1971–91, F Alistair Glenn Ltd 1977–87, Gordon's Pharmacy Ltd 1988–92, Gwynfa's (Bont) Ltd 1976–92, Gwynfa's (G C G) Ltd 1983–92, Gwynfa's (Hounslow) Ltd 1969–92, Gwynfa's Ltd 1954–92, Hammond Hopkins Ltd 1977–93, Hartleys Chemists Ltd 1938–85, S Haydock & Co Ltd 1953–90, Hillcross Pharmaceuticals Ltd 1912–88, F Holroyd (Garforth) Ltd 1976–91, F A A Jones Ltd 1951–81, Arthur Kendrick Ltd 1980–93, Lewin Peplow Ltd 1973–92, Lockwoods (Chemists) Ltd 1906–88, G W McKenzie Ltd 1986–91, E Margerrison & Co 1951–89, A F Marshall Ltd 1969–89, Pharmagen Ltd 1952–89, Pharmed Ltd 1966–89, K Newberry (Chemists) Ltd 1951–89, H E Niblett Ltd 1978–91, R G Nicklin Ltd 1972–90, Oakreads Ltd 1987–90, O T C Supplies Ltd 1966–88, Walter F Pickup Ltd 1984–89, Bernard Pitt (Seaton) Ltd 1946–90, Reappage Ltd 1982–92, Roundthorn Ltd 1976–94, Shipman Davies Ltd 1957–93, Smallwood Chemists Ltd 1921–88, Solomian Ltd 1975–88, A P Stratton Ltd 1979–92, M W & A Taylor Ltd 1983–91, G H Trott Ltd 1976–90, F B Vickers Ltd 1948–87, Charles W Waddington Ltd 1973–89, R W F Wilson & Co (Arbroath) Ltd 1985–92, R W F Wilson & Co (Inverness) Ltd 1977–90; seal registers: Briggs Cash Chemists Ltd 1976, Hartleys Chemists Ltd 1972–88, Pharmagen Ltd 1977–88, Pharmed Ltd 1967–85. (Ref: Boxes S3-7, 9-12, 16, 18-19, 21, A2, A4, current minutes, boxes 1, 3-11)

GENATOSAN LTD
Loughborough, Leicestershire

Proprietary medicine and fine chemical manufacturer

History: This company was established in 1906 at Chenies Street, London, as a wholly-owned subsidiary of Wulfing AG of Germany, manufacturers of the nerve tonic *Sanatogen*. In 1919 the company was incorporated as a limited liability company, Genatosan Ltd, an anagram of *Sanatogen*, to avoid any unpopular Germanic associations, and manufactured proprietary medicines and fine chemicals from works in Loughborough, Leicestershire. In 1946 it was acquired as a wholly-owned subsidiary of Fisons Ltd, producers of agricultural products and fertilisers which had owned a part share in the company since 1937, but it continued to trade as Genatosan Ltd. In 1947 Genatosan Trust Ltd was incorporated as a limited liability company by Fisons Ltd, to acquire the business of Whiffen & Sons Ltd, fine chemical manufacturers of London. From this point onwards, Fisons Ltd began to diversify into pharmaceutical manufacture. Bengers Ltd, producers of ethical pharmaceuticals including *Auralgicin*, a treatment for ear infections, and *Bengers Food*, a milk supplement, based at Holmes Chapel, Cheshire, was also acquired by Fisons Ltd in 1947. Following this acquisition, Genatosan Trust Ltd was renamed British Chemicals & Biologicals Ltd (BCB Ltd), a co-ordinating company for Genatosan Ltd, Whiffen & Sons Ltd and Bengers Ltd. In 1951 it was made dormant and Genatosan Ltd, Whiffen & Sons Ltd and Bengers Ltd regained control of their respective businesses. In 1964 Genatosan Ltd and Bengers Ltd were merged to form one operating company, Fisons Pharmaceuticals Ltd, a subsidiary of Fisons Ltd, with research laboratories at Loughborough and a manufacturing plant at Holmes Chapel.

M S Moss, 'Fertilisers to Pharmaceuticals: Fisons – the biography of a company 1720–1986' (Unpublished typescript, 1996, copy at Ipswich Record Office)

Records 1: Rhône-Poulenc Rorer Ltd, Rhône-Poulenc Rorer House, 50 Kings Hill Avenue, Kings Hill, West Malling ME19 4AH

Directors' meetings minutes 1948–51; memorandum and articles of association 1948; share transfer ledgers 1919–40s; balance sheets 1974–75; patent licence from Farm Products Ltd n.d.; licence agreements and correspondence: Lisle Street, Derby Road, Loughborough 1959, Dutch overseas territories 1957–60; papers re sale of *Sanatogen* in South Africa 1958–68; assignment of tenancies to and correspondence with Whiffen & Sons Ltd 1959; conveyances, Loughborough property 1960.

Records 2: History of Advertising Trust, HAT House, 12 Raveningham Centre, Raveningham NR14 6NU

Guardbooks of advertising material: Genatosan Ltd 1913–55, *Sanatogen* 1914–57; press advertisements for *Sanatogen* 1974–80s. (Ref: Ogilvy & Mather collection; AA1/2/6r; MEAL collection 1974–89, R10-80)

GENERAL APOTHECARIES CO LTD
London

Wholesale and manufacturing chemist and druggist

History: In 1855 John Gardner, surgeon and physician of 51 Mortimer Street, Cavendish Square, London, provisionally registered the Western Apothecary's Co Ltd as a limited liability company. In 1856 General Apothecaries Co Ltd was incorporated as a limited liability company, trading from 49 Berners Street, Oxford Street, London. It was established to supply the medical profession and the public with unadulterated drugs and medicines, and to trade as a dispensing chemist, dealer in photographic equipment and manufacturer of surgical appliances. It was wound up in 1860, and in the same year, a new company was incorporated, which also traded as General Apothecaries Co Ltd from 49 Berners Street, with registered offices at 5 Mitre Court, Fleet Street, London. This company was wound up in 1882. It appears that the company was reconstituted again thereafter, as records continued to be created until 1956. In 1941 the General Apothecaries Co Ltd claimed to be the only company run by medical men for the benefit of the medical profession.

Records 1: Archives & Manuscripts, Wellcome Library for the History & Understanding of Medicine, 183 Euston Road, London NW1 2BE

Minutes 1860–1942; abstract of deed of settlement 1855; share certificate books 1856, 1878–1948; annual reports and balance sheets 1882–1945; price lists 1941, n.d.; miscellaneous records 1889–1951. (Ref: MSS 5492-506)

Records 2: Public Record Office, Ruskin Avenue, Kew, Richmond TW9 4DU

Memorandum of association 1860; application for certificate of incorporation 1856; provisional registrations: Western Apothecary's Co Ltd 1855, General Apothecaries Co Ltd 1855; registration documents 1856; notice of dissolution and formation of company of same name 1860; letter of re-registration 1860; special resolution 1857; notice of additional directors 1855; list of shareholders 1856; declaration verifying list of shareholders 1856; summary of capital and shares 1857, 1859; statement of capital 1856; return of proposed capital 1955; notice of increase in nominal capital 1857; deed of settlement 1856; schedule of signatures to deed of settlement 1856; appointment of solicitor 1855; notice of situation of registered office 1860; return of the place of business 1955; correspondence with Companies Registration Office 1878–81; special resolution appointing liquidators 1860; notice of completion of winding-up 1861; notice of dissolution 1882. (Ref: BT31/466/1804, BT31/39/175)

GLAISYER & KEMP
11-12 North Street, Brighton, Brighton & Hove

Pharmaceutical chemist

History: Thomas Glaisyer and John Kemp, pharmaceutical chemists, were registered in 1852 and 1853 respectively. By 1876 they were trading from 11 & 12 North Street, Brighton, Brighton & Hove, as Glaisyer & Kemp. They were later joined in the business by Edmund Glaisyer, who registered as a pharmaceutical chemist in 1878. John Kemp died around 1894–95.

Records: East Sussex Record Office, The Maltings, Castle Precincts, Lewes BN7 1YT

Accounts 1800–65; prescription books, incl. J Weston & Co, 24 Church Road, Hove, Brighton & Hove, 1818–1927; label book c.1860–85; dispensing price lists 1886–88; certificate of registration of copyright of price book 1886; press cuttings 19th cent.; postcard of shopfront 1920; article re history 1953. (Ref: ACC 3436)

GLAXO WELLCOME PLC
Greenford Road, Greenford, London

Pharmaceutical manufacturer

History: In 1856 Joseph Edward Nathan, born in east London in 1835, travelled to New Zealand, and joined his cousin, Jacob Joseph, in his household supplies business, becoming a partner in 1861. In 1873 this partnership was dissolved, and Joseph Edward established a business, Joseph Nathan & Co, New Zealand, on his own account. In 1876 a London office was opened and in 1893 Joseph Edward moved back to London, and incorporated the business there as a limited liability company, Joseph Nathan & Co Ltd. 3 of his sons became company directors, and one, Maurice Nathan, acquired the rights to a patent for manufacturing dried milk products in 1904. By 1906 the company's most popular line was dried baby food, which was named *Glaxo* baby food. Henry Wellcome, co-founder of Burroughs Wellcome & Co Ltd, was born in 1853 in the American Midwest. During the 1860s he worked in his uncle's drug store, then took employment in a number of cities whilst studying to become a pharmacist. He graduated from the Philadelphia College of Pharmacy in 1874. In 1880 he joined his friend, Silas Burroughs, in his English pharmaceutical business, S M Burroughs & Co, which was renamed Burroughs, Wellcome & Co when he became a partner. The firm's headquarters were at Snow Hill Buildings, London, and a production plant was shortly afterwards opened at Dartford, Kent. Henry Wellcome also acquired shares in the Kepler Malt Extract Co Ltd, which had been incorporated as a limited liability company in 1879 by Silas Burroughs, to produce malt and cod-liver oil. In 1895 Silas Burroughs died and Henry Wellcome continued the business, creating research laboratories, which employed a number of distinguished scientists, including Sir Henry Dale. Early drug developments included an injection to counter the effects of tetanus, released in 1891, and a diphtheria vaccine, first produced in 1894. Between 1886 and 1912 Burroughs, Wellcome & Co established overseas subsidiaries in Australia; South Africa; Italy; the USA; Canada; Shanghai, China; Argentina; and India, and in 1913 founded the Wellcome Bureau of Scientific Research in London, as a centre for research into tropical diseases. The physiological research laboratories were re-located to Beckenham, Kent, in 1920, and in 1924 the Wellcome Foundation Ltd was incorporated as a limited liability company to co-ordinate all business and research activities. Meanwhile, Joseph Nathan & Co Ltd continued to produce dried milk products, for which demand increased during the First World War. In 1919 Harry Jephcott was appointed as a pharmaceutical chemist by Joseph Nathan & Co Ltd, and thereafter the company began a programme of research and development, which led to the introduction of its first pharmaceutical product, *Ostelin Liquid*, a vitamin D supplement, in 1924. In 1920 new headquarters were established, named Glaxo House, at Euston Road, London. During the interwar period a number of overseas subsidiary companies were established, and in 1935 construction of a much larger plant began at Greenford, Ealing, London, to which most of the business re-located during the following year. At the same time Glaxo Laboratories Ltd was incorporated as a subsidiary of Joseph Nathan & Co Ltd, to manufacture dried milk products and pharmaceuticals. In 1936 The Wellcome Foundation Ltd introduced a vaccination against yellow fever, and began production of insulin. In the same year Henry Wellcome, who had been knighted in 1932, died. His will created a charitable foundation, the Wellcome Trust, which had sole ownership of The Wellcome Foundation Ltd. All profits made by The Wellcome Foundation Ltd, were used by the Trust for investment into pharmaceutical research, and research into the history of medicine. During the Second World War Glaxo Laboratories Ltd produced large quantities of milk products, orange juice and vitamin supplements, but also engaged in pioneering research into penicillin. By 1944 the company produced 80 per cent of the country's supply of the antibiotic. In 1945 Harry Jephcott was made chairman of Joseph Nathan & Co Ltd and of Glaxo Laboratories Ltd, and shortly afterwards was knighted. In 1947 Joseph Nathan & Co Ltd was wound up, and was replaced by its subsidiary, which was incorporated as a public limited liability company, Glaxo Laboratories Ltd. Research continued, and during the 1940s a combined vaccine to combat whooping cough and diptheria, and an antibiotic, used in the treatment of tuberculosis, *streptomycin*, were released, followed in the 1950s, by a tablet form of penicillin and the production of cortisone, used in the treatment of arthritis, inflammatory and respiratory disorders. In 1958 Glaxo Laboratories Ltd acquired the business of Allen & Hanburys Ltd, a long established pharmaceutical manufacturing company, which continued to trade under its own name. In 1961 Evans Medical Ltd was acquired by Glaxo Laboratories Ltd, following which a holding company, Glaxo Group Ltd, was incorporated in London, and Glaxo Laboratories Ltd became its operating subsidiary. In 1963 Glaxo Group Ltd acquired the business of Edinburgh Pharmaceutical Industries Ltd, which comprised a number of pharmaceutical concerns, including Duncan Flockhart & Co Ltd and Macfarlan Smith Ltd. The latter was sold by the Glaxo holding company, by then renamed Glaxo Holdings plc, to its management in 1990. During the 1950s and 1960s The Wellcome Foundation Ltd conducted research which led to the development of *Purinethol*, an anti-cancer treatment, and *Marboran*, a drug which offered protection against smallpox. It also expanded research into veterinary medicines, and in 1967 acquired Calmic Ltd to increase activity in this field. By 1970 the Wellcome Foundation Ltd had increased its number of overseas subsidiaries from 8 to 58. Glaxo Group Ltd was also represented in over 100 overseas countries, through subsidiary companies or agencies. During the late 1960s Glaxo Group Ltd incorporated Sefton Bulk Pharmaceuticals Ltd as a wholly-owned subsidiary, to market fine chemicals including penicillin, which were sold to pharmaceutical companies for secondary manufacture. In 1971 Glaxo Group Ltd was renamed, Glaxo Holdings Ltd, later plc, and in 1978 acquired a small American pharmaceutical company, Meyer Laboratories Inc. This was renamed Glaxo Inc in 1980, and grew to be one of the largest pharmaceutical companies in USA. In the late 1980s Glaxo Group Research Ltd was incorporated as a limited liability company, to unify all research and development activities. During the 1980s the company's most successful product was *Zantac*, a treatment for peptic ulcers. In 1985 Wellcome plc was incorporated as a holding company and parent to The Wellcome Foundation Ltd. The terms of Henry Wellcome's will were also altered to allow the Wellcome Trust to sell 25 per cent of its shares, in order to create a more stable investment base and to increase income received. The company launched one of its most successful products, *Zovirax*, in 1981, a treatment for cold sores and herpes, and during the 1980s, marketed *Retrovir*, as a drug useful in the treatment of Acquired Immune Deficiency Syndrome (AIDS) and the Human Immuno-deficiency Virus (HIV). In 1992 the Wellcome Trust's shareholding of The Wellcome Foundation Ltd was reduced to 40 per cent. In 1995 Glaxo Holdings plc and Wellcome plc merged, forming the largest pharmaceutical company in the world, Glaxo Wellcome plc.

R Davenport-Hines and J Slinn, *Glaxo: A history to 1962* (Cambridge University Press, Cambridge, 1992); *Glaxo Wellcome: A brief history of the world's largest pharmaceutical company* (Glaxo Wellcome, London, 1995); K Holland, 'Glaxo Holdings plc', *Pharmaceutical Journal*, 5 Dec 1987; K Holland, 'The Wellcome Foundation', *Pharmaceutical Journal*, 20 Dec 1986; R R James, *Henry Wellcome* (Hodder and Stoughton, London, 1994); Sir H Jephcott, *The First Fifty Years. An account of the early life of Joseph Edward Nathan and the first fifty years of his merchandise business that eventually became the Glaxo Group* (W S Cowell Ltd, Ipswich, 1969); G Macdonald, *In Pursuit of Excellence: One hundred years Wellcome 1880–1980* (Wellcome Foundation, London, 1980); J Millen, *Glaxo from Bonnie Babies to Better Medicine* (Glaxo New Zealand Ltd, Palmerston North, 1991) C Turner, *Gold on the Green: Fifty Glaxo years at Greenford* (Glaxo, London, 1985); H Turner, *Henry Wellcome: The man, his collection and his legacy* (Heinemann, London, 1980); J Walton, *Glaxo Wellcome at Ulverston. The first fifty years* (Glaxo Wellcome Operations, Ulverston, 1989); N Watson, *Glaxo at Barnard Castle. A celebration* (Glaxo Maufacturing Services, Barnard Castle, 1994)

Records 1: Archivist (Historical Records), Records Centre, Glaxo Wellcome plc, 891-995 Greenford Road, Greenford UB6 0HE

Glaxo Export Ltd: minutes: 1983–89, general meetings 1983–87; memorandum and articles of association 1983; agendas and papers 1986–89; papers re shares 1983–84; annual accounts 1983–87; capital projects papers 1983–88; property papers 1983–85; miscellaneous papers and correspondence 1983–89.

Glaxo Group Research Ltd: minutes, agendas and papers 1963–68; agreements, share transfers and debenture correspondence 1967; annual reports and accounts 1967–68, 1975–78; consolidated accounts 1976–77; accounts 1967–79; audit papers 1967; notices to staff 1974–79; personnel records 1975–79; correspondence with University of York 1980; statutory forms 1965–78; records unlisted 20th cent.

Glaxo Holdings plc: minutes: directors' meetings 1947–75, general meetings 1950–68, 1971–81; memoranda and articles of association 1935, 1969–72; seal registers 1984–88; committee meeting minutes: executive board 1951–61, transfer 1964–68, overseas subsidiaries 1968–71; meetings, agendas and papers: directors' 1959–67, general 1975–79, educational grants 1975–86, UK commercial committee 1978; directors' papers, correspondence and internal memoranda 1940s–79, n.d.; company secretary's papers, Glaxo Holdings plc and subsidiaries 1972–85; corporate papers: company re-organisation 1961–74, mergers 1963–64, 1971–72, co-operation with Schering Corporation Inc 1960–73; preliminary announcements 1963–71; trust deed 1972; register of directors' shares 1968–75; share papers: 1961–72, rights issue and preference scheme 1965–74, stock exchange 1959–75; shareholder correspondence 1974–79; annual reports and accounts 1963–68, 1972–80; papers re banking arrangements 1977–79; legal case studies re restrictive trade practices 1945–71; papers re industrial tribunals 1974–80; chairman's conference papers 1972; interim reports 1973–75; contracts and licences with companies 1943–73; consultancy agreements 1949–85; procedure agreements 1969–72; complaints and enquiries 1958–79; papers and correspondence re overseas subsidiaries and offices 1912–83; papers re inventions offered to company 1962–68; commercial bulletins 1973–79; files re price and income control, Glaxo Holdings plc and subsidiaries 1967–78; correspondence with external parties 1954–80; promotional brochure 1971; register of deeds 1832–56; property papers, plans and correspondence 1939–82; pension papers 1971–74; commercial directorate bulletin 1975–76; papers re directors' retirements n.d.; miscellaneous papers and correspondence: 1962–82, subsidiaries 1940s–90; personal papers of L N A Planel 1978–80; records unlisted 20th cent.

Glaxo International Ltd: minutes: general meetings 1966–72, divisional meetings 1967–70; memorandum and articles of association 1965; agendas and papers: general meetings 1965–72, divisional meetings 1967–70; papers and minutes of overseas subsidiaries 1966–72; miscellaneous papers and correspondence 1961–77.

Glaxo Laboratories Ltd: minutes: directors' meetings 1935–56, 1960–79, general meetings 1970–78; memoranda and articles of association 1946–55, 1962; committee meeting minutes: executive 1947–50, 1958–67, management 1977–78, sealing 1962–77; board papers 1936–39, 1947–78; committee papers: executive 1957–62, joint advisory 1969–73; agendas, papers and minutes 1947–58; directors' attendance books 1946–64; directors' reports 1970–73; papers re mergers 1955–60, 1974; seal registers 1938–62; debenture stock register 1966–69; papers re stocks and shares 1957–58; annual accounts 1969–78; accounts: consolidated 1969–76, legal 1969–74, general 1957–67; budgets and forecasts 1968–77; capital expenditure papers 1968–77; papers re price increases 1973–77; papers and correspondence re sales 1959–68; papers re tax allowances 1969;

customs and excise papers 1950–69; duty free bonds 1935–67; papers re rating matters 1969–79; legal papers 1950–71; licences to experiment on animals 1954–70; weights and measures legislation 1958–63; papers re *Griscofulvin* 1950s–70s; inventions offered and rejected 1962–66; product advertisements 1960, 1967; property papers: Greenford 1938, Ulverston 1968–78, Montrose 1966–74, general 1945–79; wages and salaries files 1969–73; personnel statistics 1968–72; job evaluations 1969–71; safety regulations for contractors 1958–61, 1969; complaints and enquiries 1973–78; sports and social club: licences 1958–64, poisons registered 1963; correspondence re exchange control 1942–63; miscellaneous papers and correspondence 1951–79; records unlisted 20th cent.

Glaxo Operations UK Ltd: general meetings minutes 1980–86; executive committee meetings minutes 1968; minutes, agendas and papers 1962–82 (w); annual accounts 1980–87; legal accounts 1962–75; consolidated accounts 1966–77, 1980–88; capital projects 1981–82; banking records 1968–78; auditor's report 1980; customs and excise papers 1972–78; research papers 1921–67; disability pensions, board minutes 1978–87; *The Glaxo Volume* 1948–74; confidential memoranda 1963–66; biographical notes re Dr E Lester Smith 1966; miscellaneous papers and correspondence 1961–82; records unlisted 20th cent.

Glaxo-Allenburys Ltd: directors' meetings minutes 1960–72; general meetings minutes 1968–71; memoranda and articles of association 1960–62; agendas 1960–77; attendance registers 1966–72; share certificates 1960–78; accounts 1965–74, 1978; accounting papers 1959–73; audited accounts 1962–75; reports: regional 1970–71, supplies division 1971; pension scheme agenda papers 1960–64; correspondence: overseas subsidiaries and agents 1950–66, internal 1965–66; statutory forms 1960–78.

Kepler Malt Extract Co Ltd: directors' meetings: minutes 1880–1910, agenda book 1880–82; letterbook 1879–82.

Joseph Nathan & Co Ltd: minutes 1899–1924; directors' and general meetings minutes 1913–33; accounts 1940–46; balance sheet 1919–20; agreements 1906–40; papers re agencies and associated companies 1931–46; directors' papers and correspondence 1922–45; advertisement re 'Glaxo' 1908; property and miscellaneous papers early 20th cent.; records unlisted 19th–20th cents.

Sefton Bulk Pharmaceuticals Ltd: minutes: directors' meetings 1978–81, general meetings 1969–80; agendas and board papers 1968–70; annual reports and accounts 1977–83; accounts 1966–78; budgets 1978–80; capital expenditure

1978; papers re insurance 1982–83; statutory forms 1964–78; directors' correspondence 1978–83.

Wellcome Foundation Ltd: announcement of partnership 1880; partnership disputes, correspondence and legal papers of Henry Wellcome and Silas Burroughs 1879–98; general meetings minutes 1940s to date, memorandum and articles of association 1924; notices of general meetings agendas 1924–40; statutory report 1924; agreement and papers re purchase of business in New York by Henry Wellcome 1924; committee meeting minutes: management 1941–48, secretaries' 1940–49, research 1930–45, production 1941–45, war production 1940–41, distribution 1945; minutes and related papers: Wellcome Trust 1937–40, Therapeutic Research Corporation 1941–45, 1982–83, enquiry into insulin 1948; papers re overseas subsidiaries and offices: Argentina 1909, 1912, Australia 1925–42, 1980, Buenos Aires 1910, 1930–38, Cuba 1909, East Africa 1955, South Africa pre 1902, 1930–38, China 1924, Egypt 1902–04, Germany 1945–46, Ireland 1939, Italy 1900–01, 1907–12, India 1885, Mexico 1908, Milan 1932–34, Montreal 1927–43, Shanghai 1912–77, Siam 1928–30, USA 1912–56, 1978–80; share certificates 1925–43; annual reports 1940s to date; balance sheet 1887; annual summaries 1889–1908; accounts 1955; ledger, associated houses 1944–49; works journal 1935–43; cash books 1937–48 (w); cash receipts books 1940–49; accounts of overseas subsidiaries 1950–53; overseas houses monthly estimates of sales 1950–58; bills books 1922–45; bank books 1879–90; cheque books 1879–82; correspondence: tithes 1925–43, purchase tax 1946–48; litigation papers: general 1937–39, dangerous drugs 1942–45, prosecution under Milk Act 1917, trade marks with press coverage of trial 1902–04; agreements re patents 1884–1900, n.d.; trade mark papers: licences 1936–45, oppositions and consents 1899, 1904–33, infringements 1903–45, general 1885–1943, 1946–50; papers and notes: registered designs 1898–1933, copyright 1913–41; correspondence: patent certificates 1881–1938, compulsory licences 1938–39; monthly reports to managing director 1927–40; wartime memoranda and circulars re management 1939–40; post-war plans 1944; laboratory notebooks 1908–33 (w), n.d.; chemist's diaries: 1897–1909, overseas 1899–1909 (w); pharmacist's diaries: 1910–40 (w), overseas 1910–38 (w); medical diaries and visiting lists: 1889–1989 (w), war emergency editions 1917–19, 1941–47, service editions 1899–1940 (w), export edition 1923, overseas editions 1898–1967, 1984; nurses diaries: 1898–1939 (w), overseas 1898–1937 (w); formulae books and formulae 1898–1946, n.d.; research reports: 1925–41, Wellcome Bureau of Scientific Research 1913–35; reports and minutes re research into specific drugs 1900–52; handbook 1945; papers, accounts and correspondence: research laboratories 1927–43, drugs production 1892–99, 1914–56, poisons labelling 1899–1947, medicine chests 1895–1932, 1950, 1970, therapeutic research 1927–28, 1982, woodworking department 1899–1904;

standard production procedures n.d.; developmental rejects files 1948–51; record of compressed products n.d.; drugs orders and order forms 1903–08, 1922; booklet describing organisation of Laboratories of Tropical Medicine post c.1945; correspondence re sale of saccharin overseas 1910, 1933; product lists: 1956–69, 1981–88, export 1962–71, overseas 1960, 1977–80; patent certificates 1883–84; copyright agreements 1903–12; certificates of registration of designs 1902–33; price lists: general 1881–1959, retail 1960–68, wholesale 1960–66, retail and wholesale 1968–83, biologicals 1949–59, industrial 1969, reagents 1958–72, hospital 1952–53, exports 1941–77, overseas 1894, 1902–69, consumer division, Crewe 1973, medical division 1974, other companies 1878, 1892; correspondence and papers re pricing and price-cutting 1888–1943; registers of advertisements 1881–91; advertising correspondence 1946; promotional poster 1943; marketing papers 1881, 1894–1909, 1933–34, 1946–54, n.d.; publicity: sales unit annual reports 1956–65, papers 1947–50, home sales books 1936–48; press cuttings 1891–1943, 1955–58; correspondence: marketing and public relations 1929–33, 1940–43, deeds 1889–90, 1931–54; Dartford premises: conveyances 1915–42, lease and correspondence 1887–93, 1928, memorandum re acquisition 1921, plan 1928, grant of right to lay drain and cable 1916, organisation of chemical works 1898–1932, papers re print works 1937–49, valuations and inventory 1938, tenancy agreements 1948–52, rent books 1909–43, memorandum re staff safety n.d., telegram re accident 1897, correspondence and memoranda re chemical works 1946–50, correspondence re works organisation 1889, 1899, 1909, supervisor's manuals 1947, work study handbooks 1953, 1971, papers re Wellcome Club and Institute 1889–1900, press cuttings 1889–93, programmes and papers re visits to site 1890, 1905, 1932, correspondence with Dartford Urban District Council 1900–39, correspondence re land 1919–30, correspondence re water supply 1940–45, historical notes 1907–30, 1945; Gower Street premises correspondence: sale and tenancy 1920–48, proposed new building 1944–47; Beckenham premises: directors' correspondence 1923–33, lease 1898, agreements with London County Council re land 1902, 1911, 1918–20, papers re registration of physiological research laboratories 1900–01, reports re construction of penicillin factory 1944–45, visitors book 1931–46, press cuttings re anti-vivisection 1919–49; Holburn Viaduct premises, correspondence re lease 1890–91; Snow Hill premises: licence to sell wines and spirits n.d., notes 1888–89, 1925, menu 1898, notice of social events and programmes 1902–08, 1920–21; 76 High Street, St Marylebone, London premises, leases 1914, 1929; Euston Road premises, papers re laying of corner stone 1931; Wandsworth premises, papers and correspondence 1883–1930; inventories and valuations of estate 1938; press cuttings and promotional material re Wellcome building 1921–39; reports and general correspondence: Bureau of Scientific Research 1902–75, estates department 1913–39, physiological research laboratories 1895–1922, tropical research laboratories,

182   *The pharmaceutical industry – a guide to historical records*

Khartoum 1901–40, negotiations to lease Belmont and Carshalton serum laboratories from London County Council 1942–47; staff register 1879–1928; wages books: women 1902–37, men 1902–43; salaries book n.d.; salaries and wages analysis 1950–51; letters re salaries 1885–98; staff records 1919–43; contract of employment 1897; diaries: company 1980–89, 1992–93, company appointments 1957–91, consultants' appointments 1898–1958, 1966; organisational charts of chemical works and Snow Hill head office 1914–38; notes: staff roles 1924, 1948, nurses late 1920s; card re profit sharing 1892–93; pro forma contract of employment n.d.; staff accident record 1909–72; notice re female staff clothing 1904; announcement re appointment of personnel officer 1946; instructions: management 1927–37, travelling representatives 1932; correspondence: employment 1930–40, sickness 1938–39, unemployment insurance 1912–30; *The Unicorn*, magazine 1936; *Tabloid*, monthly memoranda 1947–52; Wellcome Club papers: magazine 1899, programmes 1898–1905, 1920, 1949, papers re social activities 1892–95; correspondence: drug companies 1873–1900, 1915, 1940, trade unions 1921–36, business 1880–93, 1906–41, Lederle Laboratories Inc 1935–37, internal 1927–43, foreign department 1927–40, medicine chest department 1927–40, miscellaneous 1930, 1940; list of business correspondence 1880–86; papers re medals, awards and prizes 1909–40; notices re deaths of presidents 1881, 1885; visitors' book 1947–49; stationery samples 1931; personal letterbooks of Henry Wellcome 1882–1907; private letterbooks 1878–1907; private papers: Silas Burroughs 1878–79, 1892–98, Henry Wellcome 1884–1943, Henry Wellcome's family 1913, 1933–58, Henry Hallett Dale 1906–32, Wellcome staff 1882–1937, 1951, 1979, n.d.; historical notes, articles and staff reminiscences 1905–58, 1974–80, n.d.; archives list early 20th cent.; papers, correspondence and minutes of external organisations and committees 1939–87; miscellaneous papers 1922, c.1930–36.

Records 2: Archives & Manuscripts, Wellcome Library for the History & Understanding of Medicine, 183 Euston Road, London NW1 2BE

Wellcome Bureau of Scientific Research, records in process of being listed 20th cent. (Ref: Wellcome Archives)

Records 3: Public Record Office, Ruskin Avenue, Kew, Richmond TW9 4DU

Medical Research Council committees re Burroughs, Wellcome & Co and Wellcome Foundation Ltd c.1913–54. (Ref: FD1/16/919-21, 1296, 2263, 2520 FD1/98/3702, 8614)

Records 4: The Museum Curator, Royal Pharmaceutical Society of Great Britain, 1 Lambeth High Street, London SE1 7JN

Recipe notebook, Burroughs, Wellcome & Co 1887; tape-recorded interview with Leslie G Matthews, director of The Wellcome Foundation Ltd and historian 1994. (Ref: IRA.1996.068, IRT.1996.64)

Records 5: F Maltby & Sons Ltd, Dunston House, Portland Street, Lincoln LN5 7NN

Price list, Burroughs-Wellcome Ltd 1941.

Records 6: History of Advertising Trust, HAT House, 12 Raveningham Centre, Raveningham NR14 6NU

Advertising material re Burroughs, Wellcome & Co late 19th–early 20th cents. (Ref: A1/2/4r, 7r, 11r)

GODFREY & COOKE
London

Pharmaceutical chemist

History: Ambrose Godfrey Hanckwitz, born in Germany in 1660, who on emigrating to England dropped his surname, was assistant to Robert Boyle, chemist. Boyle opened a laboratory in Maiden Lane, Covent Garden, London, in 1660 and was the first chemist to produce phosphorus and, with Frobenius, was first to manufacture ether in quantity. Godfrey received recognition for his research work by being elected a Fellow of the Royal Society. In 1680 he established a chemist's business on his own account, in Southampton Street at the sign of the Phoenix, which was later styled 'Godfrey & Cooke, chymists'. The firm's trademark featured a phoenix rising over the inscription 'Godfrey AD 1680'. Godfrey prepared all kinds of medications including cordials, 'Royal English drops', 'Powders of Kent', 'Zell', smelling salts, Glauber's salt and Epsom salts. He could also cater for more unusual requests, such as human skull, essence of ambergris, musk and citron, essence of viper, balsam for apoplexy and red spirit of purgative cochliaria. Various waters were available including honey, lavender, Queen of Hungary, orange flower and arquebusade. His laboratory remained in use after his death in 1741, until the close of the nineteenth century. During that century the business was transferred to Conduit Street, London, and in the early twentieth century to the Royal Arcade, Old Bond Street, London. In 1916 the business, still styled Godfrey & Cooke, was purchased by Savory & Moore Ltd.

R Donald, *From Ancient Alchemy to Modern Pharmacy: Bond Street 150 years ago* (Savory & Moore, n.d.) 20-4

Records 1: The Museum Curator, Royal Pharmaceutical Society of Great Britain, 1 Lambeth High Street, London SE1 7JN

Business order book 1830; formulae book n.d.; notes entitled 'a compleat course of chymistry' c.1730; memorandum of Godfrey family and firm n.d.; correspondence, Ambrose Godfrey to church wardens and overseers of St Pauls, Covent Garden 1740; Ambrose Godfrey, publication re printing a subscription 1744. (Ref: IRA.1997.066, 069, 143)

Records 2: Archives & Manuscripts, Wellcome Library for the History & Understanding of Medicine, 183 Euston Road, London NW1 2BE

Chemical and pharmaceutical formulary, in English and Latin early 18th cent. (Ref: MS 2533)

Records 3: The British Library, Department of Manuscripts, Great Russell Street, London WC1B 3DG

Medicines bill from A Seba 1717; warrant for inventor's patent 1723; papers: referral of invention to Society of Arts 1790, experiments on china bluestones 1731; correspondence: Sir Hans Sloane 1721-34, 1741, Dr J Woodward 1724-25. (Ref: Sloane MSS 4046-53, 4432, 6180, 8078)

ELLIOTT GODFREY (HOLDINGS) LTD
Manor House, Gunnersbury Drive, Ealing, London

Retail chemist

History: Elliott Godfrey (Holdings) Ltd was incorporated as a limited liability company in 1973 by Elliott and Marian Godfrey. By 1976 it owned a chain of 6 retail chemist's outlets in west and south west London, in Shepherd's Bush, Hammersmith; Ealing; Acton, Ealing; Twickenham, Richmond upon Thames; and Chessington, Kingston upon Thames. In 1993, by which time it owned 16 retail chemists businesses, the company was acquired by E Moss Ltd, the retail subsidiary of UniChem plc that became Alliance UniChem plc in 1997. By 1999 the company was dormant, its business and assets having been transferred to E Moss Ltd.

Records: Alliance UniChem plc, UniChem House, Cox Lane, Chessington KT9 1SN

Memorandum and articles of association 1973; certificate of incorporation 1973; acquisition papers 1993; combined register of members, share ledger and minutes 1973–94; issued share certificate book 1973–93.

GOGGS & OSBORNE LTD
High Street, Huntingdon, Cambridgeshire

Chemist

History: In 1932 Goggs & Osborne Ltd was incorporated as a limited liability company, to acquire the retail chemist's business at High Street, Huntingdon, Cambridgeshire. It was removed from the register of companies in 1970.

Records: Cambridgeshire County Record Office (Huntingdon), Grammar School Walk, Huntingdon PE18 6LF

Day books 1857–73 (w); prescription books 1840–1940. (Ref: Acc 1807, 818)

GRAYS PHARMACY
Castlegate Car Park, Berwick-Upon-Tweed, Northumberland

Retail chemist

History: In 1793 Robert Carr established a druggist's business at corner premises comprising 63 High Street and 2 & 4 Western Lane, Berwick-Upon-Tweed, Northumberland. He was succeeded in the business by his son, William Graham Carr, in 1837, who formed a partnership, W G Carr & Sons, with his sons, Robert and N G Carr, who were joined in partnership by another family member, Walter P Carr, in 1876. The firm specialised in the preparation of cod-liver oil emulsion. In 1891 the business was acquired by Nicol Miller Craig, also a dispensing chemist, who traded under the name Nicol Craig until 1919, when he sold his share of the business to his partner, James Rankine Hetherington. Thereafter the business was styled, J R Hetherington. In 1920 Hetherington took George Coghill Gray as an assistant, and sold the business to him in 1948. Gray continued to trade under the name J R Hetherington until 1957, when he formed a partnership with his son, William Gilbert Gray, and the business was renamed George C Gray & Son. In 1997 the firm was still trading as George C Gray &

Son, and remained in family ownership. By 1999 the pharmacy had relocated from 63 High Street, and was trading as Grays Pharmacy at Castlegate Car Park, Berwick-Upon-Tweed.

Records: Berwick-Upon-Tweed Record Office, Council Offices, Wallace Green, Berwick-Upon-Tweed TD15 1ED

Purchase ledgers 1931–54; sales ledger 1927–48; day books 1951–59; cash books 1931–46; stock book 1932–33; receipts and recipe books 1876, 1899, 1940–60s, n.d.; sale of poisons registers 1869–1904, 1919–25; prescription ledgers late 19th cent.–c.1955; leases of premises to Nicol Craig 1891, 1901–03; published reference works and formularies 1895, 1904, 1929–49.

A GREAVES & SON LTD
Sycamore House, Smeckley Wood Close, Chesterfield, Derbyshire

Dispensing chemist

History: Abraham Greaves was registered as a pharmaceutical chemist in 1853. He was in business in Ironville, Derbyshire, until sometime between 1871 and 1875 when he moved to 35 Low Pavement, Chesterfield, Derbyshire, acquiring the business of Josiah Claughton, who had traded there since 1822, and naming the business Greaves & Richardson. William Samuel Greaves was registered as a pharmaceutical chemist in 1864 and operated the Ironville business as Greaves & Sons, chemists and wholesale druggists, until after 1895. Abraham Walter Greaves was registered as a chemist and druggist in 1872 and joined his father, Abraham Greaves, in his business at Chesterfield. His son, Sydney Chater Greaves, joined the family partnership in 1902. The business continued to trade from 35 Low Pavement until 1980, when the shop was demolished and the business re-located to 3 Vicar Lane, Chesterfield. It was incorporated as a limited liability company, A Greaves & Son Ltd, in 1983. In 1997 the company was still trading with registered offices at Sycamore House, Smeckley Wood Close, Chesterfield.

'A Century-Old Chesterfield Business', *Chemist and Druggist*, 124, 23 May 1936, 605

Records 1: Chesterfield Public Library, New Beetwell Street, Chesterfield S40 1QN

Partnership agreement between Abraham Walter Greaves and Sydney Chater Greaves 1902; general meetings papers 1943–44; ledgers: 1905–43, Claughtons wholesale druggists 1849–52; accounts: wages, salaries and insurance books 1912–25, 1933–49, bills 1928–45; miscellaneous business papers 1920s; prescription books, some with press cuttings 1903–52; register of penicillin injections and account of proprietary medicines sold 1934–49; recipe books: c.1876–79, c.1900, veterinary c.1910–40; trade catalogues 1908, c.1938; trade and professional associations circulars 1933–45; correspondence 1918–46; staff Christmas boxes 1918. (Ref: GRE nos. 1-110)

Records 2: Derbyshire Record Office, New Street, Matlock. Enquiries to: County Hall, Matlock DE4 3AG

Prescription book 1867. (Ref: D1729)

Records 3: The Museum Curator, Royal Pharmaceutical Society of Great Britain, 1 Lambeth High Street, London SE1 7JN

Bills and miscellaneous papers 1860s. (Ref: IRA.1996.237)

GRIFFITH GRIFFITHS
Penygraig, Llangwnadl, Gwynedd

Chemist and shopkeeper

History: Griffith Griffiths was in business as a chemist and druggist at Penygraig, Llangwnadl, Gwynedd, prior to 1868. He traded there until 1891, when he retired from the business.

Records: Gwynedd Archives & Museums Service, Caernarfon Area Record Office, Victoria Dock, Caernarfon. Enquiries to County Offices, Shirehall Street, Caernarfon LL55 1SH

Ledger 1856–86; day books 1841–1920; miscellaneous receipts 1917–25. (Ref: XM980)

WILLIAM GRIFFITHS
Bridge Street, Aberaeron, Ceredigion

Chemist and druggist

History: William Griffiths was in business as a chemist and druggist at Bridge Street, Aberaeron, Ceredigion, from before 1868 until 1876.

Records: National Library of Wales, Department of Manuscripts & Records, Aberystwyth SY23 3BU

Accounts 1849–93; journals 1847–58; receipt book 1848; apprenticeship indenture 1844; diaries 1868–78; letters 1846–82. (Ref: Rev William Griffiths papers nos. 15, 114-43, 216-51, 255-86, Olive Mary Jones papers box 2)

W F GULLIVER
Lower Belgrave Street, Westminster, London

Retail pharmacy

History: By 1852 William Gulliver, who registered as a pharmaceutical chemist in 1851, had established a chemist and druggist's business at 33 (re-numbered 6 in 1874) Lower Belgrave Street, Westminster, London. In 1883 he assumed control of the management of Charles Anderson & Son, chemists and druggists of 23 (43 from 1878) Lower Belgrave Street, which had been trading since around 1844. During the late nineteenth century William Gulliver took his son, Walter Frederick, who registered as a pharmaceutical chemist in 1882, into partnership and from 1890, Walter Frederick assumed control of the business. Until 1909 the firm was styled William Gulliver & Son, and thereafter it was renamed Walter Frederick Gulliver. In 1922 the business was acquired by Stanley Vincent Roberts whose son, Hugh Vincent Roberts, assumed management of the pharmacy, still trading as W F Gulliver in 1937, following the death of his father in 1933. The business was sold in 1962, and incorporated as a limited liability company, John Harley Ltd. In 1997 it was trading as Keencare Ltd.

Records 1: City of Westminster Archives Centre, 10 St Ann's Street, London SW12XR

Ledgers: purchase 1837–70, sales 1851–94, 1906–14; sales journals/days books 1891–95, 1906; prescription books: Gulliver 1831–34, 1844–1912, Anderson 1844–93; recipe book 1838–78. (Ref: Acc 1553)

Records 2: Mr H V Roberts, 'Gulliver's', Main Street, Tugby LE7 9WD

Purchase ledger, S V Roberts (Totnes pharmacy) 1909–13; letterbook, W F Gulliver 1899–1904; business correspondence 1937–62; drawings of pharmacy: exterior 1952, interior 1958.

ALBERT HAGON LTD
39 Bridge Street, Cardiff

Chemist and optician

History: In 1880 Albert Hagon was registered as a chemist and druggist at 39 Great Frederick Street, Cardiff, and in 1882 was trading from 39 Bridge Street, Cardiff. In 1904 he re-located to 5 Bute Street, Cardiff, and incorporated the business as a limited liability company, Albert Hagon Ltd, shortly afterwards. In 1934 he ceased to be registered, although the company continued to trade as Albert Hagon Ltd from 5 Bute Street, and from 1938 from 5 Hayes Bridge Road, Cardiff. In 1946 the company was renamed, Albert Hagon (1946) Ltd, and in 1969 was divided into 3 limited liability companies: Hagons (Cardiff) Ltd, 27 Oxford House, The Hayes, Cardiff; Hagons (Fairwater) Ltd, 14 The Green, Fairwater, Cardiff; and Hagons (Gabalfa) Ltd, 284 North Road, Cardiff. In 1972 a further company was incorporated, Hagons (Butetown) Ltd, 59 Loudoun Street, Butetown, Cardiff. In 1974 Hagons (Cardiff) Ltd, Hagons (Gabalfa) Ltd and Hagons (Butetown) Ltd were renamed Maddock's (Cardiff) Ltd, Maddock's (Gabalfa) Ltd and Maddock's (Butetown) Ltd respectively. Hagons (Fairwater) Ltd was renamed D H Maddock & Co Ltd. All 4 companies were dissolved in 1988.

Records: Glamorgan Record Office, The Glamorgan Building, King Edward VII Avenue, Cathays Park, Cardiff CF1 3NE

Minutes: 1919, 1924, with staff salary accounts 1945–47; sales account book 1899; cash sales book 1919–28; general account books: sales and wages 1902–07, goods supplied 1903–40 (w), bank statements 1946–50, general 1885; optical account books: 1948–49, repairs and renewals 1939–47; purchases journal 1952–55; prescription books: lettered sequence 1912–56, Hagon's own prescriptions and patent medicines c.1893, 1904–14, optical 1926–51 (w); pharmaceutical notebook/exercise book n.d.; medical formulary booklets post–1911, 1925; registers: supplies purchased from wholesale drug companies, with loose papers c.1929–40, goods supplied and received c.1936–46, optical treatment, incl. correspondence and accounts with Association of Optical Practitioners 1939–48;

index of quantity of cleanser and restorer sold 1896; labels for medical and pharmaceutical preparations n.d.; promotional literature: booklets advertising business and preparations n.d., billheads n.d.; photograph of shop window display c.1920; botany notebook of L M Murray, Cardiff Technical College, Welsh College of Pharmacy 1925–26. (Ref: D/D Xql 1-45)

HALL FORSTER & CO LTD
4 Pooley Close, Stamfordham Road Industrial Estate, Westerhope, Newcastle upon Tyne

Pharmaceutical products' wholesaler

History: John Hall Forster registered as a pharmacist in 1895 and established a retail business on his own account. He sold the firm in 1903 and purchased a chemists' sundries merchant business. This firm was incorporated as a limited liability company, Hall Forster & Co Ltd, in 1908. The company began manufacturing its own brand toiletries and became a supplier of packed goods. In 1910 its stock range included some 2,500 lines. In 1920 Hall Forster & Co Ltd moved to Temple Street, Newcastle upon Tyne, where it began production of galenicals and proprietary goods. John's son, Norman Forster, joined the company in 1927, after qualifying from the London School of Pharmacy. From 1948, following the introduction of the National Health Service, the company moved towards the wholesale distribution of pharmaceutical products. It also acquired the businesses of W T Coltman, Middlesbrough, Barclay & Son, Darlington and M Baum Ltd, Sunderland. In 1972 the company re-located to a warehouse close to the Newcastle upon Tyne western by-pass. Hall Forster & Co Ltd was acquired in 1994 by UniChem plc, which merged with Alliance Sante SA in 1997 to become Alliance UniChem plc. By 1999 the company was dormant, its business and assets having been transferred to E Moss Ltd.

Records: Alliance UniChem plc, UniChem House, Cox Lane, Chessington KT9 1SN

Memorandum and articles of association 1985; acquisition papers 1993–94; combined register of members and share ledger 1986–94; share certificate books: preference 1986–94, ordinary 1964–94; share certificates: preference 1994, cumulative preference 1994.

HALLAWAY'S
5 Devonshire Street, Carlisle, Cumbria

Chemist

History: John Hallaway was registered as a pharmaceutical chemist in 1859 at 52 Castle Street, Carlisle, Cumbria. He moved to 5 Devonshire Street, Carlisle, in 1892, and in 1901 was joined in the business by Robert Railton Hallaway, who had registered as a pharmaceutical chemist in the same year. John Hallaway retired from the business in 1916, and Robert Hallaway continued to trade until 1926, when he ceased to be registered. In 1935 the business was acquired by A Holmes, who had registered as a chemist and druggist in 1913.

Records: Cumbria Record Office (Carlisle), The Castle, Carlisle CA3 8UR

Ledger 1924–36; prescription books 1858–1921 (w). (Ref: D/MIL/1-17)

ROBERT HARDY (CHEMISTS) LTD
37 Morlich Grove, Dalgety Bay, Fife

Retail chemist

History: Robert Hardy (Chemists) Ltd was incorporated as a limited liability company in 1973, by Raimes, Clark & Co Ltd, wholesale and manufacturing chemists of Smith's Place, Leith, Edinburgh. The business was a retail chemist based at 18 Roseburn Terrace, Edinburgh, from 1973, 48 Almond Green, Edinburgh, from 1980 and 37 Morlich Grove, Dalgety Bay, Fife, from 1981. The company was dissolved in 1990.

Records: The Secretary, National Register of Archives (Scotland), H M General Register House, Princes Street, Edinburgh EH1 3YY

Minutes 1973–76; combined register of members and share ledger 1973; directors' reports, balance sheets and accounts 1963–74. (Ref: NRA(S) 2974)

W G & J A HARRIES LTD
31-33 Bridge Street, Haverfordwest, Pembrokeshire

Dispensing chemist

History: W G & J A Harries Ltd was incorporated as a limited liability company in 1946, to acquire the established chemist, druggist and pharmaceutical proprietary business at 31 Bridge Street, Haverfordwest, Pembrokeshire. It traded from these premises until 1979, when it went into voluntary liquidation. In 1984 it was removed from the register of companies.

Records: Pembrokeshire Record Office, The Castle, Haverfordwest SA61 2EF

Ledgers: customer 1935–46, invoice 1957–76 (w); invoice book 1973; day books 1941–77; customers' accounts 1973–75; prescription books, with stock accounts of methylated spirits c.1870–1960; spirits stock book 1944–59; notebooks: drugs wanted n.d., 20th cent., recipes and formulae 19th cent., c.1935–40, containing price lists for garden products n.d., c.1955–56; NHS record book, supply of spectacles 1948–73. (Ref: HDB/35)

PHILIP HARRIS MEDICAL LTD
Hazelwell Lane, Stirchley, Telford

Pharmaceutical wholesaler

History: This business was established in 1817 at 102 Digbeth, Birmingham, by Thomas Ellis, a surgeon. In 1825 he was joined in partnership by Philip Harris, a chemist, and the firm moved to 1 The Bull Ring, Birmingham. The business remained there until 1830, when, after the acquisition of a second shop at 9 The Bull Ring, it began to manufacture medicines and drugs. In 1866 the firm was renamed, Philip Harris Manufacturing Chemist & Druggist Co, and in 1890 moved from The Bull Ring to Edmund Street, Birmingham. During the twentieth century the range of surgical instruments and drugs supplied by the firm expanded, and in 1963 the business was incorporated as 2 limited liability companies, Philip Harris Ltd, which specialised in sales to educational outlets, and Philip Harris Medical Ltd, which was the pharmaceutical operation. In 1963 Philip Harris Holdings Ltd was incorporated as a limited liability company to represent the interests of both companies, and in 1966, Philip Harris Medical Ltd moved to Hazelwell Lane, Stirchley, Telford. From these premises, it served doctors and chemists nationwide, and grew to become a leading independent pharmaceutical wholesaler. It was still trading in 1997.

Records 1: Philip Harris Medical Ltd, Hazelwell Lane, Stirchley, Birmingham B30 2PS

Directors' report and balance sheet 1928; surgical sales returns 1908–67; drug sales analyses 1908–16; retail sales analyses 1908–21; recipe book 1892; product catalogues: early 20th cent., 1927, 1936–38, 1948–49, 1955, surgical 1912, 1957, medical 1953, 1958, 1968, trade 1954, industrial 1956–69, retail 1963; letter from Philip Harris to London supplier 1847; Harris family bible n.d.

Records 2: Birmingham City Archives, Central Library, Chamberlain Square, Birmingham B3 3HQ

Price list late 19th–early 20th cents; photograph of laboratory late 19th–early 20th cents. (Ref: MS 565)

HARRISON BLAIR & CO LTD
Kearsley and Farnworth, Bolton

Manufacturing chemist

History: Robert Harrison was in business as a chemist and druggist at 97 Market Street, Farnworth, Bolton, prior to 1868. In 1870 James Warburton, a member of the Pharmaceutical Society since 1842, and Thomas Chester Ansdell, Kearsley, Bolton, formed a partnership of manufacturing chemists entitled Harrison Blair & Co, at Farnworth. The firm manufactured alkalis, chloride of lime, soda ash and sulphuric acid. The business was incorporated as a limited liability company, Harrison Blair & Co Ltd, in 1891 and was removed from the register of companies in 1970.

Records: Lancashire Record Office, Bow Lane, Preston PR1 2RE

Partnership agreements between James Warburton and Thomas Chester Ansdell 1870, 1885; agreements with others 1872–76, 1927; notice of sale of chemical works at Kearsley and Farnworth 1838; valuations of land and chemical works 1869–1933; plans of lands, buildings and chemical works 1840s–72, 1912, n.d.; list of employees 1870; Sick & Life Club: minutes 1918–24, rules 1874, amended rules 1921, book of receipts and payments 1918–23, cash receipt book 1924, final pay-out sheet 1924; photograph of employees 1875; James Warburton's certificate of membership of Pharmaceutical Society of Great Britain 1842. (Ref: DDX 669)

HARWOODS CHEMISTS LTD
Watford, Hertfordshire

Proprietary medicine manufacturer

History: Harwoods Laboratories Ltd was incorporated as a limited liability company in 1924 to manufacture proprietary medicines. It was acquired by Beecham Pills Ltd in 1942. After the Second World War it was amalgamated with other Beecham Group Ltd proprietary medicine subsidiaries, including Natural Chemicals Ltd and J C Eno Ltd, and was renamed Harwoods Chemists Ltd.

Records: St Helens Local History & Archives Library, Gamble Institute, Victoria Square, St Helens WA10 1DY

Memorandum and articles of association 1943; register of members 1935–42; register of members and share ledger 1942–53; share certificates books 1925–54. (Ref: BP/4/4)

H HEAPS
38 Bucks Road, Douglas, Isle of Man

Pharmacy

History: This pharmacy business at 38 Bucks Road, Douglas, Isle of Man, was operated by J S Aspell from around 1890. It was later acquired by H Heaps, and ceased trading in 1958.

Records: Manx National Heritage Library, The Manx Museum, Douglas, Isle of Man IM1 3LY

Ledgers: suppliers' accounts 1924–27, customers' accounts 1927–58; prescription books, some incl. formulae 1890–47; letter headed paper n.d. (Ref: 9744/1/1-35, 9744/2-4)

HIGGINS & MADDOCK
Church Street, Calne, Wiltshire

Chemist

History: C G Higgins, chemist, traded from Church Street, Calne, Wiltshire, from at least 1904. In 1923 the business was renamed Higgins & Maddock.

Records: Wiltshire & Swindon Record Office, County Hall, Trowbridge BA14 8JG

Customer ledger 1945–54; prescription books 1904–67. (Ref: 1553/67)

ALFRED HIGGS LTD
42 Richmond Road, Kingston upon Thames, London

Dispensing chemist and surgeon dentist

History: Alfred Higgs was registered as a chemist and druggist in 1878 in Kingston upon Thames, London, and traded from 42 Richmond Road. In 1919 he was joined in business by Stewart Clive Higgs, who had registered as a chemist and druggist in the same year, and whose registered address was 42 Richmond Road, Kingston upon Thames. He traded there, under the business name Alfred Higgs until 1935, when he re-located to 59 Sheen Lane, Mortlake, Richmond upon Thames, London. Thereafter, the business continued to trade as Alfred Higgs until 1939, when it was incorporated as a limited liability company, Alfred Higgs Ltd. The company ceased to trade under its own name in 1955.

Records: The Museum Curator, Royal Pharmaceutical Society of Great Britain, 1 Lambeth High Street, London SE1 7JN

Account books 1872–81; recipe book 1874–1936; list of patent medicines 1892; testimonial from W J Russell 1872. (Ref: IRA.1996.024, 038, 070, 195)

HILL-SMITH (WARRINGTON) LTD
77 Bridge Street, Warrington

Chemist and druggist

History: Thomas Meredith Hales was registered as a chemist and druggist in 1869, and traded from 77 Bridge Street, Warrington, until 1897. In 1898 his business was acquired by Frederick William Knowles, a Liverpool chemist and druggist registered in 1889, who traded there until around 1902. Thereafter the business was owned by Harold Miller, until around 1905, when Harold Smith acquired the business. In 1928 Smith entered into partnership with Hill's

Chemists Ltd, a local firm, and the business was incorporated as a limited liability company, Hill-Smith Ltd. In 1976 the company, renamed Hill-Smith (Warrington) Ltd, was acquired by AAH Holdings plc which became part of GEHE AG in 1995.

Records 1: GEHE UK plc, Retail Branch, Atherstone, Warwickshire. Enquiries to GEHE UK plc, Sapphire Court, Walsgrave Triangle Business Park, Coventry CV2 2TX

General meetings minutes 1946–96; combined register of members, directors and share ledger 1921–88; annual returns 1947–50; seal register 1972–88. (Ref: Box S10, S18)

Records 2: Warrington Library, Museum Street, Warrington WA1 1JB

Day books 1906–08, 1923–24; bank passbooks 1913–23; correspondence, receipts and advertising material 1926–28. (Ref: MSS 2271-4)

HILLS PHARMACEUTICALS LTD
Colne, Lancashire

Pharmaceutical wholesaler

History: In 1903 Albert Edward Hartlet and his brother Tom Hartlet established a chemist and druggist's business in Colne, Lancashire. During the 1920s branches of the business were established in Harrogate, North Yorkshire, and Sheffield, and in 1939 a further 8 pharmacies were acquired in London. By 1948 the company owned 32 pharmacies, and in 1954 established a pharmaceutical distribution company to supply these many retail outlets. The wholesale company was initially incorporated as Hills Balsam Ltd, and was later renamed Hills Pharmaceuticals Ltd. The first wholesale depot was opened at Warrington in 1965, and the retail business was scaled down. In 1972 Hills Pharmaceuticals Ltd was acquired by Crowe, Wilson & Co Ltd, Dublin, Ireland, which was renamed Fitzwilton Ltd as a result of a merger with Goulding Ltd. In 1974 Hills Pharmaceuticals Ltd acquired Henry Sykes Ltd, Huddersfield, Kirklees, and in 1976 was itself acquired by AAH Holdings plc, and became a constituent part of AAH Pharmaceuticals Ltd which was absorbed by GEHE AG in 1995.

Records: GEHE UK plc, Retail Branch, Atherstone, Warwickshire. Enquiries to GEHE UK plc, Sapphire Court, Walsgrave Triangle Business Park, Coventry CV2 2TX

General meetings minutes 1954-96; memorandum and articles of association 1954; combined register of members, directors and share ledger 1964-88; seal register 1973-88; loan agreement 1976. (Ref: S10, S18, current minutes, box 7)

EDWARD HINDLE LTD
218 & 763 Hessle Road, Kingston upon Hull

Dispensing and photographic chemist

History: Edward Hindle Ltd, dispensing and photographic chemists, was incorporated as a limited liability company in 1947. Its board of directors comprised Edward, James Edward, and Mary Hindle. Following the death of Edward in 1948, James Edward Hindle succeeded him as chairman. The company was acquired in 1993 by E Moss Ltd, the retail subsidiary of UniChem plc. The latter merged with Alliance Sante SA in 1997 to become Alliance UniChem plc. By 1999 Edward Hindle Ltd was dormant, its business and assets having been transferred to E Moss Ltd.

Records: Alliance UniChem plc, UniChem House, Cox Lane, Chessington KT9 1SN

Directors' and general meetings minutes 1948-65, 1979 to date; certification notice of incorporation (1947) 1993; combined register of members and share ledger 1948-93; share certificate books 1948-93.

HENRY HODDER & CO LTD
47-48 High Street, Bristol

Chemist

History: In 1846 Henry Hodder established himself in business in St Michael's Hill, Bristol. He moved to Broad Street, Bristol, in 1853, where he remained for 50 years. During this time Hodder pioneered the 'cash chemist' idea and was, apparently, the first chemist in the country to sell patent medicines at reduced prices. The business was incorporated as a limited liability company, Henry Hodder & Co Ltd, in 1887, the first of its branches opening in 1896 in East Street, Bedminster, City of Bristol. The Broad Street business moved to 11-12 Wine Street, Bristol, in 1903, and in 1937 to 47-48 High Street, Bristol. By this time, the company had 30 branches operating from Bristol, whilst Hodges (Chemists) Ltd, which had been acquired in 1927, controlled 27 branches in the

Birmingham area. In 1968 Henry Hodder & Co Ltd was acquired by Westons, The Chemists.

Records: Bristol Record Office, 'B' Bond Warehouse, Smeaton Road, Bristol BS1 6XN

Minutes: directors' meetings 1887–1929, general meetings 1887–1929; memorandum and articles of association 1887; resolutions 1887–1902; register of directors' 1901–1941; audited accounts 1887–1932; wages book 1891–1910; company history 1946. (Ref: Acc No.35850)

HOECHST MARION ROUSSEL LTD
Broadwater Park, Denham, Buckinghamshire

Research, development, manufacture and distribution of pharmaceutical products

History: In 1952 Fabwerke Hoechst AG was incorporated as a limited liability company in Frankfurt, Germany. Its origins were in a partnership of 1863, between 4 men, Lucius, Bruning, Meister and Muller. This firm was based on the outskirts of Hoechst, Germany, and manufactured dyestuffs. The business was incorporated as a limited liability company, Fabwerke vorm Meister Lucius & Bruning AG, in 1880, after which it began to manufacture pharmaceuticals. In 1883 the company produced the world's first safe analgesic and marketed it as *Antipyrin*. *Adrenalin* was synthesised in 1906, and the company was the first in Europe to produce insulin in 1923. In 1925 it became one of the component companies of IG Farbenindustrie AG, a huge cartel, which, after the Second World War, was charged with war crimes and collaboration with the Nazi regime in Germany. As a result, IG Farbenindustrie AG was broken down into 12 companies by the Allies in 1952, to reduce its monopoly status. Fabwerke Hoechst AG was one of these companies, and was allowed to re-occupy its Frankfurt works. In 1947 Hoechst UK Ltd was incorporated as a UK subsidiary at Hounslow, London, to distribute the products of its German parent. In 1920 in Romainville, France, Dr Gaston Roussel established the Institut de Serotherapie Hemopoietique, to conduct research into chemotherapy. In 1961 this business was incorporated as a limited liability company, Roussel Uclaf SA, and in 1968 Fabwerke Hoechst AG, which was renamed Hoechst AG in 1974, purchased 43 per cent of its shares, a figure which had risen to 54.5 per cent by 1988, and to over 99 per cent by 1997. In 1938 a subsidiary company, Roussel Laboratories Ltd, was incorporated at 1-2 Finsbury Square, London, to market and distribute the products of the Institut de Serotherapie Hemopoietique. During the 1940s and 1950s, the majority of these products were steroids and hormones. Following brief relocations to Ealing Common and Great Portland Street, Roussel Laboratories Ltd moved to new premises at Harrow Road, London, in 1951, where it began its own manufacturing programme, producing steroids and antibiotics. In 1952 Roussel Laboratories Ltd incorporated a subsidiary company, Pharmidex Ltd, to act as an investment company, and in 1956 a second subsidiary, Uclaf Ltd, was incorporated, to manufacture and deal in pharmaceutical products, and to acquire patents and copyrights. In 1962 Roussel Laboratories Ltd re-located again, to Columbus House (later Roussel House), Wembley Park, Brent, London, and in 1963 opened a packaging warehouse in Acton, Ealing, London. A further subsidiary company, Roussel Uclaf Ltd, was incorporated in 1965 to undertake management business, analytical and research work. Pharmatec Ltd was incorporated in 1970, with a similar remit, and was renamed Cassenne Ltd in 1981, but has not traded since its incorporation. In 1971 a major manufacturing plant was opened at Kingfisher Drive, Swindon, and the Harrow Road premises were closed. During the 1970s further plants were opened at Park Royal and Queen's Drive, Ealing, London, and a number of drugs were successfully launched, including *Rythmodan*, a controller of cardiac arrythmias and *Molipaxin*, an antidepressant. In 1977 Roussel Laboratories Ltd acquired Universal Nets Ltd, a company which had been incorporated in 1959 as Elastic Nets Ltd, and was renamed Roussel Medical Ltd in 1978. This company engaged primarily in the packaging, storage and distribution of pharmaceutical and hospital supplies. In 1984 Roussel Laboratories Ltd, established new headquarters at Broadwater Park, Denham, Buckinghamshire, and in 1989 the company incorporated Roussel Scientific Institute (UK) Ltd, to conduct research and development into ethical pharmaceuticals. In June 1994 Hoechst Roussel Ltd was incorporated as a limited liability company to operate the pharmaceutical businesses of Hoechst UK Ltd and Roussel Laboratories Ltd. In 1995 Hoechst AG acquired Marion Merrell Dow Inc, an American manufacturer of pharmaceutical, hospital and laboratory products, which was formed in 1989 by the merger of 2 companies, Marion Laboratories Inc and Merrell Dow Pharmaceuticals Inc. The latter was a subsidiary of the Dow Chemical Co Inc, with origins in a retail drugstore opened by William S Merrell in Cincinnati, USA, in 1828. In 1958 Merrell-National (Laboratories) Ltd was incorporated as a UK subsidiary of Merrell Dow Pharmaceuticals Inc, and was renamed Richardson-Merrell Ltd in 1968. In 1980 it was renamed Merrell Pharmaceuticals Ltd, and in 1983 Merrell Dow Pharmaceuticals Ltd. Its name changed again in 1992 to Marion Merrell Dow Ltd and in 1995 to Marion Merrell Ltd. After the acquisition of Marion Merrell Dow Inc by Hoechst AG in 1995, Hoechst Roussel Ltd was renamed Hoechst Marion Roussel Ltd, although its headquarters remained at Denham. In 1996 a subsidiary of this new company, HMR Investments Ltd, was incorporated, to acquire and protect patents, licences and property.

'Fifty Years of Patient Care: The story of Roussel in the UK 1938–88', in 8 parts, *Caroussel*, March 1988–Jan 1990; 'Hoechst' and 'Roussel Uclaf', in T Derdak (ed), *International Directory of Company Histories*, Vol. 1 (St James Press, London, 1988); *Hoechst Marion Roussel: Let's make it happen* (Hoechst, Frankfurt, 1995); K Holland, 'Roussel Laboratories Ltd', *Pharmaceutical Journal*, 10 June 1989; *In Every Walk of Life* (Hoechst, Frankfurt, 1988); *Introducing Roussel, London* (Roussel, London, 1968); T R Irwin, 'Marion Merrell Dow – historical perspective of a 'merging' company', *Pharmaceutical Historian*, 24, 2, 1994, 7-12; D Whitehead, *The Dow Story: The history of the Dow Chemical Company* (McGraw Hill, New York, 1968)

Records 1: Hoechst Marion Roussel Ltd, Broadwater Park, Denham, Uxbridge UB9 5HP

Directors' meetings minutes with correspondence 1994–96; memorandum and articles of association 1994; change of name certificate 1996; directors' letters of resignation 1994–96; notifications to registrar of companies 1995–97; register of members, directors and share ledger 1994–97; annual report and accounts 1994–95; staff magazines: *Hoechst Marion Roussel Matters* 1995, *Hoechst Marion Roussel Internet* 1996 to date, *Team Listening* 1996 to date.

Cassenne Ltd: memorandum and articles of association 1970; certificate of incorporation 1970; change of name certificate 1981; notifications to registrar of companies 1970–96; combined register of members, directors, share ledger and minutes 1970–95; share certificates 1970–73, 1980, 1991; declaration of trust with W J More 1970; annual reports and accounts 1986–95.

HMR Investments Ltd: memorandum and articles of association 1996; certificate of incorporation 1996; notifications to registrar of companies 1996–97; register of members, directors and share ledger 1996–97; share transfers 1997.

Hoechst UK Ltd: memoranda and articles of association: 1947, 1968, Hoechst Products (Nigeria) Ltd 1964; directors' meeting agenda 1991; photographs of Hounslow site 1994.

Marion Merrell Ltd: directors' meetings minutes 1981–96; memoranda and articles of association 1980, 1988; certificates of registration 1953, 1957; certificate of incorporation 1958; change of name certificates 1980–83, 1992, 1995; notifications to registrar of companies 1989–96; register of members, directors and share ledger 1981–97; accounts 1995; architectural drawings of Oakdene Farm premises 1986–87; historical notes 1991, n.d.

Medical Alginates Ltd: directors' meetings minutes 1969–78; memorandum and articles of association 1948.

Pharmidex Ltd: directors' meetings minutes 1960–95; memorandum and articles of association 1952; certificate of incorporation 1952; notifications to registrar of companies 1959–96; register of members, directors and share ledger 1960–94; issued share certificates 1952, 1960s–91; annual reports and accounts 1979, 1986–95; nominal ledger 1960–67; cash book 1960–79.

Roussel Laboratories Ltd: directors' meetings minutes 1941–96; memorandum and articles of association 1938; certificate of incorporation 1938; directors' letters of resignation 1986, 1990–94; registers of seals 1959–94; schedule of regulations n.d.; notifications to registrar of companies 1978–97; company profiles 1989; charts of board of directors and responsibilities 1981–82; registers of members, directors and share ledgers 1938–94; ordinary resolutions re share capital 1958–73; share transfer documents 1940–50, 1962, 1985; fully paid share certificates 1958–94; cancelled share certificates 1938–80s; correspondence re shares 1940–41, 1962–85; annual reports and accounts 1976–95; financial statement 1994; product catalogues 1953, 1963, 1978, 1985; promotional booklets 1960s, 1980s; press cuttings files 1988–94; press releases and statements files 1990s; priced inventory of machinery, fixtures and fittings at Wembley Park 1965; trade effluent consent papers 1997; fire certificate with architectural drawings 1992; company magazines: *Channel* 1956–60, *Contact* 1963–65, *Review* 1971–78; programme re opening ceremony of distribution and computer centre 1977; staff reports 1975–91; staff handbook 1970s; safety booklet 1985; staff magazines: *Pensions Reports* 1988–89, *Carousel* 1982–92, *Spectrum* 1968–75, *New Spectrum* 1979–82, *The Grapevine* 1983–86; photographs: senior management 1950s, 1970s, 1995, n.d., employees 1990s, n.d., premises 1951, c.1970s, 1990–96, n.d., exhibitions, presentations, visits and conferences 1946–54, n.d., 50th anniversary 1988, artwork for *Caroussel* and *Grapevine* n.d., sports and social events n.d.

Roussel Medical Ltd: general meetings minutes 1959–95; memorandum and articles of association 1959, 1977; certificate of incorporation 1959; change of name certificates 1966, 1978; notifications to registrar of companies 1977–96; register of members, directors and share ledger 1959–91; share certificates 1959–77, 1991; trust deed with G E Powderham 1977; deed of indemnity 1977; agreement with shareholders 1977; retention agreement 1977; annual reports and accounts 1979, 1986–95; bank books 1976–77, n.d.

Roussel Scientific Institute (UK) Ltd: general meetings minutes 1989–95; memorandum and articles of association 1988; change of name certificate 1989; directors' letters of resignation 1988–89; notifications to registrar of companies 1989–96; register of members, directors and share ledger 1988–94; share certificates 1989, 1991; annual reports and accounts 1989–95.

Roussel Uclaf Ltd: memorandum and articles of association 1965; annual reports and accounts 1979, 1986–90.

Roussel Uclaf SA: certificates of incorporation of overseas subsidiaries 1953–81; annual reports 1982–92 (w); photographs, premises and personnel c.1940s, 1990s, n.d.

Uclaf Ltd: directors' meetings minutes 1956–95; memorandum and articles of association 1956; notifications to registrar of companies 1959–96 (w); share certificates 1956–69, 1980–81; register of seals 1964–75; annual reports and accounts 1979, 1986–95; nominal ledger 1969–76.

Upsil Ltd: memorandum and articles of association 1959; paid-up share account book 1969–72.

Records 2: History of Advertising Trust, HAT House, 12 Raveningham Centre, Raveningham NR14 6NU

Hoechst Pharmaceuticals, papers, memoranda and advertising campaign material 1965–67. (Ref: JWT 149 (1965) 315 (1966) 407 (1967))

HOLLOWAYS PILLS LTD
Clipstone Road, London

Patent medicine manufacturer

History: In 1816 Thomas Holloway (1800–83) established a baker's and grocery shop, in partnership with his mother and brother, Henry, at Plymouth Dock (later Devonport), Plymouth. In 1828 this partnership was dissolved, and Thomas Holloway moved to London. By 1836 he was trading as a merchant and foreign agent, from 13 Broad Street Buildings, and in 1837 produced his first medicinal remedy, which he named 'Holloway's Universal Family Ointment'. By 1839 he was in business on his own account, as a patent medicine vendor, at 244 Strand, London, and began advertising his products, in particular his digestive pills, vigorously. In 1867 his business re-located to 533 (later 78) New Oxford Street, London, where it employed over 100 staff. Thomas Holloway was a generous benefactor. In 1879 he sponsored the building of Holloway College for the Higher Education of Women at Mount Lea, Egham, Surrey, which was opened, after his death, in 1886. He also sponsored the building of an asylum for the insane, the Holloway Sanatorium, at St Ann's-Hill, near Virginia Water, Surrey, which was opened in 1885. In 1884 the business was trading from 78 New Oxford Street, controlled by Henry Driver, Holloway's brother-in-law, and George Martin, under the name Thomas Holloway Patent Medicine Dealer. In 1929 the business was incorporated as a limited liability company, Holloways Pills Ltd, and in 1931 was acquired by Beecham Pills Ltd, which then acquired the rights to the licences for 'Holloways Pills' and 'Holloways Ointments'. 'Holloways Pills' were manufactured at the former factory of Holloways Pills Ltd at Clipstone Road, London, and 'Holloways Ointment' was made by Veno Drug Co Ltd at the same premises.

C Bingham, *The History of Royal Holloway College, 1886–1986* (Constable, London, 1987); T A B Corley, 'Thomas Holloway', forthcoming in *New Dictionary of National Biography* (Oxford University Press, Oxford); J Elliott, *Palaces, Patronage and Pills: Thomas Holloway, his sanatorium, college and picture gallery* (Royal Holloway, 1996); A Harrison-Barbet, *Thomas Holloway. Victorian philanthropist: A biographical essay* (Gorran, St Austell, 1990); 'The Late Mr T Holloway', *Illustrated London News*, 5 Jan 1884; F C Tring, 'Thomas Holloway and his Patent Pills', *Pharmaceutical Historian*, 7, 3, 1977, 6-7

Records 1: SmithKline Beecham plc, SmithKline Beecham House, Great West Road, Brentford TW8 9BD. Enquiries to SmithKline Beecham plc, 1 New Horizons Court, Great West Road, Brentford TW8 9EP

Power of attorney to agents for trade mark acquisitions 1901; renewals of trade marks 1890, 1935; copyright assignment re 'Health for all by Holloway's Pills' 1872; advertising leaflet 1897; press cutting re Holloway Sanatorium for mental disease 1874; paper re office staff practices 1852; correspondence with J S Driver Holloway 1953.

Records 2: The Archives, Royal Holloway, University of London, Egham TW20 0EX

Advertisements for Holloway's pills and ointments 1882–n.d.; press cuttings re Holloway's pills and ointments 1863–1968; letterbook 1874–77; correspondence with William Crossland, David Chadwick, Henry Fawcett and W Greenwell 1874–83; Royal Holloway College: rules and regulations laid down by Thomas

Holloway in deed of foundation 1883, address by Thomas Holloway on origins of college 1886, press cuttings 1886–87, golden jubilee brochure 1937, booklet containing photographs and biographical extracts of Thomas Holloway c.1968; eulogy of Thomas Holloway c.1883; photograph of statue of Thomas and Jane Holloway c.1890; historical notes and articles 1933, 1961–65. (Ref: GB 102/1, 130/1, 131/1-11; AS 903/1; RF100, 101/1-3, 110/2; PH118/1, 126/1-2, 131/7)

Records 3: Surrey History Centre, 130 Goldsworth Road, Woking GU21 1ND

Thomas Holloway, personal papers: stocks and shares ledger 1876–81, building purchase ledger, sanatorium 1881–84, diaries c.1848, 1853, letterbooks 1869–92, miscellaneous papers and correspondence late 19th cent.; Holloway Sanatorium: financial records 1885–1950, building plans n.d., sale particulars following closure of hospital 1984, medical and clerks office diaries 1927–48, registers of patients 1885–99, hospital records 1885–1980, general administrative records 1853–1965. (Ref: 2620, 2620/9/1-6, 3040, 3237NL, 3289NL, 3463NL, 3473)

Records 4: Coutts & Co, 440 Strand, London WC2R 0QS

Accounts: Thomas Holloway 1845, business 1884.

Records 5: History of Advertising Trust, HAT House, 12 Raveningham Centre, Raveningham NR14 6NU

Advertising material re Holloway's pills and ointments late 19th–early 20th cents. (Ref: AA1/2/12r)

HOWARDS & SONS LTD
Ilford, Redbridge, London

Pharmaceutical and chemical manufacturer

History: Luke Howard was apprenticed to Ollive Sims, a chemist and druggist in Stockport, in 1788. He worked with a drugs wholesaler in Bishopsgate, City of London, and started his own business at 29 Fleet Street, near Temple Bar. In 1797 William Allen, whose druggist's business at Old Plough Court Pharmacy, Lombard Street, City of London, eventually became Allen & Hanburys Ltd, took him into partnership and the business was named Allen & Howard. Allen managed the pharmacy at Plough Court, whilst Howard took charge of new manufacturing facilities located at Plaistow, Newham, London, which were re-located to Stratford, Newham, London, in 1805. Allen and Howard dissolved the partnership in 1807. Howard became sole proprietor of the Stratford factory, continuing in business as Luke Howard & Co, and Allen concentrated on his Plough Court pharmacy. In 1813 Howard took Joseph Jewell and another chemist, John Gibson, into partnership and the firm was renamed Howard, Jewell & Gibson. Robert Howard, Luke's elder son, joined the firm in 1816 as an apprentice and in 1824 as a partner. Luke Howard took charge of the firm's finances, whilst Jewell supervised and managed the growing factory until 1831, when both men retired from the business. In the same year Luke's younger son, John Eliot Howard, joined his brother Robert and one of Gibson's sons in a partnership which was styled Howard, Jewell, Gibson & Howard. The partnership was re-styled Howard, Gibson & Co between 1832 and 1841 and then Howards & Kent until 1856, when it was renamed Howards & Sons. Robert Howard's son, David, became senior partner on his father's death in 1871, and later distinguished himself by becoming founder and president of both the Institute of Chemistry and the Society of Chemical Industry. In 1888 the firm acquired the business of Hopkin & Williams (established 1850), manufacturers of fine, laboratory and photographic chemicals with offices and warehouses in Cross Street and Wandsworth, London. Howards & Sons remained at Stratford until 1898, when land at Uphall Farm, Ilford, Redbridge, London, was purchased and new premises built. The transfer of the manufacturing activities of Hopkin & Williams and of Howard & Sons began immediately and was completed by 1923. Howards & Sons was renowned as a manufacturer of fine chemicals. Quinine, an alkaloid of cinchona bark (Peruvian or Jesuits' bark), was first manufactured in 1823 following its discovery in France in 1820, and it became the firm's most profitable product in the nineteenth century. The firm also manufactured borax, ether, cocaine, citric, tartaric and benzoic acids, iodides, bromides, menthol, thymol, lactates and bicarbonate of soda. In 1903 Howards & Sons was incorporated as a limited liability company, Howards & Sons Ltd, and between 1906 and 1909 established a subsidiary, the British Camphor Co Ltd, based at Ilford, to synthesise camphor from turpentine using Behal's process. In 1914 Thorium Ltd was incorporated by Howards & Sons Ltd to process thorium, a substance under development by Hopkin & Williams, and in 1915 another subsidiary, Hopkin & Williams (Travancore) Ltd, was established to mine monazite, a raw material necessary for the production processes of Thorium Ltd. From 1916 Howards & Sons Ltd was recognised as a successful manufacturer of *Aspirin*. James Anthony & Co Ltd was incorporated as a subsidiary of Howards & Sons Ltd in 1926 to administer a Sadarehe plantation on Java in the Dutch West Indies, which its parent had purchased in order to secure supplies of cinchona bark for quinine production. This venture was successful until 1943, when the plantation was seized by the Japanese. The company had earlier acquired a concession in a company called Agatash Estates Ltd which ran a lime plantation at Agatash, Guyana. Howards & Sons Ltd's interest in this was in supplying its citric acid production, but the venture was a short-lived failure. After the First World War it became clear that the company was no longer a market leader in pharmaceutical chemicals and in 1919 a research laboratory was established to explore new fields. Thereafter, the company became a large-scale producer of solvents, organic intermediates and plasticisers and was the first UK company to manufacture the wetting agent lauryl alcohol (dodecanol). In 1953 Howards & Sons Ltd was reconstituted as a holding company and Howards of Ilford Ltd was incorporated as an operating subsidiary that conducted all manufacturing affairs. In 1961 the business was acquired by Laporte Industries Ltd, continuing to operate under its own name until 1975 when Howards of Ilford Ltd was renamed Bilstar Ltd. Thereafter, its chemical manufacturing concerns ceased.

Howards, 1797–1947 (Howards & Sons, London, 1947); D F S Scott, *Luke Howard (1772–1864): His correspondence with Goethe and his continental journey of 1816* (William Sessions, York, 1976); A W Slater, 'Howards, Chemical Manufacturers 1797–1837: A study in business history' (MSc thesis, London University, 1956)

Records 1: London Metropolitan Archives, 40 Northampton Road, London EC1R 0HB

Articles of partnership, related agreements and papers 1798–1901; memoranda and articles of association, with notices of resolutions 1903, 1919, [1949]; certificate of incorporation 1903; papers re formation, and later re-construction, of company 1903, 1919–20; directors' meetings memorandum books 1874–1905 (w); share certificate books: combined 1949–58, ordinary 1903–40, 1958–61, preference 1903–34, 1958–61, debentures 1958–61; assignment of share forms with correspondence 1903–19; share transfer correspondence 1909–14; debenture stockholders: register of trustees 1903, address register n.d., correspondence and receipts 1903–10, stock certificates with correspondence 1903–18, 1920, trustees' papers 1918–19, draft resolution approving company re-construction 1919, schedule of trust deeds 1873–1911, n.d., trust deed 1920; balance sheets, trading and profit and loss accounts 1877–1915, 1927–40 (w); statement of total income 1923–24; ledgers: private 1795–1884 (w), Luke Howard 1814–51, Robert Howard 1824–74; private ledger trial balance 1833; private account book 1825–27; cash book 1804–06; bank passbook 1835–37; bank statements 1938–41; cheques paid 1810–61, 1941–42; cheque counterfoils 1805–38, 1937–42; manufacturing account books: expenditure and income, sales of chemicals 1801–02, expenditure and income, chemical stock 1801–03, labour and transport costs 1804–06; bad debtors register 1807–48; laboratory accounts 1855, 1872–1900, 1911–30; balance sheets: foreign account 1920–34, British companies 1923-28, home journal 1932-35, foreign currency exchange rate and duty ledger 1923-26; foreign business bills book 1934-45; credit standing book 1868-c.1890; miscellaneous invoices and papers 1814-37; taxation papers and related correspondence 1811-17, 1842-56, 1899, 1910-41; deed re Joseph Jewell's calomel processing invention 1807; papers re camphor manufacture 1880s; laboratory notebooks 1800-16, 1848-51; mercurial preparations ledger 1797-1801; laboratory account book for quinine preparations 1909-56; quinine accounts 1926-34; index of chemicals n.d.; register of bark purchases 1859-75; register of [?bark] shipments 1871-78; notebook listing Java bark shipments 1898-1917; memorandum of agreement with Borax Consolidated Ltd re raw materials supply 1928; summary of diacetone alcohol quota arrangement with British Industrial Solvents Ltd and Technical Products Ltd 1942; agreement between [Dutch] quina bark producers and quinine manufacturers re supply and analysis of bark c.1918; Dutch cinchona contract 1938-39; trade agreements and correspondence re quinine 1890s-1940s; insurance policies re transport of bark c.1858, 1917; notebook re bark worked in quinine manufacture 1835-47; weekly details of quinine extractions 1913-22; catalogue of cinchona bark collection 20th cent.; stock ledger 1797-1801; stock books 1819-34, 1877-1946; register of stock purchased 1846-51; analyses of stock purchased 1934-43; sales journal 1848-53; monthly sales of chemicals analysis books 1889-94, 1913-18; tablet sales ledger 1924-27; chemicals costings book c.1867-93; office samples analysis record book 1921-47; samples analysis book 1937; letterbook and correspondence re bark supplies 1913-14, 1931-39; correspondence: patent for manufacturing sulphate of quinine 1858, cinchona 1868-85, c.1896, 1921, India Office re analysis of bark from government's Indian plantations 1881, synthetic quinine manufacture 1880s, quinine general 1945-48; price lists: 1873-82, 1907, quinine 1893-1908; product advertising c.1932-47; booklets re malaria 1930s-40s; press cuttings: quinine manufacture and trade late 19th-early 20th cents, scrapbook 1898-c.1921; property papers, with some plans: Plaistow 1796-1803, Stratford 1797-1914, n.d., Ilford 1876-1939; wages and salaries notebook 1922-46; papers re wages c.1914-23; City Mills Sick Club: rules 1900, annual financial statements 1880-1913 (w), papers re winding-up 1912; staff notices re sickness benefit 1919, 1935; Howards Pension Fund, trust deeds 1921, 1948; list of pensioners c.1919; pensions book 1944-46; notice re life pensions n.d.; miscellaneous papers re staff and works 19th-20th cents; *Uphall Works Magazine* 1930; Bureau Central: minutes 1951-52, papers and correspondence 1939-40, 1951-53; correspondence: customers' orders 1804-38, business 1805-64, John Eliot Hodgkin, Borax Works, Liverpool 1859-73, Maclaine, Watson & Co 1946-50, Etablissements Jaques Roques 1946-49, Francis Peek & Co 1946-50, Société du Traitement des Quinquinas 1946-50, James Anthony & Co 1946-52, Anglo Dutch, British Java & Francis Peek 1950-52, Comité Permanent de Propagande 1951-52; letterbooks 1804-49, 1937-40; exhibitions, papers and correspondence 1853–85; John Eliot final concord c.1744; Robert Howard, papers incl. apprenticeship indenture 1753 and letter describing fire at Plough Court 1805; Luke Howard papers: apprenticeship indenture 1788, household accounts book 1810–49, Quaker papers 1840s; Samuel Lloyd Howard, correspondence and papers re Public Health Bill 1855; Eliot Howard, papers incl. his commission as Deputy Lieutenant of Essex 1896; John Eliot Howard, letter from Duke of Argyll 1868; David Howard, papers incl. photograph issued by company on his death 1916; family papers 19th–20th cents; John Williams obituary 1948; Joseph Jewell, papers incl. amended autobiography 1957 and will 1812; correspondence of John Gibson's executors 1844; G E Howard's collection, incl. photographs and articles late 19th–20th cents; photographs and drawings of members of Howard family, staff, group meetings (quinine conventions), premises and works 19th–20th cents; papers and publications re chemical topics 20th cent.; scholarly papers and extracts from publications re quinine production and uses 19th–20th cents; company histories, incl. published articles and books 1897–1947, 1982; papers re local history 19th–20th cents; biographical accounts: Joseph Jewell n.d., Luke Howard 1865, 1894, n.d.; papers re Howard family n.d.

Agatash Estates Ltd: share certificate 1913; debenture 1917.

James Anthony & Co Ltd: memorandum and articles of association 1926; certificate of incorporation 1926.

Hopkin & Williams Ltd: annual balance sheets and trading and profit and loss accounts 1913–34 (w); summary table of annual figure 1921–29; sales and purchase agreement 1903; company assets valuation 1928; excess profits duty schedules and statements 1915–18; indemnity policy re arsenic contamination of phosphate of soda 1901; solicitors' correspondence and papers 1903–08. (Ref: Acc. 1037, Acc. 1420, Acc. 3808)

Records 2: Redbridge Central Library, Local History Room, Clements Road, Ilford, EG1 1EA

Meeting minutes: directors' 1888–1954, general 1903–55, pension board 1920–57, management committee 1949–53; management consultants' reports 1946–49; combined register of members and share ledger 1903–35; annual returns 1941–48; lists of general meetings attendees 1943, 1956; list of preference and ordinary dividends 1920–49; share and share transfer certificates 1935–49; sale and purchase agreement, Howard and Sons to Howards & Sons Ltd 1903; trust deeds with Prudential Assurance Co Ltd 1952–53; balance sheets, trading and profit and loss accounts 1901–57; statement showing increase in assets 1938–44;

taxation schedules and correspondence 1917–42; rating assessment 1944–46; ledgers: private 1884–1953, nominal 1924–46, 1955, town c.1924–46, country c.1924–42, foreign c.1920–44; journals 1903–58; cash books: payments 1947–71, receipts 1945–71; petty cash book 1954–59; petty cash disbursements 1950–51, 1966–71; overseas bills n.d.; sales records 1897–1923; sales analysis by product 1914–16; sales of products 1929–48; sales register by purchases 1940–44; invoice register 1948–50; chemical products purchases contracts 1941–45; sundries purchases c.1925–61; purchases register, by supplier c.1952–57; stock books 1947–59; quinine manufacture: 'Q' (quinine book) 1861–1908, production figures 1855–60, sales 1936–52, bark book 1927–57, quinine dermatitis, record of cases 1926–63; 'LA' books (laboratory analysis, sales and stock) 1931–56; laboratory calculation, quantities and production costs 1857–1955; wages allocation to production of chemicals 1856–86; Old Swan Works income, expenditure and production 1860–70; 'Y' (yield books): staff, products and yields 1921–50, fuel and power costs 1927–36, research laboratory bonus scheme 1941–45, 1952, yields and costing analysis by product c.1917–46, yield presents, re named staff and products 1920–43; chemical sample register 1939; advertising c.1935–61; analysis of land and buildings 1898–1945; plans, mainly of Ilford factory 1950, n.d.; correspondence and papers re plant 1938; papers re shop repairs and maintenance 1949–50; reports and correspondence re construction works 1953–54; staff record sheets 1947–49; register of hours worked 1949; alphabetical list of pay, holidays and other staff-related issues n.d.; salaries: sheets, monthly and year-end 1877–1961 (w), PAYE 1951–53, analysis 1951–54; company pension and life assurance schemes 1930s–60s; accidents record 1948–60; correspondence with Greater London Council 1965–72; private correspondence 1898–1909, 1923–52; photographs of company sports day, exhibitions, construction works at Ilford, miscellaneous c.1926, n.d.; staff magazine, *Pestle and Mortar* 1938; company histories 1847–1947, 1963; treatise by Bernard F Howard n.d.; C F Howard, executors' papers and correspondence 1947–48.

Hopkin & Williams Ltd: balance sheets and trading and profit and loss accounts 1889–1912 (w). (Ref: Howards of Ilford)

Howards of Ilford Ltd: memorandum and articles of association 1953; papers re income tax, expenses, reserves and fees 1953–66; sales analyses 1959–69; register of callers 1968; payroll sheets 1965–74; salaries, monthly tables 1962–64; wage registers 1954–58, 1968–69; papers re wages 1957–70s; manual, budgetary control and standard costs 1955; internal telephone directory 1964.

Records 3: Laporte plc, 3 Bedford Square, London WC1B 3RA

Directors' and general meetings minutes 1979–84; annual returns 1972–84; combined register of members and share ledger 1920–50; trust deed to secure debenture stock 1903; reports and accounts 1949–84 (w).

Howards of Ilford Ltd: meeting minutes: directors' 1953–89, general 1953–83, executive committee 1957–59; memorandum and articles of association 1965; combined register of members and share ledger 1953–64; annual returns 1962–87; register of seals 1964–85; reports and accounts 1963–88; financial reports 1962; company file 1964–89; entry in statutory register of subsidiary companies of Laporte Industries Ltd 1967–84; Asta patent, minutes and correspondence c.1950–56; quinine production, correspondence and reports 1952–59; cyclohexanone reports 1965–68; product survey report 1963; list of product groups manufactured n.d.; developments, reports and correspondence 1965–72; market reports 1962–80; publicity files 1975–82; war damage repairs to premises, reports and correspondence 1952–56; site investigation report 1962; Essex County Council development plan 1956; papers re Bowmans Chemicals Ltd 1952–64; correspondence re disposal of archives and furniture 1965–81. (Ref: B3/5/12, B6/3/6, B9/2/17-27, B11/2/18-22, 4/1-22)

Records 4: Manchester Central Library, Local Studies Unit Archives, St Peter's Square, Manchester M2 5PD

Correspondence re orders for drugs and payment of accounts 1824, 1836. (Ref: MISC/26, MISC/28)

Records 5: Society of Friends, Library of the Religious Society of Friends, Friends House, 173-177 Euston Road, London NW1 2BJ

Extracts of Luke Howard's journals 1811–19 compiled by Bernard F Howard 1959; biographical notes: Luke Howard 1943, 1959, Robert Howard 1863–71; Luke Howard's 'notes of a journey on the continent' 1816. (Ref: Temp MSS 900; Tract Box L16 (MIC 60); L092.3.How; MS S24 (MS Box 2/8))

Records 6: The Museum Curator, Royal Pharmaceutical Society of Great Britain, 1 Lambeth High Street, London SE1 7JN

John Eliot Howard: description and analysis of bark specimens 1850, notes re *materia medica* 1846. (Ref: IRA.1997.056-7)

ROBERT HOWDEN LTD
17-19 Southchurch Road, Southend-on-Sea

Pharmacist

History: Robert Howden was registered as a pharmaceutical chemist at 78 Gracechurch Street, London, in 1859. Between 1876 and 1887 the business was incorporated as a limited liability company, Robert Howden Ltd, and in 1898 relocated to 28 Gracechurch Street. In 1918 the company moved to 11 Fenchurch Street and in 1967 to 17-19 Southchurch Road, Southend-on-Sea, whereupon it was renamed Robert Howden (Southend) Ltd.

Records: Guildhall Library, Aldermanbury, London EC22EJ

Ledger 1911–46; prescription books 1862–1943. (Ref: Ms 23957-58)

HUNT & CO (WINCHESTER) LTD
Silver Hill, Winchester, Hampshire

Retail pharmacist

History: In 1847 George Gunner was trading from St Thomas' Street, Winchester, Hampshire, as a chemist, druggist and soda water manufacturer. In 1850 he established a chemist's business at 45 High Street, Winchester, and in 1861 leased the premises to Richard Hunt, who purchased the business in 1873, and traded as a dispensing chemist under the title Hunt & Co. The firm acquired the chemist's business of F J Barratt, 122 High Street, Winchester, in 1914, and in 1928 was incorporated as a limited liability company, Hunt & Co (Winchester) Ltd. It remained at 45 High Street until 1979 when it transferred to a site at Silver Hill, Winchester. In the same year a subsidiary, Hunt & Co (Silver Hill) Ltd, was incorporated. In 1986 Hunt & Co (Winchester) Ltd was removed from the register of companies. Hunt & Co (Silver Hill) Ltd was acquired in 1992 by AAH plc (which later became part of GEHE AG), but shortly afterwards became a dormant company.

Records 1: Hampshire Record Office, Sussex Street, Winchester SO23 8TH

Ledgers 1912–22; account books: daily 1886–87, 1904–50 (w), Winchester College 1933–50; prescription books: customer and prescriptions details 1845–1964, F J Barratt 1878–1910. (Ref: 177M85W)

Records 2: Winchester City Museums, Hyde Historic Resources Centre, 75 Hyde Street, Winchester SO23 7DW

Apprenticeship indentures 1896, 1914–19; unspecified indentures 1861; inland revenue medicine licence 1860; custom and excise office papers and stamp minutes 1898–1944; notebook of recipes for simple remedies and household products 19th cent.; photographs: chemist shop and dispensary c.1880s–1920s, stone mortar 1921; booklets, cards, prescription envelopes and miscellaneous papers 19th cent. (Ref: WINCM: LH 3034)

Records 3: GEHE UK plc, Retail Branch, Atherstone, Warwickshire. Enquiries to GEHE UK plc, Sapphire Court, Walsgrave Triangle Business Park, Coventry CV2 2TX

Hunt & Co (Silver Hill) Ltd: general meetings minutes 1985–96, combined register of members, directors and share ledger 1981–92. (Ref: Box S3, current minutes)

IRON JELLOID CO LTD
St Helens

Proprietary medicine manufacturer

History: Iron Jelloid Co Ltd was incorporated as a limited liability company in 1917, to manufacture the proprietary medicine, *Iron Jelloids* from factory premises at Watford, Hertfordshire. Around 1930, the company was acquired by Beecham Pills Ltd, and in 1953 the production of *Iron Jelloids* was transferred to the Beecham Group Ltd site at St Helens.

Records 1: St Helens Local History & Archives Library, Gamble Institute, Victoria Square, St Helens WA10 1DY

Memorandum and articles of association 1917; annual returns 1933–53; register of members 1917–49; share certificate books: ordinary 1932–49, preference n.d.; accounts and schedules 1943–52; private ledger 1946–49. (Ref: BP/4/5)

Records 2: History of Advertising Trust, HAT House, 12 Raveningham Centre, Raveningham NR14 6NU

Guardbooks of advertising material n.d.; papers, memoranda and advertising campaign material 1965–67; advertisements for *Iron Jelloids* 1974–80s. (Ref: Leo Burnett guardbooks, 30; JWT 107 (1965) 302 (1966) 404 (1967) 433; MEAL collection 1974–89, R10-80)

IZAL PHARMACEUTICALS LTD
Sterling-Winthrop House, Surbiton, Kingston upon Thames, London

Pharmaceutical distributor and manufacturer

History: In 1926 Uso Ltd was incorporated as a limited liability company at 62 London Wall, London, to operate as an agent and distributor to a range of manufacturing companies. In 1961 its registered offices moved to Thorncliffe, Chapeltown, Sheffield. In 1974 it was renamed Izal Pharmaceuticals Ltd, and began manufacture of the pharmaceutical product *Breopin*, a micro-encapsulated form of *Aspirin*. In 1976 it was acquired by Sterling Winthrop Group Ltd, and its registered offices re-located to Sterling-Winthrop House, Surbiton, Kingston upon Thames, London. The company continued to trade under its own name, until 1983, when it became dormant. It was renamed Graychurch Security Services Ltd in 1985, and was dissolved in 1986.

Records: SmithKline Beecham plc, SmithKline Beecham House, Great West Road, Brentford TW8 9BD. Enquiries to SmithKline Beecham plc, 1 New Horizons Court, Great West Road, Brentford TW8 9EP

Directors' and general meetings minutes 1974; special resolutions re change of name 1974; annual returns 1927–85; share certificates book 1926–58; annual reports and accounts 1980–84; advertisement and report for *Breoprin* n.d; internal correspondence 1974–76.

Izal Pharmaceuticals (Ireland) Ltd: annual returns 1974–85, correspondence 1974.

JANSSEN-CILAG LTD
Saunderton, High Wycombe, Buckinghamshire

Pharmaceutical manufacturer

History: In 1934 Dr Constant Janssen, a medical practitioner of Turnhout, Belgium, incorporated a limited liability company, N V Produkten Richter, to import the products of Gedeon Richter, a chemical and pharmaceutical manufacturer of Budapest, Hungary, and distribute them in Belgium, the Netherlands and the Belgian Congo (Zaire). By 1938 Dr Janssen was selling his own preparations in addition to those of Gedeon Richter and during the Second World War these products took precedence over the Hungarian imports, following the death of Gedeon Richter. In 1951 Constant Janssen's son, Paul Adriaan Jan Janssen, qualified as a doctor of medicine, and opened a small research laboratory within the premises occupied by his father's company at Statiestratt, Turnhout. He employed a team of co-workers and began research into chemical compounds and their effect upon living organisms. His laboratory was integrated into his father's company, N V Produkten Richter, which was renamed N V Laboratoria Pharmaceutica Dr C Janssen in 1956. However, his products were not marketed under the *Richter* trade mark, but under that of *Eupharma*. In 1955 N V Laboratoria Pharmaceutica Dr C Janssen launched its first compound, ambucetamide, a uterine antispasmodic, as *Neomeritine*, and in 1958 Dr Paul Janssen incorporated a company independent from his father's, styled N V Research Laboratorium Dr C Janssen. During the 1960s and 1970s specialist products were introduced which revolutionised the treatment of psychiatric patients. In 1961 N V Research Laboratorium Dr C Janssen merged with the American healthcare company, Johnson & Johnson Inc, and in 1964 was renamed Janssen Pharmaceutica N V. In 1961 a UK division of the Belgian company was established within an associate UK company, Ortho Pharmaceutical Ltd, which conducted research into contraceptives, obstetrics and gynaecology. Ortho Pharmaceutical Ltd had been incorporated as a subsidiary of Johnson & Johnson Inc in 1947, moving from Lane End, Buckinghamshire, to Saunderton, High Wycombe, Buckinghamshire, in 1955. In 1971 the UK division of Janssen Pharmaceutica N V was incorporated as a limited liability company, Janssen Pharmaceutical Ltd, which was independent from Ortho Pharmaceutical Ltd, and began trading in 1973. It was based at Marlow, Buckinghamshire, until 1984, when it moved to Grove, Oxfordshire. It conducted research into treatments for psychiatric illness, fungal and viral diseases, cancer and gastroenterology. In 1962 Ortho Pharmaceutical Ltd acquired the business of McNeil Laboratories Ltd, High Wycombe, whose parent, McNeil Laboratories Inc, was owned by Johnson & Johnson Inc. In 1982 Ortho Pharmaceutical Ltd was renamed Ortho-Cilag Pharmaceutical Ltd, and in 1988 Cilag Ltd. In 1995 this company merged with Janssen Pharmaceutical Ltd to form Janssen-Cilag Ltd. In 1997 the company, based at the former Ortho Pharmaceutical Ltd site at Saunderton, produced psychiatric, neurological, gastroenterological, anti-fungal medicines and female health care products. It also manufactured veterinary pharmaceuticals.

Brief History of Johnson & Johnson (Johnson & Johnson, New Jersey, 1995); *Dr Paul: The search for better drugs never ends* (Dirk Collier, Belgium, 1993)

Records: Janssen-Cilag Ltd, PO Box 79, Saunderton, High Wycombe HP14 4HJ

Company brochure n.d.; *Insight* magazine 1996.

Cilag Ltd: directors' and general meetings minutes 1947–75, 1991; memorandum and articles of association 1947; certificate of incorporation 1947; special resolutions 1965, 1972; notifications of changes of directors 1958–94; corporate correspondence: parent company 1983–91, directors 1964–92, general meetings, notices and agenda 1962–90; register of members and share ledger 1947–81; annual returns 1948–80 (w), 1988–90; share certificates book 1955–77; debenture share agreements 1958; share transfer forms, cancelled certificates and correspondence 1964–86; annual report 1993; accounts 1976–80, 1986–90; financial agreements and contracts 1970s–80s; cash book 1983–84; asset registers 1989; capital register 1977–88; capital expenditure: book 1970–76, application 1986; depreciation report 1989; year-end working papers 1983–86; sales: summaries and analyses 1983–88, reports and statistics 1991–92; reports and papers re pricing 1988; taxation papers 1982–83; insurance policies and papers 1974–88; correspondence with brokers 1989–91; litigation papers re drugs 1968–86; legal file 1988–91; patent and trade marks applications 1983–85, 1989–94; product royalties 1974–90; papers re product licencing 1989; files re drug developments 1980s; export file and licences 1990s; reports and papers re exports 1984–91; product liability file n.d.; individual product claims 1982–94; correspondence: drugs licences 1982–93, sales and marketing 1982–86; promotional material approvals 1988–89; title deeds, Saunderton factory n.d.; plant register 1985; factory register 1966–80; chemical plant examinations papers 1970–90; engineering inspections and certificates 1962–78; fire certificates and plans 1976–94; accidents books 1959–91; property insurance papers 1888–89; lifting machinery insurance examinations book 1979–92; papers and correspondence re discharge of trade effluent 1971–89; decoration schedule 1979–83; directors' salaries 1972 to date; wages and salaries files 1983–91; superannuation trust fund: minutes 1958–66, annual accounts 1962–65 (w); executive benefits scheme 1977–83; senior employees' life assurance 1982–91; pensions: papers 1976–91, correspondence 1983–88; Johnson & Johnson supplementary pension 1984 to date; monthly personnel reports 1973–82; staff papers: recruitment costing 1984–86, budgets 1983–86, training centre 1985–87, temporary staff 1986, shift work 1981–87, transport 1979–86, work experience 1985–86, liaison with schools and colleges 1983–91, public relations 1982–86, health and safety 1979–93, medicals 1986, security 1984–86, disaster programme 1978; European personnel conference files 1980–83; papers re local charities

1989–91; papers re sports and social club 1977–85; licence for industrial users of copyright music and related papers 1965–76; photographs: Saunderton site 1955–58, staff 1960s–80s.

Janssen Pharmaceutical Ltd: directors' and general meetings minutes 1975–94; memorandum and articles of association 1971; certificate of incorporation 1971; special resolution 1973; register of members, share ledger, directors' and general meetings minutes 1971–94; company brochures 1990, 1993; magazines: *Stag* 1978–84 (w), *The Janssen Tablet* 1986–93.

McNeil Laboratories Ltd: directors' and general meetings minutes 1959 to date; memorandum and articles of association 1958; annual returns 1959 to date. (Ref: Box 105-931 and non-referenced)

JARRET JARRETT & SONS
Glasfryn House, Glasfryn, Trawsfynydd, Gwynedd

Chemist and druggist

History: Jarret Jarrett was in business as a chemist and druggist at Glasfryn House, Glasfryn, Trawsfynydd, Gwynedd, before 1868. In 1911 he was joined in the business by Jarret Roberts Jarrett, who had registered as a chemist and druggist in 1901. In 1924 the latter ceased to be registered, and Jarret Jarrett continued to trade from Glasfryn House under the name, Jarret Jarrett & Sons. In 1929 he too ceased to be registered.

Records: Gwynedd Archives & Museums Service, Archifdy Meirion Archives, Cae Penarlag, Dolgellau LL40 2YB

Account books: 1834–44 (w), J R Jarrett 1902–09; day books 1832, 1915–20; waste book 1851–52; loose bills and list of customers' addresses 1885–1918, 1920–21; dispensing book n.d.; general bill re Jarrett's executors 1860; various records in Welsh, mainly religious 1815–77. (Ref: Z/DDC)

PHILADELPHUS JEYES & CO LTD
6 The Drapery, 4 Kingsley Park Terrace & College Street, Northampton, Northamptonshire

Wholesale and retail chemist, later photographic supplies manufacturer

History: Philadelphus Jeyes entered into partnership with a Mr Perrin during the early nineteenth century, following which he established a retail pharmacy business on his own account at 6 The Drapery, Northampton, Northamptonshire, in 1910. His eldest son, also named Philadelphus, who had been apprenticed locally, inherited the business on his father's death in 1828. He died in 1893, and the business was incorporated as a limited liability company, Philadelphus Jeyes & Co Ltd, in the same year. By 1940 it was manufacturing chemicals, including weedkiller, sheep dip and carbocide disinfectant. Among its subsidiary companies were Hardings, a tobacconist's business located at 7 The Drapery, Northampton, and Donald McKinnell Ltd, chemists, of 6 Wood Hill, Northampton, established prior to 1868. During the early 1940s the company became photographic supplies manufacturers, whilst also retaining the retail chemist side of the business. By 1955 the company had photographic supplies manufacturing plants at Kettering, Northamptonshire; Market Harborough, Leicestershire; Bedford, Bedfordshire; Towcester, Northamptonshire; Rugby, Warwickshire; Biggleswade, Bedfordshire; and Stamford, Lincolnshire. Philadelphus Jeyes & Co Ltd was removed from the register of companies in 1977.

D Palfreyman, *John Jeyes: ... the making of a household name* (Jeyes Group, Thetford, 1977)

Records: Northamptonshire Record Office, Wootton Hall Park, Northampton NN4 9BQ

Memorandum and articles of association 1893; directors' meetings notices with some agenda n.d.; directors' reports and notices of annual general meetings 1952–67; special resolutions 1908–49; annual returns and declarations 1943–60; share transfers 1901–67; share certificates n.d.; list of dividends and shareholders 1961–68; balance sheets and accounts 1899–1967; trading and profit and loss accounts: departmental 1924, branch 1925–30; summaries of turnover and expenses 1957–68; patents and trade marks 1920s, 1951; prescription books 1925–75; recipe book c.1885; papers re shops, incl. sales, purchases, stock and part report re impact of National Health Service on dispensing 1906–43, c.1950, 1971; advertisements and press cuttings c.1920–39; property leases 1923–66; mortgages and valuation of property 1930–67; staff papers, incl. pension fund and pupilage documentation 1942–57; photographs of premises c.1930; miscellaneous papers 1920–30, 1965, n.d. (Ref: PJ 1-363 and ZA 7769-93)

Donald McKinnell Ltd: directors' report and notice of annual general meeting 1966; share certificates 1965–66, n.d.; counterfoil and share certificate numbers book 1927–66; balance sheet and accounts 1946, 1965–66; papers re shop premises 1963. (Ref: 1984/59, 69)

W W JOHNSON
Llandrindod Wells, Powys

Chemist

History: William Wilson Johnson was registered as a chemist and druggist in 1886. He operated from 2 High Street, Llandrindod Wells, Powys, a business which had been established around 1878, possibly by T Davies. From 1901 Johnson had 2 chemist shops in Llandrindod Wells, one at 2 High Street and the other in Temple Street. By 1926 Johnson had vacated the High Street premises and had acquired new buildings in Park Crescent. Following his death, in around 1947, the business was purchased by George C G Hilliar, one of Johnson's former apprentices. The Temple Street premises closed in around 1953.

Records: Powys County Archives Office, County Hall, Llandrindod Wells LD1 5LG

Combined clients' accounts and prescription book 1895–1900; client sales ledger 1911–29; client sales and prescriptions ledger 1944–58; prescription books: W S Bound 1905–14, W W Johnson 1887–91, [?Temple Street] 1905–53, [?Park Crescent] 1906–60. (Ref: R/DB/1/1-83)

G FORBES JOHNSTON LTD
Dundee

Retail chemist

History: G Forbes Johnston Ltd was incorporated as a limited liability company in 1945, to acquire the chemist and optician business of Jessie K Millar, which traded as G Forbes Johnston from 148 & 154 Brook Street, Broughty Ferry, Dundee. By the mid 1960s the company owned 2 shops, the first at Brook Street, Dundee, and a second in Dunkeld, Perth & Kinross. In 1967 the company acquired the business of J B Ritchie, 103 High Street, Lochee, Dundee, and in 1970 of J Howard Johnston, 205 Brook Street, Broughty Ferry. In 1992 G Forbes Johnston Ltd was acquired by E Moss Ltd, the retail subsidiary of UniChem plc which merged in 1997 with Alliance Sante SA to become Alliance UniChem plc.

By 1999 the company was dormant, its business and assets having been transferred to E Moss Ltd.

Records: Alliance UniChem plc, UniChem House, Cox Lane, Chessington KT9 1SN

Directors' and general meetings minutes 1945 to date; memorandum and articles of association 1945; certification notice of incorporation (1945) 1992; annual returns 1946–47; acquisition papers 1992; certificate of registration of a charge 1965; combined registers of members and share ledgers 1945–92; cancelled share certificates 1965–92.

HUMPHREY JONES
Castle Street, Llangollen, Denbighshire

Pharmaceutical chemist

History: Humphrey Richard Jones was registered as a pharmaceutical chemist in 1857. He was still trading from Castle Street, Llangollen, Denbighshire, in 1895.

Records: Denbighshire Record Office, 46 Clwyd Street, Ruthin LL15 1HP

Apprenticeship indentures 1850, 1871; medicine licences 1859–60; papers incl. prescriptions, receipts and income tax returns 1858–1942; prescription books and formulary c.1860s; draft agreement with Robert Baker re exchange of lands 1865; plan of land c.1880; plan for a proposed shop 1893; tenancy agreements 1910, 1930; correspondence 1850–58, 1888, 1921; receipt for Humphrey Jones's subscriptions to the Pharmaceutical Society as an apprentice 1850–57; receipt for examination fee of H R Jones 1898; photograph of H R Jones c.1920; birth certificate of H R Jones 1874. (Ref: DD/DM/1122)

KAY BROTHERS LTD
St Petersgate, Reddish, Stockport

Chemist and druggist and manufacturing chemist

History: Samuel Kay established himself in business as a retail chemist in 1865 at 7 Lower Hillgate, Stockport. In 1866 he was joined in partnership by his brother, Thomas, and the firm, styled Kay Brothers, began manufacturing proprietary medicines. An early and profitable line was 'Kay's Compound

Essence of Linseed' for which letters patent were granted in 1873. In 1882 the firm acquired premises at St Petersgate, Stockport, in order to expand the manufacturing side of the business, whilst Lower Hillgate was retained as a retail outlet. In 1884 Kay Brothers received a royal warrant as chemists to Queen Victoria. The business was incorporated as a limited liability company, Kay Brothers Ltd, in 1887, and the following year the retail premises were sold. Towards the end of the nineteenth century the company began manufacturing non-drying sticky material for pest control and for several years the flycatcher line proved hugely successful. It was produced for use by the armed forces throughout the world during the First World War. By 1936 following research into a solid version of liquid disinfectant, the firelighter evolved and flycatchers were superseded by the production of *Zip* firelighters. The company also produced a number of pharmaceutical products. As well as packing *Mepacrine* tablets which were used in the prevention and treatment of malaria, Kay Brothers Ltd manufactured linseed cough compound, *Orbite* (grease bonding), *Tic* pills, coagulant cement and a number of toiletry products. In 1937 the company acquired new premises, Kayborough Works in Reddish, Stockport, and in 1954 purchased the business of Joshua Gibson Ltd, Manchester, a company which specialised in liquid and wax polishes. In 1957 it established a subsidiary company, Kay Brothers (Ireland) Ltd, to manufacture flycatchers and later *Zip* firelighters and linseed cough compound. During the 1950s, Kay Brothers Ltd also began to manufacture the foam plastic, polyurethane, under the trade name *Foamoprene*. In 1959 a subsidiary company, Kay Brothers Plastics Ltd, was incorporated to undertake manufacture of this product, which was used on operating tables in hospitals as well as for bandages and face masks. Gradually, Kay Brothers Ltd reduced its involvement with the manufacture of products for the retail trade and concentrated on manufacturing and wholesaling direct to industry. In 1960 it acquired factory accommodation at Marple, outside Stockport. Kay Brothers Ltd and all its subsidiaries were acquired by Reckitt & Colman Holdings Ltd in 1960, although the company continued to trade under its own name until 1988, when it was renamed Colman & Co Ltd.

'Selections from the Prose, Verse & Sketches of the Late Thomas Kay of Stockport, With Biographical Notes' (Unpublished typescript, c.1918)

Records 1: Stockport Archive Service, Central Library, Wellington Road South, Stockport SK1 3RS

Articles of partnership between Thomas and Samuel Kay 1881; minutes: directors' meetings 1876–1930, general meetings 1887–1940; articles of association 1887–1909; list of members and shareholdings 1887; share allotments 1955; share certificates 1887–1908; Thomas Kay's share dividend accounts 1891–92; papers and correspondence re share accounts and a share issue 1955–56, n.d.; annual returns 1887–1927 (w); agenda, balance sheets and directors' reports 1952–58; half-yearly balance sheets and trading accounts 1887–1926; general ledger 1893–1904; notarised bills for loans from the company 1893–1909; papers re litigations concerning 'Compound Essence of Linseed' 1872, 1893, n.d.; royal warrant as chemists and druggists 1884; trademarks, registrations and renewals 1906–15, 1934–38; 'flycatcher' patents 1898–1930; other patents: UK 1872–82, foreign 1899–1908; formulae books 1790–1913; druggists' price book 1876; notes and sales information 1865–1919; advertisements and pamphlets 1870–1925, n.d.; title deeds and related papers 1633–1925; company inventory 1887; wages book 1876–78; staff service agreements 1899–1924; testimonial letters from customers and chemists 1864–77; letterbooks 1913–32; correspondence 1922–30; photographs: Thomas Kay as mayor 1912–13, Samuel Kay n.d., factory n.d., St Peter's and Lower Hillgate premises c.1925, n.d., miscellaneous early 20th cent.; papers and correspondence re Workmen's International Exhibition 1870; literary papers of Thomas Kay 1900–14; papers re Kay brothers' vault and monument in Stockport cemetery 1879–1913; history c.1960; staff souvenir coronation fan gift 1911.

Kay Brothers Plastics Ltd: memorandum and articles of association 1959; history n.d. (Ref: B/YY)

Records 2: Reckitt's Heritage, Reckitt & Colman Products Ltd, Dansom Lane, Kingston upon Hull HU8 7DS

Product histories 20th cent.; site layout plan, Hurst Street, Reddish 1972.

E Hornby: papers re purchase of business and premises by Kay Brothers 1878–85; royal warrant granted to Alexander Shaw, chemist and druggist 1852; insurance premium receipt 1882.

KEITH HOLME
Galashiels, Scottish Borders

Pharmaceutical chemist

History: Alexander Noble was registered as a chemist and druggist at Galashiels, Scottish Borders, in 1880. The business remained in Noble family hands until 1960 when it was acquired by Keith Holme. Keith Holme retained ownership until 1995, when the business was acquired by the Lothian & Borders Co-operative Society.

Records: The Secretary, National Register of Archives (Scotland), H M General Register House, Princes Street, Edinburgh EH1 3YY

Ledgers 1880–1915; prescription books 1880–1900 (w), 1924, 1933–42; poisons register 1932–52; personal papers, education records 1910–12, c.1930, n.d. (Ref: NRA(S) 1825)

KINGSWOOD CHEMISTS
19 Market Square, Potton, Bedfordshire

Chemist

History: The business at 19 Market Square, Potton, Bedfordshire, appears to have been owned successively by W Marchant, from around 1924, E E Russell Chemists Ltd, from around 1945 and Kingswood Chemists from 1976.

Records: Bedfordshire & Luton Archives & Records Service, The Record Office, County Hall, Cauldwell Street, Bedford MK42 9AP

Sales ledger 1942–46; poisons register 1925–49; poisons list 1936; prescription books: 1932–50 (w), 1963–73, W Marchant 1924–32, E E Russell Chemists Ltd 1945–62, Charles H Ford (late E C Riley) 1950–59, E E Russell Chemists Ltd, veterinary 1973–76, E E Russell Chemists Ltd special formulae c.1959–69. (Ref: Z 585/1-16)

KNOLL LTD
25-27 Castle Gate, Nottingham

Pharmaceutical manufacture, sales and marketing

History: Badische Anilin & Soda Fabrik AG (BASF AG) was established in 1865 in Ludwigshafen, Germany, by Friedrich Engelhorn, to manufacture textile dyes. In 1897 the company pioneered the development of synthetic indigo, and by 1910 had begun production of fertilisers. In 1925 it merged with 5 other companies, creating Interessengemeinschaft Farbenindustrie AG (IG Farben AG), and ceased to trade under its own name. From this point onwards it traded as the upper Rhine branch of IG Farben AG, and was named Betriebsgemeinschaft Oberrhein. In 1952 it was re-incorporated as a separate concern, BASF AG, and in 1975 acquired a majority interest in Knoll AG, a German pharmaceutical manufacturer, also based in Ludwigshafen. By 1982

Knoll AG was a wholly-owned subsidiary of BASF AG. As a consequence, Knoll Ltd, the UK subsidiary of Knoll AG, was also acquired by BASF AG. Knoll Ltd was incorporated as a limited liability company in 1929 to manufacture bulk chemicals and pharmaceuticals, and to sell and market ethical pharmaceuticals. In 1995 BASF AG also acquired the global prescription pharmaceuticals division of The Boots Co plc, Boots Pharmaceuticals. This division included the pharmaceutical sales and marketing company, Boots Pharmaceuticals Ltd, based in Castle Quay, Nottingham, which had been incorporated as a limited liability company in 1992. This company was renamed Knoll Pharma Ltd and its entire business was transferred to Knoll Ltd. The UK pharmaceutical manufacturing operation of Boots Pharmaceuticals in Nottingham and Cramlington, Northumberland, was renamed Knoll Pharmaceuticals in 1995. In 1997 UK research and development operations were also carried out in Nottingham under the names Knoll Pharmaceuticals and Knoll Ltd.

Anon, *BASF: Milestones in its history* (BASF, Ludwigshafen, 1995)

Records 1: Knoll Ltd, 9 Castle Quay, Castle Boulevard, Nottingham NG7 1FW

Directors' and general meetings minutes 1929–96; certificate of incorporation 1929; combined registers of members, directors and share ledgers 1929–95; seal register 1988–93; debenture agreement with Savory & Moore Ltd 1940; certificate of registration of a mortgage or charge 1941; trust deed 1993; share certificate book 1956–88; share certificates 1933–50; share transfer forms 1956; corporate correspondence: minutes 1996, change of directors 1996, directors' interests and shares 1993; budget meeting minutes 1992; budget cost analysis 1994; correspondence re VAT 1989; insurance agreement 1990; lease of unit 5, King Street, Maidenhead 1991; licence to carry out alterations to Fleming House, King Street, Maidenhead 1989.

Knoll Pharma Ltd: certificate of incorporation 1992; change of name certificate 1995; combined register of members and share ledger, with directors' and general meetings minutes 1992–96; correspondence: directors' letters of resignation 1993–95, appointment of directors' alternates 1995.

Records 2: Knoll Pharmaceuticals, Pennyfoot Street, Nottingham NG1 1GF

Knoll Pharmaceuticals: clinical trial papers 1970–85; pre-clinical study papers 1964–85; laboratory notebooks n.d.–1985; research reports and notes n.d.–1985; product literature n.d.–1985; standard operating procedures n.d.–1985; policy statements n.d.; directors' correspondence n.d.

Records 3: Chemicals Operation, Knoll Pharmaceuticals, D110 Building, Main Road, Beeston, Nottingham NG9 1AD

Knoll Pharmaceuticals: laboratory reports re process development 1935–85. (Ref: TD, TDD, CP, CPD, CPS, CDG)

PETER LAWRENCE
Welwyn Garden City, Hertfordshire

Druggist and stationer

History: Philip Lawrence was trading as a druggist and stationer at Welwyn Garden City, Hertfordshire, from at least 1855 until 1864. Edmund Lawrence was registered as a chemist and druggist in Welwyn Garden City in 1869 and traded there until around 1882.

Records: Hertfordshire Archives & Local Studies, County Hall, Hertford SG13 8EJ

Ledgers 1841–50, n.d.; day books 1842–51; doctors' prescriptions 1841–44, n.d.; advertisement and stocklist, Robert Hovendon, chemist's sundriesman, 57 Crown Street, Finsbury Square, London n.d. (Ref: D/EX417 B1-8)

J C LEE
Barton-Upon-Humber, North Lincolnshire

Chemist and stationer

History: Henry Jenkins Tomlinson was in business as a chemist and druggist in Barton-Upon-Humber, North Lincolnshire, in partnership with Charles Hodgson Crowder, from before 1868 until at least 1895. The business was operated by 1876 as a chemist and druggist and wholesale druggist. Towards the end of the nineteenth century, the business was acquired by J C Lee, and became a provider of chemists' sundries and stationery.

Records: North East Lincolnshire Archives, Town Hall Square, Grimsby DN31 1HX

Ledgers: customers' accounts 1900–13, suppliers' accounts 1911–19; prescription books c.1851–66, 1884–85; bills, for supplies incl. chemists' goods, books, newspapers and groceries 1858–77; notices of auction, advertisements, local events and press cuttings 1871–84, n.d.; notes to accompany draft advertisements 1883–84. (Ref: 525, 598)

LESTERS CHEMISTS LTD
2 Bridge Street, Nuneaton, Warwickshire

Chemist

History: Henry Lester was registered as a chemist and druggist at 1 Bridge Street, Nuneaton, Warwickshire, in 1872, and in 1876 was also registered as a dentist. In 1897 William Henry Lester registered as a chemist and druggist and joined him in the business. Henry Lester ceased to be registered in 1933, and William Henry Lester moved the business to 2 Bridge Street, Nuneaton, where he traded as W H Lester. In 1941 he ceased to be registered, and thereafter the business continued to trade as W H Lester. In 1947 it re-located to 2 Market Place, Nuneaton, and was incorporated as a limited liability company, Lesters Chemists Ltd. The company continued to trade under this name until 1964, when it was acquired by Boots Pure Drug Co Ltd.

Records: Warwickshire County Record Office, Priory Park, Cape Road, Warwick CV34 4JS

Ledgers 1872–90; day books 1876–79, 1886–88; expenditure books 1898–1901; receipt books 1897–1901, 1917–28, 1951–61; bank books 1904–08; prescription books 1873–91, late 19th–20th cents; plans for new premises 1929; salaries' book 1944–47; letterbook 1915–16; diaries 1932–45; Henry Lester's certificate of qualification as a chemist and druggist 1872. (Ref: CR2207)

LEWIS & BURROWS LTD
2 Bucknall Street, New Oxford Street, London and 22 & 24 Great Portland Street, London

Chemist and druggist

History: Lewis & Burrows Drug Stores Ltd was incorporated as a limited liability company in 1895 to acquire a number of drug store businesses, all of which were located in north, west and central London. These included Burrows

Drug Stores, Lewis's Drug Stores, Mattersons Drug Stores, Griffiths Drug Stores, Bowdens Drug Stores and Trick's Drug Stores. The company was later renamed Lewis & Burrows Ltd, and was dissolved in 1993.

Records: Archives & Manuscripts, Wellcome Library for the History & Understanding of Medicine, 183 Euston Road, London NW1 2BE

Directors' meetings: minutes 1902–33 (w), agenda 1895–96; allotment book, incl. register of directors, mortgage details and prospectus 1895–1921; combined registers of members and share ledgers: preference shares 1895–c.1936, ordinary and deferred shares 1895–c.1936; register of transfers 1895–1953; journals: valuation of company for flotation 1895, accounts 1897–1910; photographs of premises, reproduced in prospectus in allotment book n.d. (Ref: CMAC/GC/134)

G LIGHTFOOT & SON LTD
Kendal and Carlisle, Cumbria

Pharmaceutical chemist

History: George Lightfoot began his pharmaceutical career as an apprentice to Joseph Cowper, pharmacist, in Penrith, Cumbria. After qualifying and managing a pharmacy in Penrith, he moved to Carlisle, Cumbria, in 1930 and purchased a small business in Wigton Road from W H Johnstone. Later, his son Maurice also served a pharmaceutical apprenticeship and joined his father in the business in 1950. They became partners in 1951. In 1952 a second pharmacy in Stanwix, Carlisle, was purchased, a business which had been established in 1888 by Messrs Ridley and had subsequently passed into the ownership of J W Errington. The business was incorporated as a limited liability company, G Lightfoot & Son Ltd, in 1953. Following this, a central distribution centre and company headquarters was established at 50 Annan Road, Gretna, Dumfries & Galloway. A long-established pharmacy, Frasers, Dumfries, Dumfries & Galloway, was also acquired in the 1950s, although it continued to trade under its own name for many years. In 1967 a town centre pharmacy in Bank Street, Carlisle, was purchased, but resold in 1970 when new premises in Botchergate were purchased, which subsequently re-located to London Road. A further pharmacy, Laidlaws, Lockerbie, Dumfries & Galloway, was also acquired at this time. In 1975 G Lightfoot & Son purchased a wine and spirits company, Keswick Wine Co, Keswick, Cumbria, and the Dumfries pharmacy was sold. The chairmanship of G Lightfoot & Son Ltd passed to Maurice Lightfoot on the death of his father in 1981. In 1982 a pharmacy and optical practice, Priestman & Humble, Penrith, was purchased and in the same year the company became involved in the setting up of a consortium-run pharmacy within the new Penrith Health Centre. In 1985 the Keswick Wine Co was wound up, but the business was retained as a pharmacy. In 1986 the Lockerbie branch was sold and a pharmacy at King Street, Wigton, Cumbria, was purchased. After 1993 the company acquired 3 additional pharmacy businesses, bringing its total number of retail outlets to 9.

Records 1: Mr Maurice Lightfoot, 'The Larches', Wetheral, Carlisle CA4 8JY

Trading accounts c.1930–90.

Records 2: Cumbria Record Office (Carlisle), The Castle, Carlisle CA3 8UR

Scotts, Bank Street, Carlisle: prescription books: 1904–22, 1962–73, Botchergate branch 1947–66; recipe books: 1911, Botchergate branch n.d.

Stewarts, Botchergate, Carlisle: recipe book c.1920.

Mounsey Robinson, Middlegate, Penrith: cash book 1902–12; prescription book 1936–38; recipe book c.1920.

Frasers, 84 High Street, Dumfries: memoranda books, goods supplied to named customers n.d. c.1930; prescription book 1949–69; recipe books c.1890, c.1910.

Laidlaws, High Street, Lockerbie: recipe book c.1920.

LINDSAY & GILMOUR
11 Elm Row, Edinburgh

Chemist

History: This business at 11 Elm Row, Edinburgh, appears initially to have been established by a Mr Lindsay in 1826. In 1867 William Gilmour was registered as a pharmaceutical chemist, and in 1870 David Gilmour was registered as a chemist and druggist. Both operated from 11 Elm Row, under the business name Lindsay & Gilmour. David Gilmour moved to 40 Bridge Street, Dunfermline, Fife, prior to 1887, but William Gilmour continued to trade at 11 Elm Row until 1906, when he ceased to be registered.

Records: The Secretary, National Register of Archives (Scotland), H M General Register House, Princes Street, Edinburgh EH1 3YY

Account books 1913–33; prescription books 1888–1978 (w). (Ref: NRA(S) 3620)

JOHN & JAMES LISTER
Shibden Hall, Halifax, Calderdale

Apothecaries

History: John Lister of Upper Brea, Yorkshire, and his brother, James Lister of Shibden Hall, established themselves in business as apothecaries in Halifax, Calderdale, in the late seventeenth century. They were subsequently joined in partnership by their younger brother, Thomas. Following the death of John Lister in 1694, James succeeded to the business in 1696. James and Thomas Lister compounded herbs and plant extracts which were sold for medicinal use, and also traded in confectioneries and other sundry goods until at least 1705.

J Lister, 'History of Shibden Hall in the Early Eighteenth Century', *Transactions of the Halifax Antiquarian Society*, 1936

Records: West Yorkshire Archive Service, Calderdale, Calderdale Central Library, Northgate House, Northgate, Halifax HX1 1UN

Ledger extracts 1689–1705; notebook and accounts of Lister family 1620s–1880s; prescription book and receipt n.d.; Shibden Hall title deeds 1710–26. (Ref: SH:1/SM; SH:3/AB/3, 5, 7, 16)

R LLOYD (CHEMIST) LTD
21 Adare Street, Bridgend, & 62 Tylacelyn Road, Penygraig, Rhondda Cynon Taff

Chemist

History: Rees Lloyd was registered as a chemist and druggist in 1874 in Penygraig, Rhondda Cynon Taff, and traded there until 1922, when he ceased to be registered. In 1894 Thomas Charles Jones registered as a chemist and druggist, and traded from Connah's Quay, Flintshire, until 1922, when he relocated to 19 Wyndham Street, Bridgend. In 1928 he moved to 21 Adare Street,

Bridgend, where he traded on his own account until 1941, when he was succeeded in the business by R Lloyd. In 1946 the business was incorporated as a limited liability company, R Lloyd (Chemist) Ltd, trading from 21 Adare Street and 62 Tylacelyn Road, Penygraig. In 1974 the business ceased trading.

Records: Museum of Welsh Life, St Fagans, Cardiff CF5 6XB

Account books 1939–69; prescription books 1883–1972; poisons registers 1950s; inventory of T C Jones' business in Bridgend n.d. (Ref: 2608/1-27)

LLOYDS PHARMACEUTICALS LTD
Clerk Green Mills, Batley, Kirklees

Manufacturing chemist

History: In the late 1920s Thomas Henry Walton's established chemist and druggist's business at Warwick Road, Batley, Kirklees, was incorporated as a limited liability company, Thomas Henry Walton & Co Ltd. In 1930 the company was renamed Walfox Ltd, and moved to Clerk Green Mills, Batley. It was acquired in 1953 by Howard Lloyd Holdings Ltd, Leicester (established as T Howard Lloyd & Son in 1890). In 1953 Walfox Ltd was renamed Howard Lloyd & Co Ltd, and traded as a pharmaceutical manufacturer from Clerk Green Mills, until it was sold to Reckitt & Colman Products Ltd in 1972 and renamed Lloyds Pharmaceuticals Ltd. The company manufactured *Bonjela*, a treatment for mouth ulcers, and *Transvasin*, an anti-rheumatic rub. Pharmaceutical manufacture ceased in 1992 and the Lloyds Pharmaceuticals Ltd factory was renamed the Howard Lloyd Special Production Unit, part of Reckitt & Colman Products Ltd.

'The Story of Clerk Green Mills', *Clerk Green Chronicle*, 1992, 8-12

Records 1: West Yorkshire Archive Service, Kirklees, Central Library, Princess Alexandra Walk, Huddersfield HD1 2SU

Minutes 1969–71; financial records 1928–78; insurance records 1939–76; product specifications 1945–72; plans c.1950–92; wages books 1929–73; photographs 1930s–92. (Ref: KC774)

Records 2: Reckitt's Heritage, Reckitt & Colman Products Ltd, Dansom Lane, Kingston upon Hull HU8 7DS

Trading and profit and loss account and balance sheet 1941–42; price lists 1909–10, early 20th cent.; staff magazine *Clerk Green Chronicle*, 1991–93; photograph of directors and sales force n.d.; Lloyds Research Ltd, memorandum and articles of association 1957.

LOFTHOUSE & SALTMER LTD
Kingston upon Hull

Wholesale druggist

History: In 1802 John Lofthouse established a druggist's business at 12 Market Place, Kingston upon Hull. He was joined in partnership by James Saltmer in 1863, and the business was styled Lofthouse & Saltmer. In 1873 warehouses were acquired at Church Lane, Kingston upon Hull. In 1910 the business was incorporated as a limited liability company, Lofthouse & Saltmer Ltd, and expanded into the wholesale distribution of drugs and galenicals, in particular, halibut liver oil. In 1941 the company's premises at Church Lane were destroyed during enemy action, prompting a move to new buildings within the city. In 1962 the company was acquired by Evans Medical Ltd, Speke, Liverpool, a subsidiary of Glaxo Laboratories Ltd. In 1965 the company re-located to Stoneferry Road, Kingston upon Hull. In 1966 the wholesale distribution interests of Glaxo Group Ltd and British Drug Houses Group Ltd, London, merged to form a limited liability company, Vestric Ltd. This combined interest created a company with 36 trading branches, amongst which were many long-established companies including James Woolley Sons & Co Ltd, Duncan Flockhart Ltd and Bradley & Bliss Ltd. Lofthouse & Saltmer Ltd became a branch of Vestric Ltd at this point, ceasing to operate under its own name. In 1984 the Kingston upon Hull branch of Vestric Ltd was closed, and amalgamated with Vestric Ltd, Leeds.

'The North of England, Vestric Hull' in M Worling, *Vestric: The first twenty years 1966–86* (Vestric, Runcorn, 1986)

Records: Kingston upon Hull City Records Office, 79 Lowgate, Kingston upon Hull HU1 1HN

Directors' meetings minutes 1910–60; register of members and transfers 1910–50; share ledger 1910–20; summary of share capital and shares 1911–17; dividend statements 1933–61; annual returns 1940–58 (w); receipts for annual returns 1942–58 (w); letter from Board of Trade re annual returns 1948; private ledgers 1910–62; private journals 1910–62. (Ref: DBLS 1-31)

J M LOVERIDGE PLC
Southbrook Road, Southampton

Manufacture, wholesale and retail of pharmaceutical products

History: John Montague Loveridge qualified as a pharmacist in 1939, and established a retail business at 439 Millbrook Road, Southampton. Shortly afterwards he established a second shop at The Corner House, Broad Street, Southampton. Although his business began as a retail operation, it soon began manufacturing galenicals and distributing the products of major drug manufacturers around the local area. In 1944 J M Loveridge Ltd was incorporated as a limited liability company to acquire the businesses at Millbrook Road and Broad Street. In the same year J M Loveridge Ltd acquired the retail pharmacy business of W E Youngman (Hythe) Ltd, The Pharmacy, New Road, Hythe, Hampshire. In 1946 this company was renamed Wessex Pharmacies Ltd and acquired the retail businesses of J M Loveridge Ltd at Millbrook Road and at Broad Street. Wessex Pharmacies Ltd also purchased properties at 6/6a Millbrook Road and at Mantle Place, Southampton, in 1946 and at Warren Avenue, Southampton, in 1947. In 1946 J M Loveridge Ltd, which was now a purely manufacturing and wholesaling operation, based at Millbrook, Southampton, organised the first medical exhibition held in England since before the Second World War. Its purpose was to publicise the range of new products that had resulted from scientific and clinical research carried out during that war. It sponsored a second exhibition in Southampton in 1948. Wessex Pharmacies Ltd sold the Warren Avenue business in 1952 and the Hythe pharmacy in 1954. The Millbrook Road business was acquired in 1958 by N J Buckingham. In 1954 J M Loveridge Ltd entered the export market, supplying packed pharmaceuticals to British Commonwealth countries. Between 1957 and 1959 it also won contracts to supply the county borough of Southampton with drugs, proprietary and non-proprietary preparations and chemists' sundries. In 1961 it purchased a distribution depot at Higher Merley Lane, Corfe Mullen, Dorset, which stocked and distributed a full range of pharmaceuticals and over-the-counter products to pharmacies and doctors throughout the south of England. By 1962 the company was organised into 4 divisions: wholesale, veterinary, pharmaceutical manufacturing and photographic. In 1963 it acquired The Standard Tablet Co Ltd, manufacturing chemists of Hove, Brighton & Hove, which had been established around 1913, and acquired by Dubarry Perfumery Co Ltd, Goldstone Laboratories, Hove, in 1924. In 1971 J M Loveridge Ltd entered into an agreement with Herbert Ferryman Ltd, Southampton, to buy Statim Pharmaceuticals Ltd, Claybank Road, Copnor, Portsmouth. This association was brief, and in 1973 J M Loveridge Ltd sold its shares in the company to Herbert Ferryman Ltd. In 1971 J M Loveridge Ltd incorporated a subsidiary company,

J M Loveridge (CI) Ltd, at 4 Lewis Street, St Helier, Jersey, to provide a wholesale distribution service to the Channel Islands. In 1973 this company was sold to Learner, Le Cocq & Co Ltd, St Helier. In 1972 J M Loveridge Ltd was floated as a public limited liability company, retaining the same name. A new warehouse in Millbrook Road, Southampton, was completed in 1976, and became the company's headquarters. By 1981 the company was organised into 3 divisions, the photographic division having been amalgamated into the wholesale division. By 1997 the headquarters of J M Loveridge plc and its manufacturing and packaging plant were at Southbrook Road, Southampton, the Millbrook Road premises having been sold.

'Soton Chemist Employs 140 in Expanding Company', *Southern Evening Echo*, 25 Oct 1962, 12

Records: J M Loveridge plc, Southbrook Road, Southampton SO15 1BH

Directors' and general meetings minutes 1944 to date; memorandum and articles of association 1944; certificate of incorporation on conversion to a public limited company 1982; special resolutions 1945, 1951; resolution 1968; combined registers of members and share registers, incl. annual returns 1944 to date; ordinary share register 1972 to date; share certificates, transfer forms and related correspondence 1944–72; balance sheets and accounts 1945–49; directors' reports and accounts 1951–58, 1965; annual reports 1972 to date; internal credit notes 1958–61; trademark certificates and related papers 1937–90; manufacturing product sheets 1972–89; 'specials' formulae books c.1940s–77; product advertisements (some with original artwork) c.1960s–70s; press cutting 1962; labels: albums 1960s–70s, printing record book 1967–80, customers' orders 1975–80; stationery sample book n.d., c.1940s–59; property papers: warehouse to rear of 6 Millbrook Road, correspondence and specifications 1958–60, Calne, Wiltshire, plans and correspondence 1972; staff time sheets 1984; photographs: John Montague Loveridge n.d., 1950s, Millbrook premises n.d., 1940s–80s, general meeting group, incl. A Loveridge and sisters n.d., mid-1980s, medical exhibitions, exhibitors' stands 1946, 1948; certificate of thanks to company for commemorative Silver Jubilee spoons 1977; letters of thanks for gifts and loans 1980s; souvenir programmes, medical exhibitions 1946, 1948; sales representative's sample case n.d.

J M Loveridge (CI) Ltd: directors' meetings minutes 1971–73; general meetings minutes 1971–72; notice of extraordinary general meeting and special resolution 1971; papers re establishment of company 1970–71; property papers: leases on Lewis Street 1968, 1970, rental receipts 1971–72, Eagle Works, Queen's Street 1972–73; correspondence 1970–73.

The Standard Tablet Co Ltd: directors' and general meetings minutes 1962–82; combined J M Loveridge Ltd and Standard Tablet Co Ltd profit and loss account (p) 1973; private ledger 1959–62; journals 1944–63; cash book 1954–63; deeds of assignment re trademarks 1963; capsule formulae book n.d., c.1920s.

Statim Pharmaceuticals Ltd: directors' meetings agenda and minutes, with monthly budgets 1967–73; draft balance sheets and profit and loss accounts 1968–70, 1973; analysis of deliveries in Portsea Island, Portsmouth 1968; confidential paper by Herbert Ferryman Ltd, with suggestion of merger of wholesaling operations with Statim Pharmaceuticals Ltd, J M Loveridge Ltd, R Cripps, Brighton, Jones & King, Portsmouth and Graham Tatford & Co Ltd, Portsmouth 1968; wage scale/staff list c.1973; quotations and rental charges for van hire c.1968–73.

Wessex Pharmacies Ltd: directors' and general meetings minutes 1942 to date; memorandum and articles of association 1942; balance sheets and accounts 1946–49; cash book 1964–70; prescription books, incl. prescriptions dispensed by N J Buckingham 1933–51, 1961–86.

MACFARLAN SMITH LTD
Wheatfield Road, Edinburgh

Manufacturer of alkaloids and fine chemicals

History: Around 1815 John Fletcher Macfarlan, a licentiate of the Royal College of Surgeons of Edinburgh and bailie of the city, acquired an apothecary's shop in North Bridge, Edinburgh, and began manufacture of the opium-based medicine, laudanum. In 1830 he took into partnership his former apprentice, David Rennie Brown, and the business was styled J F Macfarlan & Co. In 1832 the firm began to manufacture morphine acetate and hydrochloride, using the method of isolating morphine from opium, devised by Dr William Gregory of Edinburgh University. Later the firm manufactured codeine, and established a reputation as a major supplier of all opium alkaloids used in medicine, a pioneer in the production of apomorphine and ethylmorphine and a leader in the research, development and manufacture of anaesthetics, chloroform and ether. During the 1840s chemical works at Abbeyhill, Edinburgh, were acquired to aid the production of alkaloids, and in the early 1900s the firm established a further site at Northfield, Edinburgh, for the production of strychnine. In 1901 David Rennie Brown's grandson, David Rainy Brown, became a partner in the business which, from then until the 1960s, remained in family hands. The business was incorporated as a limited liability company, J F Macfarlan & Co Ltd, in 1950 and in 1960 merged with T & H Smith Ltd to form a new limited liability company, Macfarlan Smith Ltd. J F Macfarlan & Co Ltd was dissolved in 1970. T & H Smith had been established at 21 & 23 Duke Street, Edinburgh, in 1827 by Thomas Smith and his brother, Henry. In 1837 the firm began manufacture of opium alkaloids, in particular, morphine. During the 1840s Blandfield Chemicals Works, Broughton Road, Canonmills, Edinburgh, was acquired by the firm, and a London branch was established at 12 Worship Street in 1848, from which essence of coffee was also manufactured. The business was incorporated as a limited liability company, T & H Smith Ltd, in 1904 and 3 years later moved to a larger site at Gorgie, Edinburgh. In 1919 the company acquired the business of Glasgow Apothecaries Co, which had been established at Virginia Street, Glasgow, in 1805 by a group of general practitioners who wished to establish an efficient dispensary for their prescribed drugs. Shortly afterwards, Glasgow Apothecaries Co began distributing wholesale to retail druggists. In 1926 T & H Smith Ltd acquired John Mackay & Co, Edinburgh, and incorporated a number of colonial subsidiary companies in Australia, Canada and New Zealand from the 1930s. In 1962 Macfarlan Smith Ltd merged with Duncan Flockhart & Co Ltd and its subsidiary companies to form Edinburgh Pharmaceutical Industries Ltd. This group was, in turn, acquired by Glaxo Group Ltd in 1963. Macfarlan Smith Ltd continued to trade under its own name and, in 1990 was purchased from Glaxo Group plc by its management, through a newly incorporated holding company, Meconic Ltd, which was converted to a public limited liability company, Meconic plc, in 1995. Macfarlan Smith Ltd was still trading in 1999.

'Bicentenary of J F Macfarlan & Co Ltd', *Glaxo Group News*, April–May 1980; D Bolton, 'The Development of Alkaloid Manufacture in Edinburgh, 1832–1939', *Chemistry and Industry*, 1976, 701-8; L G Matthews, *History of Pharmacy in Britain* (Livingstone, Edinburgh, 1962) 229-30; *T & H Smith Ltd: Romance of 100 years* (T & H Smith Ltd, Edinburgh, 1927)

Records 1: Archivist (Historical Records), Records Centre, Glaxo Wellcome plc, 891-995 Greenford Road, Greenford UB6 0HE

Directors' meetings minutes 1958–90; general meetings minutes 1956–67, 1976; memorandum and articles of association 1960; chairman's agenda book 1964; agendas and papers 1964–65; directors' attendance books 1948–58, 1960–67, n.d.; papers: general meetings 1958–63, establishment of Macfarlan Smith (Canada) Ltd 1952–64; seal register 1960–76; register of directors' share and debenture interests 1960–65; returns of allotments of shares with correspondence 1960–62; stock valuation papers 1965; papers re shares 1952–63; annual accounts 1970–73; financial returns 1983–90; ledgers 1941–55, 1960–64;

statements of accounts: 1965-68, 1970, Macfarlan Smith (New Zealand) Ltd 1957-64, Macfarlan Smith (Australia) Ltd 1958-64; budgets 1970-72; insurance policy 1956-69; agreements on patents and trademarks 1957-64; papers: trademarks 1959-69, ethyl chloride production 1934-39, drugs production processes 1910-75; monographs re alkaloids and opiates 1813-1987; opiates processes notebooks 1941; dangerous drugs register 1961; price schedules 1961-69; advertising and promotional material, press releases and press cuttings 1944-80; plans, inventories and correspondence re building of sulphuric ether processing plant 1926-46, 1948-49; plan and notes re demolition at Blandfield Works 1988; staff salaries 1964-67; staff record cards: 1959-85, T & H Smith Ltd 1893-1964, J F Macfarlan & Co Ltd 1914-72; photographs: directors c.1920, n.d., plant, staff and exhibitions 1960s, 1977, opium processing and poppy cultivation 1930s, 1960-71, plants n.d.; portrait of Sir Austin Bide 1974; monographs re pharmacy and history of pharmacy 1906, 1939-76; historical notes and publications 1945-52, 1969, 1988; drawings of plants n.d.; office calendars 1964-84; Edinburgh maps and guides 1928-68; miscellaneous papers and agreements 1951-90.

W & R Hatrick Ltd: minutes: directors' meetings 1952-65, general meetings 1955-63; memoranda and articles of association 1929, 1934-59; profit and loss accounts and balance sheets 1936-64; papers re proposed warehouse at Blochairn Road Estate, Glasgow 1964; notes and correspondence re other Glasgow premises 1963-64; correspondence with T & H Smith Ltd 1953-61; reports on Edinburgh Pharmaceutical Industries Ltd directors' visits to company 1964-65.

J F Macfarlan & Co Ltd: partnership and co-partnership agreements 1866-1957; corporate papers: board of directors 1960-64, company registration 1926, 1935, 1951, T & H Smith Ltd's interest in the company n.d., trade with T Morson & Son 1821, 1848; share certificate issue books 1951-56; stock valuation lists 1958-60; balance sheets and profit and loss accounts 1908-63; accounting papers 1958-64; ledgers: 1926-36, private 1945-59; private journals 1951-60; taxation receipt with photograph of North Bridge premises 1896; papers re codeine patent 1886-89; papers re registration of trademark *Myelocene* n.d.; laboratory and technical notebooks re opiates 1851-82; technical notes, press cuttings and correspondence: opiates and opium trade 1850-1955, salicin 1879-1940, n.d.; papers re dressings 1889-1962; papers re ether 1914-46; recipe and process book 1906, c.1942; selling prices of opium, morphine and codeia 1855-1905; price lists 1890-1964; promotional material c.1885-1918; company scrapbook n.d.; product labels c.1880-1924; premises valuations 1875-1925; plans to build distillery 1915; property papers: Abbeyhill Works 1849-50s, 7 Hanover Street 1899-1901, 2 Grange Road 1897, 9 Moor Lane 1906,

Northfield site, Edinburgh 1909–14, 32 Bethnal Green Road 1925, Potters Bar, Hertfordshire 1939–n.d., Elstree Way, Hertfordshire 1940–61, security 1919–63; staff salaries book 1912–24; register of employees on active service 1940–45; personal papers: William Gregory 1803–58, D Rennie Brown 1808–75, D Rainy Brown 1840–1921, Alexander McDonald 1886–1920, David Brown Dott 1887, 1896–1909, 1930s–41, Lord Lister 1894–1929, A S Birnie 1936; photographs: premises c.1888–1955, staff 1911–55; papers re Paris pharmaceutical exhibition 1900; certificate of silver medal for alkaloids at Paris exhibition 1867; representatives' question and answer books c.1960; monographs: 1915–59, opiates 1882–96; office calendars 1923–39, 1948–51; agreement with other companies to form Scottish Wholesale Druggists Association 1921–36; minutes: Glasgow Druggists Early Closing Association 1854–71, company bowling club 1947–62; historical notes 1861–1952, n.d.

John Mackay & Co Ltd: balance sheets and profit and loss accounts 1927–61; recipe book 1881–1916; price lists 1953–57; product labels 1881; historical notes 1964. (Ref: Macfarlan Smith Historical Collection)

T & H Smith Ltd: minutes: directors' 1904–62, general 1904–11, 1936–47, directors' and works chemists' 1939–47, private 1946–57; memoranda and articles of association 1904–15, 1951–65; change of name certificates 1957–63; directors' meetings agenda book 1949–52; business papers: 1914–15, 1934–36, 1944–69, transition to Macfarlan Smith Ltd 1960–62, transition to Edinburgh Pharmaceutical Industries Ltd 1955–62, notes re sale of assets to John MacKay & Co Ltd 1962; registers: seals n.d., ordinary and preference shareholders 1904–51, debentures 1929–44, schedule of share bonuses 1909–25; preference stock transfers 1943–63; debenture stock books 1904–48; debenture notices and correspondence 1904–60; sealed certificates 1937–52; cancelled share certificates 1925–63; papers re stocks, shareholders and shareholdings 1904–57; mandates to pay dividends 1904–54; scrip issues 1958–59; correspondence re shares 1950–51; annual reports and accounts 1904–62; annual reports and balance sheets 1926–47; balance sheets and profit and loss accounts 1908–11, 1921, 1931–50 (w); agendas, annual reports and balance sheets 1915–36; statements of accounts 1938, 1947, 1955–62; ledgers: 1929–41, 1948–60, private 1901–36, 1941–45; journals: 1823–35 (w), 1912–21, 1943–61, cash 1964–66, private 1925–52; cash books: 1890–95, 1939–42, private 1901–37; group accounts papers 1959–60; works expense analyses 1957–59; papers re capital structure of company 1953–62; financial reports: costings at Edinburgh and Glasgow branches 1934, office organisation 1960–61; bank book 1937–60; taxation papers: income tax 1915–24, excess profits tax 1940–47, directors' tax deductions 1959–64; insurance papers 1957–70; writs 1905–47; legal agreements re drugs 1942–62; legal papers and assignments of trademarks 1880–1930;

patents and licencing papers, xylocaine hydrochloride 1949–61; codeine contracts with Ministry of Supply 1942–46; manufacturing and price regulation agreements 1915–52; research reports 1913, 1930, 1953–83; laboratory journal 1881; laboratory analyses books 1929–44; guardbook of tests and trials 1954–60; opium process books 1857–65, 1874–87, 1907–42; opium registers: receipts 1906–13, purchases 1940–53; opium operations costs book 1900–01, 1953–55; record of opium workings 1869–81; papers re opiates c.1870, c.1880, 1945–69; reports and correspondence re opium 1954–56; operations books: alkaloids department 1938–54, strychnine 1912–20, codeine 1914–53, ethyl morphine 1915–50, caffeine 1917–28, *nux vomica* 1920–46, opiates 1925–50; drugs files 1946–47; drugs production notebooks 1911–14; production and recipe books 1857–81, 1900–15, 1930–45; catalogues and price lists 1901–08, 1939–44; product catalogue 1964; despatch books 1913–42; distribution summary 1961; prescriptions log 1838; scrapbook of counter curios 1908–11; poster advertising alkaloids n.d.; promotional material 1878, 1920s–62; 150th anniversary photographs and magazine 1977; press cuttings 1947–83; guardbook incl. stationery and labels 1830s–1945; Blandfield works: inventories 1889, 1935, reports and plans 1920, 1950–55, map 1914, photographs 1920–77, visitors book 1947–65; correspondence and press cuttings re proposed site expansion 1949–55; notes re development and reorganisation plans 1956–60; papers and photographs re company premises 1893, 1907, 1944–62, 1971, n.d.; staff register 1960; staff lists 1949; salaries and wages registers 1898–1964; salaries and bonus shares register 1908–26; employment agreements: 1906–57, managing director 1952, overseas agents 1921–40; Christmas gratuities list 1905–34; review of salaries 1960–64; confidential staff files 1951–56; staff instructions 1938; *Retort*, staff magazine 1951–61; letterbook 1933–35; correspondence: G Delitsch 1876–83, C Mehta, India 1946, Allied Laboratories Ltd 1959–64, N Rainy Brown 1965–69, miscellaneous 19th cent.; photographs: buildings and works 1930s–57, 1987, n.d., drugs production 1940, 1955–60, n.d., overseas plant and drugs production 1950s–70s, n.d., personnel 1961, n.d., exhibition 1910, miscellaneous 19th–20th cents; papers re other companies 1937–65; notes: appointment of executive head 1955, drugs 1832–1942; PhD thesis re alkaloids 1939; monographs and reports 1845–1988; obituary of Dr James Watt, director 1945; historical notes 1944–69; office calendars 1951–82; T & H Smith (Australia) Ltd: memorandum and articles of association 1957, papers re incorporation 1955–59; papers re Canadian office and T & H Smith (Canada) Ltd 1934–64.

Records 2: Macfarlan Smith Ltd, Wheatfield Road, Edinburgh EH11 2QA

Directors' meetings minutes 1978–90; technical and production meetings minutes 1971–85; board papers 1974–90; formation notices n.d.; share certificates and memoranda 1970–97; accounts 1961–96; legal papers 1980 to date; enquiry papers n.d.; formula book 1940; opium processes n.d. (m); research reports 1960–70; development papers 1960–80; production papers 1974–86; manufacturing guides 1950 to date; DHSS licences 1982–84; Home Office returns 1976–93; sales reports n.d.; advertisement book 1961–65; labels and printer's blocks 1900–80; papers: Glaxo Australia 1980–85, Glaxo Group plc 1992–93, Reckitt & Colman 1959–85, Warner Lambert 1959; works reports 1969–91; alkaloid works regulations 1963–79; factory inspector's papers 1978–81; papers re fire at Wheatfield Road 1962; staff papers: former employees n.d., pension schemes n.d.; job evaluation papers 1976–88; correspondence with Dickens, Peter Smith-Deuru and Lister n.d.; miscellaneous photographs n.d.; historical articles n.d.

Glasgow Apothecaries Co Ltd: trial balance sheet, assets and liabilities on liquidation 1919.

J F Macfarlan & Co Ltd: corporate papers 1968–70s; production papers 1941, 1958–62; research papers 1951–64; notes 1904.

Meconic plc: board papers 1990–96; register of members 1990–95; share certificate books 1990–95; share transfer forms 1990–95; share option contracts 1990–95; papers re management buyout of Macfarlan Smith Ltd n.d.; floatation papers n.d.; papers re purchase of Diosynth opiate business 1993; acquisition papers 1996; accounts 1991–97; property reports 1996; correspondence with Barings and McGrigor Donald n.d.

T & H Smith Ltd: certificate of incorporation 1904; certificate of registration 1904; corporate papers 1889–20th cent.; technical meetings minutes 1951–60; accounts 1904–07, 1912–30, 1938–64; research reports 1950–70; development papers 1958–80; research and commercial papers 1968–70; papers re opiate costs 1939–60; agreements n.d.; deeds and licence agreements n.d.; work papers 1915–16; works reports 1953–63; leases and warrants n.d.; miscellaneous correspondence n.d.; company publications 1950–70.

Records 3: Dr Peter M Worling, The Grange, 29 Fernielaw Avenue, Edinburgh EH13 0EF

T & H Smith Ltd: Virginia Street, Glasgow, private formulary 1930–36.

Glasgow Apothecaries Co: centenary brochure 1905.

A G MACK & CO LTD
165 High Street, Penge, Bromley, London

Dispensing chemist

History: In 1895 Gregory Mack moved from Norfolk and established a chemist's business at 165 High Street, Penge, Bromley, London. During the 1930s his 2 sons qualified as pharmaceutical chemists, and one, Arthur Gregory Mack, succeeded to his father's business, trading as A G Mack & Co. Following the Second World War, Arthur Mack established photographic shops in London at Penge, Sidcup, Bexley, and Orpington, Bromley, which were later sold to their respective managers. During the 1950s Frank Judge was apprenticed to Arthur Mack and in 1960 qualified as a pharmaceutical chemist. In 1967 he purchased the business at 165 High Street, continuing to trade as A G Mack & Co. In 1972 he acquired Basil Smith's chemist's business at 5 The Parade, Croydon Road, Penge, and in 1974 established a branch of A G Mack & Co in the High Street, Beckenham, Bromley. In 1979 he acquired the business of Hamer & Crumpler, 121 Westmoreland Road, Bromley. In 1980 the business was incorporated as a limited liability company, A G Mack & Co Ltd. In 1981 the business of A Beaman Ltd, 77 Queensway, Petts Wood, Bromley, was acquired by the company, and sold to The Boots Co plc in 1992. In 1984 a further business was acquired, John Batten, 2 Eden Park Avenue, Elmers End, Beckenham. The Westmoreland Road, Bromley, business was sold in 1984, the 5 The Parade business in 1985, and the High Street, Beckenham, business in 1986. In 1997 Frank Judge retired, and the business was acquired by Rajnish Patel, continuing to trade as A G Mack & Co Ltd. In November 1997 the company went into liquidation.

Records: Bromley Central Library, High Street, Bromley BR1 1EX

Annual reports and accounts 1969 to date; ledgers 1950s–60s; cash books: 1920 to date, n.d., Beckenham 1976, 1983–87, Petts Wood 1989–90; customer account books 1965; VAT ledgers 1973–87, 1991–92; stock books 1962; recipe books 1950s, n.d.; F Judge's pharmaceutical notes and recipes 1950s; compendium of past formulae 1933–66; prescription books: c.1920s–50s, 1970s, 1992–94, contraceptive pills n.d., Basil Smith 1946–89; private prescriptions 1980s; script books 1980s; prescription charge notice 1971; dispensing manual 1979–80; drugs registers 1946–47, 1963–66; poisons registers 1930–80s; drug tariff 1956; architectural drawings of Penge premises 1968–69; papers re building alterations and extensions 1949–52; wages books 1940s–88; register of pharmacists and premises 1947; Basil Smith's college notebooks 1928;

certificates of registration: Arthur Mack 1930, Basil Smith n.d.; administration accounts, G H Mack's estate 1957. (Ref: Acc.1000)

MACLEANS LTD

SmithKline Beecham House, Great West Road, Brentford, Hounslow, London

Manufacture and marketing of pharmaceutical products

History: Macleans Ltd was incorporated as a limited liability company in 1919 to manufacture and market pharmaceutical products to chemists. It was initially based at Spring Street, Paddington, London. During the 1920s the company began production of medicines for the relief of stomach acidity and indigestion, under the trade name 'Macleans' Stomach Powder', as well as manufacturing peroxide toothpastes. In 1932 a new factory was built on the Great West Road, Brentford, Hounslow, London, and in 1935 Macleans Ltd was floated as a public limited liability company. It was acquired in 1938 by Beecham Pills Ltd, which had recently acquired the businesses of Dinneford & Co Ltd, manufacturers of 'Dinneford's Fluid Magnesia', and Holloways Pills Ltd, producers of 'Holloways Pills'. Both products were added to the sales portfolio of Macleans Ltd, as, in 1953, were those of J C Eno Ltd and Yeast Vite Ltd, also subsidiaries of Beecham Pills Ltd. Macleans Ltd ceased trading in 1960 and its pharmaceutical business was transferred to Beecham Group Ltd at St Helens. The name Macleans is still used as a trade name by SmithKline Beecham plc.

'Modern Methods in Pharmaceutical Manufacture', *Industrial Chemist, Pharmaceutical and Cosmetic Supplement*, Oct 1935, 118-23 and Nov 1935, 133-9

Records 1: SmithKline Beecham plc, SmithKline Beecham House, Great West Road, Brentford TW8 9BD. Enquiries to SmithKline Beecham plc, 1 New Horizons Court, Great West Road, Brentford TW8 9EP

Directors' and general meetings minutes 1931-83; register of members and share ledger 1972-74; committee meetings minutes: transfer 1948-56, formula 1938-39; seal register 1978-91; papers re company re-organisation 1959; legal actions re 'stomach powder' imitations 1938-40; legal opinion and judgement re use of trade mark *Maclean* for indigestion preparation 1937, n.d.; licence agreement with Jacq Mot Junior, Holland 1954; agreement with Bristol-Myers Co, New York 1956; representative brief re indigestion powder and tablets 1956; papers re pricing policy 1957; retail price list 1958; notice cards of representative's visit n.d.; certificate of compliance with national scheme for the employment of disabled men 1940; photographs: visit by Duchess of Kent 1958, female staff fire display n.d.; publication by Hugh Maclean 1928; historical notes 1935, 1972.

Records 2: St Helens Local History & Archives Library, Gamble Institute, Victoria Square, St Helens WA10 1DY

Papers re company re-organisation 1959–60; agreements with Beecham Pharmaceuticals Ltd re *Maclean* trade mark 1960; papers: product pricing 1960s, advertising and expenditure c.1950–61, product research conference 1959, transfer of production to St Helens 1960. (Ref: BP/4/17)

Records 3: History of Advertising Trust, HAT House, 12 Raveningham Centre, Raveningham NR14 6NU

Advertising guardbook 1970–84; advertising proofs and artwork 1980; advertisements for 'Maclean Indigestion Tablets' 1974–80s; papers, memoranda and advertising campaign material 1952–67. (Ref: Leo Burnett guardbooks, 110, proofs shelf 2; MEAL collection 1974–89, R10-80; JWT 108 (1965) 302 (1966) 404 (1967) 429, 630 (1952–67))

T McMASTER LTD
Dumbarton Road, Glasgow

Chemist and druggist

History: In 1896 Thomas McMaster was registered as a chemist and druggist at 12 Lyle Street, Greenock, Inverclyde. In 1901 he established himself in business at 322 Dumbarton Road, Glasgow, and traded under the business name T McMaster. The business was incorporated as a limited liability company, Thomas McMaster Ltd, in 1926, and by 1936 had acquired additional premises at 510 & 2354 Dumbarton Road, and at other locations in Glasgow. In 1945 Thomas McMaster moved to 10 Vanna Road, Glasgow, and in 1948 ceased to be registered. In the same year, William Crawford McMaster, who had been registered as a chemist and druggist in 1923, assumed control of the company, which continued to operate as Thomas McMaster Ltd. It ceased trading in 1952.

Records: Glasgow City Archives, Mitchell Library, North Street, Glasgow G3 7DN

Directors' meetings minutes 1928–51; combined register of members and share ledger 1928–51. (Ref: TD147/12)

JOHN McMILLAN LTD
693 Great Western Road, Glasgow

Chemist and druggist

History: John McMillan was in business as a chemist and druggist in Great Western Road, Glasgow, prior to 1868. In 1871 he was operating from 9 Breadalbane Street, Glasgow, and in 1876 from 17 Great Western Road and 8 Buckingham Buildings, Hillhead (later 693 Great Western Road), Glasgow. He also had premises at 208 St George's Road, Glasgow. In 1905 he ceased to be registered, but the business continued to trade. By 1937 it was incorporated as a limited liability company, John McMillan Ltd, operating from 17 & 693 Great Western Road, Glasgow. By 1955 it was trading only from the latter, and in 1960 ceased to operate under its own name.

Records: Glasgow City Archives, Mitchell Library, North Street, Glasgow G3 7DN

General ledger, 17 Great Western Road 1955–60; purchase ledgers: Hillhead 1955–60, Great Western Road 1955–58; sales ledger 1948–59; cash books: general 1956–58, Hillhead 1952–60; purchase invoice books: Hillhead 1905–29, 1951–60, Great Western Road 1944–56, St George's Road 1956–58; prescription books: 1941–48, Hillhead 1873–75, 1887–1960 (w), Great Western Road 1887–88, 1922–75 (w), St George's Road 1957–59. (Ref: TD698)

F MALTBY & SONS LTD
Dunston House, Portland Street, Lincoln, Lincolnshire

Pharmaceutical wholesaler and retailer

History: In 1910 Frank Maltby opened a retail pharmacy at Corporation Street, Lincoln, Lincolnshire. Later in the same year he re-located his business to 46 Silver Street, Lincoln. In co-operation with a small group of local pharmacists, Frank Maltby began to distribute pharmaceutical products and when, during the interwar period, the other pharmacists pulled out of the agreement, Frank Maltby expanded his business, becoming both a retailer and wholesaler of pharmaceutical products. Frank Maltby died in 1945, and thereafter his widow, Edith Maltby, took over the running of the business until the late 1940s, when their son, John Henry Maltby, took control of the firm. In 1949 the business was incorporated as a limited liability company, F Maltby & Sons Ltd, with John, his brother G F Maltby and their mother, Edith, as directors. John Maltby, representing the company, was a member of the Lincoln Pharmaceutical Committee from 1948. During the late 1950s, the company acquired a proportion of the shares of the Lincoln & Midland Counties Drug Co Ltd, a company with origins in the mid nineteenth century, whose most successful product was a treatment for skin ailments, 'Clark's Blood Mixture'. This company was acquired as a wholly-owned subsidiary of F Maltby & Sons Ltd in 1970, and was liquidated during the 1980s. By the 1960s F Maltby & Sons Ltd was primarily a wholesaling operation, with a small retail pharmacy attached to the premises at Silver Street. During the early 1970s John Maltby's sons, Anthony and David, entered the company as directors and the decision was taken to incorporate a subsidiary company, F Maltby Ltd, as a retail outlet. Thereafter the parent company, F Maltby & Sons Ltd, became a purely wholesale operation. In 1977 both companies re-located to more spacious premises at Dunston House, Portland Street, Lincoln, and F Maltby Ltd ceased to operate as a pharmacists' shop, but continued to function from a room at Dunston House, as a registered pharmacy, which dispensed private prescriptions to established customers and to members of staff. The area of distribution covered by F Maltby & Sons Ltd expanded by the 1980s to cover an area from Peterborough, in the south to Pickering, North Yorkshire, in the north, Norfolk and the east coast. John Maltby died in 1990, leaving the company in family hands. In 1997 the board of directors comprised his widow, J Maltby, his brother, G F Maltby and his sons, Anthony and David Maltby. The range of products which the company distributes, includes ethical pharmaceuticals, over-the-counter medicines, galenicals and generics, vaccines, toiletries and household products.

Records: F Maltby & Sons Ltd, Dunston House, Portland Street, Lincoln LN5 7NN

Certificate of incorporation 1949; ledgers 1931, 1940s; expenses account book 1926–28; invoices 1939; recipe books 1909–11, 1914–79, n.d.; stock mixtures book 1962–69; dangerous drugs and poisons registers 1930–68, 1974–87; notebook 1940s; prescription books 1911 to date; price registers 1930s, 1943–44; 46 Silver Street premises: architectural plan 1930, photographs early-mid 20th cent., 1951–52, 1970s; John Henry Maltby's certificate of fellowship of Pharmaceutical Society of Great Britain 1974; printing plate with company's name and address n.d.; published reference works and formularies 1898 to date.

Lincoln Pharmaceutical Committee: minutes 1948–72.

MARTIN & CO LTD
Lincoln, Lincolnshire

Chemist

History: Martin & Co Ltd was incorporated as a limited liability company in Lincoln, Lincolnshire, around 1899. It appears to have been wound up in the late 1960s.

Records: Lincolnshire Archives, St Rumbold Street, Lincoln LN2 5AB

Ledger and minutes c.1913–22, 1928–67; register of members and share ledger c.1899–1966. (Ref: Misc Dep 392)

W MARTINDALE
New Cavendish Street, London

Pharmaceutical manufacturer

History: The founder of this business, William Martindale (1840–1902), was apprenticed to his uncle, William Robinson Martindale, chemist and druggist of Carlisle, Cumbria, from 1856. On his uncle's death, William completed his apprenticeship with Andrew Thompson, a chemist and druggist, qualifying in 1862. In the same year William moved to north London and worked as a chemist's assistant at James Merrell's pharmacy on the corner of Camden Road and York Way. He passed the minor and major examinations of the Pharmaceutical Society of Great Britain in 1864 and 1866 respectively. Between 1866 and 1868 he worked as an assistant in T N R Morson's pharmacy, Southampton Row, London, and in 1868 joined University College Hospital (UCH) as its first qualified dispenser. He also taught pharmacy at UCH's Medical School and in 1872 edited the *UCH Pharmacopoeia*. In 1873 he acquired the business of 2 of Morson's former assistants, Hopkins & Williams. This business, situated in New Cavendish Street, London, traded thereafter as W Martindale. William Martindale also became an examiner for the Pharmaceutical Society of Great Britain, serving in this capacity for 10 years. He was elected to the Council of the Society in 1889, became Treasurer in 1898 and President from 1899 to 1900. In addition he compiled his own work, the *Extra Pharmacopoeia*, which included descriptions of drugs not covered by the *British Pharmacopoeia*. The first edition was published in 1883, and the tenth, before his death in 1902. William's son, William Harrison Martindale (1874–1932), studied at University College School, following which he was apprenticed to Charles B Allen whose chemist's business was in Kilburn, Brent, London, and worked for a family friend, Charles Umney. In 1898 he obtained his doctorate and passed both the minor and major examinations of the Pharmaceutical Society of Great Britain. Following this he assumed control of his father's firm and expanded the manufacturing side of the business. In 1928 he rebuilt the New Cavendish Street premises and erected a factory in Chenies Mews behind UCH. He continued publication of the *Extra Pharmacopoeia* until his death, whereupon, the Pharmaceutical Society of Great Britain purchased the production and selling rights. The business, W Martindale, was acquired by Savory & Moore Ltd in 1933, following which the retail operation at New Cavendish Street continued to trade as W Martindale until the mid-1970s. In 1947 Savory & Moore Ltd incorporated the manufacturing and wholesale business of W Martindale as a separate concern, William Martindale Wholesale Ltd. This name was changed in 1963 to Martindale Samoore Ltd, at which time the company had 10 wholesale depots and an ampoule factory. In 1967 Savory & Moore Ltd was acquired by Macarthys Ltd, a wholesale druggist company, established by James Macarthy as a retail pharmacy in Romford, Havering, London, in 1787. It was incorporated as a private limited liability company, Macarthys Ltd, in 1920, and converted to public limited liability status in 1961. Following the acquisition of Savory & Moore Ltd by Macarthys Ltd, W Martindale and Martindale Samoore Ltd ceased to trade in their own right. In 1959 Macarthys Ltd had incorporated a limited liability company, Romford Laboratories Ltd, to operate a pharmaceutical manufacturing plant and laboratory in Danes Road, Romford. In 1964 Romford Laboratories Ltd moved to Chesham House, Chesham Close, North Street, Romford, and in 1968 was renamed Macarthys Laboratories Ltd. In 1990 its name was changed again to Martindale Pharmaceuticals Ltd, and the company re-located to Bampton Road, Harold Hill, Romford. Macarthys plc was acquired by Lloyds Chemists plc in 1992.

W K Fitch, 'The Two Martindales', *Pharmaceutical Journal*, 29 Oct 1983, 502-6; K Holland, 'Macarthy Plc', *Pharmaceutical Journal*, 30 July 1988, 160-5; W H Martindale, 'Links with Lister', *Pharmaceutical Journal*, 28 May 1927, 616; A Wade, 'The Martindales and Their Book', *Pharmaceutical Journal*, 13 June 1992, 787-8

Records 1: Archives & Manuscripts, Wellcome Library for the History & Understanding of Medicine, 183 Euston Road, London NW1 2BE

Prescription books, incl. recipes and formulae for Sir Joseph Lister for cyanide of mercury and zinc in suspension 1885–90 (Ref: MSS 5984-5); prescription books 1936–70 (Ref: CMAC/GC/26).

Records 2: The Museum Curator, Royal Pharmaceutical Society of Great Britain, 1 Lambeth High Street, London SE1 7JN

Private account ledger 1889; cash book 1900–1905; prescription books 1896–1931. (Ref: LDPHA.MANUSCOL.1.1-37, 10.1, 26.1-2.)

Records 3: Martindale Pharmaceuticals Ltd, Bampton Road, Harold Hill, Romford RM3 8UG

Martindale Pharmaceuticals Ltd: formulae book c.1966; book containing sample packaging specifications for products manufactured under the *Ucal* brandname c.1969; portrait of William Martindale n.d.

S MAW, SON & SONS LTD
Monken Hadley, Barnet, London

Manufacturing chemist

History: The business was founded as Hornby & Maw at Fenchurch Street, London, in 1807 by George Maw, originally a Lincolnshire farmer, in joint partnership with his cousin Hornby. This was a short-lived venture and in 1814 Maw left to purchase a surgical plaster factory in Whitecross Street, London. The factory soon began to manufacture surgical instruments and later expanded to produce druggists' sundries, toiletries and pharmaceutical products. Maw's eldest son, John Hornby Maw, was sent to study under Abernethey and Stanley at St Bartholomew's Hospital, London, in order to obtain an understanding of the requirements of surgeons. John was taken into partnership by his father in 1826, and the firm was renamed George Maw & Son. George retired in 1828 and his second son, Solomon, joined his brother in partnership. In 1832 the firm was trading as J & S Maw. John retired in 1835 due to ill health and under Solomon the business expanded rapidly. The firm's first catalogue was produced in 1830, outclassing many rival publications with its lavish illustrations. Following several moves within the City, the business eventually settled at 7-12 Aldersgate Street, premises that had to be completely rebuilt following a fire in 1856. In 1860 Solomon's son, Charles, was taken into partnership and the business was re-styled S Maw & Son. On Solomon's death in 1861, Charles took sole charge of the business until 1870 when John Thompson, who had served the firm as a traveller for 10 years, was made a partner and the business was renamed S Maw Son & Thompson. In 1901 the business was incorporated as a limited liability company, styled S Maw, Son & Sons Ltd, following Thompson's retirement. By this time Charles Trentham Maw and Mowbray T Maw were directors and were joined in 1901 by Dr H T Maw. Owing to lack of space in inner London after the First World War, the company purchased a 22-acre estate at Monken Hadley, Barnet, in 1920, to which it re-located some of its manufacturing operations. The transfer was completed in 1940. Following this the company was renamed Maws Pharmacy Supplies Ltd, and in 1959 acquired the business of Felstead Manufacturing Co Ltd. In 1965 a new limited liability company, S Maw Son & Sons Ltd, was incorporated, to acquire the businesses of Maws Pharmacy Supplies Ltd and Felstead Manufacturing Co Ltd. Shares in S Maw Son & Sons Ltd were jointly owned by the holding company of the trade association, the National Pharmaceutical Union, NPU Holdings Ltd, and Norcros Ltd, Reading. In the same year a commercial agreement was signed between S Maw Son & Sons Ltd and NPU Holdings Ltd, whereby the former agreed to distribute products sponsored by the National Pharmaceutical Union. This contract operated until 1974. In 1973 Norcros Ltd sold its shares in S Maw Son & Sons to the American company, International Telephone & Telegraph Corporation Inc, which traded as ITT Inc. S Maw Son & Sons Ltd was acquired shortly afterwards as a wholly-owned subsidiary of ITT Inc, a company which, in 1973, owned 333 subsidiary companies which had no apparent corporate or technical relationship with each other and no obvious link with the pharmaceutical industry.

J Burnby, 'Pharmaceutical Connections: The Maw Family', *Pharmaceutical Historian*, 15, June 1985, 9-10; 'The House of Maw', *Indian & Eastern Druggist*, Feb 1921, 44-6; 'S Maw, Son and Sons, Ltd, New Barnet', *Pharmaceutical Journal*, 146, 12 April 1941, 159; 'Pharmaceutical Houses of London', *Chemist and Druggist*, 159, 6 June 1953, 577

Records 1: Hertfordshire Archives & Local Studies, County Hall, Hertford SG13 8EJ

Ledgers: partners' 1870–1916, personal, Charles Maw 1874–82, private 1907–53, balance, incl. partners' and later managing directors' accounts 1901–37, impersonal 1922–54, travellers' daily sales 1869–89, New Zealand customers 1913–43; commission accounts, salaries of departments and statements of sales and gross profits 1885–99; registers: comparative departmental sales figures 1913–20, annual export sales 1913–44, foreign agents 1913–20, insurance policies 1918–31; formulae book late 19th cent.; register of pharmaceutical equipment late 19th cent.; register of suppliers of glass goods and pharmaceutical fittings early 20th cent.; customer registers: London c.1875–95, n.d., Great Britain c.1875–95, n.d., foreigners c.1885–95, surgeons and doctors late 19th cent.; title deeds: Monken Hadley 1665–1919, City of London 1877–1922, Holborn, Middlesex 1918–25, St Matthew, Bethnal Green, Middlesex 1884–1916; plans, Monken Hadley 1806, 1938; wages books 1859–64, 1869–89; pay book, Feeding Bottle Department 1880-1912; account books, monthly salaries for office staff, travellers and export agents 1922-33; staff lists early 20th cent. (Ref: D/EMw)

Records 2: National Pharmaceutical Association, Mallinson House, 38-42 St Peter's Street, St Albans AL1 3NP

Memorandum and articles of association 1965; commercial agreement with National Pharmaceutical Union (NPU) for the distribution of NPU sponsored products and related statement of principles 1965; correspondence re dividend payments to NPU Holdings Ltd 1967-69; agreement re transfer of shares from NPU Holdings Ltd to Norcros Ltd 1969; correspondence between NPU Holdings Ltd and Norcros Ltd, with sale, royalty and distribution agreements and share transfer certificate 1969; report on investigation into adverse trading results 1964.

MAWSON & PROCTOR PHARMACEUTICALS LTD
Newcastle upon Tyne

Chemist and druggist and manufacturer of photographic chemicals

History: In 1768 John Proctor established an apothecary's business on his own account at Newcastle upon Tyne, and was joined in the business by his son and later, his grandson, Barnard Simpson Proctor. During the late nineteenth century, the business re-located to Grey Street, Newcastle upon Tyne and, following the death of Barnard Simpson Proctor in 1903, passed into the hands of Thomas Maltby Clague, who had been a partner in the business since 1885. The business was then styled Proctor, Son & Clague. In 1912 the firm merged with another Newcastle upon Tyne business, Mawson, Swan & Morgan Ltd, to form a limited liability company, Mawson & Proctor Ltd, located at Grainger Street, Newcastle upon Tyne. Mawson, Swan & Morgan Ltd had been established in 1828 by John Mawson, a druggist from Penrith, Cumbria, who took Joseph Wilson Swan into partnership in 1846. The firm, Mawson & Swan, compounded and dispensed tinctures and essences and during the 1850s expanded into the manufacture of photographic collodion. Following the death of Mawson in 1867, Joseph Swan conducted the business in partnership with Thomas Morgan, and incorporated the firm as a limited liability company, Mawson, Swan & Morgan Ltd, in 1900. In 1948 Mawson & Proctor Ltd was renamed Mawson & Proctor Pharmaceuticals Ltd, its primary trading activity being the wholesale distribution of pharmaceutical products. In addition, a subsidiary company, Mawson & Proctor Ltd, was incorporated to operate 3 retail pharmacies in Newcastle upon Tyne. In

1948 new premises at Low Friar Lane, Newcastle upon Tyne, were acquired to accommodate the expansion in the wholesale business and in 1965 the Grainger Street pharmacy, Mawson & Proctor Ltd, merged with around 45 local pharmacies to form a limited liability company, Mawson, Proctor (Group Pharmacy) Ltd. In 1983 Mawson & Proctor Pharmaceuticals Ltd and Mawson & Proctor (Group Pharmacy) Ltd were acquired by the wholly-owned subsidiary of AAH Holdings plc, Chemists Holdings Ltd. Mawson & Proctor Pharmaceuticals Ltd ceased to trade under its own name in 1987. AAH Holdings plc was absorbed by GEHE AG in 1995.

'Two Hundred Years Old and Still Showing the Way: A famous Tyneside business celebrates its bicentenary', *Chemist and Druggist*, 16 Nov, 1968, 1-4; 'Wholesalers Bicentenary', *Pharmaceutical Journal*, 16 Nov 1968, 523-4

Records 1: Tyne & Wear Archives Service, Blandford House, Blandford Square, Newcastle upon Tyne NE1 4JA

Directors' meetings minutes 1900–56; general meetings agenda 1901–43 (w); memorandum and articles of association 1900; certificate of incorporation 1900; estimates re proposed formation of a limited company late 19th cent.; notes re Newcastle businesses c.1910; agreement re sale and purchase of the business 1900; correspondence and agreement re sale of shares 1906–07; debenture 1916; share dividends 1940–73; trust deed 1939; balance sheets and profit and loss accounts 1885–1973 (w); liabilities and profit and loss accounts 1901–64; assets and appropriation accounts 1901–64; result of investigation into departmental accounts c.1911; private ledgers: 1875–1921, Joseph Swan 1879–95; private journal 1900–22; departmental percentage lists 1931–35; summaries of sales and purchases 1884–96; expenditure analysis booklets 1971–73; proprietary formulae book and related correspondence 1909–10; centenary exhibition: invitation to private viewing 1978, brochure 1978, *Evening Chronicle* souvenir 1978; title deeds 1878, 1906–12; mortgage papers 1899–1918, 1926; valuations: 1915, fixtures and plant 1904, Grey Street 1915–21, Grainger Street 1915–21, Melbourne Street 1921; inventory of Thomas Morgan's furniture 1886; employment agreements: G Swan 1902, J W Stobbs 1912; wages book 1918–21; staff pension fund accounts 1966–73; managers' reports: 1920–21, monthly 1923; notes for managers c.1920s; booklet re customer relations c.1920s; correspondence 1896, 1921–43; wills: Thomas Morgan 1885, Jane Dawson 1887, Peter Carr 1896; appreciation from members of the Royal family and others 1978–81. (Ref: DT/MSM/1-50)

Records 2: GEHE UK plc, Retail Branch, Atherstone, Warwickshire. Enquiries to GEHE UK plc, Sapphire Court, Walsgrave Triangle Business Park, Coventry CV2 2TX

Combined registers of directors, members and secretaries 1912 to date

Mawson & Proctor (Group Pharmacy) Ltd: general meetings minutes 1965–96; memoranda and articles of association and change of name certificates 1948, 1965, 1987; combined register of members, directors and share ledger 1965–88.

Records 3: The Museum Curator, Royal Pharmaceutical Society of Great Britain, 1 Lambeth High Street, London SE1 7JN

Formulae book 1880–85; memoranda notebook 1887–1928. (Ref: IRA.1997.052; LDPHA.LIB.382)

Records 4: Dr Peter M Worling, The Grange, 29 Fernielaw Avenue, Edinburgh EH13 0EF

Wholesale price list 1964.

MEDEVA PHARMA LTD
Evans House, Regent Park, Kingston Road, Leatherhead, Surrey

Manufacture and sale of pharmaceuticals

History: In 1809 John Evans, in partnership with his brother Edward, opened a small druggist's store in the Foregate, Worcester, Worcestershire. In 1818 the partnership was dissolved, Edward remaining in Worcester to establish himself in the vinegar trade and John travelling to London to become a partner in the firm Kempson, Yates, Evans & Parkinson, wholesale druggists of 40 King Street, Snowhill. This was a short-lived venture and in 1821 Evans formed a new partnership agreement with Daniel Stable and the business of Stable, Evans & Co was established at 62 Wood Street, Cheapside, London, and at London Wall. The partnership was dissolved in 1823, and thereafter Evans traded alone as John Evans & Co until he entered into a partnership agreement with Joseph Sidney Lescher in 1828. The new firm, Evans & Lescher, re-located to 4 Cripplegate Buildings, London. In 1833 a branch of this business was opened at 15 Fenwick Street, Liverpool, which soon moved to 8 Lord Street. Initially, Lescher managed the Liverpool business with the help of Evans' 3 sons, Thomas Bickerton, John Hilditch and Edward, but by 1835 he returned to London leaving John Hilditch in charge. The Liverpool business was renamed Evans, Sons & Co in 1840. It was primarily a manufacturing business, with drug mills and laboratories being established in Fleet Street in 1846 and at the Old Bank of England premises, Hanover Street, in 1848. The latter also served as headquarters for the business until 1941, when it was destroyed during enemy action. The London business was a separate concern, still styled Evans & Lescher, until 1845, when it was renamed Evans, Lescher & Evans after John Hilditch left Liverpool to join the partnership in London. In 1866 the firm acquired the business of Lamplough & Campbell, Montreal, Canada, and renamed it Evans, Mercer & Co, a title which it retained until 1879 when Henry Sugden Evans took control of the business and it was renamed H Sugden Evans & Co. Edward Alfred Webb, grandson of Evans the founder, was made a partner of Evans, Lescher & Evans in London in 1879, and the firm was renamed Evans, Lescher & Webb. The London and Liverpool firms worked in close co-operation up to 1902, when they amalgamated to form a limited liability company, Evans Sons, Lescher & Webb Ltd. In 1884 the Canadian business was incorporated as a limited liability company, Evans Sons & Mason Ltd, and in 1887 was renamed Evans & Son Ltd. In 1902 a group of professors from the University of Liverpool established, in joint enterprise with Evans Sons, Lescher & Webb Ltd, the Incorporated Institute of Comparative Pathology at Runcorn, Halton. This institute was acquired by the company in 1911, and in 1929 renamed the Evans Biological Institute. It was a pioneering establishment which carried out research into the treatment of human and animal diseases. In 1905 atoxyl was recognised as a useful treatment for trypanosomiasis, sleeping sickness, a discovery which was of fundamental importance to the development of chemotherapy. In 1926 *Hepatex Oral* was introduced after researchers at the Institute discovered that liver extract could be used in the treatment of pernicious anaemia. Sulphanilamide, used to treat puerperal sepsis, was manufactured by the institute in 1937 and issued under the name *Streptocide*. The Institute also manufactured diphtheria and tetanus antitoxins, vaccines to immunise against a number of contagious diseases such as cholera and typhoid, and herapin, an anti-coagulant issued as *Pularin* and *Hyaluronidase*, used to aid the absorption of injected fluids, under the trade mark *Rondase*. In 1916 the company established fine chemical works at Runcorn to supply its research laboratories with inorganic chemicals for medicinal use. By the 1950s its main products were metal salts. After the destruction of the Hanover Street premises in 1941, a new factory was built at Speke, Liverpool, and production commenced in 1943. This was a large plant which incorporated a drugs grinding mill and which manufactured drugs for administration by injection, compressed tablets, extracts and emulsions. The laboratories at Fleet Street were closed in 1958, the same year in which the company won a contract from the Ministry of Health to act as national distributors of all imported consignments of the *Salk Poliomyelitis* vaccine. In 1945 the company was re-styled Evans Medical Supplies Ltd and a number of overseas subsidiaries were established, ESL & W (South Africa) (Pty) Ltd in 1945 and Evans Medical (India) Private Ltd in 1946. Branches of Evans Medical Supplies Ltd were also established in Melbourne, Australia, in 1946 and in Karachi, Pakistan, in 1950. In 1951 Evans Medical (Northern) Ltd was incorporated at Newcastle upon Tyne, and in 1952 Evans Medical (Wales) Ltd was incorporated at Swansea. A prestigious contract was awarded to Evans Medical Supplies Ltd in 1953, to introduce and manage a pharmaceutical industry for Burma. In 1957, the company won a contract to supply the government of Liberia with its pharmaceutical requirements, which led to the incorporation of a subsidiary company, Evans Medical (Liberia) Ltd, Monrovia. In 1959 Evans Medical Supplies Ltd was renamed Evans Medical Ltd. In 1961 the company was acquired by Glaxo Laboratories Ltd, and continued to trade as Evans Medical Ltd. In 1966 the company's wholesale distribution interests, along with other wholesale distribution interests of Glaxo Group Ltd, were merged with those of British Drug Houses Group Ltd, to form a new company, Vestric Ltd. In 1968, after the acquisition of British Drug Houses Group Ltd by Glaxo Group Ltd, Vestric Ltd became a wholly-owned subsidiary of that company. In 1982 Evans Medical Ltd was bought from Glaxo Group Ltd by its management, who maintained the manufacturing plant at Speke and established new warehouses at Dunstable, Bedfordshire, and an office and manufacturing complex at Langhurst, near Horsham, West Sussex. At the same time a holding company was incorporated, Evans Healthcare Ltd. In 1990 that company was acquired by Medirace plc, of Jermyn Street, London, a pharmaceutical manufacturer engaged in the development, manufacture and sales of vaccines. It had been incorporated in 1986 as Fineasset plc and began operations in 1987 as Medirace plc, changing its name to Medeva plc when it acquired Evans Healthcare Ltd, in an attempt to reflect and give recognition to the names of both companies. Until 1998 Evans Medical Ltd continued to operate under its own name from Speke, and from administrative offices at Leatherhead, Surrey. In July 1998 Medeva plc united all its operations under a single global name and, as part of that programme, Evans Medical Ltd changed its name to Medeva Pharma Ltd.

'Evans of Liverpool', *Chemist and Druggist Export Review*, March 1947; K Holland, 'Evans Healthcare Ltd', *The Pharmaceutical Journal*, 23 Jan 1988; A E Smeeton, *Chronological History of Evans Medical 1809–1959* (Evans Medical, c.1959); 'The Sesquicentenary of Evans Medical Ltd', *The Pharmaceutical Journal*, 183, 1959, 61-2

Records 1: Archivist (Historical Records), Records Centre, Glaxo Wellcome plc, 891-995 Greenford Road, Greenford UB6 0HE

Minutes: directors' meetings 1967–91, general meetings 1902–91, n.d., executive committee meetings 1975–76, management committee meetings n.d., UK subsidiaries' meetings 1978–86, n.d., overseas subsidiaries' meetings 1948–86, n.d.; memoranda and articles of association n.d.; articles of association, Evans Medical (India) Ltd n.d.; board papers 1969–74; agenda and papers 1982–91; attendance book 1983–87, n.d.; papers re proposed acquisitions 1963; annual returns 1982–87; registers: directors' share and debenture interests n.d., shares 1942–86, n.d., members n.d., seals 1967–91, n.d.; share certificates 1944–51, 1985, n.d.; summary of outstanding issues 1989 to date; annual reports and accounts: 1955–63, 1969, n.d., overseas subsidiaries 1947–48, 1966–76; accounts: 1950–61 (w), 1985–87, n.d., overseas subsidiaries 1969, 1977–88; invoices 1986; financial plans 1980–81, 1986; budgets 1973, 1988; NHS enquiry into dextrose solutions 1967–72; patent agreements 1952–81; policy register 1958–66; project files 1983–87; medical record cards n.d.; product lists 1976, 1985–87, n.d.; products claims n.d.; sale documents n.d.; promotional material, company and drugs 1946, 1960–72, n.d.; press cuttings 1964–72; site plans 1974; tender with specification 1989; capital projects n.d.; agreements: Duncan Flockhart & Co Ltd 1961, Allied Medical Products 1971, directors' salaries 1971–72, staff n.d., consultancy n.d., appointment of agent for New Zealand 1931; employer's liability booklets 1972–76, n.d.; booklet for new employees 1960s; *Evans News*, staff newsletter 1981; files: directors 1945–49, statutory 1965–83, 1991, n.d., subsidiaries 1961–79, n.d., overseas subsidiaries 1947–49, 1963–92, n.d., communications 1990–94, general 1969 to date, n.d.; correspondence: directors 1986–88, auditors 1985, General Electric Co Ltd 1969, Lilly Industries Ltd 1969, miscellaneous 1957–69, 1987–88, n.d.; photographs: Speke laboratories 1960s–70s, Switzerland office 1967; private papers: Mrs M D C Evans n.d., Dr R M Evans n.d.; miscellaneous papers and correspondence 1961–77, 1986.

Records 2: Medeva Pharma Ltd, Medeva House, Regent Park, Kingston Road, Leatherhead KT22 7PQ

General meetings minutes 1942–78; memoranda and articles of association 1949, 1976; certification of certificate of incorporation 1945; change of name certificates 1945, 1959; combined register of members and share ledger 1941–79; share certificates and trust deeds 1965 to date; share transfer forms 1982–83; trademark certificates: *Evans' Antiseptic Throat Pastilles* 1909–92, *Minstrels* label (Heraldic)/*Evans Medicated Pastilles* 1922–90, *Lysol* 1926–82, Evans (lozenge) logo 1943–90, Evans device mark 1962–83; tuberculosis vaccine blending book 1949; information booklet re Parkinsonism drug *Clorevan* c.1960; information cards re fine chemicals c.1980s; promotional brochure c.1960s;

Evans' Medical Bulletin, monthly information booklet 1938; competition entry form featuring 1939 price list 1982; historical article 1947.

Stable, Evans & Co: indenture re Daniel Stable's co-partnership capital 1822.

Records 3: Medeva plc, 10 St James's Street, London SW1A 1EF

Directors' and general meetings minutes 1980–90; directors' meetings minutes 1990 to date; memorandum and articles of association 1995; certificate of incorporation and change of name certificate 1995; certificate stating company is a private company 1981; annual returns, related correspondence and papers 1991–92; combined register of members and share ledger 1966 to date; share certificates 1986, 1991; nominee's deed 1990; share transfer form, with declaration of trust 1990; directors' reports and accounts 1987–94.

Records 4: Dr Peter M Worling, The Grange, 29 Fernielaw Avenue, Edinburgh EH13 0EF

Dangerous drugs register 1934–57; wholesale price list 'A' 1967, 1970.

Records 5: F Maltby & Sons Ltd, Dunston House, Portland Street, Lincoln LN5 7NN

Products and price list 1952.

MEDEVALE PHARMASERVICES LTD
Vale of Bardsley, Ashton-under-Lyne, Tameside

Manufacture and sale of pharmaceutical products

History: In 1864 Thomas Kerfoot acquired a chemist's business in London Road, Manchester, established in 1797, on his own account. Initially he traded as a retail chemist, but soon began to manufacture galenicals. In 1887 he abandoned the retail side of the firm, in favour of the manufacturing business, and began production of compressed pills and tablets. In 1890 he moved to premises in Chester Street, Manchester, which were vacated after total destruction by fire in 1896. The firm re-located to a site at Bardsley Vale on the river Medlock, between Oldham and Ashton-under-Lyne, Tameside, and a warehouse was opened at 42 Lamb's Conduit Street, Holborn, London. In 1900 Thomas Kerfoot was joined in partnership by his son, Ernest Hodgson Kerfoot, and the business was styled Thomas Kerfoot & Co. A range of new pharmaceutical products was introduced, including *Salaspin* in 1914 and *Kerocain*, a synthetic local anaesthetic, in 1915. In 1918 the business was incorporated as a limited liability company, Thomas Kerfoot & Co Ltd. Ernest Kerfoot's 2 sons, Dr T H Manners Kerfoot and Henry Manners Kerfoot, entered the company in 1931, and in 1936 Thomas Kerfoot died, followed in 1944 by his son, Ernest Kerfoot. During the Second World War the company produced the anti-malarial drug *Mepacrine*, flavine antiseptics and large quantities of pills and injectables for use by the armed forces. After the war the company continued to produce pills and lozenges, and also began manufacture of penicillin cream. By the 1970s it specialised in the production of antibiotics and steroids, which it sold in unbranded form, directly to retail pharmacies, hospitals and wholesalers. In 1990 Thomas Kerfoot & Co Ltd was acquired by Medeva plc, Jermyn Street, London, and its business interests were merged with those of Evans Medical Ltd, also a subsidiary of Medeva plc. Thomas Kerfoot & Co Ltd was renamed Medevale Pharmaservices Ltd in 1993.

'Fifty Years at Bardsley Vale', *Chemist and Druggist*, 23 Nov 1946, 666-9; K Holland, 'Thomas Kerfoot & Co Ltd', *Pharmaceutical Journal*, 21 May 1988, 651-4; E H Shields, *Fifty Years at Bardsley Vale* (Thomas Kerfoot, Vale of Bardsley, 1946)

Records: Medeva plc, 10 St James's Street, London SW1A 1EF

Directors' meetings minutes 1986–95; general meetings minutes 1989–90, 1992; memoranda and articles of association 1918, 1989; certificate of incorporation 1918; change of name certificate 1993; offer document re acquisition by Medeva plc 1990; registers of members, share ledgers and annual returns 1919 to date; nominee's deed 1990; share transfer forms 1990–91, 1995; annual reports and accounts 1988–94; company secretariat correspondence and papers 1990–95.

THE MENTHOLATUM CO LTD
1 Redwood Avenue, Peel Park Campus, East Kilbride, South Lanarkshire

Marketing and manufacture of over-the-counter medicines

History: In 1889 Albert Alexander Hyde established the Yucca Co in Wichita, Kansas, USA, to manufacture soap and shaving cream. From 1889 he began research into the uses of menthol in treating colds, headaches and sore throats, and in 1893 produced *Mentholatum Ointment*, a product which derived its name from the combination of menthol and petroleum jelly used in its creation. In 1903 a factory was opened in Buffalo, and the Yucca Co was acquired by the

Mentholatum Co Inc of Wichita, Kansas in 1906. The Mentholatum Co Ltd was incorporated as a wholly-owned UK subsidiary of The Mentholatum Co Inc in 1924 to market the latter's products in Europe, the Middle East and Africa. During the Second World War its premises in Slough were commandeered by the military, forcing a temporary move to Burnham, Buckinghamshire. The Mentholatum Co Ltd re-located to Twyford, Wokingham, in 1977 and to East Kilbride, South Lanarkshire, in 1995. This move followed the acquisition of The Mentholatum Co Inc by Rohto Pharmaceutical Co Ltd, Osaka, Japan, a manufacturer of eye care and stomach pain relief pharmaceuticals, in 1988. In 1999 the company manufactured over-the-counter medicines including *Mentholatum Ointment* and *Deep Heat*, an external analgesic.

'The Mentholatum Co Ltd', *Buffalo Business Journal*, 1985, 19

Records 1: The Mentholatum Co Ltd, 1 Redwood Avenue, Peel Park Campus, East Kilbride G74 5PE

Directors' meetings minutes 1924–77; registers of members 1924–94; share certificate books 1924–93; stock transfer certificates 1934–93; special resolution re transfer of shares 1920s; register of seals 1924–83; private ledger, incl. receipts 1973–84; product information file 1984–86; promotional brochures 1987–96; press cuttings 1920s–90s; staff advertisements 1974–87; *The MC*, staff newsletter 1989–94; photograph albums: Buffalo headquarters, UK, Africa and Asia 1927–95, construction of East Kilbride site 1994, visit of Rohto Pharmaceutical Co Ltd 1988; audio and visual recordings re advertisements 1960s–70s.

Mentholatum (Nigeria) Ltd: minutes 1969–86, registers of members 1970–82, share certificates 1870–96.

The Mentholatum Co (Proprietary) Ltd: minutes 1972–82.

Mentholatum (Overseas) Ltd: register of members 1965–93, share certificates 1978, 1993.

Records 2: History of Advertising Trust, HAT House, 12 Raveningham Centre, Raveningham NR14 6NU

Advertisements: *Deep Heat* 1976–89, *Mentholatum Antiseptic Lozenge* 1977. (Ref: MEAL collection 1976–89, R10-80)

G MORGAN LTD
Woodbridge Hill, Guildford, Surrey

Dispensing chemist

History: In 1944 Gwyn Morgan, chemist, had 2 retail premises, 39 Woodbridge Hill and 75 Woodbridge Road, Guildford, Surrey. By 1959 his business had been incorporated as a limited liability company, G Morgan Ltd, and a third shop had been established at 12 Stoughton Road, Guildford. By 1970 the business was described as a chemist, ophthalmic optician and photographic dealer, and a further shop at 76 Woodbridge Road, Guildford, added to the chain.

Records: Surrey History Centre, 130 Goldsworth Road, Woking GU21 1ND

Stock sales registers 1968–78; prescription books, includes sales of methylated spirit 1932–50, 1960–73; prescription account books 1959–78. (Ref: 5191/1-13)

MORRIS E MORRIS
3 High Street, Portmadoc, Gwynedd

Dispensing chemist, druggist, grocer, tea dealer and slate merchant

History: Morris Evans Morris, brother of William Evans Morris, gentleman of Portmadoc, Gwynedd, was apprenticed to Thomas Hughes of Pwllheli, Gwynedd, chemist and druggist, for 5 years from 1846. In 1852 William Morris bought the Portmadoc druggist and grocery business of Edward Jones, and Morris Evans Morris entered the business as a qualified chemist. By 1887 his business was at 3 High Street, Portmadoc, where he remained until at least 1895. From around 1896 he expanded the business, and began selling slates. His uncle, Daniel Morris, was registered as a chemist and druggist in 1886, and his son, William Evans, was registered as a chemist and druggist in 1892. Both were operating at 3 High Street, Portmadoc, in 1895.

Records 1: Gwynedd Archives & Museums Service, Caernarfon Area Record Office, Victoria Dock, Caernarfon. Enquiries to County Offices, Shirehall Street, Caernarfon LL55 1SH

Apprenticeship indenture, M E Morris 1846; memorandum of agreement with Edward Jones, re inventory and valuation of his chemist and druggist business stock-in-trade 1852; inventory, valuation and receipt of said stock-in-trade 1852; prescription book 1866–78; advertisement n.d.; account book, slate sales

1896–1904; family papers 19th–20th cents; photographs, members of the family late 19th–20th cents; postcards, Edward VII's visit to Portmadoc 1911. (Ref: XM 2582; XS/1485/1-13 (photographs))

Records 2: National Library of Wales, Department of Manuscripts & Records, Aberystwyth SY23 3BU

Account books c.1852–93. (Ref: NLW MS 7898E)

THOMAS MORSON & SON LTD
Wharf Road, Ponders End, Enfield, London

Manufacturer of fine chemicals and proprietary medicines

History: After serving his apprenticeship at a retail chemist's shop in Fleet Market, London, and working for 2 years in the pharmacy of L A Planche, Paris, France, Thomas Newborn Robert Morson returned to London and took over the business in Fleet Market in 1821. In 1825 he moved to premises in Southampton Row, London, and began manufacture of alkaloids, fine chemicals, proprietary medicines and also medicinal creosote at a plant at Hornsey Road, north London. Another factory was established at Homerton, Hackney, London. In 1844 Thomas Morson became vice-president of the Pharmaceutical Society of Great Britain and in 1848 was made president. In 1879 Morson's son, Thomas Pierre, became a partner in the business which was styled Thomas Morson & Son, and in 1883 his younger son, Albert Robert, joined the partnership. The retail pharmacy at Southampton Row was closed in 1900, and the wholesale department moved to Elm Street, Grays Inn Road, London, in 1904. In 1901 a new manufacturing plant at Summerfield Works, Ponders End, Enfield, London, was acquired, and thereafter became the central manufacturing base for the firm. The business was incorporated as a limited liability company, Thomas Morson & Son Ltd, in 1915 and in 1957, the company was acquired as a subsidiary of Merck & Co Inc, USA. In 1997 its UK parent was Merck Sharpe & Dohme Ltd.

'A Family Occasion. Thomas Morson & Son Ltd celebrate notable events of 1848 and 1948', *Chemist and Druggist*, 159, 22 May 1948, 667-71; 'Established One Hundred Years – pen portraits of pharmaceutical wholesalers', *Pharmaceutical Journal*, 146, 12 April 1941; 'London Wholesalers in 1863 and Now', *Chemist and Druggist*, 83, 26 July 1913; A F Morson, *Operative Chemist* (Wellcome Institute Series in the History of Medicine, London, 1998); A F Morson, 'T N R Morson and his Scientific Friends', *Pharmaceutical Historian*, 20, 4, Dec 1990, 6-7

Records of pharmaceutical businesses

Records 1: Archives & Manuscripts, Wellcome Library for the History & Understanding of Medicine, 183 Euston Road, London NW1 2BE

Co-partnership agreement 1879; description of a meeting 1845; attendance list with signatures 1848–49; share capital and shareholder return 1922; list of creditors and debtors 1908; balance sheets 1878–1943; financial statement and correspondence 1948; private ledger 1892–1908; cash book 1868–71; invoices to Allen & Hanburys 1848, 1866; warehouses receipts book 1899; cheque book 1855–58, n.d.; memoranda re manufacturing 1880s, 1907, n.d.; manufacturing notes 1908–15, 1930–34, 1946; manufacturing agreement with Merck Sharpe & Dohme Ltd n.d.; technical papers 1841–44, 1856–59; analytical reports 1914, 1934–38, 1954; papers re trade effluent 1955; recipe book 1840; product catalogues and sales literature 1825, 1851, 1899–1932, 1960s, n.d.; price lists 1821, 1878; iodine purchases 1909–41; record of sales, India Office n.d.; pages from notebook n.d.; advertisements 1866–67, 1872; company brochure 1916; press cuttings 1930s–90, n.d.; product labels late 19th cent., 1921–27; papers re 'Bismuth' convention n.d.; plans: Homerton works n.d., powder and sud works 1920s; summary of expenditure on equipment and services 20th cent.; reports re factory 1914–15; valuation of powder sud works 1915; works output 1928–41; transfer agreement and history of Hornsey Road site n.d.; wages book 1878; salaries and wages cash book 1887–1909; staff references, letter of appointment and resignation n.d.; the 'M M' house pamphlet 1920; letterbook 1866–72; correspondence: incoming 1825–40, outgoing c.1860s, n.d., Jacob Bell 1841–59, n.d., Joseph Lister re surgical catgut 1907; correspondence and notes re drug developments, individuals, premises and with other companies 1837–74, 1962–73, n.d.; T N R Morson: diary 1818, portrait n.d., list of medals awarded n.d., obituary n.d., admission certificate, Société de Chimie Medicale 1834, genealogical notes 1870s; photographs: Ponders End factory 1914, powder sud works 1914, 1930s–60s, miscellaneous 1889; sketches: J Bell n.d., poster n.d., miscellaneous n.d.; articles by staff and house publications 1826, 1916–60, n.d.; report on 1855 London Exhibition n.d.; draft leader for *Pharmaceutical Journal* by Jacob Bell with comments by T N R Morson n.d.; historical notes 1927, 1930, n.d. (Ref: SA/MOR, MS 6975/7-8)

Records 2: Royal College of Surgeons, 18 Nicolson Street, Edinburgh EH8 9DW

Correspondence with Joseph Lister re antiseptic substances 1889–90, 1907.

Records 3: The Museum Curator, Royal Pharmaceutical Society of Great Britain, 1 Lambeth High Street, London SE1 7JN

List of chemical preparations 1822 (p). (Ref: IRA.1996.279)

BRUCE W MOSS LTD
367 Bowling Old Lane, Bradford

Chemist

History: Bruce W Moss was registered as a chemist and druggist in 1948, at 58 Garden Road, Brighouse, Calderdale. In 1953 he moved to 258 Bowling Old Lane, Bradford, and in 1963 acquired additional premises at 101 Little Horton Lane, Bradford. In the same year, the 2 branches were incorporated as one limited liability company, Bruce W Moss Ltd. In 1994 on Bruce W Moss's retirement, the company was sold to UniChem plc, and was renamed E Moss Ltd in 1995. It was still trading in 1997. UniChem Plc merged with Alliance Sante SA in 1997 to become Alliance UniChem plc.

Records: Alliance UniChem plc, UniChem House, Cox Lane, Chessington KT9 1SN

Directors' and general meetings minutes 1963–94; memorandum and articles of association 1963; certificate of incorporation 1963; acquisition papers 1993–94; combined register of members and share ledger 1964–94; share certificate book, with counterfoils 1963–94; share certificates: cancelled 1972, 1994, statutory declarations 1994; directors' service agreements 1972, 1979.

E MOSS LTD
Fern Grove, Feltham, Hounslow, London

Retail chemist, pharmaceutical and allied products

History: This business was established by Edgar Moss, who opened a chemist's shop on his own account in Weybridge, Surrey, in 1915. He traded as a dispensing and photographic chemist and chemist and druggist, until his son, Harold Moss, and his wife, Marjorie, assumed control of the business, which was incorporated as a limited liability company, E Moss Ltd, in 1934. The company expanded, with retail chemist shops trading throughout Surrey and Middlesex. E Moss Ltd was acquired by UniChem plc in 1991, at which time the Group had

90 retail outlets. UniChem plc merged with Alliance Sante SA in 1997 to become Alliance UniChem plc. E Moss Ltd had 571 retail outlets in 1999.

Records 1: Alliance UniChem plc, UniChem House, Cox Lane, Chessington KT9 1SN

Memorandum and articles of association 1934; certificate of incorporation 1934.

Records 2: The Museum Curator, Royal Pharmaceutical Society of Great Britain, 1 Lambeth High Street, London SE1 7JN

Order of service of thanksgiving for Harold Moss 1981. (Ref: IRA.1996.385)

WILLIAM MOSTYN (PHARMACY) LTD
Caernarfon, Gwynedd

Chemist and druggist

History: In 1916 William Mostyn registered as a chemist and druggist at 50 Borthyn Street, Ruthin, Denbighshire. In 1921 he moved to 13 Pool Street, Caernarfon, Gwynedd, where he traded as a chemist and druggist under the business name W Mostyn. In 1957 his business was incorporated as a limited liability company, William Mostyn (Pharmacy) Ltd, and in 1962 ceased trading. In the same year William Mostyn moved to Endcliffe, England Road, Caernarfon, and in 1968 ceased to be registered.

Records: Gwynedd Archives & Museums Service, Caernarfon Area Record Office, Victoria Dock, Caernarfon. Enquiries to County Offices, Shirehall Street, Caernarfon LL55 1SH

Account books 1920–27, 1939–48; cash books 1920–61; prescription books 1918–1961; prescription for cholera c.1900; register of dangerous drugs purchased and sold 1921–29, 1936–60; poisons register file 1932–60; stocktaking sheets 1925; licence to assign a lease 1920; rent book 1887–1940. (Ref: XM 9193/46 and 161-81)

MUDIE'S EXOSAC LTD
Dundee

Manufacturer of patent medicines for diabetes

History: Mudie's Exosac Ltd was incorporated as a limited liability company in 1930, to acquire the patent medicine manufacturing business of Robert Mudie, 7 Walrond Street, Dundee. The company's registered offices were at 41 Reform Street, Dundee. Mudie's Exosac Ltd specialised in the manufacture of medicinal preparations for diabetes, and traded until 1933, when it was removed from the register of companies.

Records: Dundee City Archives, Support Services, 21 City Square, Dundee DD1 3BY

Minutes 1929–31; combined register of members and share ledger 1930. (Ref: GD/Hu 11)

NATURAL CHEMICALS LTD
28 St John's Lane, Clerkenwell, London

Pharmaceutical distributor

History: In 1936 Natural Chemicals Ltd was acquired by Beecham Pills Ltd, and was attached to one of its subsidiaries, Ashton & Parsons Ltd, later renamed Phosferine Co Ltd. Natural Chemicals Ltd was initially located at Clipstone Street, London, and later re-located to St John's Lane, Clerkenwell, London. The company imported *Phyllosan* tablets from Berne, Switzerland, for packaging and distribution.

Records 1: St Helens Local History & Archives Library, Gamble Institute, Victoria Square, St Helens WA10 1DY

Directors' minutes 1953–54; memorandum and articles of association 1928; annual returns 1950–53; register of members and share ledger 1931–54; share certificate book 1930–54; share transfer certificates 1950s; private ledgers 1928–53; *Phyllosan*: research papers c.1930, reports and correspondence 1938–55, papers re labour and packaging costs 1939–42, instruction and advertising leaflet n.d., photograph of van advertising *Phyllosan* c.1930s. (Ref: BP/4/6)

Records 2: SmithKline Beecham plc, SmithKline Beecham House, Great West Road, Brentford TW8 9BD. Enquiries to SmithKline Beecham plc, 1 New Horizons Court, Great West Road, Brentford TW8 9EP

Agency agreement and deed of covenant with Chlorosan AG 1929.

Records 3: History of Advertising Trust, HAT House, 12 Raveningham Centre, Raveningham NR14 6NU

Guardbooks of advertising material re *Phyllosan* n.d.; press cuttings, advertisements for *Phyllosan* 1974–80s. (Ref: Leo Burnett guardbooks, 30; MEAL collection 1974–89, R10-80)

NEW SKIN CO LTD
SmithKline Beecham House, Great West Road, Brentford, Hounslow, London

Proprietary medicine manufacturer

History: WYT Products Ltd was incorporated as a limited liability company in 1926, to trade as a chemist and druggist. In 1937 it was renamed New Skin Co Ltd, and began manufacture of *New Skin*, a liquid product which dried to cover and protect small cuts. The company was later acquired by Beecham Group Ltd, and in 1952 went into voluntary liquidation.

Records: St Helens Local History & Archives Library, Gamble Institute, Victoria Square, St Helens WA10 1DY

Minutes 1926–53; memorandum and articles of association 1928; annual returns 1944–53; register of seals 1949–53; share certificates book 1926–52; share transfers 1935–52; private ledger 1941–42; private journal 1941–52; cash book 1940–53.

T T NICHOLSON LTD
125 Hampstead Road, London

Dispensing chemist

History: Thomas Tanner Nicholson was registered as a chemist and druggist at 15 Tremlett Grove, London, in 1886. In 1891 he moved to 125 Hampstead Road, London, and traded there until 1941, under the business name T T Nicholson. The business continued under the same name until 1948, when it was incorporated as a limited liability company, T T Nicholson Ltd. In 1966 it ceased to operate under its own name.

Records: Archives & Manuscripts, Wellcome Library for the History & Understanding of Medicine, 183 Euston Road, London NW1 2BE

Ledgers: 1893–1908 (w), Cryer & Co 1904–11; day book, Cryer & Co 1909–11; memorandum books 1899–1910; want book (fragment) n.d.; order book (fragment) n.d.; prescription book 1922–61; sale of poisons registers 1928–60; chemist and druggist diaries, annotated 1903–08, 1914. (Ref: CMAC/GC/28)

J NOBLE
20 Great Clowes Street, Salford

Chemist

History: In 1905 Harry Bellringer was registered as a chemist and druggist, at 78 Stockport Road, Denton, Tameside. In 1910 he moved to 20 Great Clowes Street, Salford, where he traded as a chemist and druggist under the name, H Bellringer. In 1948 the business was acquired by John Noble, who had registered as a chemist and druggist in 1935. He traded from 20 Great Clowes Street, under the name J Noble. In 1962 he incorporated a limited liability company, H Bellringer Ltd, to trade as a manufacturing chemist from 1 Elton Street, Great Clowes Street, Salford. This company was dissolved in 1973. J Noble at 20 Great Clowes Street, continued trading until 1977, when John Noble retired from the business. In the same year the firm was incorporated as a limited liability company, Pomshourne Ltd. It ceased trading in 1980.

Records 1: Salford City Archives, Archives Centre, 658-662 Liverpool Road, Irlam, Manchester M44 5AD

Account book, receipts and payments 1947–58; prescription books, with loose papers and list of poisons extracted from the *Chemist and Druggist* (1934) 1924–59, n.d.; recipe books 1918–19, n.d.; commonplace book 18th–20th centuries. (Ref: U38)

Records 2: Salford Local History Library, Peel Park, The Crescent, Salford M5 4WU

Photographs of shop n.d. (Ref: Local History Collection)

Records 3: Ordsall Hall Museum, Taylorson Street, Salford M5 3EX

Museum material re shop n.d. (Ref: H156-1976 to H164-1976)

NORCHEM LTD
Norchem House, Chilton Industrial Estate, Ferryhill, Durham

Pharmaceutical wholesaler

History: In 1960 6 retail pharmacists in the Ferryhill area of Durham, joined together to form a co-operative wholesale buying group, to supply their pharmacies with pharmaceutical products and to compete with the larger chains of pharmaceutical wholesalers. This buying group was incorporated as a limited liability company, Norchem Ltd, in 1960, and initially operated from premises above the retail pharmacy of one of its founding pharmacists, Thomas Dobbin, whose business, styled Banners Chemists Ltd, was located at 12 Darlington Road, Ferryhill. In 1965 the company re-located to Howlish Hall in Coundon, Durham, where it established a distribution depot, and again in 1974 to larger premises at Chilton Industrial Estate, Ferryhill. In 1980 a second warehouse was opened at Letitia Street, Middlesbrough. In 1997 the company supplied around 130 retail pharmacy businesses in a distribution area stretching from Blyth, Northumberland, in the north to York, in the south, and was largely involved in the wholesale distribution to retail pharmacists, of pharmaceutical and medical products, with a smaller line in toiletries and household goods.

Records: Norchem Ltd, Norchem House, Chilton Industrial Estate, Ferryhill DL17 0PD

Directors' meetings minutes 1960 to date; general meetings minutes 1960 to date; memorandum and articles of association 1960; certificate of incorporation 1960; combined register of directors, members and share ledger 1960 to date; unsecured loan interest book 1961 to date; share certificates books 1960 to date; annual reports and accounts 1961, 1963 to date; nominal ledger 1980 to date; expenses ledger 1972–90s; land certificate, Norchem House 1976; correspondence and planning permission certificates re building extensions at Norchem House 1976–77, 1982–84; lease agreements, Letitia Street 1980–95; architectural plans: Norchem House 1974–77, 1982–84, n.d., Letitia Street 1979.

NORTHERN PHARMACEUTICALS LTD
Galen House, 80 Gratton Road, Bradford

Pharmaceutical wholesaler

History: Northern Pharmaceuticals Ltd, a wholesaler of pharmaceutical products, with a central depot in Bradford, was incorporated as a limited liability company in 1946. Prior to its acquisition by the wholly-owned subsidiary of AAH Holdings plc, Chemists Holdings Ltd, in 1985 it was a wholly-owned subsidiary of Associated British Engineering plc. AAH Holdings was absorbed by GEHE AG in 1995.

Records 1: GEHE UK plc, Retail Branch, Atherstone, Warwickshire. Enquiries to GEHE UK plc, Sapphire Court, Walsgrave Triangle Business Park, Coventry CV2 2TX

General meetings minutes 1983–96; combined register of members, directors and share ledger 1946–89; papers and correspondence re acquisition by AAH plc 1984–85. (Ref: Boxes S10, A2)

Records 2: West Yorkshire Archive Service, Bradford, 15 Canal Road, Bradford BD1 4AT

Ledger 1946–68. (Ref: 75D89/6/1)

P D S (LEEDS) LTD
1 Howarth Place, off Camp Road, Leeds

Wholesale chemist

History: P D S (Leeds) Ltd (P D S being an abbreviation for Patents, Drugs and Sundries) was incorporated as a limited liability company at 10 Meadow Lane, Leeds, in 1930 to undertake the business of wholesale and retail chemists. As P D S (Leeds) Ltd reached the prescribed limit of 50 members for private companies at a very early stage, a separate company, P A S (Yorks) Ltd, of 5 Water Lane, Leeds, was incorporated later in the same year. In practice the 2 companies were managed as a single concern. The businesses were acquired by UniChem (Northern) Ltd in 1964, and dissolved in 1971.

Records: Alliance UniChem plc, UniChem House, Cox Lane, Chessington KT9 1SN

Directors' and general meetings minutes 1931–67; combined PDS and PAS directors' meetings minutes 1958–67; memorandum and articles of association 1930; certificate of incorporation 1930; acquisition papers 1964; notice of general meeting 1943; notice of change of directors 1965; combined register of members and share ledger 1972; annual accounts 1965–72 (w); accountants' report on PDS and PAS 1964.

P A S (Yorks) Ltd: directors' and general meetings minutes 1931–67; memorandum and articles of association 1930; certificate of incorporation 1930; notice of general meeting 1943; notice of change of directors 1965; combined register of members and share ledger 1972; accounts 1965–72 (w).

PARKE, DAVIS & CO LTD
Lambert Court, Chestnut Avenue, Eastleigh, Hampshire

Pharmaceutical manufacturer

History: In 1862 Dr Samuel Duffield established a drug store in Detroit, USA, and immediately embarked upon a manufacturing programme. In 1866 he took Hervey C Parke into partnership, and the business was styled Duffield, Parke & Co. George S Davis was taken into partnership in 1867, and in 1869 Samuel Duffield left the business. He was replaced by Dr A F Jennings, who assumed the role of head of manufacturing. Thereafter the firm was renamed Parke, Jennings & Co. In 1871 Jennings left the business, and it was re-styled Parke, Davis & Co. In 1874 the firm invented hard gelatin capsules, of which it was later to become the world's largest producer, and in the same year the business was incorporated as a limited liability company, Parke, Davis & Co Inc. By the turn of the century the company was manufacturing vaccines, serums and hormones. *Adrenalin* was synthesised in 1901, and *Pituitrin* in 1908. In 1891 the company incorporated its first overseas subsidiary, Parke, Davis & Co Ltd, at 43 Holburn Viaduct, London, to distribute the company's products in Britain, and export to the European continent. In 1899 building work began on manufacturing facilities at Hounslow, London, and the London office moved in 1900 to 111 Queen Victoria Street, London, and in 1907 to Beak Street, near Piccadilly Circus. The first factory at Hounslow was opened in 1907, and thereafter manufacturing increased rapidly. During the Second World War Parke, Davis & Co Ltd produced large quantities of drugs for the armed forces, and during the 1950s manufactured *Benylin*, an over-the-counter cough medicine, *Camoquin*, a treatment for malaria and *Quadrigen*, a vaccine against polio. In 1947 the administrative offices at Beak Street were re-located to Hounslow and in 1960 more factories and warehouses were built. In 1970 Parke, Davis & Co Inc was acquired as a wholly-owned subsidiary of Warner Lambert Inc, New Jersey, USA, a company formed by the merger during the 1950s of Warner-Hudnut Inc, Philadelphia, USA, and the Lambert Pharmacal Co Inc. Following this acquisition, Parke, Davis & Co Ltd re-located from Hounslow to Pontypool, Torfaen, where Warner Lambert Inc's UK subsidiary, Warner Lambert Ltd, was based, and continued to operate under its own name. In 1997 the company's administrative offices were at Eastleigh, Hampshire.

T Deeson, *Parke, Davis in Britain: The first hundred years* (Parke, Davis, Eastleigh, 1995)

Records 1: The Royal Society, 6 Carlton House Terrace, London SW1Y 5AG

Correspondence with Sir Henry Hallett Dale 1944–54. (Ref: 93 HD/48.5)

Records 2: F Maltby & Sons Ltd, Dunston House, Portland Street, Lincoln LN5 7NN

Price catalogue 1957.

Records 3: The Museum Curator, Royal Pharmaceutical Society of Great Britain, 1 Lambeth High Street, London SE1 7JN

Tape recorded interview with Raymond Murray Howitt, senior staff member 1996. (Ref: IRT.1997.01)

W PARKE
21 High Street, East Dereham, Norfolk

Chemist and druggist

History: William Parke was trading as a chemist and druggist at 21 High Street, East Dereham, Norfolk, prior to 1868, where he was proprietor of a solution for the extermination of turnip fly. His business was acquired by Edward Peck around 1883, who qualified as a chemist and druggist in the same year. Peck was described in 1908 as a chemist, druggist and dealer in photographic materials. He died around 1927 and his assistant, Archie Bullard, assumed control of the business until he was succeeded by H L Sturgeon in the 1940s.

Records: Norfolk Record Office, Gildengate House, Anglia Square, Upper Green Lane, Norwich NR3 1AX

Ledgers 1906–33; prescription books 1868–1966; recipe book n.d.; Edward Peck's certificate of registration with the Pharmaceutical Society of Great Britain 1883. (Ref: BR 64/1-20)

PARKER & RAWLINSON LTD
Stonebow, Lincoln, Lincolnshire

Chemist

History: William Marris Parker registered as a chemist and druggist at 344 High Street, Lincoln, Lincolnshire, in 1880, and was still trading from these premises in 1910. In 1911 the business was acquired by a Mr Rawlinson, who traded on his own account until 1919, when the firm was renamed Parker & Rawlinson. In 1922 it was incorporated as a limited liability company, Parker & Rawlinson Ltd. The company traded from 322 High Street and from St Marks Pharmacy, 344 High Street, Lincoln, until 1929, when it was dissolved.

Records 1: Lincolnshire Archives, St Rumbold Street, Lincoln LN2 5AB

Minutes 1922–24; register of members and share ledger 1922–24; ledgers: accounts with customers 1913–20, accounts with suppliers 1910–24, goods supplied locally 1912–23; day book, St Marks Pharmacy 1922; prescription books, one with formulae 1879–1923. (Ref: LPC3/2)

Records 2: Public Record Office, Ruskin Avenue, Kew, Richmond TW9 4DU

Memorandum and articles of association 1922; certificate of incorporation 1922; copy of register of directors or managers 1924; particulars re directors 1922; declaration of compliance with Companies Acts 1922; summary of share capital and shares 1924; return of allotments 1922; statement of nominal capital 1922; notice of situation of registered office 1922; correspondence with Companies Registration Office 1924–28; notice of dissolution 1929. (Ref: BT31/27256/182230)

WILLIAM PATERSON & SONS LTD
57-59 Spring Garden, Aberdeen

Wholesale and manufacturing chemist

History: During the 1820s William Paterson served a pharmaceutical apprenticeship to Thomas Black, chemist, 54 Broad Street, Aberdeen. He subsequently established a chemist's business on his own account, in Stonehaven, Aberdeenshire, relocating in the late 1830s to Broad Street, Aberdeen, and in 1844 to 134 Gallowgate. At this juncture William Paterson abandoned the retail side of his business, and focused on wholesaling. The Gallowgate premises were destroyed by fire in 1860 and rebuilt, following which he was succeeded in the business by his sons, James and Stephen. The firm re-located to Spring Garden, Aberdeen, in 1882, and by 1913 was manufacturing pharmaceuticals in addition to conducting a wholesale business. In 1928 the business was incorporated as a limited liability company, William Paterson & Sons Ltd. During the 1950s the company was acquired by Edinburgh Pharmaceutical Industries Ltd, which in turn was acquired by Glaxo Group Ltd in 1963.

'Vital Contribution to the North's Health Services', *Mirror of Enterprise*, 22 June, 1950, 11-12

Records 1: Archivist (Historical Records), Records Centre, Glaxo Wellcome plc, 891-995 Greenford Road, Greenford UB6 0HE

Directors' meeting minutes 1956–65; memoranda and articles of association 1928, 1956, 1964; reports: share accounts 1951–60, share values and purchase 1955–56; directors' report and balance sheet and profit and loss account 1957–64; statements of accounts 1957–64; price list, photographic apparatus and materials 1902; papers re proposed premises at Aberdeen 1962–68; correspondence with T & H Smith Ltd 1955–65. (Ref: Macfarlan Smith Historical Collection)

Records 2: Dr Peter M Worling, The Grange, 29 Fernielaw Avenue, Edinburgh EH13 0EF

Price catalogues 1898–1913, 1925, 1940.

PAYDENS LTD
60 High Street, Tenterden, Kent

Retail pharmacy

History: In 1790 John Breden converted premises at 60 High Street, Tenterden, Kent, into a book shop, from which he also sold patent medicines. He was succeeded by James Teasdale, a druggist and grocer in 1810 and from 1826 by William Maylam, a 'chymist and druggist'. Thereafter, the business remained a retail pharmacy, and was passed down through a succession of pharmacists. In 1856 Stephen Henry Willsher was taken as an apprentice to Thomas Bolton, and began to expand the veterinary side of the business. From 1875 he manufactured 'Willsher's Cattle Food' from premises at 64-66 High Street. In 1896 the business was acquired by Alexander Ridley and named The Pharmacy Stores.

Ridley also re-instated the book shop of 1790. In 1930 the business passed to J J Loughran and in 1952 to Mrs J Spencer. In 1962 it was acquired by H V Roberts, who again revived the book shop as a separate concern, The Tenterden Bookshop. In 1970 the business was acquired by Paydens Ltd, a chain of wholesale and retail chemists, incorporated as a limited liability company in Kent in 1956. The business was renamed Paydens Ltd, and was still trading in 1997.

Records: Mr H V Roberts, 'Gulliver's', Main Street, Tugby LE7 9WD

Notes re rent and land tax 1826–33; formulae notebooks c.1842–1900; prescription book 1847–51; private prescriptions n.d.; sale of poisons registers 1951–56, 1959–66; notebook re Willsher's cattle food manufactory 1875–82; advertising booklet, 'Haffenden's Balsamic Tincture' n.d.; advertisements n.d.; correspondence 1962–70; photographs of Ridley's postcards n.d.

FRANK PELHAM
58a High Street, Hastings, East Sussex

Dispensing chemist, ophthalmic optician and surgical instrument manufacturer

History: In 1871 James Griffiths Richards registered as a chemist and druggist in Newport. In 1873 he established himself in business at 58a High Street, Hastings, East Sussex. He ceased to be registered in 1916, but the business continued to operate. In 1934 it was acquired by Frank Skeates, who had registered as a chemist and druggist in 1894. He ceased to be registered in 1939 and in 1944 the business was acquired by Francis Spencer Elsey, who had registered as a chemist and druggist in 1923. He traded on his own account until 1946, when the business passed to Frank Pelham, who had registered as a chemist and druggist in 1931. Frank Pelham traded from 58a High Street, Hastings, as a dispensing chemist, ophthalmic optician and surgical instrument manufacturer until 1975, when he retired. At this juncture the business was acquired by Aldo Compagnone, who had registered as a pharmaceutical chemist in 1946, and was renamed the Old Town Pharmacy.

Records: East Sussex Record Office, The Maltings, Castle Precincts, Lewes BN7 1YT

Financial papers 1897–1916; prescription books 1868–1934; prescriptions under Dangerous Drugs Act 1920–51. (Ref: ACC 7545)

PEVERELL'S (CHEMISTS) LTD
Spencer Street, Eldon Lane, Bishop Auckland, Durham

Chemist

History: This company may have been established by Henry Peverell, who was in business as a chemist and druggist in Bishop Auckland, Durham, prior to 1868. He traded from Black Boy, Bishop Auckland, from at least 1871 until sometime before 1891. Subsequently, his business traded from South Church, Bishop Auckland. Arthur Peverell was trading as a chemist at Spencer Street, Eldon Lane, Bishop Auckland, from around 1910 to 1934. In 1934 his business was incorporated as a limited liability company, Peverell's (Chemists) Ltd, which traded from the same address. The company was dissolved in 1981.

Records: Durham Record Office, County Hall, Durham DH1 5UL

Minutes 1934–78; memorandum and articles of association 1934; combined register of members and share ledger 1934–76; share certificates and transfer forms 1934–40, 1950s, n.d.; correspondence and certificates re shares of Dr J McLaughlin 1957–80; particulars of directors 1943; certificates of annual returns 1956–69; copies of annual returns 1935–77 (w); directors' annual reports 1967–75; ledger 1969–78; correspondence re company certificate 1969; wills: Lillie, wife of Arthur Peverell 1933, memorandum of probate of James McLaughlin, Seaton Delaval 1976. (Ref: D/X 684)

PFIZER LTD
Ramsgate Road, Sandwich, Kent

Pharmaceutical manufacturer

History: Pfizer Inc was established in Brooklyn, New York, USA, in 1849, by 2 Germans, Charles Pfizer and Charles Erhart, to manufacture fine chemicals, including camphor, borax and acids. During the 1880s the company began to produce calcium citrate and in 1936 granted a licence to the British company, Kemball Bishop Ltd, Bromley-by-Bow, Bromley, London, which had been incorporated as a limited liability company in 1901, to manufacture calcium citrate using its fermentation processes. Kemball Bishop & Co Ltd had acquired the business of John Bennet Lawes & Co Ltd, a citric and tartaric acid producer, in 1913. During the Second World War Pfizer Inc became the first company to mass produce penicillin and by the late 1940s was the leading world producer of this antibiotic, exporting to many countries. This development led the company to establish a number of subsidiary companies in Europe, one of which, Pfizer Ltd, was incorporated as its UK subsidiary at Wear Bay Road, Folkestone, Kent, in 1953. Building work began, to re-house Pfizer Ltd, at a site in Sandwich, Kent, in 1954 and in 1958 Kemball Bishop Ltd was acquired as a subsidiary company, operating under its own name until 1968, when it was fully amalgamated into Pfizer Ltd. Laboratories, offices and workers were gradually moved to the site at Sandwich and by 1965 the removal was complete and the Folkestone plant was closed. By this time Pfizer Ltd had become the largest Pfizer operation outside the USA. Research that resulted in the discovery and manufacture of a further range of antibiotics, *Terramycin*, *Tetracycline* and *Doxycycline*, was conducted by Pfizer Ltd during the 1950s and 1960s. In addition, during the 1960s, the company manufactured a diabetic treatment, *Diabinese* and a hypertension reliever, *Hypovase*. In 1960 Pfizer Ltd began manufacture of the *Sabine* polio vaccine and was the first company to secure a licence to supply the US government and the British Ministry of Health with the vaccine in 1961. In 1964 British Alkaloids Ltd, the producer of the antiseptic *TCP*, was acquired by Pfizer Ltd and a subsidiary company, Unicliffe Ltd, was incorporated at Kingston upon Thames, London, to market *TCP* and other Pfizer products. In 1968 the Kemball Bishop Ltd factory at Bromley-by-Bow was closed, all production moved to the Sandwich site and a new plant was opened at Ringaskiddy, Cork, Ireland. In 1971 business operations diversified, and Pfizer Central Research was formed, as a centre for research and development, with sites at Sandwich and in the USA, France and Japan. Other divisions were Pharmaceuticals, Animal Health, Manufacturing, Food Science and Central Services. During the 1980s a further 8 products were licensed to the company, including *Diflucan*, an antifungal agent, and a new hypertension reliever, *Cardura*. Pfizer Ltd was awarded a Queen's Award for Technological Achievement in 1991 and for Export Achievement in 1993. In 1995 the company acquired the Animal Health Division of SmithKline Beecham plc.

Growth Through Innovation: A brief Pfizer history (Pfizer, New York, 1993); 'Pfizer Inc' in T Derdak (ed), *International Directory of Company Histories,* vol. 1 (St James Press, London, 1988); K Holland, 'Pfizer Ltd', *The Pharmaceutical Journal*, 11 Jan 1992, 55-8; J Mantle, *Pfizer at Sandwich: The story of Pfizer Ltd* (James & James, London, 1994); S Mines, *Pfizer, An Informal History* (Pfizer, New York, 1978); O Tanner, *Twenty Five Years of Innovation: The story of Pfizer Central Research* (Greenwich Publishing, 1996)

Records 1: Records Manager, Records Management Unit, Pfizer Central Research, Pfizer Ltd, Ramsgate Road, Sandwich CT13 9NJ

Letters patent re Sandwich site land 1558; publicity brochure 1955; Sandwich site plans 1917–18; leases re Folkestone properties 1955–56; income tax listing of Pfizer properties, incl. site plans for Sandwich, Folkestone and Millwall 1961–64; house magazines: *Pfizerama* 1960–71, *Pfizer Europe* 1970–75; photographs (c.25,000) of plant, offices, staff and laboratory production 19th–20th cents.

British Alkaloids Ltd: minutes 1928–66.

Kemball Bishop & Co Ltd: minutes: directors' meetings 1901–51, general meetings 1902–58; transfer of vote for extraordinary general meeting 1919; register of directors 1901–68; agreements: incorporation as a limited liability company 1901, sale and purchase of shares with A Conway Bishop 1919, Pfizer Inc 1935, 1945, 1948, Kemball Bishop (Canada) 1951, purchase by Pfizer Ltd 1959; registers of shareholders 1890, 1913–15, 1928–68; share issue 1901; share certificate transfers 1919–1963; share sale certificates with correspondence 1920; dividend book 1913–63; ledgers: 1877–82, 1965–66, private 1901–1959, interest payments 1916–57, capital expenditure 1915–59, sales 1958–59, purchase 1958–59, taxation 1958–68; journals: 1901–1918, accounts 1920–59; plant expenditure 1929; expenses 1924; shipping insurance policy 1939; laboratory notebooks 1872, 1876, 1934–57; penicillin papers: agenda, minutes and reports of General Penicillin Committee 1942–46, correspondence with Prof Florey and others at School of Pathology, Oxford 1942–45, correspondence with Ministry of Supply 1943–47, correspondence with Sir Alexander Fleming, Burroughs Wellcome, ICI and others 1942–47, internal reports and memoranda 1942–46, papers, correspondence and reports re penicillin standards, assays and the Therapeutic Substances Act Schedule 1943–46, miscellaneous papers, reports, brochures and press cuttings c.1927–72, n.d.; notes re pipe lemon juice and tartaric acid late 19th cent.; papers re sale of land in Three Mills Lane, Bromley-By-Bow 1887; leases late 19th cent.; valuations and certificates, incl. for Atlas Chemical Works, Millwall 1913, 1921–22, 1936, 1957; employment agreements with J B Lawes & Co Ltd 1914–35; superannuation fund and life assurance booklet 1953; correspondence: A C Bishop 1878–81, business dealings with Elmslie Forsyth & Sedgwick 1878–1880, E Herberts re profits 1901, Pfizer Inc re construction of fermentation works, accounting methods and citric acid production 1931–40, 1954; international exhibition awards 1904, 1906; miscellaneous company booklets and souvenir programmes 1921, 1945–53.

John Bennet Lawes & Co Ltd: minutes 1913–49; certificate of incorporation 1890; agreement with Russian Produce Importers and London Export Co 1916; debenture purchase receipts 1916; certificate re court order and minute on reduction of capital 1915; interest payments ledger 1916–47; credit and debit journal 1953–58; schedule of documents surrendered with lease of Atlas Works,

Millwall 1893; lease agreement 1896; valuation certificate 1922; plans, incl. Atlas Works late 19th cent.; historical chronology n.d.

Pfizer Inc: annual reports 1956–65; Central Research annual conference reports 1953–88 (w); publicity brochure for penicillin n.d.

Records 2: History of Advertising Trust, HAT House, 12 Raveningham Centre, Raveningham NR14 6NU

Advertisements for *TCP* 1974–89. (Ref: MEAL collection 1974–89, R10-80)

PHARMACIA & UPJOHN LTD
Davy Avenue, Knowlhill, Milton Keynes

Manufacture and marketing of pharmaceuticals

History: In 1885 the Upjohn Pill & Granule Co was established in Kalamazoo, Michigan, USA, as a partnership between Dr William Upjohn and his brother Henry. The firm began operations in 1886 and manufactured 'friable' pills, which were softer than other pills on the market and thus dissolved more effectively in the stomach. By the turn of the century the company was manufacturing compressed tablets in addition to 'friable' pills. In 1903 the business was incorporated as a private limited liability company, The Upjohn Co Inc, and increased its manufacturing and marketing activities. The company's first research laboratories were opened in 1913. Between the 1920s and 1950s the company conducted research and development into the prevention of heart disease, cancer and arthritis. In 1952 a UK subsidiary of The Upjohn Co Inc was incorporated as a limited liability company, Upjohn of England Ltd, based at 4 Alford Street in the west end of London, to manufacture and sell ethical pharmaceuticals, including corticosteroids, antibiotics, medical specialities and veterinary products. In 1956 the company re-located to a new manufacturing plant at Fleming Way, Crawley, West Sussex, and in 1961 was renamed Upjohn Ltd. In 1958 the parent company was converted to a public limited liability company, The Upjohn Co Inc. In 1961 Pharmacia AB, a manufacturer of growth hormones and drugs for the prevention of cataracts which was established in Sweden in 1911, incorporated Pharmacia GB Ltd, as its UK subsidiary. In 1995 The Upjohn Co Inc merged with Pharmacia AB, and the newly created company in the UK was renamed Pharmacia & Upjohn Ltd. Between 1995 and 1997 former Upjohn Ltd employees began to relocate from the Upjohn Ltd site at Crawley to the Pharmacia GB Ltd headquarters at Davy Avenue, Knowlhill, Milton Keynes.

R D B Carlisle, *A Century of Caring: The Upjohn story* (Upjohn, USA, 1987); 'Upjohn', in T Derdak (ed), *International Directory of Company Histories*, Vol. 1 (St James Press, London, 1988) 707-9

Records: Pharmacia & Upjohn Ltd, Fleming Way, Crawley RH10 2LZ

Upjohn Co Pte Ltd, Singapore: memorandum and articles of association 1972, certificate of incorporation 1972, certificate of appointment of corporate representative 1993, issued share certificates 1973.

Upjohn Ltd: minutes: directors' and general meetings 1952 to date, trustees of pension and life assurance scheme meetings 1960–66, 1969 to date; memoranda and articles of association 1952, 1977; certificates of incorporation 1981–82; change of name certificate 1961; correspondence re memoranda and articles of association 1972, 1977; board meeting attendance registers 1976–91; notices and proxies: directors' meetings 1974, general meetings 1974–75; registers of directors and secretaries 1954, 1967; company registration documents and correspondence: 1991–94, Upjohn (Ireland) Ltd 1978–95; registers: shareholders 1952–64, members and share ledger 1952–96, mortgages n.d.; stock transfer forms n.d.; share certificates books 1952–96; correspondence re shares 1980s; annual reports 1954–95 (w); balance sheets and profit and loss accounts 1984–95; statements of account 1991–94; balance of payments 1991; trial balances 1985, 1990, 1993; accounts 1984–95; inter-company accounts 1989–93; ledgers: sales 1990–91, 1993–94, purchases 1991; journals: costings 1991, 1993–95, sales 1988–90; expense reports: sales 1992, 1995, sales force 1993–95, external 1990–93, internal 1989–94; journals and working papers re fixed assets 1990–94; daily receipts summaries 1992–93; cash receipts 1992, 1994; cheque requisitions 1990–91, 1994–95; banking: daily summary 1990–92, journals 1989–94, receipts and statements 1991–95, transfers 1990–94, correspondence 1992, various 1986–91; forecasts: customers 1991, exports 1993; cash postings 1990–91; catering account 1991; miscellaneous accounts 1988–95; duty and VAT deferment statements 1990–95; taxation papers 1981–89; VAT review 1994–95; papers re dividend taxation relief 1968, 1991; insurance policies and correspondence 1966–95; insurance papers 1984, 1988–91; insurance claims 1990–95; correspondence: audit 1991–92, accounts 1990–95, Financial Services Act 1986; legal papers and correspondence 1983–95; affidavits re leases at Fleming Way, Crawley 1987; patent review records 1988–89; trade marks 1987–90; agreements and contracts with other companies 1960s–96; production papers and notes 1980–95; project registration files 1960, 1976–96; materials management documents 1988–95; technical support papers 1981–91; product histories and information 1986–87, 1991; correspondence with Home Office re Misuse of Drugs Act and licence to produce drugs 1990–96; advertising literature

1979–92; marketing files 1975–93, 1995; certification files 1987–91; extension works at Fleming Way, Crawley: agreement and lease 1957–64, architectural drawings 1960, 1987–91, n.d., correspondence 1982–94; warehouse at Lowfield Heath, Crawley: leases 1985, 1991, architectural drawings 1988, correspondence and papers 1985–94; 12 Park Way, Crawley: land certificate and architectural drawings 1957–58, report and valuation 1958, 1965, correspondence re Community Charge and Council Tax 1991–93, photographs n.d.; contracts and leases with related correspondence 1987–96; tenancy agreements and inventory, 8 Hatchfields, Cuckfield, West Sussex 1988–89; property papers: premises 1989, mortgages and loans 1992, construction project 1993, office expansion and renovation project 1991, 1993; inventory valuations 1991–95; pension and life assurance scheme annual accounts 1956–95; pension trust deeds and related correspondence 1955 to date; charitable trust deeds 1960, 1979, 1987–92; papers re wages 1982–89; pension records 1977–79, 1984–94; employee survey 1981–91; office services papers 1993–95; time cards 1991–94; correspondence: exports 1992–93, marketing 1992–93, forecasts for overseas subsidiaries 1989–94, office expansion project 1991–92.

PHENSIC LTD
St Helens

Pharmaceutical manufacturer

History: In 1933 Phensic Ltd was incorporated as a limited liability company to manufacture the influenza remedy *Phensic*. In the same year it was acquired by Beecham Pills Ltd. From 1955 Beecham Group Ltd began to market *Phensic*, one of its main proprietary medicines, alongside *Beechams Powders* and *Iron Jelloids*, as a headache remedy. All were manufactured at St Helens.

Records 1: St Helens Local History & Archives Library, Gamble Institute, Victoria Square, St Helens WA10 1DY

Memoranda and articles of association 1933, 1938; accounts 1935–36, 1939–54; private ledgers 1938–53; cash book 1938–55; papers re trade names *Phensic*, *Fenzic* and *Phenzic* 1932–33. (Ref: BP/4/8)

Records 2: SmithKline Beecham plc, SmithKline Beecham House, Great West Road, Brentford TW8 9BD. Enquiries to SmithKline Beecham plc, 1 New Horizons Court, Great West Road, Brentford TW8 9EP

Trade mark agreement with Veno Drug Co Ltd and Fissan Ltd 1936; advertisements for *Phensic* tablets 1950–51, n.d.

Records 3: History of Advertising Trust, HAT House, 12 Raveningham Centre, Raveningham NR14 6NU

Papers, memoranda and advertising campaign material 1965–66; advertisements for *Phensic* 1979. (Ref: JWT 108 (1965) 303 (1966) 430-3; MEAL collection 1979, R10)

S H PLATTIN
32 Derby Road, Nottingham

Dispensing and photographic chemist and ophthalmic optician

History: Around 1853 Thomas Ayre Newball, chemist and druggist, was trading at 8 Tollhouse Hill, Derby Road, Nottingham. By 1871 his business was at 36 Derby Road and Avon Terrace, 33 Shakespeare Road, Nottingham. In the early 1880s Newball was joined in partnership by Thomas Mason, who had been in business since before 1868, and the firm was styled Newball & Mason, chemists, trading from Market Place, [Southwell], and from 36 Derby Road until at least 1895. Towards the end of the nineteenth century Thomas Mason was joined in partnership by John Storer Radford, and the business was renamed Mason & Radford, chemists and druggists of 10 Derby Road. By 1908 Spencer Howard Plattin, dispensing and photographic chemist and ophthalmic optician, was in business on his own account, at 10 Derby Road, Nottingham. Some time after 1941 his business was acquired by the Burr family of Nottingham, and was re-located to 32 Derby Road. The Burr family also purchased the business of Fitzhugh & Carr, chemists of Nottingham, around 1957, closed its premises on Long Row and moved the business to 32 Derby Road when it was renamed S H Plattin.

Records: Nottinghamshire Archives & Southwell Diocesan Record Office, County House, Castle Meadow Road, Nottingham NG2 1AG

Customers' account ledger 1948–58; statement of account of Ringers of Southwell 1959; cash books 1950–58 (w); summary of monthly cash 1951; invoices: 1953–54, Dakin's Removals Ltd 1954; bank statements: 1953–56; receipts: 1953–54, Sanderson's signwriters 1954; private prescriptions 1949–57; C E Burr's appointment card c.1950. (Ref: DD 687)

J H POLLARD
113 Sneinton Road, Nottingham

Chemist

History: William Guest was trading as a chemist from 13 Carlton Street, Nottingham, from at least 1862 until 1876, by which time he was also manufacturing elastic stockings and belts. By 1885 he was trading as a poultry medicine manufacturer at 48 Church Drive, Carrington, Nottingham, and developed 'Roupills', a treatment for tuberculosis in chickens. He ceased trading some time before 1901. John Thomas Rayson registered as a chemist and druggist in Swineshead, Lincolnshire, in 1874 and by 1881 was managing Charlotte Smith's chemist business at 11 Beastmarket Hill, Nottingham, formerly owned by William Smith. By 1883 he was in business as a chemist on his own account at 273 Alfred Street Central, Nottingham. Around 1928 the business was acquired by George William Daykin, and by 1950 had been purchased by J H Pollard. Following this, the business moved from Alfred Street Central to 113 Sneinton Road, Nottingham.

Records: Nottinghamshire Archives & Southwell Diocesan Record Office, County House, Castle Meadow Road, Nottingham NG2 1AG

Ledgers, Guest's poultry and medicinal manufacturing and sales 1867–1941; cash book 1941–43; account books: 1926–46 (w), sales of stockings and support wear 1870–1912, receipts and expenditure 1922, motor running costs 1925; Daykin's personal and miscellaneous accounts 1938; address book with accounts 1894–1916; receipt book 1929–30; invoices 1938; cheque book stubs 1929–30; stock card 1938; prescription books of various named chemists 1875–80, 1894–1955; sale of poisons registers: 1899–1929, Daykin 1936–68; register of morphine 1930–36; register of dangerous drugs and poisons 1930–44; registers of purchases and sales of named drugs, Daykin 1944–68; advertising handbills and broadsheets c.1884–91, 1927–28, n.d.; property papers c.1894, 1905–26; papers and correspondence: stocking and support wear 1897–1912, n.d., delivery notes from medical suppliers 1939–62; booklet re breeding and care of poultry 1853–1901, n.d. (Ref: DD 773, DD 773 addit)

J PRESTON LTD
Wellmeadow Works, Upper Allen Street, Sheffield

Chemist and laboratory furnisher

History: George Arthur Cubley and Job Preston were both in business as chemists and druggists in Sheffield, prior to 1868. Around 1869 they acquired the business of Thomas Perry, chemist, at 4 High Street, Sheffield. In 1893, Job Preston acquired premises at 56 Fargate, and by 1896 at 33 Church Street, Sheffield. His business later moved to 105 Barkers Pool and again, around 1925, to 208 West Street. It was incorporated as a limited liability company, J Preston Ltd, in 1927, and was still trading in 1997, with registered offices at Wellmeadow Works, Upper Allen Street, Sheffield.

Records: Sheffield City Archives, 52 Shoreham Street, Sheffield S1 4SP

Account books and prescription books 1857–1955. (Ref: Acc.1988/8)

R E PRICE
High Street, Rhyl, Denbighshire

Chemist

History: Ellis Powell Jones was registered as a pharmaceutical chemist in 1853 in Rhyl, Denbighshire, and in 1856 was trading from 1 and 52 High Street. Charles Roebuck was in business as a chemist and druggist prior to 1868, in Shepley, Kirklees, and between 1876 and 1885, acquired the Rhyl business. In 1892–93, he moved to Oakbank, Honley, Kirklees, after which the business was acquired by R E Price. The business ceased trading in 1970.

Records: Flintshire Record Office, The Old Rectory, Hawarden CH5 3NR

Account books 1862–65, 1870–89; prescription books 1847–1948 (w). (Ref: D/DM/273)

PRIDMORE'S LTD
Castle Street, Hinckley, Leicestershire

Dispensing chemist and pharmaceutical wholesaler

History: Thomas Pridmore and his nephew William Pridmore were in business as chemists and druggists in Hinckley, Leicestershire, prior to 1868, trading as Thomas Pridmore & Nephew. Between 1875 and 1887 Thomas Pridmore ceased to be registered, but was replaced in the business by Sydney Spencer Pridmore, who registered as a chemist and druggist in 1882. William and Sydney Pridmore were still in business in Castle Street, Hinckley, in 1895. The business was incorporated in 1913 as a limited liability company, Pridmore's Ltd, by which time it had expanded its activities to include pharmaceutical wholesaling. The company was dissolved in 1995.

Records: Record Office for Leicestershire, Leicester & Rutland, Long Street, Wigston Magna, Leicester LE18 2AH

Day book 1879–81; ledgers, day books, cash books, purchases of materials 1857–1972; prescription books, incl. diagnoses and occasional case histories 1827–1942; J A Smith, lawyer, Smith and Pilgrim: account book 1840–42, bill book, incl. accounts for Coventry & Leicester Railway Co 1845; papers re Hinckley Gas Light and Coke Co: share certificate register 1835, share transfer register 1835–74, consumers and consumption record 1869–72; certificate of merit of British Bee-Keepers' Association presented to W S Pridmore 1883. (Ref: DE1833)

RAGG LTD
7 The Green, Edmonton, Enfield, London

Chemist

History: William Watkins Ragg (1853–1930) was registered as a chemist and druggist in 1875, and operated from The Green, Edmonton, Enfield, London. In 1920 he was joined in the business by his son, Clavell William Ragg, and later by another son, Hubert, and a daughter, Kathleen. In 1931 the business was incorporated as a limited liability company, Ragg Ltd. The company ceased trading during the 1970s, following the death of Clavell William Ragg in 1960.

J G L Burnby, 'The Raggs of Edmonton Green', *Pharmaceutical Historian*, 5, 3, Dec 1975

Records: The Museum Curator, Royal Pharmaceutical Society of Great Britain, 1 Lambeth High Street, London SE1 7JN

Account book 1934–36; stockbook and notebook 1956–58; prescription books 1876–1969. (Ref: LDPHA.MANUSCOL.16.1-14, 29.1, 30.1)

RAIMES, CLARK & CO LTD

17 Smith's Place, Leith, Edinburgh

Wholesale and manufacturing chemist

History: In 1816 John and Richard Raimes established a manufacturing druggist's business in Parliament Square, Edinburgh, styled Raimes & Co. The business moved several times from 1818 before settling at Adam's House, Smith's Place, Leith, Edinburgh, in 1832. In 1854 John and Richard Raimes were joined in partnership by George Blanshard and his brother Thomas, and the business was renamed Raimes, Blanshards & Co. During the 1840s and 1850s branches of the business were established in Glasgow, Liverpool, Dublin and York. The York branch became an independent concern, Raimes & Co, in 1892. Following the death of George Blanshard in 1882, and the retirement of Thomas Blanshard, the Edinburgh business was briefly renamed Raimes & Co until 1888, when it was styled Raimes, Clark & Co. It was controlled by John Fortune Raimes and Richard Raimes Junior, both sons of Richard Raimes, and Richard Clark, a former partner of Clark & Pinkerton, wholesale druggists of 17 Greenside Place, Edinburgh. During the 1890s Raimes, Clark & Co specialised in the manufacture of soft gelatine capsules, potassium ioxide and galenicals. Following the death of Richard Clark, the business was incorporated as a limited liability company, Raimes, Clark & Co Ltd, in 1908. During the early twentieth century the company continued to manufacture galenicals, lozenges and capsules and also began a wholesale distribution service, mainly to retail chemists. By the 1950s, following the introduction of the National Health Service, its business expanded into the manufacture and wholesale of ethical pharmaceuticals as well as proprietary medicines such as *Red Band Magnesia* and *Dr Jack's Helios*. In 1970 it incorporated a subsidiary retail chemist's company, James Dudgeon Ltd, at 134 Duke Street, Leith, Edinburgh, which was dissolved in 1989, and a management company, Pharmacy Finance Ltd, which was still trading in 1997. In 1973 another subsidiary retail chemist's company, Robert Hardy (Chemists) Ltd, was incorporated at 18 Roseburn Terrace, Edinburgh. This company was dissolved in 1990. In addition, Raimes, Clark & Co Ltd acquired a number of retail concerns. In 1974 it acquired the wholesale and retail chemist's business of H F Scott Ltd, which had been incorporated as a limited liability company in 1950, at 35 East Port, Dunfermline, Fife, and re-located to 51 High Street, Inverkeithing, Fife, in 1973. This company continued to trade under its own name until its dissolution in 1989. In 1975 Raimes, Clark & Co Ltd acquired the retail chemist's business of R & T Adam Ltd, which had been incorporated as a limited liability company in 1947. This company was based at 8 Roseneath Street, Edinburgh, and was dissolved in 1990. In 1993 it acquired J S B Heddle & Co Ltd, a pharmaceutical distributor and manufacturer of 257a Leith Walk, Edinburgh, which was incorporated as a limited liability company in 1960, and dissolved in 1989. It also acquired Red Band Chemical Co Ltd, a dispensing chemist's business, incorporated as a limited liability company in 1932. Raimes, Clark & Co Ltd was still trading, in 1997, from registered offices at 17 Smith's Place, Leith, Edinburgh.

Industries of Yorkshire. Part II. York, its capital and the great manufacturing and commercial centres of Hull, Huddersfield, Halifax, etc. (Raimes & Co, York, 1890); 'On the History of Raimes, Clark & Co Ltd', *The Scottish Pharmacist*, 1954; 'Raimes & Co Ltd, York', *Yorkshire Herald*, 3 Sept 1910, 11

Records 1: The Secretary, National Register of Archives (Scotland), H M General Register House, Princes Street, Edinburgh EH1 3YY

Deed of co-partnership, Richard Raimes and Richard Clark 1888; notices of assignment 1891–1908; list of policies assigned to Richard Clark to be assigned to new company 1894–1905; minutes 1908 to date; memorandum and articles of association 1908; memorandum on death of Richard Clark 1907; minute of meetings of company and subsidiaries 1973; signature book 1948–87; chairman's report 1968–72; annual returns 1952–68; monthly returns 1908–33; share register 1908–86; shares: debenture correspondence and convertible debentures, miscellaneous papers 1908–33, certificate counterfoils 1908–53; directors' reports, balance sheets and accounts 1963–74; balance sheets 1908–44; estimate of preliminary expenses 1908; general ledger 1948 to date; journal 1908–58; cash books: 1956–62, transfers 1962–67, loose sheets 1968–78; bill book 1910–59; patents lists: 1901–1916, Raimes, Blanshards & Co 1830–85, Sang & Barker 1830–85; trademarks, incl. register of trademark for Maclean & Sons (p) 1889, 1909; agreements: directors and trustees of Richard Clark and D B Robertson, minute 1908, wholesale chemists and druggists of Edinburgh to fix uniform prices 1906, sale of wholesale drug business, between Richard Clark, James Melrose and another 1921; chemical formulae notebook c.1924–30; drug lists 1867–1941; agreement for constituting and regulating iodine preparation combination 1898; Dr Patrick Anderson's 'True Scots Pills', testimonial, leaflets and pill boxes n.d.; price lists 1891, 1900, 1904; returns book 1856–1916; notebooks 1835, 1856–1916; advertisements c.1950–52; press cuttings re company and premises 1850–1988; papers re Smith's Place, Leith: inventory of titles of property belonging to John Raimes 1859, reports and valuations, with plans 1898–1928, pictures n.d.; plant and vehicles' register 1934–69; papers re vehicles 1919–24; salary books 1901–55; wages sheets 1956–66; staff earnings and deductions book 1956–66; employee records 1908–10; staff papers, photographs and press cuttings 1898–1954; programme of staff annual social and dance 1906; Scottish Widow Pensions Scheme 1962–63; correspondence:

Dublin, Liverpool, York and Glasgow branches n.d., Dr Alex Cumming re company re-organisation and manufacturing and scientific side of business 1920–22, miscellaneous, incl. loans and insurance policies 1891–1921, n.d.; photographs: directors and staff n.d., British Pharmaceutical Conference, Edinburgh 1938; J B Gibb, director, personal papers: order books 1900, diary excerpt 1891, photographs n.d., retirement speech n.d.; papers and articles re company history 1954–55, n.d.; profit and expense control, compiled by George S May International 1960; papers re Knowsley Investments PTY Ltd (Australia) 1969–73; Maclean & Sons: Great Exhibition medal, York 1889, Macleans Revalenta Food, papers c.1900–43.

J S B Heddle & Co Ltd: combined register of members and share ledger 1960–87.

Orr's Remedies Co: minutes 1946–48. (Ref: NRA(S) 2974)

Pharmacy Finance Ltd: minutes 1970–87; combined register of members and share ledger 1970–71; directors' reports, balance sheets and accounts 1963–74.

Records 2: Perth Museum & Art Gallery, George Street, Perth PH1 5LB

Price list of capsules 1906. (Ref: 862)

WILLIAM RANSOM & SON PLC
104 Bancroft, Hitchin, Hertfordshire

Manufacturer of pharmaceuticals and grower of crude drugs

History: William Ransom served his pharmaceutical apprenticeship in Birmingham during the early 1840s. In 1845 he established a pharmacy in Hitchin, Hertfordshire, on his own account, and in 1846 began to manufacture herbal preparations using raw materials grown at the Ransom home farm in Hitchin, and also those imported directly from overseas. He sold the pharmacy in 1849 in order to concentrate on the manufacture of drugs, tinctures and essences, operating from premises in Bancroft, Hitchin. In 1885 he was joined in partnership by his son, Francis, and the business was named William Ransom & Son. Francis was an active researcher and member of the British Pharmaceutical Conference, becoming its president in 1910. After his appointment to the business, a programme of research and development began almost immediately and the firm became the first in the UK to manufacture chlorophyll on a commercial scale. In 1913 the business was incorporated as a private limited liability company, William Ransom & Son Ltd, with Francis Ransom as chairman. In 1914 William Ransom died and in 1927 Francis Ransom's son, Richard, joined the company. By 1928 the premises in Bancroft had expanded to include a manufacturing laboratory, tincture room, vat and still rooms, and the company owned a farm at Meppershall, Bedfordshire. In 1931 the Meppershall farm was sold and one at Little Wymondley, Hertfordshire, acquired. Richard became a director in 1932 and chairman on the death of his father in 1935. In 1950 the Little Wymondley farm was sold and Wiggin Hill Farm, St Ives, Cambridgeshire, was purchased. In 1968 the company was converted to a public limited liability company, with the same name, and at the same time, Wiggin Hill Farm became an independent private partnership, although it continued to supply William Ransom & Son Ltd with lavender and camomile. In 1969 Richard Ransom passed the chairmanship to his son, Michael. Significant building works took place in 1981 to enable the company to expand its range of manufactured ethical medicines for world-wide export. Half of the company's turnover was accounted for by exports, and it had overseas agents in 50 countries. In the UK the majority of William Ransom & Son plc's pharmaceutical products were purchased by wholesale chemists. By the 1990s less than 10 per cent of the company's output was of herbal medicines, although it was one of the few UK companies still to manufacture plant-based drugs. The main products of the company in 1997 were drugs extracted from vegetable sources and liquid medicines.

'Going Strong in Galenicals: Ransom's of Hitchin Revisited', *Chemist and Druggist*, 27 Aug 1966; K Holland, 'William Ransom & Son plc', *Pharmaceutical Journal*, 14 Nov 1987, 578-9; 'The Mystery of the 'Retired' Galenical', *Chemist and Druggist*, 27 August 1955

Records 1: William Ransom & Son plc, 104 Bancroft, Hitchin SG5 1LY

Minutes: director's meetings 1913-85, general meetings 1913-59; memorandum and articles of association 1912, 1962-68, 1980; papers re incorporation of company 1912-13; notices of meetings 1920-22, 1968; resolutions to be passed at first directors' meeting 1913; special resolutions passed 1940, 1942, 1950; papers re extraordinary general meeting 1939-40; agendas and notes 1964; organisational chart c.1950s-60s; annual returns 1923-47; transferred and cancelled share certificates 1913-50; declaration of dividend: preference shares 1920, ordinary shares and debenture interest 1921, 1938-49; register of dividend payments to shareholders 1949-68; papers re registration of debentures 1925-26, 1945; share prospectus 1968; list of shareholders n.d.; correspondence re shareholding 1948-49; annual reports and accounts 1913-33, 1950-75; director's report 1951; chairman's report 1960; annual accounts 1913-58 (w);

account sheets 1886–1906; average profits 1911–13; statements of capital in business 1914–17, 1968–71; summary of liability 1918; trading and profit and loss accounts (including farm) 1960–61, 1963; farm trading and profit and loss accounts 1957–58; trading accounts 1957–58; trial balances 1958, 1960–61; statements of accounts 1970–71; ledgers: 1847–1900, 1931–71, private 1907–24, n.d., crude drugs suppliers 1882–1920, 1931–33, farm 1965–69, customers' accounts 1846–67, 1941–63, export 1943–71, orders despatched 1896–1902, town 1920s–40s, dangerous drugs 1917–84, stock 1953–62, cash analyses 1941–49, home sales 1941–77, supplier and client reconciliation 1947–63, summary balances (including farm) 1945–59, 1966–74, stationery 1950–83, currency reconciliations, overseas agents and customers 1950–79, agents' accounts 1964–71, agents' orders 1964; journals: 1879–98, 1929–70 (w), farm 1943–65, agents' accounts 1960–71, export bank charges reconciliation 1963–70, export sales 1971–72; day books: wholesale 1852–81, home 1936–46, export 1936–43, invoices 1963–65, home sales 1971, cash analyses 1975–80, cheques received 1975–78; cash books: 1855–84 (w), 1945–78, private 1942–63, farm 1938–69, receipts 1936–74 (w); notebooks: profit and loss 1884–86, accounts not rendered and owing 1895; record books: shipping 1901–44, duty paid on sales of ethanol and industrial methylated spirit 1983–87, payments received 1920–37, customers' orders 1931–38, sales 1941, credit returns, packaging and containers 1941–65; register of debtors and creditors 1941–45; invoices 1960, 1963; bank books 1889–97, 1949–59; paying-in book stubs 1942–45; bank statements 1938–43; certificate of incorporation, National Savings Movement 1940; insurance policies 1896–1904, 1941–67; deed, contract for redemption of land tax 1799; statement of excess profits duty liability 1914–17; income tax papers 1916–54; purchase tax certificates 1947, 1965; correspondence with Inland Revenue 1909–12 and legal papers re excess profits duty 1916–41; income tax and land tax receipts 1960–63; audited accounts, incl. balance sheet 1943; stock analysis for annual audit 1981; provisional patent specification 1947; letters of contract for A H Cox & Co Ltd n.d.; production meetings minutes 1953–61; laboratory journal 1851–56; notebooks: Francis Ransom c.1880–90, Marjorie Smith 1960s–70s; manufacturing diaries 1934–39; manufacturing record books 1909–13, 1926–76; papers re manufacture of galenicals 1933–46, 1958–75; stock books: dangerous drugs 1923–27, crude drugs 1929–44, industrial methylated spirit 1947–73; receipts: spirits 1960–61, ethanol 1982–89; drawback book 1895; formulation books: 1845–1950s; formulae, translated from foreign sources 1940s–50s; standards for the manufacture of tinctures 1909; product list n.d.; bonds re proper use of methylated spirit 1882–98; dangerous drugs: summary book 1970–75, record book 1922–28, register 1949–65; *Ransom's Chlorophyll*, booklets n.d.; production costs record books 1901–14; returns books: packaging and containers 1888–94, 1939, 1950s–60s, industrial methylated spirits 1925–59; waste books, orders and accounts 1859–80 (w); authority and wartime contracts on use of methylated spirits 1934–49; applications to Home Office for licences to supply dangerous drugs 1960–65; Home Office annual returns for controlled drugs 1975–85; correspondence: India Office 1893, commissioners of customs and excise 1913–29, dangerous drugs 1916–37, stills 1931–69, Ministry of Food 1946–53, manufacturing and retail chemists re orders and supplies 1946–69, private orders and supplies 1958–75 (w), bonded warehouse applications and approval 1972–73; excise licences 1940, 1945–57; shipping documentation 1940; raw materials price books 1913–40; price lists: 1937, 1952–61, n.d., concentrated extracts 1936–1947 (w), n.d., wholesale 1933, 1937–62 (w), n.d., lavender yields 1965; price regulation agreements 1910–62; client telephone index c.1950s; address books 1940s, n.d.; promotional booklets 1890s, 1962–63; press cuttings and advertisements 1950s–70s; Whinbush Road allotments: manorial court rolls 1811, 1839, 1855–57, lease 1934, valuation 1939, rental agreements between company and employees 1922, 1961, cottage maintenance payments to tenants 1963; Bancroft, Hitchin: sale of freehold with plan of lots 1855, papers and correspondence re site expansion 1969, correspondence and plans re construction of factory 1975–80; Fairview Road, Stevenage: correspondence, papers and plans with Ministry of Agriculture 1943–47, inventory and valuation of land 1943; Wymondley: builder's specifications 1934, forms re requisition of land 1942, correspondence and grant of planning permission from Hitchin District Council 1942–43, litigation papers 1940s; maps and plans of land auctioned and bought 1920; papers re factory costing, cost allocation and stock control n.d.; tender 1942; tenancy agreement, Wiggin Hill Farm 1965; lease and correspondence re Fowler's Farm, Meppershall 1916–22; correspondence and plan re land at Ickleford 1950; test certificate, Morris Worm-Gear Pulley-Block 1922; register of employees 1959–69; staff ledger 1970–75; staff employment agreements 1898, 1947; letters of application for employment 1895–98, 1939, 1948; memorandum re bonus payment 1901; termination of employment: F J Pack 1940, W A Markwell 1942; wages books: general 1897–1910, farm 1879–97, farm foreman 1916–25, works (by department) and farm 1921–30, 1938–40, works (by department) 1940–44, income tax deductions 1946–48; wages sheets 1944–46; wages and salaries books 1951–60; monthly salaries sheets 1954–63; payroll, farm and works 1969–70; wages and salaries analysis book 1969–76; payroll and wages notebook 1982–87; staff salaries, papers incl. banked cheques and letters to bank 1897, 1943–45; bonuses calculations 1920; special resolution re pensions 1942; company pension and life insurance schemes: booklet 1953, staff contributions ledger 1954–64, annual accounts 1956–57; travellers' journey cards and correspondence 1945–59; cash book, travellers' expenses 1949–76; Ministry of Labour Certificate re employment of disabled ex-servicemen 1920; in-house training records 1950s; canteen: accounts and balance sheets 1958–59, 1963, ledger 1959–64, stock-book 1959–63, dinner account balance sheets 1958–64, dinner stock book

1954-64, dinner and Christmas party programme 1953; cricket club scoring books 1934-44; correspondence: National Amalgamated Druggists Ltd 1931, Pharmaceutical Society of Great Britain 1936, 1942, death of F Ransom and J H Stott 1935-37, Royal Institute of Chemistry 1945, Association of Chemical and Allied Employees 1947, laboratory foreman 1947, employees' income tax 1940s, Sainsbury Committee 1963-68 (w), miscellaneous 1960s; photographs: staff and directors late 19th cent., 1946-51, laboratories, warehouses and staff late 19th cent.-1940s, farms, plants and agricultural workers late 19th cent., 1940s-60s, views of Hitchin 20th cent.; cartoons n.d.; censorship permit application 1944; personal papers: F Ransom 1935-36, R F Ransom 1943-69; historical notes 1960s.

Records 2: Wiggin Hill Farm, Ramsey Road, St Ives, Huntingdon PE17 4LL

Proof of a first mortgage debenture n.d.; draft profit and loss accounts, Meppershall and Wymondley Bury Farms 1928-30; ledgers 1922-47; trade ledger 1908-18; day books: 1934-44, and loose sheets 1943-50; credit books 1947-53; receipt books: carriage 1941-42, drugs containers 1949-50, parcel service 1950, haulage 1951; invoices: suppliers 1952-54, customers 1953-54; correspondence and papers re income tax 1920s-30s; diaries, Edward Ingram, farm manager, Wymondley Bury and Wiggin Hill farms 1909-65; stock books: 1922-55, and loose sheets 1942-49 (w); drawback books 1903-05; drug certificates 1943; product packaging and bottle labelling record book 1901-12; wholesale price list 1943; production correspondence: manufacturing equipment 1953, drug certification 1943-50, Herb Farm Ltd 1949, Herbal Research Institute, London 1950, HMSO 1942-50; formulae book 1937; file re supply of chloroform 1953; customer order book 1939-52; order sheets 1948-51; Belgian customer orders and account file 1951-52; correspondence and orders 1953, 1950s; wholesale export list 1941; export departmental files 1950s; suppliers' and customers' address book n.d.; consignment notebooks 1949; correspondence: shipping of drug orders 1938-52 (w), import licences 1950s, application to act as overseas agents for William Ransom & Son Ltd 1949-53, supplies and orders 1943-48, advertising 1953; insurance certificate re consignments shipped overseas 1948; wages books 1910-21, 1926-38; job applications 1940s; correspondence re staff: training courses 1948-50, employment vacancies 1944-50, job advertisements 1948-50; canteen, papers and correspondence 1953; papers and files re charities 1953.

RECKITT & COLMAN PRODUCTS LTD
Dansom Lane, Kingston upon Hull

Manufacturer of pharmaceuticals and household products

History: Following the death of his father, Thomas Reckitt, in 1819, Isaac Reckitt established a flour milling business in Boston, Lincolnshire, in partnership with his brother, Thomas. Following a succession of bad harvests, Isaac left the partnership in 1833, and moved to Nottingham, to establish himself in business as a corn factor. In 1840 he moved to Kingston upon Hull, where he first rented, and some years later purchased, a starch works on Dansom Lane. He took his son, George Reckitt, into partnership in 1848, and the business was styled I Reckitt & Son. His second son, Francis Reckitt, joined the partnership in 1852, and the firm diversified into the production of laundry blue. In 1862, following the death of Isaac Reckitt, George and Francis Reckitt took their brother James into partnership, and the business was re-styled Reckitt & Sons. In 1864 George Reckitt left the partnership. The firm was incorporated as a private limited liability company, Reckitt & Sons Ltd, in 1879, and in 1888 was converted to a public limited liability company, retaining its own name, with James and Francis Reckitt as directors. The company later began manufacturing metal polishes, including *Brasso*, introduced in 1905, and *Silvo*, introduced in 1912, and boot polishes. In 1913 the Chiswick Polish Co was established as a joint venture between Reckitt & Sons Ltd and Chiswick Soap & Polish Co. A subsidiary of the Chiswick Polish Co, Chiswick Products, was formed in 1929. Reckitt & Sons Ltd became involved in the manufacture of pharmaceuticals in 1933, when an antiseptic/disinfectant was produced, and marketed as *Dettol*. In 1938 Reckitt & Sons Ltd merged with J & J Colman Ltd, a laundry blue manufacturing company, and preparer of mustards and spices, first established in 1814. This merger created a new company, Reckitt & Colman Ltd, although each parent company continued to trade and be quoted under its own name. In the same year Reckitt & Sons Ltd acquired some shares in the business of F W Hampshire & Co Ltd, a company which was established in Derby in 1895 and incorporated as a private limited liability company in 1915. It was converted to a public limited liability company in 1927, and manufactured *Snowfire*, a treatment for chapped hands. In 1948 F W Hampshire & Co Ltd and Reckitt & Sons Ltd incorporated a jointly owned limited liability company, Sunnydale Products Ltd, to develop the overseas trades of each company. In the same year Reckitt & Sons Ltd, launched its second pharmaceutical product, *Dispirin*, a soluble form of *Aspirin*, and in 1952 introduced *Codis*, soluble *Aspirin* with codeine. In 1954 Reckitt & Sons Ltd and J & J Colman Ltd were acquired by Reckitt & Colman Holdings Ltd, thus ceasing to be independently quoted companies. In 1956 Reckitt & Sons Ltd was liquidated, and a new company of the same name was incorporated in 1957, to deal with manufacture and marketing activities. A subsidiary company, Reckitt, Colman, Chiswick (Overseas) Ltd, was incorporated in the same year, to administer the overseas trade, and new laboratories were opened at Dansom Lane. In 1960 Kay Brothers Ltd, Stockport, and Westminster Laboratories Ltd, a manufacturer of laxatives, founded in 1931, were acquired, allowing Reckitt & Sons Ltd to increase its output of pharmaceutical products, and in 1965 F W Hampshire & Co Ltd was acquired as a wholly-owned subsidiary of Reckitt & Sons Ltd. A new subsidiary company, Reckitt & Colman Products Ltd, was incorporated in 1970, comprising Reckitt & Sons Ltd, the now renamed Reckitt & Colman (Overseas) Ltd and J & J Colman Ltd. Reckitt & Colman Products Ltd was divided into divisions, of which Division C, established in 1971, was pharmaceutical. This division specialised in the manufacture of over-the-counter medicines, including *Lem-Sip* and *Senokot*, but also introduced prescription only treatments including *Gaviscon*, a treatment for heartburn, *Fybogel*, a fibre laxative, introduced in 1974, and *Temgesic*, an analgesic, launched in 1978. In 1972 Reckitt & Colman Products Ltd acquired the Carbic Ltd group of companies, which included Howard Lloyd Holdings Ltd and Lloyds Pharmaceuticals Ltd of Batley, Kirklees, manufacturers of *Bonjela*, a treatment for mouth ulcers, and *Transvasin*, an anti-rheumatic rub. In 1995 the Colman side of Reckitt & Colman plc was sold to Unilever, who in turn sold the drinks side of the business to Bass plc. In 1997 Reckitt & Colman Products Ltd continued to trade as the UK constituent of the British-based parent company, Reckitt & Colman plc.

I H Barrett (ed), *A Few Facts about Reckitt & Colman Holdings Ltd and its Ramifications* (Hull, 1965); J M Bellamy, *A Hundred Years of Pharmacy in Hull, 1868–1968* (Hull University, Hull, 1968); D Chapman-Huston, *Sir James Reckitt: A memoir* (Faber & Gwyer, London, 1927); R S Harris, 'History of Reckitt & Colman Pharmaceutical Division', *Pharmaceutical Historian*, 18, 2, June 1988, 5-6; B N Reckitt, *The History of Reckitt & Sons Ltd* (A Brown & Sons Ltd, London & Hull, 1965); 'The Story of Reckitt & Colman Ltd, Hull', *Supplement to the American and Commonwealth Visitor*, Aug 1953, 26-7

Records 1: Reckitt's Heritage, Reckitt & Colman Products Ltd, Dansom Lane, Kingston upon Hull HU8 7DS

Laboratory reports and registration documents 1978 to date; standard operating procedures 1978 to date; research data 1978 to date; 'blue book' 1970–72.

Carbic Ltd: articles of association 1951; ledger 1914–18.

F W Hampshire & Co Ltd: general meeting notice 1963; share prospectus 1965; directors' report and statement of accounts 1962; press cutting 1965.

Reckitt & Colman Holdings Ltd: private share ledger 1954–57; annual report and statements of account 1951–68; private journal 1954–61; cash book 1953–65; profit sharing audits 1957–69.

Reckitt & Colman (Insurance) Ltd: minutes 1965–71; register of members 1968–70.

Reckitt & Colman Ltd: directors' meetings minutes 1938–66; memoranda and articles of association 1938, 1952, 1969; directors' reports 1942–47, 1969–94; committee meetings minutes: organisation committee 1938–41, sales and advertising committee 1938–50; minutes of authority 1939–57 (w); Hull local board minutes 1938–57; private ledger 1940–48; royal warrant 1950; inventory and valuation of chemical works, Lancashire 1948; pension fund: minutes 1937–91 (w), register and ledger 1923–38, register of retirements 1954–89, register of deaths 1941–90, contribution records 1929–69; magazines: *Overseas Advertising News* 1938–52, *Overseas Advertising and Marketing News* 1953–65, *Overseas Marketing News* 1966–70, *Reckitt & Colman Marketing News* 1971–81, *Reckitt & Colman Marketing World* 1982–86.

Reckitt & Colman (Overseas) Ltd: directors' meetings minutes 1950–55; overseas research committee meetings minutes 1943; ledgers and journals 20th cent.

Reckitt & Sons Ltd: directors' meetings minutes 1879–1969 (w); general meetings minutes 1899–1955; minutes of authority 1943–45; memoranda and articles of association 1878, 1888, 1899–1919, 1949; certificate of incorporation 1888; register of seals 1968–71; committee meetings minutes: directors' 1896–99, 1923–69, welfare 1905–08, 1942–73, library 1927–39, fellowship fund 1928–74, research and technical 1930–44, export 1933–40 (w), long-term illness fund 1955–65, sales and advertising 1958–61, housing 1968–76, suggestions 1978–82; Hull: local board minutes 1905–49 (w), 1969–70, research committee minutes 1938–69, technical committee minutes 1948–55; works council: minutes 1932–85 (w), rules 1965–72; director's letter of resignation 1938; agreements: J & J Colman 1938, Australia office 1886, 1889; licence to carry on business in New York 1893, 1896; corporate prospectus 1888; business notebook 1912–28; transfer ledger 1904–22; stock exchange quotation 1929; correspondence re shares 1878; annual report and statement of accounts 1948; annual reports 1967–68; profit and loss accounts and balance sheets 1914–28; accounts 1827–31,

1947–55; ledgers: 1840–1912 (w), 1938–44, directors' 1879–81, private 1904–31, investments 1937–55, stocktaking 1864–78, manufacturing accounts 1869–78; journals: 1876–88, 1942–55, private 1888–99; cash books: 1814–55 (w), 1878–83, 1931–62, private 1948–55; bad debts books 1911–64; summaries of sales and profits 1889–1965, 1988; overseas subsidiaries accounts 1939–44; analysis reports of foreign houses 1892–1909; manufacturing accounts 1886–1908, 1938–60; manufacturing formulae and notes 1941–67; manufacturing and laboratory notebooks 1890–1912, 1946–64; suggestion book 1885–1902; papers re Queen's award for export achievement 1979; export terms 1941; lists of company agents world-wide 1919–39; trademark certificates and indexes 1876–1968; photographs of products 1980s–90s, n.d.; advertising resolutions and material 1879–1976; advertisements scrapbook 1948–50; advertising and promotional records: video cassettes 1962–94, films 1966–82, audio cassettes 1987–93; artwork for *Dettol* 1989–90; label books 1873–1971; promotional brochure re visit of Prince of Wales 1926; showcards and posters 20th cent., n.d.; press cuttings 1926–30; deed and mortgage agreement 1839, 1853; property register 1879–1916; Dansom Lane works: plans of garden village 1923–25, 1945, maps 1866, 1928, 1946, n.d., extension accounts re building work and plant 1899–1907; architectural plan of Francis Reckitt Institute 1915; Stoneferry: plant and labour records 1908, site plan 1973; insurance policy re dwelling houses in Dansom Lane 1852; space review 1970–71; factory notebooks 1887–88, 1925–27; Skipton factory wage rates 1962–64; agreements with employees 1859, 1900–04, 1922–35; apprenticeship indenture 1866; personnel papers: appointments register 1878–85, general records 1939–90; staff council minutes 1971–74; staff welfare accounts and papers 1950–63; staff works rules 1950–70s; staff census 1909–83; employees time book 1879–86; roll of honour n.d.; staff awards list 1921–69; staff signatures book 1927; papers re computing course c.1958; letterbooks 1850–52, 1872–1915; correspondence: George Reckitt 1848–49, c.1861, general 1844–45, 1874, visit of Duke of Kent 1977; Reckitt Employees' Hospitals and Charities Association minutes 1930–72; joint recreational committee: constitution 1948, minutes 1957–65, awards 1909, 1915; magazines: *Reckitt's Magazine* 1907–16, *Reckitt's Christmas Magazine* 1916–18, *Carrow Works Magazine* 1907–45, *Ours* 1919–70, 1990–92, *Reckitt News* 1975–90, *Roundabout* 1977–81, *Insight* 1993–95, *Chiswick News* 1976–94, *Stoneferry Special* 1985–90, *Hard News* 1987–89; visitors' book 1938–39; Reckitt's school log book 1919–67; photographs: directors 1910, Garden Village, Hull 1910, factory 1951; historical notes 19th cent.–1962, n.d.

Steradent Ltd: balance sheet and profit and loss account 1939.

Sunnydale Products Ltd: cash day book 1948–65.

Westminster Laboratories Ltd: technical committee meetings minutes 1958–61; product information and leaflets n.d.; photographs of directors and premises n.d.

Records 2: History of Advertising Trust, HAT House, 12 Raveningham Centre, Raveningham NR14 6NU

Reckitt & Sons Ltd: papers, memoranda and advertising campaign material 1952–68; advertisements: *Dispirin* 1976–78, Lloyds muscular cream 1979, *Dettol* 1979, *Senokot* 1985. (Ref: JWT 175 (1965) 176 (1965) 402 (1967) 543-5, 609 (1958–68) 610-17 (1952–68); MEAL collection 1976 R10, 1977 R10, 1978 R10, 1979 R30, R65, 1985 R60)

RED BAND CHEMICAL CO LTD
17 Smith's Place, Leith, Edinburgh

Dispensing chemist

History: Red Band Chemical Co Ltd was incorporated as a limited liability company, in Edinburgh, in 1932, to trade as a dispensing chemist. During the 1970s it was acquired by Raimes, Clark & Co Ltd, wholesale and manufacturing chemists of 17 Smith's Place, Leith, Edinburgh, and continued to trade under its own name. It was still operating in 1997.

Records: The Secretary, National Register of Archives (Scotland), H M General Register House, Princes Street, Edinburgh EH1 3YY

Minutes 1932–86; annual returns 1952–68; combined register of members and share ledger 1932–75; directors' reports, balance sheets and accounts 1963–74. (Ref: NRA(S) 2974)

ISRAEL RENSON
Classic Mansions, 30 Well Street, Hackney, London

Chemist

History: Israel Renson (1906–86), the third child of Russian Jewish immigrants, was born in Scarborough Street in the east end of London. On leaving school in 1923 he became apprenticed for 3 years to Daniel Vahrman, a chemist in Fournier Street, off Brick Lane, London, and attended evening classes at Chelsea

Polytechnic in order to sit the Pharmaceutical Society's examinations. During this time he developed strong socialist beliefs. He was employed for a short period with a large, local chemist's firm, after which he worked with a chemist in Well Street, Hackney, London, from 1927 to 1935. He then established a business, on his own account, at Classic Mansions, 30 Well Street. He sold this business to a Mr Silver in 1959.

Records: Hackney Archives Department, 43 De Beauvoir Road, London N1 5SQ

Cash book 1955–59; correspondence and papers re shop premises 1936–59; photographs of Renson outside his shop c.1936, c.1950s; Renson's Pharmaceutical Society papers: certificates issued by School of Pharmacy 1926–27, certificate of membership 1927, certificate of qualification as chemist and druggist 1927, correspondence re qualifications, Daniel Vahrman's testimonial and 50 years of membership 1927, 1977, photograph of students incl. Renson on visit to Parke, Davis & Co 1927; autobiography, edited interview with related correspondence 1977; family papers and photographs 1930s–80s; papers, notes, scrapbook, publication *Money Must Go* and correspondence re political interests c.1943–78; research papers, notes, magazines, correspondence and photographs re local societies, history and other interests n.d.; lecture slides c.1920s, c.1975–80. (Ref: HAD D/F/REN)

REYNOLDS & BRANSON LTD
13 Briggate, Leeds

Manufacturing chemist and optical instrument manufacturer

History: Richard Reynolds was a pharmaceutical chemist prior to 1852, and Richard Freshfield Reynolds was registered as a pharmaceutical chemist in 1884. Both were still operating from 13 Briggate, Leeds, in 1895. In 1948 the business was incorporated as a limited liability company, Reynolds & Branson Ltd, and in 1976 was removed from the register of companies.

Records: West Yorkshire Archive Service, Leeds, Chapeltown Road, Sheepscar, Leeds LS7 3AP

Sales and purchases ledger 1898–1954; day book, incl. orders for spectacles 1898–1900, 1935–36; prescription book 1828–30, with government posters re waste salvage c.1940. (Ref: Acc 2144)

RHÔNE-POULENC RORER LTD
Rainham Road South, Dagenham, Barking & Dagenham

Pharmaceutical manufacturer

History: In 1832 John May (1809–93) was taken into the employment of Charles John Price, a manufacturing chemist of Battersea, Wandsworth, London. He left in 1834 to establish a manufacturing chemist's business on his own account near Battersea Bridge with 2 partners, Joseph L Pickett and Thomas Ship Grimwade. Joseph Pickett died suddenly in 1835 and Grimwade left the partnership in 1839 to be replaced by William Garrard Baker. A new partnership agreement was drawn up in 1840 and the business was styled May & Baker. In 1841 premises named Garden Wharf in Battersea were purchased and became the operating centre of the business until 1934. Early fine chemical manufactures included camphor, ether, bismuth and ammonia, and in 1851 May & Baker exhibited these products and others at the Great Exhibition, receiving a medal for their acids and metallic salts. An apprentice, Thomas Tyrer, was taken on in 1862 and during the 1860s and 1870s the firm expanded its business to supply not only wholesalers, but also hospitals and boarding schools. In 1876 an abortive attempt was made to gain the rights to a patent for *Dextrine Maltose* from O'Sullivan and Valentin, and later that year May retired from the business and Baker took Richard Child Heath, a solicitor, into partnership. On May's instructions, Thomas Tyrer was also taken into partnership, and Heath's stepson, William Blenkinsop, was appointed as an assistant and, in 1878, as a partner. New products were introduced, including cadmium bromide and iodine, essences of vanilla and banana and nickel preparations. By 1886 the firm was manufacturing one of F Maxwell Lyte's patented paint products and in 1887 William Blenkinsop and Professor W N Hartley of Dublin University successfully applied for a patent to produce metallic sulphate, which was subsequently sold to May & Baker. In the same year the firm was appointed agent for 2 pharmaceutical products, *Paracetophenitidin* and methylene chloride, manufactured by the German company, Friedr Bayer & Co, and in 1889 began to manufacture *Sulphonal*, a tension reliever. In 1890 the partnership was dissolved, and the business was incorporated as a limited liability company, May & Baker Ltd. At this juncture, Tyrer retired and John May became a director, serving until his death. Dr Oscar Steinhart, a chemist, was appointed to the company in 1891, and in 1892, a second chemist, H Wood Smith, was taken on, following which, Steinhart resigned. The new company entered into an agreement in 1891 with the Vitreous Mosaic Co, a mosaic flooring manufacturer, to provide it with materials for furnaces and buildings, a partnership which lasted until the First World War. In the late 1890s a new manufacture was introduced, cyanide, based on methods used by the Cassel Co. Much of the output was exported to South Africa by

Mosenthal & Sons, until its production ceased in 1903. In the same year May & Baker Ltd began manufacture of salts of lithium, used in the treatment of gout and as antiseptics, and established a Lithia Department to manage this activity. Lithium was present in the metal mineral amblygonite, and the company arranged to receive supplies of this mineral from a Spanish mine through a French firm of manufacturing chemists, Poulenc Frères. A cobalt department was established, in 1904, to manufacture cobalt for use in the ceramics and pigments industries. However, this was an unprofitable venture and in 1913 production ceased. In the same year, Richard Heath, chairman of May & Baker Ltd, died. In 1916 his stepson, William, also died and thereafter Richard Blenkinsop became managing director of the company. In 1914 the Board of Trade issued a licence to Établissements Poulenc Frères of Paris to sell *Neo-Salversan* through their British agents, May & Baker Ltd, who subsequently began to manufacture the drug at newly acquired premises in Bell Lane, Wandsworth, London, marking the company's entry into chemotherapy. The link with Poulenc Frères was strengthened in 1916, when Georges Roche purchased 6,000 of May & Baker Ltd's shares and was elected to the board. Dr Arthur Ewins was appointed as chief chemist at the Wandsworth factory in 1917, and in 1918 George Newbery was appointed as his assistant. In the same year Richard Blenkinsop died, leaving his 2 young daughters major shareholders in the company. In 1921 they were persuaded to sell their shares to Georges Roche and in 1927, Poulenc Frères acquired 90 per cent of May & Baker Ltd's ordinary shares. Dr Roche was appointed chairman, Richard Blenkinsop's brother, Philip, vice-chairman and his cousin, Neville, managing director. In 1928 Poulenc Frères merged with the Société Chimique des Usines du Rhône and was renamed Rhône-Poulenc. In 1925 May & Baker Ltd was granted a licence to manufacture *Tryparsamide*, a treatment for trypanosomiasis, African sleeping sickness, which was obtained from arsenilic acid, and in 1927 Dr H J Barber was appointed company chemist, the fourth in a growing research and development department working with organic arsenicals. From the 1920s a number of overseas subsidiary companies were incorporated, May & Baker (India) Ltd in 1928, May & Baker (Canada) Ltd in 1929 and May & Baker (South Africa) Ltd in 1935. In 1933 building work began on land which had been purchased at Dagenham, Barking & Dagenham, in 1919, under the supervision of R V Bradshaw, an engineer. In 1934 the transfer of staff, offices and warehouses from Battersea and Wandsworth to Dagenham was completed. In the same year Garden Wharf was sold to the Morgan Crucible Co Ltd. In 1935 the specialities department, which manufactured and marketed the products of Rhône-Poulenc's Specia Co in the UK, was formed as a subsidiary company, Pharmaceutical Specialities (May & Baker) Ltd. In 1939 Neville and E K Blenkinsop relinquished the majority of their shares, marking the end of 'family' involvement in the company. Pioneering research into sulphonamides began in the 1930s, and in 1938 *M&B 693* was launched as an anti-pneumonia drug. The Dagenham factory was damaged by fire and enemy action during the Second World War, and was hampered by a shortage of raw materials. However, the company managed to maintain a good production record, partly by diversifying into plastics through the incorporation of May & Baker Plastics Ltd in 1941 and by manufacturing anti-malarial drugs. It also continued its programme of overseas expansion. In 1952 a site at Ongar, Essex, was acquired for agrochemicals and veterinary research, and in 1955, a large site was purchased at Norwich, Norfolk, for the production of agrochemicals, the company's newest products. The 1950s saw the continued production of mercurials and bismuth and also the manufacture of organic chemicals, anaesthetics, antihistamines and anti-anaerobic drugs, of which *Flagyl* was highly successful. After the granting of Indian independence in 1947 and subsequent partition of India and Pakistan, May & Baker Ltd could no longer supply the Pakistani market through May & Baker (India) Ltd. In 1966 the Pakistan Pharmaceutical Industry Ltd was incorporated, with May & Baker Ltd owning 60 per cent of its shares, and in 1976 the company was renamed May & Baker Pakistan Ltd. In 1975 the British operation was tailored to match the organisational structure of Rhône-Poulenc in France. May & Baker Ltd's activities were separated into 3 divisions: agrochemicals, fine chemicals and plastics, each of which was supported by a central administration. In 1988 the company was renamed Rhône-Poulenc Ltd and in 1990 the pharmaceutical activities of the French parent and the American company, Rorer Pharmaceuticals Ltd, merged to form Rhône-Poulenc Rorer Inc. The British affiliate became Rhône-Poulenc Rorer Ltd.

'May & Baker Ltd', *Supplement to the Chemist and Druggist* 14 April 1934; *May and Baker: The story of the organisation* (May & Baker, Dagenham, n.d.); J Slinn, *A History of May & Baker 1834–1984* (Hobsons, Cambridge, 1984); *Some Aspects of the May & Baker Organisation* (May & Baker, Dagenham, 1970)

Records 1: Rhône-Poulenc Rorer Ltd, Rainham Road South, Dagenham RM10 7XS

Partnership agreements and papers 1867, 1876–78; agreements, papers and correspondence re incorporation of company 1889–91; memorandum and articles of association 1890; memorandum of agreement with Rhône-Poulenc 1936; draft trust deed for securing debenture stock 1910; directors' agreements: R Blenkinsop 1903, Blenkinsop 1908; partners and directors' correspondence: R C Heath and W Blenkinsop 1876–88, 1904, 1906, R Blenkinsop 1903, 1905–13, W Blenkinsop and O Steinhart 1892, W Elmore 1881, amalgamation with Johnson & Sons 1896, Rhône-Poulenc 1927–46, 1965; committee meetings minutes: research directorate 1943–44, chemotherapeutic research division

1943–47, packaging 1943–45, chemists engaged in penicillin synthesis 1944–46, research policy 1956–74, library 1959–67, *Planet* editorial 1977–80, 150th anniversary working party 1983–84, Quality Circle 1984, research headquarters team 1985–89; management committees directories 1960–64, 1980; annual report and accounts 1968–80; balance sheets and profit and loss accounts: 1875–1916, 1964–67, Lithia Department 1904–08 (w), Cobalt Department 1898, 1904–09, Vitreous Mosaic Co 1899–1911; profits 1877–95; debts written off 1896; monthly returns 1877–81, 1886–88; loan ledger 1896; journals 1877–91; cash books 1884–1936 (w); receipts 1878; advertising expenses 1896; sundry expenses 1896; subscriptions and donations 1896; bank account balance 1909; overdraft guarantees 1909–12; bank correspondence 1895; auditor's report 1899; miscellaneous financial statements and memoranda 1886–1911; miscellaneous financial notes 1876, 1907–11, n.d.; litigation papers 1891–99, 1948–50; draft agreement and correspondence re patents: O'Sullivan & Valentin 1876, D Graham 1886, W N Hartley 1887–88; agreement for the right to use and work letters patent 1887; notes re work conducted by Derwent Publications' patent documentation services n.d.; correspondence re Lyte's invention 1880s; agreement for the sale of certain articles with Farbenfabriken, Germany 1887; agreements: Vitreous Mosaic Co 1891–1906, Sharland & Co 1891, Chemical Electronic Syndicate Ltd 1894, Joshua & Sons 1896, Mosenthal & Co re cyanide contract 1899, Deutsche Gold und Silber Anstalt and Cassel Co re cyanide mining 1901; correspondence re cyanide 1896–99; reports: mercurial contacts 1878, production of cyanide 1897–1908, relocation from Battersea to Dagenham (with correspondence) 1934–40, *M&B 693* 1936–41, Dr L Whitby 1937–42, warehouse department 1938, research into penicillin 1941–48, research at Oxford University 1943–46, stores and purchasing divisions 1943–47, chemotherapeutic research department 1943–49, development unit 1947, explosion in the film department (with photographs) 1951, Norwich manufacturing group 1956–71, research policy committee 1956–64, chemotherapy 1956–59, establishment of plant at Tongi, Pakistan c.1960, Sainsbury committee 1965, antioxidants 1967, promotional activities procedures 1971, information and library work course provision 1972, reorganisation of Rhône-Poulenc group and May & Baker Ltd 1974, research directorate 1981–86, Prof B J Heywood 1981–87, research sector steering committee 1983–86, Prof W D Stewart 1985–87, appointment of research associates 1985–88, inauguration of a pharmaceutical plant at Bhandup, India 1986, compounds submitted for testing n.d.; research reports: physical chemistry 1946–53, biological 1946–54, photographic 1947–53, chemical 1952–53; miscellaneous scientific reports 1942–47; price lists: pharmaceutical 1877–1971, mercurials 1894, laboratory chemicals 1948, 1960–68, medical products 1952, 1970–72; product lists: Red Book pharmaceutical products 1914, 1965–82, n.d., chemicals 1956–79, n.d., medical products 1937–66, n.d., synonyms, trade names and trade marks 1914, 1938–54; notebooks: mercurials 1904–22, n.d., Dr

G Newberry re cocaine experiments 1927–40, microanalytical department 1937–64, Dr Barber 1964–70; log books: duty research chemist 1945–48, 1960–90, shift chemist 1948–51, Mr Bradshaw, technical services 1936–42, R Broad, technical services 1977–81 (w); formulae books c.1900–19, n.d.; record sheet for first batch of tablets processed at Dagenham n.d.; treatment/dosage cards n.d.; analytical standards for chemicals 1965; reference cards re medical products n.d.; laboratory plates and smoke traces 1953; datasheets re drugs n.d.; notes re drugs 1981, n.d.; correspondence: *M&B 693* 1935–71, penicillin (including patent applications) 1943–48, 1954, research programmes (with notes) 1946–63, *Plasmosan* (with reports) 1950–56, research grants 1982–88, Ives Laboratories Inc and other pharmaceutical companies 1977–78, Smith Kline & French Laboratories Ltd 1954–55; photographs of viruses and tropical diseases n.d.; advertisement for benzoic acid late 19th cent.; promotional prospectuses: Dagenham 1951, 1962, n.d., Norwich n.d., Rhône-Poulenc 1971, 1973, n.d., Rhône-Poulenc Rorer n.d.; booklets re career opportunities 1968–69; publicity programmes 1938–39; promotional audio cassette n.d.; promotional video cassettes 1993–95; organisational chart 1945; folios outlining organisational aspects of the directorate 1975–83; visitors' book 1942–45; drug labels booklets 1930s; press cuttings booklets: 1938–74, *M&B 693* 1938–46, visit of Prince Philip to Dagenham 1962, Bombay press conference 1986, Rhône-Poulenc Rorer 1990–91; magnetic audio tapes: discovery of *M&B 693* (with transcription) 1961, Slack memorial lecture 1978, hyperlipioaenia 1979; land leases, Battersea 1876–78, 1904; contract for purchase of land 1877; property agreements: Morgan Crucible Co Ltd re windows 1886, management and maintenance of a mutual lane 1912; accounts for new plant 1899; rate valuations n.d.; notice for erection of new buildings at Bell Lane, Wandsworth 1917; conveyance of Garden Wharf, Battersea 1921; notes, correspondence and report re opening of new building 1955; tender for design of research laboratories at Bhandup, India 1985; correspondence: Battersea embankment works 1878, purchase of Pheonix Wharf Lane 1901–12, machines and buildings 1933–72, new factories at Dagenham 1936–37; architectural drawings: Battersea 1880, 1907, 1933, Dagenham 1933–46, 1972–82, n.d., Norwich 1977, Bhandup, India 1970, 1985; maps: Battersea 1838, May & Baker premises in England 1980, Hamburg n.d.; site photographs: Bell Lane 1932–33, 1947, Dagenham 1934–69, n.d., Norwich 1981, New Zealand 1963–71, overseas subsidiaries n.d.; employment agreements 1881–1901, 1911; staff appointments 1945–77; staff in Research Group 1961; staff qualifications 1968; salaries and profits 1911; staff salaries book: 1930–44, junior research group n.d.; payroll notes 1939; salary cheques: 1894, (signed by Bratton White) 1827–30; allowances for travelling expenses 1896; factory rules and regulations 1878, 1951; office procedure manual 1963; executive committee, staff briefing notes 1976–79; instructions: central administration 1945–75, publications committee 1959, 1967, research directorate 1958–66, 1979, product research group 1960–70, packaging 1952–75, n.d.; internal staff briefing notes 1981–85; staff handbook n.d.; conditions of employment 1949–79; sickness benefit scheme 1968–69, n.d.; pension scheme 1976, n.d.; safety policy 1984, n.d.; disciplinary procedures 1988; guidelines for appraisal 1989, n.d.; training policy statement 1976; correspondence and information re Chemical Workers Union 1931–69; *The Planet*, staff magazine 1946–81; staff booklets re drugs, therapies and competitive products 1957, n.d.; May & Baker scientific publications 1929–87, n.d.; indexes to May & Baker published scientific papers 1958–77; *The M & B Pharmaceutical Bulletin* 1952–79; *A Medical Bulletin* 1952–69; proceedings: annual conference of representatives 1938–41, 1968, presentation of long service awards with photographs 1948, Paris conference 1954, special medical symposium 1955, Nottingham conference 1964, hydroxybenzonitrile conference, Brighton 1968, May & Baker annual conference 1969, drug design conference, Eastbourne 1982, industry and academia conference 1985; May & Baker staff club: prospectuses c.1958, 1963, 1970, musical and dramatic section programme 1951, correspondence re golf competitions 1951–72, report, programmes and photographs re May & Baker family day 1955–70, pensioners open day programme 1973, rugby union football club 1974, railway section 1976–89; letterbooks of R Bradshaw, engineer 1934–40; letters to R Bradshaw 1934–38; correspondence: Dr V A Pertow 1944–46, H L S Atkins, production directorate 1946–74, Mr G Newbury 1943–45, Dr A J Ewins 1945–48, Dr H J Barber, research controller 1952–72, Dr R Slack 1962–67, Lord Beaverbrook 1942, Home Office re licence to test on live animals 1933–37, Greece re assistance with an earthquake disaster n.d., C G Adams, African Medical School 1955, history of May & Baker and 150th anniversary celebrations 1945–86, Queen's award for technological achievement 1982, Queen's award for export achievement 1983, research prizes 1987–88, visit of Prince Philip 1962, history of science and chemistry group 1978–81, Royal Society of Chemistry lecture 1989, graduate training 1969–80, staff employment and training 1974–80, 'flagyl' dinner 1985, May & Baker (Canada) Ltd 1936, 1943; internal correspondence: new products division 1944–47, library services division 1961, publications committee 1964–65, health and medical matters 1941–60, 1965; photographs: senior management 1942, n.d., Thomas Tyrer n.d., presentation of the Queen's award to industry 1974, delegates at the drug design conference 1982, representatives annual conference 1945–46, Paris conference 1954, visit by managing director of Rhône-Poulenc Ltd to May & Baker (India) Ltd 1980, visit to Dagenham 1965, visit to Karachi 1976, Miss Jamaica Farm Queen competition 1970, staff and laboratories 1936–83, vehicles 1955, academia and industry seminar 1985; library notebook 1978–80; internal telephone directories 1983, 1988; notes re death of John May 1893; historical notes 1945–89; family trees 1945, 1977; transcribed interviews with and letters from former employees 1970s, 1980; Dr Barber's research notes re company's history 1977-81.

Records 2: The Royal Society, 6 Carlton House Terrace, London SW1Y 5AG

Correspondence with Sir Henry Hallett Dale concerning *Plasmosan* 1951. (Ref: 93 HD/48.4)

Records 3: History of Advertising Trust, HAT House, 12 Raveningham Centre, Raveningham NR14 6NU

Advertisements: *Anthisan* 1980s, *Brulidine* 1980s. (Ref: MEAL collection 1980-89, R80)

RICHELD LTD
59 Bridge Street, Usk, Monmouthshire

Retail chemist

History: Richeld Ltd was incorporated as a limited liability company in 1968 to acquire the retail chemist's business of W J Evans (Chemists), 59 Bridge Street, Usk, Monmouthshire. In the same year it was acquired by Dudley Taylor of Warwickshire, the owner of a chain of retail pharmacies. In 1993 Dudley Taylor (Holdings) Ltd was incorporated as a holding company for Dudley Taylor's many acquired businesses, including Richeld Ltd, which was still trading under its own name in 1997.

Records: Dudley Taylor Holdings Ltd, Unit 2B, Harris Road, Wedgnock Industrial Estate, Warwick CV34 5GH

Combined register of directors' meetings, members and share register 1969-85; memorandum and articles of association 1968, certificate of incorporation 1968; application for registration as a company and related letter from Companies House 1968; annual return 1967; issued share certificates 1969; stock transfer forms 1969, 1976, n.d.; directors' reports and annual accounts 1986-88, 1991-96; letter of resignation of N F Harrison, director 1974; invoice from estate agents re sale of Newport Road premises 1986; property underlease 1972; architectural plan of proposed site at Newport Road, Caldicot, 1967; memoranda of rent reviews with covering letters 1978, 1986; correspondence: Dudley Taylor Ltd 1988, rent review 1986, estate agent re sale of Newport Road premises 1987.

J T ROBERTS (PHARMACEUTICALS) LTD
Tudhoe Park House, Spennymoor, Durham

Retail chemist

History: In 1960 N & D Chemists Ltd was incorporated as a limited liability company in Spennymoor, Durham, to trade as a retail chemist. In 1965 it was renamed J T Roberts (Pharmaceuticals) Ltd. The company owned 2 retail subsidiaries, Killingworth Chemists Ltd, Newcastle upon Tyne, which had been incorporated as Killingworth Health & Beauty Ltd in 1973 and renamed in the same year, and J T Roberts (Northern) Ltd, which had been incorporated in 1958 as E Miller Ltd and was renamed in 1972. In 1995 J T Roberts (Pharmaceuticals) Ltd and its 2 subsidiaries were acquired by E Moss Ltd, the retail arm of UniChem plc which itself merged in 1997 with Alliance Sante SA to become Alliance UniChem plc. By 1999 J T Roberts (Pharmaceuticals) Ltd was dormant, its business and assets having been transferred to E Moss Ltd.

Records: Alliance UniChem plc, UniChem House, Cox Lane, Chessington KT9 1SN

Directors' and general meetings minutes 1960 to date; certificate of incorporation 1960; change of name certificate 1965; combined register of members and share ledger 1960 to date; share certificate book 1960–95; share certificates 1995.

Killingworth Chemists Ltd: directors' and general meetings minutes 1973 to date; certification notice of change of name 1995; notices of change of directors 1970s–80s; annual returns 1978–86 (w); combined register of members and share ledger 1973 to date; share certificate 1995; stock transfer forms 1984, 1995; correspondence: registrar of companies 1970s–80s, superintendent pharmacists 1970s–80s.

J T Roberts (Northern) Ltd: directors' and general meetings minutes 1958 to date; certification notice of incorporation and change of name 1995; combined register of members and share ledger 1958 to date.

WILLIAM GRIFFITH ROBERTS
Llanfairfechan, Conwy

Pharmacist

History: William Griffith Roberts was registered as a chemist and druggist in 1893, at Hall Bank, Village Road, Llanfairfechan, Conwy. He retired in 1933, and his business was acquired by Owen Jones, who had registered as a chemist and druggist in 1920. The business traded as O Jones thereafter.

Records: Gwynedd Archives & Museums Service, Caernarfon Area Record Office, Victoria Dock, Caernarfon. Enquiries to County Offices, Shirehall Street, Caernarfon LL55 1SH

Customer account book 1908–26; prescription book 1894–1906. (Ref: XM9666, XM9742)

JOHN RODGER
Main Street West, Inveraray, Argyll & Bute

Chemist and newsagent

History: John Rodger was registered as a chemist and druggist in 1868, and traded at Main Street West, Inveraray, Argyll & Bute, until 1897, when he was succeeded by Robert Fraser. Fraser continued to trade under the name John Rodger until 1922 when he retired.

Records: Argyll & Bute Archives, Manse Brae, Lochgilphead PA31 8RT

Ledgers 1914–22; private letterbook 1879–93; diary and newspaper delivery book 1911. (Ref: DR1/86/1, 8-10)

R A ROPER
High Street, Great Dunmow, Essex

Chemist

History: It appears that this business was established by a Mr Rockhill, who was trading as a chemist in Great Dunmow, Essex, in 1848. Richard Roper probably succeeded him in the business some time prior to 1868, and remained in business in Dunmow until at least 1895.

Records: Essex Record Office, PO Box 11, County Hall, Chelmsford CM1 1LX

Ledgers 1865–85; day books 1879–86; invoice books, with details of suppliers and wholesalers 1837–65; prescription books 1846–83; recipe books, some incl. veterinary recipes 1844, n.d. (Ref: D/DU 260)

L ROWLAND & CO LTD
Dolydd Road, Wrexham

Retail and wholesale chemist

History: Edward Rowland established a chemist and druggist's business on his own account at 42 High Street, Wrexham, in 1810. Following his death in 1826, his widow took charge of the business, which in 1839 moved to 9 High Street, Wrexham. Mrs Rowland died in 1852, leaving the business to her youngest son, William, who operated the business from 9 High Street. In 1883 Langshaw Rowland was registered as a chemist and druggist and acquired the business, remaining registered until 1891–92. Sidney C Rowland was registered as a chemist and druggist in 1894. In addition to a number of retail outlets, the business comprised a wholesale distribution centre, based at Wrexham, which serviced the Rowland chain of pharmacies. The business was incorporated as a limited liability company, L Rowland & Co Ltd, in 1928. During the 1950s the wholesale distribution centre began to serve independent pharmacies, and in 1964 was appointed franchisee for the Numark Ltd sales programme for the north, mid-Wales and the Wirral peninsula. From 1964 L Rowland & Co Ltd diversified into farm supplies and veterinary products. L Rowland (Farm Supplies) Ltd was incorporated as a subsidiary company in 1980, distributing from depots in Welshpool, Powys and Oswestry, Shropshire. This company was later sold to Wynnstay Farmers, and was dormant in 1997. 2 further subsidiary companies were incorporated in 1988, L Rowland & Co (Retail) Ltd and L Rowland & Co (Wholesale) Ltd. Both of these companies, and L Rowland & Co Ltd, were still trading in 1997.

'L Rowland (of Wrexham) Celebrates 175 Years', *Pharmaceutical Journal*, 14 Sept 1985, 352

Records: Denbighshire Record Office, 46 Clwyd Street, Ruthin LL15 1HP

Ruabon branch: notice of opening 1888, accounts 1888–91, use of camera in trapping thief 1934–35; Coedpoeth branch, correspondence re appointment of manager 1924; pharmaceutical formulae and household recipes notebooks c.1828, c.1859–62; prescription books 1874–1920 (w), n.d.; tablet prescriptions and receipts 1932–33; office diaries 1892–1927; correspondence and papers, loose in diaries 1900, 1920–27; advertisements: medicinal products 1889–90, c.1920, company 1907, 1931–33; 150th anniversary booklet 1960; 175th anniversary: correspondence and papers 1984–85, press cuttings 1985; photographs, mainly staff c.1930–80s; Rowland family papers, correspondence and photographs c.1780–1979; miscellaneous papers, press cuttings and sundry items 19th–20th cents. (Ref: DD/DM/763)

ROYAL ARSENAL CO-OPERATIVE CHEMISTS LTD
Woolwich, Greenwich, London

Chemist

History: Royal Arsenal Co-operative Chemists Ltd was incorporated as a limited liability company around 1944, as a subsidiary of the Royal Arsenal Co-operative Society Ltd, which was formed by workers at Woolwich Arsenal in 1868 and named Royal Arsenal Co-operative Society in 1872.

Records: Co-operative Wholesale Society South East Region, 132-152 Powis Street, London SE18 6NL

Directors' meeting minutes 1944–85; share ledger 1944.

RUDGE ROBERTS LTD
Shrewsbury, Shropshire

Pharmaceutical wholesaler

History: In 1947 Fylde Laboratories Ltd was incorporated as a limited liability company in Shrewsbury, Shropshire, to distribute pharmaceutical products wholesale. Its name was changed to Glynwed Wholesale Chemists Ltd in 1976. The company was acquired in 1987 by AAH Pharmaceuticals Ltd and its name changed to Rudge Roberts Ltd. In 1989 it became a dormant company.

Records: GEHE UK plc, Retail Branch, Atherstone, Warwickshire. Enquiries to GEHE UK plc, Sapphire Court, Walsgrave Triangle Business Park, Coventry CV2 2TX

General meetings minutes 1970–96; notices of changes of directors 1987; combined register of members, directors and share ledger 1947–89; share purchase agreement with Vestric Ltd 1987; deed of indemnity and deed of covenant 1987; supplemental trust deed 1987; trade mark licence agreement 1985; papers and correspondence: change of name 1989, Vestric Ltd and AAH Pharmaceuticals Ltd 1986–90, acquisition by AAH Pharmaceuticals Ltd 1987–89; report on title n.d.; architectural drawings and correspondence re property 1975–87; executive employment agreement 1987. (Ref: Boxes S3, A4)

ST AMAND MANUFACTURING CO LTD
London and Belgium

Processing manufacturer of crude drug extract

History: In 1876 salicin, a bitter, crystalline substance extracted from willow-bark, was found by Dr T J MacLagen to have medicinal value in the treatment of acute rheumatism. In the same year Thomas Whiffen of Battersea, Wandsworth, London, began manufacturing the substance from the bark of a certain species of willow tree found in plentiful supply in Belgium. Groups of men from his London works were sent to Belgium to strip bark from the young shoots, after which, a concentrated extract made from the bark, was shipped to London for purification. The growth of this business led to the incorporation of the St Amand Manufacturing Co Ltd as a limited liability company in 1903, the result of a joint venture by pharmaceutical and fine chemical manufacturers T & H Smith, J F Macfarlan & Co and Thomas Whiffen. The company was incorporated to operate the Belgian end of the drug production line, organising the preliminary processing of the concentrated extract which was shipped to London for manufacture. In 1947 the trading interests of Whiffen & Sons Ltd were acquired by Fisons Ltd and in 1961 the St Amand Manufacturing Co Ltd was wound up.

R S Law, *The End of a Chapter: The story of Whiffen & Sons Limited fine chemical manufacturers* (Fisons, London, c.1973)

Records 1: London Metropolitan Archives, 40 Northampton Road, London EC1R 0HB

Directors' and general meetings attendance book 1934–47; ledgers: 1903–34, [?George Amand & Co] 1887–90; journals 1903–34; outgoing letterbooks 1907–26. (Ref: B/WHF/92-5, 119-27)

Records 2: Archivist (Historical Records), Records Centre, Glaxo Wellcome plc, 891-995 Greenford Road, Greenford UB6 0HE

Memoranda and articles of association 1903–08, 1935; share documents 1919; profit and loss accounts and balance sheets 1904–34 (w), 1940–60; correspondence with T & H Smith Ltd 1957–65. (Ref: Macfarlan Smith Historical Collection)

SANTS PLC
Wolstanton Trading Park, Newcastle-under-Lyme, Staffordshire

Pharmaceutical wholesaler

History: In 1923 the business of G W Brown, Hope Street, Hanley, Stoke-on-Trent, was acquired by Harold and Cyril Coxon, Bert Phillips and Sidney Mott, who traded as retail pharmacists from the premises, under the business name Browns Chemists. In 1933 the firm was incorporated as a limited liability company, Browns Chemists (Stoke-on-Trent) Ltd, and began a programme of retail pharmacy acquisition. Businesses acquired included Arthur Sant, W D Edge, Hardings Chemists Ltd, S J Mott and Mott & Co, all of Stoke-on-Trent, and Russell & Andress, Crewe, Cheshire. Arthur Sant, Mott & Co and Russell & Andress continued to trade under their own names, whilst the other acquired businesses were renamed Browns Chemists (Stoke-on-Trent) Ltd. The company's head offices were at 48 Piccadilly, Hanley, Stoke-on-Trent, from 1933 to 1972, when, under the directorship of Gerald Brooks, a subsidiary of Browns Chemists (Stoke-on-Trent) Ltd was incorporated, Sants Pharmaceutical Distributors Ltd, and both companies re-located to 551 Etruria Road, Stoke-on-Trent. Sants Pharmaceutical Distributors Ltd was incorporated to sell ethical pharmaceuticals and some over-the-counter medicines to pharmacies and hospitals wholesale. Its name was derived from the acquired firm, Arthur Sant, and also from the French word *santé,* meaning 'health'. From 1972 Browns Chemists (Stoke-on-Trent) Ltd sold all its retail outlets, and became involved primarily in the wholesale trade. In 1993 it was renamed Sants plc, and as such became the holding company of Sants Pharmaceutical Distributors Ltd and Browns Chemists (Stoke-on-Trent) Ltd, the remaining retail interest. All 3 companies re-located, in 1993, to Wolstanton Trading Park, Newcastle-under-Lyme, Staffordshire. In July 1997 Sants Pharmaceutical Distributors Ltd was sold to United Northwest Co-operatives Ltd and continues to trade under its own name. Sants plc was wound up in January 1999.

'A Fiftieth Anniversary Name Change', *Evening Sentinel*, 19 June 1973

Records: Sants plc, Wolstanton Trading Park, Newcastle-under-Lyme ST5 0AT

General meetings: minutes 1993–96, notice 1990, resolutions 1993; business expansion scheme prospectus 1993; proposal to form a distribution company 1971; annual reports and accounts 1972–96; interim reports 1994–95; balance sheets and profit and loss accounts 1968–88; statement of accounts 1994; sales figures of individual pharmacies 1968–80; press cuttings: company 1973, 1993, 1996, competitors 1992–96; artwork: advertising n.d., company calendars 1994–95; advertising brochures and posters 1970s–90s; company calendars 1975–77, 1988–90; architectural drawings and correspondence re Wolstanton trading estate 1992; correspondence: proposed business relationships and confidentiality agreements 1994–96, pharmaceutical companies 1970s, 1992–97, sale and purchase of premises 1972, auditors 1989; Gerald Brooks: certificate of registration as pharmaceutical chemist 1956, portrait 1987.

Sants Pharmaceutical Distributors Ltd: directors' meetings minutes 1972, 1974; general meeting notice 1989; certificate of incorporation 1972; certificate of registration 1972; list of shareholders 1973; balance sheets and profit and loss accounts 1973–87; statement of accounts 1994; sales statistics and forecasts 1972–87.

SAVORY & MOORE LTD
Strand, London

Dispensing chemist

History: In 1794 Thomas Paytherus established a retail chemist's business at 1 Norfolk Street, Strand, London. In 1797 he was joined in the business by Thomas Field Savory, who had been apprenticed to a Cheltenham, Gloucestershire, apothecary, Mr Cotter. In 1806 Savory became a partner in the business. In the same year Thomas Moore, who had traded as an apothecary from 2 Norfolk Street, was taken into partnership. Thomas Savory was the inventor of 'Seidlitz Powders', a laxative which was patented in 1815. The business was styled Paytherus Savory & Co. Shortly afterwards another retail outlet was established at 143 (originally 136) Bond Street, Mayfair. In 1788 Paytherus had founded the Gloucestershire Medical Society with Dr Edward Jenner (1749–1823), a general practitioner. As a result of this professional association, Paytherus, Savory & Co gained exclusive manufacturing and sales rights to 'Dr Jenner's Absorbent Digestive Lozenges'. When Paytherus retired in 1811, the partnership was re-named Savory Moore & Co, and Nicholas Dennys joined the business in the same year. Dennys retired in 1814 after which the firm was re-named Savory & Moore. It compounded and dispensed drugs and medicines including 'Chalybeate Aperient', 'The Nipple Liniment', 'Fullers Benedictine Pills' and 'Conkrete

Kali'. In 1815 a further retail outlet and warehouse was opened in St James's Street, Brighton, Brighton & Hove. John Davidson, a former apprentice to Savory & Moore, was made a partner from 1818 to 1826, during which time the business traded as Savory Moore & Davidson. Moore's son Adam James Moore, was taken into partnership in 1837, and the business was re-styled Savory & Moore. He withdrew from the business in 1842 to establish a chemist and druggist's firm on his own account in Cheltenham. In the first half of the nineteenth century Savory & Moore specialised in the production of medicine chests, which were supplied to, amongst others, William IV. John Savory wrote a small volume to accompany the chests, the first edition of which was published in 1836 as *A Companion to the Medicine Chest*. When Thomas Moore died in 1846, Thomas Savory's nephew, John Savory, who had been apprenticed to Thomas Moore in 1825, was taken into partnership. He became sole proprietor of the business on his uncle's death in 1847, and on his own death in 1871, his youngest son Charles Harley Savory succeeded to the business, in partnership with William Robert Barker. When Charles died in 1875, his eldest son, Arthur Ledsam Savory, joined Barker in partnership. They were joined in around 1883 by Charles Ekin. During the 1870s Savory & Moore introduced 'Datura Tatula', a remedy for asthma and bronchitis, and during the Crimean War, the War Office commissioned the firm to supply the armed forces with medicines, drugs and surgical equipment. During the Boer War Savory & Moore fitted out hospital ships and supplied field and other hospitals with vital equipment and medicines. The business was incorporated as a private limited liability company, Savory & Moore Ltd, in 1902, and was converted to a public limited liability company in 1931. During the early twentieth century the company acquired a number of London retail chemist's concerns including Dinneford & Co, established by Charles Dinneford at 180 New Bond Street, in 1920; Godfrey & Cooke, Royal Arcade, Old Bond Street, formerly at 30 Conduit Street, in 1916; and J Lloyd Bullock & Co, 3 Hanover Street, Hanover Square, in 1924. In 1928 it acquired John Bell & Croyden Ltd, Wigmore Street, London. The laboratories, manufacturing, warehousing and packaging branches of this company were transferred to Standard Works, Lawrence Road, Tottenham, Haringey, London. In addition to large-scale manufacture of tablets and ampoules at the works, the company specialised in the production of sterilised surgical dressings and had catgut, ligature, and glass-blowing departments. In 1933 Savory & Moore Ltd acquired the retail, wholesale and manufacturing chemist business, W Martindale, New Cavendish Street, London, which had been acquired from Hopkin & Williams by William Martindale in 1873. The retail concern continued to trade as W Martindale until the mid-1970s, and in 1947 the manufacturing and wholesale business was incorporated as a separate concern, William Martindale Wholesale Ltd. This name was changed in 1963 to Martindale Samoore Ltd. In 1936 Savory & Moore Ltd acquired Smith & Sons, wholesale druggists and manufacturing chemists of 44-48 Magdalen Street, Norwich, Norfolk. The wholesale chemist and druggist business was incorporated as a limited liability company, Smith & Son (Norwich) Ltd, whilst the manufacturing side of the business was incorporated as Pharmaceutical Products Ltd, with responsibility for the production of Savory & Moore's specialities. By the mid-1940s Savory & Moore Ltd had 40 retail outlets. It also held a number of royal warrants, and in 1955 was the only English company to hold warrants to the Queen, the Duke of Edinburgh and the Queen Mother simultaneously. In 1967 Savory & Moore Ltd was acquired by Macarthys Ltd, a wholesale druggist company established by James Macarthy as a retail pharmacy in Romford, Havering, London, in 1787. In 1992 Macarthys plc was acquired by Lloyds Chemists plc.

'A Chapter of History. Some particulars relating to the amalgamation of two old-established London houses', *Chemist and Druggist*, 28 Jan 1928; 'A Family Medicine Chest', *Chemist and Druggist*, 136, 1 Nov 1941, 146-7; 'A Further Chapter in the History of Savory & Moore Ltd Incorporating John Bell & Croyden, Arnold & Sons', *Chemist and Druggist*, 30 Jan 1932; 'A history of Macarthy's and Savory and Moore', *Supplement to the Chemist and Druggist*, 18 Nov 1967, 1-44; F R Brewster, 'London's Oldest Pharmacy', *Pharmacy International*, 2, 3, March 1948, 12-15, 32-3, 54; 'Chemists to the Royal Family', *Chemist and Druggist*, 4 June 1977, 810-11; L Dopson, 'Chemists to Royalty. A dip into the archives of Savory & Moore Ltd and Squire's of Oxford Street, London', *Chemist and Druggist*, 150, 6 June 1953, 570-71; 'In the Pharmaceutical Tradition', *Chemist and Druggist Export Review*, 11, 132, April 1951, 43; L G Matthews, 'The Bond Street Apothecaries', *Pharmaceutical Journal*, Aug–Dec 1983, March–Aug 1984, Jan–July 1985

Records 1: GEHE UK plc, Retail Branch, Atherstone, Warwickshire. Enquiries to GEHE UK plc, Sapphire Court, Walsgrave Triangle Business Park, Coventry CV2 2TX

Articles of co-partnership: Thomas Paytherus, Thomas Moore and T F Savory, 136 New Bond Street 1806, 1809, T F Savory, Thomas Moore and Nicholas Dennys 1811, T F Savory and Thomas Moore 1831, T F Savory and A J Moore re Cheltenham business 1846; deeds of co-partnership: T F Savory and Thomas Moore 1814, T F Savory, Thomas Moore and J Davidson 1818; deed of covenant, Paytherus, T F Savory, Thomas Moore and John Wardman re Cheltenham business 1809; deeds of dissolution of co-partnership: assigning of Paytherus' share and agreement re his relinquishment of profits and interest in the Cheltenham business 1811, Dennys, T F Savory and Thomas Moore 1814, Davidson, T F Savory and Thomas Moore 1826, T F Savory and Thomas Moore 1831, T F Savory, Thomas Moore and A J Moore 1842, T F Savory and A J

Moore 1851; assignment of assurance policy from T F Savory to A J Moore 1851; notice re purchase of J Lloyd Bullock & Co 1924; ledger 1954–67; account book 1846; papers and correspondence re capital redemption and reconstruction proposals 1944; invoices and designs for medical supplies c.1863–85; invoices, vouchers and insurance receipts re materials returned c.1861; royal warrant: association cards, rules and correspondence c.1920–70, papers 1874–c.1960; bandage design patent 1890; papers re sales of Horsley's patents 1856; recipe books 1799–1801, 1831–32, c.1880; pancreatic emulsion recipe c.1890; drugs catalogues with attached recipes 1831–32; prescription books: unidentified 1825–42, 1858–63, 1877–1904, 1953–59, T & W W Southall 1820; laboratory manufacturing notes and formulae c.1865–1920; reports re medical wagons, field hospital equipment and field dressing packets 1855–85; list of contents of medical wagons, field companions and panniers c.1882–83; director general's instructions re supplies to Crimea and China 1856; estimate of medicines required by various regiments 1835; papers re Spanish debt and supply of medicines to Spanish government c.1850–60; index to contents of drawers and cupboards aboard *Victor Emanuel* 1873; booklets re company products c.1862–78; recipes and advertisements ledger c.1865–91; papers, orders and product advertisements 1831–87; complaint and advice re advertisement 1878; counterparts of assignment: Cheltenham shop and business from Mary Anne Wardman to T F Savory, Thomas Moore and John Beavan 1813, T F Savory and Thomas Moore to Thomas G Sarel, Brighton shop manager 1818; assignment of share of leasehold premises from Dennys to T F Savory and Thomas Moore 1814; agreement between T F Savory and Thomas Moore re opening of Brighton shop 1815; leases and counterpart leases: 143 New Bond Street 1794, 15 Grosvenor Mews 1847–68; lease and architectural plan re 137 New Bond Street 1875; memorandum of lease agreement re 143 Bond Street 1847; memorandum re 220 Regent Street c.1838; tenancy agreement re 15 Grosvenor Mews 1884; papers re staff and behaviour 1877–1915; branch managers' instruction booklet n.d.; correspondence: Army Medical Department, War Office and India Office re supplies c.1860–72, William Kohler re supplies of waterproof dressings 1881–89, Princess Louise of Scleiswig Holstein re gelatine lamellas 1905, supply of pharmacy in Egypt for the Khedive 1871–81, general 1869–1969; photographs of various chemist's shops, Tottenham factory and medicine chest c.1890–1975; company medical publications 1800–1969; historical notes c.1890–1971.

Records 2: John Bell & Croyden Ltd, 50-54 Wigmore Street, London W1A 0AU

143 New Bond Street, combined prescriptions and formulae book 1862–1956; private prescriptions, recipes and formulae book, incl. for the Duke of Wellington 1824–1950.

Records 3: Oxfordshire Record Office, St Luke's Church, Temple Road, Cowley, Oxford OX4 2EX

Ledgers 1924–34; prescription books c.1850–1966. (Ref: Savory (passim))

Records 4: Suffolk Record Office, Bury St Edmunds Branch, 77 Raingate Street, Bury St Edmunds IP33 2AR

Prescription books, 58 Abbeygate Street, Bury St Edmunds 1891–1981; prescription formulary c.1896–1956. (Ref: HC 527)

Records 5: Archives & Manuscripts, Wellcome Library for the History & Understanding of Medicine, 183 Euston Road, London NW1 2BE

Prescription books, Chapel Street 1912–44; price list of Savory & Moore's *Knoll* preparations n.d. (Ref: CMAC/GC/29)

Records 6: Record Office for Leicestershire, Leicester & Rutland, Long Street, Wigston Magna, Leicester LE18 2AH

Prescription 1835. (Ref: DG39/2154)

Records 7: Falkirk Museums, History Research Centre, Callendar House, Callendar Park, Falkirk FK1 1YR

Poisons register 1936–84. (Ref: A508.01)

Records 8: Hampshire Record Office, Sussex Street, Winchester SO23 8TH

Sales ledgers 1970; prescription books of acquired companies 1887–1968. (Ref: 5M94)

Records 9: The Museum Curator, Royal Pharmaceutical Society of Great Britain, 1 Lambeth High Street, London SE1 7JN

Biographical notes, press cuttings and correspondence re Sir Hugh Linstead 1901–69. (Ref: IRA.1996.384)

SCHERING-PLOUGH LTD
Schering-Plough House, Shire Park, Welwyn Garden City, Hertfordshire

Pharmaceutical manufacturer

History: In 1884 H & T Kirby & Co Ltd was incorporated as a limited liability company to manufacture pharmaceuticals in London. In around 1890 the company acquired the business of the Soden Mineral Produce Co Ltd, 52 Bread Street, London, a firm that manufactured mineral pastilles. H & T Kirby & Co Ltd leased premises at 14 Newman Street, Oxford Street, London, until 1914, when it moved to new premises at Willesden Green, Brent, London. The company remained in family hands until the 1960s. During the 1950s H & T Kirby & Co Ltd incorporated a subsidiary, Rustat Pharmaceuticals Ltd, to oversee its overseas market. In 1965 the company leased land at Mildenhall, Suffolk, and in April and May 1967 all manufacturing departments, with the exception of the drying and granulating plants, were moved there. During the following year, Robert Blackie Ltd, manufacturing chemists, Peckham, Southwark, London, was acquired by H & T Kirby & Co Ltd. The methods of production and the products manufactured by both companies were similar, although the former produced much larger quantities than was customary for the latter. During the following year H & T Kirby & Co Ltd was acquired by Major & Fielding Ltd, Reigate, Surrey, an international company which had formerly marketed Kirby's products in West Africa. It was renamed H & T Kirby & Co Ltd in 1969 and Kirby Pharmaceuticals Ltd in 1977. The main products of the company were over-the-counter tablets, ointments, family remedies and sterile products. In 1979 Kirby Pharmaceuticals Ltd was acquired by Schering Corporation Inc, USA. Its name was changed in 1980 to Kirby-Warrick Pharmaceuticals Ltd and in 1990 to Schering-Plough Ltd. Schering-Plough Corporation Inc, owned a number of other UK companies. Its subsidiary, Scherico Ltd, Switzerland, incorporated Warrick Pharmaceuticals Ltd at Bracknell, Bracknell Forest, in 1975 to import, distribute and manufacture ethical pharmaceuticals in the UK. In 1926 White Laboratories Inc, New Jersey, USA, incorporated a UK subsidiary, White Laboratories Ltd, at Penarth Street, London. In 1952 this company was acquired by Schering Corporation (Panama) SA and in 1962 by Scherico Ltd, when it was renamed Plough Inc (UK) Ltd. Plough Inc (UK) Ltd acquired the businesses of 2 companies in 1967, Rubelle Ltd, Penarth Street, London, which was renamed Warrick Brothers Ltd in 1970, and Meggeson & Co Ltd, Ash Grove, Hackney, London, which was renamed Chand Perfume Co Ltd in 1970. This company was formerly a subsidiary of Potter & Moore Ltd, whose parent was the perfume and flavouring manufacturer, W J Bush & Co Ltd. In 1971 Plough Inc (UK) Ltd was renamed Plough (UK) Ltd and in 1980 the company was acquired by Schering Corporation Inc, USA, and in

1981 by Schering-Plough Holdings Ltd. The latter also acquired the business of Wesley-Jenssen (UK) Ltd, a manufacturer of pharmaceutical preparations and optical equipment, formerly Wigmore's Ltd in 1986 and renamed the company Wesley-Jenssen London Ltd in 1988.

'H T Kirby & Co Ltd', *The Scottish Pharmacist*, 118, 1962

Records 1: Schering-Plough Ltd, Schering-Plough House, Shire Park, Welwyn Garden City AL7 1TW

Directors' and general meetings minutes, with annual reports and accounts 1942–51, 1961–74; notice of extraordinary general meeting 1921; memoranda and articles of association 1884, 1969; certificate of incorporation 1884; change of name certificate 1969; directors' letters of resignation 1986, 1988–89; share ledger and transfer register 1885–1960; registers: members 1897–1969, members and share ledgers 1966–89; share certificates 1885–1981; share transfer forms 1952–53, 1977–79; legal opinion on share interest rate variance 1918; debentures issue trust deed 1921; cancelled debenture certificates and related papers 1927; agreement re Stanley Woodburn Kirby's purchase of debentures 1921; dividend warrant book 1963–68; instructions by individuals, payment of interest and dividends 1953–63; papers re purchase and sale of war stock 1925, 1927; register of mortgages and bonds 1914–67, n.d.; deeds of assignment 1984–92; deed appointing Horace Woodburn Kirby as manager of the Purgen branch 1904; annual reports and accounts 1908–30 (w), 1948, 1950, 1968; annual report, balance sheet and profit and loss account 1966; directors' bi-monthly reports, with correspondence 1971–72; balance sheets 1902–36 (w); export ledgers 1974–81; journals: 1976–77, home and export 1958–71, private 1967–73; cash books: export 1965–69, superannuation fund 1960–71; overseas accounts with invoices 1948–56; summary of export sales 1948–54; shipping order books 1933–64 (w); purchase tax certificate of registration 1967; insurance policies 1921, 1960s–70s; plant inspection reports and insurance policies 1970–71; affidavits re proofs of debts due to company 1937; papers re patent for Cole's World Family Pills 1884; formulae and testimonials for Cole's patent medicines n.d. c.1890s; patents, correspondence and related papers 1973; trade marks, assignment and renewal certificates 1905, 1940, 1948; papers re purchase of Cole & Co's patent medicines business by H E Kirby 1884, 1895–96; contract and correspondence with proprietor of *Purgen* trade mark 1910; agreement re manufacture and sale of *Purgen* and *Purgen tablets* 1924; factory diary re pills manufacture 1887–91; manufacturing record books 1908–12, 1916–20; private recipes and 'specials' formulae book 1941–55; price lists 1960s, 1972; international products list 1983; product code book 1961; product information booklets and leaflets c.1900–03, n.d.; booklets re medicines for home and family use 1903, 1904; supply contracts with Greater London Council 1960–73; correspondence and related papers re supply contracts: Winthrop Laboratories, Newcastle upon Tyne 1968–73, Duphar Laboratories Ltd, Southampton 1971–73; correspondence between Baiss Bros & Co and Cole & Co re orders for pills manufactured to private formula 1890–95; industrial methylated spirits and SVR licences and related correspondence 1939–64; booklet re Mildenhall site c.1967; sales and marketing papers and information packs 1968–73; label books, incl. *Cygnet* samples c.1920s–70s; loose labels early 20th cent.; original artwork for packaging and samples c.1970s–80s; leases and plans: 14 Newman Street 1773–1879, 16 Newman Street 1893, Mildenhall 1965; plant and machinery hire purchase, lease and agreements 1976–78; directors and management salaries book 1962–67; staff pension scheme, applications and correspondence 1951–66; superannuation fund cash book 1960–71; letter from Neville R Kirby to Leonard R Rose, Indonesia 1952; miscellaneous correspondence 1891–96; photographs: directors 1930s–70s, n.d., management social events 1940s–50s, staff 1914, 1920s; private papers, wills and estate papers: Edmund Thomas William Kirby 1897–1900, Mary Anne Lucy Keating 1905–11, Edmund K Kirby 1955–64, Dr Paul Ellis Rustat Kirby 1956, 1961–64.

Chand Perfume Co Ltd: directors' and general meetings minutes 1951–78; certificate of incorporation 1951; register of members and share ledger 1951–71.

Plough (UK) Ltd: directors' and general meetings minutes 1958–78; change of name certificate 1962; registers of members and share ledgers 1926–87; share transfer forms 1958, 1970–71.

Rustat Pharmaceuticals Ltd: export payments ledgers, negotiations, collections, bills of exchange and letters of credit 1960–62.

Soden Mineral Produce Co Ltd: annual reports and accounts 1890, 1892–93; balance sheet 1891; employment agreement, Herbert Edward Kirby as managing director 1892; notice of extraordinary general meeting to wind up company for purchase by H E Kirby 1890.

Warrick Brothers Ltd: directors' and general meetings minutes 1948–78; register of members and share ledger 1948–71.

Warrick Pharmaceuticals Ltd: correspondence and papers re incorporation of company 1974–77; financial statements, supplemental schedules and auditor's report 1976; external audit commentary letter 1976.

Wesley-Jenssen London Ltd: general meetings minutes and agendas 1979–88; memorandum and articles of association 1973; certificates of incorporation 1973, 1981, 1986; register of members and share ledger 1973–88; cancelled share certificates and transfer forms 1973–74, 1984, 1988; accounts 1987.

Records 2: Bush Boake Allen Ltd, Blackhorse Lane, London E17 5QP

Chand Perfume Co Ltd: directors' and general meetings minutes 1957–74; change of name certificate 1970; register of members and share ledger 1957–74; share certificate book 1957–68.

Records 3: History of Advertising Trust, HAT House, 12 Raveningham Centre, Raveningham NR14 6NU

Advertisement for *Solarcaine* sunburn treatment 1981. (Ref: MEAL collection 1981, R80)

SCOTT & BOWNE LTD
10-11 Stonecutter Street, London

Pharmaceutical manufacturer

History: Scott & Bowne Ltd was incorporated as a limited liability company in 1888 to manufacture basic pharmaceutical products. During the twentieth century the company was acquired by Beecham Group Ltd, although it continued to trade under its own name. It was dissolved in 1996.

Records 1: St Helens Local History & Archives Library, Gamble Institute, Victoria Square, St Helens WA10 1DY

Notebooks: business functions 1912–36, laboratory 1952–53; booklets re drugs c.1930s–50s; papers re formulae and sale of emulsions 1931–38; reports re emulsions 1919, 1934–35; correspondence re cod-liver oil emulsion 1934–47; advertising booklet 1930s; press cuttings 1929–32, 1974–77; building contract, factory at Southall, Ealing, London 1905; business correspondence 1904–05; photographs: factories 1920s–50s, 1973–74, staff c.1950s. (Ref: BP/4/20)

Records 2: SmithKline Beecham plc, SmithKline Beecham House, Great West Road, Brentford TW8 9BD. Enquiries to SmithKline Beecham plc, 1 New Horizons Court, Great West Road, Brentford TW8 9EP

Directors' meetings minutes 1984; registers: directors and secretaries 1930–89, directors' interests 1967–77, members 1984, share transfers 1941–79, seals 1959–79, 1991; share certificates 1878, 1984; agreements: sale of Alfred B Scott's partnership interest to Samuel W Bowne 1895, S W Scott and Scott & Bowne Ltd 1901, Scott & Bowne Inc 1912–44. (Ref: Box 97-014, unlisted)

Records 3: History of Advertising Trust, HAT House, 12 Raveningham Centre, Raveningham NR14 6NU

Papers, memoranda and advertising campaign material 1965–67. (Ref: JWT 182 (1965) 325 (1966) 402 (1967) 558-60)

H F SCOTT LTD
51 High Street, Inverkeithing, Fife

Wholesale and retail chemist

History: H F Scott Ltd was incorporated as a limited liability company in 1950 by chemists and surgeons, Alexander Scott, Gordon Islay Scott, Mary Davidson Scott, James Charles Butler and Helen Morgan. The company traded as a wholesale and retail chemist's business, and was based at 35 East Port, Dunfermline, Fife. In 1973 its registered offices re-located to 51 High Street, Inverkeithing, Fife, and in 1974 it was acquired by Raimes, Clark & Co Ltd, wholesale and manufacturing chemists, 17 Smith's Place, Leith, Edinburgh. In 1987 H F Scott Ltd went into voluntary liquidation, and in 1989 it was dissolved.

Records: The Secretary, National Register of Archives (Scotland), H M General Register House, Princes Street, Edinburgh EH1 3YY

Minutes 1950–87; directors' reports, balance sheets and accounts 1963–74. (Ref: NRA(S) 2974)

SCOTTISH CO-OPERATIVE WHOLESALE SOCIETY LTD
Glasgow

Wholesale company

History: The Scottish Co-operative Wholesale Society Ltd (SCWS Ltd) was founded in 1868 to supply goods to various retail businesses in Scotland on a wholesale basis. Initially it acted as an agent, bulk-buying goods. However, due to the failure of some suppliers to meet orders, the various businesses entered into production themselves, threatening the business of SCWS Ltd. In 1973 the society was acquired by the Co-operative Wholesale Society Ltd, Manchester, and was renamed The Co-operative Wholesale Society Ltd (Scottish Division). The Scottish Co-operative Drug Society Ltd was a subsidiary of SCWS Ltd, and was incorporated as a limited liability company in 1953.

Records: Glasgow City Archives, Mitchell Library, North Street, Glasgow G3 7DN

Recipe books 1956–68; price list of patent medicines and proprietary goods n.d.; retail drugs, cost of repairs and materials 1968–69; chemical sundries factory, milling section work specifications 1952–53, 1957, 1968.

Scottish Co-operative Drug Society Ltd: memorandum and articles of association 1953; certificate of incorporation 1953; minutes 1944–67; committee meetings minutes 1954–67; share certificates: book 1944–65, transfer forms 1953, correspondence 1954–65; annual reports and balance sheets 1954–67; liquidation accounts c.1967; licences 1953; reports and correspondence of drugs society advisor to management committee re operations of Retail Drug Society 1954–67; rules books 1944–67. (Ref: CWS 1/1/1345, 1/11, 1/13/153, 1/35/23)

SEARLE, DIVISION OF MONSANTO PLC
PO Box 53, Lane End Road, High Wycombe, Buckinghamshire

Marketing of pharmaceutical products and manufacture of pharmaceutical chemicals

History: In 1888 Gideon Daniel Searle established a small pharmacy in Omaha, Nebraska, USA, in partnership with Franklin Hereth, moving in 1890 to new premises in Chicago, USA. In 1905 the partnership was dissolved and Gideon Searle became sole owner of the business, incorporating the firm as a limited liability company, G D Searle & Co Inc, in 1908. In 1917 following the death of Gideon Searle, the chairmanship of the company passed to his son, Claude Searle. In the same year the company's first research laboratory was opened and, thereafter, G D Searle & Co Inc became a pioneer in the development and manufacture of a range of drugs. It was the first company to produce *Dramamine*, a motion sickness drug, and *Banthine*, a treatment for peptic ulcers, later replaced by *Probanthine*, during the 1940s. In 1950 G D Searle & Co Inc was converted to a public limited liability company and in 1953 G D Searle & Co Ltd was incorporated as its UK subsidiary, based in London. In 1956 this company re-located to High Wycombe, Buckinghamshire. G D Searle & Co Ltd was established primarily to market the products of its American parent, and also conducted some secondary manufacture. In 1969 a small production unit was opened at Morpeth, Northumberland, and from then onwards, all manufacturing took place at this site. In 1985 G D Searle & Co Ltd was acquired by Monsanto plc, a manufacturer of inorganic chemicals and basic pharmaceutical products which had been incorporated as a limited liability company in 1955. Thereafter G D Searle & Co Ltd traded as Searle, Division of Monsanto plc. All the research laboratories at High Wycombe were closed in 1986. During 1997 Monsanto Inc, the parent company of Monsanto plc, was divided into 2 independent publicly-owned companies, a chemicals company and a life sciences company. To facilitate this change in the UK Monsanto plc was renamed Globalstrike plc in May 1997 and went into voluntary liquidation. At the same time a new public limited company named Monsanto plc was incorporated. By November 1997 the site at High Wycombe was the UK headquarters for Monsanto plc. The Searle division also had its headquarters at this site, where it provided medical, sales and marketing support for pharmaceutical services and products, particularly in the pain and female health areas.

'Searle' in T Derdak (ed), *International Directory of Company Histories*, Vol. 1 (St James Press, London, 1988); K Holland, 'G D Searle Inc', *Pharmaceutical Journal*, 255, 29 July 1995

Records 1: Searle, Division of Monsanto plc, PO Box 53, Lane End Road, High Wycombe HP12 4HL

Canderel recipe books and leaflets n.d.; data sheets and prescribing compliances 1973–95; compliance books 1977–86, 1991–92; guardbooks of product literature 1956–78, 1988–95, n.d.; product promotional and prescribing material 1956–61, 1979–94, n.d.; price lists 1962–63; dosage cards and charts 1954–56, n.d.; papers re promotion and labelling 1985–94; company brochure 1959; audio cassette promotions n.d.; press releases 1984, 1991; advertisements 1949–69, 1987–90, n.d.; advertising and code of practice complaints 1990–92, 1995; photographs of Searle family 1956; company and other scientific journals 1988–90; patient information publications n.d.

Records 2: History of Advertising Trust, HAT House, 12 Raveningham Centre, Raveningham NR14 6NU

Guardbooks of advertising material 1923–27, 1933–55; advertisement for 'Lutussin cough suppressant' 1978. (Ref: Ogilvy & Mather collection; MEAL collection 1978, R20)

H W SELBY
Sussex Square, Haywards Heath, West Sussex

Chemist

History: This business was established in 1902 by Horace Walter Selby, chemist and druggist, who rented a house and shop named Laburnham House in Sussex Road, Haywards Heath, West Sussex. By 1939 he was registered as a chemist, trading at Sussex Square, Haywards Heath.

Records: West Sussex Record Office, Sherburne House, 3 Orchard Street, Chichester. Enquiries to County Hall, Chichester PO19 1RN

Cash book 1902–04; prescription book 1902–03; recipe book n.d., c.1902; agreement, sale of Sussex Square pharmacy 1939; shopfitter's estimates and related correspondence 1902; labels n.d.; photographs of premises c.1902–10; H W Selby's and Ruth Allen Selby's certificates of qualification n.d.; notes re H W Selby 1983. (Ref: Add MSS 30,251-3; 19,087-9; 32,697-703; PH 8088-9; MP 2203)

SELFRIDGES & CO LTD, PHARMACY DEPARTMENT
400 Oxford Street, London

Dispensing pharmacy

History: Selfridges & Co Ltd was incorporated as a limited liability company in 1908 to run a purpose-built department store at 400 Oxford Street, London. The store, established by Harry Gordon Selfridge, was opened in March 1909 and the pharmacy department was one of many departments to be established from the first day of trading. It dispensed medicines on prescription to the public and to its staff throughout the twentieth century, and was still trading in 1997.

G Honeycombe, *Selfridges, 75 Years, The Story of the Store 1909–1984* (Selfridges, London, 1984); Pound, *Selfridge, a Biography* (William Heinemann, London, 1960); A H Williams, *No Name on the Door: A memoir of Gordon Selfridge* (W H Allen, London, 1956)

Records: The Archivist, Selfridges & Co Ltd, 400 Oxford Street, London W1A 1AB

Formulae books and cards 1917–19, n.d.; prescription books 1913–62; private prescriptions 1968–69; sale of poisons register 1955–59; uncollected medicines booklet 1972–73; requisitions booklet 1967–71; labels n.d. (Ref: 1990/01/03-22, 34-5, 42, 51-2)

SELLES DISPENSING CHEMISTS LTD
PO Box 15, Great Gutter Lane, Willerby, Kingston upon Hull

Dispensing chemist

History: Selles Dispensing Chemists Ltd was incorporated as a limited liability company in Kingston upon Hull, in 1930, and began a programme of retail pharmacy acquisitions. It acquired Michael Stewart Ltd, Cottingham, East Riding of Yorkshire, a regional pharmaceutical wholesaling company incorporated in 1945, in 1959; Goodall (South Elmsall) Ltd, a chemist and optician's business of 29 Barnsley Road, South Elmsall, Wakefield, in 1965; George R Daniel & Son Ltd, a retail chemist, Linthorpe Road, Middlesbrough, incorporated 1961, in 1970; and Gordon Lock (Louth) Ltd, 61 Eastgate, Louth, Lincolnshire, a pharmaceutical dispensing and photographic retail company, incorporated in 1948, also in 1970. In 1972 Molescroft Holdings & Investments Ltd was incorporated as a limited liability company, to act as a holding company for Selles Dispensing Chemists Ltd, and its growing number of subsidiaries. In 1980 Selles Dispensing Chemists Ltd purchased J Maynard Whiteside Ltd, Bridlington, East Riding of Yorkshire, incorporated in 1964. By 1994 it owned 43 pharmacies, one pharmaceutical wholesale company and a specialist occupational health and first aid goods supplier, Selles Medical Ltd. In 1994 Molescroft Holdings & Investments Ltd and all its subsidiaries were acquired by UniChem plc which itself merged in 1997 with Alliance Sante SA to become Alliance UniChem plc. By 1999 Selles Dispensing Chemists Ltd was dormant, its business and assets having been transferred to E Moss Ltd.

Records: Alliance UniChem plc, UniChem House, Cox Lane, Chessington KT9 1SN

Directors' and general meetings minutes 1949–81, 1987, 1994–95; acquisition papers 1970s–95; combined register of members and share ledger 1930–72; share certificate books, with loose certificates, and list of staff salaries 1930–71; share certificates 1994.

George R Daniel & Son Ltd: directors' and general meetings minutes 1961–69; certificate of incorporation 1961; combined register of members and share ledger 1961–70; share certificates 1961–70.

Goodall (South Elmsall) Ltd: directors' and general meetings minutes 1960–76; combined register of members and share ledger 1960–66.

Gordon Lock (Louth) Ltd: general meetings minutes 1950–70; certificate of incorporation 1948; combined register of members and share ledger 1949–70; share certificates 1949–70.

Molescroft Holdings & Investments Ltd: combined register incl. directors' and general meetings minutes 1972–88; directors' and general meetings minutes 1989 to date; acquisition papers 1994–95; combined register of members and share ledger 1972–95; register of transfers 1977–85; share certificates 1972–94; share transfer forms 1994.

Michael Stewart Ltd: directors' and general meetings minutes 1945–82, 1987; certificate of incorporation 1945; combined register of members and share ledger 1945–59; share transfer forms 1959; share certificate 1994.

J Maynard Whiteside Ltd: certificate of incorporation 1964; combined register of members and share ledger 1964–94; share certificates 1964–94.

SELLES MEDICAL LTD
PO Box 15, Great Gutter Lane, Willerby, Kingston upon Hull

Supplier of occupational health, first aid, medical and pharmaceutical goods

History: In 1953 A C Daykin Ltd was incorporated as a limited liability company at Doncaster, to acquire the wholesale and retail chemist and druggist business of A C Daykin, 11 Church Street, Askern, Doncaster. A C Daykin Ltd was acquired by Selles Dispensing Chemists Ltd, Kingston upon Hull, in 1967 and was renamed Selles Industrial First Aid Ltd in 1974, with registered offices at Crescent Street, Cottingham, East Riding of Yorkshire. In 1986 it was renamed Selles Medical Ltd. The company traded as a supplier of specialist occupational health and first aid goods. In 1994 the holding company of Selles Dispensing Chemists Ltd, Molescroft Holdings & Investments Ltd, was acquired by UniChem plc, and Selles Medical Ltd ceased to trade in its own right. UniChem plc merged in 1997 with Alliance Sante SA to become Alliance UniChem plc.

Records: Alliance UniChem plc, UniChem House, Cox Lane, Chessington KT9 1SN

Directors' and general meetings minutes 1953-74; certificate of incorporation 1953; combined register of members and share ledger 1953-95; deed of covenant 1994.

SEQUAH MEDICINE CO LTD
46 Holborn Viaduct, London

Manufacturer of, and travelling sales operation for, patent medicines

History: In 1887 William Hartley (1857-1924) established himself in business in Portsmouth, selling various patent medicines, including prairie flower, Indian oil, Indian dentifrice and other remedies for physical complaints, under the business name Sequah Indian Medicine Firm. These 'quack' medicines were sold by travelling salesmen or mountebanks (sequahs), and sales were staged with much showmanship. One of the sequahs was a performing clairvoyant, Peter Alexander Gordon (alias James Kasper). Advertising and testimonials were placed in local newspapers, and agreements were made with pharmacists and grocers that they would maintain retail sales after Sequah representatives had moved on. A penny newspaper, *Sequah Chronicle*, was published weekly, containing advertisements, short stories and jokes. In 1889 the business was incorporated as a limited liability company, Sequah Ltd, with registered offices at 46, later 44, Farringdon Street, City of London. Hartley was managing director. By 1890 there were 23 sequahs operating in the UK, and James Kasper was posted abroad, to market the company's merchandise in the West Indies, USA, Canada and Spain. This was necessary because the Customs and Inland Revenue Act of 1890 dictated that UK medicines sales must be conducted from permanent premises. In 1890 Sequah Ltd was voluntarily wound up, and a new limited liability company with the same name was incorporated to acquire the business. This company continued to trade until 1895 when it was wound up, and the business purchased by the Sequah Medicine Co Ltd incorporated as a limited liability company in the same year. In 1907 shares in Sequah Medicine Co Ltd were purchased by John Morgan Richards & Sons Ltd, manufacturing chemists and export druggists, 46 Holborn Viaduct, London. The Sequah Medicine Co Ltd was dissolved in 1909.

Pills and Profits: The selling of medicines since 1870 (Wellcome Institute for the History of Medicine, London, 1994) 25-37; W Schupbach, 'Sequah: an English "American medicine"-man in 1890', *Medical History*, 29, 1985, 272-317

Records 1: Public Record Office, Ruskin Avenue, Kew, Richmond TW9 4DU

Memorandum and articles of association 1895; certificate of incorporation 1895; summaries of capital and shares 1896, 1901, 1906–07; registers of directors or managers 1901, 1903; statement of nominal capital 1895; certificate of dissolution 1909; notice of situation of registered office 1895; notice of change of situation of registered office 1907; John Morgan Richards & Sons Ltd, correspondence re dissolution of company 1908. (Ref: BT31/6505/45785)

Sequah Ltd: memoranda and articles of association 1889–90; certificate of incorporation 1889; notices of extraordinary general meetings 1890, 1893, 1895; special resolution 1890; agreement for purchase of Sequah Indian Medicine Firm 1889; agreement for purchase of Sequah Ltd 1890; notices of consent to take name of subsisting company 1890, 1895; summaries of capital and shares 1889–90, 1895; statements of nominal capital 1889–90; court order confirming resolutions for reduction of capital 1893; certificate of reduction of capital 1893; liquidator's statements of account 1892, 1897–98; lists of amounts paid or payable to contributors 1892, 1897–98; returns of final winding-up meetings 1891, 1898; notices of situation of registered office 1889–90; notices of change of situation of registered office 1889, 1891–92, 1894; liquidator's correspondence re dissolution of company 1891–92, 1896–97. (Ref: BT31/4793/31733, 4371/28393, BT34/700/31733, 591/28393)

Records 2: Archives & Manuscripts, Wellcome Library for the History & Understanding of Medicine, 183 Euston Road, London NW1 2BE

Accounts, receipts and expenses 1890; company booklets, handbills, posters, testimonials and pill packages (UK and West Indies) n.d.; *Sequah Annual* 1891; *Sequah Chronicle* 1890–91 (w); J Kasper's papers: ledger, containing contracts, testimonials and accounts 1890–92, personal accounts and expenses 1890–91, scrapbooks, incl. press cuttings 1890–91, letterbook, incl. stock lists, accounts and calculations 1890–92; J Kasper's correspondence, UK and overseas: Mr & Mrs James Norman 1890–91, Sequah Ltd, London, incl. from W Hartley and material about stamped medicines licences 1890–92. (Ref: CMAC/GC/69)

Records 3: The British Library, Newspaper Library, Colindale Avenue, London NW9 5HE

Sequah Chronicle (Nos.1-54: complete set) 1890–91

R J S SHEPHERD
113 Northgate Street, Gloucester, Gloucestershire

Chemist

History: Robert James Shepherd was registered as a pharmaceutical chemist in 1883 and operated from, or resided at, Townshend House, Wisbech, Cambridgeshire. For a period between 1888 and 1892, he resided at 18 Corrateree, Geneva, Switzerland, moving to 72 Northgate Street, Gloucester, Gloucestershire, in 1893. In 1907 he moved to 59 Northgate Street, and traded on his own account, until 1928, when he ceased to be registered. The business continued to trade as R J S Shepherd, moving to 113 Northgate Street by 1937. In 1979 it was closed.

Records 1: Gloucestershire Record Office, Clarence Row, Alvin Street, Gloucester GL1 3DW

Ledger, accounts with drug firms in Bristol and Cheltenham 1965–70; prescription books 1968–76; registers: poisons 1946–67, dangerous drugs purchased and supplied 1961–68, methadone purchased, sold or supplied 1968–73. (Ref: D3770)

Records 2: The Museum Curator, Royal Pharmaceutical Society of Great Britain, 1 Lambeth High Street, London SE1 7JN

Lease of premises to Robert James Shepherd 1892. (Ref: IRA.1996.117)

W E SHEPHERD
41 Litherland Road, Bootle, Sefton

Pharmacy

History: In 1893 Herbert William Shepherd was registered as a chemist and druggist in Bradford. In 1898 he moved to Burnley, Lancashire, and in 1905 to Harpenden, Hertfordshire. In 1908 he re-located to Bradford where he traded as a chemist and druggist from 64 Lumb Lane. In 1921 he moved again, acquiring the established chemist's business at 41 Litherland Road, Bootle, Sefton. In 1922 William Ellis Shepherd was registered as a chemist and druggist, and joined the business. Herbert William Shepherd retired in 1935, and William Ellis continued the Litherland Road business on his own account, trading as W E Shepherd. In 1969 the business was closed.

Records: National Museums and Galleries on Merseyside, Museum of Liverpool Life, Pier Head, Liverpool L3 1PZ

Ledger n.d.; assorted receipts and pharmaceutical formulary list n.d.; prescription books 1890–94, 1927–68; poisons registers 1936, n.d.; Liverpool chemists' price lists 1906, 1915; advertising handbills 1895–96, 1907–08, n.d.; sign announcing closure of the premises 1969; W E Shepherd's certificate of membership of Royal Pharmaceutical Society of Great Britain 1954; labels n.d.; photographs of chemists' shops n.d. (Ref: Acc.MMM1994.167.39-71, 167.148-65)

SILLETT'S
Market Place, Guisborough, Redland & Cleveland

Chemist

History: Robert Walter Fairburn was registered as a chemist and druggist in 1870 in Northallerton, North Yorkshire, where Joseph Fairburn had been in the same line of business since before 1868. Fairburn moved to Market Place, Guisborough, Redland & Cleveland, prior to 1875, where he also dealt in wines, spirits and ales. He was still in business there in 1895. Some time later the business was acquired and renamed Sillett's.

Records: Cleveland Archives, Exchange House, 6 Marton Road, Middlesbrough TS1 1DB

Ledgers 1929–41 (w); invoices 1894–1903; deeds 1778–1853. (Ref: U/SC)

EDWARD SLEE & CO
Kennington, Kensington & Chelsea; Harlington, Hillingdon; and Hounslow, London

Patent medicine manufacturer and vendor

History: In 1742 Joshua Webster MD (c.1709–1801) formulated a patent remedy, Dr Webster's diet drink, or *Cerevisia Anglicana*. Shortly before his death, Webster passed the recipe to Samuel Slee, a wine merchant of Southwark, London, who later passed the recipe to his son, Edward. In 1835 Edward Slee joined in partnership with George Pike (d 1854), who was married to his daughter, Eliza. Following Pike's death, Eliza continued the business with her son, George Pike (b 1835), under the style Edward Slee & Co. The firm traded from a number of London locations including Kennington, Kensington & Chelsea; Harlington, Hillingdon; and Hounslow, until the beginning of the twentieth century, when it appears to have ceased trading.

Records: Archives & Manuscripts, Wellcome Library for the History & Understanding of Medicine, 183 Euston Road, London NW1 2BE

Cash books 1861–68, 1881–83; financial notebooks 1885–87; miscellaneous accounts 1834–91, n.d.; legal papers and correspondence re ownership of business, incl. copy of Edward Slee's will 1835–62; records re *Cerevisia Anglicana*: endowment to S Slee 1800, recipes 1798, 19th cent., medicine-making books c.1814–86, directions re production process 1832–89, n.d., notebook n.d., 19th cent., advertising proofs c.1815–89, n.d., press cuttings 1858, 1865, n.d., correspondence with publishers re advertisements 1883, correspondence with customers, customer recommendations and advertisements 1803–96, n.d., dosage labels n.d., 19th cent., company publication 1836; delivery books 1846–52, 1882–88; memorandum book of deliveries, visitors and letters received 1859–61; suppliers' letters, invoices and circulars c.1861, 1880–1903, n.d.; miscellaneous business papers and correspondence 1835–98, n.d.; George Pike's diary 1832; private papers and correspondence of Edward Slee, Eliza Pike, George Pike junior and other members of Pike family 1825–87, 1914–31, n.d. (Ref: MSS 7164-201)

SMITH & NEPHEW PLC
PO Box 81, Hessle Road, Kingston upon Hull

Pharmaceutical manufacturer

History: In 1856 following an apprenticeship to a dispensing chemist in Grantham, Lincolnshire, Thomas James Smith opened a chemist's shop in Whitefriargate, Kingston upon Hull, on his own account. Initially he traded as a retail chemist, but in 1858 began to supply hospitals with cod-liver oil wholesale. In 1861 the business moved to larger premises at 10 North Churchside, Kingston upon Hull, and shortly afterwards, also occupied number 11. Thomas Smith was joined in partnership by his nephew, Horatio Nelson Smith, who had trained as an assistant in the wholesale textile trade, in 1896, and the firm was renamed T J Smith & Nephew. In the same year Thomas Smith died and the business passed to Horatio, who continued to trade under the established name. His interest in the textile trade led to the firm's entry into the manufacture of surgical dressings, shortly after his uncle's death. This proved a highly successful line, and demand increased sharply for such products during the First World War.

Around the turn of the century T J Smith & Nephew acquired the business of Lambert & Lambert, Kingston upon Hull, and in 1907 was incorporated as a limited liability company, T J Smith & Nephew Ltd. The company later relocated to larger premises at 5 Neptune Street, Kingston upon Hull. In 1928 T J Smith & Nephew Ltd launched the surgical dressing *Elastoplast*, which was to become one of its most successful products. In 1937 Smith & Nephew Associated Companies Ltd was incorporated as a limited liability company, with T J Smith & Nephew Ltd as a subsidiary. Smith & Nephew Associated Companies Ltd acquired Herts Pharmaceuticals Ltd in 1951, a manufacturer of the anti-tuberculosis drug *PAS* and a range of products which were marketed under the trade name *Nivea*. Herts Pharmaceuticals Ltd also operated research laboratories at Welwyn Garden City, Hertfordshire. In 1952 these research laboratories, and the technical staff of T J Smith & Nephew Ltd, merged to form a new company, Smith & Nephew Research Ltd, based at Hunsdon, Hertfordshire, and later at Harlow, Essex. This company conducted research into treatments for tuberculosis and also into surgical textiles. Pharmaceutical research and manufacture was not a major part of the overall business of Smith & Nephew Associated Companies Ltd, but it grew during the 1950s and 1960s. In 1956 Smith & Nephew Pharmaceuticals Ltd was incorporated as a limited liability company, and in 1958 began research into mental illness. This led to the launch of *Drazine*, a treatment for depression, in 1959, which was removed from the market in 1963. A drug for the treatment of insomnia, *Welldorm*, was introduced in 1962 and in the same year the company began manufacture of ophthalmic pharmaceuticals, a more successful line. This led in 1968 to a research programme into drugs to treat glaucoma, the outcome of which was *Ganda*, an adrenalin-based treatment, and *Minims*, sterile eye drops. In 1973 Smith & Nephew Pharmaceuticals Ltd became a constituent company of a newly created medical division of Smith & Nephew Associated Companies Ltd, with a factory at Bampton Road, Harold Hill, Romford, Havering, London, and head offices at Welwyn Garden City. In 1988 Smith & Nephew Associated Companies Ltd was renamed Smith & Nephew plc, and in 1989 Smith & Nephew Pharmaceuticals Ltd acquired the business of Ioptex Research Inc, California, USA, an optical lens manufacturer, which was subsequently sold in 1994. In 1991 an incontinence drug, *Ditropan*, was launched, and its licence sold to Synthelabo Groupe SA in 1995. Smith & Nephew Research Ltd was renamed Smith & Nephew Group Research Centre Ltd in 1992, and was re-located to York University Science Park. In 1993 the ophthalmic division of Smith & Nephew Pharmaceuticals Ltd was acquired by Laboratoire Chauvin SA, France, and renamed Chauvin Pharmaceuticals Ltd. The remaining business of Smith & Nephew Pharmaceuticals Ltd moved to the registered address of Smith & Nephew Medical Ltd, Hessle Road, Kingston upon Hull. In 1997 Smith & Nephew Pharmaceuticals Ltd still held a number of product licences, including

Flamazine, a treatment for burns, originally introduced in 1973, and *AmetoGel*, a skin anaesthetic, but no longer employed any staff. In 1993 Smith & Nephew Healthcare Ltd was incorporated as a subsidiary company of Smith & Nephew plc, to merge the sales and marketing functions of all its UK interests, including Smith & Nephew Pharmaceuticals Ltd, Smith & Nephew Medical Ltd and Smith & Nephew Surgical Ltd. In 1999 Smith & Nephew plc was one of the world's largest healthcare groups, developing, manufacturing and marketing a wide range of innovative and technically advanced tissue repair products, primarily in the areas of bone, joints, skin and other soft tissue. The group was the largest medical device manufacturer outside the USA, and the largest orthopaedic company in the world.

E M Bavin, 'Smith & Nephew Research Ltd, Gilston Park', *Chemistry and Industry*, 15 May 1965, 820-5; R Bennett, *Smith & Nephew, 1856–1956: A record of service to surgery and medicine* (Smith & Nephew, London, 1956); R Bennett & J A Leavey, *A History of Smith & Nephew, 1856–1981* (Smith & Nephew, 1981) Foreman-Peck, *Smith & Nephew in the Health Care Industry* (Edward Elgar, Aldershot, 1995); 'Smith & Nephew Ltd: A medical story', *Nursing Mirror*, 27 July 1978

Records 1: Smith & Nephew Medical Ltd, PO Box 81, Hessle Road, Kingston upon Hull HU3 2BN

Minutes: directors' meetings 1920–29, general meetings 1920–31; debenture certificate 1920; agreement re sale of business 1907; annual reports 1938–83 (w); balance sheet 1896; ledgers: sales 1858–1922 (w), purchase 1874–1902, sundries 1887–1903; day books: sales 1874–1910, purchase 1903–04, export sales, Smith & Nephew Manchester Ltd 1909–12, 1918–26; cash books 1869–n.d.; contracts books 1906–09, 1931–32; stock lists 1896–1903; stock order books 1875–90, 1904–10; purchase returns books 1903–09; goods inwards books 1904–07; parcel despatches book 1894–95; press cutting re speech by T J Smith 1875; lease for 10 North Churchside 1863; agreement re supply of hydraulic power to 47 Queen Street 1915; correspondence: licence for flooring 5 Neptune Street 1918, supply of electricity 1916, payment for use of London office n.d.; employee agreements 1905–14, 1931; agreement re storage of goods with James Scott 1920; office staff signing-in book 1910–11; letterbook 1898; correspondence: cod liver oil 1856–80, hospitals ordering goods 1881–86, Henrik Clasen, Copenhagen re apprenticeship of his son 1908–09; speech by T J Smith 1860; H N Smith's passport 1915.

330 *The pharmaceutical industry – a guide to historical records*

Lambert & Lambert: share register 1907–17; sales ledger 1904–10; sales day books 1905–09; cash book c.1870s; contracts book c.1930s; stock order books 1904–11.

Records 2: Chauvin Pharmaceuticals Ltd, Ashton Road, Harold Hill, Romford RM3 8SL

Smith & Nephew Pharmaceuticals Ltd: minutes: directors' meetings 1989, 1992–96, general meetings 1957–96 (w); memorandum and articles of association 1956; register of members 1957 to date; register of seals 1957 to date; share certificates n.d.; annual reports and accounts 1961–95 (w).

Records 3: Smith & Nephew Healthcare Ltd, Healthcare House, Goulton Street, Kingston upon Hull HU3 4DL

Management executive meeting minutes, papers and correspondence 1994–95; certificate of incorporation 1937; change of name certificate 1988; agreements and papers: sale of ophthalmic division 1993–94, acquisition and business of Ioptex Research Inc 1989–94, sale of Smith & Nephew Pharmaceuticals Ltd premises and transfer of business to Smith & Nephew Healthcare Ltd 1994–95; annual report and accounts 1994; annual budgets and related papers 1990–95; patent specifications and drawings 1990s; managing directors' day files 1992–96; reports: product profitability 1994, centre of excellence 1994–95, period 1994–95; general business papers and correspondence 1990s; product development files 1974–96; product licence agreements and correspondence 1983–95; manufacturing agreements 1982; product marketing plans and promotional literature 1994; agreements and papers re sale of *Ditropan* licence to Synthelabo Groupe SA 1995–96; Romford site appraisal, architectural drawings, reports and correspondence 1990–92; invitation to tender, product warehousing and distribution 1994–95; conference proceedings and papers 1994–95; customer satisfaction surveys and papers 1994–95

Records 4: History of Advertising Trust, HAT House, 12 Raveningham Centre, Raveningham NR14 6NU

Papers, memoranda and advertising campaign material 1965–67. (Ref: JWT 184 (1965) 325 (1966) 402 (1967) 562)

W SMITH (DURHAM) LTD
1 New House Road, Esh Winning, Durham

Chemist

History: William Smith was registered as a chemist and druggist in 1893, and resided at Avenue Hill, Durham. His business traded from 3 Silver Street, Durham, until 1910 and then from 34 Silver Street, Durham, until 1953. The firm also had branches at Framwellgate Moor, Durham, and Esh Winning, Durham. The business was incorporated as a limited liability company, W Smith (Durham) Ltd, in 1974, and in 1997 was still trading, with registered offices at 1 New House Road, Esh Winning.

Records: Durham Record Office, County Hall, Durham DH1 5UL

Analysis of weekly takings, bankings and cash expenses: Silver Street 1976–82, Framwellgate Moor 1976–82, Esh Winning 1979–82; monthly analyses of receipts and payments 1919–74; payments analysis books 1975–82; cash books 1974–75; VAT record books 1974, 1977–78; bank passbook 1943–45; prescription books 1897–1975 (w); stock: special orders book 1948–69, control books 1975–83, record with price lists 1978–81, valuation, Hannon Chemists Ltd, Esh Winning 1979, pills, 3 South Street n.d.; price lists, various pharmaceutical manufacturers 1962, 1970, 1974; statements of sums paid by the National Health Service for prescriptions 1972–82 (w); agency agreement with Steiner Products Ltd 1967; advertising, literature and cards 1960s–70s; accounts re building work at Silver Street 1975; wages books 1950–73; National Joint Industrial Council for Retail Pharmacy, agreement re wages and conditions of employment 1955; sales staff information n.d., c.1960s; membership certificate of the National Pharmaceutical Union and Chemists' Defence Association Ltd n.d., c.1930s; articles of pupilage, various 1929–45; Pharmaceutical Society of Great Britain, regulations and curriculum for examinations n.d., c.1942–45; title deeds and related papers, incl. copy of will of Thomas Reed of Durham, apothecary, devising a messuage and shop in Silver Street to his son Thomas 1774–1903, 1950. (Ref: D/Smi)

SMITH KENDON LTD
Bridgend

Manufacturing chemist and confectioner

History: In 1780 William Smith established a confectionery business in Fell Street, London, styled Smith & Co. In 1860 a fire destroyed the premises, and the firm moved to 128-132 Borough High Street, Southwark, London, where it remained until 1974. Samuel Smith introduced the manufacture of medicines to the firm, and by 1914 the firm's liquorice production factory in Messina, Italy, was closed, and home production of spices and jams had ceased. During the Second World War contracts for *Altoid*s were secured with the armed forces, and in 1948 the business was incorporated as a limited liability company, Smith Kendon Ltd. The name Kendon was derived from 'Ken' and 'Don', the abbreviated first names of the 2 Smith brothers. In 1974 the company re-located from Southwark to Bridgend, and won the Queen's award for industry in the same year. Subsequently, the business was acquired by an American firm, Beatrice Foods Inc, which retained 'Smith Kendon' as a trade name.

Records: London Metropolitan Archives, 40 Northampton Road, London EC1R 0HB

Articles of partnership: Joseph Chillingworth and William and Samuel Smith 1854, Samuel and Thomas Smith 1865, Samuel, Thomas and Henry Maurice Smith 1881, Samuel and Henry Maurice Smith 1891, Samuel, Henry, James and John Smith 1895; directors' meetings minutes 1951–76 (w); general meetings minutes and agenda 1970–71, 1975; agreement, sale of business to Smith Kendon Ltd 1948; certificate of registration of Smith & Co 1951; business diaries 1859–85 (w), 1950–66; memoranda authorising division of profits between Henry and John Smith 1911–16; securities book 1896–1920; annual statements of accounts 1931–77; Henry Maurice Smith's private ledgers 1881–1936; summary ledger accounts 1895–1926; summary of ledger accounts 1963; Eliza S Smith's rent and investment accounts ledgers 1899–1920; sales ledger balances 1940; sales figures 1943–50 (w); stock-in-trade account book 1826–38; proprietary product accounts 1899–1914; journey accounts 1924–39; D A L Smith's settlement accounts 1962, 1966; cash books: Ann Smith 1856–81, Thomas Smith, incl. company balance sheets 1872–85, Mrs Thomas Smith 1885–88, Samuel Smith, incl. company balance sheets 1872–99, n.d., James Nicholson Smith 1895–1900; pocket books detailing wages and sales 1912–39; miscellaneous accounts, incl. wages, rates, advertising stock and sales 1918–31; report on financial accounting and factory costing systems 1931–36; correspondence re general accounting practice 1935–37; legal papers re Finance Acts 1941; trademarks, certificate of registration of assignment to Smith Kendon Ltd 1949–50; letters patent for medicinal inventions re manufacture of liquorice and of lozenges 1863; business reports 1960s–1970s; 5 year plan 1969; proprietary product books 1849–51; mixing books 1856–[79], n.d.; recipe books 1856, 1895–1919, 1936, n.d.; recipe notebooks: 'Smith's Drop Book' 1895–

1911, 'Smith's Pellet Book', incl. note on excipients for compressed tablets 1901–13; recipe cards n.d.; productions costs book, products packaging various 1937–41; product manual 1963; product price lists 1929–32, 1958–59; product labels 20th cent.; photograph albums, product display models n.d.; stock: drugs books 1890–98, 19th cent., annual stocktaking papers 1859–85, list of stocktaking prices 1934, books 1934–35, inventory sheets 1938, 1940; sales correspondence, mainly with armed forces 1944–55; sales representatives: reports and correspondence re performance levels 1959–[67], details of incentive bonus 1961; memorandum re sales promotion programme, with special reference to 'Geeps' 1963; sales charts 1936–39, 1948–50; monthly sales summary 1953–60; summary sheets of sales forecast by product group 1961–62; advertising material 1955, n.d.; property papers: title deeds 1739–1963, accounts 1860, insurance policies 1936–75, inventories, fixtures and fittings and stock sheets 1900, 1930–36, buildings alterations 1905, 1950–61, correspondence 1931–63, re-location of business 1971–73, general and miscellaneous 1875–1937; staff papers: list of male employees 1945, pocket book, employee names and 6-months' salary 1943, Christmas gift list 1870–85, holiday book 1921–35, pocket address book, male employees 1933, proposals for staff pension and provident scheme 1955, staff handbook n.d.; correspondence: copy letterbooks 1881–1931, 1937–78, previous employees 1975, transfer of items from Southwark factory to various museums 1973–74, miscellaneous 1937–78; Second World War correspondence: defence preparations 1939–42, National Service 1940–44, renewal of deferments and lists of government contracts 1944; photographs: R Osborne, former chairman c.1965, Henry Maurice Smith n.d., Southwark factory fire damage c.1948, opening of Bridgend factory 1974; scrapbook 1840–76; address books n.d.; firewatchers' diaries 1942–44. (Ref: B/SK, Acc 2522, Acc 3085)

SMITHKLINE BEECHAM PHARMACEUTICALS (UK) LTD
Mundells, Welwyn Garden City, Hertfordshire

Pharmaceutical manufacturer

History: In 1877 an American medicine vendor, A Judson White, established a business, A J White, in London, to distribute his pharmaceutical products and to manufacture his patented medicine *Mother Seigel's Curative Syrup*. In 1884 the business was incorporated as a limited liability company, A J White Ltd, at 17 (later 39) Farringdon Road, London. In 1897 this company was voluntarily liquidated and a limited liability company of the same name, A J White Ltd, was incorporated to acquire the business. In 1907 Menley & James Ltd was incorporated as a subsidiary of A J White Ltd, to manufacture high-class pharmaceutical specialities, including *Aspirin*, *Laxol*, *Calomex* and *Gonorex*. This company rented the ground floor of 39 Farringdon Road from A J White Ltd until 1916, when it purchased a factory at Coldharbour Lane, Camberwell, Southwark, London. In 1920 A J White Ltd re-located from Farringdon Road to 64 Hatton Garden, London, which from 1927 was named Menley House. In 1940, it re-located again to Coldharbour Lane, Camberwell, Southwark, London. In 1927 A J White Ltd was appointed by Smith Kline & French Co Inc, USA, a long-established company with roots in a Philadelphia drug store of 1830, to distribute its products under licence. This relationship continued until 1956, when the former Smith Kline & French Co Inc, renamed Smith Kline & French Laboratories Inc, acquired A J White Ltd and Menley & James Ltd as UK subsidiaries. A J White Ltd was renamed Smith Kline & French Laboratories Ltd and re-located to Welwyn Garden City, Hertfordshire. This was a separate concern from Smith Kline & French Laboratories, a division of the American parent which was based in USA. Menley & James Laboratories was formed as a division of Smith Kline & French Laboratories Ltd, to market proprietary medicines. During the 1960s Smith Kline & French Laboratories Ltd, whose parent was renamed SmithKline Corporation Inc in 1970, conducted research which led to the discovery of a treatment for gastric and duodenal ulcers. This drug was marketed as *Tagamet* in 1976. It also conducted research into animal healthcare and veterinary medicines, and produced the over-the-counter cold treatment, *Contac 400*, under the trading name Menley & James in 1965. In 1961 the SmithKline Foundation was established as a charitable trust which sponsored pharmaceutical research and in 1977 Smith Kline & French Research Ltd was incorporated as a subsidiary of Smith Kline & French Laboratories Ltd in London. In 1981 SmithKline Corporation Inc acquired Beckman Instruments Inc, a manufacturer of diagnostic equipment in USA, and agreed to a change of name to SmithKline Beckman Corporation Inc. The UK subsidiary, Smith Kline & French UK Ltd, continued to trade under its existing name. In 1989 SmithKline Beckman Corporation Inc, USA, merged with Beecham Group plc, to form SmithKline Beecham plc. In the UK Beecham Group plc became SmithKline Beecham plc, and Smith Kline & French Laboratories Ltd became its subsidiary, SmithKline Beecham Pharmaceuticals (UK) Ltd.

'Smithkline Beckman Corporation', in T Derdak (ed), *International Directory of Company Histories*, Vol. 1 (St James Press, London, 1988); L Finucane, *S K & F: From Camberwell to Welwyn Garden City 1956–1989* (Smith Kline & French, Welwyn, 1989); K Holland, 'SmithKline & French Laboratories Ltd', *Pharmaceutical Journal*, 25 Feb 1989, 218-21; J F Marion, *The Fine Old House: Smithkline Corporation's first 150 years* (Smithkline Corporation, Philadelphia, 1980); D E Ward, 'History of A J White Ltd 1868–1956 and Menley & James Ltd 1908–1956' (Unpublished typescript, 1980)

Records 1: SmithKline Beecham Pharmaceuticals (UK) Ltd, Mundells, Welwyn Garden City AL7 1EY

Minutes: directors' meetings 1884–1972, general meetings 1897–1918; memoranda and articles of association 1897–1950, 1956; overseas subsidiaries certificates of incorporation 1901–56; resolution re: memorandum and articles of association 1952, increased capital 1951; papers re acquisition by Smith Kline & French Laboratories Inc 1956–58; directors' attendance books: 1918–53, overseas subsidiaries 1901–58; special resolution re directors' age 1950; general meetings reports 1908–55; subsidiary companies meeting minutes 1926–29; production committee meetings 1983–89; register of directors 1897–1904; lists of shareholders 1894–96, 1902; share ledgers: 1912–56, ordinary 1897–1912, preference 1897–1912; transfer registers 1904–57; transfer certificates 1897–1903, 1955–56; secretarial papers re share transfers 1947; share agreement 1957; dividend books 1920–56; annual summaries of share capital 1922–61; papers: distribution of dividends 1938–40, reduction of share capital 1912; share certificates 1940–57; certification reconciliation book 1900–16; fidelity bonds 1913–35; proxy forms 1910, 1946; letters of trust 1929–56; papers and correspondence: wartime dividend procedure 1939–40, Bank of England re USA securities 1941–42, shareholders 1904–05, 1939; annual reports: 1955–83, 1985–92, Smith Kline and French Laboratories 1950, SmithKline Corporation Inc 1973–80, Beckman Instruments Inc 1981, SmithKline Beckman Corporation Inc 1981–88; annual reports and accounts, company and subsidiaries 1957–90; trading profit and loss accounts and balance sheets 1898–1956; consolidated financial statements and balance sheets 1938–45, 1957–77; accounts 1957; papers, accounts and correspondence re liquidation of company 1897–98; ledgers: 1956–64, private 1899–1922, 1945–56, trading 1944–56, sales 1957–59, bought 1956–59; journals 1953–57; cash books 1946–57; export sales figures 1983–86; invoice registers 1960s–70s; cheques paid to creditors on liquidation 1898; auditors' reports 1902–03, 1907–09; correspondence with accountants 1956; power of attorney 1907; legal agreements 1940–82; assignation of trade marks 1898; overseas trade marks 1920s; letter from Mr Kidger re enemy trade marks 1916; trade mark certificates 1889, 1907–50; record of contents of parcel containing engravings for *Mother Seigel's Syrup, Tisane, Laxol* and *Iodoglidine* 1940; submission to Commission of Safety of Drugs n.d.; product development papers, laboratory data sheets and drug submissions 1961–65; clinical reports, papers and correspondence 1970s–80s; product files and formulae alteration sheets 1931–67; laboratory notebooks 1911, 1939–40; product list n.d.; price lists 1971–81; licence agreement 1928; *Iodex* promotion leaflet 1954; product advertising leaflets n.d.; product regulations 1963–75; packaging and labelling specifications booklets 1950s–60s; product labels booklets early 20th cent., 1970s, n.d.; standard procedures sheets 1977–87; drawings and photographs re drug manufacture n.d.; instruction booklet and correspondence re ampoule filling machine 1952; promotional brochures: 1950s–89, n.d., SmithKline Beckman Corporation Inc 1986; press cuttings books: neurophosphates 1928–50s, general products 19th–20th cents; press cutting re staff conditions 1970; deeds of sale and agreements 1883–85, 1897–1904; property deeds re 87 High Street, Bedford 1868–69, 1895, 1934–82; property leases 1920–45; property reports and valuations 1966, 1973–75; stock inventory 1898; building proposals with architectural drawings 1976–82, n.d.; architectural drawings, Tonbridge site 1954, 1961; salaries books 1945–57; payroll sheets 1900–32, 1957–62; pensions register 1957–61; pensions and salaries sheets 1957–62; pension papers 1964–70; careers booklet n.d.; safety code manual 1981–84; proceedings of management course 1963; company magazines: *International News* 1975–84, UK Overseas Group, *Echo* newsletters 1981–90, *Scope* 1990–91, *Microscope* 1990–91; staff magazines: *Smith Kline & French News* 1959–89, *Field Forum* 1987–90, *Field Talk* 1990–92; papers: Mexican contracts 1926, government acts 1941, 1951–65, Pakistan factory 1970–78, *Tagamet* 1974–76, telephone system 1977–84, public relations 1978–79, visit of SmithKline Beckman Corporation Inc directors to UK 1986; correspondence: directors' 1900, 1920–29, overseas subsidiaries 1900, 1913–44, 1957–79, Slaughter & May Ltd 1956–66, Dr Maurice Bloch 1973–83, company history 1957–80s, n.d., company archives 1978–83, internal 1981–85, general 1933–56; photographs: founders, M K Smith, M N Kline and H B French n.d., senior management n.d., staff, plant and offices 1950s–77, n.d., *Tagamet* 1970s, training courses 1958–64, 1972–73, social events 1950s–70s, overseas subsidiaries 1960s; company organisation charts 1970–80; corporate data manual c.1980s; subsidiary companies: registration certificates and correspondence with bank 1939–43, currency journals n.d.; certificate of membership of Hertfordshire Chamber of Commerce 1971; miscellaneous artwork and photographs 1967; slide atlas of rheumatology n.d.; company publications 1970s, n.d.; historical notes and articles 1970s, 1988, n.d.

Menley & James (Canada) Ltd: directors' and general meetings minutes 1908–25.

Menley & James (Colonial) Ltd: directors' and general meetings minutes 1942–56; share registers and summaries 1922–60; trading, profit and loss accounts and balance sheets 1914–17, 1919–53; notice of alienation 1939.

Menley & James Ltd: directors' and general meetings minutes 1908–60; memorandum and articles of association: 1956, Contac Laboratories Ltd 1966; special resolutions re articles of association 1919; certificates of incorporation of overseas subsidiaries 1901–56; chairman's agendas and accounts 1908–18;

attendance registers 1908–35, 1940–53; register of directors or managers 1930; share register and summaries: 1908–40, debentures 1919–37; share transfer certificates 1908–55; papers re shareholding in Laboratoires Julien D'Hoedt SA, Belgium 1929–47; annual reports and accounts 1973–81, 1983–85; trading profit and loss accounts and balance sheets: 1913–56, factory 1951–56; reports and financial statements 1956–59; consolidated balance sheets 1939–45; trial balances 1948–57; ledgers: 1956–57, private 1930–56, trading 1951–56; journals: 1956–57, balance sheets 1909–40, factory 1952–56; cash books 1946–57; order book 1954–57; insurance policy and papers on life of Dr Klopfer 1911–15; legal agreements 1980–83; statement of legal expenses, Bradley v company 1912–13; trade mark certificates 1907–50; product development papers, laboratory data sheets and drug submissions 1960s; product labels booklets n.d.; Coldharbour Lane: mortgage 1891–1955, agreement re electric cable 1950; correspondence re overseas subsidiaries 1931–43; photographs: staff, premises and social events 1937, 1950s–80s, n.d., overseas subsidiaries 1920s.

Menley & James (New York) Ltd: directors' and general meetings minutes 1917–25, 1940–56.

Mother Seigal's Syrup Co Ltd: directors' meetings 1901–12; certificate of incorporation 1901.

Smith Kline & French Research Ltd: annual reports and accounts 1978–84 (w).

SmithKline Foundation: minutes 1961–77; annual reports 1963–78; financial statements 1962–78, 1984.

A J White (Canada) Ltd: directors' meetings minutes 1907–25.

A J White (Colonial) Ltd: directors' and general meetings minutes 1901–56; agenda book 1901–13; share ledgers 1901–40; share certificates 1901–40; trading, profit and loss accounts and balance sheets 1915, 1938–53; ledgers 1901–39; journals 1936–45; cash books 1902–52.

A J White (New York) Ltd: directors' and general meetings minutes 1906–56.

A J White (South Africa) Ltd: minutes 1953–57.

Records 2: SmithKline Beecham plc, SmithKline Beecham House, Great West Road, Brentford TW8 9DB. Enquiries to SmithKline Beecham plc, 1 New Horizons Court, Great West Road, Brentford TW8 9EP

Directors' and general meetings minutes 1973–83.

Smith Kline & French (Ireland) Ltd: memorandum and articles of association 1972.

Smith Kline & French Research Ltd: directors' and general meetings minutes 1978–92; registers of members and share ledger 1968–88; register of seals 1956–93.

SmithKline & French Pension Trustees Ltd: minutes 1957–87; annual returns and correspondence 1967–94; annual reports and accounts 1992–94.

A J White (Colonial) Ltd: memorandum and articles of association 1901.

SMITHKLINE BEECHAM PLC
New Horizons Court, Great West Road, Brentford, Hounslow, London

Pharmaceutical manufacturer

History: Thomas Beecham was born in 1820 in Curbridge, Oxfordshire, into a relatively poor family. As a child he worked as a shepherd, and experimented with herbal veterinary medicines, which were later to provide the basis for his human medicinal preparations. By the 1840s he had qualified as a chemist, and developed a formula for the manufacture of medicinal pills. He supplemented his income with casual labour, and later established himself as a peddlar of his own wares. In 1847 Thomas Beecham moved to Liverpool, where he continued to peddle his pills, which included 'Female's Friend', 'Royal Toothpowder', 'Herbal Pills', and 'Golden Tooth Tincture'. In 1857 he moved to Wigan and opened a chemists shop, re-locating in 1860 to Milk Street, St Helens, and in 1863 to Westfield Street, St Helens, where he was joined in the business by his son, Joseph. In 1876 the firm constructed a factory in Westfield Street, for the manufacture of Beecham's pills, and in 1885 acquired new headquarters on the corner of Silver Street and Water Street, St Helens. Thomas and Joseph Beecham advertised the firm's products with vigour, and by 1890 the firm was the largest advertiser in the UK. Thomas Beecham retired from the business in 1895, and died in 1907. Joseph died 9 years later, having, in the interim, established the

Anacona Motor Co in partnership with James White, and purchased land at Covent Garden, London, where his son, Thomas Beecham, had made his mark as a music conductor. This acquisition was managed through the Covent Garden Estate Co Ltd, incorporated as a limited liability company by Joseph Beecham. After the deaths of Thomas, the elder, and Joseph, the pharmaceutical business was conducted by the executors of Joseph's will, until 1924, when it was acquired by Philip Hill, a financier, along with the Covent Garden Estate Co Ltd. He incorporated the former as a limited liability company, Beecham Estates & Pills Ltd, in the same year. In 1928 Beecham Estates & Pills Ltd was replaced by 2 limited liability companies, Beecham Pills Ltd, which was incorporated to acquire the businesses of a number of pharmaceutical manufacturing and distribution companies, and Beecham Estates Ltd, which administered the property side of the business. Companies acquired by Beecham Pills Ltd between 1928 and 1932 included Veno Drug Co Ltd, Manchester; A F Sherley & Co Ltd, Marshalsea Road, London; Yeast Vite Ltd, Cicfa Co Ltd and Iron Jelloid Co Ltd, Watford, Hertfordshire; and Holloways Pills Ltd and Dinneford & Co Ltd, London. In 1933 Phensic Ltd was incorporated as a subsidiary company of Beecham Pills Ltd, to manufacture drugs of that name. Trade expanded during the 1930s and the factory at Westfield Street was extended in 1934. More acquisitions followed, in the form of the Phosferine Co Ltd, formerly Ashton & Parsons Ltd, Watford, in 1935 and Natural Chemicals Ltd, London, 1936. Macleans Ltd, Brentford, Hounslow, London, and Eno Proprietaries Ltd, and its subsidiary, Thermogene Co Ltd, London, were acquired in 1938, and at the same time Beecham Maclean Holdings Ltd was incorporated as a subsidiary of Beecham Pills Ltd. Harwoods Laboratories Ltd, Watford, was acquired in 1942. In 1945 Beecham Pills Ltd and Beecham Estates Ltd were replaced by a public limited liability company, Beecham Group Ltd, which incorporated a subsidiary company, Beecham Research Laboratories Ltd, to conduct its research and development and manufacturing activities. Beecham Group Ltd also established a northern branch, Beecham (Northern) Ltd, which was renamed Beecham Pharmaceuticals Ltd in 1955, and Beecham Proprietary Medicines Ltd in 1962. New laboratories were opened at Brockham Park, Surrey, in 1947, and the factories at Westfield Street were extended in 1948 and in 1956. In 1959 Cephos Ltd was acquired by Beecham Group Ltd and in 1960 a factory was established at Worthington, Leicestershire. Packaging was conducted from a separate site in Crawley, West Sussex, and raw materials were processed in Irvine, North Ayrshire. From 1954 Beecham Research Laboratories Ltd conducted research into antibiotics, which led to the successful manufacture of a synthetic penicillin, *Broxil*, in 1959, and an improved version, *Celbenin*, in 1960. The company also manufactured foods, health drinks and toiletries. In 1978 the business of Scott & Bowne Ltd, manufacturers and distributors of emulsions, was acquired by Beecham Group Ltd, USA, later plc. In 1989 Beecham Group plc merged with

SmithKline Beckman Corporation Inc, USA, a manufacturer of scientific instruments and pharmaceuticals, and was renamed SmithKline Beecham plc. As a result, SmithKline Beecham plc in the UK acquired Smith Kline & French Laboratories Ltd, Welwyn Garden City, Hertfordshire, the former SmithKline Beckman Corporation Inc's largest UK subsidiary. Smith Kline & French Laboratories Ltd was renamed SmithKline Beecham Pharmaceuticals (UK) Ltd.

R Baumann, Jackson, J T Lawrence, *From Promise to Performance: A journey of transformation at SmithKline Beecham*; 'The Beecham's Pill Machine', *Chemist and Druggist*, 4 April 1987, 612; K Holland, 'Beecham Group plc', *Pharmaceutical Journal*, 30 May 1987, 675-8; H G Lazell, *From Pills to Penicillin: The Beecham story* (William Heinemann, London, 1975)

Records 1: St Helens Local History & Archives Library, Gamble Institute, Victoria Square, St Helens WA10 1DY

Notice of dissolution of partnership between Thomas and Joseph Beecham 1895; directors' meetings minutes, incl. accounts 1948–67; memoranda and articles of association 1916–62; papers re sale of Beecham Pills Ltd's pills and powder business to Beecham (Northern) 1950–55; agreements re American agency 1888, 1891; papers re company re-organisation 1949, 1952–54; summary of company matters 1937; shareholding papers and prospectuses 1918–47; papers re fixed assets 1946; directors' reports and accounts 1924–42, 1950–65; statement of accounts and correspondence 1924; annual review and summary financial statement 1992; statement re credit 1921; account books and accounts 1880–1929; ledgers: 1865–73, 1925–54, private 1924–42, African account c.1879–87; sales journals 1924–44, 1950, 1955–57; cash books 1877–90; cash received analysis book 1960–64; sales analyses books 1945–51; sales records 1856–57; papers re selling arrangements with Northern Ireland 1957–58; receipts 1883–89, 1902; banking papers: statements 1891–95, loan account 1914, books 1912–16, 1921–24, 1957–71, cheques 1888–89, 20th cent., cancelled drafts 1919–25; papers re purchase tax 1940–41, 1965; papers re stamp duty 1923–41; insurance papers 1922–36; litigation papers 1928–39; patent specification 1926; reports and papers re patent medicines 1890, 1912–24, 1935–41; Kings Council on the definition of patents and trade marks 1904; trade mark record books 1886–1966; assignment of trade marks 1923; trade mark agreements 1958; papers re use of slogan 1926–40; correspondence: *Oracle* patent 1913–28, 1937–39, *Phenosan* trade name 1940, *Frigosan* trade name 1945; product directors' meetings minutes 1940–51; laboratory notes and diary 1934–45; formulae books 1862, 1884–99, 1912–24; formularies re manufacturing processes of drugs 1933–80s; formula and correspondence 1935; product formula declarations 1961–63; recipe book 1920; product lists 1950–54, 1973; production papers: *Beechalax* laxatives c.1933–35, Beechams powders 1937–50, Beechams pills 1935–49, lung syrup 1941–44, quinine tablets 1942, *Caleno* 1943–61, importation of aloes 1935–44; reports and correspondence re 'Formula 21' 1960–66; notes re production at research laboratories 1947; packaging: specifications and samples 1957–79, booklet 1943–49, report re American packaging methods 1947, papers re assembly line packaging methods 1960–61; patent and trade mark certificates 1896–20th cent.; certificate of registration of Beecham's pills 1921–24; medicine licences 1847–64, 1916; prescription 1902; sale of pills books 1865–81; pill taking instructions booklets c.1882, 1899, 1909, n.d.; price lists 1881, 1925–29; stock papers: Pricing of Goods Act 1939, cost of drugs 1941–42, pricing of drugs 1955–69, stock valuation 1941–44; purchase reports n.d.; accounts and papers re cost of advertising 1860–1948; advertisements 1850s, 1884–1957, n.d.; advertising: schedules 1945–50, graphics and artwork 1890s–1900s, handbills 1847, 1899, booklets 1900s, 1920s, posters 1858–60s, 1890s, early 20th cent., n.d., postcards 1890s–1900, 1930s, stamps 1882–97, paper bags 1930s, jigsaw 1930s, book mark early 20th cent., competitor's brands 1850s, papers and literature 1920s–30s, proofs 1937, hoarding agreement 1921–24, audio cassettes of radio broadcasts and records 1930s–50s; legal opinion on advertising practice 1891; correspondence re advertising policy 1952, 1954; sales services guide c.1991; promotional booklets 1929–37; publicity: brochures 1902, n.d., poster n.d., calendars 1902, 1905; press cuttings books 1870s–1913; press cuttings 1892, 1931, 1945, n.d.; overseas label specimens 1945–46; stencils 1840s, n.d.; printing blocks n.d.; title deeds re factory at Brooklyn, New York 1902–27; leases: Sutton John Cross 1876, Canadian factory 1927; St Helens factory papers: articles of agreement and building contract 1946, licences 1946–48, statistical information 1949–52, plans 1947–51, scheme to prevent flooding 1938–45, wartime operations 1943–48, storage 1945–52, repairs and extension 1946–53, diesel and electricity plant 1947–48, office furniture 1949, new buildings and refurbishments 1954–57, remodelling of 'A' building 1957–61, sprinkler system 1946–48, final costings 1950, photographs of construction works 1946–49; architectural plans: 1886–87, 1934, 1948, 1956, factory at Water Street 1948; photograph survey of St Helens premises 1994; inventory of plant, machinery and equipment 1941–43; card commemorating opening of research laboratories 1947; rent book 1884; miscellaneous papers re land and property 1953–54; works of art valuation 1990, 1994; wages book 1886–90; papers re factory wages 1958–60; travellers earnings and statistics 1934–42; employees' handbook 1951; employment records 1914–19; staff advertisement 1870s; staff character reference 1915; personnel file re transfer of Maclean's Ltd staff to St Helen's 1959; information re careers exhibition 1954; induction pack 1990s; lists of employees attending pleasure excursions 1893–1901; papers re appointment and retirement of Miss Oldham, first female employee of company 1917, 1954; papers re silver jubilee dinner 1953; retirement presentation for Mr Moss 1929;

programme of miscellaneous staff function n.d.; New Year message from directors 1937; general information file 1930s; *SmithKline Beecham Communique*, managers' magazine 1989–93; *R&D News Special* 1992; staff newspapers: *Beecham Group Journal* 1960–61, *Beecham News* 1987; correspondence: employment matters and employees 1925, 1950s–60s, milk extract drinks 1925, printing contract 1884, closed shop for chemists 1914, J F Allan 1982; photographs: Philip Hill n.d., staff 1920s, 1950s, 1987–88, factories, premises and production 19th cent., 1870–1980s, overseas premises 1900, 1930s, pills and products 1890s–1970s, machinery 1926–32, 1949, 1980s, n.d., advertisements 1890s–1900s, 1930s, 1988, social events 1935–55, 1989, medicine licences 1942, miscellaneous 1900s, n.d.; private papers of Thomas Beecham senior: correspondence 1872, 1907, certificate of membership of United Society of Chemists and Druggists 1864, marriage certificate 1873, estate papers 1916–27, grave plot certificate 1907, bibles 1820, 1837; Sarah Beecham, estate papers 1877; Joseph Beecham: correspondence 1898, 1902–15, 1937, n.d., certificate from Royal Society for the Encouragement of Arts, Manufacturers and Commerce 1913, papers re divorce from Josephine Beecham c.1905, death certificate 1916, 'in memorium' booklets 1916, executors' report 1922, picture collection catalogue n.d., scrapbook n.d.; Thomas Beecham junior, correspondence, mainly re musical activities 1896–1915, n.d.; Beecham family, papers re properties 1881–99, n.d.; J C Mather, chief chemist: correspondence 1958–94, papers re Queen's award to industry 1966, inventories and valuations of equipment 1946, 1976, career booklets 1954, 1969, 1991, presss cuttings re staff 1950s–89, *Beecham Group Journal* 1960–61, *Beecham News* 1986, papers re centenary celebrations 1979–87, historical notes 1947–89, n.d.; photographs and drawings 1850s–90, 1960, n.d.; album of autographs and birthdays n.d.; historical notes 1891, 1914, 1933–68, n.d.; miscellaneous audio cassettes re company's past development, celebrations and advertising 1930s–50s, 1979, 1994–96; company music portfolios 1887–1902; packaging 20th cent.; published reference works 1903, 1913, 1927, n.d.

Anacona Motor Co: accounts book 1915–16; order book 1915–16; orders, receipts and correspondence re business transactions 1915.

Beecham (Northern) Ltd: ledgers 1950–53; sales analyses book 1951–54.

Covent Garden Estate Co Ltd: memorandum and articles of association 1918.

A F Sherley & Co Ltd: correspondence and memoranda re packaging costs and lists of products c.1942. (Ref: BP/1-3, BP/6-8)

Records 2: SmithKline Beecham plc, SmithKline Beecham House, Great West Road, Brentford TW8 9DB. Enquiries to SmithKline Beecham plc, 1 New Horizons Court, Great West Road, Brentford TW8 9EP

Minutes: directors' meetings 1928–88, general meetings 1930–59, 1990–94; committee meetings minutes 1989–95: chairman's 1964–74, executive 1949–51, 1973–88, management 1951–63, loan stock holders 1967–72, trustees of share incentive scheme 1969–78, sundry 1969–75, transfers 1970–89, sealings 1970–91, agreements under hand 1970–90, various 1972–88, banking 1973–91, marketing and technical services 1987–91, merger 1989–90; special committee of board of directors: memorandum advocating appointment of committee 1938, minutes 1939–49, resolutions 1939–62, reports 1947–49, n.d., correspondence 1939; general meeting resolutions 1936; notices of meetings 1936, 1993; chairman's general meeting speeches, proxy forms and correspondence 1936, 1954–66, n.d.; subsidiary registration certificates 1954–80; list of directors 1939–70; schedule of executive directors 1945–72; registers: directors 1930–36, 1940–89, directors' interests 1968–96, subsidiary directors' interests 1990s, members and share ledger 1966–85, shareholders 1972–96; share ledgers 1928–60s; trust deeds n.d., re unsecured loan stock 1961–72, 1978–83; summary of share transfers 1983–86; share agreement 1936; allotment letters 1936; papers re deferred and preference shares 1937–48; notices and papers sent to shareholders 1928–89; returned proxies 1936; stock exchange notice 1936, 1989–94; executive share option scheme: minutes 1983–89, option papers 1993–96; employee share scheme: minutes 1983–95 (w), seal register 1987, papers and accounts 1983–89; seal registers: 1960–67, 1986–92, subsidiaries 1980–91; papers re directors' bonus shares, interests and deaths 1936–50; annual reports and accounts 1929–96; trading and profit and loss accounts 1923; report and memorandum re organisation and financial structure 1961–62; papers re finance and capital 1989–93; certificate re profits 1928; debt recovery proceedings 1961–63; product sales analysis 1955–64; correspondence with bank 1985–89; diary extract re bank account 1928; papers re patent actions and Board of Trade 1949; representations to Pilkington Committee on broadcasting 1962; memoranda, submissions of evidence and papers to Sainsbury Committee 1960–71; agreements: W Sumner re patent pill wrapping machine 1925–29, purchase of business by Philip Hill 1928, sale of Covent Garden Estate Co Ltd 1928, *Lactopeptine* rights 1928, Holloways Pills Ltd 1929–34, advertising 1930–31, Yeast Vite Ltd 1931–34, sale of shares 1934, 1962, St Helen's Corporation 1935, Sir Thomas Beecham 1939, G S Royds 1942, Bristol-Myers Co, New York 1956, franking machine 1956–59, Prof E B Chain 1956–61, overseas subsidiaries 1956–69, various parties 1959–67, Mercedes Benz (GB) Ltd 1960, trade mark *Schlor* 1962, American Home Products Corporation 1963, Bayer AG 1973; corporate papers: proposed merger with Glaxo Laboratories Ltd 1972, group organisation and re-organisation 1961–70, 1989–95, organisation of pharmaceutical division 1962–63, UK operations 1963, 1990–92, research expenditure 1946–64, transfers and liquidations 1991–94; report on American and Canadian businesses 1888–1934; survey of changes to and growth of company since 1928, 1951; business analyses 1969, 1972; company policy and procedures 1967–70; research and manufacturing papers: steroid therapy 1961, cytotoxic drugs 1962, penicillin project 1963–64, n.d., tartaric acid 1966, chloroform in toothpaste 1970–71, future research n.d.; product leaflet 1971; prospectus advertisement 1924; advertisements for Beechams pills and powders 1955, n.d.; papers re product advertising 1938–49, 1962–65; promotional booklets 1971, n.d.; press cuttings re Sir Joseph Beecham n.d.; report and press cuttings re opening of Beecham House, Brentford 1955; mortgage bond re Beecham (Pakistan) Ltd 1965; property papers 1988–93; tenancy agreements n.d.; list of pensioners formerly employed 1961; correspondence re title deeds: organisational charts 1996–97; correspondence: shareholders 1936, W McGeorge 1962, Ministry of Health 1963–64, Prof Sir Charles Dodds 1967, history 1977, company founders 1987, Sterling Winthrop Ltd integration 1994–95, H G Lazell n.d.; general business papers and correspondence 1982–93; computer contracts 1988–93; photographs: bust of Sir Joseph Beecham n.d., Philip Hill n.d., Prof Sir Charles Dodds n.d., original pill making machine n.d., factories and workers 1920s–40s, n.d., conference c.1980s, company journals 1960–61; company publications 1898, 1906, 1953–62, n.d.; speeches and lectures given by H G Lazell 1959–69; papers re pharmaceutical industry 1965–68; historical notes 1965, 1985–87, n.d.; audio cassettes re company history 1973, n.d.; list of museum exhibits 1961; company music portfolios c.1899–1901.

Beecham Finance plc: general meetings minutes 1980–86.

Beecham Maclean Holdings Ltd: minutes: directors' and general meetings 1938–93; company prospectus 1938; register of members and share ledger 1972–74; register of members 1952–61; list of shareholders 1956; share certificates 1939–73; seal register 1979–87; agreement with Beecham Pills Ltd 1938.

Beecham Proprietary Medicines Ltd: general meetings minutes 1949–92; register of members and share ledger 1967–86; cancelled share certificates and transfer forms 1964–73; seal register 1978–91; patent documents 1964–73; correspondence file 1960–75; historical notes 1975.

Beecham Research Laboratories Ltd: general meetings minutes 1945–82; research committee meetings minutes 1948–49; proposals and correspondence re company formation 1943; register of members and share ledger 1945–84; share certificates and correspondence 1959–84; seal registers 1980–91; power of attorney 1970; accounts n.d.; memorandum and papers re organisation and costs 1943–46, 1962; company car costings 1946–47; announcement re expansion of business 1959; schedule of research programme 1944; lecture re chemotherapy 1962; paper re penicillin 1971; address by Sir Alexander Fleming at official opening 1947; catalogue offering part of Brockham Park for sale 1948; plans and papers re Worthing site 1973; correspondence: research fees 1946, salaries of directors and executive staff 1945; photographs: senior staff n.d., Brockham Park n.d, open day at Worthing factory 1967, factories and workers n.d.; memorandum re conference 1946; historical notes and articles 1958, n.d.

Bridge Pharmaceuticals Ltd: general meetings minutes 1986–92; combined register of members and share ledger 1986–88; deeds, leases, assignments, architectural drawings and correspondence re food canning business of C & E Morton Ltd acquired by Beecham Group Ltd in 1945, 1750–1940s. (Ref: Boxes 97 001-022, unlisted)

Records 3: Proprietary Association of Great Britain, Vernon House, Sicilian Avenue, London WC1A 2QH

Advertisement guardbooks: Beecham's pills 1897–1918, 1936–66, Ireland 1957–63, *Germolene* 1929–39, 1950–51, n.d., *Germaloids* 1951–67.

Records 4: History of Advertising Trust, HAT House, 12 Raveningham Centre, Raveningham NR14 6NU

Guardbooks, incl. sales figures, press cuttings, advertisements, photographs and brochures (incl. competitors) 1900–60s, n.d.; advertising material re 'Beecham's Pills' late 19th–early 20th cents; press cuttings of advertisements: proprietary medicines 1974–89, 'Dinneford's Gripe Mixture' 1976; papers, memoranda and advertising campaign material 1965–67. (Ref: SmithKline Beecham collection; Leo Burnett guardbooks, 76; AA1/1/51-2; AA1/2/14r, 19af, 24r, 28f; MEAL collection 1974–89, R10-80; JWT 107 (1965) 302 (1966) 409 (1967))

SMITHKLINE BEECHAM RESEARCH LTD
Great West Road, Brentford, Hounslow, London

Human and veterinary pharmaceutical manufacturer

History: In 1898 Ashton & Parsons Ltd was incorporated as a limited liability company to manufacture pharmaceuticals. In 1935 it was acquired by Beecham

Pills Ltd, and was renamed Phosferine Co Ltd. Its name was later changed to Phosferine Products Ltd, and in 1960 to Vitamins Ltd. In 1973 it was acquired by Beecham Group Ltd, and was renamed Beecham Research Ltd. In 1990, following the merger of Beecham Group plc and SmithKline Beckman Corporation Inc in 1989, it was renamed SmithKline Beecham Research Ltd.

Records 1: St Helens Local History & Archives Library, Gamble Institute, Victoria Square, St Helens WA10 1DY

Memoranda and articles of association 1898–1935; agreements with other companies and overseas agents 1898–1952; assignments of goodwill 1898, 1928–46; agreements re sale and directors 1929–39; register of members 1935–52; list of shareholders 1950; share certificates book 1935–46; agreement to sell shares 1936; balance sheets and trading and profit and loss accounts 1930–50; private ledgers 1935–52; cash book 1929–64; sales statistics c.1934–55; cost statements 1950–53; trade mark registration papers c.1876–1950; licences: to use trade mark *Fosforina* 1950, *Phosferine Tonic Wine* 1950; papers re trade marks 1938–49; Royalty agreements 1951; private formulae 1929–30; agreements: manufacture, exports and sales 1932–52, n.d., selling organisation of products 1951; advertising schedules 1946–50; advertisement book c.1930s–40s; advertisements 1924–25; papers re advertising costs 1929–41; correspondence: products 1938, 1952, L Rose & Co Ltd 1952–55, W E Murphy 1950–52; leases: Westfield Street, St Helens 1949, Fenwick House, High Holborn, London 1952; papers re Fenwick House lease c.1949–52; agreement re agents' commissions 1950; photograph of G H Parsons, originator of *Phosferine* 1890; miscellaneous papers 1951–55; historical notes 1946.

Records 2: SmithKline Beecham plc, SmithKline Beecham House, Great West Road, Brentford TW8 9BD. Enquiries to SmithKline Beecham plc, 1 New Horizons Court, Great West Road, Brentford TW8 9EP

General meetings minutes 1929–86; memorandum and articles of association 1990; change of name certificates 1973, 1990; agreements with Beecham Group Ltd 1952, 1964–67; annual returns 1966–70; register of members and share ledger 1967–77; share certificates and transfer forms 1964–77; seal register 1978–91; correspondence files 1947–92.

Records 3: History of Advertising Trust, HAT House, 12 Raveningham Centre, Raveningham NR14 6NU

Papers, memoranda and advertising campaign material 1966. (Ref: JWT 304 (1966) 335, 424)

SPARKS, WHITE & CO LTD
Albion Mills, East Tenter Street, London

Wholesale druggist and distillers' chemist

History: Sparks & Sons, a firm of distillers, was trading from 134 St John Street, London, in 1811. By 1818 Sparks & Evans, a firm of wholesale druggists, was trading from 14 St Peter's Hill, London. Between 1823 and 1831 the business at 134 St John Street was styled Thomas Sparks & Son, and was described variously as merchant, druggist and distillers' chemist. From 1836 until 1858 this business traded as Sparks & Co, and from 1860 as Sparks, White & Co. After 1867 the business re-located to 62 St John Street, London, and in 1909 to Albion Mills, East Tenter Street, London. It was incorporated as a limited liability company, Sparks, White & Co Ltd, in 1907, and was later acquired by Brome & Schimmer Ltd, a company of wholesale chemists. In 1993 Sparks, White & Co Ltd was renamed Brome & Schimmer Ltd, and was still trading in 1997.

Records: Guildhall Library, Aldermanbury, London EC2 2EJ

Sales ledger 1859–62, 1874–81; day books: purchases 1856–61, sales 1834–38, 1854–59; general accounts, purchases and sales arranged by drugs, spices, etc. 1836–37, 1850–57; fruit department account book, receipts and payments 1910–42; business diary 1838; outgoing letterbooks 1847–49, 1853–55. (Ref: Ms 24486-93)

SQUIRE & CO
413 Oxford Street, London

Retail chemist

History: Peter Squire (1798–1884) was apprenticed to a chemist and druggist in Peterborough from 1812 . Shortly after completing his training he was taken into the employment of Wilson, Minshull & Co, wholesale druggists of Snow Hill, London, and was soon appointed head of the wet department, and later supervisor of the manufacturing laboratory. A few years later he joined Hodgkinson, Brandram & Stead, wholesale druggists of Upper Thames Street, London, as manager of the dry department. During the 1820s he became assistant to the London operative chemist, Alexander Garden of Oxford Street, and was made temporary partner in the business until 1831, when Garden's son joined his father in partnership. Following this Peter Squire briefly moved to Paris, where he worked in M Beral's pharmacy in Rue de la Paix. In 1832 he returned to London and purchased John Scott's dispensing chemist's business at 277 (later renumbered 413) Oxford Street, trading on his own account. In 1851 he expanded his business through the purchase of Bassmead Manor, Staploe, Bedfordshire. Peter Squire was a founder member of the Pharmaceutical Society of Great Britain, and 3 times its president. Sir James Clark, physician to the Duchess of Kent and her daughter Princess Victoria, was instrumental in obtaining his appointment as chemist and druggist to the princess in 1836. He was also appointed Chemist in Ordinary to the court pharmacy by Queen Victoria in 1837, following her coronation. Peter Squire's son, Sir Peter Wyatt Squire (1847–1919), qualified at the London School of Pharmacy in Bloomsbury Square. He joined his father in the business, which was thereafter named Squire & Co, and inherited the firm when his father died. He was appointed chemist to the medical staff of the Royal household from 1867, and was knighted in 1918 for his services. Squire & Co held the formula for preparing the anointing oil that was used at the coronations of Queen Victoria, Edward VII, George V and George VI. Both Peter Squire and Sir Peter Wyatt Squire published seminal reference works relating to pharmaceutical preparations and codes of manufacturing practice. Peter Squire edited the *Companion to the British Pharmacopoeia*, which was first published in 1864, and reached its 11th edition by the time of his death, and Sir Peter Wyatt Squire edited *Pocket Companion*, which was first published in 1904. Squire & Co was acquired by Savory & Moore Ltd, dispensing chemists, London, in 1950. Savory & Moore Ltd was in turn acquired by Macarthys Ltd, later plc, in 1967. In 1992 Macarthys plc was acquired by Lloyds Chemists plc.

'Chemists to the Royal Family', *Chemist and Druggist*, 4 June 1977, 811; L Dopson, 'Chemists to Royalty. A dip into the Archives of Savory & Moore Ltd and Squire's of Oxford Street, London', *Chemist and Druggist*, 150, 6 June 1953, 570-7; R Todd, 'Peter Squire: 1798–1884', *Pharmaceutical Journal*, 232, 7 April 1984, 419-24

Records 1: GEHE UK plc, Retail Branch, Atherstone, Warwickshire. Enquiries to GEHE UK plc, Sapphire Court, Walsgrave Triangle Business Park, Coventry CV2 2TX

Prescription books for the royal family, incl. the Prince of Wales and the Empress of Russia 1835–38, 1883–87; 'royal journals', detailing purchases made by the Royal family 1893–1902.

Records 2: John Bell & Croyden Ltd, 50-54 Wigmore Street, London W1A 0AU

Royal journal for visiting royals and dignitaries 1939–48.

Records 3: Archives & Manuscripts, Wellcome Library for the History & Understanding of Medicine, 183 Euston Road, London NW1 2BE

Private ledger 1880–85; trade and personal account books 1850–54, 1870–79 (w); Peter Squire and Peter Wyatt Squire's notes on the publication of their works, incl. notes of experiments on medicinal substances 1881–1916. (Ref: MSS 4688-92)

Records 4: The Museum Curator, Royal Pharmaceutical Society of Great Britain, 1 Lambeth High Street, London SE1 7JN

Account books re Queen Victoria 1837–69 (p). (Ref: IRA.1997.060)

STABLOND LABORATORIES LTD
SmithKline Beecham House, Great West Road, Brentford, Hounslow, London

Manufacturer and distributor of drugs, medicines and other products

History: Stablond Laboratories Ltd was incorporated as a limited liability company in 1932, at Sentinel House, Southampton Row, London. Its directors were Robert Routh, Richard Millett and Alexander Kowarsky, a manufacturing chemist. It was established to manufacture and distribute cosmetics, chemicals, drugs, medicines, fertilisers and surgical appliances. In 1953 its registered offices moved to 50 Upper Brook Street, London, and in 1979 the company was acquired by Beecham Group Ltd, and its headquarters re-located to Beecham House, Great West Road, Brentford, Hounslow, London. Stablond Laboratories Ltd continued to trade under its own name until 1992, when it went into voluntary liquidation. It was dissolved in 1993.

Records: SmithKline Beecham plc, SmithKline Beecham House, Great West Road, Brentford TW8 9BD. Enquiries to SmithKline Beecham plc, 1 New Horizons Court, Great West Road, Brentford TW8 9EP

General meetings minutes 1949–92; register of members and directors n.d.; share certificates 1933–70; seal register 1991. (Ref: Box 97-014, unlisted)

STANLEYS (NOTTINGHAM) LTD
207 Radford Road, Hyson Green, Nottingham

Dispensing chemist

History: William Gill was registered as a chemist and druggist in 1883, and traded on his own account from 207 Radford Road, Nottingham, until 1935, when he retired. He was replaced in the business by Bernard William Gill, who had registered as a chemist and druggist in 1913, and who continued to trade from 207 Radford Road until 1946. In that year the business was sold and renamed Stanleys (Nottingham) Ltd.

Records: Nottinghamshire Archives & Southwell Diocesan Record Office, County House, Castle Meadow Road, Nottingham NG2 1AG

Invoices and receipts 1949–52, 1958–59; legal papers and correspondence re prosecution of Gill for incorrect drug dispensing 1900; correspondence with MPs re legal position in relation to Inland Revenue Acts and the law re drugs 1891–93; prescription books 1883–86, 1918–63; sale of poisons register 1936–78; retail price list 1904; photograph, possibly William Gill 1940. (Ref: DD 1135)

STERLING WINTHROP GROUP LTD
1 Onslow Street, Guildford, Surrey

Manufacture and marketing of pharmaceuticals, chemicals and health and hygiene products

History: In 1901 2 American pharmacists, W E Weiss and A H Diebold, established a business, Neuralgyline Co, to manufacture and market *Neuralgine*, a pain killer. The business was established at Wheeling, West Virginia, USA, and was represented in the UK by Proprietary Agencies Ltd, which imported and distributed its products. Proprietary Agencies Ltd was subsequently renamed Chas H Phillips Chemical Co Bayer Ltd. In 1907 Weiss and Diebold purchased the Sterling Remedy Co, and incorporated the 2 businesses as a limited liability company, Sterling Products Inc. During the First World War this company acquired the rights to use the name and trade marks of Friedr Bayer et Comp, Germany, including its 'miracle drug', *Aspirin*, in the USA, the UK and South America. Under the Weiss agreement of 1923, the profits of Bayer Products Ltd, the UK subsidiary company of Friedr Bayer et Comp, were divided between its German parent and Stirling Products Inc, which had been renamed Stirling Drug Inc in 1917. In 1949 the Custodian of Enemy Property disposed of the German holding of Bayer Products Ltd, which thereafter traded as a subsidiary of Sterling Drug Inc, through a UK holding company, Winthrop Group Ltd, which in 1962 was renamed Sterling Winthrop Group Ltd. In 1923 Sterling Drug Inc acquired 2 UK businesses, Scott & Turner Ltd, Newcastle upon Tyne, producers of *Andrews Liver Salts*, and Phillips Ltd, manufacturers of *Milk of Magnesia*. Claflin

Chemical Ltd was incorporated in 1953, and was subsequently renamed Sterling Drug International Ltd in 1960. It was incorporated to manufacture and deal in pharmaceutical chemicals and toiletry products. Another UK subsidiary, incorporated during the 1950s, was Winthrop Laboratories Ltd. In 1960 the business interests of Phillips Ltd and Scott & Turner Ltd were merged to form a limited liability company, Phillips, Scott & Turner Ltd which was later renamed Sterling Health Ltd, and in 1966, Winthrop Biologicals Ltd was incorporated as a limited liability company to conduct research into diagnostic agents and virological materials. In 1974 it was renamed Winthrop Pharmaceuticals Ltd and in 1981, WinPharm Ltd. In 1974 Hilton-Davis Chemicals Ltd was acquired by Sterling Winthrop Group Ltd and renamed Sterling Organics Ltd. In the same year, another subsidiary of Sterling Winthrop Group Ltd, Northern Organics Ltd, which had formerly traded as Una Pharmaceuticals Ltd, was renamed Hilton-Davis Chemicals Ltd. Other subsidiaries of Sterling-Winthrop Group Ltd were Valda Pharmaceuticals Ltd and Scientific Pharmacals Ltd. In 1992 the ethical pharmaceutical interest of Sterling Winthrop Group Ltd was acquired by the French company, Sanofi SA, and its name changed to Sanofi Winthrop Ltd. In 1995 the over-the-counter pharmaceutical business of Sterling Winthrop Group Ltd was acquired by SmithKline Beecham plc.

'Sterling Drug Inc', in T Derdak (ed), *International Directory of Company Histories*, Vol. 1 (St James Press, London, 1988) 698-700; K Holland, 'Sterling Winthrop Group Ltd, *Pharmaceutical Journal*, 19 Jan 1991, 69-72

Records 1: SmithKline Beecham plc, SmithKline Beecham House, Great West Road, Brentford TW8 9BD. Enquiries to SmithKline Beecham plc, 1 New Horizons Court, Great West Road, Brentford TW8 9EP

Minutes 1968–78, 1982–94; change of name certificate and related correspondence 1962; directors' letters of resignation 1991–94; special resolutions 1967, 1970; share transfer forms 1980–81; share certificate book n.d.; papers and agreements re sale of company to SmithKline Beecham plc 1994–95; annual reports and accounts 1980–92; accountants report 1970; papers re corporate structure 1970–71; corporate data sheets 1992–94; agreement with Tyneside Printers Ltd 1973; general correspondence 1967–76.

Bayer Products Ltd: minutes, papers and correspondence 1923–38; memorandum and articles of association 1923, 1960; combined registers of members and share ledger 1923–49; share certificates 1923–55; transferred share certificates 1929–60; private ledger n.d.; special resolutions 1960; ordinary resolutions 1955, 1959–60.

Hilton-Davis Chemicals Ltd: correspondence and papers 1961–74. (Ref: Boxes 97/012-13, 018, 022, Sterling Winthrop minutes 1-4, unlisted)

Scientific Pharmacals Ltd: minutes 1950–94; memorandum and articles of association 1938; combined register of members and directors 1981–94; annual reports and accounts 1980–92.

Scott & Turner Ltd: minutes 1908–60, memoranda and articles of association 1908–90, registers of members and share ledger 1929–60, annual returns 1960–86, annual reports and accounts 1980–87, inventory of furniture and fittings, Acton Vale 1946.

Sterling Drug International Ltd: minutes 1964–94; register of seals 1953–90; stock transfer forms and share certificates with correspondence 1961–81; annual report and accounts 1991, papers and general correspondence 1959–81.

Sterling Group Pension Trustees Ltd: minutes 1960–94, annual returns 1959–81, register of members 1957–94, combined register of members and directors 1957–94, annual reports and accounts 1980–92.

Sterling Health Ltd: minutes 1969–94, certificate of incorporation 1960, combined register of members and directors 1929–94, share transfer forms 1980–81, ordinary resolution 1961, annual reports and accounts 1980–92 (w).

Sterling Organics Ltd: annual returns 1961–82.

Valda Pharmaceuticals Ltd: share register 1923–94; share certificates book 1986; annual reports and accounts 1986–92.

WinPharm Ltd: memorandum and articles of association 1966; certificate of incorporation 1966; certificate of registration 1966; change of name certificates 1974, 1981; annual returns 1970–86; general correspondence 1965–74.

Winthrop Laboratories (Ireland) Ltd: minutes and papers 1963–74; annual returns 1956–86.

Winthrop Laboratories Ltd: directors' and general meetings minutes 1955–94; management committee meetings minutes 1957–63; memorandum and articles of association 1956; combined registers of members and share ledger 1957–94; transferred share certificates 1956–60; share certificates 1956–60; annual reports and accounts 1980–89; general correspondence 1950–54.

Records 2: History of Advertising Trust, HAT House, 12 Raveningham Centre, Raveningham NR14 6NU

Advertisements: *Andrews Liver Salts* 1979, *Milk of Magnesia* 1979–80. (Ref: MEAL collection 1979 R55, R80, 1980 R55)

STURGES
44 Market Place, Leicester

Chemist

History: William Pettifor and William Sturges were in business as chemists and druggists in Spa Place, Leicester, and Lutterworth, Leicestershire, respectively before 1868. The business at 44 Market Place, Leicester, was styled Cooper & Pettifor between 1869 and 1870, Cooper & Son by 1876 and Cooper & Sturges from 1878. Henry Cooper had been registered as a pharmaceutical chemist in 1867 and operated from 44 Market Place until sometime between 1887 and 1891, when he moved to 15 Bartholomew Place, Leicester, leaving William Sturges in sole occupancy. The Sturges family continued the business until it closed in 1961.

Records: Record Office for Leicestershire, Leicester & Rutland, Long Street, Wigston Magna, Leicester LE18 2AH

Ledger sheets 1879–84; prescription books, some incl. prescriptions for animals 1844–1928 (w); veterinary prescription book 1881–90; wages book 1878–84. (Ref: 3D61)

STURTON & SONS LTD
42 Bridge Street, Peterborough

Chemist

History: In 1833 John Sturton established a chemist's business in Bridge Street, Peterborough, on his own account. A family member, John Rowland Sturton, was registered as a pharmaceutical chemist in 1861, and by 1876 the business was styled Sturton & Sons, 42 Broad Bridge Street. John Gilbert Sturton and Frederick Sturton were registered as pharmaceutical chemists in 1888 and 1891 respectively, and thereafter the business traded as Sturton Bros. In 1937 the business was incorporated as a limited liability company, Sturton & Sons Ltd.

Shortly afterwards, a subsidiary company, Sturton (Wholesale) Journies Ltd, was incorporated, to deliver goods to shops in Norfolk, Lincolnshire and Cambridgeshire. Sturton & Sons Ltd ceased trading in 1975.

Records: Peterborough Museum & Art Gallery, Priestgate, Peterborough PE1 1LF

Balance sheet 1898; report on books and accounts 1899; accountant's report 1899; medicine orders, list of doctors supplied n.d.; prescription books, incl. mixtures and ingredients 1866–71, 1901–55 (w); composition of medicines, alphabetically indexed by compound, owned by 'Chas Hamson' n.d.

Sturton (Wholesale) Journies Ltd: list of trips taken with names and addresses of shops visited n.d.; auction catalogue, shopfittings and equipment 1975. (Ref: 1985.151)

SUMMERFIELD & SPARKES
7 Station Road, Irthlingborough, Northamptonshire

Dispensing and photographic pharmacy

History: Hugh Russell Blott was registered as a chemist and druggist in 1888, trading from High Street, Irthlingborough, Northamptonshire. In 1905 the business was acquired by a Mr Coles. In 1924 R Duncan, an agent for the Rexall Co Ltd which owned pharmacies in several towns, travelled to Irthlingborough from Aberdeen, and opened a dispensing and photographic pharmacy at 7 Station Road, named Rexall Pharmacy. He dispensed medicines for doctors in Irthlingborough, Woodford, and Little and Great Addington, Northamptonshire. Mr Coles' business in the High Street was sold to a Mr Ingham around 1949, who in turn sold the business to Summerfield & Sparkes around 1956. Rexall Pharmacy at 7 Station Road was also acquired by Summerfield & Sparkes in 1963.

Records: Northamptonshire Record Office, Wootton Hall Park, Northampton NN4 9BQ

Ledger, customers' accounts 1927–55; receipts and payments book 1930–33; purchase book 1950–63. (Ref: S 349)

HENRY SYKES & SON LTD
Huddersfield, Kirklees

Pharmaceutical wholesaler

History: In 1877 Henry Sykes registered as a chemist and druggist and established a business at Commercial Square, Moldgreen, Huddersfield, Kirklees. By 1901 the business had acquired additional premises at 218 Wakefield Road, Moldgreen, and had established a wholesale warehouse at 4 Packhorse Yard, Huddersfield. In 1910 Henry's son, Richard, joined his father in partnership, and after Henry's death, conducted the business on his own account. The business was incorporated as a limited liability company, Henry Sykes & Son Ltd, in 1944, and in 1952 Richard died. In 1960 the company moved from Packhorse Yard to larger premises at Fitzwilliam Street, and again in 1972 to warehouses at Waterloo Bridge, Huddersfield. In 1974 the company was acquired by Hills Pharmaceuticals Ltd, Burnley, Lancashire, which was itself acquired by AAH Holdings plc in 1976. Henry Sykes & Son Ltd continued to trade under its own name, as a wholesaler of pharmaceutical products, from Waterloo Bridge until 1983, when it became dormant.

Records 1: GEHE UK plc, Retail Branch, Atherstone, Warwickshire. Enquiries to GEHE UK plc, Sapphire Court, Walsgrave Triangle Business Park, Coventry CV2 2TX

General meetings minutes 1944–96; memorandum and articles of association 1944; certificate of incorporation 1944; combined register of members, directors and share ledger 1944–69; annual returns 1954–71 (w); seal register 1972–76. (Ref: Box S10, S18, current minutes, box 6)

Records 2: West Yorkshire Archive Service, Kirklees, Central Library, Princess Alexandra Walk, Huddersfield HD1 2SU

Photograph, Packhorse Yard premises c.1900; centenary dinner menu 1977. (Ref: KC423)

J A SYMONDS LTD
Ipswich, Suffolk

Chemist

History: James Alfred Symonds was registered as a chemist and druggist in 1886. He initially traded from Great Whelnetham Hall, Bury St Edmunds, Suffolk, moving to 16 Upper Brook Street, Ipswich, Suffolk, in 1893–94.

Records: Suffolk Record Office, Ipswich Branch, Gatacre Road, Ipswich IP1 2LQ

Ledgers, containing loose bills, invoices, advertisements and correspondence 1888–1919, 1931–46; prescription books 1862–94. (Ref: HC 1)

GRAHAM TATFORD & CO LTD
Grove Road, Cosham, Portsmouth

Wholesaler of pharmaceuticals and chemists' sundries

History: In 1939 Graham Tatford was employed as a pharmacist manager of a retail pharmacy in Tangere Road, Portsmouth. This shop was destroyed by a landmine in 1941, and Tatford found himself working for a year in a friend's late-night pharmacy, formulating and preparing scarce products such as hair creams and hand creams. In 1942 he established his own business, Graham Tatford & Co Ltd, which was incorporated as a limited liability company, to manufacture and distribute drugs wholesale. Retail pharmacists in the Portsmouth area were invited to subscribe for shares and around 30 did so. Initially business was carried out from Graham Tatford's house in Hayling Avenue, Portsmouth, but by 1944 larger premises had been purchased at Milford Road, Fratton, Portsmouth, incorporating offices and stock rooms. Following the establishment of the National Health Service in 1948, the company's business expanded. Graham Tatford obtained rights from a number of major manufacturers such as Allen & Hanburys Ltd and Glaxo Laboratories Ltd to distribute their growing range of modern chemotherapeutic products, and he was the first wholesaler to offer a daily delivery service in the Portsmouth area. The 1950s saw further expansion. In 1953 the company acquired Jones & King Ltd, an over-the-counter and sundries wholesaler and chief rival to Graham Tatford & Co Ltd in Portsmouth. Graham Tatford was able to capitalise on connections between Jones & King Ltd and the Isle of Wight and in 1955 established a warehouse in Ryde on the island, to supply local pharmacies with their over-the-counter and ethicals requirements. By this time, Graham Tatford & Co Ltd was no longer involved in pharmaceutical manufacture, but concentrated solely on wholesaling. By 1961 the company had again outgrown its premises and moved to a custom-built office and warehouse in Kingston Road, Portsmouth. A depot was opened at Fareham, Hampshire, in 1967, and in 1969 the company opened another warehouse at

Farnham, Surrey. Graham Tatford retired from the business in 1975, before the collapse of Resale Price Maintenance at wholesale level in 1979. This forced the company to increase its market share whilst simultaneously rationalising its physical capacity. The Farnham and Fareham depots were closed by 1981 and the company re-located to a warehouse in Cosham, Portsmouth. In 1983 the Ryde warehouse was also closed, all trade being conducted from Cosham. Sales picked up as a result of the centralisation of the business, the introduction of discounts, extended credit and territorial expansion. The company serviced an area from Brighton, Brighton & Hove, to Exeter, Devon. In the late 1980s Graham Tatford & Co Ltd diversified its services to include financial loans, the provision of computer software for organising patient medication records, and electronic point of sale and optical records storage systems. In 1992 the company joined Numark Ltd, a voluntary trading company for independent community pharmacy, and its distribution area grew to include parts of Oxfordshire, Berkshire and Buckinghamshire.

'A Pharmacist Looks at Portsmouth. Its pharmacies and pharmaceutical activities', *Chemist and Druggist*, 176, 16 Sept 1961, 302-03; M Dhalla, 'Graham Tatford & Co Ltd Celebrates its Fiftieth Anniversary', *Pharmaceutical Journal*, 24 Oct 1992, 542-3

Records 1: Graham Tatford & Co Ltd, Jackson Close, Grove Road, Cosham, Portsmouth PO6 1UII

Directors' and general meetings minutes 1942 to date; memoranda and articles of association 1979, 1981, 1989; register of directors 1942 to date; annual returns 1968 to date; register of members and share ledger 1942 to date; ledgers 1943–83; wages books 1977–78; photographs: founder, staff, premises and delivery vans 1950s–80s, 50th anniversary celebrations 1992.

Jones & King Ltd: directors' and general meetings minutes 1970–89; ledger 1978–79; photograph of handshake agreement to acquisition by Graham Tatford & Co Ltd 1953.

Records 2: City Museum & Records Office, Museum Road, Portsmouth PO1 2LJ

Business accounts ledger 1933–47. (Ref: 1426A/2)

TAYLOR BRAWN & FLOOD LTD
Bedford, Bedfordshire

Chemist

History: Robert Palgrave established a chemist's business in 1780 in the High Street, Bedford, Bedfordshire. By 1839 John and Charles Frederick Palgrave had acquired the business, and on John's death in 1840, Charles assumed sole control. Henry Stewardson, who had been Charles's assistant in the 1840s and who specialised in veterinary medicine, acquired the business in partnership with John Usher Taylor following Charles's death in 1857. This partnership was dissolved in 1866, and thereafter John Usher Taylor continued the business with John Mason Cuthbert, a dentist, as Taylor & Cuthbert. James Bennet Taylor was registered as a pharmaceutical chemist in 1879, and joined the business, which was renamed Taylor & Brawn in 1897. H S Brawn, of Stoke Goldington, Buckinghamshire, had begun an apprenticeship with Taylor in 1887. The firm acquired a number of Bedford businesses including that of Harry Thompson, registered in 1873, and Charles Hester, registered in 1875, who specialised in leather-dressing chemicals. The firm subsequently became Taylor Brawn & Flood and acquired the pharmacy of May, Allen, Brown, Ampthill, Bedfordshire, which was established prior to 1852, and that of W H Scott, Sandy, Bedfordshire, established before 1868, both of which were later sold. The business was later incorporated as a limited liability company, Taylor Brawn & Flood Ltd, and opened a mineral water factory at Kempston, Bedfordshire, which was later moved to Bedford.

H S Brawn, 'Life in an Old Bedford Pharmacy', series of 4 articles in *Bedfordshire Times*, August 1955

Records: Bedfordshire & Luton Archives & Records Service, The Record Office, County Hall, Cauldwell Street, Bedford MK42 9AP

Recipe books 19th–early 20th cents; prescription books 1831–1916 (w); indexes to prescription books n.d.; order book 1925–37; notebook of wholesalers c.1900–16; memorandum of agreement re 'Wilkinson's Ease from Pain' product sale 1912. (Ref: X 413/1-24)

DUDLEY TAYLOR (HOLDINGS) LTD
Unit 2B, Harris Road, Wedgnock Industrial Estate, Warwick, Warwickshire

Holding company for a number of retail pharmacies

History: Dudley Taylor served a pharmaceutical apprenticeship to Boots Pure Drug Co Ltd, in Truro, Cornwall, between 1934 and 1940. Following military service in the Royal Air Force during the Second World War, he purchased a small pharmacy in Brentford, Hounslow, London, in 1947, which he sold in 1948. He subsequently purchased a retail pharmacy in Kenilworth, Warwickshire, on his own account, from which he traded as Dudley Taylor Kenilworth. This business was incorporated as a limited liability company, Dudley Taylor Kenilworth Ltd, in 1984. From 1960 Dudley Taylor and his family embarked upon a programme of retail pharmacy acquisitions. Taylor acquired A H Windridge Ltd, Knowle, Solihull, incorporated as a limited liability company in 1921, in 1960 and W R Nicholas Ltd, Redruth, Cornwall, incorporated as a limited liability company in 1961, in 1961. In 1964 Taylor established a retail pharmacy in the family name, as Dudley Taylor (Bilton) Ltd. In 1963, Nicholas & Taylor Ltd, a chain of retail pharmacies in Hayle and Penzance, Cornwall, was acquired by Dudley's son, Christopher. He also incorporated his own chain of retail pharmacies, Christopher Taylor Ltd, in Cornwall, in 1976, and established a partnership, Inns & Taylor, which operated 2 more shops in Cornwall. Another of Dudley's sons, Michael Taylor, incorporated Taylors (Southam) Ltd at Southam, Warwickshire, in 1968, and in 1982, acquired Skinner & Davison Ltd of Shrewsbury, Shropshire. Further acquisitions of retail chemists by Dudley Taylor were John Adams (Chemists) Ltd, Shrewsbury, in 1966, Spackman & Mackenzie Ltd, Daventry, Northamptonshire, in 1967, Richeld Ltd, Usk, Monmouthshire, formerly W J Evans (Chemists) in 1968, N W Shillings Ltd, Torquay, Torbay, in 1971, Brian Tuck Ltd in 1976, Chappells Chemist Ltd, a chain of 3 chemist's shops in Newport in 1988 and W E Giles & Sons Ltd, a retail pharmacy of Newport, in 1913. Dudley Taylor (Holdings) Ltd was incorporated as a limited liability company in 1993, with offices at Harris Road, Wedgnock Industrial Estate, Warwick, Warwickshire, as a holding company for the many businesses the Taylor family had acquired. These subsidiaries numbered 63 in 1977. In addition, the company owns a wholesale chemist operation, Dowelhurst Ltd, which was incorporated as a limited liability company in Warwick in 1982. In 1998 the trade of A H Windridge and John Adams was taken up into Dudley Taylor Kenilworth Ltd. In 1999 the trade of Richeld was also taken up by this company.

Records: Dudley Taylor Holdings Ltd, Unit 2B, Harris Road, Wedgnock Industrial Estate, Warwick CV34 5GH

Financial statements 1993–96.

Subsidiary companies: directors' reports and annual accounts: Dowelhurst Ltd 1993–94, W E Giles & Sons Ltd 1992–96, Inns & Taylor 1987–96 (w), Maurice

Jaff Ltd 1985–87, 1991–95, W R Nicholas Ltd 1983–96 (w), N W Shillings Ltd 1983, 1986–96, Skinner & Davison Ltd 1982–92 (w), Spackman & Mackenzie Ltd 1979, 1986–96, Christopher Taylor Ltd 1985–95 (w), Dudley Taylor (Bilton) Ltd 1985–96, Taylors (Southam) Ltd 1985–96 (w), Brian Tuck Ltd 1986–87, 1991–93.

Dudley Taylor Kenilworth Ltd: directors' reports and annual accounts 1983–96 (w); prescription book 1948–58; photographs: Dudley Taylor 1938, premises 1950s.

Chappells Chemist Ltd: report and financial statements 1986.

Nicholas & Taylor Ltd: directors' reports and annual accounts 1982–96 (w); architectural drawings 1988.

TAYLOR, GIBSONS LTD
Newcastle upon Tyne

Chemist and druggist

History: Taylor Gibson and Christopher Myers formed a partnership, styled Taylor, Gibson & Myers, in Newcastle upon Tyne, to trade as chemists and druggists in 1800. By 1876 the firm was named Gibson Taylor & Co and was trading from Biggmarket, Newcastle upon Tyne. The business was subsequently incorporated as a limited liability company, Taylor, Gibsons Ltd and was still trading in 1959.

Records: Tyne & Wear Archives Service, Blandford House, Blandford Square, Newcastle upon Tyne NE1 4JA

Deed of co-partnership between Taylor Gibson and Christopher Myers 1800; prescription books 1879–1959; recipe books 1876–79, 1908–14. (Ref: 113)

TEUCER LTD
165-167 High Street & 52 Alexandra Street, Southend-on-Sea

Manufacturing and retail chemist

History: Between 1906 and 1907 Sydney Francis Body acquired the chemist's business of A G Doble, Station Road, Westcliff-on-Sea, Southend-on-Sea. He traded as a chemist and druggist from these premises, under the business name S F Body, and also began manufacturing pharmaceutical products under the brand name Teucer. In 1920 Teucer Ltd was incorporated as a limited liability company, and traded from 165 High Street, Southend-on-Sea. In 1928 S F Body was re-located to 52 Alexandra Street, Southend-on-Sea. Sydney Francis Body was president of the Southend-on-Sea Association of Pharmacists from around 1917, and was also a member of the Pharmaceutical Society Organisation Committee during and after the First World War.

Records: Essex Record Office, Southend Branch, Central Library, Victoria Avenue, Southend-on-Sea SS2 6EX

Papers re formation of company incl. draft name and articles of association 1920; ledger 1954–55; bank passbook 1920–23; formula books containing product labels, product descriptions, costings and retail prices 1924–53; prescription books: Station Road 1906–12, High Street 1911–14, 1931–69, Alexandra Street 1932–40, patients of Dr Gordon Hopkins, Ditton Court Road, Westcliff 1920–40; rules, with lists of officers and members, Southend-on-Sea Association of Pharmacists 1917; papers re re-organisation of the Pharmaceutical Society of Great Britain 1917; Pharmaceutical Society Organisation Committee: minutes 1917–19, report 1918; photographs: first and subsequent annual dinners of the Southend Chemists Association 1911, c.1935, S H Body c.1955; S H Body's memoirs of pupilage with James George Netting, Plymouth, pharmaceutical chemist 1896–1900. (Ref: D/F 41)

THERMOGENE CO LTD
St Helens

Proprietary medicine manufacturer

History: Thermogene Co Ltd was incorporated as a limited liability company in 1909, to acquire the business of Thermogene Co, Queen's Road, Haywards Heath, West Sussex, which manufactured the medicated wool *Thermogene*. In 1929 Thermogene Co Ltd was acquired jointly by J C Eno Ltd and International Proprietaries Ltd, whereupon its registered offices re-located to 160 Piccadilly, London. In 1938 it was acquired by Beecham Pills Ltd, following that company's acquisition of J C Eno Ltd in the same year, and its registered offices moved again, to 68 Pall Mall, London. *Thermogene* was manufactured at Haywards Heath until 1953, when production moved to the St Helen's plant of Beecham Group Ltd. Thermogene Co Ltd was dissolved in 1956.

Records 1: St Helens Local History & Archives Library, Gamble Institute, Victoria Square, St Helens WA10 1DY

Minutes 1927–35; particulars of directors and managers 1939–53; papers re liquidation of company 1954; annual returns books 1935–51; register of members 1919–53; share certificate book 1926–53; private ledgers 1938–52; notes re debits and credits 1949–53; papers re manufacturing processes 1950–53; report re visit to Brussels 1949–55; papers: overseas trade 1953–62, Haywards Heath premises c.1954–63. (Ref: BP/4/10)

Records 2: Public Record Office, Ruskin Avenue, Kew, Richmond TW9 4DU

Memorandum and articles of association 1909; certificate of incorporation 1909; agreement to purchase Thermogene Co 1909; special resolutions 1909–56 (w); annual returns 1931–53 (w); declaration of compliance with Companies Acts 1909; copies of registers of directors or managers 1909, 1919–20, 1935; particulars of changes of directors or managers 1935–53 (w); notices of location of registers of members 1948, 1953; summaries of share capital and shares 1910–30; agreement re shares 1919; extraordinary resolution re dividends 1929; returns of allotments 1910, 1919; register of particulars of mortgages and charges n.d.; notice of debentures created 1927; certificate of registration of debentures 1921; directors' reports, profit and loss accounts and balance sheets 1948–52; statement of nominal capital 1909; statement of increase in nominal capital 1919; declaration of solvency 1954; notice of situation of registered office 1909; notices of change in situation of registered office 1929, 1939; notice of appointment of liquidator 1954; liquidator's statement of account 1956; affidavits verifying liquidators' statements 1955–56; list of amounts payable to contributors 1955; return of final winding-up meeting 1956. (Ref: BT31/36871/101072)

THOMAS FAMILY
Penrallt Street, Machynlleth, Powys

Chemist, grocer and draper

History: This was the family business of Owen and Susanah Thomas and their son John. John Thomas was trading as a chemist and druggist in Machynlleth, Powys, from prior to 1868 until at least 1895.

Records: National Library of Wales, Department of Manuscripts & Records, Aberystwyth SY23 3BU

Ledgers and account books 1800–86; day books 1830–92; miscellaneous accounts and memoranda of Owen Thomas and Susanah Thomas 1807–32; miscellaneous accounts 1812–80 (w); invoice book 1855–64; stock book 1860; credit book 1871–84; register of licenses 1872–74; list of books lent 1814–15; particulars of money borrowed n.d.; notebook containing recipes 1829–30; exercise books of John Thomas and others, 1793, 1831–64; invoices and receipts, incl. letters 1839–1901; poetry and anecdotes book compiled by John Thomas 1860.

R McLAREN TODD LTD
Syston, Leicestershire

Chemist

History: Robert Alexander McLaren Todd was apprenticed to Alfred Berridge, chemist and druggist of 11 Cheapside, Leicester, in 1892. Following this, he established himself in business in Syston, Leicestershire, in 1905, at premises which had been occupied by chemists or druggists since John Wilde established a chemist and grocer's business there in 1849. McLaren remained in business at Syston until 1947, when he was succeeded by his son, Douglas. In 1977 the business was incorporated as a limited liability company, R McLaren Todd Ltd, and ceased trading in 1983. In 1985 it was removed from the register of companies.

Records: Record Office for Leicestershire, Leicester & Rutland, Long Street, Wigston Magna, Leicester LE18 2AH

Ledger 1963–65; day book 1905–13; cash book 1905–13; accounts 1944–46; bills for shopfittings 1924–37; agreement for supply of Rexall remedies in Syston with United Drug Co, Boston, USA 1914; buyer's order book n.d., c.1930; prescription books 1905–68; prescription envelopes, personal notes and miscellaneous papers 1919–41; sale of poisons register 1901–26; dangerous drugs registers 1926–78; apprenticeship indentures: R A McLaren Todd 1892, George Henry Rimmington 1908; apprenticeship rules 1881; advertisements: R A McLaren Todd's medicines n.d., c.1900–10, A Berridge c.1900; photographs: R A McLaren Todd c.1900, chemist's shop c.1921–22, Syston 1907–71, Leicester Insurance Committee, pre-inauguration of NHS 1948; National Health Insurance Committee: accounts 1913–15, drug tariff c.1940; religious notes/sermons of R A McLaren Todd 1912; pamphlets and press cuttings re history of local area and history of pharmacy 1932–39, 1954–74; record of grants of burial rights in Leicester Corporation Cemetery freehold graves 1895–1950;

auction details and history of Sturges' chemist's shop in Market Street 1960, n.d. (Ref: DE 2547)

TREMLETT HOLDINGS LTD
94-98 Fratton Road, Fratton, Portsmouth

Retail chemist and dispensing pharmacist

History: Percy Gordon Tremlett came to Fratton, Portsmouth, from the Isle of Wight in the late nineteenth century to serve his apprenticeship with the firm of Brews & Macintosh, pharmacists. In 1901, once qualified, he opened his own shop at 2a Fratton Road, Fratton, where he worked as a dispensing pharmacist, optician and dentist. Tremlett's son, Richard Gordon Tremlett, began his apprenticeship in his father's shop in 1925 at the age of 18. In 1932 he too opened a shop in Portsmouth, at 1 New Road East, Copnor. In addition to managing his own business, he assumed control of his father's shop from 1934, when his father fell ill, and in 1945 acquired a third shop at 117 Winter Road, Southsea, Portsmouth. In 1947 the business was incorporated as a limited liability company, Tremlett (Chemists) Ltd, under the tripartite directorship of Richard, his mother Annie May Tremlett and the family solicitor, Kenneth Frederick Allen. A second family company, R G Tremlett Ltd, was incorporated in 1952 with Richard and his wife, Molly Doreen Tremlett, as directors. During the 1950s and 1960s this company acquired a number of premises, including a stock room at 2b Fratton Road. In 1969 a subsidiary of R G Tremlett Ltd was incorporated, Tremletts Pharmacies Ltd, to acquire 3 chemist's shops in the Portsmouth area. All were purchased in 1969, although one, in Queen's Parade, was subsequently sold in 1971. In 1974 the New Road East business was sold to Ian Tremlett, who traded from that address as Tempo Drug Store. Tremlett (Chemists) Ltd also established a chemist's shop at 20 West Street, Porchester, Portsmouth, in 1974, and purchased 90-98 Fratton Road, Fratton. In the same year the business and premises of R G Tremlett Ltd at 2a Fratton Road were sold to Tremlett (Chemists) Ltd. In 1975 Richard Tremlett transferred his shares in Tremlett (Chemists) Ltd to his sons, Ian and William, and Annie May Tremlett retired as company secretary. The company re-located from 20 to 44 West Street, Porchester, in 1980. In 1983 a major re-structuring of the family business resulted in the acquisition by Tremlett (Chemists) Ltd of the shares of R G Tremlett Ltd and its subsidiary, Tremlett Pharmacies Ltd. Richard Tremlett and his wife Molly retired from the business at this juncture. Tremlett (Chemists) Ltd was renamed Tremlett Holdings Ltd, and R G Tremlett Ltd was renamed Tremletts Chemists Ltd operating as the trading company for the group. The 2 retail chemist shops at 15 Albert Road, Southsea, and 144-146 Forton Road,

Gosport, Hampshire, which had been owned by Tremletts Pharmacies Ltd, were transferred to Tremletts Chemists Ltd, and Tremletts Pharmacies Ltd became a dormant company. In 1985 Tremletts Chemists Ltd acquired the business of Bridgemary Pharmacies Ltd of 182 Nobles Avenue, Bridgemary, Gosport, Hampshire, and at about the same time sold the 144-146 Forton Road business. Three further premises were acquired by the company after 1991.

R Tremlett, *Sixty Two Years a Fratton Pharmacist* (WEA Local History Group, Portsmouth, c.1985); 'A Pharmacist Looks at Portsmouth. Its pharmacies and pharmaceutical activities', *Chemist and Druggist*, 176, 16 Sept 1961, 301

Records: Tremletts Chemists Ltd, 94-98 Fratton Road, Fratton, Portsmouth PO1 5BZ

Directors' and general meetings minutes 1947 to date; memorandum and articles of association 1947; certificate of incorporation 1947; combined register of members and share ledger 1947-77; annual returns 1981-82; share certificate book 1947-82; list of securities, with correspondence 1980; statements of account, incl. profit and loss account and balance sheet 1962-79 (w); private ledgers 1967-82; formulae book late 1940s; dangerous drugs registers 1950-71; salaries and wages book 1964-65; photographs, mainly shopfronts and interiors c.1940s-60s.

Tempo Drug Store: statements of account, incl. trading and profit and loss account, and balance sheet 1974-79 (w); ledger 1973-74.

R G Tremlett: trading account and balance sheet 1946.

Tremletts Chemists Ltd: directors' and general meetings minutes 1952 to date; memorandum and articles of association 1952; combined register of members and share ledger 1952-84; annual returns 1981-82; share certificate book 1952-53, 1978; list of securities, with correspondence 1980; statements of account, incl. trading and profit and loss account and balance sheet 1962-79 (w); private ledgers 1967-85; recipe book c.1970s; prescription books 1957-73; private prescriptions 1986-91; daily and monthly prescription numbers books 1974-86; branch purchase, insurance, building and repair work with related correspondence and plans 20th cent.; miscellaneous papers, press cuttings, correspondence and photographs 1927 to date.

Tremletts Pharmacies Ltd: directors' and general meetings minutes 1969-80; memorandum and articles of association 1969; certificate of incorporation 1969;

combined register of members and share register 1969–82; annual returns 1981–82; share certificate book 1969–70, 1982; statements of account, incl. trading and profit and loss account and balance sheet 1969–79 (w); private ledgers 1970–82.

G TURNER (BIGGLESWADE) LTD
63 High Street, Biggleswade, Bedfordshire

Chemist

History: William Henry Barker traded as a 'chymist and druggist, oil and colourman, inventor and proprietor of Barker's sheep and lamb dip' from 63 High Street, Biggleswade, Bedfordshire, between 1830 and the early 1850s. By 1853 he had taken Henry Newbery into partnership. In 1864 Newbery assumed control of the business, which traded as a wholesale and retail chemist. The business was acquired by Reuben Caborn, chemist and druggist, oil and colourman, during the late 1860s, and by 1876 was owned by George Neal Maxwell, who registered as a chemist and druggist in Northampton, Northamptonshire, in 1868. He operated as a dispensing and family chemist, dentist, wholesale druggist, agricultural, veterinary and manufacturing chemist, homeopathic medicine vendor, pharmaceutical manufacturer, drysalter, oil and colourman and photographic material dealer. By 1877 George Maxwell had moved to Finsbury Park, London, and the business at High Street, Biggleswade, was operated by John Evans, who registered as a pharmaceutical chemist in 1880. The firm was styled Evans & Son from 1892. Thomas Dexter Robinson, who was registered as a pharmaceutical chemist in Northfleet, Kent, in 1876, acquired the business around 1894, and in 1898 ownership passed to George Turner, who moved to Biggleswade from Longton, Stoke-on-Trent. In 1948 the business was incorporated as a limited liability company, G Turner (Biggleswade) Ltd, and was dissolved in 1968.

Records: Bedfordshire & Luton Archives & Records Service, The Record Office, County Hall, Cauldwell Street, Bedford MK42 9AP

Directors' meetings minutes 1949–68; account books: annual accounts and summarised receipts and payments 1949–66, accounts, with balance sheets 1959–68; ledgers: individuals' accounts 1855–60, 1880–88, 1918–42, institutions' accounts 1915–41; day books, credit sales 1869–1908 (w); cash books, daily sales 1877–1910; receipt and payment books: Biggleswade 1880–1906, 1925–39, Turner, Staffordshire 1892–97; purchases notebook c.1890–95; wholesalers' vouchers, Turner: Staffordshire 1895–98, Biggleswade 1898–1904; wholesalers account book, Turner, Staffordshire 1891–96; prescription books: Biggleswade and district 1825–1966 (w), Cheadle, Longton, etc., Staffordshire 1872–98; recipe books c.1821–33, 1881, early–20th cent.; notebooks, recipes for prescriptions n.d., 20th cent.; catalogue of photographic apparatus, materials and chemicals, Thomas Turner, Longton n.d.; product advertisements n.d.; letter requesting ointment 1911; label albums: 1824–n.d., Turner, Staffordshire 1864–n.d., Turner, Biggleswade 1898–1966, non-customised pharmaceutical bottling and packaging c.1960, box for sundries and non-pharmaceuticals n.d.; memorandum, Thomas Turner to Longton public n.d.; dental certificate of Thomas Turner, Longton 1878; letter of condolence to Mr Turner on son's death [18]73; probate of will of Charles Henry Smith of Manchester 1869; printed miscellanea 1890, 1900, n.d. (Ref: X 346/1-115)

R C TURNER
Quinton Pharmacy, 67 Halesowen Road, Quinton, Dudley

Pharmacist

History: Ronald Charles Turner was born in 1916 in Harborne, Birmingham. He qualified as a pharmaceutical chemist in 1937 and then worked briefly with 5 chemists in the West Midlands area before purchasing his own pharmacy at 67 Halesowen Road, Quinton, Dudley, in 1939. He continued to trade from the premises until 1988 when he retired. He died in 1995.

Records: Dudley Archives & Local History Service, Mount Pleasant Street, Coseley, Dudley WV14 9JR

Statements of account 1951–86; weekly account books 1960–87; day books 1953–59; account book of tax calculations 1981–87; invoices and receipts 1975–87; bank statements 1958–60, 1976–87 (w); valuation of stock certificate 1987; statement of sums payable for prescription orders 1986–87; register of controlled drugs and poisons 1939–87; prescription registers 1939–69; private prescriptions 1981–87; specifications and estimate for shopfront 1967; plan for shopfront 1967. (Ref: RCT/1-3)

TURTON'S CHEMISTS LTD
Greenside House, Tudhoe, Spennymoor, Durham

Chemist

History: In 1939 R Cubey Ltd was incorporated as a limited liability company at 17 Church Street, Bowland Terrace, Blaydon, Gateshead, to trade as a retail chemist. In 1954 the company was acquired by Joseph Cecil Turton Roberts, and renamed Turton's Chemists Ltd in 1955. In 1995 the company was acquired by UniChem plc which itself merged in 1997 with Alliance Sante SA to become Alliance UniChem plc. By 1999 Turton's Chemists Ltd was dormant, its business and assets having been transferred to E Moss Ltd.

Records: Alliance UniChem plc, UniChem House, Cox Lane, Chessington KT9 1SN

Directors' and general meetings minutes 1940–95; change of name certificate 1955; combined register of members and share ledger 1940–95; share transfer forms 1974; share certificate book 1940–95; share certificates 1995.

C E UNDERHILL & SONS LTD
17-18 Fore Street, Callington, Cornwall

Retail pharmacy and pharmaceutical distributor

History: The founder of this business, Cyril Edgar Underhill, was apprenticed between 1893 and 1898 to the firm W Woods & Son, chemists and druggists, 50 Bedford Street, Plymouth. Upon qualifying, he joined R D Doble in partnership, in his firm, H T Doble & Son, Tavistock, Devon. This firm owned 4 retail chemist shops, 2 in Devon, at Tavistock and Yelverton, and 2 in Cornwall, at Gunnislake and Callington. The Gunnislake business, which was based in Commercial Street, traded under the name, Siviour. In 1904 C E Underhill acquired the businesses of Siviour at Gunnislake and H T Doble & Son at Callington on his own account. From the latter, he traded as a chemist, veterinary chemist and dentist. In 1908 the Callington business was incorporated as a limited liability company, C E Underhill & Co Ltd, following which C E Underhill's sons, Cyril Edgar and Ernest Russell, joined their father as company directors. In 1927 C E Underhill, the younger, established a chemist's business on his own account at 107 Fore Street, Saltash, Cornwall, which was renumbered 19 Fore Street in 1986. His father and Ernest Russell managed C E Underhill & Co Ltd at Fore Street, Callington and Siviour at Gunnislake. In 1930 C E Underhill & Co Ltd was renamed C E Underhill & Sons Ltd, incorporating the Callington and Saltash businesses, and Siviour was sold. In 1947 the Callington premises were expanded with the purchase of a tobacconist shop and until 1975 C E Underhill & Sons Ltd traded as wholesalers of tobacco as well as retail pharmacists. In addition, the company operated as pharmaceutical wholesalers, supplying drugs to rural doctors. During the 1960s Siviour was re-acquired by C E Underhill & Sons Ltd, having been incorporated as a limited liability company, Siviour Ltd. This company traded as a drug store, without a dispensary, and was supplied with stock by C E Underhill & Sons Ltd at Callington. Siviour Ltd was something of a liability, receiving a warning in 1967 for using counter bags carrying the title 'chemist' without due licence, and in 1972 the business was sold to William Price. In 1957 C E Underhill & Sons Ltd acquired a pharmacy at 139 Callington Road, Burraton, Saltash, and from 1962 operated an off-licence at the back of the chemist shop in Fore Street, Callington. In 1978 David John Underhill, the son of Cyril Edger, the younger, replaced his father as manager of the 19 Fore Street, Saltash branch, and following the death of his uncle in 1989 and of his father in 1990, became sole director of C E Underhill & Sons Ltd.

Records 1: C E Underhill & Sons Ltd, 17-18 Fore Street, Callington PL17 7AE

Directors' and general meetings minutes 1908 to date; directors' meetings minutes 1978; memorandum and articles of association 1908, 1930; special resolution re change of name 1930; correspondence re acquisition of businesses and accommodation 1957–58; combined share register 1908 to date; share certificates 1977–78, 1986, 1989; correspondence and valuations re C E Underhill's shareholdings 1956–60; letter re transfer of shares from C E Underhill to his son 1977, directors' reports, trading and profit and loss accounts and balance sheets, Callington and Saltash 1960–83 (w); ledgers 1958–61, 1968–79; journal 1953–82; day books 1963–93; customer account book 1954–61; bank statements: Burraton and Saltash 1961–63, Callington 1960–63, 1969–84; bank deposit books, Callington and Saltash 1980–81; VAT book, Callington, Saltash and Burraton 1973–83; certificate of registration for VAT 1973, 1976; income tax remittance cards 1957–74; correspondence re taxation and compilation of annual accounts 1950–60; insurance policies 1947–61; drug room book n.d.; dangerous drugs registers 1948–74; sale of poisons registers. 1968–87, n.d.; prescription books 1933–92; NHS prescription number forms with correspondence 1949–77; sources of supplies book 1962; oxygen supplies records 1968–93; suppliers' bills and invoices 1962–63; valuations of stock in doctors' dispensaries 1957s–80s; doctors' day books 1986–93; medicine labels 1940s–50s; correspondence: distribution of pharmaceuticals 1960s, Pharmaceutical Society of Great Britain re labelling of medicines 1967, application to operate off-licence 1962; press cuttings 1970s–90s; mortgage deeds re Callington, Saltash and Gunnislake shops 1905, 1924–33, 1947–58, 1976; lease with plans and correspondence 1989–90; notice that Callington premises are listed historic buildings 1986; correspondence: valuations of properties 1955, building works at Saltash 1950–51, adjoining accommodation at

Commercial Street 1960s, renaming and renumbering 1986; maps of Callington 1906–07, 1952; agreements: Western National Omnibus Co Ltd 1964, insurance committee for the county of Cornwall 1913; staff books 1982–90; salaries cheques 1960–63; correspondence: staff recruitment 1957, 1960s–80s, wages 1966, Siviour Ltd 1968; photographs: Underhill family 1940s, 1952, 60th anniversary window display 1980s; C E Underhill's private papers: apprenticeship indenture 1893, testimonials 1917, birth certificate 1878, will 1955, private bank book n.d.; E R Underhill's private papers: certificate of registration with Pharmaceutical Society of Great Britain 1927, certificate of qualification as chemist and druggist 1927; D R Wakeford's certificate of registration as pharmaceutical chemist 1956; D J Underhill's personal papers and student notebooks 1961–66; papers re wills and estates: C E Underhill 1966–67, Mrs A F Underhill 1940.

Siviour Ltd: trading, profit and loss account and balance sheet 1950–55, 1961–72; accounts 1967; monthly accounts sheets for goods supplied by C E Underhill & Sons Ltd 1961–63, 1969–70; invoices and correspondence from Plymouth accountants 1961–62, 1970–71; bank statements 1960–62, 1969–70; bills and invoices: contractors 1961–63, 1969–70, Tamar Brewery, Devonport 1961–62, utilities 1961–64, 1969–70; financial correspondence: sale of company 1968, 1972, annual accounts 1962–70; notice of assessment for corporation tax 1969; income tax remittance cards 1962–70; tax inspectors' receipts re national insurance contributions 1961–63, 1969–70; excise licence for retailer's off-licence 1963–72; retail licences for methylated spirits 1963–70; certificates and list of persons entitled to sell poisons 1961–70; correspondence re contravention of Pharmaceutical Society of Great Britain's rules re labelling 1961, 1967; certificate of valuation of stock 1963; staff recruitment: records 1960s, correspondence 1969–70.

Records 2: C E Underhill & Sons Ltd, 19 Fore Street, Saltash PL12 6AF

Prescription books 1927 to date; medicines labels c.1940s–70s; photograph of premises c.1980s; certificate of registration of D J Underhill as pharmaceutical chemist 1966.

UNICHEM (SHEFFIELD) LTD
3 Snow Lane, Sheffield

Wholesale chemist

History: The firm originated as the wholesale chemist business of John Henry and Nellie Holden, trading from 39 Carver Street, Sheffield. The business was incorporated as a limited liability company, J H Holden Ltd, in 1958 and was acquired by UniChem Ltd in 1971. In 1973 the company was renamed UniChem (Sheffield) Ltd and was wound up in 1982. It was removed from the register of companies in 1985.

Records: Alliance UniChem plc, UniChem House, Cox Lane, Chessington KT9 1SN

Directors' and general meetings minutes 1958–82; notice of an extraordinary general meeting 1971; memorandum and articles of association 1958; certificate of incorporation 1958; change of name certificate 1973; acquisition papers 1971; combined register of members and share ledger 1958–71; annual accounts 1980.

VENO DRUG CO LTD
55-56 Pall Mall, London

Proprietary medicine manufacturer

History: Veno Drug Co Ltd was incorporated as a limited liability company in 1924, and in 1925 was acquired by Beecham Pills Ltd. It manufactured proprietary medicines including 'Dr Cassells Tablets', 'Venos Lightning Cough Cure' and *Germolene*. Its factory and offices were situated in Manchester, and Beecham Pills Ltd acted as selling agents for its products. During the 1940s its head office re-located to Pall Mall, London.

Records 1: St Helens Local History & Archives Library, Gamble Institute, Victoria Square, St Helens WA10 1DY

Directors' meetings minutes 1939–49; memoranda and articles of association 1925–48; certificate of incorporation 1932; business papers 1908, 1924–27; agreements: shareholdings 1927, sale of assets 1924; applications: ordinary shares 1925, deferred shares 1925; accounts 1948–49; private ledgers 1929–50; net profit certificates 1914–24; sales summary book 1949–51; register of trade marks and trade names c.1905–60s; assignment of trade marks and patents 1922, 1925, 1939; licence for use of unpatented secret 1919; notice of opposition to trade marks 1921; undertakings re use of trade names 1924, 1927; agreement re sale of Lady Veno's rights 1924; agreement of rights to agency for sale of Phensic Ltd's products 1951; certificates of analysis of drugs 1937; information sheets re use of *Germolene* n.d.; pamphlet re *Phensic* n.d.; advice leaflet re home treatments n.d.; notes re formula for Dr Cassell's tablets 1940; advertising graphics n.d.; advertisement 1919; papers re premises: Lund Street, Cornbrook, Manchester 1943–53, Chester Road, Stretford, Manchester 1949–52; claim forms for properties at Lund Street and Chester Road 1949; report re possible amalgamation with Beechams Pills Ltd at Chester Road, Manchester or Westfield Street, St Helens 1949; agreements: lights and building 1927, service 1926, 1929, appointment of chief chemist 1925; photographs: plant and premises 1920–40, 1949, n.d., advertisements n.d.; extract from Act of Parliament re Middlesex Hospital 1836; agreement with Middlesex hospital re gift for cancer research 1922. (Ref: BP/4/11)

Records 2: SmithKline Beecham plc, SmithKline Beecham House, Great West Road, Brentford TW8 9BD. Enquiries to SmithKline Beecham plc, 1 New Horizons Court, Great West Road, Brentford TW8 9EP

Trade mark agreement with Phensic Ltd and Fissan Ltd 1936; advertising agreements with G S Royds 1937; insurance assignment 1937.

Records 3: Proprietary Association of Great Britain, Vernon House, Sicilian Avenue, London WC1A 2QH

Advertisements 1935–48.

Records 4: History of Advertising Trust, HAT House, 12 Raveningham Centre, Raveningham NR14 6NU

Advertisements: *Germolene* and *Germaloids* 1974–89, *Venos* 1979. (Ref: MEAL collection 1974–89, R10-80)

VESTRIC LTD
Hampton Court, Tudor Road, Manor Park, Runcorn, Halton

Pharmaceutical wholesaler

History: Vestric Ltd was incorporated as a limited liability company in 1966, following the merger of the wholesale distribution interests of Glaxo Group Ltd and British Drug Houses Group Ltd. This combined interest created a company with 36 trading branches, amongst which were many long-established companies including James Woolley Sons & Co Ltd, Lofthouse & Saltmer Ltd and Bradley & Bliss Ltd. Following the acquisition of British Drug Houses Group Ltd by Glaxo Group Ltd in 1968, Vestric Ltd became a wholly-owned subsidiary of

Glaxo Group Ltd until 1985, when it was sold to AAH Holdings plc. Before this acquisition, AAH Holdings plc was concerned primarily with the distribution of solid fuel, but was taking an increasing interest in developing a national wholesale pharmaceutical group. At the time of its purchase of Vestric Ltd, AAH Holdings plc owned 4 pharmaceutical wholesaling companies, Hills Pharmaceuticals Ltd, Northern Pharmaceuticals Ltd, Herbert Ferryman Ltd and Mawson & Proctor Pharmaceuticals Ltd. The purchase of Vestric Ltd gave AAH plc national coverage, and created a large group of subsidiary wholesaling companies, which were merged to form AAH Pharmaceuticals Ltd, with head offices at West Lane, Runcorn, Halton. In 1995 AAH plc was acquired by GEHE AG, Germany, and Vestric Ltd became a wholly-owned subsidiary of this company. By 1999 Vestric Ltd was a dormant company.

M Worling, *Vestric, The First Twenty Years 1966–86* (Vestric, Runcorn, 1986)

Records 1: GEHE UK plc, Retail Branch, Atherstone, Warwickshire. Enquiries to GEHE UK plc, Sapphire Court, Walsgrave Triangle Business Park, Coventry CV2 2TX

General meetings minutes 1966–96; combined register of members, directors and share ledger 1977–88; register of seals 1965–80; sealing committee meetings minutes 1985–89; Vestric Pensions Ltd, combined register of members, directors and share ledger 1985–91. (Ref: Box S18)

Records 2: Dr Peter M Worling, The Grange, 29 Fernielaw Avenue, Edinburgh EH13 0EF

Publicity brochure 1965; price list n.d.; draft report re use of Ford vans n.d.

G E WAKEFIELD
55 High Street, Hucknall & 576 Mansfield Road, Sherwood, Nottingham & 7 Guildhall Street, Lincoln, Lincolnshire

Chemist

History: Edwin Widdowson established a chemist and druggist's business in Market Place, Bulwell, Nottingham, prior to 1868. By 1877 he had opened a second shop at 55 High Street, Hucknall, Nottingham, which between 1888 and 1891 was acquired by Josiah Wedgwood Heath, who registered as a chemist and druggist in 1886, at High Street, Alcester, Warwickshire. Heath remained at 55 High Street until the business was acquired by Geoffrey E Wakefield some time between 1928 and 1932. Shortly afterwards, Wakefield acquired the business of William Meakin, FPS, a chemist and druggist at 538a Mansfield Road, Sherwood, Nottingham, by 1910, who had moved to 576 Mansfield Road by 1928. This business ceased trading during the early 1950s. Wakefield also acquired the business of George J Walker, 7 Guildhall Street, Lincoln, Lincolnshire, in 1971. This business had been acquired by E R Baines in 1924.

Records: Nottinghamshire Archives & Southwell Diocesan Record Office, County House, Castle Meadow Road, Nottingham NG2 1AG

55 High Street: ledgers 1871–90, day books 1888–1917 (w), stock record of purchases 1891–95, 1930, prescription books, incl. stocklists 1882–1906, prescriptions 1930–60; 576 Mansfield Road, prescription books 1928–52; 7 Guildhall Street, prescription books 1906–73. (Ref: DD673)

WALWINS OF GLOUCESTER LTD
127 Southgate Street, Gloucester, Gloucestershire

Chemist

History: James Tucker was registered as a pharmaceutical chemist in 1853, and traded from 86 Northgate Street, Gloucester, Gloucestershire, until around 1879, when his business was acquired by Evan Gresmond Hughes of Llandeilo, who registered as a chemist and druggist in 1871. The Walwin family were in business as general chemists and suppliers of photographic equipment at 127 Southgate Street, Gloucester, from around 1906. This business was incorporated as a limited liability company, Walwins (Chemists) Ltd, in 1937, and was later renamed Walwins of Gloucester Ltd. It appears to have acquired the business of Evan Hughes at 86 Northgate Street, and in 1997 was still trading.

Records 1: Gloucestershire Record Office, Clarence Row, Alvin Street, Gloucester GL1 3DW

Ledgers: sales of chemists' and photographic goods and services 1946–63, customers' accounts 1936–38; day books: Evan G Hughes 1876–77, other 1947–48; prescription books: first series, incl. J Tucker 1835–1940 (w), second series 1847–90, 1914–28, third series 1921–36; photographs of Gloucestershire buildings c.1870–1900, 1913. (Ref: D2752)

Records 2: The Museum Curator, Royal Pharmaceutical Society of Great Britain, 1 Lambeth High Street, London SE1 7JN

Agreement of Evan G Hughes to supply Ancient Order of Druids with prescriptions 1890. (Ref: IRA.1996.102)

WARD & WOODMAN LTD
39 Eastgate Street, Gloucester, Gloucestershire

Pharmaceutical chemist

History: Joseph Ward was registered as a pharmaceutical chemist in 1862 and traded at 45 Eastgate Street, Gloucester, Gloucestershire, moving to 39 Eastgate Street by 1887. In 1917 he moved to 29 Park Road, Gloucester, where he remained until he ceased to be registered in 1925. He was replaced in the Eastgate Street business by William Arthur Gelsthorpe Woodman, who had registered as a chemist and druggist in 1908, and who traded under the business name W A G Woodman. In 1935 he moved to 17 Eastgate Street, and in 1940 renamed the business Ward & Woodman. It was incorporated as a limited liability company, Ward & Woodman Ltd, in 1942, and in 1972 ceased trading.

Records: Gloucestershire Record Office, Clarence Row, Alvin Street, Gloucester GL1 3DW

Cash books, incl. wages 1914–56; petty cash book, incl. notes about business, staff and topical events 1927–41; account/order book for St Bartholomew's Hospital, London 1936–49; stock books 1920–46; stock sheets 1934–35, 1940; stock order book 1934–41; prescription books 1835–65, 1902–43 (w); papers and correspondence re shopfront alterations 1951–52; photographs of shop c.1920–57; shop window competition certificate 1950. (Ref: D3096)

WARD LABORATORIES (UK) LTD
4 New Horizons Court, Great West Road, Brentford, Hounslow, London

Importer and manufacturer of pharmaceutical products

History: Ward Laboratories (UK) Ltd was incorporated as a limited liability company in 1964, to import and manufacture pharmaceutical products. It was later acquired by Beecham Group Ltd, and continued to trade under its own name. It was dissolved in 1996.

Records: SmithKline Beecham plc, SmithKline Beecham House, Great West Road, Brentford TW8 9BD. Enquiries to SmithKline Beecham plc, 1 New Horizons Court, Great West Road, Brentford TW8 9EP

Directors' and general meetings minutes 1965–81; memorandum and articles of association 1964; register of members and directors 1970–89; seal register 1983–91; accounts 1978.

ARTHUR WEDDELL
105 High Street, Colchester, Essex

Dispensing chemist

History: Samuel Manthorp, opened a chemist's shop at 105 High Street, Colchester, Essex, in 1834. He died in 1874 and was succeeded by his son Frederic William Manthorp, who sold the business to Arthur Weddell in 1881. Arthur Weddell had registered as a pharmaceutical chemist at 29 Austen Street, Stamford, Lincolnshire, in 1873. Galenicals, pills and ointments were manufactured on the premises, 2 of the most successful were Weddell's bronchial mixture and Weddell's worm powders. Arthur Weddell died in 1925, and thereafter his widow ran the business. After a short time she handed management over to W Whyte, formerly an apprentice to Arthur Weddell, and in 1941, he became sole owner of the business. The business continued to trade under the name Arthur Weddell until its closure in 1964.

W H A C Whyte, 'Apprenticeship and all That: A record of 47 years in pharmacy', *Chemist and Druggist*, 18 May 1968, 448-9; W H A C Whyte, 'A Tendency Towards Healing', *Pharmaceutical Journal*, 21 and 28 Dec 1974, 608-9; W H A C Whyte, 'History of Pharmacy: fading facets', *Pharmaceutical Journal*, 18 Feb 1961, 137-8; W H A C Whyte, 'Memoir: A Colchester chemist and analyst', *Pharmaceutical Journal*, 26 Dec 1959, 442-3; W H A C Whyte, 'Town Centre Casualty: more memories of a Colchester pharmacy now no more', *Chemist and Druggist*, 30 Nov 1968, 512-13

Records: Essex Record Office, Colchester & North-East Essex Branch, Stanwell House, Stanwell Street, Colchester CO2 7DL

Prescription books 1877–95, 1905–22; recipe books c.1872–1925; analyses books 1881–1909, 1922–36. (Ref: D/F 67)

WHIFFEN & SONS LTD
Fulham, Hammersmith & Fulham, London

Fine chemical manufacturer

History: In 1854 Thomas Whiffen (1819–1904) joined Edward Herring, whose family had been wholesale druggists for many years at 40 Aldersgate Street, London, and Jacob Hulle, in their alkaloid and fine chemical manufacturing business, believed to have been named the British & Foreign Alkaloid Co, at Trinity Square, Borough, Southwark, London. In 1858 Hulle bought Herring's share in the business and in 1859 the factory re-located to Thomas Whiffen's home in Lombard Road, Battersea, Wandsworth, London, where quinine and strychnine were manufactured. Hulle retired in 1868, leaving the business and the rights to strychnine manufacture to Whiffen, who continued the business on his own account. In the same year, Thomas Whiffen was joined in business by his second son, William George (1852–1934), who, at the age of 17, took charge of the works. His eldest son, Thomas Joseph (1850–1931), entered the business in 1873. In 1887 both sons were taken into partnership, and the business was styled Whiffen & Sons. In the same year the firm acquired the business of George Atkinson & Co, chemical manufacturers of 66 Aldersgate Street, London. This firm had been established in 1703, when a Mr Primatt began compounding drugs at that address. During the early eighteenth century his son, Humphrey Primatt, was joined in partnership by John Maud, and the business was styled Primatt & Maud by 1744, and Maud & Primatt Chymists by 1753. The firm's product range included iodine, bromides and camphor. Following the death of John Maud in 1782, his son, also named John Maud, assumed control of the business on his own account from 1798 to 1820. Between 1821 and 1865, the business passed through a succession of partners, Biggar, Atkinson, Dell and Chippendale, until styled George Atkinson & Co in 1865. In 1884 the production of certain kinds of chemicals was banned in the City of London, hence the firm moved to factory premises at Southall, Ealing, London, which were named Aldersgate Chemical Works, and warehouses and offices at 31-32 St Andrews Hill, London. In 1903 Thomas Whiffen & Sons incorporated, as a limited liability company, the St Amand Manufacturing Co Ltd, as a joint venture with fine chemical manufacturers T & H Smith and J F Macfarlan & Co, to process Belgian willow tree bark in order to produce salicin, which had been discovered as an effective treatment for rheumatism in 1876. In 1904 Thomas Whiffen's 2 sons assumed control of their father's business, which, from around 1900, specialised in the production of alkaloids. In 1908 Thomas Joseph Whiffen's son, George Goodman Whiffen, joined the firm, followed by his brother, Stanley White Whiffen, in 1912. In the same year the business was incorporated as a private limited liability company, Whiffen & Sons Ltd. A third brother, Noel Hardy

Whiffen, joined the company in 1921. In 1923 Whiffen & Sons Ltd re-located to a new warehouse, which retained the name Aldersgate Chemical Works, at Carnwath Road, Fulham, Hammersmith & Fulham, London. The company also owned a factory at Battersea which was closed in 1933, following which all operations were centralised on the Fulham site. In 1935 a research department was opened at Fulham, in premises named the Jubilee Laboratory. From this point onwards, the company moved into organic research, beginning manufacture of bromine compounds and iodine derivatives. In 1947 the trading interests of the company were acquired by Fisons Ltd, following which the Whiffen family maintained its interest in the company for a short while: George Goodman and Noel Hardy Whiffen both retired in 1948, whilst Stanley White Whiffen continued as managing director until 1950 and remained a director until 1958, when the Fulham site was sold off and fine chemical production was moved to the Willows Works, Loughborough, Leicestershire. In 1966 Whiffen & Sons Ltd was renamed Fisons Industrial Chemicals Ltd. From then onwards the company had little connection with fine chemicals, the last of which were manufactured in 1972.

R S Law, *The End of a Chapter: The story of Whiffen & Sons Limited, fine chemical manufacturers* (Fisons, London, c.1973); J T W Mann & R E Lewkowitsch, 'A Short History of Whiffen & Sons Ltd 1654–1947', reprinted from *Fisons Journal*, Jan 1948; G McGuire, 'Whiffen & Sons Limited', *Fisons Journal*, 73, Aug 1962, 19-23

Records 1: London Metropolitan Archives, 40 Northampton Road, London EC1R 0HB

Articles of partnership: Herring & Hulle 1850s, Thomas, Thomas Joseph and William George Whiffen 1887; memorandum and articles of association 1912; agreement re formation of a new company 1910; contract for sale and purchase of Battersea business 1912; papers re formation n.d.; annual returns 1913–36; lists and appointments of directors 1921–25; report and list of members, first statutory meeting 1912; lists of shareholders, cancelled share certificates, transfers and dividends 1912–46; share transfer certificates 1935; profit and loss account and balance sheet 1912; canteen trading and profit and loss account 1941–43; ledgers: 1887–99, 1917–40, private 1872–1934 (w), Bennet estate 1874–81, company war savings group 1940–47, national savings group 1940–42; accounts 1867–68, 1934–46; insurance documents, incl. for goods shipments and exhibition stands 1939; agreements: various parties with reports of conventions 1892–1934, Staniform Ltd re products manufacture 1929; papers: legislation governing the chemical industry 1851, 1901–49, Imperial Economic Conference, Ottawa 1932; report of chartered patent agents re protection provided by

Mr Vautin's patents 1928; patent registrations and renewals 1894–1950; trademark registration papers 1926; laboratory notebooks: strychnine production 1858, Frank Moul 1884–96, coffee, atropine etc. sampling record 1908–32, T J Waitt's nicotine sampling record 1915–47, T J Waitt's and D Lowdell's henbane sampling record 1918–47, nux vomica received 1921–35, soda iodide 1919–26, preparation of 'DA' or 'ZA' 1927–48; chemical analyses books 1905–30; caffeine and production of decaffeinated coffee, papers, agreements and correspondence 1879–1915; stock balance sheets, various chemicals 1889–90, 1916–23; stocktaking books 1895–1928; Hampton warehouse stock record 1940–45; notes and correspondence re quinine compounds 1840s; correspondence and agreements: iodine preparations and compounds 1888, 1911, 1928–29, camphor 1890–1927, vermilion 1904, 1931–34, lysoform preparations 1906–10, bromides 1908–49, plianol, with Dr Reginald T Brain 1929–47, strychnine sales 1936–40, atrophine 1939–50, emetine 1939–50, quinine 1949–53, euphyllin, with Dutch, German and Australian parties and the Custodian of Enemy Property 1932–39, cardophylin 1931, 1939–50, gelozone 1940s, n.d.; price lists: 1931–54, quinine 1873–77; T S R Gillett Ltd and others, Calcutta, orders 1931–41; orders and correspondence 1937–43; representatives' records of visits and orders: [? Thomas Joseph Whiffen's] notebook 1890–93, Charles Jackson 1909, 1922, A G Campbell 1939–47, W W Churchill 1940–41; advertisements: gelozone 1940–47, proofs, notes, correspondence and cuttings 1939–55; press cuttings books 1875–88, 1904–57; labels registers 1933, c.1936–41, n.d.; letter re labelling, with samples of poison products 1936; samples, and boxes used for packaging n.d.; packaging record book c.1907–27; cable code books c.1901–15; exhibitions 1932–49; title deeds, legal papers and correspondence re property 1859–1948; papers and correspondence re Aldersgate Chemical Works, Carnwath Road, Fulham 1920–47; plan of Woldingham n.d.; wages books 1918–19, 1933–44; canteen staff wages 1944–47; lists of employees 1935–47; staff income tax returns 1917–24; pensioners' names and addresses 1944; trustees of superannuation fund meetings minutes 1922–38; pension cash books: 1913–32, 1948–51, widows of employees 1926–33; pension and life assurance scheme: booklets 1933–34, circulars 1947–48; staff letters, agreements, cuttings and reminiscences 1886–1948; welfare pamphlets, cuttings and circulars 1941–48; rules and regulations: Aldersgate friendly society 1893, Lombard friendly society 1910; Lombard social club, later Aldersgate works club: minutes 1932–47, statements and letters 1932–47; Aldersgate social club minutes 1953–58; Aldersgate sports and social club papers: cash book 1957–58, receipted accounts and notes of payments 1957–58, notebook re social events 1951–53, newsletter 1949–51, miscellaneous notices and circulars 1911, 1947–52; Aldersgate football club minutes 1954–55; company personnel home guard parade attendances, correspondence and orders 1940–45; air raid precautions staff data book c.1941–42; fire guard duty book

1941–43; firewatchers' payments and allowances 1941–45; air raid precautions, papers, correspondence and awards of Defence Medal 1938–46; general papers re civil defence 1952–55; correspondence: Thomas Joseph Whiffen, from Canada 1910, Sir Alfred Chatterton re sandalwood oil visits to India 1924–29 with valuations and reports re war damage 1940–47, sales promotions 1947–49; photographs: family members 1867–1945, Lombard football club 1922, Lombard social and athletic club 1911–12, staff and factory (Fulham, Battersea and Southall) 1865–1956; photograph album of Mysore sandalwood oil factory n.d. and posters of exhibition stands 1888–1949; obituaries: Thomas Joseph Whiffen 1931, Jessie Anne Whiffen 1934, William George Whiffen 1934; letters of condolence on death of William George Whiffen 1934; sales catalogue, Thomas Joseph Whiffen's home n.d.; correspondence re Stanley White Whiffen's retirement 1950; historical notes and articles 1936, 20th cent.; miscellaneous papers 1883–1951; stationery, Whiffen and subsidiary companies n.d.; Mysore, India, sandalwood oil factories: annual reports 1919–22, shipments to Whiffen & Sons Ltd 1920–23, sales 1916–24, correspondence re Whiffen & Sons Ltd as agents 1915–17, correspondence and papers 1917–24.

Staniform Ltd: directors' and general meetings minutes 1929–47; memorandum and articles of association 1929; directors' and general meetings attendance book 1929–46 (w); share register 1929–38; legal papers and share certificates 1928–44; agreements: Whiffen & Sons Ltd re products manufacture 1929, Butler & Thompson Ltd re manufacture of compound lotion containing *Staniform* powder n.d.; account book 1928–36; scientific report/notes on coefficients 1927, 1930. (Ref: B/WHF/1-245)

Records 2: Archives & Manuscripts, Wellcome Library for the History & Understanding of Medicine, 183 Euston Road, London NW1 2BE

Laboratory books, containing notes on production, development and testing of fine chemicals 1896–1951; emetine record books 1916–52; Whiffen family correspondence 1802–60; miscellaneous company papers 1935–58; correspondence, research notes and papers of Dr Elsa Lewkowitsch re company history 1947–71. (Ref: MSS 5887-94)

Records 3: Rhône-Poulenc Rorer Ltd, Rhône-Poulenc Rorer House, 50 Kings Hill Avenue, Kings Hill, West Malling ME19 4AH

Memoranda and articles of association 1948, 1966; litigation papers, company v tenant, Z Onions & Sons Ltd and architectural drawing of Z Onions Yard 1966–67; scientific reports 1963; product lists 1953–55, 1963; sales catalogue 1962; product booklets and leaflets 1957–70s; promotional brochures n.d.; conveyance of Willow Works, Derby Road, Loughborough 1965; licence agreement and correspondence re Lisle Street allotments 1959–65; correspondence re proposed new road 1965–66; proceedings of international conference on *Hydrazine* 1957; *Technical News*, newsletter 1963–68.

Records 4: History of Advertising Trust, HAT House, 12 Raveningham Centre, Raveningham NR14 6NU

Guardbook of advertising material 1954. (Ref: Ogilvy & Mather collection)

M WHITFIELD LTD
St Aidan's Terrace, Trimdon Station, Durham

Retail chemist

History: M Whitfield Ltd, a retail chemist's business, was incorporated as a limited liability company in 1935 at Sunderland Road, Horden, Durham, by Joseph S Whitfield, a poor law relieving officer and his wife Margaret. Joseph Whitfield was unable to register the company in his own name whilst holding public office, and thus the company was named after his wife. In 1936 a second shop was opened by the company at 1-2 Hartlepool Street, Thornley, Durham and in 1937 a third business was established in Newsham, Blyth, Northumberland, but later sold in 1947. All traded as M Whitfield Ltd. In 1941 a retail chemist's shop was opened at Empire Buildings, Durham, and was managed by Joseph and Margaret Whitfield's daughter, Mary Ann. In the following year Mary Whitfield married John Grundy, who became a company director. Between 1945 and 1958 the company acquired a number of other chemist's shops, including 22 Alexander Terrace, Wheatley Hill, 18 Sunderland Road, Gilesgate, and 28 Middle Street, Blackhall Colliery, Durham, and 107 King's Road, North Ormesby, Middlesbrough. Whitfield Drug Stores Ltd was incorporated as a wholly-owned subsidiary of M Whitfield Ltd in 1947, to operate former M Whitfield Ltd businesses which no longer had trained pharmacists in post and thus could not trade officially as retail chemists. This company was wound up during the 1970s. In 1950 West Hartlepool Drug Co Ltd was incorporated as a limited liability company, to distribute pharmaceutical products wholesale. It was incorporated as a joint venture between M Whitfield Ltd and G Whitfield Ltd. George Whitfield, the owner of G Whitfield Ltd, was also a son of Joseph Whitfield. West Hartlepool Drug Co Ltd was renamed Durham Pharmaceuticals Ltd in 1979, and continued to trade in 1997. In 1965 M Whitfield Ltd re-located its head offices from the Horden to the Middle Street shop and in the same year, a plan to relocate the Gilesgate premises was turned down by Durham County Council, following which the company lodged and won an appeal against this decision in 1966. In 1974 Peter R W Grundy and John W Grundy, sons of Mary Ann and John Grundy, joined the company as directors, and in 1979 the company re-located its headquarters to its current address, St Aidan's Terrace, Trimdon Station, Durham. Durham Pharmaceuticals Ltd was also accommodated at St Aidan's Terrace from 1979. In 1985 M Whitfield Ltd acquired an 18 per cent share in Victoria Pharmacy Ltd, a retail pharmacy within a health centre in Hartlepool, and in 1993 Adaptability was established as a division of M Whitfield Ltd, to supply disability aids to retail pharmacies, nursing homes and hospitals.

Records: M Whitfield Ltd, St Aidan's Terrace, Trimdon Station TS29 6BT

Memorandum and articles of association 1935; annual reports and accounts 1935 to date; purchase ledgers 1946 to date; cash books 1984 to date; branch account books 1954–71; dangerous drugs register 1949–68; stock book 1941–58; press cuttings re company 1964–67, n.d.; legal charge re Alnwick Street premises 1987; approval of building plans certificates, Sunderland Road, Horden 1960, 1967; architectural drawings: Gilesgate 1953, 1966–67, Front Street, Coxhoe, Durham 1953, 1963, Hartlepool Street 1957, 107 Kings Road 1958, Sunderland Road, Horden 1960, Alexandra Terrace 1964, Middle Street 1964, n.d., St Aidan's Terrace 1987, 93 High Street, Easington Lane, Durham n.d.; appeal re Gilesgate building plans 1966; correspondence: premises at Gilesgate 1960s, property 1962, 1966–73; telegram to J S Whitfield re planning appeal 1966; photographs of premises and staff c.1950s–70s; *Whitfield Times*, staff magazine 1988 to date; certificates of qualification as chemist and druggist: John Grundy 1941, Mary Ann Whitfield 1941; certificates of qualification as pharmaceutical chemist: John Grundy 1954, Mary Ann Grundy 1954, Peter Robert Whitfield Grundy 1973; portraits: Joseph Whitfield n.d., Margaret Whitfield n.d.

Durham Pharmaceuticals Ltd: memorandum and articles of association 1950; annual reports and accounts 1950 to date; purchase ledgers 1972 to date; sales ledgers 1980 to date; cash books 1984 to date; sale of poisons register 1969–72.

Whitfield Drug Stores Ltd: certificate of incorporation 1947; ledger 1948–57; receipts and payments ledger 1958.

TIMOTHY WHITES & TAYLORS LTD
53 South Street, Dorchester, Dorset

Chemist and retailer

History: Taylor's Drug Co was established by W B Mason during the late nineteenth century as a chain of chemist's shops based around West Yorkshire and Lancashire. In 1888 the business was incorporated as a limited liability company, Taylor's Drug Co Ltd. Between 1911 and 1915 it purchased the chemist's business of W How(e), established in South Street, Dorchester, Dorset, in 1865, and operated a number of other subsidiaries under the style Taylors (Cash Chemists). In 1848 Timothy White established a chemist's business on his own account in Portsmouth. In 1869 he qualified as a pharmacist and in 1904 his business was incorporated as a limited liability company, Timothy Whites Ltd. In 1908 Timothy White died, and his son, Woolmer White, assumed control of the business. In 1935 Timothy Whites Ltd merged with Taylor's Drug Co Ltd, forming a new limited liability company, Timothy Whites & Taylors Ltd, with headquarters in Portsmouth and a large number of branches across Great Britain. In 1968 Timothy Whites & Taylors Ltd was acquired by Boots Pure Drug Co Ltd.

Records 1: Company Archivist, The Boots Co plc, Company Archives (D31), Nottingham NG2 3AA

Photographs of shopfronts c.1900–60; miscellaneous papers incl. price lists and branch lists, unlisted 20th cent.

Taylors (Cash Chemists) London Ltd: directors' meetings minutes 1928–69; general meetings minutes 1928–94; register of directors, members and share ledger 1928–89; seal books 1928–72.

Taylor's Drug Co Ltd: directors' meetings minutes 1895–1916; management meetings minutes, incl. advertising committee minutes 1912–20; private ledger 1885–93.

Records 2: Dorset Record Office, 9 Bridport Road, Dorchester DT1 1RP

South Street, Dorchester branch, prescription books 1932–67. (Ref: D/DSE/C1, C2[MS27], C3[MS28], C4)

Records 3: Museum of the History of Science, University of Oxford, Old Ashmolean Building, Broad Street, Oxford OX1 3AZ

Prescription/recipe 1938. (Ref: MS Museum 284)

Records 4: History of Advertising Trust, HAT House, 12 Raveningham Centre, Raveningham NR14 6NU

Guardbooks of advertising material 1952–59. (Ref: Ogilvy & Mather collection)

WILSON'S (STOWMARKET) LTD
Old Market Place, Sudbury, Suffolk

Dispensing chemist

History: Thomas Wilson was registered as a pharmaceutical chemist in 1863. He traded at Walsham-le-Willows, Ixworth, Suffolk, until 1879, when he entered into partnership with William Harvey, chemist, Stowmarket, Suffolk. Thomas Wilson was still in business in 1895, and in 1934 the business was incorporated as a limited liability company, Wilson's Ltd. It was later renamed Wilson's (Stowmarket) Ltd, with trading premises in Old Market Place, Sudbury, Suffolk. The company ceased trading in 1980.

Records: Suffolk Record Office, Ipswich Branch, Gatacre Road, Ipswich IP1 2LQ

Articles of partnership, Thomas Wilson and William Harvey 1879; sales day book 1937–52; prescription books: 1877–1969 (w), veterinary 1924–51; poisons registers 1938–54; letter re award from International Fisheries Exhibition, London 1883; T Wilson's and W Harvey's executors' acknowledgement of receipt of money from F M Wilson 1931. (Ref: HC 408 and 455/1-3)

A H WINDRIDGE LTD
Knowle, Solihull

Retail chemist

History: A H Windridge Ltd, a retail chemist's business, was incorporated as a limited liability company at Knowle, Solihull, in 1921. In 1960 it was acquired by Dudley Taylor, Warwick, Warwickshire, the owner of a chain of retail pharmacies. In 1993 Dudley Taylor (Holdings) Ltd was incorporated as a holding company for Dudley Taylor's many acquired businesses, including A H Windridge Ltd, which was still trading under its own name in 1997.

Records: Dudley Taylor Holdings Ltd, Unit 2B, Harris Road, Wedgnock Industrial Estate, Warwick CV34 5GH

Directors' and general meetings minutes 1921–70; directors' reports and annual accounts 1985–96 (w).

R WOOLLATT & J BOYD
Fore Street, Taunton, Somerset

Chemist

History: Richard Woollatt was in business as a chemist and druggist at 17 Fore Street, Taunton, Somerset, prior to 1868. He continued to operate there until 1906, after which J Boyd assumed control of the business.

Records: Archives & Manuscripts, Wellcome Library for the History & Understanding of Medicine, 183 Euston Road, London NW1 2BE

Ledgers containing customer accounts 1917–44 (w); account book, with advertisements for 'Woollatt's wonderful embrocation' and 'Woollatt's wonderful pills' 1891–1907; day book fragment 1939; notebook containing a record of Woollatt's product advertisements placed in West Country newspapers 1904–05; prescription books 1880–1918 (w). (Ref: MSS 5661-73)

JAMES WOOLLEY, SONS & CO LTD
Manchester

Manufacturing chemist and druggist and pharmaceutical wholesaler

History: Following his apprenticeship to Samuel Dean, druggist, of 4 Piccadilly, Manchester, James Woolley (1811–58) opened a chemist and druggist's business on his own account in King Street, Manchester, in 1833. In 1840 he acquired R H Hargreaves' druggist and drysalter's business in Market Street, which had been established since 1796. He was a founder member of the Pharmaceutical Society of Great Britain, formed in 1841, and became a Council member in 1843. On his death he was succeeded by his eldest son, George Stephen Woolley (c.1837–1918), who developed the manufacturing side of the business. George's brother, Herman Woolley, was placed in charge of the manufacturing section in 1867, and in 1872 a third brother, Harold Woolley (1850–89), was taken into partnership, and took responsibility for the manufacture of scientific equipment and surgical instruments. The business traded as James Woolley, Sons & Co. In 1872 due to a fire at King Street, the firm re-located to premises at Knowsley Street, Cheetham Hill, Manchester, which housed drug mills and laboratories. By 1889 the business was concerned primarily with the wholesale distribution of drugs, and as a result, warehouse accommodation was acquired at Victoria Bridge, Manchester, in 1892. In 1895 the business was incorporated as a limited liability company, James Woolley, Sons & Co Ltd. In 1936 the company acquired J C Arnfield & Sons Ltd, Stockport, a retail and wholesale chemist's business, which was established by Ollive Sims in 1786, renamed Kay Brothers in 1867, and incorporated as a limited liability company, Kay Brothers Ltd, in 1887. In 1909 following its acquisition by J C Arnfield, it was renamed J C Arnfield & Sons Ltd. In 1950 James Woolley, Sons & Co Ltd was converted to a public limited liability company, retaining its own name. In 1962 it was acquired, along with its subsidiary, J C Arnfield & Sons Ltd, by British Drug Houses Group Ltd, whereupon the 2 companies were merged to form one limited liability company, BDH (Woolley & Arnfield) Ltd. In 1966 the wholesale distribution interests of British Drug Houses Group Ltd and Glaxo Group Ltd, merged to form a limited liability company, Vestric Ltd. This combined interest created a company with 36 trading branches, amongst which were many long-established companies including Lofthouse & Saltmer Ltd, Duncan Flockhart Ltd and Bradley & Bliss Ltd. BDH (Woolley & Arnfield) Ltd became the Manchester branch of Vestric, and ceased to trade under its own name.

'The House of Woolley, 1844–1944', *Chemist and Druggist*, 141, 20 May 1944, 568-71; 'A Manchester Showroom. Notes on a reorganisation carried out by James Woolley, Sons & Co Ltd', *Chemist and Druggist*, 122, 4 May 1935, 548-9; H T Milliken, *Saga of a Family: The story behind the House of Woolley* (BDH, Poole, 1967); *Woolleys of Manchester: A record of 150 years in pharmacy* (James Woolley, Manchester, 1946)

Records 1: John Rylands Library, University of Manchester, 150 Deansgate, Manchester M3 3EH

Articles of agreement 1872; articles of partnership 1890; articles of association 1950; ledgers: 1868, private, incl. trade accounts, balance sheet and profit and loss accounts 1881–91; cash books 1844–83; agreement re division of profits 1890; references and accounts, Pochin & Woolley, Stretford Road, Manchester n.d.; invoices: R H Hargreaves, 69 Market Street 1838, Peake, Earlestown 1876; correspondence re disputed trademark names n.d.; price lists: 1872–94, William Langton & Co, wholesalers, London 1855; speciality product lists, advertisements and testimonial 1878, 1896–1903; scrapbook of pharmaceutical advertisements and periodical articles 1883–1908; deeds, some relating to

Market Street premises 1864–74, 1891–95, 1917; income tax assessments for 69 Market Street 1847–57; lists of assets 1850–54 (w); insurance papers re fire at 69 Market Street and cost of re-building new laboratories at Knowsley Street 1867–72; salaries book 1845–83; wages books 1874–83, 1908–13; salaries and expenses ledger 1865–70; staff papers: concessions re working hours and conditions 1876–81, dinners and picnics, with programmes 1879–1938, national service register 1914; golden anniversary: lists of directors and staff, 1854–1962, correspondence and photographs of presentations to staff 1946, illuminated address by George Stephen Woolley 1908; staff magazines 1934–52 (w); company history scrapbook with illustrations and photographs 1796–1951; photographs 1900–n.d.; photograph album, fleet of lorries 1927; personal papers of James Woolley: attendance certificate, Manchester Infirmary classes 1829, membership certificate, Literary & Philosophical Society of Manchester 1860, membership certificate, National Anti-Corn League n.d., school bills for son, Percy Woolley 1856–57, executorship papers 1848, shareholdings 1847–57; Hermann Woolley's certificates, Owens College 1863–65; William Woolley of Mottram's will 1728; agreements: Whitehead of Newton, machine printer, with Yates, Yates & Kilgrow, Bank Ridge 1813, Samuel and Robert Kay and J C Arnfield 1888; assignment of goodwill of business of E Hornby, chemist of Stockport, to Kay Brothers, chemist of Stockport 1883; miscellaneous papers and publications, incl. minutes of Pharmaceutical Association, Manchester branch 1841–45; medals, International Health Exhibition 1884, 1895–96; anatomy lantern slides n.d. (Ref: James Woolley papers)

Records 2: Manchester Central Library, Local Studies Unit, St Peter's Square, Manchester M2 5PD

Prescriptions 1870. (Ref: M367/5/9/3-6)

Trade organisations and pharmacy schools: lists of records

ASSOCIATION OF THE BRITISH PHARMACEUTICAL INDUSTRY
12 Whitehall, London

Trade association representing the interests of manufacturing pharmacists

History: This Association was established in London as the Drug Club, to represent the interests of wholesale druggists and to offer a venue for social intercourse, 18 firms being represented at its opening meeting on 17 December 1891. In 1929 a new organisation was founded, the Wholesale Drug Trade Association, at Gordon Square, London, and in 1930 the Drug Club was wound up and its assets transferred to the new Association, which sought to ensure that medicinal products of the highest quality were readily available. The Association's premises were destroyed by enemy action in 1940, following which it moved briefly to BMA House, Tavistock Square, London, and then to 2 other London locations before settling at its current address, 12 Whitehall, London. It was renamed the Association of the British Pharmaceutical Industry in 1948, to reflect the fact that the bulk of its membership by then comprised manufacturing chemists, although wholesaling chemists continued to be represented through Division D of the Association. The increased representation of manufacturing chemists was a consequence of the expansion in research, development and manufacture of pharmaceutical products during the 1940s, as the industry became more scientifically based. In 1949 the Association merged with the Pharmaceutical Export Group, a government body established in 1940, after which its primary objectives were to represent the pharmaceutical industry before government departments and to develop exports of pharmaceutical products. In 1961 the Association changed its name, slightly, to the Association of the British Pharmaceutical Industry. By the 1960s the Association's main interest was the representation of manufacturing rather than wholesaling chemists. The latter established an independent organisation, the National Association of Pharmaceutical Distributors in 1966, which was renamed the British Association of Pharmaceutical Wholesalers in 1991. By 1980 the Association of the British Pharmaceutical Industry had 154 manufacturing member companies, a figure which had fallen to 100 by 1992. In 1997 the Association provided education and training, held conferences and examinations and offered an export information service.

D W F Hardie & J Davidson Pratt, *A History of the Modern British Chemical Industry* (Pergamon, Oxford and London, 1966), 332-3; N Wells, *Medicines: 50 years of progress, a celebration of the 50th anniversary of the Association of the British Pharmaceutical Industry* (Office of Health Economics, London, 1980)

Records 1: Association of the British Pharmaceutical Industry, 12 Whitehall, London SW1A 2DY

Annual reports 1949 to date.

Records 2: William Ransom & Son plc, 104 Bancroft, Hitchin SG5 1LY

General meetings minutes: 1962–79 (w); Division A annual meetings minutes 1963, 1969, 1971; annual reports 1953–55, 1964–80 (w); press release re election results following new constitution 1961–62; membership directory 1960; list of overseas pharmaceutical manufacturing associations 1966; conference programmes and dinner attendee lists 1959–70s; weekly service sheets 1968.

Records 3: British Association of Pharmaceutical Wholesalers, 19a South Street, Farnham GU9 7QU

Minutes: Wholesale Drug Trade Association and Division D of Association of the British Pharmaceutical Industry committee meetings 1939–61 (w), Wholesale Drug Trade Association and Division D of Association of the British Pharmaceutical Industry general meetings 1940–65 (w), Division D council meetings 1961–65.

Records 4: The Worshipful Society of Apothecaries, Apothecaries' Hall, Black Friars Lane, London EC4V 6EJ

Memoranda 1962–63.

Records 5: Dr Peter M Worling, The Grange, 29 Fernielaw Avenue, Edinburgh EH13 0EF

Minutes of meeting to discuss formation of National Association of Pharmaceutical Distributors 1965.

BIRKENHEAD & WIRRAL PHARMACISTS' ASSOCIATION
Birkenhead, Wirral

Provincial branch of the Pharmaceutical Society of Great Britain

History: In 1905 the Birkenhead & Wirral Chemists' Association was founded, as a local branch of the Pharmaceutical Society of Great Britain, at Birkenhead, Wirral. In 1907 its president was A H Ellithorne, and the Association met monthly. In 1910 it was renamed the Birkenhead & Wirral Association of Pharmacists, and in 1917 the Birkenhead, Wallasey & Wirral Association of Pharmacists. By 1920 it was named the Birkenhead & Wirral Pharmacists' Association, and continued to operate under this name until at least 1992.

Records: Wirral Archives Service, Birkenhead Central Library, Borough Road, Birkenhead L41 2XB

Minutes: 1919–35, 1950–72, committee meetings 1953–66; annual reports 1925–34 (w); rules, circulars and membership cards 1976–78. (Ref: YPA)

BRITISH ASSOCIATION OF PHARMACEUTICAL WHOLESALERS
19a South Street, Farnham, Surrey

National trade association representing the interests of pharmaceutical wholesalers

History: This trade association was founded in 1966 as the National Association of Pharmaceutical Distributors. It originated from Division D, the wholesaling division of the Association of the British Pharmaceutical Industry. The Association of the British Pharmaceutical Industry, established as the Drug Club in 1891, initially represented wholesaling chemists, but throughout the course of the twentieth century, came to promote the interests, predominantly, of manufacturing pharmacists. It was this change in emphasis which prompted pharmaceutical wholesalers to consider the formation of a trade association to represent their interests alone. Prior to 1966 wholesale druggists were represented either through the Association of the British Pharmaceutical Industry at national level, or through one of 4 regional organisations: the London Wholesale, Druggists, Sundries & Proprietaries Association, the Northern Wholesale Druggists' Association, the Scottish Wholesale Druggist Association or the Ulster Wholesale Chemists' Association. In 1965, at a meeting of the Northern Wholesale Druggists' Association in Southport, Sefton, the first plans for a national wholesale organisation were proposed and a steering committee established. In 1966 the National Association of Pharmaceutical Distributors was founded and Division D of the Association of the British Pharmaceutical Industry was dissolved. In 1967 the National Association of Pharmaceutical Distributors incorporated a limited liability company, Sales Data Analysis Pharmaceuticals Ltd, which operated under the name SDA Pharmaceuticals Ltd, at Northolt Lane, South Harrow, Harrow, London, to administer a contract between National Association of Pharmaceutical Distributors and International Medical Statistics Ltd, a limited liability company which traded under the title IMS Ltd. Under the terms of this contract, pharmaceutical wholesalers sold pharmaceutical data to IMS Ltd, who, in turn, forwarded the information to pharmaceutical manufacturers for medical research purposes. The income received from manufacturers on receipt of this information was returned to wholesalers via IMS Ltd and SDA Ltd. In 1991 the National Association of Pharmaceutical Distributors was renamed the British Association of Pharmaceutical Wholesalers, and in 1993 launched an Associate Members' Scheme, allowing pharmaceutical manufacturers to become members of British Association of Pharmaceutical Wholesalers in order to increase co-operation and communication between the 2 groups.

P M Worling, 'The History of the National Association of Pharmaceutical Distributors', *NAPD 25th Anniversary* (NAPD, 1991); P M Worling, 'Pharmaceutical Wholesale Distribution: The influence of the National Health Service and growing market competition on the development of the wholesale distribution of pharmaceuticals in the United Kingdom' (Unpublished PhD thesis, University of Bradford, 1988)

Records 1: British Association of Pharmaceutical Wholesalers, 19a South Street, Farnham GU9 7QU

Meetings minutes: general 1965 to date, council 1965 to date, associate members general 1993–94, associate members council 1993–96; attendance registers: general meetings 1966–87, various committees 1966–78; register of members and directors 1967–80s; *BAPW: The Vital Link*, news bulletin 1993–94.

SDA Ltd: general meetings minutes, incl. inaugural meeting 1967 to date.

Records 2: Dr Peter M Worling, The Grange, 29 Fernielaw Avenue, Edinburgh EH13 0EF

Inaugural general meeting minutes 1966; lists of members and code of practice c.1960s, 1971.

Records 3: Mr E H Butler, Galen Management Services Ltd, Galen House, 66 Commercial Square, Freemans Common, Leicester LE27 7SR

Photograph of inaugural meeting 1966.

BRITISH MEDICAL ASSOCIATION
BMA House, Tavistock Square, London

Voluntary professional association of doctors and independent trade union

History: The British Medical Association was founded in Worcester, Worcestershire, in 1832 as the Provincial Medical & Surgical Association. Initially it was established to counter the dominance of London over medical matters, but gradually membership was extended to London doctors and, in 1856, the organisation was renamed the British Medical Association. Its publication, the *Provincial Medical and Surgical Journal*, later became the *British Medical Journal*. The Association lobbied Parliament on a range of medical issues. The Medical Act of 1858, which established the General Medical Council, resulted from pressure brought on governments by the British Medical Association. In the early 1900s the Association campaigned against 'quack' patent medicines and, after the creation of the National Health Service in 1948, actively represented Health Service doctors. The Association continues to carry out these functions, and is also a registered trade union, presenting evidence on behalf of National Health Service doctors and providing legal advice. It also continues to lobby and advise governments on medical issues. British Medical Association committees which have been particularly concerned with matters relating to pharmacy include the Pharmacopoeia Committee, whose remit is to oversee any revisions to the *British Pharmacopoeia* and to nominate witnesses in the event that a revision committee be appointed, and the Joint Committee of the British Medical Association and the Pharmaceutical Society of Great Britain. This latter committee's inital terms of reference were to liaise on matters of common interest, later specified as matters of common interest relating to the National Health Service. The Joint Formulary Committee was established in 1947 following a recommendation from the afore-mentioned Joint Committee, that representatives of the medical and pharmaceutical professions should join together to produce a Standard Prescribers' Formulary based on the formulary section of the British Pharmaceutical Codex. After 1949 the committee was charged with the duty of reviewing the National Formulary as and when required.

P Bartrip, *Mirror of Medicine: A history of the BMJ* (BMJ and Clarendon Press, Oxford, 1990); P Bartrip, *'Themselves Writ Large', The British Medical*

Association 1832–1966 (BMJ, London, 1996); E Grey-Turner and F M Sutherland, *History of the British Medical Association, Vol. 2, 1932–1981* (BMA, London, 1982); E Muirhead Little, *History of the British Medical Association, Vol. 1, 1832–1932* (BMA, London, 1932); P Vaughan, *Doctors' Commons: A short history of the British Medical Association* (Heinemann, London, 1959)

Records: The Archivist, British Medical Association, BMA House, Tavistock Square, London WC1H 9JP

Pharmacopoeia Committee, minutes, agendas and meeting papers 1926–27; Joint Committee of the British Medical Association and the Pharmaceutical Society of Great Britain, minutes, agendas and meeting papers 1959–61, 1964–67; Joint Formulary Committee, minutes, agendas and meeting papers, incl. lists of preparations 1946 to date; correspondence re range of dispensing and prescribing issues 1950s to date. (Ref: B/46, B/363, B/213)

BRITISH SOCIETY FOR THE HISTORY OF PHARMACY
36 York Place, Edinburgh

Society for advancing education in the history of pharmacy

History: The British Society for the History of Pharmacy was established in 1952 as the History of Pharmacy Committee of the Council of the Pharmaceutical Society of Great Britain. Its main activities were the holding of exhibitions, meetings and lectures, and the production of newsletters to stimulate interest in the history of pharmacy. Membership of the Committee was open only to members of the Pharmaceutical Society, and hence its activities were somewhat limited. Increased concern about the lack of access to the History of Pharmacy Committee for historians of medicine and pharmacists who were not members of the Pharmaceutical Society, led to a decision in May 1967 to promote a British Society for the History of Pharmacy, which would be independent of the Pharmaceutical Society of Great Britain and thus able to broaden its membership. In the interim the History of Pharmacy Committee remained functional, in order to agree the constitution of the British Society for the History of Pharmacy. The newly constituted Society held its inaugural meeting on 14 June 1967, independently of the Pharmaceutical Society, although the bond between the 2 remained strong. Secretarial and accommodation facilities for the newly founded Society continued to be provided by the Pharmaceutical Society. Since 1967 the British Society for the History of Pharmacy has promoted research into the history of pharmacy through publications, in particular through its own journal, the *Pharmaceutical Historian*, and through meetings and annual conferences. The Society also encourages its members to collect and preserve historical archives and artifacts.

Records: Royal Pharmaceutical Society of Great Britain, 36 York Place, Edinburgh EH1 3HU

Minutes: committee meetings 1952–96 (incl. newsletters 1956–62), inaugural meeting 1967; reports of annual general meetings 1968–96; transactions 1970–77; provisional committee papers and reprints of articles c.1956–67; papers: meeting attendance lists, agendas, spare minutes, reports, rules and newsletters c.1956–67, lists of members, annual reports, constitution and rules 1970s–80s; correspondence: general 1956–64, conferences 1967–96; membership list 1997.

COLCHESTER ASSOCIATION OF CHEMISTS & DRUGGISTS
Colchester, Essex

Provincial trade association

History: The Colchester Association of Chemists & Druggists was founded in 1841, immediately after the Pharmaceutical Society of Great Britain was established. Its purpose was to provide a provincial trade association for members of the pharmaceutical profession and to counter the dominance of London in the Pharmaceutical Society of Great Britain. The Association held quarterly meetings and established a library of scientific books. It also considered and debated proposed legislation relating to the pharmaceutical industry, for example, the 1863 bill which sought to introduce decimalisation of weights and measures. Between 1894 and 1909 meetings of the Association ceased, but were re-instituted thereafter. In 1953 the Colchester Association of Chemists & Druggists was merged into the local branch of the National Pharmaceutical Union, and ceased to exist in its own right.

W H A C Whyte, 'Pharmaceutical Predecessors in Colchester', *Chemist and Druggist*, 18 May 1974, 621

Records: Essex Record Office, Colchester & North-East Essex Branch, Stanwell House, Stanwell Street, Colchester CO2 7DL

Minutes 1841–1953; accounts 1841–1953. (Ref: D/Z 285)

DEPARTMENT OF PHARMACOLOGY & THERAPEUTICS, UNIVERSITY OF LIVERPOOL
University of Liverpool, Liverpool

Pharmacy school

History: Before 1896 pharmaceutical education in Liverpool was conducted solely by the Liverpool Chemists' Association, which established a school for this purpose in 1849. In 1885 this school was closed, and the Liverpool Chemists' Association licenced the formation of a private institution, the Liverpool School of Pharmacy, at 6 Sandon Terrace, Upper Duke Street, which prepared students for the examinations of the Pharmaceutical Society of Great Britain. In 1895 the Faculty of Medicine at University College Liverpool (which in 1903 became the University of Liverpool) instigated the establishment of a separate School of Pharmacy within the College. Until the early twentieth century the Liverpool School of Pharmacy, controlled by the Liverpool Chemists' Association, remained the leading institution in the training of pharmacists, whilst the University's School of Pharmacy largely offered courses in pharmacy to medical students. At various times between 1900 and 1906, abortive attempts were made to merge the 2 schools. In 1908 a new lectureship in pharmacology was established at the University's Faculty of Medicine, and in 1930 W J Dilling was appointed as the first professor of pharmacology in the Department of Materia Medica, Pharmacy, Pharmacology & General Therapeutics. In 1951 he was succeeded by Andrew Wilson, who held the chair in pharmacology until 1974. In 1955 the department was renamed the Department of Pharmacology & General Therapeutics. The Liverpool School of Pharmacy, formerly operated by the Liverpool Chemists' Association, was acquired by the Liverpool College of Technology in 1950, which was a predecessor of Liverpool Polytechnic, latterly Liverpool John Moores University. The Department of Pharmacology & Therapeutics at the University of Liverpool was still in operation in 1997.

'A History of Liverpool Pharmacy', supplement to *Pharmaceutical Journal*, 135, 14 July 1962, 44-5; 'Pharmaceutical Education in Liverpool', supplement to *Pharmaceutical Journal*, 135, 14 July 1962, 46; B R Edwards, 'The Origins and Early Development of Pharmaceutical Education in Liverpool' (Unpublished MEd thesis, University of Liverpool, 1975); T Kelly, *For Advancement of Learning, the University of Liverpool 1881–1981* (Liverpool University Press, Liverpool, 1981) 104-5, 159

Records: Department of Special Collections & Archives, Sydney Jones Library, University of Liverpool, PO Box 123, Liverpool L69 3DA

Faculty of medicine meetings minutes: pharmaceutical committee 1896–97, committee re teaching of *materia medica* 1908; pharmacology department meetings minutes 1956–73; pharmacology department papers 1893–1974; faculty of medicine: student attendance lists in department of *materia medica* 1911–20, report of sub-committee on pharmacology 1913; memoranda, reports and correspondence: proposed amalgamation of Liverpool School of Pharmacy with university 1900–05, proposed amalgamation of School of Pharmacy and degree courses 1905–11; advertisement for pharmaceutical courses 1898; Prosper H Marsden (lecturer in pharmacy 1896–1931): list of lecture fees 1902–05, correspondence re remuneration and entitlement to wear academic dress 1902, 1908; Andrew Wilson (professor of pharmacology 1951–74): research papers 1930–69, addresses, lectures and lecture notes 1944–73, draft articles and reprints of papers 1938–72, papers re teaching and examinations 1947–74, instructions to students 1938, 1946–60, correspondence 1946–70, photographs and slides of research, experiments and university 1932–36, 1952–62, correspondence re establishment of endowed lectureship in pharmacology 1913. (Refs: P4/1/7, P5A/13-14, 16, D106/1-14, FM1/6.1, 7.1)

THE DRUG & FINE CHEMICAL MANUFACTURERS' ASSOCIATION
Tavistock Square, London

Employers' association

History: The Drug & Fine Chemical Manufacturers' Association, in existence from at least 1919, was established to represent the interests of employers within the drug and fine chemical industries. In 1920 the Association attempted to secure the right for its Edinburgh members to pay lower wage rates than its London members, on the grounds that average wages in Edinburgh were lower than in London. A petition by the National Warehouse & General Workers' Union before the Industrial Court in 1920 prevented this move. During the 1920s the Association continued to negotiate with trade unions which represented drug and fine chemical workers.

Records: William Ransom & Son plc, 104 Bancroft, Hitchin SG5 1LY

Minutes: general meetings 1922–26, executive committee meeting 1924, proceedings before the Industrial Court 1922; trades unions' action, secretary's report 1924; memorandum of agreement with National Drug & Chemical Union and papers re revision 1925; lists of members 1924–26.

GOVERNMENT LYMPH ESTABLISHMENT
Hendon, Barnet, London

Preparation, storage and supply of lymph for vaccinations

History: In 1871 the Local Government Board assumed responsibility for vaccinations from the Privy Council. In 1881 it founded an Animal Vaccine Station in order to produce lymph for vaccinations. By 1898 all vaccinations had to be administered with lymph issued by the Board, the arm-to-arm method of vaccination having been eradicated. In 1907 the Government Lymph Establishment was founded at Hendon, Barnet, London, to co-ordinate the preparation, storage and supply of lymph, and to conduct research and testing. In 1919 the Establishment became the responsibility of the Ministry of Health, and remained operative until 1946 when it was dissolved. From this date the preparation of vaccines was conducted at the Lister Institute and the supply of lymph was organised by the Public Health Laboratory Service.

Records: Public Record Office, Ruskin Avenue, Kew, Richmond TW9 4DU

Government Lymph Establishment, correspondence and papers re production and testing of vaccinations for immunisation against smallpox 1897–1946; Ministry of Health, files of Ministry and subordinate departments incl. Government Lymph Establishment 1862–1985. (Ref: MH70, MH78)

LABORATORY OF THE GOVERNMENT CHEMIST
London

Laboratory for analysis of chemical substances

History: In 1894 the Government Laboratory was established, following the merger of the laboratories of the Board of Customs and the Board of Inland Revenue. The Government Laboratory was responsible for conducting chemical analysis of samples for various government departments. In 1911 the post of Government Chemist was created, and the Laboratory was renamed the Government Chemist's Laboratory. The Government Chemist was responsible for overseeing cases brought under the various food and drugs acts, as well as acts concerning dangerous industrial chemicals. In 1959 the Laboratory was placed under the control of the Department of Scientific & Industrial Research, and was re-styled the Laboratory of the Government Chemist. It has since passed into the control of various ministries and in 1997 was an executive agency of the Department of Trade & Industry.

Records: Public Record Office, Ruskin Avenue, Kew, Richmond TW9 4DU

Papers and correspondence 1803–1992. (Ref: DSIR26)

LEICESTER & LEICESTERSHIRE CHEMISTS' ASSOCIATION
Leicester

Local trade association and examination centre

History: The Leicester Chemists' Assistants & Apprentices Association was a local educational organisation, established in 1869, to provide basic courses in pharmacy, following the foundation of the Pharmaceutical Society of Great Britain in 1841 and the introduction of compulsory examinations for apprentices who wished to be registered as chemists and druggists in 1868. The Association provided lectures, formal classes and a library for its members. The Association was wound up in 1886 and replaced by the Leicester & Leicestershire Chemists' Association in the same year. This Association also served as an education and examination centre, whilst promoting the interests of pharmacists more generally. It remained operative until the development of local educational facilities in Leicestershire forced its closure after 1893.

Records: Record Office for Leicestershire, Leicester & Rutland, Long Street, Wigston Magna, Leicester LE18 2AH

Minutes 1869–75; notice of closure and of meeting to promote a chemists' trade association 1886; notice of meeting to form a chemist's association in Leicester 1886; notice of winding-up of Association and sale of assets n.d.; notices of meetings or classes 1886–88; ballot paper for election to council n.d.; year and rule book 1886; cards listing subjects of lectures and Association rules 1880–81; card listing subjects of lectures and treasurer's report 1884; card with treasurer's report and advertisement for *materia medica* class 1885; annual subscription receipt, Mr [S F] Burford 1893; blank membership card n.d.; advertising handbills 1887–88. (Ref: DE 5170/1-24)

LIVERPOOL CHEMISTS' ASSOCIATION
Liverpool

Local trade association and examination centre

History: The Liverpool Chemists' Association was founded in the early nineteenth century, and in 1849 established a pharmacy school to instruct students who wished to take the examinations of the Pharmaceutical Society of Great Britain. In 1885 this school was closed, and the Liverpool Chemists' Association licenced the formation of a private institution, the Liverpool School of Pharmacy, at 6 Sandon Terrace, Upper Duke Street, which continued to train pharmacists until the early twentieth century.

Records 1: The Museum Curator, Royal Pharmaceutical Society of Great Britain, 1 Lambeth High Street, London SE1 7JN

Dispensing and retail price lists 1880–98, 1909. (Ref: IRA.1996.077-079)

Records 2: Nottinghamshire Archives & Southwell Diocesan Record Office, County House, Castle Meadow Road, Nottingham NG2 1AG

Annual report 1902. (Ref: DD 1135 addit/100)

MANUFACTURING, SCIENCE, FINANCE
33-37 Moreland Street, London

Trade union

History: In 1988 the trade union, Manufacturing, Science, Finance, was formed, following the merger of the Association of Scientific, Technical & Managerial Staff, founded in 1968, and Technical, Administrative & Supervisory Staffs, established in 1986, both having been formed through the merger of a number of trade unions and staff associations. The earliest predecessor of the Association of Scientific, Technical & Managerial Staff was the National Union of Scientific Workers, founded in 1917, and renamed the Association of Scientific Workers in 1927. In 1968 the Association of Scientific Workers merged with the Association of Supervisory Staffs, Executives & Technicians, which had also been founded in 1917, as the National Foreman's Association. This merger created the Association of Scientific, Technical & Managerial Staff. In 1997 Manufacturing, Science, Finance was the largest trade union in the UK representing the interests of professional and skilled workers. Amongst those represented by the union were pharmacists and pharmaceutical workers.

Records: Modern Records Centre, University Library, University of Warwick, Coventry CV4 7AL

Association of Scientific, Technical & Managerial Staffs: national executive committee meetings minutes 1968–71; national officer's files re dealings with Shell, Unilever and ICI 1967–74; circulars 1968–77; subject files incl. relations with other unions, health and safety issues 1968–83; press cuttings 1968–79.

National Association of Scientific Workers: minutes 1918–68; branch minutes Harpenden 1943–57, Hayes 1942–46, RAF Farnborough 1918–27, South Farnborough 1942–45; subject files 1960s–70s; *Scientific Worker* 1920–54; *Journal* 1955–68.

Association of Supervisory Staffs, Executives & Technicians: minutes 1942–68; annual delegate conference proceedings 1941–68 (w); circulars 1955–68; subject files n.d.; agreement files n.d.; National Industrial Relations Court papers n.d. (Ref: MSS.79)

MEDICAL RESEARCH COUNCIL
20 Park Crescent, London

Council promoting research into medicine and biological science and government adviser

History: The Medical Research Council, founded in 1920, was successor to the Medical Research Committee, set up in 1913. This Committee was established by the National Insurance Act of 1911 which, in addition to creating a contributory health and unemployment insurance scheme, introduced a national fund for medical research. The Medical Research Committee administered this fund. Following the First World War the Committee was renamed the Medical Research Council and was granted a royal charter in 1920. It was responsible to a committee of the Privy Council, until 1965, when powers were transferred to the Secretary of State for Education and Science, and in 1966 a new royal charter was issued. Responsibility for the Medical Research Council again changed hands in 1992, passing to the Office of Public Service and Science, a department of the Cabinet Office. The Medical Research Council's main source of funding is an annual parliamentary grant with which it employs its own research staff, and awards grants and fellowships to external researchers in academia and in hospitals, some tenable abroad. It conducts its own research and responds to matters concerning medicine brought to its attention by government departments. A significant portion of the Medical Research Council's research is conducted by the National Institute for Medical Research, founded in 1914, which conducts research and consultancy into the basic biomedical sciences including pharmacology. The Clinical Research Centre, established in 1967, also undertook a large amount of the Medical Research Council's research until 1994, when it was closed. In addition a number of the Medical Research Council staff are posted in establishments outside the Council's control.

A Landsborough Thomson, *Half a Century of Medical Research* (HMSO, London, 1973-75)

Records: Public Record Office, Ruskin Avenue, Kew, Richmond TW9 4DU

Minutes and meeting papers: 1913-89, n.d., Drugs Advisory Committee 1913-54; annual reports 1914-95; reports of special research projects incl. re antibiotics, cinchona, cocaine, insulin, poliomyelitis, morphine, penicillin, sulphonamides 1915-71; papers re quinine clinical trials and malaria 1913-54; legislation: Therapeutic Substances Act 1925, Dangerous Drugs Act 1932, Food and Drugs Acts 1938, Penicillin Act 1947; files: general 1910-86, committees, working parties and conferences 1946-94. (Ref: FD1-2, 4-7, 13)

NATIONAL ASSOCIATION OF WOMEN PHARMACISTS
1 Lambeth High Street, London

Professional body

History: The Association of Women Pharmacists was established in 1905, with Isabella Skinner Clarke as president and Margaret Buchanan as vice-president. It was established to provide a support network for women pharmacists who, although having received the right to qualify as pharmaceutical chemists or chemists and druggists under the provisions of the 1868 Pharmacy Act, had been excluded from membership of the Pharmaceutical Society of Great Britain until 1879. Even after their admission, women did not have equal rights with men, being obliged to enter the lecture theatre by a separate door, for example. The Association of Women Pharmacists was established to improve the image and treatment of female pharmacists, and to expand their employment opportunities. In the early twentieth century the vast majority of women pharmacists were employed in hospitals or as dispensing assistants. Very few owned their own businesses, and most were managed by men. The Association of Women Pharmacists kept registers of members who required locums, and put them in touch with other members who were seeking employment. It housed an employment bureau, which maintained a 'black list' of poorly paid posts, and put pressure on these employers to improve their female employment opportunities, and also encouraged its members to join in partnership and establish their own businesses. In addition it provided a social support network and an insurance and annuity scheme for its members. Membership of the Association of Women Pharmacists was confined to women who had passed the major or minor examination of the Pharmaceutical Society of Great Britain. By the 1920s the Association was renamed the National Association of Women Pharmacists. During the Second World War the employment bureau worked with the Central Pharmaceutical War Committee, resulting in a maximum utilisation of female pharmacists during the war. During the 1940s a Merseyside branch of the National Association of Women Pharmacists was established in Liverpool, and in 1965 a Welsh branch was founded in Cardiff. Meetings were held at 46 Cardiff Road, Llandaff, attracting a small, but increasing, number of women pharmacists. By 1997 the Merseyside branch had been disbanded, but the National Association of Women Pharmacists, and branches in Blackpool, Leicester and Nottingham, were still active.

S W F Holloway, *Royal Pharmaceutical Society of Great Britain 1841–1991: A political and social history* (Pharmaceutical Press, London, 1991), 262-8

Records 1: The Museum Curator, Royal Pharmaceutical Society of Great Britain, 1 Lambeth High Street, London SE1 7JN

Minutes, incl. committee minutes, notices of meetings and social events 1937–58, 1982–96; cash books 1924–54; press cuttings book 1935–47; regular women's pharmacy column titled 'Pharmacist A', extracted from the *British and Colonial Druggist* 1933–51; Merseyside branch: general meeting minutes 1959–71, collective meetings minutes 1971–95, committee meeting minutes 1946–68, branch meetings minutes 1946–59, attendance book 1965–91, membership list 1950–89, annual reports 1946–71, accounts 1986–95; newsletters 1948–n.d.; miscellaneous accounts, correspondence, meetings notices, membership cards, press cuttings, photographs and lists of female pharmacy students n.d.; papers of Liverpool Standing Conference on Women's Organisations & British Federation of Business and Professional Women n.d. (Ref: IRA.1996.389; IRA.1997.153)

Records 2: Mrs C Vining, 21 Wingfield Road, Whitchurch, Cardiff CF4 1NJ

Welsh branch: general meeting minutes c.1965 to date.

Records 3: Mrs P Baker, 24 Cae Garw, Thornhill, Cardiff CF4 9DX

Welsh branch: silver jubilee newsletter 1991, photographs of silver jubilee dinner 1991.

NATIONAL PHARMACEUTICAL ASSOCIATION
Mallinson House, 38-42 St Peter's Street, St Albans, Hertfordshire

Trade association representing the interests of retail pharmacists

History: Following the National Health Insurance Act of 1911, the Pharmaceutical Society of Great Britain established a Local Associations Executive in 1913 to conduct negotiations with the government on behalf of retail pharmacists who participated in the National Health Insurance scheme. However, the Jenkin Judgement of 1920 ruled that the Pharmaceutical Society of Great Britain did not have the legal status to represent the trading interests of retail pharmacists, and paved the way for the establishment of a separate society. The Retail Pharmacists' Union was founded in 1921 to represent the interests of retail pharmacists, to regulate prices and terms of employment and to arrange insurance for its members, superseding the Local Associations Executive. Those who took out membership of the Retail Pharmacists' Union, also qualified for membership of the Proprietary Articles Trade Association, founded in 1896, and Chemists' Defence Association Ltd, incorporated as a limited liability company in 1899. The Retail Pharmacists' Union offered trademark registration, a debt collection service, assistance with stocktaking and regular 'union letters', short reports, including circulars and press releases, distributed to branch officers and members. In 1922 the Retail Pharmacists' Union incorporated the Chemists' Mutual Insurance Co Ltd, as a limited liability company, to provide low premium insurance cover for retail pharmacists. This company was later renamed the Pharmacists' Mutual Insurance Co Ltd. In 1928 the Chemists' Sickness & Provident Society, later renamed the Pharmaceutical & General Provident Society, was formed, to provide sickness insurance and subscription investment for pharmacists. The Retail Pharmacists' Union was located initially at the offices of the Proprietary Articles Trade Association and the Chemists' Defence Association Ltd in Temple Avenue, London, but relocated shortly afterwards, with the Chemists' Defence Association Ltd, which by then, was its wholly-owned subsidiary, to 19 Tavistock Square, London, and again in 1926, to 4-6 Queen Square, London. The Chemists' Defence Association Ltd provided legal advice and defence against prosecutions, free of charge, to all Retail Pharmacists' Union members. By 1931 90 per cent of retail chemists across the country had taken out membership of the Retail Pharmacists' Union, which in 1932 was renamed the National Pharmaceutical Union to reflect this trend. In 1935 the National Pharmaceutical Union launched and financed the Chemists' Friends Scheme, which sought to combat the sale of medicines by traders other than pharmacists. This was followed shortly afterwards by the incorporation of NPU Ltd, a limited liability company which supported the activities of the Chemists' Friends Scheme and the business activities of the National Pharmaceutical Union.

In 1938 the Chemists' Friends Scheme was renamed the Chemists' Friends Association, and after the Second World War it was known as the Chemists' Federation. It was dissolved in 1958, following the passing of the Restrictive Trade Practices Act. During the Second World War the National Pharmaceutical Union established a War Distress Fund, supported by members' contributions and registered under the War Charities Act, to protect retail chemists from financial losses as a result of evacuations. In 1945 a Business Purchase Fund was introduced, which granted loans to retail pharmacists who wished to purchase businesses. Shortly afterwards a Joint Industrial Council was founded, which consisted of employer and employee representatives, and aimed to encourage good industrial relations within the pharmaceutical industry. Following the establishment of the National Health Service in 1948 the dispensing of medicines became increasingly important, and the National Pharmaceutical Union secured a place on a number of government committees. One such committee was the National Health Insurance Committee, formed in 1947 and renamed the Pharmaceutical Services Negotiating Committee in 1976. This Committee was recognised by the Secretary of State for Health and Social Security as representative of British chemists, for negotiations within the National Health Service. The National Pharmaceutical Union also promoted the interests of its members against the sale of over-the-counter medicines by supermarkets and multiple stores, through its Marketing Policy Committee, established in 1956. In 1965 a limited liability company, NPU Holdings Ltd, was incorporated to finance this marketing operation. During the 1960s the Marketing Policy Committee sponsored, jointly with UniChem Ltd, a Modern Pharmacy Exhibition in London, and NPU Holdings Ltd, incorporated a subsidiary company, NPU Marketing Ltd, to acquire the business of the Marketing Policy Committee. In 1965 the National Pharmaceutical Union relocated to Mallinson House, 321 Chase Road, Southgate, Enfield, London, and members of the Scottish Pharmaceutical Federation and the Ulster Chemists' Association were taken into membership. In 1972 Independent Chemists Marketing Ltd was incorporated as a subsidiary of the National Pharmaceutical Union to produce a range of chemists' sundries, which were marketed under the title 'NUMARK', and to capitalise on the buying and selling power of its members. Later the company was renamed Care Chemists Ltd, and was sold by the National Pharmaceutical Union to its management. In 1974 it was renamed Numark Ltd, still operating from Mallinson House, but as an independent company, operating as a voluntary marketing and buying organisation for independent chemists. In 1977 the National Pharmaceutical Union was renamed the National Pharmaceutical Association and NPU Ltd was renamed NPA Ltd. In 1978 the National Pharmaceutical Association moved to premises in St Peter's Street, St Albans, Hertfordshire, and in 1982, launched the 'Ask Your Pharmacist' campaign, which sought to enhance the expertise and importance of the community pharmacist, and which remained an important feature of marketing policy during the 1990s. In 1997 the National Pharmaceutical Association continued to represent the interests of retail pharmacists, offer training courses and publish a range of information leaflets.

The National Pharmaceutical Union: Fifty years' service to independent pharmacy (Newman Neame Ltd, London, 1971); 'Seventy Five Years of the National Pharmaceutical Association', supplement to *Pharmaceutical Journal*, 27 Jan 1996; H Cowen, 'The Strategy of NPU Holdings Ltd is Based on Realism', *Pharmaceutical Journal*, 6 March, 1965; J Vatistas, 'Here's to the Next 75 Years: looking ahead with confidence', *Pharmacy Today*, Jan–Feb 1996, 10-11

Records 1: National Pharmaceutical Association, Mallinson House, 38-42 St Peter's Street, St Albans AL1 3NP

Executive committee meetings minutes 1920–76; Pharmaceutical Society of Great Britain letters and schedules re proposed Retail Pharmacists' Union 1914–21; Local Associations Executive papers re formation of Retail Pharmacists' Union 1920; proceedings of inaugural meeting 1920; invitation for nominations for election to first committee meeting 1921; draft constitution and rules c.1920; statement of policy 1982; membership registers 1915–26, 1935–47; statement of benefits and membership material 1960s; annual report 1974; ledgers: 1951–83, clearing house 1971–82; journal 1967–82; cash book sheets 1974–82 (w); draft accounts 1976–79; show expenses 1979; business purchase fund, register of loans, deeds and documents 1946–82; Joint Industrial Council: council meetings minutes 1943–55, joint negotiating and general purposes committee meetings minutes 1944, employers' agendas and year books 1966–71, papers re industrial disputes tribunal 1956; committee and sub-committee minutes: board of management meetings 1977–95, business services meetings 1943–47, National Health Insurance meetings 1922–24, 1927–47, finance meetings 1955–76, marketing policy meetings 1957–67 (w), pharmacy assistants training board meetings 1963–84, training assistants meetings 1964–66, training meetings 1985–94, local organisations meetings 1962–66, Drug Trade Council meetings 1941–45, Pharmaceutical Whitley Council meetings 1948–49, organisation meetings 1923–31, general purposes meetings 1928–39, medicine stamp duty meetings 1936–39, publicity meetings 1933–34, 1959–60, price protection meetings 1927–35, price list revision meetings 1923, photographic dealers meetings 1933–35, silver jubilee meetings 1946, distress fund meetings 1959–74, Mallinson banquet meetings 1949, miscellaneous meetings 1947–95; committee agendas: executive meetings 1947–76, business services meetings 1947–95 (w), local organisations meetings 1963–67, finance meetings 1965–95 (w), publications meetings 1959–67, general purposes meetings 1968–95 (w);

reports: enquiry into costs of National Health Service dispensing 1956, Joint Working Party on the Medical and Pharmaceutical Professions 1970, public relations recommendations 1973; investigation into proprietary frequency 1958; enquiry into consultancy services in the distributive trades 1969; speeches and addresses: splinter groups in pharmacy 1970, Joseph Wright, director 1967, 1975; union letters 1921–72; papers: National Pharmaceutical Service Joint Committee 1944–48, Restrictive Trade Practices Act 1957–65, proposed venture with UniChem 1963–65, Pharmaceutical Committee representatives conference 1964, 1968, National Chamber of Trade 1966, 1975–77, Pharmaceutical Society of Great Britain's planned pharmaceutical service 1967–69, failed launch of retailer-controlled wholesaling organisation for pharmacists 1968–69, Public Relations Working Party of the Pharmaceutical Society of Great Britain 1960s–72, EEC countries and pharmacy 1972–75, Pharmaceutical Services Negotiating Committee 1974–77; survey of wholesalers 1965; registers of sales and receipt of methylated spirits n.d.; formulae lists 1933–57, with revision notes 1968; formulae booklets 1961, 1963; *NPU Bulletin*, products catalogue 1965–69; leaflet re retail prices 1968; retail price lists 1924–61; price list supplements 1921–30, 1962–92, 1994; advertising material n.d.; publicity campaign guardbooks 1957–58; publicity leaflets and related papers 1946, 1960s–82; press cutting 1970; architectural plans n.d.; renovation records and plans 1990; plans, correspondence and papers re move from Southgate to St Albans 1975–79; enquiries into management salaries 1963, 1967; pension fund: ledgers 1938–80, registers of subscribers 1938–49, papers 1961–71; booklets and leaflets re training courses 1960s, n.d.; leaflets re pharmacy as a career 1959, 1970s–80s; circular letters 1969–73; correspondence and papers: formation of Retail Pharmacists' Union 1920, Pharmaceutical Society of Great Britain 1937, 1951, resale price maintenance 1950–56, 1965–69, Institute of Health Education, Sheffield re National Pharmaceutical Union membership 1969, British Medical Association Working Party 1970–72, Department of Health and Social Security 1971–76, Company Chemists' Association 1972, National Chamber of Trade 1972–75, Government re Boots Co Ltd 1975, miscellaneous 1940s–60s; photographs: executives c.1920s, 1940s–50s, staff 1940s, Mallinson House 1920s, 1976–79; notes re discussion at executive committee meeting re proposed meeting with representatives of Council 1960s; research papers and articles 1965, 1970s; booklets of other companies and associations 19th cent–1905, 1953–70s; historical notes n.d.

Chemists' Defence Association Ltd: directors' and general meetings minute books 1899–1966; agendas and year books 1947–93; annual reports and accounts 1921–59, 1971–80; annual accounts 1973–74, 1981–83; estimated accounts 1977–81; ledger 1971–83; journal 1952–82; investments papers 1973–78;

Department of Trade returns 1982–84; case books 1921–28, 1938–48; membership list 1959; analysis of dispensing scheme registers 1926–36.

Chemists' Federation: minutes: committee meetings 1936–58, council and sub-committee meetings 1958; revised constitution and rules 1956; ledger 1947–58; cash book 1957–58; defence fund, declaration of trust 1958; statement to Monopolies and Restrictive Practices Commission 1953; judgement re Restrictive Practices Act 1956, and agreement between members of Chemists' Federation 1958; code of standards for proprietary medical products 1950; lists of members 1946–58 (w).

NPA Ltd: directors' meetings minute books, incl. minutes of inaugural meeting 1935–59; general meetings agenda 1978; annual report and accounts 1977–78; ledgers 1947–82; day book 1976–83; cash books 1975–85; accounts 1977–78; estimated accounts 1980.

NPU Holdings Ltd: minutes: directors' meetings 1965–84, general meetings 1969–72, directors' and general meetings 1972–83; general meeting agendas 1974–76; share purchases and unclaimed dividends 1973–78; annual reports and accounts 1965–80; accounts 1972–76.

NPU Marketing Ltd: annual reports and accounts 1974–76; review of organisation 1970; reports: order processing 1971, future planning 1971, establishment of trading organisation for retail pharmacy 1971, proposed study of independent chemist trade 1974, corporate structure and strategy n.d.; distributors' lists c.1969; handbook, with commentary on draft n.d.; guide to promotional activity 1969–70; proposals and reports re implementation of computing system 1971, n.d.; *Nutimes*, news bulletin 1969.

NPUH Development Ltd: memorandum and articles of association 1966; ledger 1966–77.

Numark Ltd: directors' meetings minutes 1977; records re corporate structure n.d.; stock control record 1970s; sales statistics 1977; price list and order form 1970s; distributors' circulars 1976–77; report re study tour to USA 1980; papers and programmes re wholesaler seminars 1977; merchandising material 1974; brochure n.d.

Pharmacists' Mutual Insurance Co Ltd: directors' and general meetings minutes 1922–63; directors' agenda books 1977–95; annual returns and related correspondence 1975–76; ledgers 1958–82; journal 1966–82; cash books 1962–69, 1971–85; investment papers 1978–87; Golden Jubilee dinner menu 1972.

Pharmaceutical & General Provident Society: minutes: management committee and general meetings 1928–65, 1975–85, executive committee meetings 1947–95 (w); ledgers 1928–87; publicity brochure n.d.

Records 2: The Museum Curator, Royal Pharmaceutical Society of Great Britain, 1 Lambeth High Street, London SE1 7JN

Statement of benefits of membership of NPU and CDA Ltd 1946; display card showing metric/imperial conversion tables for prescriptions n.d; Company Chemists' Association, representations to privy council 1964. (Ref: IRA.1996.129, 161, 363)

NORTHERN WHOLESALE DRUGGISTS' ASSOCIATION
North of England

Regional trade association representing the interests of wholesale druggists and pharmacists

History: The Northern Wholesale Druggists' Association was established in 1902, to represent the interests of pharmaceutical wholesalers in the North of England, due to their frustration at the increasing dominance of manufacturing pharmacists within the Association of British Pharmaceutical Industry. The Association was peripatetic, its meetings being held twice yearly in various northern cities. During the following years companies from the south of the country were increasingly taken into membership, and the Association began to represent the interests of English wholesale companies in a national context. Pressure from this organisation and other regional wholesale trade associations contributed to the foundation of the National Association of Pharmaceutical Distributors in 1966, which was renamed the British Association of Pharmaceutical Wholesalers in 1991. The Northern Wholesale Druggists' Association was dissolved in 1966.

P M Worling, 'The History of the National Association of Pharmaceutical Distributors' in *NAPD 25th Anniversary* (NAPD, 1991)

Records 1: British Association of Pharmaceutical Wholesalers, 19a South Street, Farnham GU9 7QU

Minutes 1902–65; attendance registers 1955–65.

Records 2: Dr Peter M Worling, The Grange, 29 Fernielaw Avenue, Edinburgh EH13 0EF

Agenda and notes re costings n.d.; annual conference papers: meeting and conference programmes 1948, 1955, correspondence and costings 1965, invitation lists 1957, 1965; correspondence with Southport conference organiser 1957, 1964–65.

NOTTINGHAM PHARMACEUTICAL ASSOCIATION
11 Exchange Row, Nottingham

Association promoting pharmaceutical education

History: In 1868 the Nottingham & Nottinghamshire Chemists' Association was founded, for the purpose of inter-communication of opinion, better scientific education of assistants and apprentices and to form a professional library. The first meeting was held on 12 February 1869 at 11 Exchange Row, Nottingham. The Association was renamed the Nottingham & Nottinghamshire Pharmaceutical Association in 1905, and the Nottingham Pharmaceutical Association in 1907 by which date it had 60 members. It continued to operate until 1924.

Records: Nottinghamshire Archives & Southwell Diocesan Record Office, County House, Castle Meadow Road, Nottingham NG2 1AG

Minutes: general meetings, incl. balance sheets, press cuttings and notices of meetings 1887–1903, ordinary or monthly meetings 1869–78, council meetings 1884–1908, temporary meetings 1869; rules: 1905, with list of officers 1869, with list of officers and members 1882–83; annual report 1891–92; balance sheet 1891–92; registers of attendance at meetings 1890–93; lists of members and associates 1870–84 (w); membership card 1904–05; attendance register, University College pharmaceutical classes 1886–90; draft speech re minor examination 1883; library: regulations n.d., users' record book 1869–89, catalogue 1882–83, advertisements 1874, 1905; correspondence and papers: Association business, incl. administration of the Medicine Stamp Acts 1871–73, 1890–93, 1905–06, education 1869–74, 1905, n.d.; Nottingham School of

Pharmacy prospectus c.1902; annual dinner menus and tickets 1898–1905; programme of events 1904–05; reports and papers of other chemists/pharmaceutical associations, incl. a list of pharmaceutical associations in the Nottingham district 1898–1902; press cuttings re Pharmaceutical Society 1905; book of pressed lichens and mosses c.1870s. (Ref: DD 1135 addit, DD 1830/3-5)

PHARMACOPOEIA COMMISSION
Market Towers, 1 Nine Elms Lane, London

Government commission

History: The *British Pharmacopoeia* was first published in 1864, under the auspices of the General Council of Medical Education & Registration of the United Kingdom. It was a formulary, containing a list of all known drugs, with descriptions and formulae for preparation. In 1928 the Pharmacopoeia Commission was established to oversee the preparation of the *British Pharmacopoeia*, following recommendations made in the same year by a subcommittee of the Committee of Civil Research. Until 1969 the Commission was appointed by the General Medical Council, but following the passing of the Medicines Act of that year, responsibility was transferred to the Secretary of State and the operation was managed by the Department of Health and Social Security. The Pharmacopoeia Commission remains responsible for the preparation of the *British Pharmacopoeia*, which is normally issued every 5 years.

H Singh, 'History of the British Pharmacopoeia', *Pharmatimes*, 22, 11-12, 1990; 23, 1-3, 1991

Records: Royal Botanic Gardens, Library & Archives, Kew, Richmond TW9 3AE

Registered file 1930–51. (Ref: PRO/4/P/9)

PROPRIETARY ARTICLES TRADE ASSOCIATION
5 Caxton Way, Watford Business Park, Watford, Hertfordshire

Association monitoring retail price maintenance on over-the-counter medicines

History: The Proprietary Articles Trade Association was founded in 1896 by William Samuel Glyn-Jones, to protect sales of proprietary medicines from price-cutting, and thereby maintain fair competition. William Samuel Glyn-Jones also founded the Chemists' Defence Association Ltd, a limited liability company which offered legal advice and defence for chemists who faced legal action. At an inaugural meeting at Anderton's Hotel, Fleet Street, London, the association was founded with the title, The Association of Manufacturers, Retailers & Wholesalers of Proprietary Articles. This title was found too cumbersome and was shortly afterwards amended to the Proprietary Articles Trade Association. The Association drew its membership from all sectors of the pharmaceutical industry, whom it sought to protect from price undercutting by multiple branch chemists, a practice which was becoming widespread during the late nineteenth century. The Proprietary Articles Trade Association issued its first list of protected proprietary articles in 1896, and the proprietors of these 15 articles, agreed, along with pharmaceutical wholesalers, not to sell their goods to traders whom the Association had listed as price-cutters in its 'Stop-List'. By 1897 the list comprised 142 articles. In 1896 the Proprietary Articles Trade Association's offices were situated in the back room of Glyn-Jones' pharmacy, East India Dock Road, London, following which they were re-located to a number of London destinations before settling, in 1926, at 43 Gordon Square, London. In the same year the Association incorporated, as a limited liability company, PATA Trust Co Ltd, to act as trustee of the assets of the Proprietary Articles Trade Association and to collect investment income on its behalf. In 1919 a sub-committee of the Central Profiteering Committee reported in favour of the Proprietary Articles Trade Association's policy of price protection, on the grounds that price maintenance was in the public interest, preventing inflation of prices during periods of scarcity. In 1930 the Proprietary Articles Trade Association again came under public scrutiny through the Restraint of Trade Committee. However, the committee ruled that price maintenance was not unlawful, and indeed protected wage and labour conditions within the industry. Following this ruling, the Proprietary Articles Trade Association strengthened its rules and constitution. In 1956 the Restrictive Trade Practices Act was passed, which abolished collective resale price maintenance. However, it allowed manufacturers to take legal action in order to dictate selling prices. This was taken one stage further in 1949 when the Lloyd Jacob Committee criticised the practice of resale price maintenance by collective action. In 1964 the Resale Prices Act abolished resale price maintenance in total, unless manufacturers could prove that it was in the public interest for their prices to be protected. Between 1964 and 1970 the Proprietary Articles Trade Association, together with other interested organisations, worked on this legislation and, in 1970, at the Restrictive Practices Court, achieved an exemption for medicines, on the grounds that excessive price competition would lead to a squeezing out of small independent pharmacies, which often served remote communities, by multiple stores.

The Story of a Crusade: PATA 50th anniversary 1896–1946 (PATA, London, 1946); 'A Century of Proprietary Medicines', *Pharmaceutical Journal*, 146, 12 April 1941,138-40; 'Fifty Years of Price Protection: Jubilee of the PATA 1896–1946', reprinted from *Chemist and Druggist*, 16 March 1946, 1-15; 'Glyn-Jones' Portrait Loaned to Society', *Pharmaceutical Journal*, 256, 9 March 1996; G Harroway, 'RPM and the PATA' in *The Scottish Pharmaceutical Federation: 75th anniversary review, 1919–1994* (Atalink, London, 1994) 20; S W F Holloway, 'Cutting Remarks: reflections on the origins of the PATA', *Pharmaceutical Journal*, 256, 10 Feb 1996; A Hunt, 'Sir William Glyn-Jones, a Pharmaceutical Colossus', *Pharmaceutical Journal*, 255, 23 & 30 Dec 1995

Records 1: Proprietary Articles Trade Association, 5 Caxton Way, Watford Business Park, Watford WD1 8UA

Minutes: general meetings incl. annual reports 1896 to date, sub-committee meetings 1926, Fair Trading Congress meetings 1931–65; notice of general meeting 1960; annual report 1959; handbooks 1971–74; year books, incl. annual reports and accounts 1904–61; cash book 1962–87; Pharmaceutical Trade Fund: trustees meetings minutes 1964–71, annual accounts 1964–70, papers and correspondence 1963–70; Resale Price Maintenance Defence Fund: trustees meetings minutes 1952–77, declaration of trust 1952; papers re future of Proprietary Articles Trade Association 1944; resale price maintenance: statement 1955, papers and minutes 1948, 1950, campaign leaflets 1951–52, 1961–64, n.d.; statements: constitution and objectives 1930, Restraint of Trade Committee 1930–31, Lloyd Jacob Committee 1947–49; price lists issued by various dispensing chemists 1888, 1895–1900; press cuttings booklet 1895–96; correspondence: deputation to Board of Trade 1950–52, Association of the British Pharmaceutical Industry and Proprietary Association of Great Britain re Resale Prices Act 1964–67, Monopolies and Restrictive Practices Commission n.d.; journals: *The Anti-Cutting Record* 1895–1937, *PATA Quarterly Record* 1946–65; golden jubilee dinner programme 1947; photographs of directors and premises 20th cent.

PATA Trust Co Ltd: directors' and general meetings minutes 1927 to date; certificate of incorporation 1926; share register 1927 to date; financial papers and related correspondence 1920s–30s.

Records 2: Mr E H Butler, Galen Management Services Ltd, Galen House, 66 Commercial Square, Freemen's Common, Leicester LE2 7SR

Memorandum and articles of association 1965; handbook 1973-74; newsletter 1981.

Records 3: The Museum Curator, Royal Pharmaceutical Society of Great Britain, 1 Lambeth High Street, London SE1 7JN

PATA Quarterly Record 1946, 1964; birth certificate of William Samuel Glyn-Jones 1869; order of service for funeral of Sir Hildreth Glyn-Jones 1980. (Ref: IRA.1996.379-81)

PROPRIETARY ASSOCIATION OF GREAT BRITAIN
Vernon House, Sicilian Avenue, London

Trade association for the owners and manufacturers of proprietary medicines

History: The Proprietary Association of Great Britain was established in 1919 as the Association of Manufacturers of British Proprietaries to provide the services of a trade association to the owners and manufacturers of proprietary medicines and foods, to form government contacts, and to contribute to the raising of standards and working conditions within the industry. In particular it sought to distinguish its members from those who manufactured and marketed 'quack' medicines. In 1920 when the Proprietary Medicines Bill was brought before Parliament, proposing that all proprietary medicines which claimed to cure or relieve illness should be registered and their ingredients disclosed, the Association of Manufacturers of British Proprietaries offered support, but objected to the disclosure clause, which threatened loss of trade marks. As a result the bill was re-drafted, omitting this clause. Pressure of parliamentary business stalled the passing of the bill, and by 1926 there was still no law relating to proprietary medicines. In this year the Association of Manufacturers of British Proprietaries was renamed the Proprietary Association of Great Britain. During the interwar period the Association turned its attention to the regulation of proprietary medicine advertising. Many outrageous claims were being made by manufacturers of patent medicines, mainly those who did not hold Proprietary Association of Great Britain membership, and thus the Association embarked upon a campaign of encouraging newspaper editors only to accept advertisements from its members. From 1937 the Association launched a Code of Standards for advertising practice, which was formally adopted by the Advertising Association in 1939. The 1942 Pharmacy and Medicines Act, which provided for the control of medicines advertising, also used the Code of Standards as a guide. By 1948 the Proprietary Association of Great Britain was self-regulator for the industry and in 1962 was influential in the formation of the Advertising Standards Authority. The Medicines Act was passed in 1968 after considerable discussion with the Association, which advised on the need for statutory controls on licencing and advertising, in addition to those voluntary controls already practised. More recently the Proprietary Association of Great Britain has advised its members on trade related issues and has actively helped its members to export their products. It liaises with the Medicines Control Agency, the Department of Trade & Industry and the Ministry of Agriculture in this respect.

Fifty Years of Home Medicines: The story of the PAGB (PAGB, London, 1969); 'Proprietary Medicines', supplement to *Pharmaceutical Journal*, 19 Sept 1994, M1-M15

Records: Proprietary Association of Great Britain, Vernon House, Sicilian Avenue, London WC1A 2QH

Minutes: executive committee and general meetings 1919–42, 1946–96, finance committee meetings 1951–71, proprietary remedies export group meetings 1940–51; memorandum and articles of association 1955, 1989; certificate of incorporation 1942; special resolution re articles of association 1965; report of the select committee 1914; annual reports 1920–42, 1946–96; annual accounts 1922–47 (w), 1959–96 (w); accounts ledger 1971–74; list of members 1965–67; membership subscriptions registers 1958–88; annual subscription fees 1955; membership application forms 1919–20; poisons booklet 1923; patent medicine manufacturers': price lists 1936–39, 1971, n.d., product booklets 1940s, n.d.; applications for product licences 1971; survey re child safety packaging 1984–94; code of standards of advertising practice 1950–94; code of practice for advertising 1994; guidance notes re advertising 1964; advertising bills n.d.; over-the-counter directories 1993–95; correspondence: executive committee members 1984–95, E C de Witt & Co Ltd 1960s–70s; photographs, exporters' seminars 1980–81; publications 1947, 1980s–94; historical notes and tributes 1977, 1984; catalogue, London Medical Exhibition, Westminster 1959.

ROYAL PHARMACEUTICAL SOCIETY OF GREAT BRITAIN
1 Lambeth High Street, London

Society registering pharmacists and regulating the pharmaceutical profession

History: In 1815 Parliament passed the Apothecary Act. This legislation fully recognised apothecaries as medical practitioners, whilst also allowing them to continue their role as dispensers of medicines. In addition, the Act recognised a new group of specialist suppliers, chemists and druggists, who were awarded the right to prepare and dispense medicines but not to prescribe them. Chemists and druggists had been operating since the eighteenth century and, in contrast to the apothecaries, required no training. In 1794 this had prompted the foundation of a short-lived organisation, the General Pharmaceutical Association of Great Britain, a body of apothecaries who attempted to discredit the chemists and druggists. This objective failed, however, as indicated by the enactment of the 1815 legislation. Nevertheless, continued campaigning by the apothecaries brought the lack of training and qualifications of the chemists and druggists to the public eye. In 1841 Jacob Bell, proprietor of John Bell & Co, dispensing chemists, 20 Haymarket, London, led discussions which culminated in the formation of the Pharmaceutical Society of Great Britain in the same year. The Society was based at 17 Bloomsbury Square, London, and was established to regulate the pharmaceutical profession and to set up a system of registration for pharmacists. It received a royal charter in 1843, but was not granted the use of the word 'Royal' in its title until 1988. From 1841 Jacob Bell began to publish papers in a periodical called *Pharmaceutical Transactions*, which became the *Pharmaceutical Journal* in 1842. In the same year the Pharmaceutical Society of Great Britain School of Pharmacy was also established at 17 Bloomsbury Square and began examining chemists and druggists immediately. The Pharmaceutical Society of Great Britain also established a library at 17 Bloomsbury Square. 2 courses were available, one leading to a rudimentary minor examination, for assistants employed by chemists and druggists, and the other to the major examination, intended for established chemists and druggists who were already, or aspired, to be members of the Pharmaceutical Society of Great Britain. In 1851 a North British branch of the Society, later renamed the Scottish Department, was established in Edinburgh, to ease the pressure on Scottish pharmacists who were required to travel to London to sit examinations. The branch rented various premises in Edinburgh between 1851 and 1884 when it settled at 36 York Place, and was responsible for appointing Scottish examiners and regulating the conduct of examinations in Scotland. Applications for registration were submitted to the Scottish Department, but final registration was conducted in London. Under the 1852 Pharmacy Act, the Register of Pharmaceutical Chemists, the first statutory register of pharmacists, was established. It included those who were already members of the Pharmaceutical Society of Great Britain in 1852, and those who had passed the major examination. Prior to 1852 membership was limited to those who had both passed the major examination and were proprietor chemists and druggists. It was granted additionally to some unexamined proprietor chemists and druggists who had been admitted as members in the early years. Those who had passed either of the Society's examinations and were not proprietors were called associates prior to 1852, and non-proprietor individuals who had passed the minor examination retained this status until 1898, from which year they were eligible for membership. Between 1852 and 1872 the names of all who passed the major examination were added to the Register of Pharmaceutical Chemists, but only those who were proprietors were admitted to membership of the Society. From 1872 all pharmaceutical chemists were granted membership. Compulsory registration for all practising pharmacists was introduced by the Pharmacy Act of 1868. Passing the minor examination now became the legal minimum requirement to practice, and those who qualified were listed in the new Register of Chemists and Druggists. Those already established in business in 1868 were exempt from taking the minor examination. The major examination and the Register of Pharmaceutical Chemists continued to be produced annually after 1868. The Pharmaceutical Society of Great Britain was charged with the responsibility of examining all intending examination candidates and registering them once qualified. An annual yearly fee was paid for registration. In 1925 its School of Pharmacy became a recognised school of the University of London, and from this date a number of students chose to study for a degree in pharmacy rather than to take the major examination. In 1933 membership of the Society for registered pharmacists became compulsory and in 1954 the minor examination was phased out. Qualification as a pharmacist could now be achieved through the major examination, renamed the Diploma in Pharmaceutical Chemistry (PhC), or a degree in pharmacy (BPharm). In the same year the Pharmaceutical Society of Great Britain ceased to produce separate registers of pharmaceutical chemists and chemists and druggists, instead producing one register of pharmaceutical chemists. In 1967 the PhC was phased out, and the sole route to qualification was by degree. The Society moved to new premises at 1 Lambeth High Street, London, in 1976, and at the same time established a Welsh Executive, to implement its policy for Wales. Unlike the Scottish Department, the secretariat for the Welsh Executive was based at Lambeth. In 1997 the Royal Pharmaceutical Society continued to register pharmacists in community and hospital pharmacy and to regulate and promote the profession. It also had responsibility for enforcing legislation concerning pharmacy and the sale of medicines and poisons. It carried out these functions through a council and a series of committees. The council governed the Society, and was comprised of pharmacists elected by the membership and 3 non-elected Privy Councillors. It operated through a series of committees and specialist departments that reported to it. Departments included, pharmaceutical sciences, practice, law, ethics, inspectorate, education and publications amongst others. The Society also had 136 local branches.

'Pharmaceutical Society in Pictures', *Chemist and Druggist*, 1941, 12 April, 227; I M Caldwell, *36 York Place: Pharmacy and the New Town 1884* (Pharmaceutical Society, Edinburgh, 1884); S W F Holloway, *Royal Pharmaceutical Society of Great Britain 1841–1991: A political and social history* (Pharmaceutical Press, London, 1991); N Tallis and K Arnold-Foster, *Pharmacy History: A pictorial record* (Pharmaceutical Press, London, 1991)

Records 1: The Museum Curator, Royal Pharmaceutical Society of Great Britain, 1 Lambeth High Street, London SE1 7JN

Memorandum of association 1840; charter and bye-laws 1862–96, 1935–81; supplemental charters 1948, 1953, 1975; grant of arms 1844, 1993; register of seals 1900–40s; special general meeting minutes 1965; presidents' general meeting speech 1980; general meetings attendance books 1867–1918; council papers: agendas 1842–1914 (w), handbill and circular letter re election 1937, orders re appointment of examiners 1919–70, petition from chemists and druggists 1964, statement upon advertising 1971; annual reports: 1870, 1922–83 (w), North British branch 1931–32; balance sheets 1956–75; accounts 1841–1975, 1991; ledgers: general 1841–68, 1937–67, purchase 1959–72, expenses 1889–1921; journal 1942–67; day book 1938–64 (w); cash books 1864–1947, 1959–67; abstracts of statistics 1841–1920, 1954–77; cash sales analysis book 1944–54; receipts 1948–73; benevolent fund: register 1865–1950, accounts 1865–1976, ledgers 1900–58, subscriptions 1873; orphan fund papers 1892–1960, provident fund payments ledger 1910–27; parliamentary fund journal 1927–46; memorial funds: account books 1928–60, correspondence 1919–76; Russia x-ray fund accounts and correspondence 1942; emergency fund account book 1954–60; papers re Jenkins v Society test case 1920; evidence to Royal Commission on the National Health Service 1976; litigation papers 1855, 1965–68, 1979; enquiry committee survey 1939; correspondence re case against Potter & Clarke 1926–29; papers re legislation 1844–1986; committee meetings minutes: examiners 1842–61, 1943, 1960–62, laboratory class 1850–53, laboratory student's society 1852–56, 1874–1918, British pharmaceutical conference 1863–1983, journal 1866–69, general purposes 1875–1919, house 1875–90, law and parliamentary 1878–83, British Pharmaceutical Codex formulary 1886–1903, finance 1903–78 (w), drug tariff 1914–16, British pharmaceutical codex revision 1914–34, various 1914–80s, research 1915–23, Harrison Memorial Fund 1919–21, British Pharmaceutical Codex 1921–28, University of London, board of studies in pharmacy 1924–32, science 1924, 1960–77, 1982, British pharmaceutical conference executive 1925–45, league of ex-service pharmacists 1925–31 1939–45, dinner 1926–36, establishment 1927–62, parliamentary fund 1927–42, department of pharmaceutical sciences 1928, pharmacy sub-committee 1930–33, poisons board 1933–36, statutory 1934–91, special 1936-44, enquiry 1937-41, pharmaceutical trust 1938-56, war 1939-46, vegetable drugs 1941-46, public services 1942-1962, record of notable pharmacists 1942, planning 1942-43, nomination of examiners 1943, joint school 1943-48, national pharmaceutical service 1944-48, law 1944-53, 1960-65, n.d., Birdsgrove House 1946-52, formulary 1946-49, 1952-75, publications 1946-72, educational policy c.1947-58, films 1949-67, staff association 1950-68, co-ordinating committee of the Society and the Guild of Public Pharmacists 1951-54, history of pharmacy 1952-67, general practice of pharmacy 1960-63, pharmaceutics and pharmacognosy 1960-75, methods for the evaluation of drugs 1960-1970s, scientific advisory 1960-65, working parties 1960s-80s, co-ordinating committee for pharmacy 1962-66, practice 1963-81, council constitution 1963, adjudicating 1963-91, methods for the evaluation of drugs 1963-77, pharmaceutical analysis 1965-71, pharmaceutics 1965-70, education 1966-84 (w), Welsh executive 1969, 1976, Federation International Pharmaceutique 1969, new legislation 1970-77, audio-visual aids 1970-87, analytical methods 1976-77, biological safety 1976-81, assay on Crude Drugs 1977, laboratory library and museum n.d., organisation n.d., Pharmacy and Poisons Bill n.d.; committee meetings attendance books: education 1925-81, examiners 1928-39, parliamentary fund 1928-50, benevolent fund 1931-76, law 1935-45, enquiry 1937-41, council 1937-81, emergency 1939-44, joint school 1945-48; working party papers: drug developments 1960s-82, National Health Service pharmaceutical services 1970-72, computers 1978-79, information to patients 1982-83, child resistant containers 1983, 150th anniversary celebrations 1991; Scottish central pharmaceutical war committee constitution and terms of reference 1939-46; examination reports: board of examiners 1868-1900, examining syllabus committee 1934, post-graduate education committee 1985, general 1848-1953, external organisations 1918, 1945, 1972; examination regulations and papers 1888-1970; preliminary examination papers and notices of privileges/prizes 1888-93; examination results 1848-53, 1899-1970; papers re examinations, registration and prizes 1842-47, 1878, 1889-1960, 1980s; papers re student associates 1904-15; student opinions 1920; examination receipts 1843-53; certificates of qualification n.d.; School of Pharmacy laboratory: accounts 1926-35, reports 1961-88, day book 1926-35, sale of poisons register 1956-70, notebooks c.1877, 1927-28; correspondence: examinations 1916-25, 1942, Hanbury medal 1943-47; membership lists: Society 1868-1993, council and auditors 1850-1900, British pharmaceutical conference committee 1947-64; registers: members 1844-1933, chemists and druggists 1868-c.1907, pharmacy superintendent 1926-74, offenders 1879-1910 (w), students n.d., diplomas 1844-57, 1875-1933, apprentices 1885-1905, assistants 1852-n.d.; membership cards 1880-1973; papers re national register of pharmacists 1938-56; files re drugs 1977-79, 1991; catalogue of pharmaceutical apparatus 1861, 1880-81; retail price list of Edinburgh price list committee

1875; papers re pharmaceutical manpower in armed forces 1942–62; papers re demobilisation of pharmacists 1943–44; prospectuses and promotional material 1891, 1937–69; centenary celebration order of service 1941; jubilee programme and congratulation scroll 1891; programme for presentation of presidential chair to the Pharmaceutical Society of Great Britain by Pharmaceutical Associations of Australia and New Zealand 1933; press cuttings 1901–74; speech by Sir Joseph Swan 1868; Bloomsbury Square: deeds 1840–1957, leases n.d., architectural plans 1858–68, 1896, 1956–60, insurance policies c.1951–65, inventory of furniture and fittings 1861, papers 1899, 1948; Brunswick Square: architectural survey and plans 1936, papers re sale to University of London 1947–51, correspondence 1948–56; Bedford Place, tenancy agreement 1943, 1951; Birdsgrove House: architectural plans n.d., cash books and ledger 1949–59, gifts received 1949–60; Great Russell Street, leases and correspondence 1840–1964; 9 Galen Place, lease and licence 1950; Lambeth High Street: architectural plans and briefings 1944–77, 1986–89, press cuttings and programmes 1960–82, photographs 1974–75; staff wages book 1943–63, 1967; record of salaries 1842–74; staff payment sheets 1962–63; personnel files 1968–80; staff association, minutes and papers 1947–68; papers re holiday payment and taxation 1957–62; rules re superannuation scheme 1951; papers re manpower survey 1950–84; instructions to typists 1936; visitors' books 1877–1985; outgoing letterbook 1856–62; correspondence: Dr Jonathan Pereira to Professor Guibount 1830–53, Jacob Bell 1839–67, transfer of *Pharmaceutical Journal* from Jacob Bell to Society 1858, Belgian pharmacists 1919, poisons 1923–30, enquiry into advertising 1947–50, training 1964–67, drug warning codes 1972–73; lectures: Dr George Fordyce on chemistry 1780, De Pereira on *materia medica* 1847; departmental records: secretary and registrar, minutes, papers, reports, cash books, legal files and letterbook 1852–63, 1892–1985, British pharmaceutical conference, minutes, financial records, proceedings, papers, press cutting and subscription books c.1863–1987, publications, cash books, files and ethical guidelines 1873–1984, school of pharmacy, annual reports, papers, prospectuses and notes 1873–1902, 1937–53, library and museum, accounts, files re history and buildings, notes re 1952 exhibition, correspondence and visitors books 1877–1980, Liverpool school of pharmacy, lists of students, prospectuses, press cuttings 1887–1958, pharmaceutical journal, list of members, circulation figures, conditions, correspondence and notes 1899–1961, 1973, journal of pharmacy and pharmacology, reports and papers 1950–77, pharmaceutical sciences, papers, reports and lecture 1968–82, law department, minutes, papers, correspondence and leaflet re registration 1933–85, Welsh executive, minutes, balance sheets and correspondence 1969–76, college of pharmacy practice, annual reports and newsletters 1981–89, public relations, publications and press cuttings 1980–95; local branches: annual reports, anniversary booklets and brochures 1953, 1961, 1973, minutes, expenses and reports 1935–79, list of branch secretaries 1936–72, circular letters from London 1923–78; Bath & District branch, membership cards, press cuttings, notes and correspondence 1905–62; Leicester & Leicestershire branch: account book 1915–50, press cuttings 1950s; West London branch, syllabus 1938–39; Bedfordshire branch, golden jubilee brochure 1973; pharmacy club: minutes 1897–1922, minutes and accounts 1934–38; membership of cricket and football clubs n.d.; calendar 1877; musical score in honour of first female president 1947; album of signatures of subscribers to portrait of Walter Hills 1910; applications for annual dinner 1921, 1924; historical notes c.1885–1974; publications: Society 1862–90s, 1921–82, Society and external organisations 1912–83. (Refs: IRA.1996.007, 012, 014, 029, 032, 076, 103-4, 106-8, 112-13, 116, 122, 130, 133, 135-8, 143-9, 154-8, 161-2, 164-5, 172-99, 201-4, 206, 208, 211, 213-19, 221-6, 235-6, 238-9, 254, 259, 284, 299, 374, 377, 386, 388, 400-72; IRA.1997.001, 003, 007, 038-9, 077-8, 082, 133, 142; RPSGB-Co, RPSGB-Ge; LDPHA.MANUSCOL.25.1, 27.1-2)

Records 2: National Pharmaceutical Association, Mallinson House, 38-42 St Peter's Street, St Albans AL1 3NP

Papers and correspondence re proposed new charter 1951; report of committee of enquiry into the practice and organisation of pharmacy in Great Britain 1937; reports and papers of committee considering a planned pharmaceutical service 1967–69.

Records 3: Royal Botanic Gardens, Library & Archives, Kew, Richmond TW9 3AE

General file 1928–48. (Ref: PRO 4/P/8)

Records 4: Public Record Office, Ruskin Avenue, Kew, Richmond TW9 4DU

Medical Research Council Committees concerning the Pharmaceutical Society of Great Britain n.d. (Ref: FD1/2021-22, 5089)

Records 5: National Archives of Scotland, H M General Register House, Princes Street, Edinburgh EH1 3YY

Applications for charter 1952–64. (Ref: HH/41/356)

Records 6: Museum of Welsh Life, St Fagans, Cardiff CF5 6XB

Letter to John Griffith, Pencaerau, Caernarfonshire, informing him of his success in preliminary examination 1873. (Ref: 3179/3)

ST ALBANS MEDICAL CLUB
London

Dining club for surgeons, physicians and apothecaries

History: This London dining club met at the St Albans tavern near Pall Mall from 1797. At the time of his death in 1815, John Birch was described as the father of the club. Before 1832 its membership was restricted to 5 physicians, 5 surgeons and 5 apothecaries. Sir Frederick Stanley Hewitt (1880–1954), surgeon apothecary to the Royal family, was treasurer from 1942 until 1954.

John Bull, *History of the St Albans Medical Club* (Unpublished typescript, 1967); Robin Price, 'St Albans Medical Club Treasurer's Book 1798–1829', *Journal of the International Food and Wine Society*, 1979, 6, 1, 7-12

Records: Archives & Manuscripts, Wellcome Library for the History & Understanding of Medicine, 183 Euston Road, London NW1 2DE

Club rules and membership lists 1901–72; treasurer's books, some containing monthly and annual accounts for dinners, details of elections, attendances, bets and occasional minutes 1789–1954; statements of financial account 1938–65; minor cash and receipt books 1936–72; invoices, receipts and other financial records 1914–62; attendance books 1840–1933; betting books, some with wine accounts 1840–1954; correspondence: treasurers' 1933–1968, president's 1946–59; dinner menus 1922–90, n.d.; club histories 1869–1973, n.d.; James W D Bull's research notes and photographs of club's history 1966–87, n.d.; photograph albums of members 1846–1927, n.d.; photographs of members and dinners n.d. (Ref: MSS 6216, 6994-7017)

SCHOOL OF PHARMACY, UNIVERSITY OF STRATHCLYDE
University of Strathclyde, Glasgow

Pharmacy school

History: In 1796 a higher education institution, named Anderson's Institution, was established in Glasgow. Amongst the many subjects taught were classes in *materia medica*, marking an early association with pharmacy. From 1870 the Glasgow Chemists & Druggists Association operated a specialist pharmacy library from Anderson's Institution. The demand for pharmacy education was taken up by the Glasgow & West of Scotland Technical College, which was the predecessor of the Royal Technical College, where a School of Pharmacy was established in 1920, with Robert Lind as lecturer from 1927 to 1931. From 1934 students who studied at the Royal Technical College were eligible to graduate with honours degrees from the University of Glasgow. In 1956 the Royal Technical College was renamed the Royal College of Science and Technology, and was granted university status in 1964, when it was renamed the University of Strathclyde. In 1968 the Pharmacy Department was separated into 3 divisions, Pharmaceutical Chemistry, Pharmaceutical Technology and Pharmacology. In 1982 the Pharmaceutical Chemistry and Pharmaceutical Technology Divisions merged, creating the Department of Pharmaceutical Sciences. Pharmacology remained a separate department. In 1997 the Departments of Pharmaceutical Sciences and Pharmacology constituted the School of Pharmacy at the University of Strathclyde.

Records 1: University Archives, University of Strathclyde, McCance Building, 16 Richmond Street, Glasgow G1 1XQ

Committee meetings minutes 1922–50; special prospectus 1911–12, 1953–58; open day brochure and invitation card 1967; teaching hand-outs 1958; leaflet re pharmaceutical technology c.1980; certificate awarded to Robert Douglas Wellwood 1904; final year dinner menu and song sheet 1967; university institutional records 1920 to date. (Ref: OE, OF 13/1-4, T-MIN8)

Records 2: Glasgow University Archives & Business Records Centre, 13 Thurso Street, Glasgow G11 6PE

Papers of Robert Lind: lecture notes and examination papers 1927–31, laboratory notebooks 1927–32. (Ref: DC416)

SCOTTISH PHARMACEUTICAL FEDERATION
135 Wellington Street, Glasgow

Trade association regulating business and trading matters of Scottish community pharmacists

History: From the early twentieth century Scottish chemists began to campaign for an organisation to represent their business interests. Although there was a North British branch of the Pharmaceutical Society of Great Britain, at Edinburgh, later to become the Scottish Department, this organisation concerned itself with registration, educational and legal issues, and not with trade matters. In April 1919 a meeting of the Glasgow and Edinburgh Chemists' Associations and the North British branch of the Pharmaceutical Society was held, to consider the possibility of establishing a federation of Scottish pharmacists. It was proposed that an organisation should be founded which would regulate profits, sale of goods, working conditions and apprenticeships and which would provide an employment bureau. In May of the same year the Scottish Pharmaceutical Federation was established, and its first meeting was held at the offices of the North British branch of the Pharmaceutical Society. Throughout the following year relations with the Pharmaceutical Society of Great Britain, which claimed to have the same powers as the Scottish Pharmaceutical Federation to 'protect those who carried out the business of chemist and druggist', were strained. It was not until 1920, and the case of Jenkin *v.* The Pharmaceutical Society, that the Scottish Pharmaceutical Federation was proven to be the only Scottish organisation with the power to regulate conditions of employment, wages, opening hours and prices within the pharmaceutical industry. Following this judgement, the Retail Pharmacists' Union was established in England in 1921, to protect the business interests of English pharmacists, later acquiring the business of Chemists' Defence Association Ltd, which had been incorporated as a limited liability company in 1898, and being renamed the National Pharmaceutical Union. The Scottish Pharmaceutical Federation was affiliated to the National Pharmaceutical Union in 1965. For a time branches of Scottish Pharmaceutical Federation were also opened in Aberdeen and Perth, Perth & Kinross. In 1969 a business purchase and guarantee fund was introduced, offering loans to chemists and pharmacists to enable them to purchase businesses. The National Pharmaceutical Union was renamed the National Pharmaceutical Association in 1977, following which it was proposed that the Scottish Pharmaceutical Federation should be renamed the Scottish Pharmaceutical Association, in line with its English equivalent. This motion was defeated, although the Scottish Pharmaceutical Federation remained affiliated to the National Pharmaceutical Association. Recently the Scottish Pharmaceutical Federation has promoted the concerns of its members on matters such as the introduction of statutory sick pay, minimum wage legislation, the negative effect on community pharmacy of loss of resale price maintenance, and continues to represent the interests of community pharmacists. In 1954 the Scottish Pharmaceutical Federation established a clearing house for payment of chemists' accounts, to save both administrative time and cost for members, which by 1997 had grown to an annual turnover of over £9 million.

R P Marr, 'The Scottish Pharmaceutical Federation' in M Harrington (ed), *The Scottish Pharmaceutical Federation, 1919–1994, 75th anniversary review* (Atalink, London, 1994) 7-18

Records: Scottish Pharmaceutical Federation, 135 Wellington Street, Glasgow G2 2XD

Executive council meetings minutes 1951–97; finance and general purposes committee meetings minutes 1951–97; financial statements 1920–97.

THERAPEUTIC RESEARCH CORPORATION
National

Co-ordinating organisation for pharmaceutical research and development

History: The Therapeutic Research Corporation was founded in 1941 as a joint venture between pharmaceutical manufacturers May & Baker Ltd, British Drug Houses Ltd, Glaxo Laboratories Ltd, Burroughs Wellcome & Co Ltd and Boots Pure Drug Co Ltd. The Pharmaceutical Division of Imperial Chemical Industries Ltd (ICI Ltd) was a member from 1942. The Corporation was established to promote pharmaceutical research and development, in an attempt to compete with German advances in this field. It set out to achieve these objectives by combining the research expertise and facilities of Britain's largest manufacturing and research and development companies, funding pharmaceutical research projects and representing the concerns of the pharmaceutical industry before government. During and after the Second World War the most significant advance in pharmaceutical research resulting from the work of the Therapeutic Research Corporation was the development of penicillin. It also funded a number of research groups at various academic institutions in the UK. It was wound up in 1972 by voluntary liquidation.

R Davenport-Hines & J Slinn, *Glaxo: A history to 1962* (Cambridge University Press, Cambridge, 1992), 138-41; J Liebenau, 'The British Success with Penicillin', in *Social Studies of Science* (1987), 17, 69-86

Records: Archivist (Historical Records), Records Centre, Glaxo Wellcome plc, 891-995 Greenford Road, Greenford UB6 0HE

Directors' meeting minutes 1951–53; minutes and related papers 1941–45 of the TRC board and the following sub-committees: Biological Committee (Biol); Biological Standardisation Committee (BS); Carragin Progress Reports (AC);

Central Biological Institute (BI); Clinical Advisory Sub-Committee (CL); General Penicillin Committee; Mould Metabolic Products Sub-Committee (MMP); Patents Sub-Committee (PS); Penicillin Pharmacological Sub-Committee (Pen Pharm); Penicillin Producers Research Conference; Penicillin Synthesis Sub-Committee; Pharmacological Sub-Committee; Tuberculosis Sub-Committee; publications, TRC research papers; progress and production reports relating to penicillin, tercinin and other TRC products; TRC patent and trade mark applications – UK and overseas; TRC and IC(P) photographs of stages of penicillin production; press cuttings related to the formation of activities of TRC and development and uses of penicillin; financial and legal correspondence and papers relating to the formation of TRC, incl. balance sheets, accounts 1952–65, articles of association and research expenses; correspondence files – TRC Chairman and Secretary to member companies, research workers, chemical suppliers and others; printing blocks – TRC logo and letterheads; property papers n.d.

VEGETABLE DRUGS COMMITTEE
National

Government committee

History: As a result of severe shortages of organic drugs during the Second World War due to overseas trade restrictions, a Vegetable Drugs Committee was appointed by the Ministry of Health in 1941. Its remit was to analyse and encourage the cultivation of vegetable drugs within the Empire, and in particular, to oversee the collection of medicinal plants. The committee comprised representatives from the Ministry of Agriculture & Fisheries, the Pharmaceutical Society of Great Britain and the Wholesale Drug Trade Association, amongst others. It produced a list of British plants, categorised by their pharmaceutical usefulness, and also provided instructions regarding their identification, collection and distribution. Foxglove and deadly nightshade were found to be particularly beneficial. In 1942 responsibility for the Vegetable Drugs Committee passed to the Ministry of Supply, and Dr R W Butcher was appointed chief organiser. The Committee's work was overseen by the Therapeutic Requirements Committee of the Medical Research Council. In 1945, due to a storage surplus, the collection of foxglove was restricted, although the Vegetable Drugs Committee continued to operate in the immediate post-war period.

L Hastings, 'The Botanic Gardens at Kew and the Wartime Need for Medicines', *Pharmaceutical Journal*, 257, Dec 1996, 923-7

Records: Royal Botanic Gardens, Library & Archives, Kew, Richmond TW9 3AE

Minutes 1941–47; reports 1941–47; correspondence 1941–47; registered files 1928–57. (Ref: PRO 1/MUS/28/1-7)

WORLD FEDERATION OF SCIENTIFIC WORKERS
London

Trade union

History: The World Federation of Scientific Workers was founded in 1946, and was recognised by UNESCO as a non-governmental organisation. It represented scientific workers worldwide. In 1992 its London offices closed.

Records: Modern Records Centre, University Library, University of Warwick, Coventry CV4 7AL

Minutes 1946–94; treasurer's papers 1946–78; correspondence, subject files and circulars 1947–79; journal, *Scientific World* 1957–92; photographs 1940s–70s. (Ref: MSS.270)

THE WORSHIPFUL SOCIETY OF APOTHECARIES
Apothecaries' Hall, Black Friars Lane, London

City livery company, examining and licensing body for medical practitioners

History: Prior to 1617 City of London apothecaries were required to be members of the Grocers' Company of the City of London. Following a decree by James I in 1614, the City apothecaries were granted independence from the Grocers, and in 1617, received a charter to form the Worshipful Society of Apothecaries of London. Initially, the Society had no permanent premises and scant funds. However, the Master and the 2 Wardens, who comprised the Private Court of the Society, and the Court of Assistants, took oath immediately. The main functions of the Society were to improve the quality of drugs available to the public and to regulate the qualifications of dispensers. Those who wished to become apothecaries were required to serve a 7 or 8 year apprenticeship with a qualified apothecary. Once this apprenticeship was completed, the former apprentice could apply for full membership (freedom) of the Society, and for the freedom of the City of London. Some could later be elected to the Livery, which allowed them to vote in the elections for the Lord Mayor and Sheriffs of London, and a select few were elected to the Court of Assistants, from which they might rise to Junior and then Senior Warden, and, ultimately, to Master. In 1632 premises at Black Friars in the City of London were acquired by the Society, but these were destroyed during the Great Fire of London of 1666. Building work on Apothecaries' Hall recommenced in 1668 and was completed by 1671. In 1672 a joint stock company, the Laboratory Stock, was incorporated at the Hall. This company manufactured pure drugs, for the Society's members initially, and later for general sale. It also gained a monopoly over supply to the East India Company, the Army and the Crown Colonies. A further monopoly was granted by Queen Anne to a second joint stock company, the Navy Stock, to supply the Royal Navy with its medical requirements. The 2 companies amalgamated to form the United Stock in 1823, and by the 1880s, the Society's trading operations were organised by management committees. In 1673 the Society established a Physic Garden at Chelsea, London, where plants were grown to aid apprentices with their studies and for compounding in the laboratories. The garden remained in the hands of the Society until 1899. From 1518 the College of Physicians had exercised a monopoly on medical practice in London. However, during the Great Plague of 1666 the apothecaries gained widespread support by remaining in London to tend to the sick while the physicians retreated to the countryside. Unlike the physicians, the apothecaries were not permitted to charge for their medical advice, only for the medicines that they dispensed. Legally, an apothecary was licensed only to compound and dispense medicines that had been prescribed by a physician. This was altered in 1704, following a ruling in the House of Lords, the result of the 'Rose Case', which recognised apothecaries as legitimate medical practitioners. The ensuing legislation did not, however, permit them to charge fees for this role. In 1748 Parliament failed to grant the apothecaries sole rights to the compounding and selling of drugs. This marked the emergence of unqualified chemists and druggists as pharmaceutical dispensers, a group that later organised, in 1841, to form the Pharmaceutical Society of Great Britain. The transition of the apothecary from dispenser to medical practitioner was consolidated by the Apothecaries' Act of 1815, which effectively placed the Worshipful Society of Apothecaries in charge of general medical practice across England and Wales and established the Society as the chief regulating and qualifying body for general practitioners. The old-style dispensing apothecary was abolished by the Medical Act of 1886, the responsibility for the regulation of chemists and druggists and pharmacists passing to the Pharmaceutical Society of Great Britain. It was not until 1922, however, that drugs manufacture in the Society of Apothecaries' chemical laboratories and all trading activities ceased, and that the Society became a purely professional body. The 1815 Act empowered the Society to appoint a Court of Examiners which was responsible for conducting and regulating Society examinations. The major qualification awarded by the

Society was the Licence of the Society of Apothecaries, renamed the Licence in Medicine, Surgery and Midwifery in 1907. Completion of an apprenticeship ceased to be a requirement for entry to the Licence of the Society of Apothecaries examinations in 1874. However, members of the Society were distinct from licenciates, and for the former, apprenticeship remains one of the 3 means (the others being by patrimony or redemption) of becoming a member or freeman of the Society. From 1815 the Society also established a certificate entitled Assistant to an Apothecary, which later became a certificate for pharmacy, and then dispensing, technicians. This certificate ceased to be awarded in 1998. In 1865 Elizabeth Garrett became the first woman in Britain to qualify as a medical practitioner, by obtaining the Licence of the Society of Apothecaries. Having failed to exclude her from its examinations, as had other medical licencing bodies, the Court of Examiners altered its regulations in 1867 in such a way that women could no longer be admitted. This policy remained in force until 1888. Indeed women were not granted the right to become 'freemen' until 1947. In 1858 the General Medical Council was founded by Act of Parliament, and the regulatory role initiated by the Society passed to the General Medical Council. However, the Society continued to award a range of professional qualifications. From 1928 to 1963 it offered a Mastery of Midwifery, and in 1959 established a Faculty for the History of Medicine that in 1973 became the Faculty of the History and Philosophy of Medicine and Pharmacy. By 1997 diplomas continued to be awarded in both disciplines, and the Society still awarded its Licence, and also offered specialist postgraduate diplomas, including Clinical Pharmacology, Regulatory Toxicology and Medical Jurisprudence. In addition, it continued to award a number of prizes and scholarships for original work and research in pathology, therapeutics and cardiology, including the Rogers Prize, the Gillson Scholarship and the Galen Medal, as well as administering charitable funds.

W Carew Hazlitt, *The Livery Companies of the City of London* (Swann Sonnenschein, London, c.1882); W S C Copeman, *The Worshipful Society of Apothecaries of London: A history 1617–1967* (Worshipful Society of Apothecaries, London, 1980); G Corfe, *The Apothecary Ancient and Modern of the City of London* (Elliott Stock, London, 1885); C Newman, *The Evolution of Medical Education in the Nineteenth Century* (Oxford University Press, Oxford, 1957), especially chapters 2 and 3; C Wall, H Charles Cameron & E Ashworth Underwood, *A History of the Worshipful Society of Apothecaries of London, Vol. 1, 1617–1815* (Oxford University Press, Oxford, 1963); C Wall, *The London Apothecaries, Their Society and Their Hall* (Worshipful Society of Apothecaries, London, 1932); T D Whittet, 'The Barges of the Society of Apothecaries', *Pharmaceutical Historian*, 10, 1, 1980, 4-7

Records 1: The Clerk, The Worshipful Society of Apothecaries, Apothecaries' Hall, Black Friars Lane, London EC4V 6EJ

Records unlisted, incl. over 1,000 bundles of loose papers, in the following categories: foundational and constitutional records, incl. charters 1617, 1685, rules and ordinances 1618, grant of arms 1617; records of governance, incl. Court minutes 1926 to date; records re Masters, Wardens, Court of Assistants, Society officers and members of staff, incl. membership lists and/or year books 1702, 1719, 1727–41 (w), 1745 to date; financial records, incl. insurance policies 18th–20th cents; records of trade, craft and professional activities, such as Court of Examiners 1815 to date; incl. question papers of Arts examination, 1864–95, LSA/LMSSA 1860–81, 1890–1920 (w), and returned diplomas and certificates 1822–20th cent.; stock companies and retail pharmacy 1702–1922 (w), incl. laboratory plan 1823; Chelsea Physic Garden, incl. minute books 1862–91, 1896–98 and plans 1725, 1732, 1871; administrative records, incl. Clerks' letterbooks 1876–1953; records of gifts and charities, incl. wills and bequests; Hall contents and property papers, incl. inventories 19th–20th cents, plans 1771, c.1860, c.1911, leases and deeds 17th cent. to date.

Records 2: Guildhall Library, Aldermanbury, London EC2P 2EJ

Minutes: court meetings 1617–1926, special committee meetings 1814–50, 1883–1920; memorandum books 1606–1870; copy charters 1614, 1617; copy ordinance 1618; ordinances 1717–24, 1818–24, 1842, 1878; mayoral precepts and orders 1661–1747; description of arms granted 1617; account books 1626–1931; record of donations 1621–1831; bills and receipts 1783–85, 1807–46, 1930–36; legal papers: disputes with other societies 1606–1724, 1746, apothecaries' legislation 1747, 1812–17, 1844–47; Laboratory Stock: managers' committee meetings minutes 1741–51, 1760–67, agreements 1712–1822, subscriptions book 1728–1817, receipt books 1772–87, general papers 1671–72, 1730–72, 1827–28, dispensing book 1868–72; United and Navy Stock: committee meetings minutes 1822–66, agreements 1703, 1745–66, deeds 1822–79, accounts 1812–81; therapeutic and pharmacological common place book late 17th cent.; examination papers: minutes 1815–99, reports 1820–67, 1882–93, papers re curriculum 1835, 1844–47, fee books 1846–97, cash books 1860–99, student/candidate books 1815–1939, registers of licentiates and assistants 1815–1954; apprentice bindings 1617–1836 (w); freedom admissions 1617–1890 (w); quarterage books 1667–80, 1703–43, 1804–83; membership bonds 1672–96; lists: membership 1674–80, 1755–71, livery 1685, 1688, assistants 1693–1714; information against unqualified practitioners 1825–35; Chelsea Physic Garden: committee meetings minutes 1731–1862, administrative papers 1722–1846, rules and orders 1722–1829, building work accounts 1676, 1841–43, catalogue of plants presented to the Royal Society 1722–99; papers re building works 1632–34, 1667–82 (w), 1727, 1781–83, 1828–43 (w); inventories 1654–1817 (w); library catalogues 1783–1817; miscellaneous administrative papers 1674–1870; Friendly Medical Society: minutes 1775–1844, 1875–1917, copy constitution 1725, cash books 1774–1922, membership lists 1876–1913. (Ref: Mss 8200-305, 10809, 10979-90, 14276, 14472-4, 21744-7 [24052])

Records 3: Archives & Manuscripts, Wellcome Library for the History & Understanding of Medicine, 183 Euston Road, London NW1 2BE

Minute books (p) 1629–75; books registering persons admitted to freedom (p) 1694–1814. (Ref: MSS 8022-4, MS 8596)

Records 4: The Museum Curator, Royal Pharmaceutical Society of Great Britain, 1 Lambeth High Street, London SE1 7JN

Bill for syrup of poppies 1822; correspondence re acquisition of Society's wholesale trading activities by Randall & Wilson Ltd, Southampton 1922. (Ref: IRA.1996.142, 263)

Appendix 1
Geographical guide to minor collections of records relating to pharmaceutical companies and pharmacies which have been publicly deposited

ENGLAND

BATH & NORTH EAST SOMERSET
BATH & NORTH EAST SOMERSET COUNCIL
Archive & Record Office, Guildhall, Bath BA1 5AW

Apothecary/chemist, Bath, prescriptions day book 1866–68 (Ref: Acc 328).

BEDFORDSHIRE
BEDFORDSHIRE & LUTON ARCHIVES & RECORDS SERVICE
The Record Office, County Hall, Cauldwell Street, Bedford MK42 9AP

John W Biss, 48 High Street, Bedford, chemist and druggist, later surgeon and dentist, sales ledgers 1888–89 (Ref: Z447/142-6).

BIRMINGHAM
BIRMINGHAM CITY ARCHIVES
Central Library, Chamberlain Square, Birmingham B3 3HQ

Atkinson's, Birchfield Road, Handsworth, chemist, prescription book 1927–35 (Ref: Z 440); R S Dyer, MPS, Coventry Road, Hay Mills, Yardley, dispensing chemist, prescription book 1935–49, private recipe book 1934, draft of business card n.d. (Ref: MS 1238); M G Hewitt, 165 Hagley Road, Birmingham, chemist, prescription books 1862–1940 (w) (Ref: MS 308); M Latham, MPS, and A H Moseley, MPS, 1116 Coventry Road, Hay Mills, stamped prescriptions 1944–49 (Ref: MS 1238/6).

BOLTON
BOLTON ARCHIVE & LOCAL STUDIES SERVICE
Central Library, Civic Centre, Le Mans Crescent, Bolton BL1 1SE

K Melling & Son, 341 Chorley New Road, Horwich, pharmaceutical chemist, poison book 1934–67 (Ref: ZZ/332).

BRADFORD

WEST YORKSHIRE ARCHIVE SERVICE, BRADFORD
15 Canal Road, Bradford BD1 4AT

Harrison, Parkinson & Co, Sunbridge Road, Bradford, chemist, bills and receipts 1845, 1883, 1904–05, drugs catalogue 1864, advertisement 1864, bill head n.d., press cuttings re history of the business n.d., notes re Benjamin Baynes, foreman, who drowned in 1822, n.d., Thomas Richardson's will 1876, Herbert Richardson's will n.d., Jackson's will 1948, executor's accounts 1904–05, 1927, executor's ledgers 1876–93, correspondence re H R Jackson, deceased 1948–49, deed of release for the estate of Edith Mary Jackson 1958 (Ref: 9D79/1-2).

BRISTOL

BRISTOL RECORD OFFICE
'B' Bond Warehouse, Smeaton Road, Bristol BS1 6XN

John Morse & Thomas Martin, apothecaries, articles of partnership, letters and account 1738–60 (Ref: 12879 (19-21)); A L Thomson, Long Street, Tetbury, Gloucestershire, chemist and druggist, tradesmen's vouchers for goods supplied, incl. illustrated letterheads 1879–91 (Ref: Acc 40437).

UNIVERSITY OF BRISTOL LIBRARY SPECIAL COLLECTIONS
Tyndall Avenue, Bristol BS8 1TJ

'B.J.', [?Westminster, London], doctor, prescription book 1876–77 (Ref: 1560).

BUCKINGHAMSHIRE

BUCKINGHAMSHIRE RECORD OFFICE
County Hall, Aylesbury HP20 1UA

Arthur Mortimer, copy agreement with British Felsol Co for manufacture of *Culpus*, invented by Mortimer for treatment of multiple sclerosis 1956 (Ref: D/X 920).

CALDERDALE

CALDERDALE MUSEUMS & ARTS
Shibden Hall, Lister's Road, Halifax HX3 6XG

Dyers Chemists, Halifax, dispensing chemist, business premises photographs n.d.

CAMBRIDGESHIRE

CAMBRIDGESHIRE RECORD OFFICE, CAMBRIDGE BRANCH
Shire Hall, Castle Street, Cambridge CB3 0AP

G E Beall & Son Ltd, 25 Sidney Street, Cambridge, pharmacist, prescription book 1950–66 (Ref: R80/60: 888); Brain Brothers, 7 Abbey Gate Street, Bury St Edmunds, Suffolk, chemist, business sales particulars with plans 1887 (Ref: 296/SP471); James Fernie, Newport-on-Tay, Fife, chemist, formulary 1901–n.d. (Ref: R80/60: 888); Thomas & John Healy, Oakham, Rutland, apothecaries, counterpart deed of partnership 1737 (Ref: L100/22); Messrs E Matthews, High Street, Royston, Hertfordshire, chemist, stock incl. showcases and fittings 1911 (Ref: 296/SP880); G F Rogers Ltd, 92a Mill Road and 25 Sidney Street, Cambridge, pharmacist, prescription book 1941–67 (Ref: R80/60: 888); Joseph Sturton, Cambridge, chemist, memorandum of agreement with Ebenezer Field, chemist, to relinquish chemist's shop 1859 (Ref: R59/4/7/1).

CAMBRIDGESHIRE RECORD OFFICE, HUNTINGDON BRANCH
Grammar School Walk, Huntingdon PE18 6LF

Chemist, Cambridgeshire, account books 1858–1900 (w), prescription books 1863–73, 1890–1942, notebook containing recipes for special mixtures in constant use such as cough mixture, gout pills and tooth powder n.d., c.1850, printed booklet entitled 'Cox's Companion to the Medicine Chest', giving instructions for the use of various drugs and medicines 1851 (Ref: Acc 2140).

CHESHIRE

CHESHIRE RECORD OFFICE & CHESTER DIOCESAN RECORD OFFICE
Duke Street, Chester CH1 1RL

W A Brearey, Hill & Co, R B Roberts, T H W Simmons, J Rymer Young, chemists, invoices 1897–1900 (Ref: D 3702/7); E C Earlam, 7 Church Street, Frodsham, pharmacist, combined ledger and prescription book 1875–1913, deeds 1770–1905 (Ref: D 2572); Francis Horden, Cheadle, chemist, druggist and grocer, illustrated bill 1822 (Ref: DDX 339/1); Samuel Hulme, Market Place, Sandbach, chemist and druggist, ledger 1865–71 (Ref: DDX 602); Alec Hutton, articles of pupilage to Charles Charnley, Grove Pharmacy, Wilmslow, dispensing chemist 1927 (Ref: D 4470/2).

CHESTER ARCHIVES
Town Hall, Chester CH1 2HJ

J P Craine & Son, 104 and 106 Northgate Street, Chester, dispensing chemist, prescription books 1903–47 (w) (Ref: CR 491); Milling Johnson Ltd, 48 Northgate Street, Chester, chemist, recipe books 19th–20th cents. (Ref: CR 731).

CORNWALL

CORNWALL RECORD OFFICE
County Hall, Truro TR1 3AY

William Henry Bucher, 31 Boscawen Street, Truro, recipe book early 20th cent. (Ref: X763/1); Co-operative Chemists, 35 Fore Street, St Austell, chemist and druggist, prescription books 1903–67 (Ref: AD303/1/1-4).

COVENTRY

COVENTRY CITY ARCHIVES
Mandela House, Bayley Lane, Coventry CV1 5RG

Weltons, 13 High Street, Coventry, dispensing chemist, prescription books 1902–48 (Ref: PA 657).

CUMBRIA

CUMBRIA RECORD OFFICE, BARROW IN FURNESS
140 Duke Street, Barrow in Furness LA14 1XW

George Bennett, Horsfields (Barrow) Ltd and J N Murray Ltd, Barrow in Furness, dispensing chemists, prescription books (m) 1874–1975 (Ref: BMF 11-12).

CUMBRIA RECORD OFFICE, CARLISLE
The Castle, Carlisle CA3 8UR

William Donken (d.1764), 'Dr Donken', Penrith, bills for medicines, attendances etc. on Hudleston family 1744–51 (Ref: D/Hud/82/12); John Martin, Penrith, apothecary, bill 1781 (Ref: D/Van 6 Household records); Pape's, Keswick, chemist, prescription books 1906–55, veterinary cures c.1910 (Ref: DB 102/1-57); J W Pickering, Maryport, chemist, day books, sales 1930–36, alphabetical memoranda book, containing the composition of various pharmaceutical products n.d., c.1900 (Ref: DX 1192/5-9); Richard Story, Penrith, apothecary, bills for visits, medicines and cosmetics supplied to Fletcher Vane family and servants 1780–84 (Ref: D/Van 6 Household records); Wilson & Kitchin, 27 King Street, James Street and Catherine Street, Whitehaven, chemist, volume containing price lists, historical notes and details of apprentices 1902–25 (Ref: DH 22 Daniel Hay Collection from Whitehaven Library).

CUMBRIA RECORD OFFICE, KENDAL
County Offices, Stricklandgate, Kendal LA9 4RQ

F W Boon & Son Ltd, Kendal, chemist, ledgers 1959–86(w), day books 1969–80(w), purchase ledgers 1968–78 (Ref: WDB116); W Doherty, Windermere, chemist, prescription books 1940–47, 1957–65 (Ref: WDB/51); Eden Pharmacy, Appleby, pharmacist, ledger 1951–55, small order books 1918–24, order book 1948–50, prescription books 1911–46 (w), dangerous drugs and sale of poisons register 1948–53, student's note books on pharmacy mid 20th cent. (Ref: WDB/42); Highgate Pharmacy, Kendal, prescription book, 1876–1965 (Ref: WDB/49 Microfilm JAC 165); Lakeland Pharmacy, Bowness-on-Windermere, prescription book 1935–38, photographs of premises n.d. (Ref: WDB/37 Microfilm JAC 165-6); N K Mitchell, Kendal, chemist, account and prescription book 1930–58, photograph of premises n.d. (Ref: WDB 41); R Moorhouse, Kendal, chemist, ledgers 1947–49, 1957, sales books 1950–57, day books 1954–57 (Ref: WDB/36); Severs & Bateson, Kendal, chemist and druggist, articles of agreement between Joseph Severs and Thomas Bateson 1882, cash books 1878–1901, bank passbook (Thomas Bateson) 1872–1900 (Ref: WDX859/3-8).

DERBYSHIRE

DERBYSHIRE RECORD OFFICE
New Street, Matlock. Enquiries to County Hall, Matlock DE4 3AG

Adams' patent medicines price list 1884 (Ref: D1602); S Coates, Ilkeston/Alfreton, chemist, correspondence and invoices 1851–63 (Ref: D842); W Elmitt, Derby, chemist, account books 20th cent. (Ref: D1595); T Hollingsworth, 28 Queen Street, Derby, chemist, account book 1842–49 (Ref: D2074); Samson Augustus Robey, Clay Cross, chemist, prescription registers 1915–78, recipe book c.1930, poisons and drugs registers 1949–78 (Ref: D4673); G Saxton, Smedley Street, Matlock, chemist and optician, prescription book 1952–63 (Ref: D4634).

Unnamed apothecary, account books 1675–1740 (Ref: D77); unnamed chemist, Matlock, invoices late 19th cent. (Ref: D281).

DEVON

DEVON RECORD OFFICE
Castle Street, Exeter EX4 3PU

John Arnold, Exeter, doctor of physic, and John May, Dunsford, yeoman, articles of agreement concerning medicine called 'The Cordial of Health' n.d. (Ref: 53/6 Box 104); Ball, West Teignmouth, apothecary, assignment re bankruptcy 1756

(Ref: 924B/B8/12); Lewis Judah Cohen, alias Eljaysee, Plymouth, gentleman, and Henry Matthews, Exeter, chemist, articles of agreement concerning medical mixture 'Eljaysee's Aqua Elysii' and 'Eljaysee's Vegetable Toothpowder' cures for toothache n.d. (Ref: 53/6 Box 104); Collins, Bampton, surgeon and apothecary, apprenticeship indenture 1879 (Ref: 1044B add 2/B3/1); Thomas Fisher, Buckfastleigh, surgeon and apothecary, and John Francis Cookson, Ugborough, surgeon and apothecary, articles of partnership 1852 (Ref: 2461Z/B 1); Hinton Lake & Son Ltd, 41 High Street, Exeter, dispensing chemist, prescription books, some belonging to other named chemists 1832–1930, correspondence with rubber manufacturers 1928 (Ref: 3021B); Hole, apothecary, and Edworthy, farmer, Hulmleigh, legal case papers 1794 (Ref: 1292M/Legal/H10); Holman, Ham & Co Ltd, Exmouth, chemist and druggist, deed of co-partnership between Holman & Ham 1850 (Ref: 53/6 Box 93), prescription books 1880–1905 (Ref: 2893B); Howard & Summers, Cullompton, apothecaries, partnership agreement 1859 (Ref: 74B/MT 1993); W B Phillips, chemist, druggist and stationer, bills 1836–42, Phillips & Cooper, late Matthews & Co, wholesale chemist and druggist, bill 1843 (Ref: 1044B/M/F 22); William Quicke, Ottery St Mary, correspondence and legal papers arising from Quicke's application for post of clerk and traveller to Henry Matthews, Exeter, chemist (Ref: 2461Z/B4); Ridd, Coleridge, apprenticeship indenture to Legg, North Tawton, surgeon and apothecary 1792 (Ref: 1292M/Family III/1); William Venn, Thelbridge, apprenticeship indenture to Richard Bryan, South Molton, apothecary 1712 (Ref: 2309B/F 29/1); Charles Wheaton, Honiton, apprentice indenture to George Huggins, Exeter, chemist and druggist 1844 (Ref: 282M/AI 4).

Apothecary's account book, fragment with index 1859–61 (Ref: 74B/Z 22); apothecary's bill 1753 (Ref: CC 216/65); chemist and grocer, account books 1856–70 (Ref: 337B/10/23); chemist, wine merchant, shoemaker and ironmonger, Torquay and Barnstaple, bills 1824–53 (Ref: 318Z/B 38-42); surgeon and apothecary's bill 1807–08 (Ref: 474M/F 12).

NORTH DEVON RECORD OFFICE
Library & Record Office, Tuly Street, Barnstaple EX31 1EL

Barnstaple Pharmacy, 65 Boutport Street, Barnstaple, pharmacist, prescription books 1893–1910, 1922–70, recipe book, with historical notes 1837–1932 (Ref: B 111); Sydney J Buckle, 1 High Street, Great Torrington, chemist, prescription books 1866–1947 (Ref: B 157); D W Turner, The Square, Holsworthy, chemist, prescription books 1919–46 (Ref: B 299).

DONCASTER

DONCASTER ARCHIVES
King Edward Road, Doncaster DN4 0NA

Doncaster pharmacist, prescription book 1923–32 (Ref: DZ.MD.387).

H I WELDRICK LTD
Highfield House, 11-13 Highfield Road, Doncaster DN1 2LA

H I Weldrick Ltd, retail pharmaceutical chemist, Doncaster, prescription books 1879–1929.

DORSET

DORSET RECORD OFFICE
9 Bridport Road, Dorchester DT1 1RP

Beach & Co, East Street, Bridport, retail chemist, prescription 1949 (Ref: D/BTM: 7/2/1); Durden, Pearce & Spicer, 13 Cornhill and High East Street, Dorchester, chemist, prescription books, some containing loose papers 1863–1948 (w) (Ref: D/DSE/B1-15); Evans, 33 High Street, Dorchester, chemist, prescription books 1863–1906 (w), advertisement for an assistant n.d., correspondence n.d. (Ref: D/DSE A1-4); William J Gregory, Weymouth, dispensing chemist, prescription books 1891–1936 (Ref: D/GGY); Hine & Son, Beaminster Square, Beaminster, retail chemist, deed of co-partnership 1859, deed of dissolution 1968, advertisement for Richard Hine, pharmacist 1923 (Ref: D1/LN 39, Ph 512); Albert Edgar and Charles Sydney Prideaux, High West Street, Dorchester, surgeons, prescription books 1903–12 (Ref: D.561/1); F Stennet, chemist, prescription books 1762–69, 1773–91 (Ref: D/WLC:Z24-6).

Apothecary, fragments of prescription book 1776–79 (Ref: D/BTM: 7/1/1); chemists, Doncaster, prescription books 1946–47 (Ref: D. 561/2); chemists, Weymouth and Dorchester, prescription books 1903–12, 1946–47 (Ref: D.561/1-2); chemists, Wimborne, reception books 1898–1952 (Ref: D/WMM: unlisted).

DURHAM

DURHAM RECORD OFFICE
County Hall, Durham DH1 5UL

Brandon & Byshottles Co-operative Chemists Ltd, Durham, chemist, committee meeting minutes 1951–68 (Ref: D/Co/BB); Robert Brown, 19 High Row, Darlington, chemist, druggist and grocer, and James Crosby Robson, Darlington, retired druggist and grocer, assignment of share in stock of partnership and indemnity 1876 (Ref: D/XD 83/14); John Burdon, 14 Claypath, Durham, chemist and druggist, accounts 1855–65, 1867–82, advertisements, correspondence and receipts 1852–75 (Ref: D/X 159/1-3); East Durham Co-operative Chemists, Durham, chemist, committee meetings minute book 1951–65 (Ref: D/Co/EDC); Philip Harrison, Darlington, chemist and druggist, will 1808 (Ref: D/DL/8/16); John Edward Hodgson, 14 High Row, Darlington, chemist, prescription books of Hodgson and predecessors 1856–1945, J Robinson's prescriptions and letters requesting prescriptions 1886–96, J E Hodgson's recipe book, medical and cosmetic preparations n.d (Ref: D/Hg); Waters The Chemists, High Northgate and 2 Prebend Row, Darlington, chemist, prescription books, incl. list of industrial spirits dispensed c.1924–50, medicinal, cosmetic and veterinary preparations recipe books incl. some advertisements (mainly for Bainbridge & Finlayson of Stockton-on-Tees) n.d (Ref: D/XD 38); Masons, Saddler Street, Durham, chemist, drugs register 1921–39 (Ref: D/X 62/1).

Chemist, Durham, prescription book early 20th cent. (Ref: D/X 205/1).

EAST RIDING OF YORKSHIRE

EAST RIDING OF YORKSHIRE ARCHIVE & RECORDS SERVICE
County Hall, Beverley HU17 9BA

John Albin, Newport, Isle of Wight, chemist and druggist and printer, general ledger 1802–39 (Ref: DDCL 3371); Merkins, Cottingham, chemist, prescription books 1907–85; formula books pre 1920 (Ref: DDX 636); Robinson & Co, Market Place, Beverley, chemist and druggist, account book 1817–20, receipt books 1869–74 (Ref: DDX 579).

EAST SUSSEX

EAST SUSSEX RECORD OFFICE
The Maltings, Castle Precincts, Lewes BN7 1YT

Baker's, 44 High Street, Lewes, chemist, prescription book 1840–84 (Ref: ACC 6077/28/1); Eastbourne Pharmaceutical Committee (National Health Service) and Panel Chemists, minutes 1947–48; Eastbourne Pharmaceutical Committee and Panel Chemists: minutes 1927–47, combined minutes with Eastbourne District Pharmaceutical War Committee 1941–45; Eastbourne Pharmaceutical (National Health Service), minutes 1958–71 (Ref: ACC 6700); Hastings Insurance Committee, East Sussex, registers of payments to chemists 1918–44 (Ref: INS 2/9); Thomas Martin, 16 and 17 High Street, Cliffe, Lewes, pharmaceutical chemist, notebook detailing Rev J Constable of Ringmer's account 1862–66 (Ref: MOB 1610).

ESSEX
ESSEX RECORD OFFICE, CHELMSFORD BRANCH
PO Box 11, County Hall, Chelmsford CM1 1LX

Philip Gardiner, Marine Square, Wapping and Great Clacton, apothecary, accounts books 1674–78, 1699–1704, bills, receipts and accounts 1669–1703, deeds 1673–98, correspondence 1670–1711 (Ref: D/DC1); John Gilling, Market Hill, Saffron Walden, pharmaceutical chemist, prescription books 1862–1909 (Ref: D/F 20); G C Key & Charles B Thacker, 21 High Street, Saffron Walden, chemist, dispensary register 1897–1937 (Ref: D/F 15); W Metcalfe, Chelmsford, chemist, account books 1893–1919, day books 1884–90 (w), prescription books 1883–1903, H R Plattin's formulae book c.1858, H R Plattin junior's Westminster College notebook c.1877, dairyman's account book, with enclosures re Fakenham 1894–98 (Ref: D/F 29).

ESSEX RECORD OFFICE, COLCHESTER & NORTH-EAST ESSEX BRANCH
Stanwell House, Stanwell Street, Colchester CO2 7DL

Baker & Fairhead Ltd, Head Street, Colchester, chemist, prescription books 1838–1943 (Ref: D/F 119); William Byfield, St Botolph Street, Colchester, apprenticeship indenture 1813, diary 1834–59, notebook n.d. early 19th cent., scrapbook c.1827–40, certificate of marriage of Ann Carthew Rawle 1838, astrological prediction 1827 (Ref: Acc C81, Acc C175).

GLOUCESTERSHIRE
GLOUCESTERSHIRE RECORD OFFICE
Clarence Row, Alvin Street, Gloucester GL1 3DW

John Day, Upton-Upon-Severn, valuation of property incl. medicines 1813 (Ref: D2080/134); Waldron Griffiths, Cirencester, chemist, prescription 1900 (Ref: D4457/Z1); Hamptons Ltd, Gloucester, chemist, prescription books 19th–20th cents. (Ref: D2418, unlisted); H J Hands, Chipping Campden, dispensing chemist, prescription books, Hands and successors late 19th cent.–1930 (Ref: D5119); Andrew Hingston, Cheltenham, chemist, day book 1837–38, trustee's receipt book 1838–39, bankruptcy papers, incl. appointment of commissioners, correspondence, sales particulars, accounts and legal documents 1837–39; press cutting 1838 (Ref: D2025 Box 132); John Marston, Tewkesbury, druggist and grocer, sale of shop contents 1837 (Ref: D2080/501); Mrs Sarah Roberts, Cheltenham, chemist and druggist, bill 1818 (Ref: D3893/6/3); Rose's Pharmacy, 23 Southgate Street, Gloucester, pharmacist, prescription book n.d., mid 19th cent., short memoir of James Dudfield Rose (1868–1947) n.d. (Ref: D5529); F B Sellors, 145 High Street, Tewkesbury, chemist and druggist, notebook of medical recipes, many accompanied by appropriate pill box or bottle labels c.1870–85 (Ref: D5792); Messrs Smith, Blockley, village store proprietors, stock list of drugs sold 1826–34, illustrated billheads of Evesham drug dealers 1843–55, stocklists, accounts and receipted bills from wholesalers 1817–53 (Ref: D4220/2-3, D3471/718); Spa Pharmacy, Montpellier, Cheltenham, pharmacist, prescription books, some with loose papers 1904–76 (w) (Ref: D3893/14/1-7); John Staight, Toddington, sale of property incl. drugs 1811 (Ref: D2080/103); A L Thomson, Long Street, Tetbury, chemist and druggist, customers' orders for pharmaceutical supplies, incl. occasional details of illnesses and complaints 1878–1904 (Ref: D4457/1).

Chemists' vouchers 1825–27 (Ref: D245 I 86); pharmaceutical prescription n.d. c.19th cent. (Ref: D3471/244).

HAMPSHIRE

HAMPSHIRE RECORD OFFICE
Sussex Street, Winchester SO23 8TH

Frederick James Barratt, 122 High Street, Winchester, chemist and druggist, prescription books 1878–1910 (Ref: 177M85W/75-82); R W Cooke, 48 Andover Road, Winchester, dispensing chemist, prescription books 1935–54 (Ref: 156M85W/1-6); Robert Dolling, Beaulieu, apothecary, diary 1801–03 (Ref: photocopy 444); Hunt & Co, Winchester, pharmacist, prescription books 1845–1964 (Ref: 177M85W/1-74); Overseers of Holybourne, record of medicines purchased 1793–94 (p) (Ref: 649); Edward Powell, 95 High Street, Winchester, pharmacy, title deeds 1779–1883 (Ref: 102M93W/1-11); Mr Ward, photograph of his chemist's shop c.1960s–70s (Ref: 217M84/16); Whitchurch Pharmacy, Newbury Street, Whitchurch, pharmacist, account books 1923–31, dangerous drugs register 1923–39, prescription books: T P Liggins 1917–22, E A Cox 1923–36, J Weeks 1937–40, 1944–45 (Ref: 175M88); George Woodman, Odiham, chemist and druggist, personal diaries with business references 1862–1932, notebook incl. medical preparations late 19th cent. (Ref: 78M89/1-11).

Pharmacy Committee of the Winchester Group Hospital Management Committee, minutes 1958–71 (Ref: 106M90/3).

Agreement for sale of chemist's business, Alton 1856 (Ref: 4M51/217); article re George Shenton, chemist, Winchester (Ref: Top. Winchester 1/299); bill of indictment for theft of beeswax from a Winchester chemist 1752 (Ref: W/D3/175); medicinal and culinary recipes early 19th cent. (Ref: 383M87/1); prescription book, Alton 1804–50 (Ref: 4M51/216); prescription for pills 1831 (Ref: 23M93/87/2/16); prescription for William Heathcote 1749 (Ref: 63M84/355); prescriptions for Emma Austen-Leigh 1873–75 (Ref:

23M93/87/2/45); tenancy agreement for chemist and druggist's premises in High Street, Winchester 1907 (Ref: W/F1/27/7).

HERTFORDSHIRE
HERTFORDSHIRE ARCHIVES & LOCAL STUDIES
County Hall, Hertford SG13 8EJ

James Busby Ltd, 12a High Street, Harpenden, prescription book, incl. prescription and dosage instructions 1869–1902 (Ref: D/EX 631 B1); James Lewis, 168 High Street, Ware, prescription books c.1840–50s, 1896–1900 (Ref: Acc 2601); George Lines & Co, Market Place, Hertford, chemist, prescription books, incl. occasional veterinary scripts c.1817–1922, 1925–87, recipe books for medicinal, toiletry and household preparations late 18th–early 20th cents., executors' papers, incl. inventory of stock-in-trade 1900 (Ref: D/ELi, D/EL B244); Benjamin Medcalf, Ware, pharmaceutical chemist, prescription books 1849–59, 1871–91 (Ref: D/EX 425 B1-3); George Ringrose, MPS, papers relating to his estate 1865, 1876–87 (Ref: D/EL 3557/1-71).

Chemist, Hoddesdon, prescription book 1864 (Ref: 63679-80).

NATIONAL PHARMACEUTICAL ASSOCIATION
Mallinson House, 38-42 St Peter's Street, St Albans AL1 3NP

Evans, Gadd & Co Ltd, annual report and accounts 1968, correspondence with National Pharmaceutical Union re repayments on loan and interest charges 1967–73.

ISLE OF WIGHT
ISLE OF WIGHT COUNTY & DIOCESAN RECORD OFFICE
26 Hillside, Newport PO30 2EB

Thomas S Flower, Pier Street, Ryde, pharmaceutical chemist, almanac 1879 (Ref: 94/36); Gibbs & Gurnell, 34 Union Street, Ryde, chemist, advertisements late 19th cent. (p) (Ref: RYD/77); William Thomas Smith, Bembridge, chemist, prescription books 1903–80 (Ref: WTS 1-19).

KENT
CENTRE FOR KENTISH STUDIES
County Hall, Maidstone ME14 1XQ

Thomas Gilbert Batting, 98 Calverley Road, Tunbridge Wells, chemist and druggist, prescription book, incl. firework preparations and notes of Batting's patent medicines c.1876–1912, loose notes of remedies, prescriptions and labels for pill boxes and bottles c.1857–1907.(Ref: U2944/B1-2); J H Bishop Ltd, 14 Mount Pleasant, Royal Tunbridge Wells, apothecary/chemist and druggist, prescription books 1868–1975 (w) (Ref: U1922/B1-31); Jeremiah Cliff, Tenterden, physician and apothecary, diary listing deaths at Tenterden c.1713–41 (Ref: P364 28/4); A E Hobbs Ltd, 72 Mount Pleasant Road and 20 St John Road, Tunbridge Wells, prescription books 1872–1953 (Ref: U2353/B1/1-B5/8); Hope family, Cranbrook, barber-surgeons and apothecaries, account books, Richard Hope 1688–1716, 1751, bills 1798–99, price list of drugs c.1730, title deed 1659, papers, Richard Hope 1724–26, pre-1786, papers, Thomas Hope 1713–46, 1797–1802 (Ref: U442/F5/1-15); [T Isherwood], Cobham Street, Gravesend, retail pharmacy, account book, income and expenditure 1971–72, statement of sums payable for monthly prescriptions 1971–72, bank statements 1970–72 (Ref: U2551/B1-3); Anthony Kingley & Edward Pincke, London, druggist, articles of partnership 1710 (Ref: U145 B1); Sittingbourne Pharmacy, 139 High Street, Sittingbourne, prescription books 1827–1974, receipt books 1864–1968 (Ref: U1914/B1-24); Starling & Vine, Hadlow, surgeon apothecaries, articles of partnership 1841 (Ref: U442 B18/1); Thomas G Stonham & Son, 70-71 Bank Street, Maidstone, pharmaceutical chemist, prescription books, incl. customers, prescription ingredients and some price lists for different types of medicines 1833–1908 (w) (Ref: U1823/46/B1-26); Benjamin Wood, New Romney, surgeon apothecary, income tax papers 1844–46, insurance receipts 1837–68, conveyance to Benjamin Wood of surgeon and apothecary practice 1831, agreements with assistants 1844, 1847, agreements to purchase land 1852, certificate of his entry on the medical register 1859 (Ref: U1045/B1).

EAST KENT ARCHIVES CENTRE
Enterprise Business Park, Honeywood Road, Whitfield, Dover CT16 3EH

Richard Hammon, Beach Street and Rendezvous Street, Folkestone, pharmaceutical chemist, prescription books 1845–55, 1862–65 (Ref: F1975/8).

KINGSTON UPON HULL

UNIVERSITY OF HULL
Brynmor Jones Library, Cottingham Road, Kingston upon Hull HU6 7RX

William Hay, 4 Regent's Terrace, Anlaby Road, Kingston upon Hull, chemist and druggist, diaries, incl. accounts re takings and expenses 1865–71 (w), 1898–1901 (Ref: DX/95).

KIRKLEES

WEST YORKSHIRE ARCHIVE SERVICE, KIRKLEES
Central Library, Princess Alexandra Walk, Huddersfield HD1 2SU

Heckmondwike & District Co-operative Pharmacy Ltd, Heckmondwike, pharmacist, board of management and committees minutes 1956–66 (Ref: KC95/100); Benjamin Redfearn, Wellington Street, Batley, druggist and grocer, recipe book, for bowel trouble preparations, gargle for sore throat, whooping cough mixture, liquor morphia, mist for cholera, sprain liniment, tooth powder and pills for asthmatic fits 1860s (Ref: KC678); John Walker (Cleckheaton) Ltd, 26 Market Street, Cleckheaton, chemist, deeds 1940 (Ref: KC669/Box 11).

LANCASHIRE

LANCASHIRE RECORD OFFICE
Bow Lane, Preston PR1 2RE

Briggs family, Garstang, surgeon apothecaries, records unlisted 1695–1831 (Ref: DDX 901); Burnley Co-operative Chemists Ltd, Burnley, minute book 1945–59 (Ref: DDX 1101 acc. 7803); Fisher & Fisher, 6 Orchard Street, Preston, chemist, day books 1912–55, prescription books 1870–1967 (Ref: DDX 684); T B Patch Ltd, Chadderton, Oldham, chemist and optician, memorandum and articles of association 1926, balance sheets 1947–68 (w), accounts (optical) 1953–61, vouchers 1961–69 (w) (Ref: DDX 653); Frank Pick, Burnley, chemist, prescription books 1833–96, 1914–15 (Ref: DDX 1101 acc. 7803).

LEEDS

WEST YORKSHIRE ARCHIVE SERVICE, LEEDS DISTRICT ARCHIVES
Chapeltown Road, Sheepscar, Leeds LS7 3AP

Bell's Pharmacy, 85 Kirkgate, Leeds, pharmacist, prescription books 1843–71, 1905–09 (Ref: Acc 1545); Joseph Brooks Bilborough, 73 Briggate, Leeds, druggist and oil merchant, bills, receipts and correspondence 1804–54, licences 1808–54, price lists n.d., bond to discharge a debt n.d., billheads 1915, trade advertisements n.d., premises photograph n.d., family papers: probate papers n.d., investments 1846, 1868–69, expenses 1849, papers relating to properties owned by Samuel Glover n.d., library ticket of Samuel Glover 1825 (Ref: GL/A/1-37, GL/B/1-5); William Henry Fleck, Masbrough, chemist and druggist, papers re bankruptcy 1843 (Ref: DB215/197); Robert Goodall & Henry Backhouse, Leeds, drysalter and druggist, partnership deeds 1858 (Ref: B N & G 17/2/17); J C Reinhardt & Sons, 76 Briggate, Leeds, chemist, prescription book 1832–34, photograph of shop late 19th cent. (Ref: Acc 1373); Charles F Thackray Ltd, Great George Street, Leeds, chemist, prescription books 1870–1941 (Ref: Acc 1094); Walkers of Doncaster, chemist and druggist, papers re bankruptcy 1854 (Ref: DB215/211).

WEST YORKSHIRE ARCHIVE SERVICE, YORKSHIRE ARCHAEOLOGICAL SOCIETY
Claremont, 23 Clarendon Road, Leeds LS2 9NZ

Albert Benn, Bramley, chemist, ledgers c.1890, 1892–1935, diary containing recipes for medicine 1900, notebook containing prices of medicines late 19th cent., family photograph c.1900 (Ref: MD361); William James Blyth, 8 High Street, Sunderland, chemist, apprenticeship indenture, W J Blyth to Thomas Botrill Hurworth 1849, cash books 1863–89, certificate of registration with Pharmaceutical Society 1850, personal papers, incl. receipts re legal costs for deed of separation from wife Isabella, alimony payments and executorship documentation re Henry Markham, ship owner of Stockton late 19th cent., Bucktrout and Blyth family papers, incl. wills and property papers 18th–19th cents. (Ref: MD315).

LEICESTERSHIRE

RECORD OFFICE FOR LEICESTERSHIRE, LEICESTER & RUTLAND
Long Street, Wigston Magna, Leicester LE18 2AH

Cornelius Bayley, High Street, Uppingham, Rutland, chemist and druggist, prescription books 1920–33 (Ref: DE2772); Brownlows, Melton Mowbray, chemist, prescription book 1883–99 (Ref: DE645); Cheney, Lutterworth, chemist, prescription books 1850–95 (Ref: 20D61); Francis Corrall, Lutterworth, chemist and druggist, bill 1831–32 (Ref: DE1267/8); W H Dennis Ltd, 8 Halford Street, Leicester, dispensing chemist, prescription books of S F Burford 1885–1913 and Sidney Palmer 1913–35 (w) (Ref: 3D50); F W Goodess, Market Street, Leicester, chemist, prescription books 1884–1931, miscellaneous indexes c.1912–16 (Ref: 14D69); William Goodess Higginson, chemist and druggist, agreement for sale and valuation of 6 Gallowtree Gate, Leicester to Samuel Cox, Market Harborough, chemist 1868 (Ref: 14D60); Thomas Healy, Oakham, Rutland, apothecary, account for medicines 1719–20 (Ref: DE1262), partnership deed 1736–37 (Ref: DE1797/2/22); William Tom Hind, Queen's Road, Clarendon Park, Leicester, chemist and druggist, prescription books 1894–1951 (Ref: DE3827); Ludlow, Griffiths & Smith, Hinkley and Burbage, surgeons and apothecaries, partnership agreements 1875–94 (Ref: DE451); John Mason and Thomas Paget, Leicester, surgeons, apothecaries and male midwives, dissolution of partnership 1792 (Ref: 2D71/1018); Nedham & Benfield, chemist, valuation of contents of shop at expiration of partnership 19th cent. (DE66(Box 3506)); Oldacres & Geary, Market Bosworth, apothecaries, partnership agreement and dissolution of partnership 1849, 1852 (Ref: DE319/278); T W Palmer, Highcross Street, Leicester, chemist and druggist, recipe book c.1834, apprenticeship indenture, Tom Cooke to Charles Edward Furnival, Leicester, chemist and druggist 1895 (Ref: 16D55); A H Preston, 9 Cattle Market and 16 Leicester Road, Loughborough, chemist, prescriptions books 1882–1927, 1935–50, notes re prescriptions 1892–1926, 1946–51, n.d., correspondence re prescriptions 1880–1928, n.d.; animal prescriptions ledger and papers 1900s–29, registered reference card for repeat order 1935 (Ref: DE3711); Mr Redfern, Ashby-de-la-Zouch, chemist, account of drugs and medicines sold 1855–56 (Ref: DE41/1/155); K Scotney, Allandale Road, Leicester, pharmacist, dangerous drugs register 1939–73, files and papers re dangerous drugs acts, pharmaceutical products, use of spirits, employment guidelines c.1935–76, requisition books 1960–71, Leicestershire Area Health Authority lists 1975 (Ref: DE3061); John Sowerby, English Street, Carlisle, Cumbria, chemist, list of medicines with their doses and uses n.d. (Ref: 3D42/2/260); John Spender, apothecary, bills and accounts 1787–94 (Ref: DE107); Stiles, Market Harborough, chemist, prescription books 1857–1925 (Ref: 8D73); Lacey A Vincent, notice of take-over of the chemist and druggist business of John Watson, High Street, Market Harborough c.1863 (Ref: DE513/35).

LINCOLNSHIRE

LINCOLNSHIRE ARCHIVES
St Rumbold Street, Lincoln LN2 5AB

Thomas Anderson Goodall, Epworth, North Lincolnshire, chemist, accounts c.1871–75 (Ref: TGH 2/G).

Apothecary, prescription books 18th cent. (Ref: 2LCL).

LIVERPOOL

LIVERPOOL RECORD OFFICE & LOCAL HISTORY SERVICE
City Libraries, William Brown Street, Liverpool L3 8EW

J J Blaby, 9 and 11 Allerton Road, Woolton, chemist and druggist, prescription books, covering clients in Woolton, Childwall and Gateacre, 1892–n.d. (Ref: 380MD/125); William C Fergusson, Liverpool, chemist and druggist, prescription book 1837–n.d. (Ref: 380MD/113); [John Steel], Atherton Street and Gloucester Street, Liverpool, chemist and druggist, prescription book c.1800–50 (Ref: 380MD/132).

Chemists and pharmacists, Liverpool, prescription books 1848–50, 1883–1969 (Accs 1893, 1943, 3504, 4683, 4859, 4936).

NATIONAL MUSEUMS & GALLERIES ON MERSEYSIDE
Museum of Liverpool Life, Pier Head, Liverpool L3 1PZ

Augustus Hardings, chemist, notebook n.d. (Ref: Acc. 1981.955); Leigh's Pharmacy, Walton Village, Liverpool, pharmacy, business advertising cards c.1950–60, business advertising pad and calendar 1950, fly papers c.1930–60, drugs labels c.1950–60, sheets of assorted pharmacy bottle labels c.1950–60 (Ref: Acc.MMM1993.166.38-99); John Lawrence Moxon, 252 Park Road, Liverpool, chemist, prescription n.d. (Ref: Acc.1982.719.5); L W Mussell, Garston, dispensing chemist, prescription n.d. (Ref: Acc.1985.574).

Miscellaneous chemists' envelope n.d. (Ref: Acc. 1975.21.4), document 1911–13 (Ref: Acc.1966.296.1).

LONDON

BRENT LEISURE SERVICES
Community History Library & Archive, Cricklewood Library, Olive Road, Cricklewood, London NW2 6UY

G Zeidemann, 10 Handel Parade, Whitechurch Lane, Edgware, Harrow, retail chemist, ledger, with entries for drugs dispensed 1930–49 (Ref: A3/1982).

BRITISH LIBRARY DEPARTMENT OF MANUSCRIPTS
96 Euston Road, London NW1 2DB

The Department of Manuscripts holds much material relating to medicine, chemistry, botany and pharmaceutics in the early modern period, both in terms of theoretical study and commercial practice. The collections of Sir Hans Sloane are particularly rich in these areas.

BRITISH LIBRARY NATIONAL SOUND ARCHIVE
96 Euston Road, London NW1 2DB

Tape recorded interviews with 50 community pharmacists and chemists 1995 (Ref: C816/01-50); tape recorded interviews with 40 hospital pharmacists 1997–98 (Ref: C917)

CAMDEN LOCAL STUDIES & ARCHIVES CENTRE
Holborn Library, 32-38 Theobalds Road, London WC1X 8PA

Evans, Hampstead, chemist, prescription books 1895–1912, 1922–43 (Ref: JM/10/9C); Adam Hilger, manufacturer of laboratory and technical equipment, accounts and order books 1900s–20s (Ref: JM/10/9A-9C).

CITY OF WESTMINSTER ARCHIVES CENTRE
10 St Ann's Street, London SW1P 2XR

Blake, Sandford & Blake, 47 Piccadilly, Westminster, London, pharmaceutical chemist and druggist, assignment of goodwill in business, M A E Blake to G W

Sandford 1870, covenants for payments of annuities, G W Sandford to M A E Blake 1870, C A Blake to M A E Blake 1883, partnership agreement, G W Sandford and C A Blake 1883 (Ref: Acc 784); Ebenezer Sheldon & John Pryor Peregrine, Mount Street, Westminster, surgeons, apothecaries and male midwives, partnership agreements, E Sheldon and J P Peregrine 1831–32, cash receipt book 1817–35, legal and family papers, mainly probate records of E Sheldon incl. executors' accounts and inventories of 17 Mount Street (1829) and 45 Green Street (1835) 1832–69 (Ref: Acc 929).

CORPORATION OF LONDON RECORD OFFICE
PO Box 270, Guildhall, London EC2P 2EJ

Dr Hodges and William Edwards, apothecaries, order for payment for care of sick prisoners in Wood Street Compter 1680 (Ref: Misc. Mss. 158.25).

Apothecary/grocer, schedule of goods and wares 1655 (Ref: MC1/85 No.202), apothecary's shop, schedule of wares 1630 (Ref: MC1/47 No.128), 1676 (Ref: MC1/230 No.154); bills for treatment of sick prisoners in Wood Street Compter 1675, 1704–05 (Ref: Misc. Mss. 200.3); bills and orders for payment of apothecaries for treatment and medicine 1719–20 (Ref: Misc. Mss. 158.25).

GUILDHALL LIBRARY
Aldermanbury, London EC2P 2EJ

Thomas Henry Hodder, Staines, Surrey, chemist and druggist, recipe book with medical remedies and drug prescriptions 1830–58 (Ref Ms 16262).

Churchwardens' accounts with bills and vouchers for medicines supplied to the poor 1690–1825 (Ref: Ms 20786), 1753–56 (Ref: Ms 11948), 1695–1775 (Ref: Ms 8867).

GUNNERSBURY PARK MUSEUM
Gunnersbury Park, London W3 8LQ

K M Carr, weight cards 1921, 1924, n.d. (Ref: 96.52/3.4, 5-6); Robert Dawkes Ltd, 17 Horn Lane, London, pharmacist, prescription ledger 1934–37 (Ref: 94.338); Stockwells Chemists, Ealing Green, London, prescription books 1930–92 (Ref: 96.210-11), Pharmaceutical Society certificate of Charles James Stockwell 1954 (Ref: L0028); E F Tilson Ltd, 286 High Street, Brentford, Hounslow, chemist, prescription book 1881–1916 (Ref: 72.39/1); A H Walker (Acton) Ltd, 6 Broadway, Acton, Ealing, delivery note 1969 (Ref: 94.176).

HACKNEY ARCHIVES DEPARTMENT
43 De Beauvoir Road, London N1 5SQ

Robert Debenham, Upper Clapton Road, chemist's shop lease 1840–62 (Ref: HAD M 1574); John Goodwin, 223 Lower Clapton Road, pharmaceutical chemist, lease of premises 1893 (Ref: HAD M 4003); E Lambert & Son, 60 Queens Road, Dalston, trade catalogues relating to domestic and surgical specialities, incl. contraceptive devices 1890s (Ref: 331.95 library); MD, Hackney, apothecary, letter concerning medicines ordered 1745 (Ref: HAD M 2586); Mr Westbrook, High Street, Stoke Newington, retail chemist, sale catalogue 1846 (Ref: HAD M 3987).

HILLINGDON LOCAL HERITAGE SERVICE
Central Library, 14-15 High Street, Uxbridge UB8 1HD

William G Carter, 114 Pinner Road, Northwood, chemist, prescription books 1938–61 (Ref: MC3 - 7264).

ISLINGTON LOCAL HISTORY COLLECTION
Islington Central Reference Library, 2 Fieldway Crescent, Islington, London N5 1PF

J T de Peare Ltd, Highbury Park, Islington, chemist, ledgers 1874–1987 (Ref: YL855 G440).

LEWISHAM LOCAL STUDIES CENTRE
Lewisham Library, 199-201 Lewisham High Street, London SE13 6LG

Robert Blackie Ltd, Peckham and New Cross, manufacturing chemist, stock record ledger 1960–63, export packing index book 1948–54, shipping despatch book 1966–69, formulae cards for products c.1949–63, dangerous drug requisition slips 1962, 1968, plans and drawings of machinery 1945–69, outers and cartons book 1940–60 (Ref: Acc83/32, Acc69/19).

LONDON METROPOLITAN ARCHIVES
40 Northampton Road, London EC1R 0HB

Stephen Green Ltd, Princes Street and 192-212 Lambeth Road, London, ointment manufacturer, business accounts, summaries 19th cent., papers re litigation concerning ointment business and personal estates 19th cent., ointment recipes n.d., correspondence, bills and testimonials re Singleton's Eye Ointment n.d., title deeds, property papers and plans 1784–1894, photograph of Stephen Green n.d., family papers of proprietors 18th–19th cents., miscellaneous papers n.d. (Ref: B/SIN); Lambert & Son, London, druggist, employment agreement 1893 (Ref: 0/470).

PUBLIC RECORD OFFICE
Ruskin Avenue, Kew, Richmond TW9 4DU

Thomas Bridge, London, druggist, diary 1760–1811 (Ref: J90/12-14); Nightingale & Scott, London, drysalter, correspondence 1761–69 (Ref: C109/1-14).

Apothecary, London, petty cash and receipt book 1667–85 (Ref: C104/126-31); chemist, account books 1800–05 (Ref: C108/118); wholesale druggist, account books 1674–83 (Ref: C114/59).

ROYAL BOROUGH OF KENSINGTON & CHELSEA LIBRARIES & ARTS SERVICE
Central Library, Phillimore Walk, London W8 7RX

H B Alexander and J Pritchard, deed of licence to carry out the business of chemist 1871 (Ref: 22517); Cowards of Kensington, 4 Stratford Road, Kensington, chemist, prescription books 1875–1957 (w) (Ref: 24458-66); Gamble & Co, 347 Kensington High Street, London, chemist, prescription books 1921–73, photographs of premises 1972 (Ref: 23397-434, K73/300-5).

ROYAL BOTANIC GARDENS
Library & Archives, Kew, Richmond TW9 3AE

Ronald Melville, Kew, pharmaceutical researcher, papers, incl. notes on drugs and on Crude Drugs Committee 1934–40, miscellaneous papers re drugs 1939–44 (Ref: Melville Papers).

ROYAL COLLEGE OF PHYSICIANS
11 St Andrews Place, Regent's Park, London NW1 4LE

List of apothecaries' shops visited by the censors of the Royal College of Physicians c.1791 (Ref: MS 2184); records of visitations to apothecaries' shops, made by the censors of the Royal College of Physicians 1724–1856 (Ref: MSS 2151-83).

ROYAL COLLEGE OF SURGEONS OF ENGLAND
35-43 Lincoln's Inn Fields, London WC2A 3PN

Charles Bayley, Edinburgh, chemist, day book, with references to Sir Walter Scott's household 1823–25 (Ref: ADD.Mss.270).

ROYAL PHARMACEUTICAL SOCIETY OF GREAT BRITAIN
Museum Curator, 1 Lambeth High Street, London SE1 7JN

Named businesses: J D Aldcock, recipe book 1856 (Ref: IRA.1997.047); Jacob Anthony, Bedford, Bedfordshire, chemist and druggist, invoices 1829–39 (Ref: IRA.1997.151); Arnold & Foster, Maidstone, Kent, surgeons, invoice for medicines supplied 1784 (Ref: IRA.1996.264); William Babington, St Guy's Hospital, lectures on *materia medica* n.d. (Ref: IRA.1997.030); Charles Stuart

Bailey, manufacturing chemist, receipt book 1896–1901 (Ref: IRA.1997.053); Barclay & Sons Ltd, patent certificate 1897 (Ref: IRA.1996.019); Benjamin & William Batley, 22 Barbican, London, bill and correspondence 1830 (Ref: IRA.1996.265); William Baxter, Bromley, pharmaceutical chemist, prescription late 19th–early 20th cents. (Ref: IRA.1996.261); Timothy Bevans Ltd, stock inventory 1773–76 (Ref: IRA.1997.011); Mr Blaxland, Wandsworth, London, surgeon and apothecary, appeals against land tax 1806 (Ref: IRA.1996.016); Peter Boa, 64 Morningside Drive, Edinburgh, papers re purchase of business by John O Russell 1935 (Ref: IRA.1996.240); Elizabeth Boothe, receipt book 1649–1848 (Ref: IRA.1997.018); R Bright & John B[--]ster, 29 Broad Bridge Street, Peterborough, inventory and valuation of stock 1854 (Ref: IRA.1996.266); Murdoch Cameron, 130 Parliamentary Road, Glasgow, poisons register 1872–1936 (Ref: IRA.1996.009); Mr Cann, apothecary, bills for visits and medicines 1767–92 (Ref: IRA.1996.286); J C Chubb, recipe book 20th cent. (Ref: IRA.1996.005); Edward Chute, Exeter, Devon, apothecary, coat-of-arms late 18th cent. (Ref: IRA.1996.141); Clay & Abraham, 87 Bold Street, Liverpool, pharmaceutical chemist, recipe books 1852–1924 (Ref: IRA.1996.054), stock of shop 1845 (Ref: IRA.1996.075), press cuttings and price lists (Ref: IRA.1997.013), instructions to staff re duties and wages 1854–1911 (Ref: IRA.1997.012); Dr W Clayton, recipe book with advertisements and accounts 1861–87 (Ref: IRA.1997.097); Frederick Thomas Cooper, Ross-on-Wye, Herefordshire, recipe book and diary mid 19th cent. (Ref: IRA.1996.045); Cope & Taylor, 3 Market Place, Derby, apothecaries, photographs, historical notes and press cuttings n.d. (Ref: IRA.1996.171, 247); Thomas Davy, Gould Square, London, druggist, price list early 19th cent. (Ref: IRA.1996.267); John & Anne Dyssryn, recipe book 1794 (Ref: IRA.1997.049); Joseph Evans, letter regarding bill for wines 1779 (Ref: IRA.1996.091); Thomas Evens, 8 Edgecombe Street, Stonehouse, Gloucestershire, chemist, letterbook 1831–36 (Ref: IRA.1996.011); Frank Fish, School of Pharmacy, London University, Dean, tape recorded interview 1995 (Ref: IRT.1996.50); R Gregory Ltd, 347 Kensington High Street, London, chemist, formulary c.1929 (Ref: LDPHA.LIB.41972); Giles, Schacht & Co, Clifton, rules 1890 (Ref: IRA.1996.248); Francis Gordon, surgeon, accounts for drugs supplied to him by London wholesale druggists 1737–84 (Ref: IRA.1997.080); Richard Greene, Lichfield, Staffordshire, apothecary, bookplate 1716–93 (Ref: IRA.1996.100); W J Hallett & Co, 10 Stall Street, Bath, chemist, recipe book 1923 (Ref: IRA.1996.052); Richard Hampson, receipt book 15th–16th cents. (Ref: IRA.1997.065); J Hart, St Sampson's, Guernsey, pharmaceutical chemist, prescription 1941 (Ref: IRA.1996.244); Hearon, McCulloch & Squire, 95 Bishopsgate Street, London, price list 1859 (Ref: IRA.1996.271); Norman Heatley, key figure in development of penicillin, tape recorded interview 1994 (Ref: IRT.1996.56); Herring Bros, price list 1840 (Ref: IRA.1996.272); C W Heslop, East Dulwich, London, notebook 20th cent. (Ref:

IRA.1996.004); Ricardo Hill, recipe book 1807 (Ref: IRA.1997.064); Samuel Hinde, drug bill and prescription 17th cent. (Ref: IRA.1996.273); David Hooper, notebooks 1930–49 (Ref: IRA.1996.008, 030); Sidney Charles Hudson, 601 Green Lane, London, pharmacy, notebook 1901–13 (Ref: LDPHA.LIB.36320); Samuel Huskisson, apothecary, account book 1835–39 (Ref: IRA.1997.022); Charles Cater Islip, Orlingbury, Wellingborough, Northamptonshire, chemist and druggist, recipe book 1880s (Ref: IRA.1996.044); David Jack, tape recorded interview 1995 (Ref: IRT.1996.57); John F James, 2 King Street, Sheffield, chemist and druggist, drugs catalogue 1823 (Ref: IRA.1996.274); Jenner family, correspondence, invoices and orders 1841–61 (Ref: IRA.1997.145); John Wesley Jones, Llanelly, recipe book incl. labels 1877 (Ref: IRA.1997.094); Holmes Keall, Bury St Edmunds, Suffolk, chemist and druggist, recipe notebook 1859–68 (Ref: IRA.1996.053); Langton, Langton & Wheatley, Laurence Pountney Lane, London Bridge, price list 1838 (Ref: IRA.1996.275); William Henry Lenton, Oakham, Rutland, pharmaceutical chemist, recipe book and miscellaneous papers 1866–1940 (Ref: IRA.1996.046); Long & Strickland, Bognor Regis, West Sussex, pharmaceutical chemist, account book 1904–14 (Ref: IRA.1996.006); Prosper Henry Marsden, Liverpool, pharmacist, press cuttings scrapbook 1886–1913 (Ref: IRA.1997.073); George Meggeson, 147 Cannon Street, London, druggist and manufacturer, price list mid 19th cent. (Ref: IRA.1996.277); James Metcalfe & Sons, 5 Old Fish Street, London, price list 1839 (Ref: IRA.1996.278); Johnathan Middleton, lectures re physiology and *materia medica* 1796–1803 (Ref: IRA.1997.037); Mr Mitchell, page from ledger 1828 (Ref: IRA.1996.092); John Moor, Yeovil, Somerset, recipe notebook 1825 (Ref: IRA.1996.055); Eyre & Henry Moses, 4 Little St Mary Avenue, London, drysalter and drug merchant, deed of co-partnership 1846 (Ref: IRA.1997.152); John Thomas Newby, recipe book 1830 (Ref: IRA.1996.058); John Oldham, formulae book 1825 (Ref: IRA.1997.041); John Buxton Payne, scrapbook of documents, incl. indenture to Mark Cooper, chemist 17th–18th cents. (Ref: IRA.1997.075); James Puech, Oxinden Street, near Haymarket, catalogue 1684 (Ref: IRA.1997.033); Robert Pierce, Hurst, Sussex, account of pharmacy apprenticeship 1930s (Ref: IRA.1997.002); S Powell Jones and Thomas Wilson, accounts 1815, 1871–1916 (Ref: IRA.1996.065); G Price, Portland Place, London, recipe book 1844 (Ref: IRA.1997.020); Cornelius Walter Reeves, recipe book 1871–78 (Ref: IRA.1996.043); Reinhardt & Sons, 76 Briggate, Leeds, pharmaceutical chemist, recipe book 1836 (Ref: IRA.1996.060); T Roberts & Co, 12 Crane Court, Fleet Street, London, advertisement and pamphlet late 19th–early 20th cents. (Ref: IRA.1996.255); John Roper, Market Place, Ulverston, Cumbria, chemist and druggist, products list early 19th cent. (Ref: IRA.1996.281); Shaw & Edwards, 66 St Paul's Church Yard, London, price list early 19th cent. (Ref: IRA.1996.285); Thomas Simpson & Son, Market Place, Stowmarket, Suffolk, chemist, recipe books mid 19th cent. (Ref:

IRA.1996.039), labels scrapbook 1886 (Ref: IRA.1997.106); Robert Small, receipts in physic and surgery 1783 (Ref: IRA.1997.028); Charles Henry Snell, formulae in Latin n.d. (Ref: IRA.1997.005); John Steadman & Co, Walworth, London, chemist, scrapbook of labels, packing circulars and letterheads 1913–28 (Ref: IRA.1997.074); Mr Taylor, notebook 1846–57 (Ref: IRA.1996.069); Dr Charles John Samuel Thompson, 157 Lodge Lane, Liverpool, chemist and druggist, recipe book c.1878–1911 (Ref: IRA.1996.066), notebook 20th cent. (Ref: IRA.1996.015); Townson & Mercer, 89 Bishopsgate Street, London, manufacturing chemist, bill for apparatus and chemicals 1885 (Ref: IRA.1996.291); Robert Turlington, Chancery, drugs specification 1744 (Ref: IRA.1996.253); S J Turner chemist's labels book n.d. (Ref: IRA.1997.091); G F Watts, 17 The Strand, London, chemist and perfumer, handbill n.d.(Ref: IRA.1996.228); Stanley Wedgewood, tape recorded interview 1996 (Ref: IRT.1996.81); Wiggin & Son, Ipswich, Suffolk, prescription book n.d. (Ref: LDPHA.LIB.36030); Stephen Williams, tape recorded interview 1996 (Ref: IRT.1996.83); Wilson & Dickinson, 11 George Street, Bath, dispensing chemist, advertisements booklet 1925 (Ref: IRA.1996.229); Henry Wood, High Street, Brentford, Hounslow, pharmaceutical chemist, recipe books late 19th cent. (Ref: IRA.1996.041); W Wyatt, Whitwell, Chesterfield, Derbyshire, recipe book late 19th cent. (Ref: IRA.1996.047); Francis H Yates, 64 St Martins Lane, Liscard, Wirral, dispensing and photographic chemist, labels books 1900–06 (Ref: IRA.1997.084, 086).

Official bodies: Aberdeen, North of Scotland Society of Chemists & Druggists, minutes 1885–1909 (p) (Ref: IRA.1997.089); Aberdeen Pharmaceutical Association, minutes 1908–19 (Ref: IRA.1997.081); Association of Chemists & Druggists of Great Britain, correspondence 1830 (Ref: IRA.1996.159); Excise Office, general order re unlicensed selling of spirits and wines by apothecaries and chemists and druggists 1843 (Ref: IRA.1996.114); provisional committee of the Birmingham Trade Conference of Chemists & Druggists, notice of conference 1876 (Ref: IRA.1996.205); fifth international pharmaceutical congress, photograph of excursion 1881 (Ref: IRA.1996.209); British Pharmaceutical Students' Association, proceedings of second annual conference 1944 (Ref: IRA.1996.210); Guild of Hospital Pharmacists, minutes and reports 1942–70, 1985–88 (Ref: IRA.1996.311-13); Manchester Chemists' & Druggists' Association, trade association, retail price list 1882 (Ref: IRA.1996.074); Plymouth, Devonport, Stonehouse & District Chemists' Association, trade association, notices, press cuttings and dinner menus 1868–99 (Ref: IRA.1996.028); Registered Pharmacists' Union, rules and objects 1946–47 (Ref: IRA 1996.086); Wakefield Chemists' Association, trade association, minute books 1879, 1901–14 (Ref: IRA.1996.031).

Miscellaneous: formulary 1844–51 (Ref: LDPHA.LIB.37396); prescription books: 19th–20th cents. (Ref: LDPHA.LIB.41971, LDPHA.MANUSCOL.18.1, LDPHA.LIB.38455, IRA.1997.087, IRA.1996.245); recipe books 15th–20th cents. (Ref: IRA.1996.093, IRA.1997.019, IRA.1997.149, IRA.1997.050, IRA.1997.092, IRA.1997.093.1, IRA.1996.042, IRA.1996.040, IRA.1996.059, IRA.1996.056, 061, IRA.1996.057, IRA.1997.032, 040, 062, 096, 098-9, 101, IRA.1997.095); account books 1817 (Ref: IRA.1997.024), 1832–84 (Ref: IRA.1997.083), n.d. (Ref: IRA.1997.104); ledger 1920–32 (Ref: IRA.1997.085); apothecaries cash book 1796–1808 (Ref: IRA.1997.103); medical bill book of Queen Victoria (p) c.1861–69 (Ref: IRA.1997.060); receipt books 15th–20th cents. (Ref: IRA.1997.023, IRA.1997.079, IRA.1997.042, IRA.1997.048, IRA.1997.100, IRA.1997.036); apprenticeship indentures 1802–1923 (Ref: IRA.1997.144); patent 1698 (Ref: IRA.1996.249); sale of poisons register, Exmouth, Devon, 1923–34 (Ref: IRA.1996.010); price list 1844 (Ref: IRA.1996.280); apothecaries bills and letters 1719–65 (Ref: IRA.1996.276); notebooks 1545–94 (Ref: IRA.1997.043), 1920–46 (Ref: IRA.1996.036); sales registers 1844–45, 1953–54, prescription books 1819–1971, formulary n.d., notebooks 1904–09, 1932 (Ref: LDPHA.LIB.20785-5085, MANUSCOL.1. 1-30.1); prescriptions, advertisements, almanacs and deeds 17th–19th cents. (Ref: IRA.1997.146); prescriptions and labels n.d. (Ref: IRA.1997.055); labels and crests n.d. (Ref: IRA.1997.058); pharmacy labels designed by Suttley & Silverlock Ltd 1840 (Ref: IRA.1997.070), 1920s (Ref: IRA.1997.071); chemist's labels book n.d. (Ref: IRA.1997.102); press cuttings re pharmacy 1658–1816 (Ref: IRA.1997.107); formulae notebook, 16 Dunstable Road, Luton, n.d. (IRA.1997.003); reminiscences of various chemists 1895–1907 (Ref: IRA.1997.051); photographs: apothecaries tokens 17th cent. (Ref: IRA.1996.371), medicinal plants mid 20th cent. (Ref: IRA.1996.293).

SCIENCE MUSEUM LIBRARY
South Kensington, London SW7 5NH

John Brameld, apothecary, memorandum book, containing lists of drugs and their prices, common ailments of humans and animals, and cures c.1762–95 (Ref: MS 381); Pars & Co, Bournemouth, dispensing chemist, prescription books 1876–1978 (Ref: ARCH : PARS); John Walker, Stockton-on-Tees, chemist, day book 1825–29 (Ref: MS 209).

VESTRY HOUSE MUSEUM
London Borough of Waltham Forest, Vestry Road, London E17 9NH

London Rubber Company Ltd, Chingford, Waltham Forest, manufacturer of latex, rubber equipment and oral contraceptives, photographs (over 400 images) of products, incl. gloves, condoms and diaphragms 1930s–80s, and factories, at

Hackney, Chingford, Wales and several unidentified sites 1930s–80s (Ref: LDVHM 1994.68, 1994.80.1-414).

Pharmaceutical manufacture, photographs 20th cent. (Ref: 4.334); pharmacists, photographs 20th cent. (Ref: 4.830).

WALTHAM FOREST ARCHIVES
Vestry House Museum, London Borough of Waltham Forest, Vestry Road, London E17 9NH

Leyton Urban District Council, printed tenders for hospital supplies (incl. chemists' sundries) 1910 (Ref: Acc.10108); contracts for supplies to Leyton Isolation Hospital 1893–1914 (Ref: L52.2Ms).

ARCHIVES & MANUSCRIPTS, WELLCOME LIBRARY FOR THE HISTORY & UNDERSTANDING OF MEDICINE
183 Euston Road, London NW1 2BE

Armitage Dispensing Chemist, Blackheath, Lewisham, prescription books, incl. prescriptions dispensed for particular doctors 1899–1940 (Ref: CMAC/GC/100); William Armitage, Thorne, Doncaster, retail chemist, account book 1847–99 (Ref: MS 978); Bartlett & Goodall, 37 Crawford Street, Bryanston Square, London, dispensing chemist, prescription books 1937–61 (Ref: MSS 1080-4); Batt family, Witney, Oxfordshire, surgeon apothecaries, ledgers, accounts for medical treatment and drugs dispensed 1774–99 (Ref: MSS 5201-2); John Bell, London, chemist, prescriptions 1928–29; James Brocklehurst, Hyde, Tameside, chemist and druggist, invoice books, containing pasted-in bills 1835–45, prescription book, incl. some veterinary prescriptions and recipes 1844–73 (Ref: MSS 5946-8); Thomas Burden & Co, 41 Store Street, Bedford Square, London, dispensing chemist, prescription books 1863–71 (w), 1909–11 (Ref: MSS 6217-9); Carr family, Settle, North Yorkshire, and Gomersal, Kirklees, apothecaries, medical notebooks, incl. prescriptions, diaries, notes from reference works, lists of medical bills, household and estate accounts 1739–1861 (Ref: MSS 5203-7); Thomas Acraman Coate, 106 Strand, London and 19 Clare Street, Bristol, dispensing chemist, recipe book 1863 (Ref: MS 6954); William Coyney, Holywell, Flintshire, surgeon and apothecary, account books 1746–73 (Ref: MSS 1899-1901); H C Croadsell, Cockermouth, Cumbria, wholesale and retail chemist, prescription books incl. rough accounts, notes, correspondence and advertising material 1923–51 (Ref: CMAC/GC/75); G Daniel, 680 Holloway Road, London, chemist, prescription book 1864–83, notebook, containing prescriptions, medical and domestic receipts and loose chemists' labels (mainly of Robert Green) 1878 (Ref: MS 2033-4); English Royal Apothecaries, medicines dispensing allowance claims: George Shiers 1604, 1608, Adrian Metcalfe (whose claim was authorised by William Harvey, royal physician) 1636

(Ref: MS 5137); John Evans, 49 Dawson Street, Dublin, Ireland, apothecary, prescription books 1752–53, 1768–69, 1802–03 (Ref: MSS 2312-4); Faller's Pharmacy, Lymington, Hampshire, retail pharmacy, prescription books 1932–79 (Ref: CMAC/GC/13); Nicholas Gaynsford, Hartfield, East Sussex, apothecary, case notes and medical recipes 1712–13 (Ref: MS 6919); Gordon family, Fochabers, Moray, medical practice, accounts for medicines purchased 1733–73, 1789, accounts for optical instruments purchased from Benjamin Martin and P & J Dollond, optician, London 1761–81, account for postage 1741–46 (Ref: MS 5268); [?R Greaves], notebook, recording recipes and accounts 1893–95, n.d. (Ref: MS 7118); Thomas Grimshaw, Preston, Lancashire, and London, chemist and druggist, recipe book 1887–97 (Ref: MS 7144); Harrods Ltd Pharmacy Department, Knightsbridge, London, dispensing pharmacy, prescription registers 1935–77 (w) (Ref: CMAC/GC/214); Charles Heygate, [?West Haddon], Northamptonshire, pharmaceutical chemist, account book 1752–73 (Ref: MS 2833); Thomas Henry Holberton, Hampton Court, apothecary, account book 1829–33 (Ref: MS 2862); Thomas Howitt, Lancaster, surgeon and pharmacist, apprenticeship indenture 1825, University of London attendance and examination certificates 1829–31 (Ref: MS 5196); Imperial Pharmacy, South Croydon, Croydon, ledgers 1907–10, 1920s, 1938, cash analysis books 1923–43, cheque analysis book 1931–42 (Ref: CMAC/GC/101); Lloyd Kenyon, 3rd Lord Kenyon, prescriptions 1835–66 (Ref: MSS 5296-303); Gilbert Laurie & Co, Edinburgh, druggist, combined letterbook and accounts re drugs purchased or supplied 1768–97 (Ref: MS 3181); William Lee, surgeon apothecary, Odiham, Hampshire, account book 1774–80 (Ref: MS 3974); W J Manktelow, pharmacist, student's pharmacy notebooks 1937–38 (Ref: CMAC/GC/118); Moore & Co, London, chemist, prescriptions 1934 (Ref: CMAC/GC/61); Morgan family, Lichfield, Staffordshire, surgeon apothecaries, articles of dissolution of partnership between Thomas Salt and Simon Morgan 1815, apprenticeship indenture, Major Butler Morgan to Francis Newbold and William Binley Dickinson, Macclesfield, Cheshire 1820, Herbert Major Morgan's examination certificates, from Society of Apothecaries and Royal College of Physicians 1860–61 (Ref: MS 6884); Pope Roach & Son, London, chemist, prescriptions 1933; William John Charles Richards, New Bridge Street, Blackfriars, London, chemist, Freedom of the City of London, copy certificate 1857 (Ref: MS 6955); Thomas Roots, Kingston upon Thames, apothecary, account book 1749–52, post book containing copies of bills sent for medical supplies, bleeding, dressing issues, ulcers and similar treatments 1750–53 (Ref: MSS 4254, 6033); M Sheridan, 207 & 307 Fulham Road, London, dispensing chemist, prescription registers 1887–1984 (Ref: CMAC/GC/189); Spencer, Dakers & Co, Newcastle upon Tyne, pharmacist, purchases account book 1896–1914 (Ref: MS 7162); Peter Taylor, 18 Park Road, London, chemist and druggist, prescription books 1914–37 (Ref: MSS 4760-1); Mrs Torbock, Crackenthorpe Hall, Cumbria, patient, medical prescriptions made out by various dispensing chemists 1880–1910, n.d. (Ref: MS 7045); Tylers, 87 Abingdon Road, London, dispensing chemist, cash books, general sales 1951–57 (w), dangerous drugs registers 1945–55, specification for war damage 1948 (Ref: CMAC/GC/102); William Waylett, William Waylett & Thomas Sargent, Lydd, Kent, surgeon apothecaries, patients' bills 1777–1821, account of medicines supplied to poor of Kenardington, Kent 1738–39, medical recipes in English and Latin, and list of women delivered by Waylett the younger 1757–1815, Waylett's estate, accounts, receipts, correspondence and miscellaneous papers 1717–1826, F R Cock, Waylett's biographer, correspondence, papers, prints and photographs 1887–1935 (Ref: MSS 4979-80, 5625-30); Woody & Thompson, Tamworth, Staffordshire, pharmacist, prescription book 1824–65 (Ref: MS 5094).

Apothecary, Leeds, combined cash and recipe book 19th cent. (Ref: MS 7111); apothecary or chemist, [London], production books recording batches of compound medicines manufactured, with the cost of each ingredient and overall manufacturing costs 1741–95 (Ref: MSS 5940-1); chemist, [?Islington, London], prescription books 1845–88 (Ref: MSS 3975-93); chemist, Scarborough, North Yorkshire, prescription book c.1875–1900 (Ref: MS 3994); druggist and general stores trader, England, sales ledger 1847–58 (Ref: MS 833); medical accounts, individuals' accounts with surgeons and apothecaries 1584–1864 (Ref: MS 5269); hundreds of miscellaneous medical recipe books, many accompanying household, culinary or veterinary recipes 14th–19th cents. (Ref: Western Manuscripts collection); retail chemist, Norwich, Norfolk, dangerous drugs register, diamorphine 1933–52, note on Smith & Son (Norwich) Ltd letterhead n.d.; miscellaneous pharmacists, day book 1943–46, cash books, sales n.d., daily records 1914–19, prescription books 1873–76, 1913–17, batch books 1925–51 (Ref: CMAC/GC/103).

MANCHESTER

MANCHESTER CENTRAL LIBRARY, LOCAL STUDIES UNIT ARCHIVES
St Peter's Square, Manchester M2 5PD

J H Adams, Stoke-on-Trent, chemist, prescriptions made up 1837, n.d. (Ref: M207/2/1-3); William Barker, Derby, prescriptions (with chemists' stamps) and letters concerning a consumptive patient 1831–44, n.d. (Ref: M35/5/17/1-24); Thomas Cross, Manchester, chemist, order for drugs 1824 (Ref: MISC/26); George Danson, Manchester, chemist and druggist, order for drugs and return of empty packages n.d. (Ref: MISC/28); Walter Edwards, Northern Moor, Manchester, pharmacist, account books, daily trading figures 1953–81 (w) (Ref: M517); Mr Farrer, apothecary, bill for medicines supplied to Duchess of

Newcastle, incl. cost of embalming John Holles, Duke of Newcastle 1707–11 (Ref: L1/3/1); Thomas Gilks Gibbons, papers incl. apprenticeship indenture to Samuel Davies, chemist and druggist, Chester, Cheshire, 1833, testimonials supporting application for post of dispenser at Birmingham Infirmary 1840, lease and correspondence re dwelling house and shop, [4] Market Street, Manchester 1840–73 (Ref: MISC/35); Gerald E Hurst, 727 Wilmslow Road, Didsbury, Manchester, chemist, prescription books 1940–69 (w), register of spirits received and despatched 1954–57, press cutting re Wilmslow Road c.1968 (Ref: M482); Parry family, miscellaneous chemist's prescriptions 1870–71 (Ref: M367/5/9/ 1-9); Pritchards Ltd, 67 Chorlton Road, Hulme, Manchester, and High Street, Cheadle, Salford, chemist, prescriptions included in circular from vicar of St Mary's, Hulme, advising parishioners of precautions against cholera epidemic 1866, prescription on reverse of election leaflet n.d., family and miscellaneous papers 19th–20th cents. (Ref: M375); Woodall family, Stalybridge, Tameside and Didsbury, Manchester, chemist, apprenticeship indenture, John Woodall 1833, apprenticeship indenture, John Leigh Woodall 1870, day books, John Woodall 1846–48, family papers 1834–1908 (Ref: MISC/621).

NEWCASTLE UPON TYNE

NORTHUMBERLAND RECORD OFFICE
Melton Park, North Gosforth, Newcastle upon Tyne NE3 5QX

William Davison, chemist, list of shop contents n.d. (Ref: ZMD 167); John Dymond, surgeon, apothecary and male midwife, and Robert Dymond, apothecary, articles of co-partnership 1779 (Ref: ZAN B1/1/40); Hexham Chemists, prescriptions 1889 (Ref: NRO 1635/271-4); Ralph Stamp, Alnwick, chemist, correspondence 1846 (Ref: NRO 530 20/242).

Apothecary's business, Holborn, London, deed of partnership 1800 (Ref: ZAN B1/1/51); chemist and druggist, deed of co-partnership 1838 (Ref: ZNI 22).

TYNE & WEAR ARCHIVES SERVICE
Blandford House, Blandford Square, Newcastle upon Tyne NE1 4JA

R Sheel, 8-12 Durham Road, Low Fell, Gateshead, chemist and druggist, sale of poisons register 1872–1905 (Ref: DX140/1); Wallsend Co-operative Chemists Society Ltd, Wallsend, North Tyneside. chemists' supplier, directors' and general meetings minutes 1953–70 (Ref: DT/COP13); Wilkinson & Simpson Ltd, 24 Newgate Street, Newcastle, wholesale druggist, photograph of shop and offices c.1905 (Ref: DX276/1); B Williamson & Co, 18 Market Place, South Shields, South Tyneside, chemist, prescription books 1875–1930 (w) (Ref: DX699/1-8).

NORFOLK

THE BRIDEWELL MUSEUM
Bridewell Alley, Norwich NR2 1AQ

Named businesses: S C Bobby, Soham, Cambridgeshire, chemist, dangerous drugs registers 1921–61 (Ref: 1994.78.453, 455), sale of poisons registers 1936–59 (Ref: 1994.78.456-8); William Boor, Wisbech, Cambridgeshire, nostrum diary n.d. (Ref: 1994.78.403); P H Davies, March, Cambridgeshire, nostrums book n.d. (Ref: 1994.78.394); Gardiner & Lacey, The Guildhall Pharmacy, 13 St Giles Street, Norwich, prescription books 1881, 1934–43, nostrums books n.d. (Ref: 1994.78.392-3, 407, 483); Alf J Grand, 2 Alexandra Road, Norwich, dangerous drugs register 1931–55 (Ref: 1994.78.454); James William Hart, Worthing, receipt book 1849 (Ref: 1994.78.390); Edgar H Judge, 20 North Street, Boston, Lincolnshire, chemist, prescription books 1855–90, nostrums book 1900 (Ref: 1994.78.400, 488-9); Pain & Bayles, Ipswich and Felixstowe, Suffolk, prescription books 1873–78, 1894–98, n.d. (Ref: 1994.78.345, 373, 484); L Piper (late Edwards), Wolsey Pharmacy, 47 St Nicholas Street, Ipswich, Suffolk, day book 1889–94, correspondence c.1940s–50s, wages book 1928–46 (Ref: 1994.78.475, 479, 1736), Guy Robinson, East Dereham, day books 1916–19, 1928–31, 1949–43, prescription book 1938–44, audio cassette re his pharmacist father, Alfred Robinson n.d. (Ref: 1994.78); Chas F Shewell, 36 Church Street, Cromer, dispensing chemist, prescription books 1900–01, 1910–12, 1924–26, 1946–48 (Ref: 1994.78.344, 346-8); G Shreeve & Son, Coldwell's Drug Stores, Essex, day book 1894–99 (Ref: 1994.78.476); G Shreeve & Son, Imperial Pharmacy, Hamlet Court Road, Westcliff-on-Sea, prescription books 1903–35, 1946–65 (Ref: 1994.78.480-1, 485-7), correspondence 1906–30s (Ref: 1994.78.1736); Smith & Wesley, Market Place, Downham Market, prescription forms 1918 (Ref: 1994.78.411); James M Weller, Long Stratton, nostrums books late 19th–early 20th cents. (Ref: 1994,78.391, 395, 408); Wiles & Holman, 135 Hamilton Road, Felixstowe, Suffolk, sale of poisons registers 1909–13, 1923–35 (Ref: 1994.78.451-2).

Trade association: Ipswich Chemists' Association, minute book 1917–31 (Ref: 1994.78.477).

Miscellaneous: invoices 1890s–early 20th cent. (Ref: 1994.78.1733); prescription book 1862–67 (Ref: 1994.78.373); nostrums book n.d. (Ref: 1994.78.403); advertising material and press cuttings 1870, 1930s–40s (Ref: 1994.78.1734); correspondence with chemists 1940s–50s (Ref: 1994.78.1736); photographs of chemists' shops n.d. (Ref: 1994.78.1735).

THE HISTORY OF ADVERTISING TRUST
HAT House, 12 Raveningham Centre, Raveningham NR14 6NU

W A Bell, East Southsea, store chemist, advertising material late 19th–early 20th cents. (Ref: AA1/1/44); Proctor & Gamble Ltd, papers and memoranda with agents re advertising 1985–90 (Ref: Leo Burnett research papers).

Guardbooks of advertising material for various pharmaceutical products 1984–85 (Ref: Leo Burnett guardbooks, 5, 12); product advertising press cuttings for various proprietary medicines, incl. *Aspirin* 1974–89 (Ref: MEAL collection, R10-80); portfolio of advertising material, incl. pharmaceutical products late 19th–early 20th cents. (Ref: AA1/1); scrapbook of advertising material, incl. pharmaceutical products late 19th–early 20th cents. (Ref: AA1/2); papers and memoranda with agents re advertising of analgesics, cold remedies and indigestion remedies 1992, n.d. (Ref: Leo Burnett research material).

NORFOLK RECORD OFFICE
Gildengate House, Anglia Square, Upper Green Lane, Norwich NR3 1AX

Thomas Preston Gostling, Market Hill, Diss, pharmacist, prescription book 1874–1904 (Ref: MC 362/8); Row & Taylor Ltd, St Stephens Street, Norwich, dispensing chemist and optician, prescription book 1915–18 (Ref: BR 222/1).

NORTH EAST LINCOLNSHIRE

NORTH EAST LINCOLNSHIRE ARCHIVES
Town Hall Square, Grimsby D31 1HX

Richard Alcock, Ulceby, Lincoln, grocer and druggist, ledger 1817–40, papers re crops and purchase of property, incl. farm stock 1823 (Ref: 515); Walter E Humphrey, Cleethorpes, dispensing chemist, prescription book 1876–1907 (Ref: 296).

NORTHAMPTONSHIRE

NORTHAMPTONSHIRE RECORD OFFICE
Wootton Hall Park, Northampton NN4 8BQ

George Armfield, Sheep Street, Northampton, prescription book 1825 (Ref: YZ 253); John Clower, 22 Bridge Street, Northampton, pharmaceutical chemist, prescription book 1888–99 (Ref: ML 2037-9); Charles A Hedley, 10 Market Square, Higham Ferrers, chemist, prescription books 1919–59 (Ref 'Acc 1978/59); Herbert Henry Newitt, Market Place, Long Buckby, chemist, prescription books c.1869–99, c.1916–22, estate papers 1898–1902 (Ref: ZA 4615-8, MKM 124/3); E Simms, 15 Market Place, Kettering, pharmacist, prescription book, Henry Hitchman 1879–94 (Ref: ZB 1099); Robert W Willson & Co, 6 Long Causeway, Peterborough, chemist, prescription books 1886–91,

1896–1942 (w), J E Saunders, Market Place 1901–33, M Heanley, Market Place 1896–1915 (Ref: ZB 89).

NORTHUMBERLAND

BERWICK-UPON-TWEED RECORD OFFICE
Council Offices, Wallace Green, Berwick-Upon-Tweed TD15 1ED

John Brown, 5 High Street, Berwick-Upon-Tweed, pharmacist, labels for products sold in Brown's shop late 19th cent. (Ref: BRO.479).

NORTH YORKSHIRE

NORTH YORKSHIRE COUNTY RECORD OFFICE
Malpas Road, Northallerton, North Yorkshire (correspondence address, County Record Office, County Hall, Northallerton DL7 8AF)

Chemist, Bedale, prescription books 1892–1929 (Ref: ZRX (MIC 3328)).

YORK CITY ARCHIVES DEPARTMENT
Art Gallery Building, Exhibition Square, York YO1 2EW

Dispensing chemist, forerunner of Mark F Burgin, Coney Street, York, prescription books 1826–40 (w) (Ref: ACC 119).

NOTTINGHAM

NOTTINGHAMSHIRE ARCHIVES & SOUTHWELL DIOCESAN RECORD OFFICE
County House, Castle Meadow Road, Nottingham NG2 1AG

Bradford & District Chemists' Association, Bradford, trade association, rules 1900 (Ref: DD 135 addit/103); George William Briggs, Low Street, Sutton-in-Ashfield, Nottinghamshire, pharmaceutical chemist, prescription book c.1885–95 (Ref: DD 757); Edward Dales, 37 Beech Avenue, Nottingham, pharmaceutical chemist, annual financial statements and related correspondence 1933–50, receipts 1924–26, 1942–51, handbills advertising cough medicine and other shop items c.1920s, correspondence 1951, certificate of Fellowship of Royal Pharmaceutical Society with covering letter 1954, 1957, educational certificates 1888–1905, birth and death details re Edward and Elizabeth Dales 1989, print, competition prize n.d., c.1950s (Ref: DD 1524, DD 1900); Davis & Son, Northbrook Street, Newbury, West Berkshire, chemist, account to J L Franklin for medicines 1871 (Ref: DD 96/3); George Fox, Worksop, chemist, prescription book incl. printed recipes and remedies c.1840 (Ref: DD 1269/1); Midland Pharmaceutical Association, trade association, programme of events 1898–99, 1904–05 (Ref: DD 1135 addit/101-2); Edmund Monck, Southwell,

Nottinghamshire, apothecary, will inventory 1712, admon bond 1712 (Ref: PRSW 114/24); Matthew Needham, Nottingham, surgeon and apothecary, will 1781 (Ref: DDCB 67); J Pickard, Low Street, Sutton-in-Ashfield, Nottinghamshire, dispensing chemist, prescription books 1886–1915, 1925–66, recipe book n.d., c.20th cent., repeat prescription request 1911, circular re supply of laudanum to suspected addicts 1937, advertisement for Radford's medications for humans and animals n.d., c.1930s, J Pickard's pharmacology notebook n.d., 20th cent., stationery n.d., 20th cent. (Ref: DD 1184); Ross Sergeant, Cheapside, Nottingham, dispensing chemist, prescription books 1853–58, 1898–1963 (Ref: DD 929); James Stephenson, 72 Hartley Road, Radford, Nottingham, chemist, invoices 1948–49, prescriptions 1907–19, certificate of insurance against death as result of facial anthrax contracted through use of Anti-Thrax shaving brush 1932, postcard of shopfront n.d. (Ref: DD 1102).

Apothecary, Nottinghamshire, itemised bill incl. pills, powders, drops and 'bleeding' 1821 (Ref: DD 877/6); pharmacist, Nottinghamshire, symptom and treatment book 1914 (Ref: DD 1232/1).

NOTTINGHAM CITY LIBRARY
Oral History Collection, Local Studies Library, Angel Row, Nottingham NG1 6HP

Tape recorded interviews with pharmacists: Wilfred Aynes, Nottingham, chemist 1992–93 (Ref: C490, C519 b), Mary Burr, Mould, community pharmacist 1992–93 (Ref: C521 a), Dr Frank Cooper, Woollaton, academic pharmacist 1992–93 (Ref: C520 a), Robert Onley, Woollaton, community pharmacist 1992–93 (Ref: C517 b), Trevor R Roberts, West Bridgford, Nottingham, hospital pharmacist 1992–93 (Ref: C518 b), John Rushworth, Mapperley, community pharmacist 1992–93 (Ref: C518 a), Denis R Shaw, industrial pharmacist 1992–93 (Ref: C519 a), Walter Smith, Woodthorpe, hospital pharmacist 1992–93 (Ref: C517 a), Gertrude Watson, Beeston, academic pharmacist 1992–93 (Ref: C520 b), Reginald Scott Wood, Reigate 1992–93 (Ref: C521 b).

Tape recorded memoirs of a variety of Nottingham pharmacists, entitled 'Dusting and Dispensing' 1992 (Ref: C495).

UNIVERSITY OF NOTTINGHAM, HALLWARD LIBRARY,
Department of Manuscripts & Special Collections, University Park, Nottingham NG7 2RD

Sir Theodore Mayerne, physician, receipts book c.1643–65 (Ref: Pw V 90); Park Pharmacy, Derby Road, Nottingham, dispensing chemist, prescription books 1920–29 (Ref: Acc.739).

OXFORDSHIRE

OXFORDSHIRE RECORD OFFICE
St Luke's Church, Temple Road, Cowley, Oxford OX4 2EX

Thomas Houghton & Co, St Clements, Oxford, chemist, ledger 1865–92 (Ref: Acc 3172); F L Loxley, Oxford, chemist, prescription books 1898–1940 (Ref: Lox (passim)); Mountain Ltd, Sheep Street, Bicester, chemist and optician, prescription books 1848–81 (Ref: Mount (passim)).

UNIVERSITY OF OXFORD, MUSEUM OF THE HISTORY OF SCIENCE
Old Ashmolean Building, Broad Street, Oxford OX1 3AZ

George C Druce, 118 High Street, Oxford, pharmacist and botanist, scrapbook, containing correspondence, press cuttings and ephemera re pharmacy, botany, Oxford scientific societies and Oxford City Council c.1882–1902 (Ref: MS Museum 110); Francis Newbery & Sons Ltd, 45 St Pauls' Church Yard, London, medicine vendor, bookseller and publisher, Dr James's Fever Powder sales account book 1768–98, unopened packet signed by Francis Newbery n.d. (Ref: MS Museum 30-1, 46); Daniel Price, [Abergavenny], apothecary, bill 1718 (MS Museum 48).

Billheads, French, of various trades incl. pharmacist early 19th cent. (MS Museum 23); colour-printed cards advertising patent medicines, mainly American but incl. Thomas Holloway of London late 19th cent. (Ref: MS Gabb 7 (2)); list, Portuguese, of oriental herbs and *material medica* written in Indo-China in 1516, 1869 (p) (Ref: MS Museum 14).

PLYMOUTH

PLYMOUTH & WEST DEVON RECORD OFFICE
Unit 3, Clare Place, Coxside, Plymouth PL4 0JW

Edwin Patchett, retail chemist, recipes and remedies notebook with some costs 1885–87 (Ref: Acc 560/2).

PORTSMOUTH

CITY MUSEUM & RECORDS OFFICE
Museum Road, Portsmouth PO1 2LJ

Bloomfields Chemists, Portsmouth, prescription book 1941–49 (Ref: 1386A/1/2); N V Humphrey, 402 London Road, Hilsea, Portsmouth, recipes and prescriptions ledger 1930–54 (Ref: 1288A); National Co-operative Chemists Ltd, 179 Albert Road, Southsea, chemists' co-operative, Margnard & Co, prescription books 1902–27, W J Page, prescription books c.1912–26, Portsea Island Co-operative Chemists Ltd: prescription books 1902–78, sale of poisons register 1936–68, Shuttlock Dangerous Drugs Act register 1951–72 (Ref: 1525A/1/1/1-18).

READING

BERKSHIRE RECORD OFFICE
9 Coley Avenue, Reading RG1 6AF

J P Bate Ltd, Reading, chemist, prescription books 1878–87, 1949–50, 1960–64 (Ref: D/EX 970); Hickman & Son Ltd, 5 The Mall, Newbury, prescription books 1901–05, 1911–79 (Ref: D/EX 1164); deeds of 6 & 7 High Street, Windsor, 1735–1954 incl. sale particulars of 7 High Street, let to Russell & Co chemists 1922 (Ref: D/EX 1268).

ROCHDALE

ROCHDALE LOCAL STUDIES LIBRARY
Esplanade Arts and Heritage Centre, Esplanade, Rochdale OL16 1AQ

J J Thomas & Son, 24 Yorkshire Street, 54 Drake Street and 10 St Mary's Gate, Rochdale, chemist, prescription books 1902–28, 1944–63, prescription records, human and veterinary n.d., c.1937–63 (Ref: M/CPR/1-7).

ROTHERHAM

ROTHERHAM METROPOLITAN BOROUGH ARCHIVES & LOCAL STUDIES SECTION
Brian O'Malley Central Library, Walker Place, Rotherham S65 1JH

Henry Laycock, 11 High Street, Rotherham, chemist and druggist, private domestic and business diary, with accounts c.1830–57 (m) (Ref: 9/Z).

ST HELENS

DR JEAN HUGH-JONES
36 Laurel Drive, St Helens WA10 5JD

William Pilkington, St Helens, general practitioner, recipe and preparation book 1789–early 20th cent. (Ref: microfilm copy available at St Helens Local History & Archives Library, Gamble Institute, Victoria Square, St Helens WA10 1DY).

SALFORD

SALFORD CITY ARCHIVES
Archives Centre, 658-662 Liverpool Road, Irlam, Manchester M44 5AD

Joseph Faulkner, [?Eccles, Salford], chemist and general provisions retailer, account book, containing debtors' names and charges for goods and services supplied, medicines in particular 1862-89, recipe books, medical and household, with loose press cuttings 1859, late 19th cent., 1906-15, n.d. (Ref: U311/B1); C S Fletcher Ltd, 263 Eccles New Road, Weaste, Salford, chemist, bills and receipts 1955, 1961-63 (Ref: U186/F1).

SHEFFIELD

SHEFFIELD CITY ARCHIVES
52 Shoreham Street, Sheffield S1 4SP

Dr Gilbert Heathcote, Sheffield, prescription books 1700-19 (Ref: BHD 310); Cadman Hodgkinson, Sheffield, apothecary, prescription book 1777 (Ref: MD 3498); Charles O Morrison, 137 West Street, Sheffield, pharmaceutical chemist, recipe book c.1891 (Ref: MD 6794); Newham & Pickard, Shude Lane, Sheffield, manufacturing chemist and wholesale druggist, articles of partnership 1888, memorandum re debt due 1888, lease 1887 (Ref: MD 6384/1-3); D W Slinn, Glossop Road, Sheffield, chemist, prescription books 1948-71 (Ref: 201/B1/21); Bruce Smith, Sheffield, manufacturing chemist and ophthalmic optician, trade mark certificate 1924 and renewal 1928, recipe books 1920s (Ref: 1996/102); Levi Turner, Glossop Road, Sheffield, chemist, prescription books 1928-48 (Ref: 201/B1/19-20); R E Wardell, Glossop Road, Sheffield, chemist, prescription books 1919-28 (Ref: 201/B1/16-18); G D Wreaks, J S Burnell, 321 Glossop Road, Sheffield, chemist and druggist, prescription books 1869-1919 (Ref: 201/B1/1-15).

SHROPSHIRE

IRONBRIDGE GORGE MUSEUM TRUST
Telford, Shropshire TF8 7AW

H Foster, Birmingham, chemist, records 19-20 cents. (Ref: 1997.3149)

SHROPSHIRE RECORDS & RESEARCH CENTRE
Castle Gates, Shrewsbury SY1 2AQ

John Adams, Shrewsbury, chemist, prescription books 1872-75, 1911-78, formulae book c.1900 (Ref: 6232/1-16W, 76232/17/1); G Cross & Son, 70 Mardol, Shrewsbury, agricultural and pharmaceutical chemist, correspondence re orders and supplies 1915, advertising circulars n.d., miscellaneous records 1885,

1898 (Ref: 5207); Alfred Morgan, Shropshire Street, Market Drayton, chemist and grocer, combined day and cash books 1895–1900 (Ref: 1051/1-2).

SOMERSET
MR A BOND
Schmaltings, Martin Street, Baltonsborough BA6 8QY

A O Bond Ltd, Eddystone House, West Street, Somerton, dispensing chemist, prescription book 1864–1922

SOMERSET ARCHIVE & RECORD SERVICE
Obridge Road, Taunton TA2 7PU

Adcocks, 18 Fore Street, Taunton, chemist, prescription books 1893–1960 (Ref: DD/ADK); [?Dr Bronington], Chard, prescription book 1839–41 (Ref: DD/UK); Davey of Wiveliscombe, chemist, prescription for pills for Mrs Woodhouse 1852 (Ref: DD/TBL); Henry Handford, Taunton, Great Torrington and Thornton Heath, chemist and druggist, prescription books 1862–92 (Ref: DD/SAS(C/795/TN164)); Keeble's, Crewkerne, chemist, price lists and handbills for remedies 1902 (Ref: DD/X/FWL); Arthur John Smith, 47 North Street, Taunton, chemist and druggist, prescription books 1875–1915 (Ref: DD/X/MNR); Fred Wellington, Taunton, chemist, prescription note 1872 (Ref: DD/X/BES); Wiveliscombe Pharmacy, prescription book 1894–1927 (Ref: DD/X/WHS).

SOUTHEND-ON-SEA
ESSEX RECORD OFFICE, SOUTHEND BRANCH
Central Library, Victoria Avenue, Southend-on-Sea SS2 6EX

Eastwood Pharmacy, Rayleigh Road, Eastwood, sale catalogue 1937 (Ref: D/F 36/17/15); Harrington & Sons, Rochford and 40 Alexandra Street, Southend-on-Sea, dispensing chemist, ledger of toiletries, household and pharmaceutical products sold 1912–23, Harrington's 50th anniversary products booklet 1891, prescription books 1873–94, 1920–26 (Ref: D/F 41, D/DS 313/5/11/10); William Pearce Kernot, Rochford, Essex, chemist and druggist, probate copy of will [1841] (Ref: D/DJe F9).

Deeds of tenement in High Street, Rayleigh, Essex, used as apothecary's shop 1791–94 (Ref: D/DJe T50).

STAFFORDSHIRE
STAFFORDSHIRE RECORD OFFICE
Eastgate Street, Stafford ST16 2LZ

Victor Cartwright, High Street, Uttoxeter, dispensing chemist, purchase ledgers 1902–14, sales ledgers 1893–96, day books 1912–15, prescription books 1871–1920, bundle of notices re Shops Act 1950 (Ref: D1349); Lewis Dickenson, Stafford, apothecary, apothecary's account books 1715–58, account book with some apothecary's accounts 1741–53 (Ref: D1798/HM29/7-9); Fowke & Son, 46 Greengate Street, Stafford, dispensing and photographic chemist, ledgers 1927–28, private ledgers, B S Jones 1927–28, personal papers of W F Fowke, incl. title deeds to shops and lands 1889, 1909, 1916, sale of business agreement 1936, birth certificate 1869, marriage settlement 1896, probate papers, incl. a cash book 1936–41, and miscellaneous papers n.d. (Ref: D4338/A/24, D4338/G/3); David Hatfield Ltd, South End Pharmacy, Wolverhampton Road, Stafford, chemist, general meeting minutes 1932, general ledger, incl. capital accounts and annual balance sheets 1927–30, day book 1927–36, prescription book 1927–45 (Ref: D4338/A/27, D3292); Marson & Son, 53 Greengate Street and 27 Earl Street, Stafford, dispensing and photographic chemist and optician, general ledger incl. capital accounts and balance sheets 1919–24, accounts 1908–18, 1926–34 (Ref: D4338/A/21, G/4-5).

Apothecary, Stafford, account books 1707–22, 1736–55 (Ref: D1798/HM27/3-4).

SUFFOLK

SUFFOLK RECORD OFFICE, BURY ST EDMUNDS BRANCH
77 Raingate Street, Bury St Edmunds IP33 2AR

Brain Brothers, 7 Abbeygate Street, Bury St Edmunds, chemist and druggist, sales particulars and plans for druggist's shop 1887 (Ref: HE 500/6/7); Nunn, Hinnell, Clark & Burdon Ltd, 12-13 Abbeygate Street, Bury St Edmunds, chemist and druggist, prescription books 1837–96, 1914–18 (Ref: 2195).

SUFFOLK RECORD OFFICE, IPSWICH BRANCH
Gatacre Road, Ipswich IP1 2LQ

John Betts & Son, 64 Thoroughfare, Woodbridge, chemists and druggists, prescription books 1885–1960 (Ref: HC460); A Harrington, Needham Market, chemist, day book, credits 1897–1901, notes and photographs re business and premises in Needham Market 1984 (Ref: HC 421); Dr Lay, Peasenhall, chemist, account book 1885–1912 (Ref: HC 24/1); Thomas Matthew, London, apothecary, and Thomas Neale, London, surgeon, deed of partnership 1751 (Ref: X1/8/2.8); Sir John Rous, 5th Bt, Henham Hall, prescription book, household recipes and medicinal remedies 1754 (Ref: HA11/C47/24); Stearn Bros Ltd, 3 Market Place, Stowmarket, chemist, notebooks, sales of game paste manufactured by Simpson's 1888–1900 (Ref: HC 16); Noel G Stow, Ipswich, apprentice chemist, articles of pupilage 1944–46, employers' letters of reference 1946–47, father's letter of congratulation 1949, book of preparations made during apprenticeship 1944–47, Stow's notes to accompany written apprenticeship record 1993 (Ref: HC 450:10,348); M E Wilderspin, East Bergholt, dispensing chemist, ledgers, detailing patients' and doctors' accounts 1957–71, day book 1970–71, quarterly account book 1969–71, patient's quarterly bills 1967, 1971, Wilderspin's London College of Pharmacy notebook on plant structure n.d. (Ref: HC 436: 8813).

SUFFOLK RECORD OFFICE, LOWESTOFT BRANCH
Central Library, Clapham Road South, Lowestoft NR32 1DR

John Colby, Lowestoft, apothecary, probate inventory 1719 (p) (Ref: 535/3/7/5); George Staffe Crisp, Lowestoft, medicine licence 1851 (p) (Ref: 264/1/2/7).

Bill for medicines supplied 1782–86 (Ref: 89/4/9).

SURREY

SURREY HISTORY CENTRE
130 Goldsworth Road, Woking GU21 1ND

Bishops Chemist, High Street, Thames Ditton, chemist, prescription books 1905–78 (Ref: 2613/1); John Pierce Boyce & Son, 132-134 Guildford Street, Chertsey, chemist and druggist, prescription book 1823–37, order book, composed of letters for 'Mr Boyce's Infallible Chilblain Remedy' 1878–91, miscellaneous papers 1954, n.d. (Ref: 374); John Bristed, Cliff Terrace and High Street, Margate, Kent, chemist, ledger, business and private accounts 1890–94 (Ref: 2613/2/1); The Ripley Pharmacy, Ripley, pharmacy, prescription books 1939–78 (w) (Ref: 5249/1-7); John Salter, Weybridge, apothecary, will 1745, title deeds 1720 (Ref: 256/3/1-3).

WAKEFIELD

WEST YORKSHIRE ARCHIVE SERVICE, WAKEFIELD HEADQUARTERS
Registry of Deeds, Newstead Road, Wakefield WF1 2DE

Belks Court Practice, Pontefract, pharmacy books 1945–71 (Ref: C474); C S Chalinor, Castleford, pharmaceutical notebook c.1940 (Ref: B268); Horbury Industrial Co-operative Society, drugs and dispensary stock books c.1940 (Ref: C504); J Judge, Northgate and Kirkgate, Wakefield, pharmacist, ledgers 1857–61, 1946–48, 1952–69 (Ref: C861, Box 21); Nicholson & Sons, Leeds, manufacturing chemist, deeds, patent specifications and other papers 1829–92

(Ref: C158); E P Shaw, Wakefield, chemical books 1868-72, 1900-04 (Ref: C971).

Miscellaneous book of remedies and medical notes, Yorkshire, pharmacist c.1830-80 (Ref: C696).

WARWICKSHIRE

GEHE UK PLC
Retail Branch, Atherstone, Warwickshire. Enquiries to GEHE UK plc, Sapphire Court, Walsgrave Triangle Business Park, Coventry CV2 2TX

W Aston & Co Ltd, Westgate House, 39-41 Romsey Road, Winchester, Hampshire, dispensing chemist, prescription books 1937-40, 1942-63; Brooks & Warburton Ltd, 232-240 Vauxhall Bridge Road, London, pharmaceutical price list 1939-40.

SHAKESPEARE BIRTHPLACE TRUST RECORDS OFFICE
The Shakespeare Centre, Stratford-upon-Avon CV37 6QW

Richard Hawkes, 33 High Street, Stratford-upon-Avon, chemist, recipe book 1827, prescription books 1869-1904, notice of change of premises 1838, visiting cards 1868-80, F Kendall, personal papers: notebooks n.d., mayor's dinner speech 1854, correspondence 1861-67; family photographs c.1880s-1920s (Ref: DR 152, DR 197/286-90, 315, DR 315/2-14); Loggins Ltd, 3 High Street, Stratford-upon-Avon, chemist, prescription books 1913-60 (Ref: DR 292).

WARWICKSHIRE COUNTY RECORD OFFICE
Priory Park, Cape Road, Warwick CV34 4JS

W A Ball, 29 Smith Street, Warwick, chemist, prescription book 1939-42 (Ref: CR3058); John Newton, Kenilworth, chemist and druggist, letters, not all connected to his business 1824-45 (Ref: Z774).

Dispensing chemist, Leamington, prescription books 1902-09 (Ref: CR2301, 2308, 2410).

WEST SUSSEX

WEST SUSSEX RECORD OFFICE
Sherburne House, 3 Orchard Street, Chichester. Enquiries to County Hall, Chichester PO19 1RN

Sidney Barstow Ltd, 9 North Street, Chichester, chemist and druggist, apprenticeship indenture of Sidney Barstow 1889, prescription books 1786-1846, recipe book early 20th cent. (Ref: Add MSS 19,545-19,551); Henry James Berry, 6 Montague Street, Worthing, pharmaceutical chemist, day book, containing record of articles purchased, prices and purchasers' names 1865–67, suppliers' bills 1854–78 (Ref: Add MSS 27,510-5); Harry Holland, 80 Aldwick Road, Bognor Regis, chemist, prescription books 1933–63 (Ref: Add MSS 24,152-5); Nyewood Pharmacy, Aldwick Road, Bognor Regis, pharmacist, account books, weekly receipts and payments 1950–59 (Ref: Add MSS 18,195-203); E Thorp & Son, 47 Aldwick Road, Bognor Regis, pharmaceutical chemist, purchase journal 1943–51, prescription books: 1910–72, 'own prescribing' 1936–66 (Ref: Add MSS 24,129-51).

WILTSHIRE
BRADFORD-ON-AVON MUSEUM
Bridge Street, Bradford-on-Avon BA15 1BY

R T Christopher, Bradford-on-Avon, pharmacist, prescription books 1863–1986 (Ref: Acc. 1990.1).

WILTSHIRE & SWINDON RECORD OFFICE
County Hall, Trowbridge BA14 8JG

Edgar Neale's, High Street, Chippenham, chemist, prescription books 1872–1922 (w), 1944–66 (Ref: 1759); James Talbot, 56-60 Milford Street, Salisbury, drysalter and wholesale druggist, ledger 1899–1928 (Ref: 1928); James Woodman, High Street, Malmesbury, shopkeeper, ironmonger, draper and apothecary, day books 1827–38 (Ref: 988/1).

WIRRAL
WIRRAL ARCHIVES SERVICE
Birkenhead Central Library, Borough Road, Birkenhead L41 2XB

C H Cranshaw, Central Station Pharmacy, Birkenhead, chemist, prescription books 1935–69 (Ref: ZCR); Woodfield Cooke Ltd, Hoylake and Birkenhead, pharmacist, prescription books 1898–1947 (w), dangerous drugs register 1929–48 (Ref: ZWC).

WOLVERHAMPTON
WOLVERHAMPTON ARCHIVES & LOCAL STUDIES
42-50 Snow Hill, Wolverhampton WV2 4AG

William Bailey & Son, Horseley Fields Chemical Works, Wolverhampton and 2-3 Abchurch Yard, Cannon Street, London, wholesale and manufacturing chemist and druggist, insurance policy for chemical works, with schedule of laboratories and shops 1862, title deeds, property papers and plans re land at Horseley Fields 1751–1912, valuations of chemical works and mortgage 1866, schedule of repairs at chemical works 1918, papers and plan re land purchase by Wolverhampton & Walsall Railway 1868–69, Henry Wood, distiller of Oaken and tenant of Horseley Fields, will 1814 (Ref: DX-573, D/BRA/6 Acc 398).

WORCESTERSHIRE

WORCESTERSHIRE RECORD OFFICE
St Helen's Branch, Fish Street, Worcester WR1 2HN

Anderson & Virgo, 12 The Foregate, Worcester, chemist, prescription books c.1805–1913, 1950, 1960–64 (Ref: 705:422 BA 3089); S C Hawkswood & Son Ltd, Stourbridge, Dudley, chemist, prescription books 1895–1968 (Ref: 899:958 BA 10272); Horniblow & Son, 50 Sidbury, Worcester, chemist, prescription book 1870–76 (Ref: b 705:547 BA 4755); E J Kitson Ltd, 1 Broad Street, Worcester, chemist, prescription books 1894–1948 (Ref: b 705:814 BA 7391); Lea, Perrins & Smith, Worcester, chemist (later sauce manufacturer), prescription books 1836–41 (Ref: b 705:291 BA 9440); Manders, Belle View Terrace, Great Malvern, chemist, prescription books 1837–1980 (w), poisons registers 1936–80 (Ref: 705: 1231 BA11135); Roxall Pharmacy, 136 High Street, Stourbridge, pharmacist, account book 1924–32 (Ref: 705:260 BA 6123); Steward family, High Street, Worcester, chemist, order book and files 1890–94, 1915–19 (w), receipts 1969, C C Steward's pharmacognoscy notebook c.1931–33, family papers, incl. correspondence, press cuttings and photographs 20th cent. (Ref: 705:781 BA 7537).

NORTHERN IRELAND

ANTRIM

PUBLIC RECORD OFFICE OF NORTHERN IRELAND
66 Balmoral Avenue, Belfast, BT9 6NY

Named businesses: Apothecary Hall of Ireland, address of governors to the Earl of Kimberley and the text of his reply 1804 (Ref: T.2541/VR/19); Alfred Bishop Ltd, London, manufacturing chemist, case papers re use of trade mark 'Yamba' by Orzone (Ireland) Ltd 1933 (Ref: D.971/39/1/50); Robert F Black, Belfast, public analyst for Northern Ireland, medical analysis book incl. analysis of drugs from various Northern Irish dispensaries 1899–1944, notebook recording drugs sent from various Northern Irish dispensaries for analysis 1899–1906, draft and printed letters re appointment of analysts in Northern Ireland 1911–27, letters, circulars and press cuttings relating mainly to the salaries and conditions of analysts in Ireland c.1887–1930 (Ref: D.2682/1); Board of Guardians, Ballygawley, Tyrone, dispensary, alphabetical index to registers and casebook

1852–59, photograph of shop c.1910 (Ref: D.971/1&8); J P Bowden, Belfast, pharmaceutical chemist, prescription book 1931–60 (Ref: D.3629/1-3); Alexander Boyd, Lisburn, chemist, prescription books 1891–1935 (Ref: D.2937/1/1-77); Butler Medical Hall, Belturbet, receipt for medical goods and prescriptions 1828 (Ref: D.2359/5&25); James A Campbell and Francis Campbell, Belfast, partnership agreement 1895 (Ref: D.3552/2B); John Clarke & Co Ltd, wholesale druggist, statement of affairs 1911–13 (Ref: D.1372); Dr Patrick Connor, Newry, Down, druggist, apprenticeship indenture and bond with Henry McBride 1837 (Ref: T.3064/1A&B); Samuel Daspaignoll & Co, apothecaries, account 1739–40 (Ref: T.1732/6); Davidson & Hardy, Belfast, laboratory supplies, prescription books 1868–1921 (Ref: D.1008/1-9); Eglinton Chemical Co, legal correspondence 1883–94 (Ref: D.1769/61/3); Thomas Ferguson, Tandragee, Armagh, chemist, licence to practice as a chemist 1792, admittance card to lectures at the University of Edinburgh and certificate of attendance 1824 (Ref: D.1918/1&2/2&11); John Grattan, Edenderry, apothecary and druggist, apprenticeship agreements 1825–30, 1851 (Ref: D.2068/2A&B/3&4, D.3667/3); Gratton Chemists Ltd, Belfast, pharmaceutical chemist, prescription books 1827–1959, National Health Insurance Scheme prescription books 1944–58, dangerous drugs registers 1921–59 (Ref: D1072/1-5); Alfred Gray, Ogle Street, Armagh, chemist, photographs of shop c.1900 (Ref: D.1667/1-4); W J Hamilton, Gortin, Tyrone, chemist and grocery merchant, account books and labels of medicine bottles 1899–1927 (Ref: D.2462/1-4); John W Haslett, Belfast, chemist and druggist, business records 1905–71 (Rcf: D.3795); Kilwaughter Chemical Co, Larne, accounts and stock books 1889–1947 (Ref: D.1190); Dr William Moore, Ballymoney, Antrim, dispensary book and diary 1837–48, 1851–70 (Ref: D.2171/131&132); C Morrison Ltd, Belfast, wholesale chemist, ledgers 1947–62 (Ref; D.2443/13); Adam [Reys?], Derry, Londonderry, surgeon and apothecary, deed of apprenticeship with Thomas Rogers 1796 (Ref: D.2854/1); Tate's Medical Hall, Belfast, files and account books 1923–73 (Ref: D.3090); William S Taylor, Enniskillen, Fermanagh, chemist, deeds, case papers, test papers and correspondence 1810–1945, miscellaneous papers re estates of Charles Edward Taylor, chemist's apprentice 1881–1910 (Ref: D.3336/3); Wilson & Colville, chemist, legal correspondence 1890 (Ref: D.1769/35/3).

Official records: Belfast Corporation, bills incl. a clause allowing establishment of municipally owned chemists' shops 1923 (Ref: CAB.8J/4); Dervock Dispensary Committee, rules regulations and a report 1839 (Ref: T.2310/3&4); transcript state papers, Ireland, referring to petitions from Dublin City apothecaries for incorporation by royal charter 1745 (Ref: T.1060(1)p.61).

Miscellaneous: apothecary or doctor, Dublin, Ireland, medical prescription book 1747–49 (Ref: D.3480/32/1); dispensary, Portadown, Armagh, annual report

1850 (Ref: D.1248/0/20); letter re apothecary's apprentice 1805 (Ref: D.572/18/106); register of dangerous drugs and poisons 1954–73 (Ref: D.2973).

SCOTLAND

ABERDEEN

ABERDEEN UNIVERSITY, DISS: HERITAGE DIVISION, DEPARTMENT OF SPECIAL COLLECTIONS & ARCHIVES
King's College, Aberdeen AB24 3SW

George Innes, Aberdeen, druggist, personal papers 1823–25 (Ref: MS 2769/II/70).

Medical diaries 1765–66, remedies c.1800 (Ref: AUL MS 3470).

ARGYLL & BUTE

ARGYLL & BUTE ARCHIVES
Manse Brae, Lochgilphead PA31 8QU

George Stirling, Argyll Street, Dunoon, chemist and druggist, plans for reconstruction of shop 1887 (Ref: BD/12/D3).

DUMFRIES & GALLOWAY

DUMFRIES & GALLOWAY ARCHIVES
Archive Centre, 33 Burns Street, Dumfries DG1 2PS

Thomas Hunter, MD, Sanquhar, inventory and valuation of goods and chattels incl. stock of medicine 1844 (Ref: RI5/50/4); David Know, Edinburgh, chirurgeon and apothecary, action for non-payment of medicines supplied against Agnes Maxwell n.d. (Ref: GGD 56/21); Thomas Paxtoun, Lockerbie, surgeon, petition to justices of the peace against Jean Irving for stealing medicines from his shop n.d. (Ref: RB2/2/180); Robert Stewart of the Stewarts of Shambellie, payment to Nathaniel Firmin for medicines 1723 (Ref: GGD 37/1/9).

Orders and regulations governing shops in Dumfries Burgh, incl. regulations under the 1908 Poisons and Pharmacy Act 1908–38 (Ref: BH2/2/18).

DUNDEE

DUNDEE UNIVERSITY LIBRARY
Archives & Manuscripts Department, Dundee DD1 4HN

L P Michie, 276 Perth Road, Dundee, chemist, cash book 1907–20, prescription book 1907–10 (Ref: MS 15/82).

EDINBURGH

NATIONAL ARCHIVES OF SCOTLAND
H M General Register House, Princes Street, Edinburgh EH1 3YY

Court of Session productions (CS96/): Matthew Allen, Edinburgh, chemist and druggist, sederunt book 1814–22 (Ref: 3586); British Tar Co, Culross, Fife, tar and related medicinal chemicals manufacturer, sal-ammoniac works account book 1785–89 (Ref: 3335); John Gib, Castleton, Dunfermline, Fife, surgeon and druggist, sederunt books 1827–29 (Ref: 4211-12); John Swan, Bo'ness, Falkirk, seedsman and druggist, day books 1861–63 (Ref: 2966-7); Dr John Thomson, Edinburgh, physician and druggist, sederunt book 1830 (Ref: 4564); William Thomson & Co, Edinburgh, druggist, account book 1783–85 (Ref: 1086); John Threshie, Dumfries, Dumfries & Galloway, surgeon, druggist and apothecary, sederunt book 1816–17 (Ref: 433); James Whyte, Edinburgh, druggist, ledger 1786–93 (Ref: 1614).

Deposited collections (GD/)
Named businesses: William Ainslie, apprenticeship indenture to Robert Carr, apothecary, chemist and druggist of Berwick-Upon-Tweed 1831, contract of co-partnership, as manufacturing chemist and wholesale and retail chemist and druggist, 5-8 George Street, Edinburgh, with eldest son 1891 (Ref: 374/11, /17/1); William, Alexander and Hugh Nisbet, surgeons' and apothecaries' accounts n.d. (14) (Ref: 6/2082); John Balfour, Edinburgh, accounts due for medicine and attendance 1766, doctors' bills for medicines 1704–53, Duncan Campbell of Glenure, letter with account for medicines from John Aitkin 1780 and account for medicines and a prescription for his sons 1765–71, Ivie Campbell, apothecary, letter to Alexander Campbell of Barcaldine regarding the sending of medicine 1785–88, Donald MacLaine, surgeon, account for medicines for Alexander and Hugh Campbell 1796, A Anderson, letter to Mary Campbell regarding supply of pectoral and laxative pills 1814, J Gregory MD, prescriptions for Mary Campbell for asthma 1814, Dr McNab, letter to Mary Campbell regarding quinine and tincture of myrrh n.d., recipes and medical prescriptions 18th–19th cents, William Cleland, letter to Thomas Baillie relating his cure of 40 doses of Jesuits' bark for his Kentish fever and ague 1741 (Refs: 70/295, /218, 257, 333, 365, 413, 482 & 557, /1035 & 1436, /1665A, /1934, /2099, /2164, /2180, /3500, /3570); James Brown, surgeon, apothecary burgess of Edinburgh, decree for payment of sums due for specified drugs and medical services 1701 (Ref: 5/347); James Campbell, apprenticeship indenture, to Thomas Wood, surgeon apothecary of Edinburgh n.d. (Ref: 64/2/19); John Cathcart, account for

garden seeds and medicines 1727 (Ref: 180/462); John Clark, Dunkeld and London, surgeon, correspondence with Col Allan Macpherson about his practice and patent medicine 1793–1804 (Ref: 80/932); William Douglas, Forfar, Angus, chirurgeon apothecary, accounts due 1718–30 (Ref: 205/Baldovan 164); Robert Grahame, Callingad, copy act of admissions allowing him to practise chirurgery and pharmacy 1688, medical recipes n.d. (Ref: 22/1/597, /3/816-17); Dr James Hall, account book, drugs purchased 1791–95 (Ref: 113/436); Sir William Knighton, medical prescriptioner 1818, receipts for medicines for Mrs Nelly Kerr 1751–52 (Ref: 150/2692, /2980); Daniel McDonald, Culrose, surgeon and apothecary, bill n.d. (Ref: 29/1977); James Pringell, Coupar Angus, surgeon apothecary, account for medicines supplied to David Bittone 1667 (Ref: 7/2/52); David Pringle, Edinburgh, chirurgeon apothecary, account due 1676–81 (Ref: 40/2/xviii/1); David Pringle, chirurgeon, detailed account for drugs supplied to Mary Erskine 1678–82, David Erskine, letter to Earl of Mar containing signature in favour of Peter Hepburn as chirurgeon and apothecary to the Queen 1707 (Ref: 124/16/14, /513/7); Dr Willliam Sinclair, accounts due for drugs to Edinburgh druggists 1751–61 and William Leslie 1793, medical prescriptions for Sinclair and Ferryman families 1842–74, part of advertising testimonials, Lignum's antiscorbutic drops 1812, miscellaneous recipes 19th cent. (Ref: 136/1075 & 1115, /1202, /1297, /1390); Dr John Stedman, Kinross, Perth & Kinross, medical prescriptions 1770 (Ref: 242/Box 40); Alexander Walker, Haddington, East Lothian, surgeon, letters concerning payment for medicines 1745–56, pharmacopoeia n.d. (Ref: 110/976, /1178); Drs J Weir and William Burnett, Medical Commissioners, letter re prices charged for medicines supplied to the Navy by the Apothecaries Company 1823, Royal College of Surgeons and A Mundell, correspondence re Apothecaries Bill 1825, President, Royal College of Surgeons of Edinburgh, letter opposing Apothecaries Bill 1825 (Ref: 51/2/656, /5/709 & 711, /5/714).

Miscellaneous accounts: account for medicines 1653–1710 (Ref: 268/17/1-24, /60); apothecaries' and surgeons' accounts 1663–1764 and medical prescriptions n.d. (Ref: 25/9/44); accounts for medicines 1666, 1704, 1736 (Ref: 75/302, 316 & 325); accounts for medicines, 1678, 1693, 1696–98, 1700 (Ref: 109/2846, /2887 & 2889, /2896, /2911); chemists' accounts 1746–78 (Ref: 203/11/5/17, 19 & 23); accounts for medical attendance and medicines 1780–91 (Ref: GD88/1/58-9 & 71); physician's fee book and book of prescriptions 18th cent. (Ref: 385).

Miscellaneous prescriptions and recipes: medical prescriptions 1661–1702 (Ref: 26/6/207); medical prescriptions 17th cent., 1797 (Ref: 16/58/3-4); medical prescriptions 1717 (Ref: 44/33/19); medical prescriptions 1746 (Ref: 157/1717); medical prescriptions for cure of lumbago and rheumatism, treatment of cholera, etc. n.d. (Ref: 71/332); medical prescriptions 18th cent. (Ref: 267);

book of prescriptions and recipes late 18th cent. (Ref: 1/384/26); medical prescriptions 1833 (Ref: 82/263); medical prescriptions for Hope family, Luffnmess 20th cent. (Ref: 364/1/748), medical recipes and prescriptions 1647–1859, medical recipes 1693–1734, medical recipes and notes 1740–51, accounts for medicines 1655–1891, memoranda book containing medical recipes 1750–74 (Ref: 18/2125, /2130, /2142, /2175, /2336); medical recipes 17th cent. (Ref: 103/2/311); medical recipes 17th cent. (Ref: 1/32, 345); recipes and prescriptions c.1730–40 (Ref: 10/911); medical recipes and case book 1739–43 (Ref: 1/126/2); medical remedies n.d. (Ref: 34/997); recipes, incl. ointment for sores n.d. and an external cure for sore throat n.d. (Ref: 158/564, /596, /925).

Miscellaneous: advertisement, Dixon's Antibilious Pills n.d. (Ref: 99/229/18/7); apothecary's apprenticeship indenture 1758 (Ref: 241); return of medical officers, apothecaries and purveyors in Crimea 1855 (Ref: 45/8/190), letters of advice and prescriptions for preventing miscarriage 1689–94 (Ref 45/26/131), medical prescriptions 17th–18th cents. (Ref: 45/26/137); letters to an Inverness apothecary 1716 (Ref: 305); letter with medical prescription 1697 (Ref: 233).

The Scottish Home and Health Department (HH/): Executive Council (Scotland) (pharmaceutical) circulars 1963–74 (Ref: 48/85); Local Authority Health Services (Food & Drugs) 20th cent. (Ref: 64).

Register House Series (RH/): Francis Congalton, chirurgian, apothecary, account for medicines supplied to Sir William Dick of Prestonfield 1729 (Ref: 15/36/31); Dr James Gregory, accounts for medicines supplied to the Gordon of Carnoustie family 1720–24 (Ref: 15/1/18/3); Alexander Munro, Edinburgh, surgeon, account for medicines supplied to Mr Geddes of Kirkurd 1738–45 (Ref: 15/70/7); Dr Walter Stuart, letters to Arthur Gordon of Carnoustie and wife, with medical prescriptions (Ref: 15/1/160).

Apothecary's bills, Lady Cobb and Robert Seton 1680–1704 (Ref: 15/22/14); bottle of Battley's Sedative Solution, produced in the trial of Dr E W Pritchard 1865 (Ref: 19/35); list of drugs in a medicine chest 1742 (Ref: 15/1/95); medical prescriptions 1712 (Ref: 15/70/47); medical prescriptions for Mrs Geddes 1716 (Ref: 15/70/38); medical prescription n.d. (Ref: 15/1/41); prescriptions n.d. (Ref: 15/19/77).

NATIONAL LIBRARY OF SCOTLAND
George IV Bridge, Edinburgh EH1 1EW

Named businesses: Dr Anderson, transcript of certificate relating to his pills 1694 (Ref: MS 6295, f 1); W Blackhall & Co, Brechin, Angus, chemist, receipted bill for medicines 1863 (Ref: MS 15443, f 160); James Borthwick, apothecary burgess of Edinburgh, accounts 1666–67 (Ref: MS 5291, ff 1-6);

Martha Bruce, Countess of Elgin, medical recipes 18th cent. (Ref: MS 10282); William Castlelaw, apothecary, bill to 1st Earl of Tweeddale 1642 (Ref: MS 14618, f 157); R[obert] Collins, medical recipes late 18th cent. (Ref: MS 10964); William Cullen, MD, Edinburgh, 'Lectures upon Pharmacy' 18th cent. (Ref: MS 3759); Joshua Drayner, London, apothecary, bills 1687 (Ref: MS 7025, ff 151-2); Robert Ellison, Newcastle upon Tyne, apothecary, accounts 1658, 1661 (Ref: MS 5414, ff 18-19, 23); Erskine family accounts, incl. medical accounts 1602–1749 (Ref: MS 5100); John Ford, London, apothecary, accounts 1679 (Ref: MS 14629, ff 71, 355); John Ford, apothecary to 2nd Marquess of Tweeddale, account 1679 (Ref: MS 14648, f 52); Neil M Gunn, article entitled, 'Prescriptions' 1933 (Ref: Dep 209, Box 9); Neil M Gunn 'The Health Service We Want', 1944 (Ref: Dep 209, Box 8); David Hodgeton, Brechin, chemist, receipted bills 1865 (Ref: MS 15440, f 221); Robert Hope, Edinburgh, surgeon apothecary, receipted account 1723 (Ref: MS 5100, f 193); S Houston, apothecary, account 1788 (Ref: MS 5035, f 173); Dr Edward Jenner (discoverer of vaccination), prescription 1814 (Ref: MS 7178, no 94); Andrew and John Johnston, commonplace book containing medical notes and recipes late 18th–early 19th cents. (Ref: Acc 5811, no 11a); Sir Edmund King, prescriptions 1685–86, n.d. (Ref: MS 7108/98-107); R V Knight, London, apothecary, accounts and receipts 1775–76 (Ref: 5029, ff 128, 154, 183, 208-9, 230); Robert Lowis, prescriptions 1701 (Ref: MS 2077); medical recipe 1701 (Ref: Ch 3174); William Maginn, review of William Thomas Brande's *Pharmacy* (London, 1825) 1825 (Ref: MS 3551, f 50); Francis Masterton, Edinburgh, apothecary, receipted account 1716 (Ref: MS 5100, f 157); David Murray, Perth, Perth & Kinross, apothecary, account 1678 (Ref: MS 9949, f 127); James Murray, Perth, Perth & Kinross, apothecary, receipted account 1689 (Ref: MS 5100, f 103); Hugh Paterson, burgess of Edinburgh, surgeon-apothecary, discharged account 1693 (Ref: MS 5100, f 130); Walter Porterfield, apothecary, account 1695 (Ref: MS 976, f 133); Walter Scott, Jedburgh, Scottish Borders, apothecary, accounts 1668–76 (Ref: MS 5414, ff 33, 50, 62); John Stevenson, burgess of Banff, Aberdeenshire, surgeon apothecary, bill 1702 (Ref: MS 8134, f 14); George Stirling, Perth, Perth & Kinross, surgeon apothecary, receipted account 1718 (Ref: MS 5100, f 161).

Miscellaneous accounts: physicians' and apothecaries' accounts 1617–47 (Ref: Adv MS 80-2.5, f 172); surgeons' and apothecaries' accounts 1636–49 (Ref: MS 16852, ff 52, 66, 110, 258); surgeons' and apothecaries' accounts 1652–65 (Ref: MS 16853, ff 10-11, 86, 113, 141-2, 149, 170, 211-14); accounts for medicine 1656 (Ref: MS 17606, ff 125-7); surgeons' and apothecaries' accounts 1665–91 (Ref: MS 14636, ff 23-44); surgeons' and apothecaries' accounts 1668–1720 (Ref: MS 16854, ff 4, 20, 30, 68, 73, 93, 138, 161, 206); apothecary's account 1673–74 (Ref: MS 8198, f 69); apothecary's accounts 1674 (Ref: MS 5370, ff 139–40); apothecary's account 1676 (Ref: MS 6145, f 43); accounts for medicines 1679–84 (Ref: MS 17457, ff 162-3); apothecary's account 1680 (Ref: MS 5324, no 8); apothecary's account 1689 (Ref: MS 6146, f 54); accounts for medicine 1693–94 (Ref: MS 17458, ff 105, 217, 311-14); accounts for medicine 1699–1700 (Ref: MS 6487, ff 39, 45); estate account book containing accounts for medicines 1703–46 (Ref: MS 6456 *passim*); accounts for drugs 1708 (Ref: MS 15916, f 241); accounts for medicine 1714 (Ref: MS 17708, ff 121, 124, 146); account concerning medicine 1717 (Ref: MS 6433, f 73); accounts for medicine 1723 (Ref: Adv MS 82.3.3., ff 57, 59, 64, 78); accounts for medicine 1723–28 (Ref: MS 17696, ff 148-55); account for medicine 1731 (Ref: MS 17454, f 175); account for medicine 1733 (Ref: MS 6445, f 111); account for medicine 1733 (Ref: Adv MS 82.3.4, f 164); surgeons, Edinburgh and Haddington, East Lothian accounts for medical treatment and medicines 1734–59 (Ref: MS 14663, ff 135-47); account for medicine 1738 (Ref: 16865, f 22); account for medicine 1744 (Ref: MS 17617, f 84); accounts for medicine 1748, 1774–75 (Ref: MS 17608, ff 60, 98, 173); account for medicine 1754 (Ref: MS 17685, f 145); account for medicine 1755 (Ref: MS 17667, f 32); account for medicine 1756 (Ref: MS 17626, f 160); account for medicine 1761 (Ref: MS 17725, f 95); accounts for medicine 1768, 1770 (Ref: MS 17607, ff 140, 189, 205); apothecary's account 1771–72 (Ref: MS 14685, f 21); volume incl. accounts for medicines 1780–1814 (Ref: MS 5472); accounts for medicine 1803–11 (Ref: MS 9968, ff 96, 101, 114, 194, 213, 223, 238); accounts for medicines and medical attendance 1820–22 (Ref: MS 11958, ff 41, 135-6); accounts for medicine 1822, 1830 (Ref: MS 6474, ff 65, 226, 239-40); accounts for medicines and medical attendance 1825 (Ref: MS 11959, ff 8-12, 182, 193-7); apothecaries' and surgeons' accounts 1826, 1904 (Ref: MS 16898, ff 6-7, 209); accounts for medicines and medical attendance 1829–32 (Ref: MS 11960, ff 88, 183); accounts for medicine 1831–32 (Ref: MS 6475, ff 89, 96, 121-2, 226, 266); accounts for medicine 1833–34 (Ref: MS 6476, ff 32, 138, 170, 227); accounts for medicine 1835–36 (Ref: MS 6477, ff 11-12, 31-3, 36-7, 75, 119, 139, 150, 154, 157, 186, 233, 316); accounts for medicine, with related letter 1846–48 (Ref: MS 17413, ff 113-16); accounts for medicines 1892–93 (Ref: MS 21374, ff 82-3, 241-5); account for medicine n.d. (Ref: MS 6478, f 206).

Miscellaneous prescriptions: medical treatises and prescriptions, in Gaelic 16th–17th cents. (Ref: Adv MS 72.1.2); medical prescriptions and notes 1685–86, late 17th cent., c.1754 (Ref: MS 7108, ff 98-110); medical prescription 1689 (Ref: MS 14407, f 130); medical prescriptions and instructions on medical practice 1698 (Ref: MS 16468, ff 186-249); medical treatises and prescriptions, in Gaelic 17th cent. (Ref: Adv MS 72.1.20); medical prescriptions 17th–18th cents. (Ref: MS 3031); medical prescriptions 17th–18th cents. (Ref: MS 6503, ff 22-5); medical prescriptions and recipes 1727, n.d. (Ref: MS 1498); medical prescriptions 18th cent. (Ref: MS 3004, f 27v); medical prescriptions 18th–19th cents. (Ref: Acc 7228, no 606); medical prescriptions 1858, 1861 (Ref: MS 20037, ff 8, 44-5); medical prescription 1865 (Ref: MS 20039, f 30); medical prescription 1865 (Ref: MS 20208, f 176); medical prescriptions early 19th cent. (Ref: MS 10326, f 102); prescription for rheumatism, lumbago, chilblains and insect bites 19th cent. (Ref: MS 3871, f 311); medical prescriptions 19th cent. (Ref: MS 10311, f 160).

Miscellaneous recipes: medical recipes c.1540, n.d. (Ref: Adv MS 29.2.5, ff 188-90); medical opinions and recipes 1614–1905, n.d. (Ref: MS 17851); medical recipes and treatise on making of plasters 1656 (Ref: MS 5112, ff 1-59); medical recipes 1656, c.1660 (Ref: MS 8207, ff 1-2); medical recipe book 1688–89 (Ref: Acc 6605); medical recipes [?17th cent.] (Ref: MS 5008, ff 195-202); medical recipes 17th cent. (Ref: MS 5407, f 79, Adv MS 22.2.11, Adv MS 23.1.10, Adv MS 29.2.10, ff 93-8, Adv MS 31.2.1, f 19); household and medicinal recipes 17th cent. (Ref: Adv MS 23.6.5); recipes for itch and deafness 17th cent. (Ref: Adv MS 31.4.6, f 89); medical recipes 17th–18th cents. (Ref: MS 165, 5112,15912, ff 48-80, 6-33 inverted, Adv MS 80.7.2, ff 56-8); medical recipes late 17th–18th cents. (Ref: MS 10978 *passim*); medical recipe 1702 (Ref: Ch 3178); book of medical recipes compiled by 3rd Duke of Argyll 1709–32 (Ref: MS 3773); letters and recipes concerning conception 1713 (Ref: MS 20772, ff 52-6); medical recipes 1714, 1716 (Ref: MS 16503, ff 73, 139v); medical recipes 1718 (Ref: Dep 221, Blair MS 15); medical recipe 1723 (Ref: Adv MS 82.3.3, f 61); medical recipes 1757–58 (Ref: Adv MS 23.5.12); medicinal recipes c.1769 (Ref: MS 8325, ff 171-7); medical recipes c.1785 (Ref: 24547, pp 76, 96); medical recipes [?1786] (Ref: 3635, f 25); medical recipes 18th cent. (Ref: MS 9478, ff 51-124, 10281,17832, f 43, 17889,17892, 20800, ff 61-2, Adv MS 5.2.16); notebook containing domestic and medical recipes 18th cent. (Ref: Acc 4713); medicinal recipes late 18th cent. (Ref: MS 1881, ff 1-56 inverted); medical recipes late 18th cent. (Ref: MS 19215); medical recipes 18th and 19th cents. (Ref: MS 19238, f 13); commonplace book containing medical recipes (p) 18th–19th cents. (Ref: Acc 8862); medical recipes 1806, 1820–23 (Ref: MS 14275, ff 21v, 24-5, 27v, 29, 34, inverted ff 5v-9); medical recipes 1811–12 (Ref: MS 2806); medical recipes 1812, 1815 (Ref: MS 19930, ff 67-8); recipe for making medicine to treat gout 1813 (Ref: MS 15385, f 3); medical recipes and prescriptions 1813–30, n.d. (Ref: Acc 6684, no 28); household and medical recipes c.1822 (Ref: MS 14276, pp 27, 34-40); medical recipes 1825 (Ref: MS 9479); household and medicinal recipes 1831 (Ref: MS 10388, ff 10-11); medical recipe 1840 (Ref: MS 10779 (15), f 1); volume containing pharmacist's notes and recipes from Germany 1840 (Ref: Acc 10078); medical recipes 1847 (Ref: MS 5065, ff 63v-71v); medical and household recipes 1856–61 (Ref: MS 15393, ff 138v-42, 148v-54, 156v-57, 162-6); medical recipe 1860

(Ref: MS 10778, f 752); medical recipe c.1865 (Ref: MS 10779 (10). f 59); medical recipes early 19th cent. (Ref: MS 10965); medical recipes 19th cent. (Ref: MS 1887, ff 1-12 inverted); household and pharmaceutical recipes 19th cent. (Ref: MS 9240); recipe for Pitch pills 19th cent. (Ref: MS 10376, f 99); miscellaneous medical and culinary recipes 19th cent. (Ref: MS 13420, ff 1-10); recipes for tooth powder 19th cent. (Ref: MS 14193B, f 81); notebook containing household and medical recipes 1902–36 (Ref: MS 14272).

Miscellaneous: apothecary's list of medicines 1680 (Ref: MS 2987, f 5); bill for medicines and attendance 1674 (Ref: MS 500, f 6B); bills for medicines and miscellaneous items 1688, 1708, 1722–24 (Ref: Adv MS 29.1.2 (viii), ff 176, 179–84, 213); bills, apothecaries, 1764–79 (Ref: MS 12947, f 1); bills, surgeons and apothecaries, Edinburgh and Haddington, East Lothian, 1791–1802 (Ref: MS 14692, ff 1-22); glossary of medical terms 18th cent. (Ref: Adv MS 81.1.19, f 144); list of drugs 1726 (Ref: MS 2974, f 9); list of medicinal plants 18th cent. (Ref: MS 17829, f 99); notebook containing list of illnesses and their remedies 17th cent. (Ref: Acc 7228, no 525); notes on pharmaceutical preparations 1692 (Ref: MS 2185).

NATIONAL REGISTER OF ARCHIVES (SCOTLAND)
H M General Register House, Princes Street, Edinburgh EH1 3YY

Named businesses: William King & Son, Edinburgh, chemist, account book 1938–47, drug accounts 1948–53, 1960–63, prescription books: William King 1881–83, 1930–76, J Hindes 1881–94 (Ref: NRA(S) 3616); R S McPherson, Broughty Ferry, Dundee, pharmaceutical chemist, prescription books 1906–69 (w), leaflet 'Emergency Powers (Defence): Shortage of Drugs No.709' 1942 (Ref: NRA(S) 2534); James Marshall, Dunoon, Argyll & Bute, dispensing chemist, prescription books 1912–30 (Ref: NRA(S) 939); A Y Barrie, Morgan Tower Pharmacy, Dundee, pharmacy, prescription books 1905–59, 6-monthly files n.d., sale of poisons register 1886–1934, dangerous drugs register 1940–49, Butler & Crispe catalogue 1939; account book of own anaesthetic 'veracain' sold to doctors, dentists and chemists c.1923–34; account book of own anaesthetic 'Erad' sold to doctors, dentists and chemists c.1949–57. (Ref: NRA(S) 1642, GD/AYB 1-13); R M Park, Edinburgh, chemist, prescription books 1920–46, 1951–54, 1974–93 (Ref: NRA(S) 3617); Porteous Vegetable Ointment Co, minute book 1895–1906 (Ref: NRA(S) 412); Alexander Kennedy Stewart, Edinburgh, dispensing chemist and druggist, prescription books 1898–1969 (Ref: NRA(S) 3543); George Stirling, Dunoon, Argyll & Bute, chemist and druggist, cash book 1933–34 (Ref: NRA(S) 574).

Miscellaneous prescriptions and recipes: medical prescriptions 1608–1713, prescriptions 1697–1736 (Ref: NRA(S) 3666); medical prescriptions n.d. (Ref:

NRA(S) 2654); medical receipts 18th cent. and prescriptions n.d. (Ref: NRA(S) 104); medical recipes 18th cent. (Ref: NRA(S) 852); medical recipes 18th cent. (Ref: NRA(S) 428); medical recipes 18th–19th cents. (Ref: NRA(S) 16); letters with medical advice and recipes 1795–1811 (Ref: NRA(S) 783).

Miscellaneous: chemists' accounts 1764–95 (Ref: NRA(S) 2383); letter opposing the use of drugs 1807 (Ref: NRA(S) 63).

ROYAL COLLEGE OF PHYSICIANS
9 Queen Street, Edinburgh, EH2 1JQ

H B Wyllie, Edinburgh, pharmaceutical chemist, prescription book 1932–44 (Ref: RCPE/W).

Loose prescriptions c.1730 (no ref).

UNIVERSITY OF EDINBURGH LIBRARY
Special Collections Department, George Square, Edinburgh EH8 9LJ

William Cullen (1710–90), lecture notes on chemistry and pharmacy 1773 (ref: MS 3143)

DR PETER M WORLING
The Grange, 29 Fernielaw Avenue, Edinburgh EH13 0EF

Carnegies of Welwyn Ltd, Welwyn Garden City, Hertfordshire, products lists 1954–54; Clay & Abraham, 87 Bold Street, Liverpool, invoice 1862; Knights (Manufacturing Chemists) Ltd, Perry Bar, Birmingham, change of name certificate to BDH (Knights) Ltd 1963, contract to purchase 'Six-in-One' bleach 1961; John Knox (Stoke on Trent) Ltd, press cutting 1960; W H Legat, products list 1930s; R Sumner, Liverpool, accounts 1963.

Manufacturing chemists, miscellaneous formulae 1900–30.

FALKIRK

FALKIRK MUSEUMS
History Research Centre, Callendar House, Callendar Park, Falkirk FK1 1YR

John W Bennie, Polmont, dispensing chemist, prescription and quarterly account 1926, 1928 (Ref: A558.08-09); Campbells, High Street, Falkirk, chemist, photograph of shop 20th cent. (Ref: P18149); Alexander Cochrane, Falkirk, pharmacist, articles of apprenticeship of Elizabeth M MacDonald 1933–39, photographs of shop 1927, 1930s (Ref: A521.004, P00395, P14960); Cochrane & Marshall, 190 High Street, Falkirk, chemist and druggist, account books 1846–47 (Ref: A037.056); Cockburns, Falkirk, chemist, photograph of shop 20th cent. (Ref: P03655); Drummonds, High Street, Main Street and Callendar Riggs,

Falkirk, South Street, Bo'ness, chemist, photographs of shops 1970–77, 1982, 20th cent. (Ref: P12896-7, P15288, P15565, P17475, P18152, P21267, P21296, P21306, P21749-50); William Forgie, 106 High Street, Falkirk, dispensing chemist, invoice 1892 (Ref: A208.021); Haighs, Hope Street, Bo'ness, photograph of shop 20th cent. (Ref: P19394); Lyons, Falkirk, chemist, photograph of shop 20th cent. (Ref: P15605); Yule The Chemist Ltd, chemist, directors reports and accounts 1970–82 (Ref: A623.157-65).

Photograph of chemist's shop, High Street, Falkirk 20th cent. (Ref: P17764).

FIFE

FIFE LIBRARY SERVICE, ST ANDREWS BRANCH LIBRARY
Hay Fleming Library, Church Square, St Andrews. Enquiries to Fife Library Service, County Buildings, St Catherine Street, Cupar KY15 4TA

Charles Brown, Edinburgh, druggist, diary, containing his thoughts on religion 1764–65, and brief notes re his family genealogy 1863 (Ref: DA809.4M: 0.11575).

GLASGOW

GLASGOW CITY ARCHIVES
Mitchell Library, North Street, Glasgow G3 7DN

James Allen, 5 Skirving Street and 240 Kilmarnock Road, Newlands, Glasgow, pharmacist, prescription books 1911–58 (Ref: TD335).

Account for medicine 1789–90 (T/CL/miscellaneous bundle 42); Greenock apothecary, papers 1835–44 (T/ARD).

GLASGOW UNIVERSITY ARCHIVES & BUSINESS RECORDS CENTRE
13 Thurso Street, Glasgow G11 6PE

John W Miller (Chemist) Ltd, Glasgow, dispensing chemist, prescription books 1929–70, recipe books c.1877–78, n.d., Glasgow & West of Scotland Formulary 1908 (Ref: UGD 209); Andrew Dysart Ltd, 11 Byres Road, Glasgow, chemist, prescription books 1893–1944 (Ref: UGD 38).

GREATER GLASGOW HEALTH BOARD
Glasgow University Archives & Business Records Centre, 13 Thurso Street, Glasgow G11 6PE

Regional Infusion Fluids Laboratory, Knightswood Hospital, Glasgow, supplier of infusion fluids to hospitals, production and stock records 1949–84, correspondence files and related architectural drawings re proposed upgrading of laboratory 1971-78 (Ref: HB85).

UNIVERSITY OF STRATHCLYDE ARCHIVES
University of Strathclyde, Glasgow G1 1XQ

Glasgow Chemists & Druggists Association, Andersonian Building, Glasgow, trade association, list of office bearers and rules of association 1870-77, library catalogue 1880-86 (Ref: T-MIN/5).

ORKNEY

ORKNEY ARCHIVES
The Orkney Library, Laing Street, Kirkwall KW15 1NW

Medical accounts and prescriptions c.1723-19th cent. (Ref: D13/4/9).

PERTH & KINROSS

PERTH MUSEUM & ART GALLERY
George Street, Perth PH1 5LB

John Brydon, 39 South Methven Street, Perth, Perth & Kinross, chemist and druggist, handbills and invoices, notes for medicinal preparations and correspondence c.1900-10 (Ref: 850, 860-1); Peter Strang, 154 High Street, Perth, Perth & Kinross, chemist, prescription books 1921-48 (Ref: 896).

SCOTTISH BORDERS

SCOTTISH BORDERS ARCHIVE & LOCAL HISTORY CENTRE
Library Headquarters, St Mary's Mill, Selkirk TD7 5EW

C Hounam, Berwickshire, chemist, prescription books 1869-1974 (Ref: SC/B/31/1-14); W Mitchell & Son, C L Hutchinson, Exchange Buildings, Earlston, chemist and pharmacist, prescription books 1911-19, 1930-84 (Ref: D/86/1-5).

SOUTH LANARKSHIRE

BIGGAR MUSEUM TRUST
Moat Park, Biggar ML12 6DT

Aaron Whitfield, 58 High Street, Biggar, chemist, unlisted business papers, incl. property papers, licences and bills 1865-77 (Ref: GC/5/68).

MR T MATTHEWS
T/A John S Dempster, 54 High Street, Biggar ML12 6BJ

John S Dempster, 54 High Street, Biggar, dispensing chemist, prescription book of unnamed predecessor c.1889–90.

WALES

CAERPHILLY

GWENT COUNTY RECORD OFFICE
County Hall, Cwmbran NP44 2XH

John Brace, chemist, ledger(s?) 1835–40 (Ref: Q/IDP 30); Abraham Clements, Newport, druggist, papers re damage to property during riots 1840 (Ref: Q.Misc.P.T.Acc); John Crosswell, 3 Morgan Street, Tredegar, chemist and druggist, Petty Sessions order for compensation payment for damage sustained during election riots 1868 (Ref: Q.C.C.O.4.0003); George Deakin, Blaenavon, druggist, letter to Clerk of Peace re death by poisoning court case 1850 (Ref: Q.C.of P.C. 0013-23); Edward Waites, Tredegar, Blaenau Gwent, chemist and druggist, Petty Sessions order for compensation payment for damage sustained during election riots 1868 (Ref: Q.C.C.O.4.0003); R M Williams Ltd, 51 Cross Street, Abergavenny, Monmouthshire, chemist, sale of chemist's business agreement 1916, articles of association n.d. (Ref: Misc.Mss.1602.5/6).

Monmouthshire County Council, General Purposes Committee, lists of persons entitled to sell poisons 20th cent. (Ref: C.GP.); chemist's bill 1961 (Ref: Dpa 111-68).

CARDIFF

GLAMORGAN RECORD OFFICE
The Glamorgan Building, King Edward VII Avenue, Cathays Park, Cardiff CF1 3NE

Robert Drane, 8 Queen Street, Cardiff, chemist, receipted bill 1903, diaries 1881–1914 (w), letters to Joshua John Neale, Penarth, Vale of Glamorgan, friend and fellow naturalist 1896–1911, photographs 1913–14, c.1900–27, will 1914, press cuttings re Drane's death 1914, 1927, memoir 1916, Drane's poems 1902–07, papers and booklets re Drane's interests in pottery and natural history, and examples of his lectures 18th–early 20th cents., list of Drane's books n.d., c.1914 (Ref: D/D Xib 1-31; D/D Xib 28/1-33; D/D Xgb; D/D X 89/1-10); J Francis, Merthyr Tydfil, chemist, requests for chemist's preparations c.1904–40, photograph of son J L Francis c.1910 (Ref: D/D X 425/4, 58); E G Howell & Sons, Cardiff, chemist, prescription books: issued under doctors' authorisation 1891–1952 (w), made up by chemists 1929–55 (w) (Ref: D/D Xqb 1-66).

Cardiff & District Pharmacists' Association, minute books 1945–88 (Ref: D/D PA/C 1/1-3).

MUSEUM OF WELSH LIFE
St. Fagans, Cardiff CF5 6XB

E Glyn Jones, Gaerwen, Isle of Anglesey, dispensing chemist and ophthalmic optician, prescription books 1933–74, poisons register 1933–36, chemist's notebook, entitled *Materia Medica* n.d. (Ref: 3432/1-5); William A Peter Ltd, Barry, Vale of Glamorgan, dispensing chemist, prescription book 1890–1904 (Ref: 2914).

CARMARTHENSHIRE

CARMARTHENSHIRE ARCHIVE OFFICE
County Hall, Carmarthen SA31 1JP

R M Davies, Carmarthen, chemist, day book 1844–45 (Ref: Mus.371); G R Thomas, Woods Row, Carmarthen, 20th cent. notes taken from medicine bottle c.1868 (Ref: Acc 485); William Thomas & William Tollerton, Llandeilo, apothecaries, bills and receipts 1798–99 (Ref: Cawdor/Vaughan 34/4108, 4285); Chemist, 14 Vaughan Street, Llanelli, prescription books 1891–1979, ledgers 1923–30, 1957–73, account books 1953–66, cash book 1912–29, wages book 1947–79, scrap book of recipes and press cuttings c.1899–1916 (DB111).

CEREDIGION

NATIONAL LIBRARY OF WALES
Department of Manuscripts & Records, Aberystwyth SY23 3BU

Named businesses: Hugh Davies & Co, Machynlleth, Powys, chemist, prescription books 1885–1930 (Ref: NLW Minor Deposits 1414-17B); Lewis Evans, 17 High Street, Cardigan, Ceredigion, chemist and druggist, ledger 1883–1907 (Ref: MS 12543); Captain Foley, Ridgeway, Pembrokeshire, notes on medical and other prescriptions early 19th cent. (Ref: Lucas MSS and Records, nos 1978-9); John Harries, Pant-coy, 'medicine man', prescription book 1809, medical prescriptions 1849, 1870 (Ref: Cwrtmawr MS 97A, NLW MS 11704A); Robert Owen Hughes, Caernarfon, Gwynedd, druggist, apprenticeship indenture with Ellis Roberts 1829 (Ref: Henry Rumsey Williams Deeds and Documents, no. 997); Dr Hugh Davies Jones, prescription book 1888–90 (Ref: NLW MS 20935B); Hugh Parry Jones, Llannerch-y-medd, Isle of Anglesey, doctor, day books 1880–91 (Ref: NLW MSS 21759-72D); Daniel Lewis, Plas Llangeitho, MD, prescription book early 19th cent. (Ref: NLW MS 4944B); Dr Mead, prescription 1715 (Ref: Chirk Castle, Group F, no. 6751); Sir John Philipps, notebook containing medical recipes 1701–28 (Ref: Picton Castle, no. 584);

Thomas Price, druggist, extracts from notebook c.1830-34, account book 1831-39 (Ref: NLW Facs 567, NLW Facs 594); Dan Thomas, Penarth Road, Cardiff, chemist and druggist, prescription book 1892-99 (Ref: NLW MS 16837D).

Trade association: Cardiganshire Pharmaceutical Society, minutes 1950-93 (Ref: NLW ex 1693, NLW Minor Deposit 1255B).

Miscellaneous accounts: accounts for drugs and medical attention 1787-1843 (Ref: D T M Jones Collection, nos. 6934, 6950, 6988, 7048 and 7146).

Miscellaneous prescriptions: medical prescriptions late 17th cent. (Ref: Tredegar Park Muniments 117/125-6); medical prescriptions c.1729-31 (Ref: Cilymaenllwyd, nos 137-8); doctor's diagnosis and prescription book 1774-80 (Ref: Harri Williams Collection, no. 14); day books recording prescriptions 1815-29 (Ref: NLW MS 11703E); pharmacist, Aberaeron, Ceredigion, prescription books 1885-1951 (Ref: NLW Misc Vols 269, 314, 315); prescriptions c.1900 (Ref: Harpton Court, no. 3981).

Miscellaneous recipes: medical recipes 16th cent. (Ref: Edwinsford, no. 3240); letter re powder to cure blindness, called 'eyebright' 1628 (p) (Ref: Gwysaney, Group I: NLW Facs 371); remedies 1666-1730 (Ref: Peniarth MSS & Documents, no. 511); recipes 17th cent. (Ref: Chirk Castle, Group A, no. 23); recipes 17th-18th cents. (Ref: Chirk Castle, Group.F, no. 9343, Glansevern, no. 14866); medical and household recipes 17th-19th cents. (Ref: Esgair and Pantperthog, nos 4, 9); account book containing a medical recipe 1697-1702 (Ref: Llwyngwair, no. 4), reference to 'receit' for the eyes 1721 (Ref: Picton Castle, no. 1473); remedy 1721 (Ref: Picton Castle, no. 1475); remedy for 'hectick fever' 1722 (Ref: Picton Castle, no. 1478); recipes 1756-61 (Ref: D T M Jones, nos 562-3); medical recipes 18th cent. (Ref: Llanfair Brynodol, MS 12, Trovarth & Coed Coch Deeds, no. 669, Sir Leonard Twiston Davies, nos 9022-36, Eriviat Estate Deeds, nos 508-9, Llanfair Brynodol, nos X29, X31, X34); medical recipes late 18th cent. (Ref: Penty Park, no. 68, Glansevern, no. 14566); recipes 18th or 19th cent. (Ref: Dol'rhyd, no. 14); medicinal and cylinary recipes c.1834 (Ref: Downes Evans, no. 199); folk medicine and recipes 1837-1937 (Ref: W R Jones, 'Gwenith Gwyn', nos 112-30); medicinal recipes c.1844 (Ref: Edwinsford, no. 4176); recipes 1849 (Ref: John Jenkins, no. 190); medical recipes 19th cent. (Ref: Aston Hall, nos 8012-21, 8288-94, Maesnewydd Deeds, no. 383, Poyston, no. 404, Lucas, nos 1548-80, Paul Diverres, no. 45 (MS 69A), J R Hughes, no. 7, D Teifigar Davies MSS, p. 1); medicinal recipes late 19th cent. (Ref: NLW Minor Deposit 1343B); household and medical recipes early 20th cent. (Ref: Rev. William Griffiths, no. 15); recipes n.d. (Ref: NLW MSS 13146, 11452, 11471, 11516-17, 11758, 11792, 11816, 11896, 11990, 11995, 11998, 12031, 12350, 12395, 12419, 12435, 12470, 12518, 12634, 12746,

13077, 13081, 13094, 13111-12, 13120, 13122, 13130, 13138-9, 13141, 13144, 13146, 13153-4, 13158-60, 13166, 13178, 13237).

Miscellaneous: advice on rheumatism 1859–60 (Ref: Aston Hall Correspondence, nos 4384, 4393); drugs catalogue 1824 (Ref: Tredegar Park Muniments, 57/457); lectures re cholera in England 1829, 1854 (Ref: Aston Hall Correspondence, nos 6343, 6481, 7027).

DENBIGHSHIRE
DENBIGHSHIRE RECORD OFFICE
46 Clwyd Street, Ruthin LL15 1HP

I J Edisbury, High Street, Wrexham, pharmacist, prescription book 1888 (Ref: DD/DM/801); J Wynne Williams, 10 Wrexham Street, Mold, Flintshire, chemist, photographs c.1890–1900 (Ref: DD/DM/798/4-5).

FLINTSHIRE
FLINTSHIRE RECORD OFFICE
The Old Rectory, Hawarden CH5 3NR

Dann & Buttling, The Highway, Hawarden, chemist, prescription books 1917–43 (Ref: D/DM/878); J Wynne Williams, 10 Wrexham Street, Mold, chemist, prescription book 1915–42, recipe and formulae book c.1882 (Ref: D/DM/475).

GWYNEDD
DEPARTMENT OF MANUSCRIPTS
The Library, University of Wales, Bangor LL57 2DG

J Griffith, Old Colwyn, dispensing chemist, prescription books 1923–40 (Ref: 25754-7); E A Neill Ltd, Rhos-on-Sea, Conwy, dispensing chemist, prescription book 1913–14 (Ref: 25749); B Roberts, Llanfairfechan, dispensing chemist, prescription books 1877–84 (Ref: 10127-8); John Thompson Ltd, Penrhyn Avenue, Rhos-on-Sea, dispensing chemist, prescription books 1917–21 (Ref: 25750-2).

Chemist, Beaumaris, Anglesey, prescription books 1839–43 (Ref: 10485); chemist, Bethesda, poisons register 1875–1939 (Ref: 10251); chemist, Colwyn Bay area, prescription book 1922–25 (Ref: 25753); chemist, Penmaenmawr, prescription books 1886–1904 (Ref: 10252-4).

GWYNEDD ARCHIVES & MUSEUMS SERVICE
Caernarfon Area Record Office, Victoria Dock, Caernarfon. Enquiries to County Offices, Shirehall Street, Caernarfon LL55 1SH

Caernarvonshire & Anglesey Dispensary, Bangor, report 1822 (Ref: XM3475); Castle Pharmacy, Y Maes, Caernarfon, pharmacist, ledgers 1923–36, account books 1935–36, prescription book 1880–1907, exercise note books, Liverpool School of Pharmacy (R Emlyn Roberts) 1932 (J Glyn Jones) 1932–33 (Ref: XM9813); W Bowen Davies, Radnorshire, physician, prescription 1895 (Ref: XM1105/4/28); James Francis, 13 Pool Street, Caernarfon, dispensing chemist, prescription book late 19th–early 20th cents. (Ref: XM6203); Evan Emrys Jones, Caernarfon, chemist, tape recorded interview re time as an employee of Humphrey Jones & Sons n.d. (Ref: XMT/413); Humphrey Jones & Son, 24 Market Place, Penygroes, dispensing chemist, articles of agreement, 1934 (Ref: XM5088/7); Llanberis & Drws y Coed Copper Mines, druggist, accounts 1831 (Ref: X Vaynol/5857,5858); Griffith Owen, 25 and 27 High Street, Caernarfon, chemist and wine merchant, labels, advertising leaflet, billhead and card c.1883–1942 (Ref: XM7088, XM1395/211); Owen Parry, Medical Hall, 142 High Street, Portmadoc, ledger 1929–58, prescription books 1893–1904, 1911–64 (Ref: XM 7458); Robert B Roberts, Llanfairfechan, Conway, chemist, prescription book 1894–1906 (Ref: XM9666/3); Thomas Webster, 241 High Street, Bangor, dispensing chemist, advertisement n.d. (Ref: XM6639/8); John Lewis Williams, Mona Pharmacy, High Street, Pwllheli, dispensing chemist and optician, optical prescription books 1947, 1957–58, price list and prescriptions book, William Williams, chemist, Llangybi n.d., notebook, record of NHS prescriptions sent to Cardiff 1949 (Ref: XM 2905); R M Williams, Llys Menai, Menai Bridge, Isle of Anglesey, ledger and prescriptions book 1899–1907 (Ref: XD14/8/1).

Chemist, receipt for Moriah Chapel 1907 (Ref: XM309/28); envelope for a trial supply of Dr Singh's catarrh treatment n.d. (Ref: XM1395/84/33).

PEMBROKESHIRE

PEMBROKESHIRE RECORD OFFICE
The Castle, Haverfordwest, SA61 2EF

Phillips the Chemist, Victoria Place, Haverfordwest, chemist, credit accounts on behalf of Picton Castle Estate 1851–1926 (Ref: HDB/3).

SWANSEA

WEST GLAMORGAN ARCHIVE SERVICE
County Hall, Oystermouth Road, Swansea SA1 3SN

John T Davies, Uplands, Swansea, dispensing chemist, prescription books 1877–1951 (Ref: D/D JTD 1-74); Hibbert & Son, New Street Square, Neath, Port Talbot, pharmaceutical chemist, prescription book 1855–64, prescription for George Jones 1909 (Ref: D/D Xln, D/D Z 138/1).

Appendix 2

Guide to public records

BOARD OF TRADE (BT)
Company registration records, files of dissolved companies 1844–1990s (BT31, 34, 41); Bankruptcy Department, papers 1844–1972 (BT37-40, 221, 226); Industry and Manufacturers Department, correspondence and papers 1919–66 (BT64); Companies Department, papers 1904– (BT15), apprenticeship papers (BT19).

Medical and dental objections to Companies Acts, petitions from chemists 1900 (BT6/297).

COURT OF BANKRUPTCY (B)
Order books 1710–1877 (B1), commissions books and files 1710–1911 (B3-4), enrolment books 1710–1859 (B5), registers 1733–1925 (B6), minute books 1714–1875 (B7), proceedings 1832–1958 (B9-10).

COURT OF CHANCERY (C)
Company liquidation proceedings 1849–1915 (C26, J13), debenture actions 1891–1956 (J13, J14, J137), registers of petitions 1892–1949 (J119).

DEPARTMENT OF ECONOMIC AFFAIRS (EW)
Economic Development Committee for the Chemical Industry, Committee of Enquiry into the Relationship of the Pharmaceutical Industry with the National Health Service (Sainsbury Committee), papers 1965–68 (EW27/78).

Papers re incomes policy: remuneration of chemists for dispensing National Health Service prescriptions, remuneration of hospital pharmacists (EW8/159-60).

DEPARTMENT OF HEALTH AND SOCIAL SECURITY (BN)
Medicines Commission, minutes 1969–81 (closed for 30 years) (BN38).

DEPARTMENT OF SCIENTIFIC AND INDUSTRIAL RESEARCH (DSIR)
Joint Committee on Chemotherapy: progress reports 1929–34, applications for tests 1927, programmes 1926–28, general papers 1926–34 (DSIR36/3565-8).

Records Bureau, registers of scientific research in the UK 1915, 1948 (DSIR36/1791).

HOME OFFICE (HO)
Dangerous drugs entry books 1920–21, dangerous drugs (DDA symbol series) and drugs record cases (DRC symbol series) files 1950–67 (HO177, 319).

Miscellaneous (E) Division, papers re dangerous drugs and poisons 1855–1956 (HO45).

INDUSTRIAL RELATIONS (IR)
Apprenticeship books 1710–1811 (IR1), apprenticeship indexes (IR17).

MINISTRY OF HEALTH (MH)
Cohen Committee on the Definition of Drugs, papers and correspondence 1950–62 (MH133/76-82).

Committee of Enquiry into the Relationship of the Pharmaceutical Industry with the National Health Service (Sainsbury Committee), Committee and Figures Sub-committee: minutes and agenda, evidence submitted, drafts of reports, committee members' correspondence 1964–67 (MH104).

Committee on Prescribing, papers and correspondence 1949–62 (MH133/71-5).

Committee on the Cost of Prescribing, papers and correspondence 1950–63 (MH133/83-114).

Correspondence and papers re numerous subjects incl. chemists, drugs, medical appliances, poisons, therapeutic substances, prescription pricing and provision of medical, surgical and dental equipment to National Health Service 1910–72 (MH58, 62, 81, 135-6); subject files and papers of File Offices A–D re Pharmaceutical Section, chemists' remuneration, named diseases, medicines prescribing, complaints against medical, dental and pharmaceutical professions, vaccination and immunisation (MH117, 148-9, 153-4).

Joint Committee on a National Pharmaceutical Service, papers and correspondence 1947–53 (MH135/576).

Standing Committee on Operational Research in the Pharmaceutical Services, papers and correspondence (MH135/96-7).

Standing Pharmaceutical Advisory Committee, committee papers and reports 1947–63 (MH133/366-82).

Working Party on Differences in Dispensing Practices Between England, Wales and Scotland, papers and correspondence 1947–48 (MH135/596-8).

PUBLIC RECORD OFFICE (PRO)
Ruskin Avenue, Kew, Richmond TW9 4DU

REGISTRAR GENERAL (RG)
Smallpox vaccination returns 1898–1921, 1938–41 (RG56).

SCIENCE RESEARCH COUNCIL (EV)
Science and Engineering Research Council: Chemical Sub-committee meetings minutes 1959–65 (EV1/26-9), Chemical Technology Sub-committee meetings papers (EV1/22-5), Research Grants Committee meetings minutes 1956–65 (w) (EV1/1-10).

Index of names

Page numbers in bold indicate main entries for pharmaceutical businesses and organisation

AAH Holdings plc, 140, 144, 162, 169, 196, 249, 266, 355, 373
AAH Pharmaceuticals Ltd, 162, 169, 170, 196, 305, 373
AAH plc, 27, 97, 99, 117, 140, 169, 170, 211, 373
AAH Retail Pharmacy Ltd, 169
Abbott, Wallace Calvin, 73
Abbott Alkaloidal Co Inc, 73
Abbott Chemical Co Ltd, 73, 74
Abbott Laboratories Eire Ltd, 73
Abbott Laboratories (England) Ltd, 73
Abbott Laboratories Inc, 73
Abbott Laboratories Ireland Ltd, 73, 74
Abbott Laboratories Ltd, **73-4**
Aberdeen, North of Scotland Society of Chemists & Druggists, 452
Aberdeen Pharmaceutical Association, 452
Acklam & Wood Ltd, 170, 171
Actons Chemists Ltd, 170, 171
Adam, Jeanie Whitson, 75
Adam, John Cruikshank, 75
Adam, R & T Ltd, **75**, 282
Adam, Richard Dickson, 75
Adam, Thomas Chalmers, 75
Adams, Hubert, 75
Adams, J H, 456
Adams, John, 75, 359, 464

Adams, John (Chemists) Ltd, **75-6**, 359
Adams, John Hubert, 75
Adams, William, 75
Adams, William & Son, 75
Adcock, Herbert Dickson, 76
Adcock, Isaac Dickson, 76
Adcock, Walter James, 76
Adcock Ltd, **76-7**
Adcocks, 465
Agatash Estates Ltd, 205, 208
Ainslie, William, 473
Aitkin, John, 473
Alan, George (Chemists) Ltd, 170, 171
Albin, John, 438
Albright & Wilson Ltd, 84, 118, 131, 133
Alcock, Richard, 459
Aldcock, J D, 449
Aldo Compagnone, 271
Alexander, H B, 449
Allan, Dr James, 77
Allen, A H, 77
Allen, A H & Partners, **77**
Allen, Charles B, 245
Allen, Edward Ransome, 83
Allen, George, 3, 83
Allen, George & Co, 83, 85
Allen, Hanburys & Barry, 78
Allen, James, 481
Allen, Kenneth Frederick, 364

Allen, Matthew, 473
Allen, S & G, 83
Allen, Stafford, 83
Allen, Stafford & Sons, 83
Allen, Stafford & Sons Ltd, **83-5**, 118, 131, 133
Allen, William, 33, 41, 78, 80, 82, 83, 204
Allen, William & Co, 78
Allen, William Clarkson, 83
Allen & Hanburys, 1, 5, 6, 9, 16, 20, 25, 34, 38, 46, 78, 83
Allen & Hanburys Co Ltd (Canada), 79
Allen & Hanburys (Farms) Ltd, 81
Allen & Hanburys Ltd, **77-83**, 78, 79, 80, 82, 135, 176, 204, 356
Allen & Hanburys (Research) Ltd, 81
Allen & Hanburys (Russia) Ltd, 79
Allen & Hanburys (South America) Ltd, 79
Allen & Hanburys (Surgical Engineering) Ltd, 79
Allen & Howard, 78, 204
Allen Chlorophyll Co Ltd, 84, 85
Alliance Sante SA, 27, 87, 125, 130, 190, 197, 218, 260, 261, 302, 321, 322, 368
Alliance UniChem plc, **85-8**, 130, 184, 190, 197, 218, 260, 261, 302, 321, 322, 368
Allied Laboratories Ltd, 79, 81
Alpharma Inc, 146
Amalgamated Anthracite Collieries Ltd, 169
American Home Products, 27
Anacona Motor Co, 339, 342
Anderson, 152

Anderson, A, 474
Anderson, Charles & Son, 188
Anderson, Dr, 476
Anderson & Virgo, 470
Anderson's Institution, 422
Animal Vaccine Station, 397
Annison, Philip J, **88**
Ansdell, Thomas Chester, 193
Anthony, Jacob, 450
Anthony, James & Co Ltd, 205, 208
Aplin, John Henry, 89
Aplin, Robert John, 89
Aplin Chemist, **89**
Aplins, 89
Aplins (Chemists) Ltd, 89
Apothecaries' Hall, 4, 5
Apothecary Hall of Ireland, 470
Arbuckle, William, 5
Armfield, George, 460
Armitage, William, 454
Armitage Dispensing Chemist, 454
Arnfield, J C, 386
Arnfield, J C & Sons Ltd, 386
Arnold, John, 436
Arnold & Foster, 450
Arnold & Son, 107
Arnold & Sons Basildon Ltd, 108
Arnold & Sons Ltd, 108, 109
Arnold & Sons Veterinary Instruments Ltd, 108
Ash Grove Perfumery Ltd, 132, 134
Ashley, E Ltd, **89-90**
Ashley, William, 89
Ashton & Parsons Ltd, 262, 339, 345
Asker, John Ltd, **90**
Aspell, J S, 194
Associated British Engineering plc, 266

Index of names

Associated Electrical Industries, 20
Association of Chemists & Druggists of Great Britain, 452
Association of Manufacturers of British Proprietaries, 413
Association of Manufacturers, Retailers & Wholesalers of Proprietary Articles, 411
Association of Scientific, Technical & Managerial Staff, 399, 400
Association of Supervisory Staffs, Executives & Technicians, 399, 400
Association of the British Pharmaceutical Industry, 23, 28, **388-9**, 390, 391, 408
Association of Women Pharmacists, 401, 402
Aston & Co Ltd, W 468
Astra, 27, 91
Astra Pharmaceuticals Ltd, 114
AstraZeneca Pharmaceuticals Ltd, **90-6**
Atkinson, George & Co, 6, 7, **96-7**, 377
Atkinson's, 431
Attenburrow, E, 131
Attenburrow, Ellen, 131
Attenburrow, J, 131
Attenburrow, James the elder, 131
Attenburrow, James the younger, 131
Attenburrow, Joseph, 131
Aynes, Wilfred, 462
Ayrton, F, 97
Ayrton, Saunders & Co Ltd, 97
Ayrton, Saunders & Co plc, **97-8**
Ayrton, Saunders & Kemp Ltd, 97
Ayrton Saunders Ltd, 97

Ayrton Saunders (Midland) Ltd, 98

Babington, William, 450
Badische Anilin & Soda Fabrik AG *see* BASF AG
Bailey, Charles Stuart, 450
Bailey, William & Son, 469
Baines, E R, 374
Baker, Cyril, 99
Baker, Edward, 154
Baker, Samuel, 154
Baker, Thomas B, 99
Baker, William Garrard, 8, 11, 295
Baker & Fairhead Ltd, 439
Baker & Son, 154
Baker & Son (Chemists), 99
Baker & Son (Chemists) Ltd, **98-9**
Baker's, 438
Balfour, John, 474
Ball, 436
Ball, W A, 468
Banners Chemists Ltd, 265
Bannister & Thatcher Ltd, **99-100**
Barber, Dr H J, 296
Barclay & Son, 190
Barclay & Sons, 9, 18
Barclay & Sons Ltd, 450
Barclay family, 11
Barker, William, 457
Barker, William Henry, 366
Barker, William Robert, 309
Barlow family, 100
Barnes, James, 100
Barnes, James & Son, 100
Barnes, Lawrence Robert, 100
Barnes & Crompton Ltd, **100-1**
Barnstaple Pharmacy, 436
Barr, M & J Ltd, 170, 171
Barratt, Frederick James, 211, 440
Barrie, A Y, 479
Barringer, J & E Ltd, 83, 85

Barron Harvey & Co, 128
Barry, John Thomas, 78
Barstow, Sidney Ltd, 468
Bartlett & Goodall, 454
Barwis, Thomas, 11
BASF AG, 27, 121, 222, 223
Bass, Charles Murfleet, 99
Bass, C M & Son, 99
Bass, Wilfred Raymond, 99
Bass, W R, 99
Bass & Son, 99
Batchelor, Alfred Ernest, 142
Batchelor, Charles, 142
Batchelors Ltd, 142
Bate, J P Ltd, 463
Bateson, Thomas, 435
Batley, Benjamin & William, 450
Batt family, 454
Batten, John, 239
Batting, Thomas Gilbert, 441
Battiscombe, Robert, **101**
Battle, John Scoley, 101
Battle, Son & Maltby, 101
Battles Ltd, **101-2**
Baum, M Ltd, 190
Baxendale, Lily, 113, 114
Baxter, William, 450
Bayer, Frederick & Co, 295
Bayer, Friedr et Comp, 102, 350
Bayer, Friedrich, 102
Bayer Chemicals Ltd, 102
Bayer Diagnostic Production Ltd, 103
Bayer Dyestuffs Ltd, 102
Bayer Pharmaceuticals Ltd, 102, 103
Bayer plc, **102-104**
Bayer Products Ltd, 102, 350, 351
Bayer UK Ltd, 102, 103
Bayley, Charles, 449
Bayley, Cornelius, 444

BCB Ltd, 111, 163, 172
BDH (Knights) Ltd, 480
BDH (Woolley & Arnfield) Ltd, 386
Beach & Co, 437
Beall, G E & Son Ltd, 433
Beaman, A Ltd, 239
Beatrice Foods Inc, 332
Beaumont, John, 142
Beckett, William, 134
Beckman Instruments Inc, 334, 335
Beecham, 1, 21, 25, 26, 27, 37, 45
Beecham, Joseph, 338, 339
Beecham, Thomas, 15, 338, 339, 342
Beecham Estates & Pills Ltd, 339
Beecham Estates Ltd, 339
Beecham Finance plc, 344
Beecham Foods Ltd, **104-5**
Beecham Group Ltd, 104, 105, 110, 137, 139, 141, 194, 212, 240, 263, 277, 316, 339, 346, 349, 361, 375
Beecham Group plc, 334, 339, 345
Beecham Maclean Holdings Ltd, 339, 344
Beecham (Northern) Ltd, 339, 342
Beecham Pharmaceuticals Ltd, 157, 241, 339
Beecham Pills Ltd, 104, 105, 157, 194, 203, 212, 240, 262, 277, 339, 340, 344, 345, 361, 371
Beecham Proprietary Medicines Ltd, **105-6**, 339, 344
Beecham Research Laboratories Ltd, 45, 110, 339, 344
Beecham Research Ltd, 346
Beechams Pills Ltd, 104
Belks Court Practice, 467
Bell, Frederick John, 107

Index of names

Bell, Jacob, 33, 107, 415
Bell, John, 454
Bell, John & Co, 4, 106, 109, 415
Bell, John & Croyden Ltd, 5, **106-9**, 309
Bell, John Hills & Lucas Ltd, 5, 107, 109
Bell, Thomas, 106
Bell, W A, 459
Bell, William Henry, 117
Bell's Chemists, **106**
Bell's Pharmacy, 443
Bellamy, John, 109
Bellamy & Wakefield, 109
Bellamy & Wakefield Ltd, **109-10**
Bellringer, H, 110, 264
Bellringer, Harry, 264
Bellringer, H Ltd, **110**, 264
Bencard, C L Ltd, 110
Bencard Pharmaceuticals Ltd, **110-11**
Benger, F B & Co Ltd, 111, 163
Benger, Frederick Baden, 111, 163
Bengers Food Ltd, 111, 163
Bengers Ltd, **111-12**, 163, 172
Benn, Albert, 444
Bennett, George Horsfields (Barrow) Ltd, 434
Bennie, John W, 480
Beral, M, 347
Berk Pharmaceuticals, 114
Berridge, Alfred, 363
Berry, Henry James, 469
Betriebsgemeinschaft Oberrhein, 222
Betts, John & Son, 466
Bevan, 39
Bevan, Edward, **112**
Bevan, Joseph Gurney, 6, 11, 77, 80
Bevan, Silvanus, 1, 77, 80

Bevan, Silvanus & Timothy, 77
Bevan, Timothy, 77
Bevan, Timothy & Sons, 77
Bevans, 5, 38
Bevans, Timothy Ltd, 450
Beverley, E
Bevis, 154
Bevis, George, 154
Bevis, G F Ltd, 154
Biggar, Atkinson & Dale, 7
Biggar, Robert, 8
Bilborough, Joseph Brooks, 443
Bilson, Frederick Eastall, 113
Bilson & Friendship Ltd, **112-13**
Bilstar Ltd, 206
Biorex Laboratories Ltd, **113-15**
Biorex (Marketing) Ltd, 113, 114, 115
Birch, John, 421
Birkenhead, Wallasey & Wirral Association of Pharmacists, 390
Birkenhead & Wirral Association of Pharmacists, **390**
Birkenhead & Wirral Chemists' Association, 390
Birkenhead & Wirral Pharmacists' Association, 390
Birmingham Trade Conference of Chemists & Druggists, 452
Bishop, Alfred, 9
Bishop, Alfred Ltd, 470
Bishop, J H Ltd, 442
Bishops Chemist, 467
Biss, John W, 431
Blaby, J J, 445
Black, Robert F, 470
Black, Thomas, 269
Blackhall, W & Co, 475
Blackie, Robert Ltd, 313, 448
Blades Chemist, 115

Blades Chemist Ltd, **115-16**
Blain, Alfred Lucas, 116
Blain, William, 116
Blain, William & Sons, 116
Blain, William & Sons Ltd, **116-17**
Blain, William Rushton, 116
Blake, C A, 447
Blake, M A E, 447
Blake, Sandford & Blake, 446
Blake & Son, 3
Blanshard, George, 282
Blanshard, Thomas, 282
Blaxland, Mr, 450
Bleasdale, W & Co, 117
Bleasdale, William, 117
Bleasdale Ltd, **117-18**
Blenkinsop, E K, 296
Blenkinsop, Neville, 296
Blenkinsop, Philip, 296
Blenkinsop, Richard, 296
Blenkinsop, William, 295
Bliss, William Thomas, 126
Bloomfields Chemists, 462
Blott, Hugh Russell, 354
Blyth, William James, 444
Boa, Peter, 450
Boake, A & Co, 118
Boake, A Roberts & Co, 84, 118
Boake, A Roberts & Co (Holding) Ltd, 118, 119
Boake, A Roberts & Co Ltd, 84, **118-19**, 131, 133
Boake, A Roberts & Co (Manufacturing) Ltd, 118
Boake, Arthur, 118
Bobby, S C, 458
Body, S F, 361
Body, Sydney Francis, 361
Bolton, Thomas, 270
Bond, A O Ltd, 465
Boon, F W & Son Ltd, 435

Boor, William, 458
Boot, Jesse, 19, 20, 45, 120, 121
Boot, John, 120, 121
Boot, Mary, 120
Boot & Co Ltd, 120
Booth, R L, **120**
Boothe, Elizabeth, 450
Boots, 19, 20, 21, 22, 26, 27, 45, 46
Boots Cash Chemists, 120
Boots Co Ltd, The, 121
Boots Contract Manufacturing, 121
Boots Co plc, The, **120-5**, 223, 239
Boots Healthcare International, 121
Boots of Nottingham, 18
Boots Opticians, 121
Boots Pharmaceuticals, 223
Boots Pharmaceuticals Ltd, 223
Boots Properties, 121
Boots Pure Drug Co Ltd, 93, 120, 145, 225, 359, 383, 424
Boots the Chemists, 121, 493
Borthwick, James, 475
Bound, W S, 218
Bowden, J P, 471
Bowdens Drug Stores, 226
Boyce, John Pierce & Son, 467
Boyd, Alexander, 471
Boyd, J, 385
Boyd, J & R Woollatt, **385**
Boyle, Robert, 4, 183
Brace, John, 483
Bradford & District Chemists' Association, 460
Bradford Chemists' Alliance Ltd, 87, **125-6**
Bradley, Charles Reginald, 126
Bradley, George, 126
Bradley & Bliss, 126
Bradley & Bliss Ltd, **126-7**, 128, 230, 372, 386
Brain Brothers, 466, 433

Brameld, John, 453
Brandon & Byshottles Co-operative Chemists Ltd, 437
Brawn, H S, 358
Brearey, W A Hill & Co, 433
Breden, John, 270
Brews & Macintosh, 364
Bridge, Thomas, 449
Bridgemary Pharmacies Ltd, 365
Bridge Pharmaceuticals Ltd, 345
Briggs, George William, 461
Briggs Cash Chemists Ltd, 171
Briggs family, 443
Bright, R & B[--]ster, John, 450
Brint, D F (Portishead) Ltd, 170, 171
Bristed, John, 468
British Alkaloids Ltd, 273, 274
British & Foreign Alkaloid Co, 377
British Association of Pharmaceutical Wholesalers, 25, 388, **390-2**, 408
British Camphor Co Ltd, **127**, 205
British Chemicals & Biologicals Ltd, 111, 163, 172
British Drug Houses Group Ltd, 126, **127-9**, 153, 230, 252, 372, 386
British Drug Houses Ltd, 20, 22, 25, 79, 92, 93, 127, 128, 135, 424
British Dyestuffs Corporation Ltd, 90
British Felsol Co, 432
British Medical Association, 15, **392-3**
British Pharmaceutical Conference, 136, 284
British Pharmaceutical Students' Association, 452

British Society for the History of Pharmacy, **393-4**
British Tar Co, 473
Broadwater Properties Ltd, 86, 87
Brocklehurst, E A Ltd, **129**
Brocklehurst, James, 454
Brocklehurst's, 129
Brome & Schimmer Ltd, 347
Bronington, Dr, 465
Brooks, Gerald, 307
Brooks & Warburton Ltd, 468
Brothers, William, 168
Brothers & Williams, 168
Brown, Charles, 481
Brown, David Rainy, 233, 236
Brown, David Rennie, 233, 236
Brown, Edward, 130
Brown, Edward Oliver, 130
Brown, G W, 307
Brown, James, 473
Brown, J & Son Chemists (Walker) Ltd, **130**
Brown, John, 142, 460
Brown, Robert, 437
Brown's Pharmacy, **130**
Brownlow, Alan Foster, 90
Brownlows, 444
Browns Chemists, 307
Browns Chemists (Stoke-on-Trent) Ltd, 307
Bruning, 198
Brunner Mond & Co Ltd, 90
Brunton, Alfred Melvin, 99
Bryan, Richard, 436
Brydon, John, 482
Buchanan, Margaret, 401
Bucher, William Henry, 434
Buckingham, N J, 231, 233
Buckle, Sydney J, 436
Bucklee, W H, 143

Bullalow Ltd, 135, 136
Bullard, Archie, 268
Bullock, J Lloyd & Co, 309
Bullock, John Lloyd, 4
Burbage, 444
Burden, Thomas & Co, 454
Burdon, John, 438
Bureau of Scientific Research, 181
Burford, S F, 444
Burgin, Mark F, 460
Burgoyne, Burbridge, 8
Burnell, J S, 464
Burnett, William, 474
Burnley Co-operative Chemists Ltd, 443
Burr, E F, 168
Burr, G E, 168
Burr, J C N W Ltd, 170, 171
Burr, Mary, 461
Burr family, 278
Burroughs, Silas, 16, 175, 180, 182
Burroughs, S M & Co, 175
Burroughs Wellcome, 16, 19, 34, 38, 43, 44
Burroughs, Wellcome & Co, 175, 182, 183
Burroughs Wellcome & Co Ltd, 174, 424
Burrows, Graham Ltd, 131
Burrows & Close Ltd, **130-1**
Burrows Drug Stores, 225
Busby, James Ltd, 441
Bush, James Mortimer, 133
Bush, William Ernest, 132
Bush, William John, 132
Bush, W J & Co, 84, 118, 131, 132
Bush, W J & Co Ltd, 84, 118, 131, **132-4**, 313
Bush, W J Pension Trustees Ltd, 134

Bush Boake Allen Ltd, 84, 118, **131-2**, 133
Butcher, Dr R W 425
Butler, Edward Henry, 134
Butler, Edwin Harold, 135
Butler, Edwin Henry, 134
Butler, Edwin Hugh, 135
Butler, E H & Son, 134, 135
Butler, E H & Son Ltd, **134-6**
Butler, George, 143
Butler, James Charles, 317
Butler, John, 134
Butler, Pickering & Beckett, 134
Butler Medical Hall, 471
Butterfield, James Moore, 117
Butterfield & Clarke, 117
Buychem (S W London) Ltd, **136-7**
Byfield, William, 439

Caernarvonshire & Anglesey Dispensary, 487
Caley, A J, 2
Calmic Ltd, 176
Cameron, Murdoch, 450
Cameron Pharmaceuticals Ltd, 134
Campbell, Francis, 471
Campbell, Ivie, 473
Campbell, James A, 471
Campbell, James, 473
Campbells, 480
Cann, Mr, 450
Caplan, C P & Sons Ltd, 170, 171
Capsuloid Co, The, 137
Capsuloid Co Ltd, The, **137**
Capsuloids (1909) Ltd, **137-8**
Carbic Ltd, 290
Cardiff & District Pharmacists' Association, 484
Cardiganshire Pharmaceutical Society, 485

Care Chemists Ltd, 404
Carnegies of Welwyn Ltd, 480
Carr, K M, 447
Carr, N G, 185
Carr, P & J (Chemists) Ltd, 170, 171
Carr, Robert, 185, 473
Carr, Walter P, 185
Carr, W G & Sons, 185
Carr, William Graham, 185
Carr family, 454
Carter, William G, 448
Carter & Sons, 138
Carter & Sons (Sheffield), 138
Carter & Sons (Sheffield) Ltd, **138**
Cartwright, J H, 107
Cartwright, Victor, 466
Cassel Co, 295, 298
Cassenne Ltd, 199, 200
Castlelaw, William, 476
Castle Pharmacy, 487
Castlereagh Pharmaceuticals Ltd, 170, 171
Cathcart, John, 474
Cave, J R Ltd, **138-9**
Central Pharmaceutical War Committee, 402
Central Station Pharmacy, 470
Cephos Ltd, **139**, 339
Chalinor, C S, 467
Chand Perfume Co Ltd, 313, 315, 316
Chappells Chemist Ltd, 359, 360
Charnley, Charles, 433
Charnwood Pharmaceuticals Ltd, 135, 136
Chauvin Pharmaceuticals Ltd, 328
Cheers, Samuel, 140
Cheers & Hopley, 140
Cheers & Hopley Ltd, **139-40**
Chelsea Physic Garden, 427, 429

Chemists' Defence Association Ltd, 331, 403, 406, 411, 423
Chemists' Federation, 404, 407
Chemists' Friends Association, 404
Chemists' Friends Scheme, 403, 404
Chemists Holdings (London) Ltd, 140
Chemists Holdings Ltd, **140-1**, 162, 169, 249, 266
Chemists' Mutual Insurance Co Ltd, 403
Chemists' Sickness & Provident Society, 403
Cheney, 444
Chester, J F (Roughton) Ltd, **141**
Chiddingfold Pharmacy, **141-2**
Chiswick Polish Co, 289
Chiswick Products, 289
Chiswick Soap & Polish Co, 289
Christopher, R T, 469
Chubb, J C, 450
Chute, Edward, 450
CIBA, 21
Cicfa Co Ltd, 137, 339
Cilag Ltd, 214, 215
Claflin Chemical Ltd, 350
Clague, Thomas Maltby, 248
Clark, A H (Allington) Ltd, 170, 171
Clark, A H (Maidstone) Ltd, 170, 171
Clark, A H (Park Wood) Ltd, 170, 171
Clark, John, 474
Clark, Richard, 282
Clark & Howes Ltd, **142**
Clark & Pinkerton, 282
Clarke, Isabella Skinner, 401
Clarke, John & Co Ltd, 471
Clarke, Joseph, 117

Claughton, Josiah, 186
Claughtons, 187
Clay & Abraham, 450, 480
Clayton, Dr W 450
Cleaver & Walker, 8
Cleland, William, 473
Clements, Abraham, 483
Cliff, Jeremiah, 442
Clotabs Ltd, 110
Clower, John , 459
Clutton, Joseph, 5, 142, 144
Clutton, Mary, 142
Clutton, Morris, 5, 6, 142
Coate, Thomas Acraman, 454
Coates, S, 435
Cochrane, Alexander, 480
Cochrane & Marshall, 480
Cockburns, 480
Cocker, 115
Cohen, Lewis Judah, 436
Colby, John, 467
Colchester Association of Chemists & Druggists, **394**
Coldwell's Drug Stores, 459
Cole, Francis, 90
Coleridge, 436
Coles, Mr, 354
Collins, 436
Collins, R, 476
Colman, J & J Ltd, 289, 290
Coltman, W T, 190
Colman & Co Ltd, 220
Congalton, Francis, 476
Connor, Dr Patrick, 471
Contabs Ltd, 145
Continental Laboratories Ltd, 145
Cooke, R W, 440
Cooke, Tom, 444
Cookson, John Francis, 436
Cooper, Dr Frank, 461
Cooper, Frederick Thomas, 450

Cooper, George, 126
Cooper, George & Co, 126
Cooper, Gordon, 141
Cooper, Henry, 353
Cooper, Mark, 451
Cooper & Pettifor, 353
Cooper & Son, 353
Cooper & Sturges, 353
Co-operative Chemists, 434
Co-operative Wholesale Society Ltd, 318
Cope & Biddle, 9
Cope & Taylor, 450
Corbyn, 5, 6, 38, 39
Corbyn, John, 142
Corbyn, Stacey & Co, 5, 143
Corbyn, Stacey & Co Ltd, **142-4**
Corbyn, Thomas, 5, 6, 142
Corbyn, Thomas & Co, 6, 142, 143
Corbyn & Stacey, 5
Corbyn family, 36
Corrall, Francis, 444
Co-Tabs Ltd, 146, 147
Cotter, Mr, 308
Coulson, Horace & Sons, 144
Coulson, Horace & Sons Ltd, **144**
Coulthard, Charles Edward, 123
Covent Garden Estate Co Ltd, 339, 342
Cowards of Kensington, 449
Cowper, Joseph, 226
Cox, A H, 9
Cox, Anthony, 145
Cox, Arthur H & Co Ltd, **145-7**
Cox, Arthur Hawker, jnr, 145
Cox, Arthur Hawker, snr, 1, 145
Cox, E A, 440
Cox, Edward Edwards, 145
Cox, Homersham Edward, 145
Cox, Peter, 161
Cox, Roy, 145

Cox, Samuel, 444
Cox, Tom, 145
Cox, Valentine, 45
Cox, W M, 161
Cox Continental Ltd, 145, 147
Cox family, 161
Cox Pharmaceuticals, 146
Coxon, Cyril, 307
Coxon, Harold, 307
Coyney, William, 454
Craig, Nicol, 185
Craig, Nicol Miller, 185
Craine, J P & Son, 434
Cranfordian Ltd, 161
Cranshaw, C H, 470
Crisp, George Staffe, 467
Croadsell, H C, 454
Crompton, H G, 100
Cross, G & Son, 464
Cross, Thomas, 457
Cross & Herbert Ltd, **147-8**
Crosswell, John, 483
Crowder, Charles Hodgson, 224
Crowe, Wilson & Co Ltd, 196
Crowther, James, 149
Croyden, Charles, 107
Croyden & Co, 106
Croyden & Co Ltd, 107
Cruttenden, Joseph, 5
Cryer & Co, 264
Cubey, R Ltd, 368
Cubley, George Arthur, 280
Cullen, William, 476, 480
Culrose, 475
Cummins, E & F Ltd, 170, 171
Cundall, Edward, 148
Cundall, Robert, 148
Cundall, T B, 148
Cundall, Thomas Bowser, 148
Cundall, R & Co, **148**
Cuthbert, John Mason, 358

Dale, Henry Hallett, 182
Dale, Sir Henry, 175
Dales, Edward, 460
Dales, John, 117
Dalmahoy, Alexander, 3
Daniel, G, 455
Daniel, George R & Son Ltd, 321, 322
Daniel, Richard & Son Ltd, 135
Dann & Buttling, 486
Danson, George, 456
Daspaignoll, Samuel & Co, 471
Davey of Wiveliscombe, 465
Davidson, John, 309
Davidson & Hardy, 471
Davies, D E Ltd, 170, 171
Davies, Hugh & Co, 484
Davies, John T, 487
Davies, P H, 458
Davies, R M, 484
Davies, Samuel, 457
Davies, T, 218
Davies, W Bowen, 487
Davis, George S, 267
Davis & Son, 460
Davison, William, 2, 457
Davy, A S Ltd, 170, 171
Davy, Douglas Edward, 149
Davy, Edward Josiah, 149
Davy, Hill & Co, 127
Davy, Hill & Hodgkinson Ltd, 127
Davy, Humphrey, 149
Davy, Humphrey & Son Ltd, 149
Davy, Humphry, 41
Davy, Kathleen, 149
Davy, Percy, 149
Davy, Thomas, 450
Davy, Yates & Hicks, 127
Davy's, H Exors Ltd, **148-9**
Dawe, R J (Park Parade) Ltd, 170, 171

Dawkes, Robert Ltd, 447
Day, John, 439
Daykin, A C, 322
Daykin, A C Ltd, 322
Daykin, George William, 279
Deakin, George, 483
Dean, Samuel, 385
Deane, James, 149, 150
Deane, Henry & Co, 150
Deane, W H (High Wycombe) Ltd, 79
Deane & Co, **149-50**
Debenham, Robert, 448
Dempster, John S, 483
Dennis, W H Ltd, 444
Dennys, Nicholas, 308
Department of Materia Medica, Pharmacy, Pharmacology & General Therapeutics, University of Liverpool, 395
Department of Pharmaceutical Sciences, University of Strathclyde, 422
Department of Pharmacology, University of Strathclyde, 422
Department of Pharmacology & Therapeutics at the University of Liverpool, **395-6**
de Peare, J T Ltd, 448
Dervock Dispensary Committee, 471
Diceys, 11
Dickenson, Lewis, 466
Dickinson, William Binley, 455
Diebold, A H, 350
Dilling, W J, 395
Dinneford, Charles, 4, 309
Dinneford & Co, 240, 309, 339
Dinneford & Co Ltd, 240, 339

Dixon, George E, 137
Dobbin, Thomas, 265
Doble, A G, 360
Doble, H T & Son, 368
Doble, R D, 368
Dobson & Stokoe Ltd, 170, 171
Dodds, Sir Charles, 21
Doherty, W, 435
Doll, Dr Richard 113
Dolling, Robert, 440
Donken, William, 434
Dott, David Brown, 236
Douglas, William, 474
Dow Chemical Co Inc, 199
Dowelhurst Ltd, 359
Downer, George Frederick Arthur, 150
Downer, G F A, 150
Downer & Walker, **150**
Dr MacKenzies Laboratories Ltd, 146
Dr Miles Medical Co Inc, 103
Drane, Robert, 483
Drayner, Joshua, 476
Dreifuss, R B Ltd, **150-1**
Driver, Henry, 203
Druce, George C, 462
Drug & Fine Chemical Manufacturers' Association, The, **396**
Drugs Advisory Committee, 401
Drummond, Jack (Sir), 21
Drummonds, 480
Dubarry Perfumery Co Ltd, 231
Dudgeon, James Ltd, **151**, 282
Duffield, Dr Samuel 267
Duffield, Parke & Co, 267
Duisberg, Carl, 102
Duncan, Anderson & Flockhart, 152
Duncan, John, 151

Duncan, R, 354
Duncan & Flockhart, 152
Duncan & Ogilvie, 152
Duncan Flockhart & Co, 152
Duncan Flockhart & Co Ltd, **151-4**, 155, 176, 234
Duncan Flockhart Evans Ltd, 153
Duncan Flockhart Ltd, 230, 386
Durbin, Henry, 3
Durden, Pearce & Spicer, 437
Durham Pharmaceuticals Ltd, 381, 382
Dyer, R S, 431
Dyers Chemists, 432
Dymond, John, 457
Dymond, Robert, 457
Dysart, Andrew Ltd, 481
Dyssryn, John & Anne, 450

Earlam, E C, 433
Eastbourne District Pharmaceutical War Committee, 438
Eastbourne Pharmaceutical Committee and Panel Chemists, 438
Eastbourne Pharmaceutical Committee (National Health Service) and Panel Chemists, 438
Eastbourne Pharmaceutical (National Health Service), 438
East Durham Co-operative Chemists, 438
Eastgate Pharmacy, **154**
Eastwood Pharmacy, 465
Eden Pharmacy, 435
Edgar, Albert, 437
Edge, W D, 307
Edinburgh Chemists Association, 423
Edinburgh Pharmaceutical Industries Ltd, 79, 82, 153, **155-6**, 176, 234, 270
Edisbury, I J, 486
Edmondson, William, 156
Edmondson & Vogt Ltd, 156
Edwards, 458
Edwards, Samuel & Sons, 141
Edwards, Walter, 456
Edwards, William, 447
Eglinton Chemical Co, 471
Ehrlich, Paul, 17, 28
Ekin, Charles, 309
Elastic Nets Ltd, 199
Eli Lilly, 21
Elliotts Pharmacy Ltd, 170, 171
Ellis, Thomas, 192
Ellison, Robert, 476
Elmhirst, William, **156-7**
Elmitt, W, 435
Elsey, Francis Spencer, 271
Engelhorn, Friedrich, 222
English Royal Apothecaries, 454
Eno, James Crossley, 37, 45, 157
Eno, J C Ltd, **157-8**, 194, 240, 361
Eno Proprietaries Ltd, 157, 339
Erhart, Charles, 272
Errington, J W, 226
Eschmann Bros & Walsh Ltd, 79
ESL & W (South Africa) (Pty) Ltd, 252
Établissements Poulenc Frères, 296
Eucryl Ltd, 162
Evans, 437, 446
Evans, Edward, 250
Evans, Gadd & Co Ltd, 441
Evans, Henry Sugden, 251
Evans, H Sugden & Co, 251
Evans, John, 250, 366, 455
Evans, John & Co, 250
Evans, John Hilditch, 250, 251

Evans, Joseph, 450
Evans, Lescher & Evans, 251
Evans, Lescher & Webb, 251
Evans, Lewis, 484
Evans, Mercer & Co, 251
Evans, Ronald, 159
Evans, Ronald H, **159-60**
Evans, Thomas Bickerton, 250
Evans, William, 257
Evans, W J (Chemists), 301, 359
Evans & Lescher, 250, 251
Evans & Son, 366
Evans & Son Ltd, 251
Evans Biological Institute, 251
Evans Healthcare Ltd, **159**, 252
Evans Medical (India) Private Ltd, 252
Evans Medical (Liberia) Ltd, 252
Evans Medical Ltd, 16, 25, 43, 159, 176, 230, 252, 255
Evans Medical (Northern) Ltd, 252
Evans Medical Pensions Ltd, 159
Evans Medical Supplies Ltd, 252
Evans Medical (Wales) Ltd, 252
Evans Sons, Lescher & Webb Ltd, 16, 18, 19, 43, 251
Evans Sons & Co, 251
Evans Sons & Mason Ltd, 251
Evens, Thomas, 450
Ewins, Dr Arthur, 296

Fabwerke Hoechst AG, 198
Fabwerke vorm Meister Lucius & Bruning AG, 198
Fairburn, Joseph, 326
Fairburn, Robert Walter, 326
Faller's Pharmacy, 455
Farbenfabriken Bayer AG, 102
Farquhar, **160**
Farquhar, James, 160
Farquhar, James Marshall, 160

Farquhar, J M, 160
Farrer, Mr, 456
Faulkner, Joseph, 464
FBA Pharmaceuticals Ltd, 102
Felstead Manufacturing Co Ltd, 247
Fennings, Dr Alfred, 160
Fennings Pharmaceuticals, **160-1**
Ferguson, Thomas, 471
Fergusson, William C, 445
Fernie, James, 433
Ferris & Williams, 83
Ferryman, Herbert, 140, 161
Ferryman, Herbert Ltd, 140, **161-2**, 169, 231, 373
Field, Ebenezer, 433
Fineasset plc, 159, 252
Fish, Frank, 450
Fisher, Thomas, 436
Fisher & Fisher, 443
Fison, Joseph & Co Ltd, 162
Fison, Packard & Prentice Ltd, 162
Fison's Chemicals (Export) Ltd, 167
Fisons Chemicals Ltd, 163
Fisons Industrial Chemicals Ltd, 163, 378
Fisons Ltd, 111, 135, 162, 163, 172, 306, 378
Fisons Pension Trust Ltd, 166
Fisons Pharmaceuticals Ltd, 27, 111, **162-7**, 172
Fisons plc, 164-167
Fitzhugh, Richard, 168
Fitzhugh & Carr, **167-8**, 278
Fitzwilton Ltd, 196
Fleck, William Henry, 443
Fletcher, C S Ltd, 464
Flockhart, William, 152
Flower, Thomas S, 441
Foggitt, John B, 120

Foggitt, W T, 120
Foley, Captain, 484
Ford, Charles H, 222
Ford, John, 476
Forgie, William, 481
Forster, John Hall, 190
Forster, Norman, 190
Foster, H, 464
Foster Pharmaceuticals Ltd, 170, 171
Fowke, W F, 466
Fowke & Son, 466
Fox, George, 460
Francis, J, 483
Francis, James, 487
Francis, James Bridge, 168
Francis, John, 168
Francis, John Herbert, 168
Francis & Co (Wrexham) Ltd, **168-9**
Fraser, Robert, 303
Frasers, 226, 227
Friendly Medical Society, 430
Fulford, C E Ltd, 145, 163
Furnival, Charles Edward, 444
Fylde Laboratories Ltd, 305
Fynmore, Thomas, 8

Gabbetis, T H, **88**
Gale, Samuel, 107
Galen Management Services Ltd, 135
Gamble & Co, 449
Gane, E Inge & Co, 141
Garden, Alexander, 347
Gardiner, Philip, 439
Gardiner & Lacey, 458
Gardner, John, 173
Gattey, Joseph, 11
Gaynsford, Nicholas, 455

GEHE AG, 27, 97, 140, 169, 196, 211, 249, 266, 373
GEHE UK plc, 97, 117, 162, **169-71**, 355
Geigy, 134
Genatosan Ltd, 111, 162, 163, **171-3**
Genatosan Trust Ltd, 111, 163, 172
General Apothecaries Co Ltd, 10, **173-4**
General Council of Medical Education & Registration of the United Kingdom, 410
General Medical Council, 49, 392, 410, 428
General Pharmaceutical Association of Great Britain, 415
Gib, John, 473
Gibbons, Thomas Gilks, 457
Gibbs, J R, 128
Gibbs & Gurnell, 441
Gibson, John, 205
Gibson, Joshua Ltd, 220
Gibson Taylor & Co, 360
Gilbertsons, Henry Ltd, 97
Gilchrists (Chemists) Ltd, 170, 171
Giles, Schacht & Co, 450
Giles, W E & Sons Ltd, 359
Gill, Bernard William, 350
Gill, William, 350
Gilling, John, 439
Gilmour, David, 227
Gilmour, William, 227
Glaisyer, Edmund, 174
Glaisyer, Thomas, 174
Glaisyer & Kemp, **174**
Glasgow & West of Scotland Technical College, The, 422

Glasgow Apothecaries Co, 10, 234, 238
Glasgow Chemists & Druggists Association, 422, 482
Glasgow Chemists Association, 423
Glasgow Druggists Early Closing Association, 236
Glaxo, 22, 23, 24, 25, 26, 27, 29, 43, 44
Glaxo-Allenburys Ltd, 179
Glaxo Australia, 238
Glaxo Export Ltd, 177
Glaxo Group Ltd, 79, 126, 128, 153, 155, 156, 176, 230, 234, 252, 270, 373, 386
Glaxo Group plc, 234, 238
Glaxo Group Research Ltd, 80, 176, 177
Glaxo Holdings Ltd, 176
Glaxo Holdings plc, 159, 169, 176, 177
Glaxo Inc, 176
Glaxo International Ltd, 178
Glaxo Laboratories Ltd, 20, 79, 81, 175, 176, 178, 230, 252, 356, 424
Glaxo Operations UK Ltd, 179
Glaxo SmithKline, 29
Glaxo Wellcome plc, 1, 27, 29, 34, **174-83**
Glenn, F Alistair Ltd, 170, 171
Globalstrike plc, 319
Gloucestershire Medical Society, 308
Glyn-Jones, William Samuel, 411
Glynwed Wholesale Chemists Ltd, 305
Godfrey, Elliott, 184
Godfrey, Elliott (Holdings) Ltd, **184-5**
Godfrey, Marian, 184

Godfrey & Cooke, 4, **183-4**, 309
Goggs & Osborne Ltd, **185**
Golden Key Pharmacy, 160
Goodall, Robert & Henry Backhouse, 443
Goodall, Thomas Anderson, 445
Goodall (South Elmsall) Ltd, 321, 322
Goodess, F W, 444
Goodwin, John, 448
Gordon, Francis, 450
Gordon, Peter Alexander, 323
Gordon family, 455
Gordon's Pharmacy Ltd, 170, 171
Gostling, Thomas Preston, 459
Gottfried, Dr Siegfried, 113, 114
Goulding Ltd, 196
Gourlay, H H, 100
Government Chemist, 397
Government Chemist's Laboratory, 397
Government Laboratory, 397
Government Lymph Establishment, **397**
Grahame, Robert, 474
Grand, Alf J, 458
Grattan, John, 471
Gratton Chemists Ltd, 471
Gray, Alfred, 471
Gray, George C & Son, 185
Gray, George Coghill, 185
Gray, William Gilbert, 185
Graychurch Security Services Ltd, 213
Grays Pharmacy, **185-6**
Greaves, A & Son Ltd, **186-7**
Greaves, Abraham, 186
Greaves, Abraham Walter, 186
Greaves, R, 455
Greaves, Sydney Chater, 186
Greaves, William Samuel, 186

Index of names

Greaves & Richardson, 186
Greaves & Sons, 186
Green, Robert, 454
Green, Stephen Ltd, 448
Greene, Richard, 450
Gregory, Dr James, 475
Gregory, Dr William, 233
Gregory, J, 473
Gregory, R Ltd, 450
Gregory, William, 236
Gregory, William J, 437
Grew, Nehemiah, 1
Grierson, G A, 117
Griffith, J, 486
Griffiths Drug Stores, 226
Griffiths, Griffith, **187**
Griffiths, Waldron, 439
Griffiths, William, **187-8**
Grimshaw, Thomas, 455
Grimwade, Thomas Ship, 8, 295
Grindley, John, 140
Grindley, William, 140
Grindley & Son, 140
Grocers' Company of the City of London, 49, 426
Grove Pharmacy, 433
Grundy, John, 381, 382
Grundy, John W, 382
Grundy, Peter R W, 382
Guest, William, 279
Guild of Hospital Pharmacists, 452
Guildhall Pharmacy, The, 458
Gulliver, Walter Frederick, 188
Gulliver, W F, **188-9**
Gulliver, William, 188
Gulliver, William & Son, 188
Gunner, George, 211
Gwynfa's (Bont) Ltd, 170, 171
Gwynfa's (G C G) Ltd, 170, 171
Gwynfa's (Hounslow) Ltd, 170, 171

Gwynfa's Ltd, 170, 171
Hagon, Albert, 189
Hagon, Albert Ltd, **189-90**
Hagon, Albert (1946) Ltd, 189
Hagons (Butetown) Ltd, 189
Hagons (Cardiff) Ltd, 189
Hagons (Fairwater) Ltd, 189
Hagons (Gabalfa) Ltd, 189
Haighs, 481
Hales, Thomas Meredith, 195
Halfords, 121
Hall, Dr James, 474
Hall Forster & Co, 87
Hall Forster & Co Ltd, **190**
Hallaway, John, 191
Hallaway, Robert Railton, 191
Hallaway's, **191**
Hallett, W J & Co, 450
Hamer & Crumpler, 239
Hamilton, W J, 471
Hammon, Richard, 442
Hammond Hopkins Ltd, 170, 171
Hampshire, F W & Co Ltd, 289, 290, 291
Hampson, Richard, 450
Hamptons Ltd, 439
Hanbury, Cecil, 82
Hanbury, Charlotte, 78
Hanbury, Cornelius, 78, 80, 81
Hanbury, Cornelius, jnr, 78
Hanbury, Daniel, 78, 80, 82
Hanbury, Daniel Bell, 78
Hanbury, Frederick Janson, 78, 79, 82
Hanbury, Sir Thomas, 82
Hanckwitz, Ambrose Godfrey, 4, 183

Handford, Henry, 465
Hands, 439
Hands, H J, 439

Handsworth, 431
Hardings, 217
Hardings, Augustus, 446
Hardings Chemists Ltd, 307
Hardy, Robert (Chemists) Ltd, **191**, 282
Hargreaves, R H, 385
Harley, John Ltd, 188
Harries, John, 484
Harries, W G & J A Ltd, **191-2**
Harrington, A, 466
Harrington & Sons, 465
Harris, Philip, 192
Harris, Philip Holdings Ltd, 192
Harris, Philip Ltd, 192
Harris, Philip Manufacturing Chemist & Druggist Co, 192
Harris, Philip Medical Ltd, **192-3**
Harrison, John & Co, 109
Harrison, Parkinson & Co, 432
Harrison, Robert, 193
Harrison & Scott, 109
Harrison Blair & Co, 193
Harrison Blair & Co Ltd, **193**
Harrods Ltd, Pharmacy Department, 455
Hart, J, 450
Hart, James, 116
Hart, James William, 458
Hartlet, Albert Edward, 196
Hartlet, Tom, 196
Hartley, Professor W N, 295
Hartley, William, 323
Hartleys Chemists Ltd, 170, 171
Harvey, William, 384
Harwoods Chemists Ltd, **194**
Harwoods Laboratories Ltd, 194, 339
Haslett, John W, 471
Hatfield, David Ltd, 466
Hatrick, W & R & Sons Ltd, 155

Hatrick, W & R Ltd, 235
Hawkes, Richard, 468
Hawkswood, S C & Son Ltd, 470
Hay, William, 442
Haydock, S & Co Ltd, 170, 171
Hazelwell Products Ltd, 104
Healy, Thomas, 444
Healy, Thomas & John, 433
Heanley, M, 460
Heaps, H, **194**
Hearon, McCulloch & Squire, 450
Hearon, Squire & Francis, 128
Heath, Josiah Wedgwood, 373
Heath, Richard, 296
Heath, Richard Child, 295
Heathcote, Dr Gilbert, 464
Heathfield, Harold George, 150
Heatley, Norman, 450
Heckmondwike & District Co-operative Pharmacy Ltd, 443
Heddle, J S B & Co Ltd, 282, 284
Hedley, Charles A, 459
Henry, Thomas, 8, 9, 456
Henry, William, 9
Hereth, Franklin, 318
Herring, Edward, 7, 377
Herring, Thomas, 9
Herring Bros, 450
Herts Pharmaceuticals Ltd, 328
Heslop, C W, 450
Hester, Charles, 358
Hetherington, James Rankine, 185
Hetherington, J R, 185
Hewitt, M G, 431
Hexham Chemists, 457
Heygate, Charles, 455
Hibbert & Son, 487
Hickman & Son Ltd, 463
Higgins, C G, 195
Higgins, William Clement, 148
Higgins & Maddock, **194-5**

Higgins Chemists, 148
Higginson, William Goodess, 444
Higgs, Alfred, 195
Higgs, Alfred Ltd, **195**
Higgs, Stewart Clive, 195
Highgate Pharmacy, 435
Hilger, Adam, 446
Hill, Arthur S & Sons, 127
Hill, Charles Alexander, 127
Hill, Philip, 21, 25, 339
Hill, Ricardo, 451
Hillcross Pharmaceuticals Ltd, 170, 171
Hilliar, George C G, 218
Hills, Thomas Hyde, 107
Hills, Walter, 107
Hills Balsam Ltd, 196
Hill's Chemists Ltd, 195
Hill-Smith Ltd, 196
Hill-Smith (Warrington) Ltd, 140, 169, **195-6**
Hills Pharmaceuticals Ltd, 140, 169, **196-7**, 355, 373
Hilton-Davis Chemicals Ltd, 352
Hind, William Tom, 445
Hinde, Samuel, 451
Hindes, J, 479
Hindle, Edward, 197
Hindle, Edward Ltd, **197**
Hindle, James Edward, 197
Hindle, Mary, 197
Hine, Richard, 437
Hine & Son, 437
Hingston, Andrew, 439
Hinsberg, Dr Oskar, 102
Hinton Lake & Son Ltd, 436
History of Pharmacy Committee of the Council of the Pharmaceutical Society of Great Britain, 393
Hitchman, Henry, 459

HMR Investments Ltd, 199, 200
Hobbs, A E Ltd, 442
Hodder, Henry, 197
Hodder, Henry & Co Ltd, **197-8**
Hodder, Thomas Henry, 447
Hodges, Dr, 447
Hodges (Chemists) Ltd, 197
Hodgeton, David, 476
Hodgkinson, Brandram & Stead, 347
Hodgkinson, Cadman, 464
Hodgkinson, Clark & Ward, 127
Hodgson, J E, 438
Hodgson, John Edward, 438
Hoechst AG, 1, 18, 198, 199
Hoechst Marion Roussel Ltd, **198-202**
Hoechst Pharmaceuticals, 202
Hoechst Products (Nigeria) Ltd, 200
Hoechst Roussel Ltd, 199
Hoechst/Roussel-Uclaf, 1
Hoechst UK Ltd, 18, 146, 198, 199, 200
Hoffmann, Dr Felix, 102
Hoffmann-La Roche, 18
Holberton, Thomas Henry, 455
Holden, J H Ltd, 371
Holden, John Henry, 371
Holden, Nellie, 371
Hole, 436
Holland, Harry, 469
Hollingsworth, T, 435
Holloway, Thomas, 15, 37, 45, 202, 203, 204, 462
Holloway College for the Higher Education of Women, 203
Holloway Sanatorium, 203
Holloways Pills Ltd, **202-4**, 240, 339
Holman, Ham & Co Ltd, 436

Holman & Ham, 436
Holme, Keith, **221-2**
Holmes, A, 191
Holmes Keall, 451
Holroyd, F (Garforth) Ltd, 170, 171
Hooper, 4
Hooper, David, 451
Hooper, Struve & Co, 2
Hooper, William, (Pall Mall), 2
Hooper, William, 4
Hope family, 442
Hope, Richard, 442
Hope, Robert, 476
Hope, Thomas, 442
Hopkin & Williams, 205, 309
Hopkin & Williams Ltd, 127, 208, 209
Hopkin & Williams (Travancore) Ltd, 205
Hopkins & Williams, 244
Hopley, John Henry, 140
Horbury Industrial Co-operative Society, 467
Horden, Francis, 433
Hornby, 246
Hornby, E, 221
Hornby & Maw, 246
Horner & Sons, 83
Horniblow & Son, 470
Houghton, Thomas & Co, 462
Hounam, C, 482
Houston, S, 476
How(e), W, 383
Howard, David, 205
Howard, Gibson & Co, 205
Howard, Jewell, Gibson & Howard, 205
Howard, Jewell & Gibson, 205
Howard, John Eliot, 205, 210
Howard, Luke, 8, 9, 10, 33, 78, 204, 205, 206, 208

Howard, Luke & Co, 205
Howard, Robert, 205, 206, 208
Howard & Sons, 78, 205
Howard & Summers, 436
Howard Lloyd & Co Ltd, 229
Howard Lloyd Holdings Ltd, 229, 290
Howards, 8, 9, 10, 16, 38
Howards & Kent, 205
Howards & Sons, 127, 205, 206
Howards & Sons Ltd, 127, **204-10**
Howards of Ilford Ltd, 206, 209, 210
Howden, Robert, 211
Howden, Robert Ltd, **211**
Howden, Robert (Southend) Ltd, 211
Howell & Sons, E G, 483
Howitt, Thomas, 455
Hudson, Sidney Charles, 451
Huggins, George, 436
Hughes, Evan Gresmond, 374
Hughes, Robert Owen, 484
Hughes, Thomas, 257
Hulle, Jacob, 7, 377
Hulme, Samuel, 433
Human Genome Sciences Co, 29
Humphrey, N V, 462
Humphrey, Walter E, 459
Hunt, Richard, 211
Hunt & Co, 211, 440
Hunt & Co (Silver Hill) Ltd, 211, 212
Hunt & Co (Winchester) Ltd, **211-12**
Hunter, Thomas, 472
Hurst, Gerald E, 457
Hurworth, Thomas Botrill, 444
Huskisson, Samuel, 8, 451
Huskisson, Thomas, 8
Hutchinson, C L, 482

Hutton, Alec, 433
Hyde, Albert Alexander, 255
Hyde, F W, 107

ICI, 20, 21, 22, 24, 26, 95, 91, 400
  see also Imperial Chemical Industries
ICI Ltd, 90, 91, 145
ICI Pharmaceuticals Division, 92, 424
ICI plc, 91, 92
IG Farben AG, 222
IG Farbenindustrie AG, 198
Imperial Chemical Industries Ltd, 90, 424
Imperial Chemical (Pharmaceuticals) Ltd, 21, 91, 93
Imperial Pharmacy, 455, 458
IMS Ltd, 391
Incorporated Institute of Comparative Pathology, 251
Incorporated Liverpool Institute of Comparative Pathology, 16
Independent Chemists Marketing Ltd, 404
Ingham, Mr, 354
Innes, George, 472
Inns & Taylor, 359
Institut de Serotherapie Hemopoietique, 198
Institute of Chemistry, 205
Insulin AB Ltd, 79, 82
Inter City Computer Bureau Ltd, 135
Interessengemeinschaft Farbenindustrie AG, 222
International Medical Statistics Ltd, 391
International Proprietaries Ltd, 157, 361

Ioptex Research Inc, 328
Ipswich Chemists Association, 458
Iron Jelloid Co Ltd, **212-13**, 339
Isherwood, T, 442
Islip, Charles Cater, 451
ITT Inc, 247
Izal Pharmaceuticals (Ireland) Ltd, 213
Izal Pharmaceuticals Ltd, **213**

Jack, David, 451
Jack, Sir David, 46
Jackson, Thomas, 11
Jaff, Maurice Ltd, 359
James, John F, 451
James, Robert, 37
Janson, Frederick, 78
Janssen, Dr, 214
Janssen, Dr Constant, 213
Janssen, Paul Adriaan Jan, 214
Janssen-Cilag Ltd, **213-16**
Janssen Pharmaceutical Ltd, 214, 216
Janssen Pharmaceutica N V, 214
Jarrett, Jarret & Sons, **216**
Jarrett, Jarret Roberts, 216
Jarrett, Jarret, 216
Jarrett, J R, 216
Jenner, Dr Edward, 308, 476
Jenner family, 451
Jennings, Dr A F, 267
Jephcott, Harry (Sir), 20, 24, 46, 175, 176
Jewell, Joseph, 205, 208
Jeyes, Philadelphus, 217
Jeyes, Philadelphus & Co Ltd, **216-18**
Johnson, William Wilson, 218
Johnson, W W, **218**
Johnson & Johnson Inc, 214
Johnston, Andrew & John, 476

Johnston, G Forbes, 218
Johnston, G Forbes Ltd, **218-19**
Johnstone, W H, 226
Jones, 4
Jones, B S, 466
Jones, Dr Hugh Davies, 484
Jones, Edward, 257
Jones, E Glyn, 484
Jones, Ellis Powell, 280
Jones, Evan Emrys, 487
Jones, F A A Ltd, 170, 171
Jones, Hugh Parry, 485
Jones, Humphrey, **219**
Jones, Humphrey & Son, 487
Jones, Humphrey Richard, 219
Jones, J Glyn, 487
Jones, John Wesley, 451
Jones, J Rees, 141
Jones, O, 303
Jones, Owen, 303
Jones, S Powell, 451
Jones, Thomas Charles, 228
Jones, William, 3
Jones & King Ltd, 356, 357
Joseph, Jacob, 174
Judge, Edgar H, 458
Judge, F, 239
Judge, Frank, 239
Judge, J, 467

Kasper, J, 324
Kasper, James, 323
Kay, Thomas, 219
Kay Brothers, 219, 220, 386
Kay Brothers (Ireland) Ltd, 220
Kay Brothers Ltd, **219-21**, 290, 386
Kay Brothers Plastics Ltd, 220, 221
Keeble's, 465
Keencare Ltd, 188
Kemball Bishop & Co Ltd, 274
Kemball Bishop Ltd, 272, 273

Kemp, John, 174
Kemp, W H & Sons, 97
Kempson, Yates, Evans & Parkinson, 250
Kendale Dispensing Chemists, 113, 114
Kendall, F, 468
Kendrick, Arthur Ltd, 170, 171
Kenyon, Lloyd, 455
Kepler Malt Extract Co Ltd, 175, 179
Kerfoot, Dr T H Manners, 255
Kerfoot, Ernest, 255
Kerfoot, Ernest Hodgson, 254
Kerfoot, Henry Manners, 255
Kerfoot, Thomas, 254, 255
Kerfoot, Thomas & Co Ltd, 255
Kernot, William Pearce, 465
Kernoth, 151
Keswick Wine Co, 226, 227
Key, G C, 439
Killingworth Chemists Ltd, 302
Kilwaughter Chemical Co, 471
King, Sir Edmund, 476
King, William, 480
King, William & Son, 480
Kingley, Anthony & Edward Pincke, 442
Kingswood Chemists, **222**
Kingswood Chemists Ltd, 89
Kirby, H & T & Co Ltd, 313
Kirby Pharmaceuticals Ltd, 313
Kirby-Warrick Pharmaceuticals Ltd, 313
Kitson, E J Ltd, 470
Knight, R V, 476
Knighton, Sir William, 474
Knights (Manufacturing Chemists) Ltd, 480
Knoll AG, 222, 223
Knoll Ltd, **222-3**

Knoll Pharma Ltd, 223
Knoll Pharmaceuticals, 223, 224
Know, David, 472
Knowles, Frederick William, 195
Knox, John (Stoke on Trent) Ltd, 480
Kowarsky, Alexander, 349

Laboratoire Chauvin SA, 328
Laboratory of the Government Chemist, **397-8**
Laboratory Stock, 427, 429
Lactic Ferments Ltd, 145, 147
Laidlaws, 226, 227
Lakeland Pharmacy, 435
Lambert, E & Son, 448
Lambert & Lambert, 328, 330
Lambert & Son, 448
Lambert Pharmacal Co Inc, 267
Lamplough & Campbell, 251
Langham Bros, 107
Langton, Langton & Wheatley, 451
Laporte Industries Ltd, 206
Latham, M, 431
Laurie, Gilbert & Co, 455
Lawes, John Bennet & Co Ltd, 272, 274
Lawrence, Edmund, 224
Lawrence, Peter, **224**
Lawrence, Philip, 224
Lawson, John, 120, 122
Lay, Dr, 466
Laycock, Henry, 463
Lazell, Leslie, 25
Lea, Perrins & Smith, 470
Learner, Le Cocq & Co Ltd, 232
Lee, J C, **224-5**
Lee, William, 455
Leeson, R, 161
Legat, W H, 480
Legg, 436

Leicester & Leicestershire Chemists' Association, **398**
Leicester Chemists' Assistants & Apprentices Association, 398
Leigh's Pharmacy, 446
Lenton, William Henry, 451
Lescher, Joseph Sidney, 250
Leslie, William, 474
Lestar Laboratories Ltd, 146
Lester, Henry, 225
Lester, W H, 225
Lester, William Henry, 225
Lesters Chemists Ltd, **225**
Levmedic Ltd, 102
Lewin Peplow Ltd, 170, 171
Lewis, Daniel, 484
Lewis, James, 441
Lewis & Burrows Drug Stores Ltd, 225
Lewis & Burrows Ltd, **225-6**
Lewis's Drug Stores, 226
Liebreich, Oscar, 8
Liggins, T P, 440
Lightfoot, G & Son Ltd, **226-7**
Lightfoot, George, 226
Lightfoot, Maurice, 226
Lincoln & Midland Counties Drug Co Ltd, 243
Lincoln Pharmaceutical Committee, 243
Lindsay, Mr, 227
Lindsay & Gilmour, **227**
Lines, George & Co, 441
Lister, James, 228
Lister, John, 228
Lister, John & James, **228**
Lister, Joseph (Lord Lister), 41, 245, 236
Lister, Thomas, 228
Lister Institute, 397

Liverpool Apothecaries Company, 10
Liverpool Chemists' Association, 395, **398-9**
Liverpool College of Technology, 395
Liverpool John Moores University, 395
Liverpool Polytechnic, 395
Liverpool School of Pharmacy, 395, 399, 487
Liverpool University Medical School, 16
Lloyd, R, 229
Lloyd, R (Chemist) Ltd, **228-9**
Lloyd, Rees, 228
Lloyd, Thomas, 140
Lloyd, T Howard & Son, 229
Lloyds Chemists Ltd, 89
Lloyds Chemists plc, 108, 117, 245, 310, 348
Lloyds Pharmaceuticals Ltd, **229-30**, 290
Lloyds Research Ltd, 230
Lloyds Retail Chemists Ltd, 89
Local Associations Executive, 403
Local Government Board, 397
Lock, Gordon (Louth) Ltd, 321, 322
Lockwoods (Chemists) Ltd, 170, 171
Lofthouse, John, 230
Lofthouse & Saltmer, 230
Lofthouse & Saltmer Ltd, **230**, 372, 386
Loggins Ltd, 469
London Apothecaries' Society, 5
London Rubber Company Ltd, 453
London School of Hygiene & Tropical Medicine, 46

London Society of Apothecaries, 10
London University, 450
London Wholesale Drug and Chemical Protection Society, 18
London Wholesale, Druggists, Sundries & Proprietaries Association, 390
Long & Strickland, 451
Lothian & Borders Co-operative Society, 221
Loughran, J J, 271
Loveridge, J M (CI) Ltd, 232
Loveridge, J M Ltd, 231, 232, 233
Loveridge, J M plc, **231-3**
Loveridge, John Montague, 231
Lowis, Robert, 476
Loxley, F L, 462
Lucas, E W, 107
Lucius, 198
Ludlow, Griffiths & Smith, 444
Lyons, 481

Macarthy, James 245, 310
Macarthys Laboratories Ltd, 245
Macarthys Ltd, 245, 310, 348
Macarthys Pharmaceuticals Ltd, 108
Macarthys plc, 245, 310, 348
McDonald, Alexander, 236
McDonald, Daniel, 474
MacDonald, Elizabeth M, 480
Macfarlan, J F & Co, 233, 234, 235, 239, 306, 377
Macfarlan, J F & Co Ltd, 234, 235, 238
Macfarlan, John Fletcher, 11, 233
Macfarlan Smith (Australia) Ltd, 235
Macfarlan Smith (Canada) Ltd, 234
Macfarlan Smith Ltd, 176, **233-8**

Index of names

Macfarlan Smith (New Zealand) Ltd, 235
Mack, A G & Co, 239
Mack, A G & Co Ltd, **239-40**
Mack, Arthur Gregory, 239
Mack, Gregory, 239
Mackay, John & Co, 234
Mackay, John & Co Ltd, 236
McKenzie, G W Ltd, 170, 171
McKinnell, Donald Ltd, 217
MacLagen, Dr T J, 306
MacLaine, Donald, 473
Macleans, 21, 25
Macleans Ltd, 110, 157, **240-1**, 339
McMaster, Thomas, 241
McMaster, Thomas Ltd, 241
McMaster, T Ltd, **241**
McMaster, William Crawford, **241**
McMillan, John, 242
McMillan, John Ltd, 242
MacMurdo & Co, 9
McNab, Dr, 473
McNeil Laboratories Inc, 214
McNeil Laboratories Ltd, 214, 216
McPherson, R S, 479
Maddock, D H & Co Ltd, 189
Maddock's (Butetown) Ltd, 189
Maddock's (Cardiff) Ltd, 189
Maddock's (Gabalfa) Ltd, 189
Major & Fielding Ltd, 313
Maltby, Anthony, 243
Maltby, David, 243
Maltby, Edith, 242
Maltby, F & Sons Ltd, **242-3**
Maltby, F Ltd, 243
Maltby, Frank, 242
Maltby, John, 242
Maltby, John Henry, 242
Maltby, Joseph, 101
Maltby, William Battle, 101
Mander, Bacon & Weaver, 8

Manders, 470
Manktelow, W J, 455
Manthorp, Frederic William, 376
Manthorp, Samuel, 376
Manufacturing, Science, Finance, **399-400**
Marchant, W, 222
Margnard & Co, 463
Marion Laboratories Inc, 199
Marion Merrell Dow Inc, 1, 199
Marion Merrell Dow Ltd, 199
Marion Merrell Ltd, 199, 200
Marns, Thomas & Co Ltd, 146, 147
Marsden, Prosper H, 396
Marsden, Prosper Henry, 451
Marshall, A F Ltd, 170, 171
Marshall, James, 479
Marshall, John, 107
Marshall, John D, 106
Marshall, Nicholas, 142
Marshall, Thomas, 88
Marson & Son, 466
Marston, John, 439
Martin, George, 203
Martin, John, 434
Martin, Thomas, 432, 438
Martin & Co Ltd, **244**
Martindale, W, **244-6**, 309
Martindale, William, 244, 309
Martindale, William Harrison, 244
Martindale, William Robinson, 244
Martindale, William Wholesale Ltd, 245, 309
Martindale Pharmaceuticals Ltd, 245, 246
Martindale Samoore Ltd, 245, 309
Mason, John & Thomas Paget, 444
Mason, Thomas, 278
Mason, W B, 383
Mason & Radford, 278
Masons, 438

Masterton, Francis, 477
Mattersons Drug Stores, 226
Matthew, Thomas, 466
Matthews, E, 433
Matthews, Henry, 436
Matthews & Co, 436
Mattion, H B Ltd, 170
Maud, Gamaliel, 7
Maud, John, I, 6, 7, 8, 96, 377
Maud, John, II, 7, 96, 377
Maud, John, III, 7, 377
Maud, John & Co, 7
Maud & Primatt, 7, 96, 377
Maw, Charles, 246, 247
Maw, Charles Trentham, 246
Maw, Dr H T, 247
Maw, George, 246
Maw, George & Son, 246
Maw, J & S, 246
Maw, John Hornby, 246
Maw, Mowbray T, 246
Maw, S & Son, 246
Maw, Solomon, 246
Maw, S Son & Sons Ltd, **246-8**
Maw, S Son & Thompson, 246
Mawson, John, 248
Mawson, Proctor (Group Pharmacy) Ltd, 249
Mawson & Proctor (Group Pharmacy) Ltd, 250
Mawson & Proctor Ltd, 248, 249
Mawson & Proctor Pharmaceuticals Ltd, 140, 169, **248-50**, 373
Mawson & Swan, 248
Mawson, Swan & Morgan Ltd, 248
Maws Pharmacy Supplies Ltd, 247
Maxwell, George Neal, 366
May, Allen, Brown, 358
May, Charles, 83
May, John, 8, 295

May & Baker, 8, 16, 19, 20, 21, 22, 23, 44, 295, 298
May & Baker (Canada) Ltd, 296
May & Baker (India) Ltd, 296, 297
May & Baker Ltd, 135, 295, 296, 297, 424
May & Baker Pakistan Ltd, 297
May & Baker Plastics Ltd, 297
May & Baker (South Africa) Ltd, 296
Mayerne, Sir Theodore, 461
Maylam, William, 270
Mayne Nickless, 135
Mead Johnson Inc, 128
Mead, Dr, 484
Meakin, William, 374
Meconic Ltd, 234
Meconic plc, 234, 238
Medcalf, Benjamin, 441
Medeva Pharma Ltd, **250-4**
Medeva plc, 159, 252, 255
Medevale Pharmaservices Ltd, **254-5**
Medical Alginates Ltd, 201
Medical Research Committee, 400
Medical Research Council, 22, **400-1**, 425
Medicopharma Ltd, 135
Medirace plc, 159, 252
Meggeson, George, 9, 451
Meggeson & Co Ltd, 313
Meister, 198
Melling, K & Son, 432
Melville, Ronald, 449
Menley & James, 334
Menley & James (Canada) Ltd, 336
Menley & James (Colonial) Ltd, 336
Menley & James Laboratories, 334
Menley & James Ltd, 333, 334, 336

Index of names

Menley & James (New York) Ltd, 337
Mentholatum Co Inc, The, 256
Mentholatum Co Ltd, The, **255-6**
Mentholatum Co (Proprietary) Ltd, The, 256
Mentholatum (Nigeria) Ltd, 256
Mentholatum (Overseas) Ltd, 256
Merck, Fredrish Jacob, 128
Merck & Co Inc, 27, 258
Merck KgaA, 128
Merck Ltd, 128
Merck Sharp & Dohme, 21
Merck Sharpe & Dohme Ltd, 258
Merkins, 438
Merrell, James, 244
Merrell Dow Pharmaceuticals Inc, 199
Merrell Dow Pharmaceuticals Ltd, 199
Merrell Pharmaceuticals Ltd, 199
Merrell-National (Laboratories) Ltd, 199
Metcalfe, Adrian, 454
Metcalfe, James & Sons, 451
Metcalfe, W, 439
Meyer Laboratories Inc, 176
Michie, L P, 473
Middleton, Johathan, 451
Midland Pharmaceutical Association, 460
Mildred, Samuel, 78
Mildred & Allen, 78
Miles Laboratories Inc, 103
Miles Laboratories Ltd, 103
Miles Ltd, 103, 104
Millais, Thomas, 116
Millar, Jessie K, 218
Miller, E Ltd, 302
Miller, Harold, 195
Miller, John W (Chemist) Ltd, 481

Miller, Patrick, 9
Millett, Richard, 349
Milling Johnson Ltd, 434
Ministry of Health, 397
Mitchell, Mr, 451
Mitchell, N K, 435
Mitchell, W & Son, 482
Molescroft Holdings & Investments Ltd, 321, 322
Mona Pharmacy, 487
Monck, Edmund, 460
Monsanto plc, 319
Moor, John, 451
Moore, Adam James, 309
Moore, Dr William 471
Moore, Thomas, 4, 308
Moore & Co, 455
Moorhouse, R, 435
Morgan, Alfred, 465
Morgan, Butler, 455
Morgan, G Ltd, **257**
Morgan, Gwyn, 257
Morgan, Helen, 317
Morgan, Simon, 455
Morgan, Thomas, 248
Morgan family, 455
Morgan Tower Pharmacy, 479
Morison, James, 1, 15, 37
Morris, Benjamin, 5
Morris, Daniel, 257
Morris, Morris E, **257-8**
Morris, Morris Evans, 257
Morris, William Evans, 257
Morrison, Charles O, 464
Morrison, C Ltd, 471
Morse, John, 432
Morson, Albert Robert, 258
Morson, T & Son, 235
Morson, Thomas & Son, 258
Morson, Thomas & Son Ltd, **258-60**

Morson, Thomas Newborn Robert, 258
Morson, Thomas Pierre, 258
Morson, Thomas, 16, 33
Morson, T N R, 10, 11, 244
Mortimer, Arthur, 432
Moseley, A H, 431
Mosenthal & Sons, 296
Moses, Eyre & Henry, 451
Moss, Bruce W, 260
Moss, Bruce W Ltd, **260**
Moss, Edgar, 260
Moss, E Ltd, 86, 125, 129, 130, 135, 151, 184, 190, 197, 218, 219, **260-1**, 302, 321, 368
Moss, Harold, 260
Moss, Marjorie, 260
Mostyn, W, 261
Mostyn, William, 261
Mostyn, William (Pharmacy) Ltd, **261**
Mother Seigal's Syrup Co Ltd, 337
Mott, Sidney, 307
Mott, S J, 307
Mott & Co, 307
Mottershead & Co, 111, 163
Moult brothers, 1
Mounsey Robinson, 227
Mountain Ltd, 462
Moxon, John Lawrence, 446
Mudie, Robert, 262
Mudie's Exosac Ltd, **261-2**
Muller, 198
Munro, Alexander, 475
Murray, David, 476
Murray, James, 476
Murray, J N Ltd, 434
Murray, Sir James, 152
Mussell, L W, 446

Myers, Christopher, 360
N & D Chemists Ltd, 302
Nathan, Joseph, 34
Nathan, Joseph & Co, 20, 174
Nathan, Joseph & Co Ltd, 174, 175, 176, 179
Nathan, Joseph Edward, 174
Nathan, Maurice, 174
National Association of Pharmaceutical Distributors, 25, 388, 389, 390, 391, 408
National Association of Scientific Workers, 400
National Association of Women Pharmacists, **401-2**
National Co-operative Chemists Ltd, 462
National Foreman's Association, 399
National Institute for Medical Research, 400
National Pharmaceutical Association, 47, **403-8**
National Pharmaceutical Union, 247, 394, 403, 404, 423
National Union of Scientific Workers, 399
National Warehouse & General Workers' Union, 396
Natural Chemicals Ltd, 194, **262-3**, 339
Neale, Thomas, 466
Neale's, Edgar, 469
Nedham & Benfield, 444
Needham, Matthew, 461
Neill, E A Ltd, 486
Netting, James George, 361
Neuralgyline Co, 350
New, Thomas Cheney, 90
Newball, Thomas Ayre, 278

Newball & Mason, 278
Newberry, K (Chemists) Ltd, 170, 171
Newbery, Francis & Sons Ltd, 462
Newbery, George, 296
Newbery, Henry, 366
Newbery & Co, 15
Newberys, 3, 11
Newbold, Francis, 455
Newham & Pickard, 464
Newitt, Herbert Henry, 459
New Skin Co Ltd, **263**
Newton, John, 468
Niblett, H E Ltd, 170, 171
Nicholas, W R Ltd, 359, 360
Nicholas & Taylor Ltd, 359, 360
Nicholson, Thomas Tanner, 263
Nicholson, T T, 263
Nicholson, T T Ltd, **263-4**
Nicholson & Sons, 467
Nicklin, R G Ltd, 170, 171
Nightingale & Scott, 449
Nisbet, Alexander, 473
Nisbet, Hugh, 473
Nisbet, William, 473
Nobel Industries Ltd, 90
Noble, Alexander, 221
Noble, J, 110, **264**
Noble, John, 110, 264
Noble family, 221
Norchem Ltd, **265**
Norcros Ltd, 247
Northern Organics Ltd, 351
Northern Pharmaceuticals Ltd, 140, 169, **265-6**, 373
Northern Wholesale Druggists' Association, 135, 390, **408-9**
Nottingham & Nottinghamshire Chemists' Association, 409

Nottingham & Nottinghamshire Pharmaceutical Association, 409
Nottingham Pharmaceutical Association, **409-410**
Nottingham School of Pharmacy, 409
NPA Ltd, 404, 407
NPUH Development Ltd, 407
NPU Holdings Ltd, 247, 404, 407
NPU Marketing Ltd, 404, 407
Numark Ltd, 304, 357, 404, 407
Nunn, Hinnell, Clark & Burdon Ltd, 467
N V Laboratoria Pharmaceutica Dr C Janssen, 214
N V Produkten Richter, 213, 214
N V Research Laboratorium Dr C Janssen, 214
Nyewood Pharmacy, 469

Oakreads Ltd, 171
Ogilvie, 152
Oldacres & Geary, 444
Oldham, John, 451
Old Town Pharmacy, 271
Onley, Robert, 461
Onward Pharmaceutical Services Ltd, 135, 136
Orr's Remedies Co, 284
Ortho-Cilag Pharmaceutical, 214
Ortho Pharmaceutical Ltd, 214
O T C Supplies Ltd, 170, 171
Oubridge, Murray Dinsdale, 130
Owen, Griffith, 487
Owen Owen Ltd, 140

Packard & James Fison (Thetford) Ltd, 162
Page, W J, 463
Pain & Bayles, 458

Pakistan Pharmaceutical Industry
    Ltd, 297
Palgrave, Charles Frederick, 358
Palgrave, John, 358
Palgrave, Robert, 358
Palmer, Edward, 8
Palmer, Sidney, 444
Palmer, T W, 444
Pape's, 434
Park, R M, 479
Park Pharmacy, 461
Parke, Davis, 18, 19
Parke, Davis & Co, 135, 267
Parke, Davis & Co Ltd, 135, **267-8**
Parke, Hervey C, 267
Parke, Jennings & Co, 267
Parke, W, **268**
Parke, William, 268
Parker, C, 120
Parker, William Marris, 269
Parker & Rawlinson, 269
Parker & Rawlinson Ltd, **269**
Parkinson, John, 99
Parry, Owen, 487
Parry family, 457
Pars & Co, 453
P A S (Yorks) Ltd, 86, 266, 267
PATA Trust Co Ltd, 411, 412
Patch, T B Ltd, 443
Patchett, Edwin, 462
Patel, Rajnish, 239
Paterson, Hugh, 476
Paterson, James, 270
Paterson, Stephen, 270
Paterson, William, 155, 269
Paterson, William & Sons Ltd, 155, **269-70**
Pattison, R W, 150
Paxtoun, Thomas, 473
Paydens Ltd, **270-1**
Payne, John Buxton, 451

Paytherus, Thomas, 4, 308
Paytherus Savory & Co, 308
P D S (Leeds) Ltd, 86, **266-7**
Peck, Edward, 268
Pelham, Frank, **271**
Penrith Health Centre, 227
Peregrine, John Pryor, 447
Perrin, Mr, 217
Perrin, Sir Michael, 25
Perry, Thomas, 280
Peter, William A Ltd, 484
Pettifor, William, 53
Peverell, Arthur, 272
Peverell, Henry, 272
Peverell's (Chemists) Ltd, **272**
Pfizer, Charles, 272
Pfizer Central Research, 273
Pfizer Inc, 272, 275
Pfizer Ltd, **272-5**
Pharmaceutical & General
    Provident Society, 403, 408
Pharmaceutical Association,
    Manchester branch, 387
Pharmaceutical Export Group, 23, 388
Pharmaceutical Products Ltd, 310
Pharmaceutical Services
    Negotiating Committee, 404
Pharmaceutical Society of Great
    Britain, 8, 18, 21, 33, 35, 46,
    49, 50, 51, 66, 67, 78, 107,
    109, 193, 243, 244, 245,
    258, 348, 361, 385, 390,
    392, 393, 394, 395, 398,
    399, 401, 402, 403, 405,
    415, 416, 423, 425, 427
    see also Royal
    Pharmaceutical Society of
    Great Britain
Pharmaceutical Specialities (May &
    Baker) Ltd, 296

Pharmaceutical Trade Fund, 412
Pharmacia AB, 275
Pharmacia & Upjohn Ltd, **275-7**
Pharmacia GB Ltd, 275
Pharmacists' Mutual Insurance Co Ltd, 403, 407
Pharmacopoeia Commission, 93, **410**
Pharmacy Committee of the Winchester Group Hospital Management Committee, 440
Pharmacy Finance Ltd, 282, 284
Pharmacy Stores, The, 270
Pharmagen Ltd, 171
Pharmatec Ltd, 199
Pharmed Ltd, 171
Pharmidex Ltd, 199, 201
Phensic Ltd, **277-8**, 339
Philipps, Sir John, 484
Phillips, Bert, 307
Phillips, Chas H Chemical Co Bayer Ltd, 350
Phillips, Scott & Turner Ltd, 351
Phillips, W B, 436
Phillips & Cooper, 436
Phillips Ltd, 351
Phillips the Chemist, 487
Phosferine Co Ltd, 262, 339, 346
Phosferine Products Ltd, 346
Physiological Research Laboratories, 44
Pick, Frank, 443
Pickard, J, 461
Pickering, Henry, 134
Pickering, J W, 434
Pickett, Joseph L, 295
Pickup, Walter F Ltd, 171
Pierce, Robert, 451
Pigeon, Richard Hotham, 8
Pike, Eliza, 326

Pike, George, 326
Pilkington, William, 463
Piper, L, 458
Pipes, William, 88
Pitt, Bernard (Seaton) Ltd, 171
Planche, L A, 258
Plattin, S H, 168, **278**
Plattin, Spencer Howard, 278
Plough Inc (UK) Ltd, 313
Plough (UK) Ltd, 313, 315
Plymouth, Devonport, Stonehouse & District Chemists' Association, 452
Pollard, J H, **279**
Pomshourne Ltd, 264
Pope Roach & Son, 456
Porteous Vegetable Ointment Co, 479
Porterfield, Walter, 476
Portsea Island Co-operative Chemists Ltd, 463
Potter & Moore, 132
Potter & Moore Ltd, 132, 313
Poulenc Frérés, 19, 20, 296
Powell, Edward, 440
Precis (497) Ltd, 159
Prentice Bros Ltd, 162
Preston, A H, 445
Preston, B M, 90
Preston, J Ltd, **279-80**
Preston, Job, 280
Price, Charles John, 295
Price, Daniel, 462
Price, G, 451
Price, R E, **280**
Price, Thomas, 485
Price, William, 369
Prickett, Joseph L, 8
Prideaux, Charles Sydney, 437
Pridmore, Sydney Spencer, 280
Pridmore, Thomas, 280

Pridmore, Thomas & Nephew, 280
Pridmore, William, 280
Pridmore's Ltd, **280-1**
Priestman & Humble, 226
Primatt, Humphrey, 96, 377
Primatt, Lacey, 7
Primatt, Mr, 96
Primatt, Nathaniel, 7
Primatt & Maud, 96, 377
Pringell, James, 474
Pringle, David 474
Pritchard, J, 449
Pritchards Ltd, 457
Proctor, Barnard Simpson, 248
Proctor, John, 248
Proctor, Son & Clague, 248
Proctor & Gamble Ltd, 459
Products (Beechams) Ltd, 104
Proprietary Agencies Ltd, 350
Proprietary Articles Trade Association, 18, 47, 403, **410-13**
Proprietary Association of Great Britain, 47, **413-14**
Provincial Medical & Surgical Association, 392
Public Health Laboratory Service, 397
Puech, James, 451

Quicke, William, 436

Radford, John Storer, 278
Ragg, Clavell William, 281
Ragg, Hubert, 281
Ragg, Kathleen, 281
Ragg, William Watkins, 281
Ragg Ltd, **281**
Raimes, Blanshards & Co, 282
Raimes, Clark & Co, 75, 151, 191, 282

Raimes, Clark & Co Ltd, 75, 135, 151, 191, **282-4**, 293, 317
Raimes, John, 282
Raimes, John Fortune, 282
Raimes, Richard, 282
Raimes, Richard, jnr, 282
Raimes & Co, 282
Randall, William, 3
Randall & Wilson Ltd, 161, 430
Ransom, Francis, 284, 285
Ransom, Michael, 285
Ransom, Richard, 285
Ransom, William, 85, 284, 285
Ransom, William & Son, 85, 284
Ransom, William & Son Ltd, 285
Ransom, William & Son plc, **284-8**
Rawlings, Marion, 88
Rawlinson, Mr, 269
Rayson, John Thomas, 279
Read, James & Co, 148
Read & Orchard, 148
Reappage Ltd, 171
Reckitt, Colman, Chiswick (Overseas) Ltd, 290
Reckitt, Francis, 289
Reckitt, George, 289
Reckitt, I & Son, 289
Reckitt, Isaac, 289
Reckitt, James, 289
Reckitt, Thomas, 289
Reckitt & Colman, 238
Reckitt & Colman Holdings Ltd, 220, 289, 291
Reckitt & Colman (Insurance) Ltd, 291
Reckitt & Colman Ltd, 289, 291
Reckitt & Colman (Overseas) Ltd, 290, 291
Reckitt & Colman plc, 290
Reckitt & Colman Products Ltd, 229, **289-93**

Reckitt & Sons, 289, 290
Reckitt & Sons Ltd, 289, 290, 291, 293
Red Band Chemical Co Ltd, 283, **293**
Redfearn, Benjamin, 443
Redfern, Mr, 445
Reeves, Cornelius Walter, 451
Regional Infusion Fluids Laboratory, 481
Register of Chemists and Druggists, 416
Register of Pharmaceutical Chemists, 415, 416
Registered Pharmacists' Union, 452
Reinhardt, J C & Sons, 443
Reinhardt & Sons, 451
Renson, Israel, **293-4**
Resale Price Maintenance Defence Fund, 412
Retail Pharmacists' Union, 403, 423
Rexall Co Ltd, 20, 354
Reynolds, Richard, 294
Reynolds, Richard Freshfield, 294
Reynolds & Branson Ltd, **294**
Reys, Adam, 471
Rhône-Poulenc, 20, 27, 44, 296
Rhône-Poulenc Ltd, 297
Rhône-Poulenc Rorer Inc, 163, 297
Rhône-Poulenc Rorer Ltd, 163, **295-301**
Richards, James Griffiths, 271
Richards, John Morgan & Sons Ltd, 323
Richards, William John Charles, 455
Richardson-Merrell Ltd, 199
Richeld Ltd, **301**, 359
Richter, Gedeon, 214
Ridd, 436

Ridley, Alexander, 270
Ridley, Messrs, 226
Ridley (Wholesale Chemists) Ltd, 135
Righton, James, 138
Riley, E C, 222
Ringrose, George, 441
Ripley Pharmacy, 467
Roberts, B, 486
Roberts, Francis George Adair, 118
Roberts, Hugh Vincent, 188
Roberts, J T (Northern) Ltd, 302
Roberts, J T (Pharmaceuticals) Ltd, **302**
Roberts, Joseph Cecil Turton, 368
Roberts, Mrs Sarah, 439
Roberts, R B, 433
Roberts, R Emlyn, 487
Roberts, Robert B, 487
Roberts, Stanley Vincent, 188, 189
Roberts, T & Co, 451
Roberts, Trevor R, 461
Roberts, William Griffith, **302-3**
Robertson, James, 152
Robey, Samson Augustus, 435
Robinson, Alfred, 458
Robinson, Guy, 458
Robinson, J, 438
Robinson, Thomas Dexter, 366
Robinson & Co, 438
Robson, James Crosby, 437
Roche, Georges, 296
Rockhill, Mr, 303
Rodger, John, **303**
Roebuck, Charles, 280
Rogers, F A, 143
Rogers, G F Ltd, 433
Rohto Pharmaceutical Co Ltd, 256
Romford Laboratories Ltd, 245
Roots, Thomas, 455
Roper, John, 451

Roper, R A, **303-4**
Roper, Richard, 303
Rorer Pharmaceuticals Ltd, 297
Rose, Dr Frank, 91
Rose, James Dudfield, 439
Rose's Pharmacy, 439
Roundthorn Ltd, 171
Rous, Sir John, 466
Roussel, Dr Gaston, 198
Roussel Laboratories Ltd, 198, 199, 201
Roussel Medical Ltd, 199, 201
Roussel Scientific Institute (UK) Ltd, 199, 202
Roussel Uclaf Ltd, 199, 202
Roussel Uclaf SA, 198, 202
Routh, Robert, 349
Row & Taylor Ltd, 459
Rowland, Edward, 304
Rowland, Langshaw, 304
Rowland, Mrs, 304
Rowland, Sidney C, 304
Rowland, William, 304
Rowland, L & Co Ltd, **304-5**
Rowland, L & Co (Retail) Ltd, 304
Rowland, L & Co (Wholesale) Ltd, 304
Rowland, L (Farm Supplies) Ltd, 304
Roxall Pharmacy, 470
Royal Arsenal Co-operative Chemists Ltd, **305**
Royal Arsenal Co-operative Society, 305
Royal Arsenal Co-operative Society Ltd, 305
Royal College of Physicians, London, 39
Royal Pharmaceutical Society of Great Britain, 46, 47, **414-21**

see also Pharmaceutical Society of Great Britain
Royal Technical College, 422
Rubelle Ltd, 313
Rudge Roberts Ltd, **305-6**
Rushworth, John, 461
Russell, E E Chemists Ltd, 222
Russell, John O, 450
Russell & Andress, 307
Russell & Co, 463
Rust, Nancy, 130
Rustat Pharmaceuticals Ltd, 313, 315

St Albans Medical Club, **421**
St Amand Manufacturing Co Ltd, **306-7**, 377
St Marks Pharmacy, 269
Sales Data Analysis Pharmaceuticals Ltd, 391
Salt, Thomas, 455
Salter, John, 467
Saltmer, James, 230
Sandford, G W, 447
Sandoz, 21
Sangers, 18, 27
Sanofi SA, 351
Sanofi Winthrop Ltd, 351
Sant, Arthur, 307
Sants Pharmaceutical Distributors Ltd, 307, 308
Sants plc, **307-8**
Saunders, A H, 97
Saunders, J E, 460
Saunderson, Matthew, 3
Savory, Arthur Ledsam, 309
Savory, Charles Harley, 309
Savory, John, 4, 33, 309
Savory, Thomas, 4, 308
Savory, Thomas Field, 4, 36, 308

Index of names

Savory & Moore, 4, 38, 40, 45, 106, 308
Savory & Moore Ltd, 36, 76, 108, 183, 245, **308-12**, 348
Savory Moore & Co, 308
Savory Moore & Davidson, 309
Saxton, G, 435
Schacht, George, 11
Scherico Ltd, 313
Schering Corporation Inc, 178, 313
Schering Corporation (Panama) SA, 313
Schering-Plough Corporation Inc, 313
Schering-Plough Holdings Ltd, 314
Schering-Plough Ltd, **313-16**
School of Pharmacy, 190, 294, 348, 395, 396, 415, 416, 422, 450
Scientific Pharmacals Ltd, 352
Scotney, K, 445
Scott, Alexander, 317
Scott, Gordon Islay, 317
Scott, H F Ltd, 282, **317**
Scott, John, 348
Scott, Mary Davidson, 317
Scott, Walter, 476
Scott, W H, 358
Scott & Bowne Ltd, **316-17**, 339
Scott & Turner Ltd, 351, 352
Scott Chemists Ltd, 86, 87
Scottish Co-operative Drug Society Ltd, 318
Scottish Co-operative Wholesale Society Ltd, **317-18**
Scottish Pharmaceutical Federation, 404, **422-4**
Scottish Wholesale Druggist Association, 390
Scotts, 227
SCWS Ltd, 317, 318
SDA Ltd, 391

SDA Pharmaceuticals Ltd, 391
Searle, Claude, 318
Searle, Division of Monsanto plc, **318-19**
Searle, G D & Co Inc, 318
Searle, G D & Co Ltd, 318, 319
Searle, Gideon Daniel, 318
Sefton Bulk Pharmaceuticals Ltd, 176, 179
Selby, Horace Walter, 320
Selby, H W, **320**
Selfridges & Co Ltd, 20, **320-1**
Selles Dispensing Chemists Ltd, **321-2**
Selles Industrial First Aid Ltd, 322
Selles Medical Ltd, 321, **322-3**
Sellors, F B, 439
Sequah Ltd, 323, 324
Sequah Medicine Co, 45
Sequah Medicine Co Ltd, **323-4**
Sergeant, Ross, 461
Severs, Joseph, 435
Severs & Bateson, 435
Shaw, Denis R, 461
Shaw, E P, 468
Shaw & Edwards, 11, 451
Sheel, R, 457
Sheldon, Ebenezer, 447
Sheldon family, 139
Shepherd, Herbert William, 325
Shepherd, R J S, **325**
Shepherd, Robert James, 325
Shepherd, W E, **325-6**
Shepherd, William Ellis, 325
Sheridan, M, 455
Sherley, A F & Co Ltd, 339, 342
Shewell, Chas F, 458
Shiers, George, 454
Shillings, N W Ltd, 359, 360
Shipman Davies Ltd, 171
Shreeve, G & Son, 458

Sillett's, **326**
Silve, Mr, 294
Simmons, T H W, 433
Simms, E, 459
Simpson, Thomas & Son, 451
Sims, Ollive, 204, 386
Sinclair, Dr Willliam, 474
Sinclair, James, 115
Sinclair, Matilda Anne, 115
Sittingbourne Pharmacy, 442
Siviour, 368, 369
Siviour Ltd, 369, 370
Skeates, Frank, 271
Skinner & Davison Ltd, 359, 360
Skues, Ernest, 86
Slee, Edward, 326
Slee, Edward & Co, **326-7**
Slee, Samuel, 326
Slinn, D W, 464
Small, Robert, 452
Smallwood Chemists Ltd, 171
Smith, Arthur John, 465
Smith, Basil, 239
Smith, Bruce, 464
Smith, Charlotte, 279
Smith, Frederick, 106
Smith, Harold, 195
Smith, Henry, 234
Smith, Horatio Nelson, 327
Smith, H Wood, 295
Smith, Messrs, 440
Smith, Samuel, 332
Smith, T & H, 11, 155, 234, 306, 377
Smith, T & H (Australia) Ltd, 237
Smith, T & H (Canada) Ltd, 237
Smith, T & H Ltd, 155, 234, 235, 236, 238
Smith, T H, 16
Smith, Thomas, 234
Smith, Thomas James, 327

Smith, T J & Nephew, 327, 328
Smith, T J & Nephew Ltd, 328
Smith, Walter, 461
Smith, W (Durham) Ltd, **331**
Smith, William, 330, 331, 332
Smith, William Thomas, 441
Smith & Co, 332
Smith & Nephew Associated Companies Ltd, 328
Smith & Nephew Group Research Centre Ltd, 328
Smith & Nephew Manchester Ltd, 329
Smith & Nephew Medical Ltd, 328, 329
Smith & Nephew Pharmaceuticals Ltd, 328, 329, 330
Smith & Nephew plc, **327-30**
Smith & Nephew Research Ltd, 328
Smith & Nephew Surgical Ltd, 329
Smith & Son (Norwich) Ltd, 310, 456
Smith & Sons, 309
Smith & Wesley, 458
Smith Kendon Ltd, **331-3**
Smith Kline & French, 21
Smith Kline & French Co Inc, 334
Smith Kline & French (Ireland) Ltd, 338
Smith Kline & French Laboratories Inc, 334
Smith Kline & French Laboratories Ltd, 340
SmithKline & French Pension Trustees Ltd, 338
Smith Kline & French Research Ltd, 334, 337, 338
Smith Kline & French UK Ltd, 334
Smith Kline Beckman, 26

SmithKline Beckman Corporation Inc, 334, 335, 340, 346
SmithKline Beckman Inc, 339
SmithKline Beecham, 26, 27, 29
SmithKline Beecham Pharmaceuticals (UK) Ltd, **333-8**, 339
SmithKline Beecham plc, 240, 273, 334, **338-45**, 351
SmithKline Beecham Research Ltd, **345-6**
SmithKline Corporation Inc, 334, 335
SmithKline Foundation, 334, 337
Snell, Charles Henry, 452
Société Chimique des Usines du Rhône, 296
Society of Chemical Industry, 205
Soden Mineral Produce Co Ltd,, 313, 315
Solomian Ltd, 171
South End Pharmacy, 466
Southend-on-Sea Association of Pharmacists, 361
Sowerby, John, 445
Spa Pharmacy, 440
Spackman & Mackenzie Ltd, 359, 360
Sparks, Thomas & Son, 347
Sparks, White & Co, 347
Sparks, White & Co Ltd, **347**
Sparks & Co, 347
Sparks & Evans, 347
Sparks & Sons, 347
Specia Co, 296
Spencer, Dakers & Co, 455
Spencer, Mrs J, 271
Spender, John, 445
Spicers, Pepperers & Grocers' Company, 36
Squire, Peter, 2, 347, 348

Squire, Sir Peter Wyatt, 348
Squire & Co, **347-9**
Stable, Daniel, 250
Stable, Evans & Co, 250, 254
Stablond Laboratories Ltd, **349**
Stacey, George, 142
Staight, John, 440
Stamp, Ralph, 457
Standard Tablet Co Ltd, The, 231, 233
Staniform Ltd, 380
Stanleys (Nottingham) Ltd, **349-50**
Stanser, John, 88
Starling & Vine, 442
Statim Pharmaceuticals Ltd, 231, 233
Steadman, John & Co, 452
Stearn Bros Ltd, 466
Stedman, Dr John, 474
Steedman, John, 1
Steel, John, 445
Steinhart, Dr Oscar, 295
Stennet, F, 437
Stephenson, James, 461
Steradent Ltd, 292
Sterling Drug International Ltd, 351, 352
Sterling Group Pension Trustees Ltd, 352
Sterling Health Ltd, 351, 352
Sterling Organics Ltd, 351, 352
Sterling Products Inc, 102, 350
Sterling Remedy Co, 350
Sterling Winthrop Group Ltd, 213, **350-2**
Stevenson, John, 476
Steward, C C, 470
Steward family, 470
Stewardson, Henry, 358
Stewart, Alexander Kennedy, 479
Stewart, Michael Ltd, 321, 322

Stewarts, 227
Stiles, 445
Stirling, George, 472, 476, 479
Stirling Drug Inc, 102, 350
Stockwells Chemists, 447
Stonham, Thomas G & Son, 442
Story, Richard, 434
Stow, Noel G, 466
Strang, Peter, 482
Stratton, A P Ltd, 171
Struve, Friedrich, 2
Stuart, Dr Walter 475
Sturgeon, H L, 268
Sturges, **353**, 363
Sturges, William, 353
Sturges family, 353
Sturton, Frederick, 353
Sturton, John, 353
Sturton, John Gilbert, 353
Sturton, John Rowland, 353
Sturton, Joseph, 433
Sturton & Sons, 353
Sturton & Sons Ltd, **353-4**
Sturton Bros, 353
Sturton (Wholesale) Journies Ltd, 354
Summerfield & Sparkes, **354**
Sumner, R, 480
Sunnydale Products Ltd, 289, 292
Swan, John, 473
Swan, Joseph, 249
Swan, Joseph Wilson, 248
Swanbrig Engineers Ltd, 79
Sykes, Henry, 196, 355
Sykes, Henry & Son Ltd, **354-5**
Sykes, Henry Ltd, 196
Sykes, Richard, 355
Symonds, J A Ltd, **355-6**
Symonds, James Alfred, 356
Synthelabo Groupe SA, 328
Talbot, James, 469

Tate's Medical Hall, 471
Tatford, Graham, 233, 356, 357
Tatford, Graham & Co Ltd, **356-7**
Taylor, Christopher, 359
Taylor, Christopher Ltd, 359, 360
Taylor, Dudley, 75, 76, 301, 359, 384
Taylor, Dudley (Bilton) Ltd, 359, 360
Taylor, Dudley (Holdings) Ltd, 75, 301, **358-60**, 384
Taylor, Dudley Kenilworth, 359
Taylor, Dudley Kenilworth Ltd, 359, 360
Taylor, Gibson, 360
Taylor, Gibson & Myers, 360
Taylor, Gibsons Ltd, **360**
Taylor, James Bennet, 358
Taylor, John Usher, 358
Taylor, Michael, 359
Taylor, Mr, 452
Taylor, M W & A Ltd, 171
Taylor, Peter, 455
Taylor, R T, 2
Taylor, William S, 471
Taylor & Brawn, 358
Taylor & Cuthbert, 357
Taylor Brawn & Flood, 358
Taylor Brawn & Flood Ltd, **358**
Taylor Brothers, 143
Taylor family, 359
Taylors (Cash Chemists), 383
Taylors (Cash Chemists) London Ltd, 383
Taylor's Drug Co, 18, 383
Taylor's Drug Co Ltd, 383
Taylors (Southam) Ltd, 359, 360
Teasdale, James, 270
Technical, Administrative & Supervisory Staffs, 399
Tempo Drug Store, 364, 365

Tenterden Bookshop, The, 271
Teucer, 361
Teucer Ltd, **360-1**
Thacker, Charles B, 439
Thackray, Charles F Ltd, 443
Therapeutic Research Corporation, 22, 180, **424-5**
Thermogene Co, 361
Thermogene Co Ltd, 339, **361-2**
Thexton, George W, 120
Thomas, Alfred E, 149
Thomas, Dan, 485
Thomas, G R, 484
Thomas, J J & Son, 463
Thomas, John, 78, 279, 362, 451
Thomas, Owen, 362
Thomas, Susanah, 362
Thomas, William & Tollerton, William, 484
Thomas family, **362-3**
Thompson, Andrew, 244
Thompson, Dr Charles John Samuel, 452
Thompson, Harry, 358
Thompson, John, 112, 246
Thompson, John Ltd, 486
Thompson & Capper, 38
Thomson, A L, 432, 440
Thomson, Dr John, 473
Thomson, William & Co, 473
Thorium Ltd, 205
Thorp, E & Son, 469
Threshie, John, 473

Tilson, E F Ltd, 447

Tobal Products Ltd, 73
Todd, Douglas, 363
Todd, R McLaren Ltd, **363-4**
Todd, Robert Alexander McLaren, 363

Tollington, Richard B, 117
Tomlinson, Henry Jenkins, 224
Towers, George, 9
Towers, John, 8, 9
Townson & Mercer, 452
Tremlett, Annie May, 364
Tremlett, Ian, 364
Tremlett, Molly Doreen, 364
Tremlett, Percy Gordon, 364
Tremlett, R G, 365
Tremlett, R G Ltd, 364
Tremlett, Richard Gordon, 364
Tremletts Chemists Ltd, 364, 365
Tremlett (Chemists) Ltd, 364
Tremlett Holdings Ltd, **364-6**
Tremletts Pharmacies Ltd, 45, 364, 365
Trick's Drug Stores, 226
Trott, G H Ltd, 171
Tuck, Brian Ltd, 359, 360
Tucker, J, 374
Turlington, Robert, 452
Turner, D W, 436
Turner, G (Biggleswade) Ltd, **366-7**
Turner, George, 366
Turner, Levi, 464
Turner, R C, **367**
Turner, Ronald Charles, 367
Turner, S J, 452
Turton's Chemists Ltd, **367-8**
Tylers, 456
Tyrer, Thomas, 295

Uclaf Ltd, 199, 202
Ulster Chemists' Association, 404
Ulster Wholesale Chemists' Association, 390
Umney, Charles, 245
Una Pharmaceuticals Ltd, 351
Underhill, C E, 369
Underhill, C E, the younger, 368

Underhill, C E & Co Ltd, 368
Underhill, C E & Sons Ltd, **368-70**
Underhill, Cyril Edgar, 368, 369
Underhill, David John, 369
Underhill, E R, 369
Underhill, Ernest Russell, 368
UniChem, 27, 151
UniChem (Investments) Ltd, 86, 87
UniChem Ltd, 86, 100, 136, 371, 404
UniChem (Northern) Ltd, 86, 88, 266
UniChem plc, 86, 87, 125, 129, 130, 151, 184, 190, 197, 218, 260, 261, 302, 321, 322, 368
UniChem (Sheffield) Ltd, **370-1**
Unicliffe Ltd, 273
Unilever, 20, 73, 290, 400
Union Camp Corporation Inc, 131
United Alkali Co Ltd, 90
United Drug Co Inc, 18, 20, 121
United Northwest Co-operatives Ltd, 307
Universal Nets Ltd, 199
University College Liverpool, 395
University of Liverpool, 251, 395
University of London, 416
University of Strathclyde, 422
    School of Pharmacy, **421-2**
Upjohn, Dr William 275
Upjohn, Henry, 275
Upjohn Co Inc, The, 275
Upjohn Co Pte Ltd, 276
Upjohn (Ireland) Ltd, 276
Upjohn Ltd, 275, 276
Upjohn of England Ltd, 275
Upjohn Pill & Granule Co, 275
Upsil Ltd, 202
Uso Ltd, 213
Uxbridge Cotton Mills Ltd, 107

Vahrman, Daniel, 293
Valda Pharmaceuticals Ltd, 351, 352
Vantage Chemists, 169
Vegetable Drugs Committee, **425-6**
Venn, William, 436
Veno Drug Co Ltd, 203, 339, **371-2**
Vestric Ltd, 25, 27, 126, 128, 140, 155, 169, 230, 252, **372-3**, 386
Vestric Pensions Ltd, 373
Vickers, F B Ltd, 171
Victoria Pharmacy Ltd, 382
Vincent, Lacey A, 445
Vitamins Ltd, 346
Vitapointe (UK) Ltd, 163
Vitreous Mosaic Co, 295, 298

Waddington, Charles W Ltd, 171
Wain, Cecil Alexander, 149
Waites, Edward, 483
Wakefield, G E, **373-4**
Wakefield, Geoffrey E, 373, 374
Wakefield, John, 109
Wakefield Chemists' Association, 452
Walduck, John H, 106
Walfox Ltd, 229
Walker, A H (Acton) Ltd, 447
Walker, Alexander, 474
Walker, Elim, 3
Walker, George J, 374
Walker, Helen Emily, 150
Walker, John, 453
Walker, John (Cleckheaton) Ltd, 443
Walkers of Doncaster, 443
Waller, William, 11
Wallsend Co-operative Chemists Society Ltd, 457
Walton, Thomas Henry, 229

Index of names

Walton, Thomas Henry & Co Ltd, 229
Walwin family, 374
Walwins (Chemists) Ltd, 374
Walwins of Gloucester Ltd, **374-5**
Warburton, James, 193
Ward, Joseph, 375
Ward, Joshua, 37
Ward & Woodman, 375
Ward & Woodman Ltd, **375**
Ward Laboratories (UK) Ltd, **375-6**
Wardell, R E, 464
Waring, A W, 143
Waring, E S, 120
Warner, W R, 21
Warner-Hudnut Inc, 267
Warner Lambert, 238
Warner Lambert Inc, 267
Warner Lambert Ltd, 267
Warrick Brothers Ltd, 84, 85, 313, 315
Warrick Pharmaceuticals Ltd, 313, 315
Waters The Chemists, 438
Watson, Gertrude, 461
Watson, John, 445
Watts, G F, 452
Waylett, William, 456
Waylett, William & Sargent, Thomas, 456
Webb, Edward Alfred, 251
Webster, Joshua, 326
Webster, Thomas, 487
Weddell, Arthur, **376**
Wedgewood, Stanley, 452
Weeks, J, 440
Weir, Dr J, 474
Weiss, W E, 350
Weldrick, H I Ltd, 437
Wellcome, 22, 26, 27, 29
Wellcome, Henry, 16, 20, 25, 38, 41, 44, 175, 176, 180, 182
Wellcome Bureau of Scientific Research, 16, 175, 180, 182
Wellcome Foundation, 20, 25
Wellcome Foundation Ltd, 175, 176, 177, 180
Wellcome Physiological Laboratory, 16, 19
Wellcome plc, 27, 176, 177
Wellcome Trust, 175, 176, 177, 180
Weller, James M, 458
Wellington, Fred, 465
Weltons, 434
Weskott, Johann Friedrich, 102
Wesley-Jenssen London Ltd, 314, 316
Wesley-Jenssen (UK) Ltd, 314
Wessex Pharmacies Ltd, 231, 233
Westbrook, Mr, 448
Western Apothecary's Co Ltd, 173
West Hartlepool Drug Co Ltd, 381
Westminster Laboratories Ltd, 290, 293
Weston, J & Co, 174
Westons, The Chemists, 198
Wheaton, Charles, 436
Whiffen, George Goodman, 377, 378
Whiffen, Noel Hardy, 377, 378
Whiffen, Stanley White, 377, 378
Whiffen, Thomas, 7, 306, 377
Whiffen, Thomas & Sons, 377
Whiffen, Thomas Joseph, 377
Whiffen, William George, 377
Whiffen & Sons, 96, 172, 306, 377
Whiffen & Sons Ltd, 111, 163, 172, **377-81**
Whiffen family, 378, 380
Whitchurch Pharmacy, 440

White, A J, 333
White, A J (Canada) Ltd, 337
White, A J (Colonial) Ltd, 337, 338
White, A J Ltd, 21, 333, 334
White, A J (New York) Ltd, 337
White, A J (South Africa) Ltd, 337
White, A Judson, 333
White, James, 339
White, Timothy 383
White, Woolmer, 383
White Laboratories Inc, 313
White Laboratories Ltd, 313
Whites, Timothy & Taylors Ltd, 121, **382-4**
Whites, Timothy Ltd, 18, 383
Whiteside, J Maynard Ltd, 321, 322
Whitfield, Aaron, 482
Whitfield, George, 381
Whitfield, G Ltd, 381
Whitfield, Joseph S, 381
Whitfield, Margaret, 381
Whitfield, Mary Ann, 381
Whitfield, M Ltd, **381-2**
Whitfield Drug Stores Ltd, 381, 382
Wholesale Drug Trade Association, 21, 23, 388, 389, 425
Whyte, James, 473
Whyte, W, 376
Widdowson, Edwin, 373
Wiggin & Son, 452
Wiggin Hill Farm, 285
Wigmore's Ltd, 314
Wilde, John, 363
Wilderspin, M E, 467
Wiles & Holman, 141, 458
Wilkinson & Simpson Ltd, 457
William, Alexander, 473
Williams, Elizabeth, 168
Williams, Harold, 100
Williams, J Wynne, 486

Williams, John Lewis, 487
Williams, John Thompson, 112
Williams, R M, 487
Williams, R M Ltd, 483
Williams, Stephen, 452
Williams, William, 168, 487
Williams & Fitzhugh, 168
Williamson, B & Co, 457
Willsher, Stephen Henry, 270
Willson, Robert W & Co, 459
Wilson, Andrew, 395, 396
Wilson, Minshull & Co, 347
Wilson, R W F & Co (Arbroath) Ltd, 171
Wilson, R W F & Co (Inverness) Ltd, 171
Wilson, Thomas, 384, 451
Wilson & Colville, 471
Wilson & Dickinson, 452
Wilson & Kitchin, 434
Wilson's Ltd, 384
Wilson's (Stowmarket) Ltd, **384**
Windridge, A H, 359
Windridge, A H Ltd, 359, **384-5**
WinPharm Ltd, 351, 352
Winstanley & Son, 143
Winthrop Biologicals Ltd, 351
Winthrop Group Ltd, 350
Winthrop Laboratories (Ireland) Ltd, 352
Winthrop Laboratories Ltd, 351, 352
Winthrop Pharmaceuticals Ltd, 351
Wiveliscombe Pharmacy, 465
Wolsey Pharmacy, 458
Wood, Benjamin, 442
Wood, Henry, 452, 470
Wood, Reginald Scott, 461
Wood, Thomas, 473
Woodall, John, 457
Woodall, John Leigh, 457

Index of names

Woodall family, 457
Woodfield Cooke Ltd, 469
Woodman, George, 440
Woodman, James, 469
Woodman, W A G, 375
Woodman, William Arthur Gelsthorpe, 375
Woods, W & Son, 368
Woodthorpe, 461
Woody & Thompson, 456
Woollaton, 461
Woollatt, R & J Boyd, **385**
Woollatt, Richard, 385
Woolley, George Stephen, 385
Woolley, Harold, 385
Woolley, Herman, 385
Woolley, James, 385
Woolley, James Sons & Co, 386
Woolley, James Sons & Co Ltd, 230, 372, **385-7**
World Federation of Scientific Workers, **426**
Worshipful Society of Apothecaries, The, 36, 47, 49, **426-30**
Wray, Hilton, 11
Wrays, 11
Wreaks, G D, 464
Wright, E A, 168
Wright, Robert, 154
Wulfing AG, 163, 172
Wyatt, W, 452
Wye, John, 11
Wyeth, 21
Wyllie, H B, 480
Wynnstay Farmers, 304
WYT Products Ltd, 263

Yates, Francis H, 452
Yeast Vite Ltd, 105, 240, 339
Young, J Rymer, 433
Young, Sir James, 152
Youngman, W E (Hythe) Ltd, 231
Yucca Co, 255
Yule The Chemist Ltd, 481

Zachary, Thomas, 106
Zeidemann, G, 446
Zeneca, 29
Zeneca Pharmaceuticals Ltd, 91
Zeneca plc, 27, 91

Index of places

Aberaeron, Ceredigion, 187, 188, 485
Aberdeen, City of Aberdeen 78, 155, 269, 270, 354, 423, 452, 472
Abergavenny, Monmouthshire, 462, 483
Africa, 35, 172, 180, 252, 256, 313
Alcester, Warwickshire, 76, 373
Alfreton, Derbyshire, 435
Alnwick, Northumberland, 2, 457
Alton, Hampshire, 440
Ambleside, Cumbria, 106, 123
Ampthill, Bedfordshire, 83, 358
Appleby, Cumbria, 435
Argentina, 175, 180
Armagh, Armagh, 471
Ashbourne, Derbyshire, 126
Ashby-de-la-Zouch, Leicestershire, 445
Ashton-under-Lyne, Tameside, 161, 254
Askern, Doncaster, 322
Australia, 19, 43, 175, 180, 234, 252
Aylesbury, Buckinghamshire, 123

Ballygawley, Tyrone, 470
Ballymoney, Antrim, 471
Bampton, Devon, 436
Banff, Aberdeenshire, 476
Bangor, Gwynedd, 487
Barnstaple, Devon, 1, 125, 145, 146, 436, 436
Barrow in Furness, Cumbria, 434

Barry, The Vale of Glamorgan, 484
Barton-Upon-Humber, North Lincolnshire, 224
Basildon, Essex, 108
Bath, Bath & North East Somerset, 431, 450, 452
Batley, Kirklees, 229, 290, 443
Beaminster, Dorset, 437
Beaulieu, Hampshire, 440
Beaumaris, Isle of Anglesey, 486
Bedale, North Yorkshire, 460
Bedford, Bedfordshire, 217, 358, 431, 449
Bedminster, City of Bristol, 197
Beeston, Nottinghamshire, 461
Belfast, Antrim, 470, 471, 472
Belgium, 213, 214, 306
Bembridge, Isle of Wight, 441
Berwick-Upon-Tweed, Northumberland, 185, 460, 473
Bethesda, Gwynedd, 487
Beverley, East Riding of Yorkshire, 88, 438
Bexhill, East Sussex, 126
Bicester, Oxfordshire, 462
Biggar, South Lanarkshire, 482
Biggleswade, Bedfordshire, 217, 366
Birkenhead, Wirral, 390, 469
Birkenshaw, Kirklees, 2
Birmingham, Birmingham, 9, 10, 73, 76, 109, 126, 135, 192, 198, 284, 431, 453, 464
Bishop Auckland, Durham, 272

Blackburn, Lancashire, 139
Blackhall Colliery, Durham, 381
Blackley, Manchester, 91
Blackpool, Lancashire, 402
Blaenavon, Torfaen, 483
Blaydon, Gateshead, 367
Blockley, Gloucestershire, 440
Blyth, Northumberland, 265, 381
Bo'ness, Falkirk, 473, 481
Bognor Regis, West Sussex, 451, 469
Bolton, Bolton, 116, 193
Bootle, Sefton, 325
Boston, Lincolnshire, 289, 458
Bournemouth, Bournemouth, 112, 113, 453
Bowness-on-Windermere, Cumbria, 123, 435
Bracknell, Bracknell Forest, 313
Bradford, Bradford, 87, 125, 260, 265, 325, 432, 460
Bradford-on-Avon, Wiltshire, 469
Bramley, Rotherham, 444
Brazil, 35
Brechin, Angus, 476
Bridgend, Bridgend, 103, 104, 228, 229, 331, 332
Bridlington, East Riding of Yorkshire, 321
Bridport, Dorset, 437
Brighouse, Calderdale, 260
Brighton, Brighton & Hove, 1, 2, 4, 145, 174, 309, 357
Bristol, City of Bristol, 3, 73, 91, 128, 197, 432, 454
Brockham, Surrey, 339
Buckfastleigh, Devon, 436
Buckingham, Buckinghamshire, 150
Burbage, Leicestershire, 444
Burma, 180, 252

Burnham, Buckinghamshire, 256
Burnley, Lancashire, 123, 325, 355, 443
Bury, Bury, 123
Bury St Edmunds, Suffolk, 356, 433, 451, 466

Caernarfon, Gwynedd, 261, 484, 487
Callington, Cornwall, 368, 369
Calne, Wiltshire, 194, 195
Cambridge, Cambridgeshire, 144, 433
Canada, 3, 6, 43, 78, 79, 175, 180, 234, 251, 323, 336
Cardiff, 189, 402, 483, 485, 487
Cardigan, Ceredigion, 484
Carlisle, Cumbria, 135, 191, 226, 244, 445
Carmarthen, Carmarthenshire, 484
Carrington, Nottinghamshire, 279
Castleford, Wakefield, 467
Channel Islands, 116, 232, 450
Chard, Somerset, 465
Cheadle, Salford, 433, 457
Cheetham Hill, Manchester, 385
Chelmsford, Essex, 439
Cheltenham, Gloucestershire, 4, 36, 123, 308, 439, 440
Chertsey, Surrey, 467
Chester, Cheshire, 139, 140, 434, 457
Chesterfield, Derbyshire, 186, 452
Chichester, West Sussex, 154, 468
Chiddingfold, Surrey, 141
China, 175, 180
Chippenham, Wiltshire, 469
Chipping Campden, Gloucestershire, 439
Cirencester, Gloucestershire, 439
Claughton, Lancashire, 90

Clay Cross, Derbyshire, 435
Cleckheaton, Kirklees, 443
Cleethorpes, North East Lincolnshire, 459
Clifton, North Somerset, 11, 450
Cockermouth, Cumbria, 454
Colchester, Essex, 150, 376, 394, 439
Colne, Lancashire, 196
Colwyn Bay, Conwy, 486
Connah's Quay, Flintshire, 228
Copnor, City of Portsmouth, 231, 364
Corfe Mullen, Dorset, 231
Cosham, City of Portsmouth, 98, 99, 357
Cottingham, East Riding of Yorkshire, 321, 322, 438
Coundon, Durham, 265
Coupar Angus, Perth & Kinross, 474
Coventry, 169, 170, 434
Cowes, Isle of Wight, 160
Cramlington, Northumberland, 223
Cranbrook, Kent, 5
Crawley, West Sussex, 275, 339
Crewe, Cheshire, 307
Crewkerne, Somerset, 101, 465
Cromer, Norfolk, 458
Cuba, 180
Cullompton, Devon, 436
Culross, Fife, 473
Curbridge, Oxfordshire, 338
Curdworth, Birmingham, 138

Dalgety Bay, Fife, 191
Darlington, Darlington, 190, 437, 438
Dartford, Kent, 175
Daventry, Northamptonshire, 359
Denham, Buckinghamshire, 199

Denton, Tameside, 264
Derby, Derbyshire, 89, 135, 289, 435, 450, 456
Derry, Londonderry, 471
Devonport, City of Plymouth, 202, 452
Didsbury, Manchester, 457
Diss, Norfolk, 459
Doncaster, Doncaster, 322, 437
Dorchester, Dorset, 383, 437
Dorking, Surrey, 124
Dosthill, Staffordshire, 170
Douglas, Isle of Man, 194
Downham Market, Norfolk, 458
Dumfries, Dumfries & Galloway, 226, 473
Dundee, City of Dundee, 218, 261, 262, 473, 479
Dunfermline, Fife, 227, 282, 317, 473
Dunkeld, Perth & Kinross, 218, 474
Dunoon, Argyll & Bute, 472, 479
Dunstable, Bedfordshire, 252
Durham, Durham, 265, 331, 381, 382, 437, 438

Earlston, Scottish Borders, 482
East Bergholt, Suffolk, 467
East Dereham, Norfolk, 268, 458
East Kilbride, South Lanarkshire, 255, 256
Eastleigh, Hampshire, 267
Eastwood, Essex, 465
Eccles, Salford, 464
Edenderry, Offaly, 471
Edgbaston, Birmingham, 76
Edinburgh, City of Edinburgh, 11, 16, 75, 135, 136, 151, 152, 155, 227, 233, 234, 282, 283, 293, 393, 396, 415, 423, 449, 450, 455, 472,

473, 474, 475, 476, 477, 479, 480, 481
Egham, Surrey, 203
Egypt, 180
Enniskillen, Fermanagh, 471
Epworth, North Lincolnshire, 445
Europe, 25, 26, 27, 39, 198, 256, 273
Evesham, Worcestershire, 90, 440
Exeter, Devon, 86, 357, 435, 436, 450
Exmouth, Devon, 436, 453

Falkirk, Falkirk, 480, 481
Fareham, Hampshire, 142, 356, 357
Farnham, Surrey, 357, 390
Farnworth, Bolton, 193
Felixstowe, Suffolk, 458
Ferryhill, Durham, 265
Fochabers, Moray, 455
Folkestone, Kent, 273, 442
Forfar, Angus, 474
Framwellgate Moor, Durham, 331
France, 7, 10, 19, 24, 198, 258, 273, 296, 297, 328, 347
Fratton, City of Portsmouth, 356, 364
Frodsham, Cheshire, 433

Galashiels, Scottish Borders, 221
Garstang, Lancashire, 443
Garston, Liverpool, 446
Gateshead, Gateshead, 457
Germany, 4, 7, 17, 18, 19, 23, 26, 27, 28, 43, 44, 97, 102, 128, 163, 172, 180, 183, 198, 222, 298, 350, 373
Glasgow, City of Glasgow, 9, 10, 73, 234, 239, 241, 242, 282, 317, 421, 422, 450, 481, 482
Glastonbury, Somerset, 79

Gloucester, Gloucestershire, 325, 374, 375, 439
Godalming, Surrey, 141
Gomersal, Kirklees, 454
Gortin, Tyrone, 471
Gosport, Hampshire, 365
Grantham, Lincolnshire, 327
Gravesend, Kent, 442
Great Addington, Northamptonshire, 354
Great Clacton, Essex, 439
Great Dunmow, Essex, 303
Great Haywood, Staffordshire, 99
Great Malvern, Worcestershire, 75, 470
Great Torrington, Devon, 436, 465
Greenock, Inverclyde, 241, 481
Gretna, Dumfries & Galloway, 226
Grove, Oxfordshire, 214
Guernsey, Channel Islands, 116
Guildford, Surrey, 257, 350
Guisborough, Redland & Cleveland, 326
Gunnislake, Cornwall, 368
Guyana, 205

Haddington, East Lothian, 474, 477, 479
Hadlow, Kent, 442
Halifax, Calderdale, 228, 432
Handsworth, Birmingham, 431
Hanley, City of Stoke-on-Trent, 307
Harborne, Birmingham, 367
Harpenden, Hertfordshire, 325, 441
Harrogate, North Yorkshire, 196
Hartfield, East Sussex, 455
Hartlepool, Hartlepool, 382
Haslemere, Surrey, 141
Hastings, East Sussex, 271, 438
Haverfordwest, Pembrokeshire, 487

Hawarden, Flintshire, 486
Hayle, Cornwall, 359
Haywards Heath, West Sussex, 102, 320, 361
Heckmondwike, Kirklees, 443
Hertford, Hertfordshire, 441
High Wycombe, Buckinghamshire, 213, 214, 318, 319
Higham Ferrers, Northamptonshire, 459
Hilsea, City of Portsmouth, 462
Hinkley, Leicestershire, 280, 444
Hitchin, Hertfordshire, 85, 284
Hoddesdon, Hertfordshire, 441
Holland, 7 see also Netherlands
Holmes Chapel, Cheshire, 111, 163, 172
Holsworthy, Devon, 436
Holywell, Flintshire, 454
Honiton, Devon, 436
Honley, West Yorkshire, 280
Horden, Durham, 381
Horley, Surrey, 124
Horsham, West Sussex, 160, 161
Horwich, Bolton, 432
Hove, Brighton & Hove, 174, 231
Howden, East Riding of Yorkshire, 129
Hoylake, Wirral, 469
Hucknall, Nottinghamshire, 373
Huddersfield, Kirklees, 196, 355
Hulme, Manchester, 457
Hungary, 214
Hunsdon, Hertfordshire, 328
Huntingdon, Cambridgeshire, 185
Hyde, Tameside, 454
Hythe, Hampshire, 231

Ilfracombe, Devon, 125
Ilkeston, Derbyshire, 435
India, 43, 175, 180

Inveraray, Argyll & Bute, 303
Inverkeithing, Fife, 282, 317
Inverness, Highland, 475
Ipswich, Suffolk, 8, 111, 162, 355, 356, 452, 458, 466
Ireland, 68, 73, 74, 103, 118, 120, 180, 196, 273, 282, 337, 345, 352, 455, 471
Ironville, Derbyshire, 186
Irthlingborough, Northamptonshire, 354
Irvine, North Ayrshire, 339
Isle of Wight, 356, 363
Italy, 7, 175, 180, 332

Jamaica, 5, 6
Japan, 25, 26, 256, 273
Jarrow, South Tyneside, 73
Java, 205
Jedburgh, Scottish Borders, 476

Kearsley, Bolton, 193
Kempston, Bedfordshire, 358
Kendal, Cumbria, 156, 226, 435
Kenilworth, Warwickshire, 359, 468
Keswick, Cumbria, 226, 434
Kettering, Northamptonshire, 217, 459
Kingston upon Hull, City of Kingston Upon Hull, 78, 129, 197, 230, 289, 321, 322, 327, 328, 442
Kinross, Perth & Kinross, 151, 474
Kirkby Lonsdale, Cumbria, 120
Knowle, Solihull, 359, 384

Lancaster, Lancashire, 455
Lane End, Buckinghamshire, 214
Larne, Antrim, 471
Leatherhead, Surrey, 250, 252

Index of places

Leeds, Leeds, 18, 86, 120, 130, 145, 230, 266, 294, 443, 451, 456, 467
Leicester, City of Leicester, 131, 134, 135, 229, 312, 353, 363, 398, 402, 444, 445
Leith, City of Edinburgh, 75, 151, 191, 282, 283, 293, 317
Letchworth, Hertfordshire, 4, 118
Lewes, East Sussex, 438
Liberia, 252
Lichfield, Staffordshire, 450, 455
Lincoln, Lincolnshire, 101, 120, 140, 169, 242, 244, 269, 374
Lisburn, Lisburn, 471
Liscard, Wirral, 452
Little Addington, Northamptonshire, 354
Liverpool, Liverpool, 16, 18, 97, 195, 250, 251, 282, 338, 395, 398, 402, 445, 446, 450, 451, 452, 480
Livingston, West Lothian, 86
Llandeilo, Carmarthenshire, 374, 484
Llandrindod Wells, Powys, 218
Llandudno, Conwy, 115
Llanelli, Carmarthenshire, 484
Llanfairfechan, Conwy, 302, 303, 486
Llangeitho, Ceredigion, 485
Llangollen, Denbighshire, 219
Llangwnadl, Gwynedd, 187
Llangybi, Gwynedd, 487
Lockerbie, Dumfries & Galloway, 226, 472
London, 1, 3, 4, 5, 6, 7, 8, 9, 10, 11, 15, 16, 18, 19, 21, 27, 36, 38, 39, 40, 49, 77, 78, 79, 83, 84, 86, 90, 96, 97, 102, 104, 106, 107, 108, 111, 113, 118, 127, 128, 132, 137, 140, 141, 142, 143, 150, 151, 152, 159, 163, 169, 172, 173, 174, 175, 176, 183, 184, 196, 198, 199, 202, 203, 204, 211, 213, 225, 230, 234, 244, 246, 247, 250, 258, 262, 263, 267, 275, 293, 306, 308, 313, 316, 318, 320, 323, 332, 333, 334, 339, 347, 348, 349, 361, 366, 371, 376, 377, 388, 392, 394, 396, 397, 399, 400, 401, 403, 410, 411, 413, 414, 415, 421, 426, 432, 442, 447, 448, 449, 450, 451, 452, 453, 454, 455, 456, 457, 462, 466, 468, 469, 470, 476
Acton, 184, 199, 447
Barnet, 246, 247
Battersea, 7, 8, 16, 96, 295, 306, 378
Beckenham, 175, 239
Bethnal Green, 78
Blackheath, 454
Brentford, 104, 105, 110, 157, 240, 338, 339, 345, 349, 359, 375, 447, 452
Bromley, 239, 272, 450
Camberwell, 334
Chelsea, 427
Chessington, 184
Chingford, 453
Clerkenwell, 262
Colliers Wood, 86
Dagenham, 295, 296
Dalston, 448
Ealing, 73, 184, 199, 447
East Dulwich, 450

Edgware, 446
Edmonton, 281
Enfield, 113, 114, 128
Feltham, 260
Foots Cray, 128
Fulham, 377, 378
Greenford, 80, 175
Hackney Wick, 83
Hackney, 132, 293, 294, 313, 448, 454
Hammersmith, 160
Hampstead, 446
Harlington, 326, 327
Hendon, 397
Highbury, 448
Hillingdon, 77
Holborn, 142, 254
Homerton, 258
Hounslow, 139, 146, 198, 263, 267, 326, 327
Ilford, 16, 127, 204, 205
Islington, 114, 456
Kennington, 326, 327
Kensington, 449
Kew, 449
Kilburn, 245
Kingston upon Thames, 195, 273, 455
Knightsbridge, 455
Lambeth, 149
Mitcham, 132
Morden, 86, 136, 150
Mortlake, 195
New Cross, 157, 448
Northwood, 448
Orpington, 239
Paddington, 240
Peckham, 313, 448
Penge, 239
Perivale, 73, 107
Plaistow, 78, 204

Ponders End, 258
Putney, 150
Richmond, 103
Romford, 135, 245, 310, 328
Ruislip, 128
Shepherd's Bush, 184
Shoreditch, 83
Sidcup, 239
South Croydon, 455
South Harrow, 391
Southall, 7, 96, 316, 377
Southgate, 404
Southwark, 76, 137, 326, 332
Stoke Newington, 448
Stratford, 78, 118, 204, 205
Surbiton, 213
Sydenham, 73, 107
Thornton Heath, 465
Twickenham, 184
Walworth, 452
Walthamstow, 86, 118, 131
Wandsworth, 11, 205, 296, 450
Wapping, 439
Westminster, 188, 446, 447
Willesden Green, 313
Woolwich, 305
Long Buckby, Northamptonshire, 459
Long Melford, Suffolk, 83
Long Stratton, Norfolk, 458
Longton, Stoke-on-Trent, 366
Loughborough, Leicestershire, 111, 162, 171, 172, 378, 445
Louth, Lincolnshire, 321
Lowestoft, Suffolk, 467
Luton, Luton, 453
Lutterworth, Leicestershire, 353, 444
Lydd, Kent, 456
Lymington, Hampshire, 455
Lytham, Lancashire, 100

Index of places

Mabelthorpe, Lincolnshire, 161
Macclesfield, Cheshire, 90, 91, 455
Machynlleth, Powys, 362, 484
Maidenhead, Windsor & Maidenhead, 74
Maidstone, Kent, 442, 449
Malmesbury, Wiltshire, 469
Manchester, Manchester, 8, 73, 104, 111, 120, 163, 220, 254, 318, 339, 371, 385, 386, 452, 456
Mapperley, Nottinghamshire, 461
March, Cambridgeshire, 458
Margate, Kent, 467
Market Drayton, Shropshire, 465
Market Harborough, Leicestershire, 217, 444, 445
Marlow, Buckinghamshire, 214
Maryport, Cumbria, 434
Masbrough, Sheffield, 443
Matlock, Derbyshire, 435
Melton Mowbray, Leicestershire, 130, 131, 444
Menai Bridge, Isle of Anglesey, 487
Meppershall, Bedfordshire, 285
Merthyr Tydfil, Merthyr Tydfil, 483
Mexico, 35, 180
Middlesbrough, Middlesbrough, 190, 265, 321
Mildenhall, Suffolk, 313
Milton Keynes, Milton Keynes, 275
Mold, Flintshire, 486
Morpeth, Northumberland, 319

Neath, Neath Port Talbot, 487
Needham Market, Suffolk, 466
Netherlands, 214 *see also* Holland
Newark-on-Trent, Nottinghamshire, 123

Newbury, West Berkshire, 103, 461, 460
Newcastle-under-Lyme, Staffordshire, 307
Newcastle upon Tyne, Newcastle upon Tyne, 37, 86, 130, 157, 190, 248, 249, 252, 302, 350, 360, 455, 457, 476
Newport, Isle of Wight, 438
Newport, Newport, 101, 271, 359, 483
Newport-on-Tay, Fife, 433
New Romney, Kent, 442
Newry, Down, 471
New Zealand, 174, 234
Northallerton, North Yorkshire, 326
Northampton, Northamptonshire, 135, 216, 217, 366, 459
Northfleet, Kent, 366
North Ormesby, Middlesbrough, 381
North Tawton, Devon, 436
Norway, 78
Norwich, Norfolk, 2, 83, 297, 310, 456, 458, 459
Nottingham, Nottinghamshire, 46, 120, 121, 123, 135, 159, 167, 168, 222, 223, 278, 279, 289, 350, 402, 409, 460, 461
Nuneaton, Warwickshire, 86, 225

Oakham, Rutland, 433, 444, 451
Odiham, Hampshire, 440, 455
Old Colwyn, Conwy, 486
Oldham, Oldham, 254, 443
Oswestry, Shropshire, 304
Ottery St Mary, Devon, 436
Oxford, Oxfordshire, 462
Pakistan, 252, 297, 298, 336
Peasenhall, Suffolk, 466

Penmaenmawr, Conwy, 486
Penrith, Cumbria, 226, 248, 434
Penygraig, Rhondda Cynon Taff, 228
Penygroes, Gwynedd, 487
Penzance, Cornwall, 359
Perry Bar, Birmingham, 480
Perth, Perth & Kinross, 151, 160, 423, 476, 482
Peterborough, City of Peterborough, 243, 347, 353, 450, 459
Pickering, North Yorkshire, 243
Plymouth, City of Plymouth, 361, 368, 436, 452
Pocklington, East Riding of Yorkshire, 148
Polmont, Falkirk, 481
Pontefract, Wakefield, 467
Pontypool, Torfaen, 267
Portadown, Armagh, 471
Portmadoc, Gwynedd, 257, 487
Portsmouth, City of Portsmouth, 45, 79, 323, 356, 364, 383, 462
Potton, Bedfordshire, 222
Prenton, Wirral, 97
Preston, Lancashire, 86, 100, 116, 443, 455
Pwllheli, Gwynedd, 257, 487

Queenborough, Kent, 73
Quinton, Dudley, 367

Radford, Dudley, 461
Rainham, Havering, 118
Rayleigh, Essex, 465
Reading, 126, 128, 247, 463
Reddish, Stockport, 219, 220
Redruth, Cornwall, 359
Reigate, Surrey, 313, 461

Rhos-on-Sea, Conwy, 486
Rhyl, Denbighshire, 280
Ripley, Surrey, 467
Rochdale, Rochdale, 463
Rochester, Medway Towns, 3
Rochford, Essex, 465
Romania, 113
Ross-on-Wye, Herefordshire, 450
Rotherham, Rotherham, 148, 149, 463
Royal Leamington Spa, Warwickshire, 468
Royal Tunbridge Wells, Kent, 442
Royston, Hertfordshire, 433
Rugby, Warwickshire, 217
Rugeley, Staffordshire, 99
Runcorn, Halton, 97, 100, 170, 251, 373
Russia, 43
Rustington, West Sussex, 146
Ruthin, Denbighshire, 261
Ryde, Isle of Wight, 356, 357, 441

Saffron Walden, Essex, 439
St Albans, Hertfordshire, 135, 403, 404
St Austell, Cornwall, 434
St Helens, St Helens, 104, 139, 157, 212, 240, 277, 338, 361, 463
St Helier, Jersey, 232
St Ives, Cambridgeshire, 285
St Leonards, East Sussex, 126
St Sampson's, Guernsey, 450
Salford, Salford, 110, 264
Salisbury, Wiltshire, 147, 148, 469
Saltash, Cornwall, 369
Sandbach, Cheshire, 433
Sandwich, Kent, 126, 272, 273
Sandy, Bedfordshire, 358
Sanquhar, Dumfries & Galloway, 472

Index of places

Scarborough, North Yorkshire, 456
Scotland, 151, 317, 415, 423
Settle, North Yorkshire, 454
Sheffield, Sheffield, 2, 3, 77, 86, 120, 138, 196, 213, 279, 280, 371, 451, 464
Shepley, Kirklees, 280
Sherwood, Nottinghamshire, 374
Shirley, City of Southampton, 161, 162
Shrewsbury, Shropshire, 75, 305, 359, 464
Singapore, 276
Sittingbourne, Kent, 442
Slough, Slough, 256
Soham, Cambridgeshire, 458
Somerton, Somerset, 465
South Africa, 43, 74, 175, 180, 295
Southam, Warwickshire, 359
South America, 43, 67, 79, 350
Southampton, City of Southampton, 3, 161, 170, 231, 232, 430
South Elmsall, Wakefield, 321
Southend-on-Sea, Southend-on-Sea, 211, 360, 465
South Molton, Devon, 436
Southport, Sefton, 138, 139
Southsea, City of Portsmouth, 99, 364, 462
South Shields, South Tyneside, 457
Southwell, Nottinghamshire, 460
Spain, 7, 323
Speke, Liverpool, 230, 251
Stafford, Stafordshire, 466
Staines, Surrey, 447
Stalybridge, Tameside, 457
Stamford, Lincolnshire, 217, 376
Staploe, Bedfordshire, 348
Stirchley, Telford, 192
Stockport, Stockport, 124, 204, 219, 220, 290, 386

Stockton-on-Tees, Stockton-on-Tees, 453
Stoke Goldington, Milton Keynes, 358
Stoke Poges, Buckinghamshire, 103
Stoke-on-Trent, City of Stoke-on-Trent, 97, 456
Stonehaven, Aberdeenshire, 269
Stonehouse, Gloucestershire, 450, 452
Stourbridge, Dudley, 470
Stowmarket, Suffolk, 384, 451, 466
Stratford-upon-Avon, Warwickshire, 90, 468
Sudbury, Suffolk, 384
Sunderland, Sunderland, 190, 444
Sutton-in-Ashfield, Nottinghamshire, 460, 461
Swansea, Swansea, 86, 112, 252, 487
Sweden, 27, 91, 275
Swindon, Wiltshire, 199
Swineshead, Lincolnshire, 279
Switzerland, 23, 253, 262, 313, 325
Syston, Leicestershire, 363

Tamworth, Staffordshire, 456
Tandragee, Armagh, 471
Taunton, Somerset, 125, 385, 465
Tenterden, Kent, 270, 442
Tetbury, Gloucestershire, 432, 440
Tewkesbury, Gloucestershire, 439
Thames Ditton, Surrey, 467
Thelbridge, Devon, 436
Thorne, Doncaster, 454
Thornley, Durham, 381
Torquay, Devon, 359
Towcester, Northamptonshire, 217
Trafford Park, Trafford, 91
Trawsfynydd, Gwynedd, 216
Tredegar, Blaenau Gwent, 483

Trimdon Station, Durham, 381
Trowbridge, Wiltshire, 89
Truro, Cornwall, 359, 434
Twyford, Wokingham, 256

Ugborough, Devon, 436
Ulceby, Lincolnshire, 459
Ulverston, Cumbria, 451
United States of America, 5, 6, 18, 20, 22, 23, 24, 25, 26, 27, 28, 29, 39, 43, 44, 73, 102, 103, 121, 128, 131, 143, 145, 146, 164, 175, 176, 180, 199, 255, 258, 267, 272, 273, 275, 297, 313, 318, 323, 328, 329, 334, 339, 340, 350
Uppingham, Rutland, 444
Upton-upon-Severn, Worcestershire, 439
Usk, Monmouthshire, 301, 359
Uttoxeter, Staffordshire, 466

Virginia Water, Surrey, 203

Wakefield, Wakefield, 452, 467
Wales, 304, 416, 454
Walker, Newcastle upon Tyne, 130
Wallsend, Newcastle upon Tyne, 457
Ware, Hertfordshire, 79, 441
Warrington, Warington, 140, 169, 195, 196
Warwick, Warwickshire, 75, 124, 358, 359, 384, 468
Watford, Hertfordshire, 105, 137, 157, 194, 212, 340, 410
Weaste, Salford, 464
Wellingborough, Northamptonshire, 451
Welshpool, Powys, 304

Welwyn Garden City, Hertfordshire, 224, 313, 328, 333, 334, 339, 480
West Bridgford, Nottinghamshire, 461
Westcliff-on-Sea, Southend-on-Sea, 360, 458
West Haddon, Northamptonshire, 455
West Indies, 3, 5, 39, 143, 205, 323
Weston-super-Mare, North Somerset, 125
West Teignmouth, Devon, 435
Weybridge, Surrey, 260, 467
Weymouth, Dorset, 437
Whitchurch, Hampshire, 440
Whitehaven, Cumbria, 434
Widnes, Halton, 118
Wigan, Wigan, 338
Wigton, Cumbria, 227
Wilmslow, Cheshire, 433
Wimborne, Dorset, 437
Winchester, Hampshire, 5, 211, 440, 441, 468
Windermere, Cumbria, 123, 435
Windsor, Windsor & Maidenhead, 101, 463
Wisbech, Cambridgeshire, 325, 458
Witney, Oxfordshire, 454
Wiveliscombe, Somerset, 465
Wolverhampton, Wolverhampton, 8, 469
Woodbridge, Suffolk, 466
Woodford, Northamptonshire, 354
Woodthorpe, Nottinghamshire, 461
Woollaton, Devon, 461
Woolton, Liverpool, 445
Worcester, Worcestershire, 250, 392, 470
Worksop, Nottinghamshire, 460
Worsbrough, Barnsley, 156

Worthing, West Sussex, 458, 468
Worthington, Leicestershire, 339
Wrexham, Wrexham, 164, 168, 304, 486
Yardley, Birmingham, 431

Yelverton, Devon, 368
York, York, 117, 265, 282, 328, 460

Zaire, 214

Index of subjects

acetanilid, 11
acetophenetidine, 102
Acquired Immune Deficiency
    Syndrome *see* AIDS
acriflavine, 91
adrenalin, 328
agricultural chemist *see* chemist,
    agricultural
AIDS, 27, 33, 177
alkali, 90, 193
alkaloid, 7, 10, 11, 16, 73, 233, 258,
    377
ambucetamide, 214
ammonia, 295
anaemia, 251
anaesthetic, 11, 19, 24, 91, 151,
    152, 153, 233, 255, 297, 329
analgesic, 21, 22, 198, 256, 290
analyst, 4, 77, 470
animal healthcare, 334
antibacterial, 103
anti-bilious pill, 157
antibiotic, 23, 26, 33, 50, 51, 73,
    176, 199, 255, 272, 273,
    275, 339
anti-cancer product, 91, 176
antidepressant, 199
antifungal agent, 214, 273
antihistamine, 297
anti-rheumatic rub, 229, 290
antiseptic, 273, 289, 296
anti-ulcerant, 26
apomorphine, 233
apothecary, 1, 3, 4, 5, 6, 8, 10, 33,
    34, 35, 36, 37, 38, 39, 49,
    66, 71, 77, 99, 101, 142,
    156, 228, 233, 248, 308,
    415, 426, 431, 432, 433,
    434, 435, 436, 440, 442,
    444, 445, 447, 448, 449,
    450, 451, 453, 454, 455,
    456, 457, 461, 462, 464,
    466, 467, 470, 471, 472,
    473, 474, 475, 476, 477,
    479, 481
apothecaries' company, 10
arsenical, organic, 19, 296
arthritis, 121, 176, 275
asthma, 79, 309
atoxyl, 251

baby food, 174
balsalazide, 114
barber-surgeon, 442
barbiturate, 73
benzoic acid, 205
bicarbonate of soda, 9, 205
bismuth, 8, 19, 295, 297
borax, 7, 205, 272
botanist, 462
Bright's disease, 50
bromide, 96, 205, 377
bromine compounds, 378
bronchitis, 309
builders' supplies, 169
burns, 329

cadmium bromide, 295
calcium citrate, 272
camomile, 285

camphor, 7, 8, 96, 127, 205, 272, 295, 377
cancer, 33, 50, 91, 92, 214, 275
carbenoxolone, 113, 114
carbocide disinfectant, 217
cardiac arrythmias, 199
cardiovascular product, 91, 103
cataract, 50, 275
cephaeline emetamine, 69
chemical, 118, 163, 205, 217, 223, 350, 358
    agricultural, 163, 297
    fine, 7, 17, 19, 21, 84, 90, 96, 111, 162, 163, 171, 172, 176, 205, 233, 258, 272, 377, 378, 396
    industrial, 84, 118, 131, 133, 163
    manufacture of, 78, 318, 350
    manufacturer of, 90, 96, 118, 171, 204, 214, 233, 258
    pharmaceutical, 66, 118, 163, 318, 351
    photographic, 205, 248
chemist, 1, 2, 3, 11, 18, 20, 25, 27, 33, 34, 35, 36, 37, 38, 39, 40, 41, 43, 44, 45, 46, 49, 50, 51, 67, 75, 76, 77, 78, 85, 86, 88, 89, 90, 97, 98, 99, 100, 101, 105, 106, 107, 109, 112, 113, 115, 120, 126, 130, 131, 134, 138, 140, 141, 142, 144, 145, 148, 149, 150, 156, 157, 160, 161, 167, 168, 174, 185, 186, 187, 188, 189, 191, 192, 193, 194, 195, 196, 197, 204, 216, 217, 218, 219, 220, 221, 222, 224, 225, 227, 228, 229, 241, 242, 244, 248, 257, 260, 261, 263, 264, 268, 269, 270, 271, 272, 278, 279, 280, 281, 293, 303, 304, 305, 309, 310, 317, 320, 321, 325, 326, 330, 346, 347, 350, 353, 355, 356, 358, 360, 362, 363, 366, 367, 368, 373, 374, 375, 382, 383, 384, 385, 398, 401, 415, 416, 423, 427, 431, 432, 433, 434, 435, 436, 437, 438, 439, 440, 441, 442, 443, 444, 445, 446, 447, 448, 449, 450, 451, 452, 453, 454, 455, 456, 457, 458, 459, 460, 461, 462, 463, 464, 465, 466, 467, 468, 469, 470, 471, 472, 473, 474, 477, 480, 481, 482, 483, 484, 485, 486, 487, 488, 489
    agricultural, 366, 464
    dispensing, 36, 66, 67, 89, 110, 115, 130, 139, 142, 143, 144, 147, 160, 168, 173, 185, 186, 191, 195, 197, 211, 239, 257, 260, 263, 271, 278, 280, 283, 293, 308, 321, 327, 347, 349, 366, 376, 384, 415, 431, 432, 433, 434, 436, 437, 439, 440, 444, 446, 452, 454, 455, 456, 458, 459, 460, 461, 465, 466, 467, 468, 470, 480, 481, 483, 484, 486, 487, 488
    manufacturing, 3, 4, 8, 66, 75, 97, 100, 110, 116, 117, 136, 138, 142, 143, 148, 149, 151, 162, 173, 191, 193,

219, 229, 231, 246, 264, 269, 282, 293, 294, 295, 323, 331, 349, 366, 385, 388, 448, 450, 452, 464, 467, 470, 473
  pharmaceutical, 18, 49, 50, 51, 66, 67, 75, 100, 101, 109, 112, 115, 116, 117, 129, 130, 138, 140, 142, 149, 150, 168, 174, 175, 183, 186, 188, 191, 211, 219, 221, 226, 227, 239, 271, 280, 294, 325, 353, 358, 361, 366, 367, 374, 375, 376, 384, 401, 416, 431, 437, 439, 441, 442, 443, 447, 448, 450, 451, 452, 455, 460, 464, 465, 469, 471, 480, 487
  photographic, 90, 168, 197, 260, 278, 374, 452, 466
  research, 102, 113, 299
  retail, 14, 19, 47, 67, 75, 85, 100, 107, 120, 126, 134, 136, 150, 151, 159, 161, 184, 185, 191, 216, 217, 218, 219, 254, 260, 266, 271, 282, 301, 302, 304, 308, 309, 317, 321, 322, 327, 347, 359, 360, 364, 366, 368, 381, 384, 386, 403, 437, 446, 448, 454, 455, 456, 462, 473
  veterinary, 366, 368
  wholesale, 15, 67, 75, 100, 116, 117, 126, 127, 136, 142, 151, 161, 173, 191, 216, 266, 269, 271, 282, 293, 304, 317, 322, 359, 366, 371, 386, 436, 469, 471, 473
chemists' sundries, 100, 190, 224, 231
chemists' supplier, 457
chemotherapeutic product, 356
chemotherapy, 17, 198, 251, 296
chirurgeon *see* surgeon
chloride of lime, 193
chlorine, 90
chloroform, 8, 91, 133, 152, 233
chlorophyl, 284
chocolate, 138
cholera, 160, 251
chymist *see* chemist
cinchona, 6, 67
  bark, 16, 22, 205
cinchonidine, 67
citric acid, 134, 205, 206, 272
coagulant cement, 220
cobalt, 296
cocaine, 8, 50, 205
cocoa butter, 10
codeine, 233, 289
cold, 160, 255
cold sore, 176
colour merchant, 101, 366
confectioner, 331
confectionery, 138, 228, 332
contraceptive, 214, 453
corticosteroid, 275
cortisone, 24, 102, 176
cosmetic, 163, 349
cough, 160
  medicine, 73, 220, 267
creosote, medicinal, 258
cyanide, 295

dentist, 358, 366, 364, 368, 431
depression, 328
diabetes, 50, 261, 262
diabetic, 273
diagnostic product, 73
digestive granule, 157

digestive pill, 37, 202
dining club, 421
diptheria, 16, 175, 176, 251
disability aid, 382
disinfectant, 90, 289
dispensing chemist *see* chemist,
    dispensing
distiller, 347
distributor,
    of drugs and medicines, 349
    of pharmaceuticals, 73, 159,
        213, 262, 368
doctor, 392, 432, 435
dragon's blood, 134
draper, 362, 469
dressing, 125
drug,
    anti-allergic, 163
    anti-anaerobic, 297
    anti-epileptic, 73
    anti-malarial, 19, 22, 35, 255,
        297
    anti-pneumonia, 297
    crude, 284, 289, 306
    industry, 396
    manufacture of, 152, 349
    milling, 83, 84, 118, 131, 133
    motion sickness, 318
    non-proprietary, 231
    organic, 425
    proprietary, 231
druggist, 1, 2, 3, 18, , 33, 34, 35,
        36, 37, 38, 39, 40, 41, 43,
        49, 50, 51, 67, 68, 76, 88,
        89, 90, 99, 100, 101, 106,
        112, 113, 115, 120, 126,
        130, 131, 134, 136, 138,
        140, 142, 145, 148, 149,
        150, 151, 156, 157, 160,
        161, 168, 173, 185, 186,
        187, 188, 189, 191, 193,
        195, 196, 204, 211, 216,
        218, 219, 221, 224, 225,
        227, 228, 229, 230, 241,
        242, 244, 248, 257, 260,
        261, 263, 264, 268, 269,
        270, 271, 272, 278, 279,
        280, 281, 303, 304, 309,
        310, 320, 322, 323, 325,
        326, 330, 347, 350, 353,
        354, 355, 356, 360, 362,
        363, 366, 368, 373, 374,
        375, 385, 398, 401, 415,
        416, 423, 427, 431, 432,
        433, 434, 435, 436, 437,
        438, 440, 441, 442, 443,
        444, 445, 446, 447, 448,
        449, 450, 451, 452, 455,
        456, 457, 459, 464, 465,
        466, 467, 468, 469, 471,
        472, 473, 474, 480, 481,
        483, 484, 485, 487
    wholesale, 101, 128, 148, 149,
        161, 186, 187, 224, 230,
        245, 250, 282, 310, 347,
        366, 377, 388, 408, 449,
        450, 457, 464, 469
druggists' sundries, 246
drysalter, 68, 366, 385, 443, 449,
    451, 469
dyestuff, 21, 90, 91, 97, 198

ear infection, 111, 163, 172
elastic stocking, 279
embrocation, 68
emetine, 10, 69
employers' association, 396
emulsion, 339
epilepsy, 50
essence, 248
    flavouring, 118
    manufacturer of, 131

of coffee, 234
of vanilla, 295
of banana, 295
prepared, 132
ether, 2, 8, 67, 91, 152, 183, 205, 233, 295
ethyl chloride, 152
ethylmorphine, 233
explosive, 90
eye care, 256

farm supplies, 304
fertiliser, 111, 162, 163, 172, 222, 349
first aid goods, 321, 322
flavouring, 131, 132, 133
food manufacturer, 339
fragrance, 131
fuel company, 169, 373
fungal disease, 214

galenical, 9, 15, 40, 61, 69, 78, 79, 84, 86, 100, 106, 135, 161, 190, 230, 231, 243, 254, 282, 376
gastroenterology, 214
gelatine capsule, 282
general practitioner, 308, 463
generic, 243
glaucoma, 50, 328
glycyrrhetic acid, 113
glycyrrhizin, 113
gout, 296
grocer, 257, 270, 362, 363, 433, 436, 437, 439, 443, 459, 465, 471
gynaecology, 214

hair cream, 356
hand cream, 356
hay fever, 80

headache, 255
healthcare,
    product, 214
    service, 169
health product, 339, 350
heartburn, 290
heart disease, 91, 275
herapin, 251
herb,
    compounded, 228
    distiller, 132
    extractor, 83
    farm, 83
    grower, 83
    prepared, 132
    preparation, 284
    remedy, 15, 120
herbalist shop, 120
herpes, 177
HIV, 27, 177 *see also* AIDS
homeopathic medicine vendor, 366
hormone, 267
hospital furniture, 79, 107
hospital product, 73
hospital pharmacist *see* pharmacist, hospital
household product, 21, 23, 25, 174, 212, 243, 265, 289
Human Immuno-deficiency Virus *see* HIV
hydrochloride, 11, 233
hygiene product, 350
hypertension reliever, 273

importer, 375
incontinence, 328
indigestion, 240
inflammatory disorder, 176
insomnia, 328
insulin, 20, 23, 79, 175, 198
intramuscular injection, 163

iodide, 8, 205
iodine, 9, 96, 295, 378
ipecacuanha, 35, 69
   root, 134
   acid, 69
ironmonger, 469
iron tonic, 157

jalap, 35

laboratory, 397
   equipment, 446
   furnisher of, 279
lactate, 205
lactucarium, 152
latex, 453
laudanum, 233
laundry blue, 289
lauryl alcohol, 206
lavender, 285
laxative, 79, 290, 308
leech, 2
liquorice, 332
livery company, 426
lymph, 397

malaria, 16, 22, 91, 220, 267
malt, 175
manufacturer of,
   fine chemicals, 84, 90, 96, 111, 163, 171, 172, 233, 258 376, 377
   patent medicines, 104, 202, 261, 323, 326
   pharmaceuticals, 67, 73, 77, 90, 110, 111, 120, 134, 141, 145, 151, 155, 157, 159, 160, 162, 163, 174, 204, 213, 214, 222, 229, 231, 244, 252, 267, 272, 277, 284, 289, 295, 313, 316, 327, 333, 338, 345, 366, 375
   proprietary medicines, 105, 137, 139, 171, 194, 212, 258, 263, 361, 371
manufacturing chemist *see* chemist, manufacturing
medical goods supplier, 322
medical practitioner, 427
medicated wool, 361
medicine
   antifungal, 214
   chest, 309
   ethical, 70
   homeopathic, 366
   manufacturer of, 255, 258, 323, 332
   over-the-counter, 70, 86, 243, 255, 256, 290, 307, 313, 334, 356, 404, 410
   patent, 2, 9, 19, 37, 38, 45, 61, 70, 100, 104, 105, 120, 128, 197, 202, 261, 270, 323, 326, 333, 392, 413
   poultry, 279
   proprietary, 2, 4, 15, 17, 26, 37, 40, 70, 100, 105, 106, 111, 137, 139, 162, 163, 171, 172, 190, 194, 212, 219, 258, 263, 277, 282, 334, 361, 371, 411, 413, 459
   quack, 11, 70, 323, 413
   vendor, 462
   veterinary, 21, 176, 334, 338, 357
mental illness, 328
menthol, 205, 255
mercurial, 8, 297
metallic sulphate, 295
methylene chloride, 295
midwife, 444, 447, 457
milk,

infant, 79
product, 79, 174, 175
supplement, 111, 163, 172
monazite, 205
morphia, 16
morphine, 10, 11, 50, 152, 234
morphine acetate, 233
moss, Iceland, 134
mountebank, 323
mouth ulcer, 114, 229, 290

nerve tonic, 163, 172
neurological product, 214
newsagent, 303
nickel preparation, 295
nutritional product, 73

obstetrics, 214
occupational health, 321, 322
oil,
    anointing, 348
    cod liver, 16, 78, 79, 97, 152, 175, 185, 327
    distillation, 84
    essential, 118, 131, 133
    halibut liver, 230
    merchant, 366, 443
    opium alkaloid, 11, 233, 234
optical instrument, 294, 314, 328
optician, 101, 189, 218, 321, 364, 435, 443, 459, 462, 466, 487
    ophthalmic, 257, 271, 278, 484
organic intermediate, 206
orthopaedic company, 329

pain killer, 350
paralysis, 50
patent medicine *see* medicine, patent
penicillin, 22, 23, 25, 44, 51, 91, 176, 255, 272

pepper mill, 83
peptic ulcer, 176, 318
perfume, 132
pest control, 220
pharmaceutical,
    bulk, 223
    dispenser of, 321, 427
    distributor of, 73, 159, 213, 262, 368
    ethical, 73, 111, 163, 172, 199, 223, 243, 275, 282, 307, 313, 351
    export dealer, 97
    hospital and laboratory products, 199
    manufacture of, 102, 222, 240, 250, 254, 275, 318, 350
    manufacturer of, 67, 73, 77, 90, 110, 111, 120, 134, 141, 145, 151, 155, 157, 159, 160, 162, 163, 174, 204, 213, 214, 222, 229, 244, 252, 267, 272, 277, 284, 289, 295, 313, 316, 327, 333, 338, 340, 345, 366, 375
    marketing of, 222, 240, 275, 318, 350
    opthalmic, 328
    over-the-counter, 351
    research and development, 121, 424
    retailer, 97, 100, 169, 242
    sale of, 222, 250, 254
    supplier of, 322
    synthetic, 91, 102
    veterinary, 214, 345
pharmaceutical chemist *see* chemist, pharmaceutical
pharmaceutical wholesaler *see* wholesaler, of pharmaceuticals

pharmacist, 4, 70, 90, 100, 112, 141, 144, 154, 211, 226, 231, 302, 367, 408, 414, 427, 433, 435, 436, 439, 440, 443, 445, 447, 451, 455, 456, 458, 459, 460, 461, 462, 467, 469, 470, 482, 485, 486, 487
   community, 88, 404, 422, 423, 446, 461
   dispensing, 106, 244, 364, 457
   hospital, 446, 461
   industrial, 461
   manufacturing, 388
   opthalmic, 226
   retail, 106, 211, 265, 307, 356, 403
   women, 401, 402
pharmacy, 141, 194, 226, 325, 369, 467, 479
   dispensing, 320, 354, 455
   photographic, 354
   retail, 8, 75, 113, 114, 135, 140, 169, 188, 248, 270, 301, 358, 359, 368, 382, 384, 442, 455
pharmacology, professor of, 395, 396
phenacetin, 11
phosphorous manufacturer, 84, 118, 131, 133
phosphorus, 4, 183
photographic chemist *see* chemist, photographic
photographic dealer, 101, 173, 257, 366, 374
photographic retailer, 239, 321
photographic supplies manufacturer, 216, 217
physician, 37, 173, 442, 461, 474
plasticiser, 206

plant extract, compounded, 228
poison, rat, 73
polio, 267, 273
polish, 289
polyurethane, 220
potassium ioxide, 282
printer, 438
proprietary article, 100, 190, 411
proprietary medicine *see* medicine, proprietary
protein therapy, 153
psychiatric illness, 214
psychiatric product, 214
publisher, 15
puerperal sepsis, 251

quack, 37, 38, 70, 392
   medicines of, 11, 323, 413
Quaker, 38, 106, 142, 208
quinine, 7, 10, 16, 19, 22, 67, 157, 205, 377
quinoline, 67, 103

research chemist *see* chemist, research
respiratory disorder, 176
retail chemist *see* chemist, retail
retail pharmacist *see* pharmacist, retail
retailer, 231, 382, 464
rheumatism, 377
rubber equipment, 453

salicin, 306, 377
salicylic acid, 133
salts,
   Epsom, 1, 9
   lithium, 296
   mercury, 19
   metal, 251
   Rochelle, 8

smelling, 2, 146, 183
school of pharmacy, 190, 294, 348, 395, 396, 399, 415, 416, 421, 422, 450
scientific instrument, 340
seed merchant, 148
senna, 3, 5, 6, 35
sequah, 323
serum, 267
shampoo, 163
sheep dip, 217, 366
shopkeeper, 187, 439, 469
skin, 243, 329
slate merchant, 257
smallpox, 72, 176
soda ash, 193
solvent, 206
sore throats, 40, 255
spice, 132
stationer, 224, 436
sterile eye drop, 328
sterile product, 313
steroids, 198, 199, 255
stomach acidity, 240
stomach pain relief, 256
strychnine, 7, 8, 10, 233, 377
sulphamezathine, 145
sulphanilamide, 145, 251
sulphonamide, 20, 22, 296
sulphuric acid, 193
surgeon, 4, 72, 99, 156, 168, 173, 192, 317, 431, 436, 437, 444, 447, 449, 450, 455, 456, 457, 461, 466, 472, 473, 474, 475, 476, 477, 479
surgeon apothecary, 11, 421, 442, 443, 454, 455, 456, 473, 476
surgeon dentist, 195
surgical appliance, 173, 349
surgical dressing, 309
surgical instrument, 16, 39, 43, 46, 79, 97, 107, 192, 246, 271, 385
surgical plaster factory, 246
surgical textile, 328
synthetic dye, 102
synthetic indigo, 222

tartaric acid, 205, 272
tea dealer, 257
teething, 160
tension reliever, 295
tetanus, 16, 175, 251
textile dye, 222
thorium, 205
thymol, 205
tincture, 132, 248
tissue repair products, 329
tobacco, 368
toiletries, 84, 163, 169, 190, 220, 243, 246, 265, 339, 351
toothpaste, 240
trade association, 388, 390, 392, 394, 403, 408, 413, 422, 452, 460, 482
trade union, 392, 399, 426
tropical disease, 16, 19, 175
trypanosomiasis, 251, 296
tuberculosis, 50, 176, 279, 328
typhoid, 19, 160, 251

uterine antispasmodic, 214

vaccination, 153, 397
vaccine, 16, 19, 20, 50, 72, 153, 175, 243, 251, 252, 267, 273, 397
veterinary business, 231, 270
veterinary chemist *see* chemist, veterinary
veterinary product, 275, 304
veterinary research, 297

vinegar, 250
viral disease, 214
vitamin, 23, 175

water,
   aerated, 2
   soda, 211
weedkiller, 217
wholesale chemist *see* chemist, wholesale
wholesale druggist *see* druggist, wholesale
wholesaler, 125, 317, 356, 368
   pharmaceuticals, 85, 97, 100, 128, 134, 140, 155, 161, 169, 190, 192, 196, 231, 242, 248, 265, 280, 305, 307, 355, 356, 369, 373, 385, 390, 408, 411
   chemists' sundries, 85, 356
   drugs, 169, 230
   ethical medical products, 125, 356
   see also chemist, wholesale
   see also druggist, wholesale
wholesaling, pharmaceutical, 25, 86, 97, 281, 321, 372
whooping cough, 176
wine, 226, 326, 487

yellow fever, 175

Index of archive repositories

Abbott Laboratories Ltd, 74
Alliance UniChem plc, 87, 100, 125, 129, 136, 185, 219, 266, 323, 368, 371
Argyll & Bute Archives, 303, 472
Association of the British Pharmaceutical Industry, 389
AstraZeneca Pharmaceuticals Ltd, 93

Baker, Mrs P, Cardiff, 402
Bath & North East Somerset Council Archive & Record Office, 431
Bayer Diagnostic Production Ltd, 104
Bedfordshire & Luton Archives & Records Service, 222, 358, 366, 431
Bell, John & Croyden Ltd, 311, 348
Berkshire Record Office, 463
Berwick-Upon-Tweed Record Office, 186, 460
Biggar Museum Trust, 482
Birmingham City Archives, 110, 193, 431
Bolton Archive & Local Studies Service, 117, 431
Bond, Mr A, 465
Boots Co plc, The, 121, 383
Bradford-On-Avon Museum, 469
Brent Leisure Services, 446
Bridewell Museum, Norwich, 458
Bristol Record Office, 198, 432

British Association of Pharmaceutical Wholesalers, 389, 409
British Library, 37, 184, 446
  Newspaper Library, 324
  National Sound Archive, 446
British Medical Association, 393
Bromley Central Library, 239
Buckinghamshire Record Office, 123, 150, 432
Bury Archive Service, 123
Bush Boake Allen Ltd, 132, 133, 316

Calderdale Museums & Arts, 432
Cambridgeshire Record Office,
  Cambridge branch, 144, 433
  Huntingdon branch, 185, 433
Camden Local Studies & Archives Centre, 446
Carmarthenshire Archive Office, 484
Chauvin Pharmaceuticals Ltd, 330
Cheshire Record Office & Chester Diocesan Record Office, 433
Chester Archives, 140, 433
Chesterfield Public Library, 186
City of Westminster Archives Centre, 188, 446
Cleveland Archives, 326
Co-operative Wholesale Society South East Region, 305
Cornwall Record Office, 434
Corporation of London Record Office, 447

Index of archive repositories

Coutts & Co, 204
Coventry City Archives, 434
Cumbria Record Office,
   Barrow in Furness branch, 434
   Carlisle branch, 191, 227, 434
   Kendal branch, 106, 120, 123, 156, 435

Denbighshire Record Office, 169, 219, 304, 486
Derby Local Studies Library, 90
Derbyshire Record Office, 187, 435
Devon Record Office, 435
Doncaster Archives, 437
Dorset Record Office, 101, 382, 437
Dudley Archives & Local History Service, 367
Dumfries & Galloway Archives, 472
Dundee City Archives, 262
Dundee University, Library, Archives & Manuscripts Department, 472
Durham Record Office, 272, 331, 437

East Kent Archives Centre, 442
East Riding of Yorkshire Archive & Records Service, 148, 438
East Sussex Record Office, 174, 271, 438
Essex Record Office,
   Chelmsford branch, 303, 439
   Colchester & North-East Essex branch, 376, 394, 439
   Southend branch, 361, 465

Falkirk Museums, 312, 480
Fife Library Service, St Andrews, 481

Flintshire Record Office, 280, 486

Galen Management Services Ltd, 392, 413
GEHE UK plc, 98, 109, 140, 144, 196, 212, 250, 266, 305, 310, 348, 355, 373, 468
Glamorgan Record Office, 189, 483
Glasgow City Archives, 241, 242, 318, 481
Glasgow University Archives & Business Records Centre, 422, 482
Glaxo Wellcome plc, 80, 126, 128, 153, 155, 234, 252, 270, 306, 424
Gloucestershire Record Office, 123, 325, 374, 375, 439
Greater Glasgow Health Board, 481
Guildhall Library, London, 211, 347, 429, 447
Gunnersbury Park Museum, 447
Gwent County Record Office, 101, 483
Gwynedd Archives & Museums Service, 116, 129, 187, 216, 257, 261, 303, 486

Hackney Archives Department, 294, 447
Hampshire Record Office, 142, 211, 312, 440
Hertfordshire Archives & Local Studies, 224, 247, 441
Hillingdon Local Heritage Service, 448
History of Advertising Trust, 83, 95, 104, 106, 112, 124, 158, 167, 172, 183, 202, 204, 212, 241, 256, 263, 275, 278, 293, 301, 316, 317,

319, 330, 345, 346, 353, 372, 381, 384, 458
Hugh-Jones, Dr Jean, 463

ICI plc, 92
Ironbridge Gorge Museum Trust, 464
Isle of Wight & Diocesan County Record Office, 161, 441
Islington Local History Collection, 448

Janssen-Cilag Ltd, 215

Kingston upon Hull City Records Office, 230
Knoll Pharmaceuticals, 224

Lambeth Archives Department, 150
Lancashire Record Office, 123, 193, 443
Laporte plc, 210
Leicestershire, Leicester & Rutland Record Office, 131, 281, 312, 353, 363, 398, 444
Leicestershire Record Office, 398
Lewisham Local Studies Centre, 448
Library of the Religious Society of Friends, 82, 210
Lightfoot, Mr Maurice, Carlisle, 227
Lincolnshire Archives, 102, 244, 269, 445
Liverpool Record Office & Local History Service, 445
London Metropolitan Archives, 96, 127, 167, 206, 306, 332, 378, 448

Macfarlan Smith Ltd, 154, 156, 237

Maltby, F & Sons Ltd, 74, 147, 183, 243, 254, 268
Manchester Central Library, 210, 387, 456
Manx National Heritage Library, 194
Martindale Pharmaceuticals Ltd, 246
Matthews, Mr T, Biggar, 482
Medeva Pharma Ltd, 253
Medeva plc, 254
Merseyside Record Office, 139
Museum of Welsh Life, 229, 421, 484

National Archives of Scotland, 420, 473
National Library of Scotland, 475
National Library of Wales, 188, 258, 362, 484
National Museums & Galleries on Merseyside
  Maritime Records Centre, 97
  Museum of Liverpool Life, 326, 445
National Pharmaceutical Association, 248, 420, 423, 441
National Register of Archives (Scotland), 75, 151, 191, 222, 228, 283, 293, 317, 479
Norfolk Record Office, 268, 459
North Devon Record Office, 125, 436
North East Lincolnshire Archives, 224, 459
North Yorkshire County Record Office, 460
Northamptonshire Record Office, 217, 354, 459

Index of archive repositories

Northumberland Record Office, 457
Nottingham City Library, 122, 461
Nottinghamshire Archives, 123, 160, 168, 278, 279, 350, 374, 399, 409
Nottinghamshire Archives & Southwell Diocesan Record Office, 123, 160, 168, 278, 279, 350, 373, 460

Ordsall Hall Museum, 264
Orkney Archives, 482
Oxfordshire Record Office, 312, 462

Pembrokeshire Record Office, 487
Perth Museum & Art Gallery, 160, 284, 482
Peterborough Museum & Art Gallery, 354
Pharmacia & Upjohn Ltd, 276
Plymouth & West Devon Record Office, 462
Portsmouth City Museum & Records Office, 99, 357, 462
Powys County Archives Office, 218
Proprietary Articles Trade Association, 412
Proprietary Association of Great Britain, 158, 161, 345, 372, 414
Public Record Office, 124, 137, 173, 182, 269, 324, 362, 397, 398, 401, 420, 448, 490
Public Record Office of Northern Ireland, 470

Ransom, William & Son plc, 85, 389, 396

Reckitt's Heritage, Reckitt & Colman Products Ltd, 221, 229, 290
Redbridge Central Library, Ilford, 208
Rhône-Poulenc Rorer Ltd, 112, 164, 172, 297, 380
Roberts, Mr H V, Tugby, 189, 271
Rochdale Local Studies Library, 463
Rotherham Metropolitan Borough Archives & Local Studies Section, 149, 463
Royal Borough of Kensington & Chelsea Libraries & Arts Service, 449
Royal Botanic Gardens, Kew, 82, 410, 420, 426, 449
Royal College of Physicians, Edinburgh, 480
London, 449
Royal College of Surgeons, of England, 449
Edinburgh, 259
Royal Pharmaceutical Society of Great Britain, 77, 82, 88, 95, 109, 124, 126, 144, 182, 184, 187, 195, 210, 246, 250, 260, 261, 268, 281, 312, 325, 349, 374, 394, 399, 402, 408, 413, 417, 430, 449
Royal Society, The, 19, 95, 124, 268, 301

St Helens Local History & Archives Library, 105, 138, 139, 158, 194, 212, 241, 262, 263, 277, 316, 334, 340, 346, 351, 362, 371

Salford City Archives, 110, 264, 464
Salford Local History Library, 264
Science Museum Library, 453
Scottish Borders Archive & Local History Centre, 482
Scottish Pharmaceutical Federation, 424
Shakespeare Birthplace Trust Records Office, 90, 468
Sheffield City Archives, 77, 138, 157, 280, 464
Shering-Plough Ltd, 314
Shropshire Records & Research Centre, 76, 464
Smith & Nephew Healthcare Ltd, 330
SmithKline Beecham plc, 105, 111, 141, 158, 203, 213, 240, 262, 277, 316, 335, 338, 343, 346, 349, 372, 376
Somerset Archive & Record Service, 125, 465
Staffordshire Record Office, 100, 465
Stockport Archive Service, 124, 220
Sturton (Wholesale) Journies Ltd, 354
Suffolk Record Office,
  Bury St Edmunds branch, 312, 466
  Ipswich branch, 356, 384, 466
  Lowestoft branch, 467
Surrey History Centre, 124, 141, 204, 257, 467

Tatford, Graham & Co Ltd, 357
Taylor, Dudley Holdings Ltd, 76, 301, 359, 385
Tremletts Chemists Ltd, 365
Tyne & Wear Archives Service, 249, 360, 457

Underhill, C E & Sons Ltd, 370
University of Aberden, Department of Special Collections & Archives, 472
University of Bristol Library Special Collections, 432
University of Edinburgh Library, Special Collections Department, 480
University of Hull, Brynmor Jones Library, 442
University of Liverpool, Sydney Jones Library, 395
University of London, Royal Holloway, 203
University of Manchester, John Rylands Library, 386
University of Nottingham, Hallward Library, 122, 461
University of Oxford,
  Bodleian Library, Department of Western Manuscripts, 113
  Museum of the History of Science, 82, 144, 382, 462
University of Strathclyde Archives, 422, 482
University of Wales, Bangor, Library, Department of Manuscripts, 116, 487
University of Wales, Swansea, Library & Information Services, 112
University of Warwick, Modern Records Centre, 399, 426

Vestry House Museum, London, 453
Vining, Mrs C, Cardiff, 402

Waltham Forest Archives, 454
Warrington Library, 196
Warwickshire County Record Office, 76, 124, 225, 468
Weldrick, H I Ltd, 437
Wellcome Library for the History & Understanding of Medicine, London, 82, 97, 143, 173, 184, 226, 245, 259, 263, 312, 324, 327, 349, 380, 385, 421, 430, 454
West Glamorgan Archive Service, 487
West Sussex Record Office, 154, 320, 468
West Yorkshire Archive Service,
  Bradford, 266, 432
  Calderdale, 228
  Kirklees, 229, 355, 442
  Leeds, 130, 294, 443
  Wakefield, 467

Yorkshire Archaeological Society, 444
Whitfield, M Ltd, 382
Wiggin Hill Farm, St Ives, 288
Wiltshire & Swindon Record Office, 89, 148, 195, 469
Winchester City Museums, 212
Wirral Archives Service, 390, 469
Wolverhampton Archives & Local Studies, 469
Worcestershire Record Office, 470
Worling, Dr Peter M, Edinburgh, 88, 98, 127, 129, 136, 239, 250, 254, 270, 373, 389, 391, 409, 480
Worshipful Society of Apothecaries, 389, 429

York City Archives Department, 117, 460